Fodor's
BUCKET LIST
USA

TOP REASONS TO GO

★ **Wild landscapes:** Mountain peaks, lakes, beaches, forests, and prairies all reward travelers with stunning views.

★ **History:** Monuments tell the American story, from Philly to Mt. Rushmore and beyond.

★ **Adventure:** White-water rafting, hiking, skiing, and more get the blood pumping.

★ **National Parks:** Grand Canyon, Zion, Yellowstone, Great Smoky Mountains: check them all off the list.

★ **Cool cities:** Get wonderfully lost among the skyscrapers of New York, Chicago, and more.

Welcome to the USA

The trip of a lifetime is around every corner of the USA, whatever your travel style may be. Maybe it's the eye-popping natural scenery of national parks, the vast arts and cultural riches of fast-paced cities, or the endearing personalities and quirky attractions of off-the-beaten-path small towns. Just remember that a bucket list never needs to be literal list of boxes to check, and that the true key to this type of travel is to always be open to discovering America's quintessential experiences.

What makes something worthy of appearing on a bucket list? In asking our team of passionate local experts to share their must-see recommendations for each U.S. state, we encouraged the inclusion of both iconic sites (looking at you, San Diego Zoo and Art Institute of Chicago) and idiosyncratic adventures, like canoeing through an old-growth bottomland hardwood forest in South Carolina's underrated Congaree National Park and gazing up at the aerial spectacle that is the Albuquerque International Balloon Fiesta.

Bucket list experiences are as much about wowing us with their superlative features—say, the Grand Canyon or Seattle's Space Needle—as they are about capturing the cultural or historical essence of a place. In this latter category, consider taking a tour of the Birmingham Civil Rights Institute or learning about Cherokee culture at the Cherokee National Historic Museum in Oklahoma.

And while bigger isn't always better, you're still encouraged to hike at least a stretch of the nearly 2,200-mile Appalachian Trail and drive beneath the magnificent orange piers of the Golden Gate Bridge. Also take time to smell the flowers—perhaps in the gardens of Asheville's Biltmore Estate or the brilliantly colorful fields of Washington State's Skagit Valley Tulip Festival. There are few more quintessential outdoor adventures than surfing in Hawaii, skiing in the Colorado Rockies, or hiking in Yosemite National Park. And attending a renowned annual event is another memorable way to get to know what's special about a place. Consider Mardi Gras in New Orleans, the Maine Lobster Festival in Rockland, or the Iowa State Fair in Des Moines.

As you plan your travels, please confirm that places are still open, and let us know when we need to make updates by writing to us at ✉ *corrections@fodors.com*.

Contents

MAPS

Chapter 1

EXPERIENCE BUCKET LIST USA

130° W
120° W
110° W
100° W
50° N
30° N
WEST COAST, ALASKA, AND HAWAII
THE ROCKIES
GREAT PLAINS
SOUTHWEST
WASHINGTON
OREGON
CALIFORNIA
NEVADA
IDAHO
MONTANA
WYOMING
UTAH
COLORADO
ARIZONA
NEW MEXICO
NORTH DAKOTA
SOUTH DAKOTA
NEBRASKA
KANSAS
OKLAHOMA
TEXAS
MEXICO
PACIFIC OCEAN
Seattle
Olympia
Spokane
Vancouver
Portland
Salem
Great Falls
Missoula
Helena
Billings
Minot
Bismarck
Boise
Pierre
Eureka
Casper
Reno
Elko
Salt Lake City
Cheyenne
Sacramento
San Francisco
San Jose
Denver
Fresno
Colorado Springs
Las Vegas
Santa Barbara
Los Angeles
San Bernardino
Flagstaff
Santa Fe
Albuquerque
Amarillo
Oklahoma City
San Diego
Phoenix
Tucson
El Paso
Ft. Worth
Austin
San Antonio
Corpus Christi
Laredo
90
15
5
84
94
29
25
80
70
35
40
10
8
20
37
ALASKA
Fairbanks
Anchorage
Juneau
1
2
3
HAWAII
KAUA'I
NI'IHAU
O'AHU
MOLOKA'I
Honolulu
LANAI
MAUI
KAHO'OLAWE
Waimea
HAWAI'I

Bucket List USA
Regional Areas
90° W
80° W
70° W
CANADA
GREAT LAKES
NEW ENGLAND
MID-ATLANTIC
SOUTHEAST
Lake Superior
Lake Michigan
Lake Huron
Lake Ontario
Lake Erie
ATLANTIC OCEAN
GULF OF MEXICO
Caribbean Sea
BAHAMAS
CUBA
MAINE
NH
VT
MA
CT
RI
NEW YORK
PENNSYLVANIA
NJ
MD
DE
WEST VIRGINIA
VIRGINIA
NORTH CAROLINA
SOUTH CAROLINA
GEORGIA
FLORIDA
ALABAMA
MISSISSIPPI
LOUISIANA
ARKANSAS
TENNESSEE
KENTUCKY
OHIO
INDIANA
ILLINOIS
MICHIGAN
WISCONSIN
MINNESOTA
IOWA
MISSOURI
International Falls
Sault Ste. Marie
Fargo
Minneapolis
St. Paul
Sioux Falls
Milwaukee
Detroit
Chicago
Des Moines
Omaha
Indianapolis
Cincinnati
Cleveland
Pittsburgh
Buffalo
Rochester
Syracuse
Burlington
Augusta
Portland
Boston
Providence
Bridgeport
New York
Philadelphia
Baltimore
WASHINGTON, D.C.
Richmond
Norfolk
Charleston
Kansas City
Topeka
St. Louis
Tulsa
Nashville
Knoxville
Raleigh
Charlotte
Wilmington
Memphis
Little Rock
Atlanta
Columbia
Savannah
Dallas
Shreveport
Jackson
Montgomery
Jacksonville
Tallahassee
Baton Rouge
New Orleans
Houston
Orlando
Tampa
Miami
0
200 mi
0
200 km

The Best Landmarks in the USA

GOLDEN GATE BRIDGE
Named for the mile-long strait at the mouth of San Francisco Bay that it crosses, this suspension bridge is known around the world for its graceful towers and rusty orange color—it was originally intended to be blue and yellow, but the color of the primer stuck. (*p. 477*)

MT. RUSHMORE
South Dakota's Black Hills would still be famous without it, but this colossal sculpture of four presidents—Washington, Jefferson, Lincoln, and, slightly behind the others, Theodore Roosevelt—makes them iconic. By artist Gutzon Borglum, Mt. Rushmore's design changed several times before debuting in 1941. (*p. 446*)

THE CHICAGO BEAN
No trip to downtown Chicago is complete without snapping a selfie of yourself reflected in this striking polished–stainless steel sculpture by Anish Kapoor. Anchoring flower-filled Millennium Park, its official name is *Cloud Gate.* (*p. 709*)

STATUE OF LIBERTY
People throw the word "iconic" around a lot these days, but New York's Statue of Liberty is perhaps the one landmark that truly represents the United States in the eyes of the world. You can visit the island, but the best way to enjoy the statue is standing on the deck of the (free) Staten Island Ferry. (*p. 162*)

SPACE NEEDLE

Built for the World's Fair in 1962, Seattle's 604-foot Space Needle is an unforgettable beacon of the city's skyline. The futuristic design was a compromise between two powerful men, one who wanted it to look like a balloon, the other like a flying saucer. (*p. 545*)

EDMUND PETTUS BRIDGE

The most powerfully disturbing symbol of America's civil rights struggle is this bridge in downtown Selma, Alabama. In 1965, state troopers brutally attacked 400 mostly African American demonstrators peacefully marching across it to Montgomery. (*p. 241*)

MIAMI BEACH

More than 800 historic buildings in Miami Beach's Art Deco District make up the biggest collection of 1920s and 1930s resort architecture in the world. Don't miss the baby-blue, neon-lit Colony Hotel on Ocean Drive. (*p. 260*)

THE WASHINGTON MONUMENT

The world is full of similarly shaped obelisks, but something about the 1884 Washington Monument—maybe its location on top of a small hill, or the ring of flags surrounding its base—inspires. It's Washington, D.C.'s compass: east is the Capitol, north is the White House, and west is the Lincoln Memorial. (*p. 210*)

GATEWAY ARCH

The nation's tallest monument, the 630-foot St. Louis Gateway Arch treats you to sweeping views of the Mississippi River. (A futuristic tram whisks you to the top.) Don't miss the museum, which strives to weave in the stories of the region's Indigenous people. (*p. 396*)

HOLLYWOOD SIGN

Fun fact: these 50-foot letters didn't originally spell "Hollywood." They advertised "Hollywood-land," an upscale real estate development. When they fell into disrepair, the city of Los Angeles came to its rescue with a new coat of paint, removing the last four letters in the process. (*p. 478*)

The Best National Parks in the USA

GRAND CANYON

You'll never forget your first visit to Arizona's Grand Canyon, gazing down at the seemingly endless expanse from the South Rim. Repeat visitors come for hiking, horseback riding, or white-water rafting. *(p. 567)*

ACADIA

It comprises more than a dozen other islands, but most visitors to this coastal paradise in Maine stick to easily accessible Mount Desert Island. Bike the carriage roads, hike lofty Cadillac Mountain, or trek to Bass Harbor Head Lighthouse. *(p. 49)*

ARCHES

It took millions of years for erosion to form the sandstone arches that give this Utah park its name. Delicate Arch is the most famous and Landscape Arch is the longest, but there are more than 2,000 others to grab your attention, making this the largest collection of natural arches in the world. *(p. 633)*

OLYMPIC

Covering nearly 1 million acres, western Washington's peninsular jewel offers what is essentially three parks in one, with glacier-topped mountains, misty primeval forests filled with evergreens, and driftwood-strewn beaches where you can set up camp and watch the waves roll in past towering sea stacks. *(p. 547)*

GREAT SMOKY MOUNTAINS
The country's most visited national park—accessed from popular vacation towns in Tennessee (Gatlinburg and Pigeon Forge) and North Carolina (Bryson City and Cherokee)—the densely forested Great Smoky Mountains is especially beautiful for hiking and camping in spring and fall. (*p. 331*)

YELLOWSTONE
Occupying the northwest corner of Wyoming and parts of Montana and Idaho, the country's first national park is known for its geothermal features, including Old Faithful geyser, but it also contains a stunning alpine lake and herds of free-roaming bison. (*p. 689*)

DEATH VALLEY
Straddling the border of California and Nevada, Death Valley is the hottest place in the United States. It sets other records, being the driest (barely 2 inches of rain a year) and the lowest (282 feet below sea level) national park. (*p. 487*)

ROCKY MOUNTAIN
Since it's bisected by the Continental Divide, the eastern half of this Colorado park is craggy mountains, while the western half is lush, green forests. Both offer endless opportunities for hiking and wildlife viewing. (*p. 649*)

YOSEMITE
The granite peak of El Capitan draws extreme climbers and receives star billing, but this 1,200-square-mile park in California's Sierra Nevada mountains has plenty of superlatives, including Bridalveil Fall, the country's tallest waterfall, and arguably the most striking hotel in any national park, the Ahwahnee. (*p. 480*)

ZION
Utah's Zion offers a diverse array of breathtaking spots like the Narrows, a slot canyon that often narrows to less than 20 feet wide, and the thrillingly steep and dramatic hike atop Angel's Landing. Its soaring red cliffs attract casual hikers and serious rock climbers. (*p. 631*)

The Best Outdoor Adventures in the USA

CRUISING THROUGH GLACIER BAY
Brown bears lumber along the shore of Alaska's Glacier Bay while bald eagles soar overhead and sea otters swim alongside your boat. Calving glaciers and the snowcapped Fairweather Range complete the scene. (*p. 677*)

MOUNTAIN BIKING IN MOAB
Considered by many to be the ultimate mountain-biking experience, Slick-rock Trail in Moab, Utah, is a 10-mile trek through delightful desert terrain. There are also plenty of easier rides through Moab. (*p. 638*)

HIKING THE APPALACHIAN TRAIL
Running for 2,200 miles from Georgia to Maine, the Appalachian Trail is the Holy Grail for serious hikers. Challenge yourself on the most mountainous part of the route, in North Carolina. (*p. 337*)

SKIING IN ASPEN
Home to four world-class ski areas that comprise more than 5,600 acres of breathtaking terrain—all of them accessed with one lift ticket—Aspen offers prime conditions, fluffy powder, and trails for every style and ability. The town's tony resorts and scene-y night-life are legendary. (*p. 653*)

BACKPACKING IN MT. RAINIER NATIONAL PARK
Washington's Mt. Rainier is a magnet for backpackers, with dozens of off-the-beaten-path routes like the challenging 17-mile Mother Mountain Loop. Wildlife like marmots and black bears share the evergreen-shaded and wildflower-bordered trails. (*p. 544*)

SNORKELING IN THE CHANNEL ISLANDS
The kelp forests just off the coast of California's Santa Cruz Island, part of famous Channel Islands National Park, make for some of the country's most seductive underwater scenery. (*p. 496*)

ROCK CLIMBING IN NEW RIVER GORGE
One of the nation's newest national parks, West Virginia's New River Gorge ranks among the country's top destinations for climbing. The park's sheer sandstone cliffs create quite a challenge even for pros. (*p. 222*)

Rafting in the Grand Canyon

RAFTING IN THE GRAND CANYON

Riding the rapids through the Grand Canyon on the Colorado River is one of the greatest thrills imaginable. It's not all white water, though: there are long, relaxing stretches where you can drift amid grandiose rock formations on a multiday adventure. *(p. 567)*

SNOWSHOEING IN MICHIGAN

Michigan's Upper Peninsula is prime snowshoeing territory, especially in the towering old-growth forests of the remote Porcupine Mountains (aka Porkies). There's a 110-mile hut-to-hut trail where you can warm yourself up next to a wood-burning stove. Or, try the activity at Pictured Rocks National Lakeshore, also known for its ice climbing. *(p. 734)*

SURFING ON THE NORTH SHORE OF OAHU

From November to February, only experienced surfers should take on the towering waves along Hawaii's famous North Shore on Oahu. This area is often called the "seven-mile miracle" for its long stretch of breaks. *(p. 516)*

SWIMMING WITH MANATEES

Florida's gentle giants are surprisingly easy to spot from December to March, when they congregate in the warmer waters of freshwater springs. You can legally swim with them in Crystal River, and kayak among them in South Florida, but remember to respect all rules and maintain your distance. *(p. 266)*

SKYDIVING IN SNOHOMISH

Take on the ultimate bucket list activity in Snohomish, Washington, considered one of the top skydiving destinations in the world. As you soar through the fresh mountain air you can spot dense evergreens and snowcapped peaks. *(p. 557)*

The Best Historical Sites in the USA

INDEPENDENCE HALL

A UNESCO World Heritage site, this 18th-century landmark is where the Declaration of Independence and the Constitution were adopted. It's the centerpiece of Philadelphia's Independence National Historical Park, home to the Liberty Bell, Congress Hall, and more. (*p. 184*)

CLIFF PALACE

In Colorado's Mesa Verde National Park, this is the largest cliff dwelling in North America. Carved in the 12th century by Ancestral Puebloan people beneath rocky overhangs, they are extraordinarily well preserved. (*p. 655*)

BILTMORE ESTATE

The largest private house in the country, the 19th-century Biltmore Estate remains one of the most prominent mansions of the Gilded Age. It sits on an 8,000-acre estate in Asheville, North Carolina's Blue Ridge Mountains. On view are antiques and art, 75 acres of gardens, a conservatory, hiking and horseback trails, and America's most visited winery. (*p. 332*)

THE FREEDOM TRAIL

A bronze plaque embedded in a cobblestone street marks the beginning of Boston's Freedom Trail, which runs for more than 2 miles past some of the city's most historic American Revolutionary War–era sites, including Faneuil Hall, the Old North Church, and the Paul Revere House. (*p. 66*)

HOT SPRINGS NATIONAL PARK

For centuries, Indigenous peoples and later settlers soaked in the healing waters of these warm, mineral-rich springs in Arkansas's Ouachita Mountains. The compact national park preserves a row of eight ornately designed historic bathhouses where you can still soak, plus hiking and biking trails. *(p. 248)*

ELLIS ISLAND

In the shadow of the Statue of Liberty, this tiny island in New York Harbor was once the busiest immigration center in the country. Many visitors look up ancestors who passed through while they are here. *(p. 162)*

CASTILLO DE SAN MARCOS

Construction began on St. Augustine's fortress more than three centuries ago, when the Spanish wanted to shore up their defenses in what is now known as Florida. Its waterfront perch is dazzling. *(p. 263)*

EBENEZER BAPTIST CHURCH

The Rev. Martin Luther King Jr. was pastor at this two-towered brick church in Atlanta until he was assassinated in 1968. To this day the church still has a strong focus on civil rights and racial justice. *(p. 280)*

HISTORIC JAMESTOWNE

The first successful English settlement in North America, Virginia's Historic Jamestowne includes some of the country's oldest buildings, including a 17th-century brick church tower and nearby cemetery. *(p. 201)*

THE ALAMO

This restored though surprisingly modest 18th-century Spanish Colonial mission was the site of the storied Battle of the Alamo, when Mexican troops routed frontiersman Davy Crockett and roughly 200 others during the Texas Revolution in 1836. *(p. 610)*

The Best Natural Attractions in the USA

CRATER LAKE

In a caldera formed nearly 8,000 years ago by a massive volcanic eruption, Oregon's brilliant blue lake has a depth of 1,943 feet, making it the nation's deepest. It's fed by snowfall from the dramatic peaks that ring its shores. (*p. 530*)

NIAGARA FALLS

It's not the tallest (that's Angel Falls in Venezuela) or the widest (that's Khone Falls in Laos), but with more than 20 million visitors a year, Niagara, located in both New York and Canada, is by far the world's most celebrated waterfall. Catch a glimpse from above at Niagara Falls Observation Tower or on a boat tour. (*p. 163*)

MENDENHALL GLACIER

One of the most accessible glaciers in the world, this enormous 13-mile-long glacier is just a short drive from downtown Juneau. It's an astounding sight viewed across a lake from the visitor center, but the real fun is actually walking on its icy-blue surface via a helicopter or hiking tour. (*p. 462*)

CAPE COD NATIONAL SEASHORE

Stretching almost 40 miles around the crooked arm of Outer Cape Cod, this breezy expanse of rolling sand dunes, wildlife-rich ponds and estuaries, sweeping beaches, and shady pine barrens captivates enthusiasts of recreation and conservation alike. (*p. 72*)

MAMMOTH CAVE

Central Kentucky's Mammoth Cave is sometimes overlooked by visitors from beyond the region. That's a shame, because these otherworldly caverns make up the world's longest cave system (at 426 miles), a wonderland for spelunking and subterranean tours. (*p. 295*)

HELLS CANYON

The deepest canyon in North America—2,000 feet deeper than the more famous Grand Canyon—this remote and lightly traveled area straddles the border of Oregon and Idaho. It's best experienced on a white-water rafting tour on the Snake River. (*p. 668*)

California's redwood trees

TALL TREES GROVE
The discovery of the world's tallest tree led to the creation of California's Redwood National Park in 1968. A moderately strenuous hike takes you to these tall wonders. (*p. 485*)

KILAUEA
Erupting almost continually since 1983, Hawaii's Kilauea is the world's most active volcanic mass. When lava pools in the Halema'uma'u crater, it's possible to catch a glimpse on a hike or drive along the crater's rim. (*p. 508*)

DENALI
From miles away on clear days, you can behold the icy peak of 20,310-foot-tall Denali, North America's tallest mountain peak. It soars above 6 million acres of virtually untouched Alaskan wilderness. (*p. 461*)

BLACK HILLS
In North America's oldest mountain range, located in South Dakota, bison graze in the grasslands beneath the impressive spires of Custer State Park. (*p. 443*)

WHITE SANDS
One of country's most remarkable geological sights, this 275-square-mile tract of undulating gypsum sand dunes in New Mexico is the world's largest. Some of its desert animals are found nowhere else. (*p. 597*)

THE EVERGLADES
Called the "River of Grass," the Everglades is the largest mangrove forest in the Western Hemisphere. Florida's subtropical wetlands are the only place where the American alligator and crocodile coexist. (*p. 261*)

The Best Museums in the USA

TACOMA'S MUSEUM OF GLASS

Designed with a soaring conical tower that houses a working hot shop and reached via a pedestrian overpass lined with colorful glassworks, this striking museum showcases western Washington's reputation as one of the world's foremost hubs of contemporary glass art. *(p. 551)*

THE GETTY MUSEUM

Few museums enjoy a more memorable setting than the Getty, perched high on a hill overlooking Los Angeles. The modern architecture is stunning, the sculpture gardens are gorgeous, and the collection unequaled on the West Coast. *(p. 488)*

ISABELLA STEWART GARDNER MUSEUM

The art at this Boston landmark—think Rembrandt, Michelangelo, Matisse, and Manet—is impressive, but the museum's location in a Venetian-style palazzo around a light-filled courtyard is equally enthralling. See masterpieces like Titian's *Europa* and John Singer Sargent's *El Jaleo*. *(p. 69)*

ART INSTITUTE OF CHICAGO

It may contain modern must-sees like Pablo Picasso's *The Old Guitarist*, Marc Chagall's *America Windows*, and Grant Wood's *American Gothic*, but the vast collection here spans many eras and cultures. *(p. 707)*

BIRMINGHAM CIVIL RIGHTS INSTITUTE

Set beneath a breathtaking glass dome, this interpretive museum and research center in Birmingham, Alabama, tells the story of the ongoing struggle for racial equality in the United States and traces African Americans' struggle for equality back to the 1800s. (*p. 239*)

GEORGIA O'KEEFFE MUSEUM

In Santa Fe, about an hour from her beloved rural New Mexico home and studio, the only museum dedicated to groundbreaking painter Georgia O'Keeffe occupies a contemporary pueblo-style building that makes the perfect backdrop for her art. (*p. 596*)

NEGRO LEAGUE BASEBALL MUSEUM

A real game changer, this Kansas City, Missouri, museum chronicles the rich legacy of the historic baseball league, formed in 1920 because players were banned from all-white major league teams until Jackie Robinson broke the color barrier in 1947. (*p. 399*)

NATIONAL MUSEUM OF AFRICAN AMERICAN HISTORY AND CULTURE

Among the more recent additions to Washington, D.C.'s incomparable collection of Smithsonian Institution museums, NMAAHC occupies a dramatic building shaped like an inverted pyramid and contains more than 40,000 objects. Watch for the always compelling rotating exhibits. (*p. 211*)

METROPOLITAN MUSEUM OF ART

You could take a week to explore this sprawling museum in New York City, which includes an Egyptian temple dating back 2,050 years and the living room of a house designed by Frank Lloyd Wright. (*p. 164*)

THE 9/11 MEMORIAL MUSEUM

On the site of New York's Twin Towers, which were felled in a terrorist attack on September 11, 2001, this poignant museum memorializes the event with home videos, news camera footage, and interviews with survivors. (*p. 168*)

The Best Festivals and Events in the USA

ART BASEL MIAMI BEACH

Every December, Miami Beach becomes the center of the art world when it hosts the massive Art Basel, an international festival that originated in Switzerland, and the swanky parties that come along with it. *(p. 258)*

BURNING MAN

Tens of thousands of avid "burners" return each summer to northern Nevada's Black Rock Desert for Burning Man, a "temporary metropolis dedicated to community, art, self-expression, and self-reliance." *(p. 591)*

KENTUCKY DERBY

The nation's preeminent see-and-be-seen Thoroughbred race has been a fixture in spring at Churchill Downs in Louisville since 1875. In addition to races, Derby Week features glamorous parties where attendees dress in their finest threads. *(p. 296)*

SKAGIT VALLEY TULIP FESTIVAL

The fertile fields of this lush valley in northwest Washington State burst with color throughout April, as millions of tulips as well as daffodils, irises, crocuses, and other stunning blooms carpet the landscape. Other events include a parade, art shows, and a street fair. *(p. 556)*

SOUTH BY SOUTHWEST

In March, Austin, Texas, pretty much surrenders to this weeklong event that literally fills the streets with outdoor concerts by musicians of every possible genre. Indoors are film screenings and interactive media demonstrations. *(p. 611)*

IOWA STATE FAIR

Begun in 1854 and known as a high-profile campaign stop for U.S. presidential hopefuls, this 11-day agricultural showcase is one of the country's largest and most beloved, featuring classic fair food, kids' rides, and dozens of rock and country concerts. *(p. 373)*

MAINE LOBSTER FESTIVAL

In Maine, summer isn't summer without lobster. This celebration of the state's famous shellfish, held in the dapper coastal town of Rockland, has a parade, cooking contests, and the crowning of the Maine Sea Goddess. *(p. 61)*

Coney Island Mermaid Parade

CONEY ISLAND MERMAID PARADE

Manhattan parades might be bigger, but none of them are as fun as this Brooklyn street festival smack in the middle of Coney Island's amusement park, with thousands of mermaids, mermen, and every conceivable creature from under the sea. *(p. 171)*

MARDI GRAS

With its riotously colorful krewe parades and balls, the legendary Carnival celebration includes festivities over several weeks throughout Southern Louisiana but it's most famous for its Fat Tuesday culmination in New Orleans. *(p. 308)*

OREGON SHAKESPEARE FESTIVAL

The Bard isn't the only playwright whose works are brought to life during this venerable eight-month showcase in Ashland that dates back to 1935. Hundreds of performances take place in outdoor and indoor venues. *(p. 536)*

ALBUQUERQUE INTERNATIONAL BALLOON FIESTA

From morning to night, the skies over New Mexico are filled with every conceivable shape and color of hot air balloon. Whimsical designs include astronauts, swarms of bumblebees, and even *Star Wars* characters. *(p. 599)*

CHERRY BLOSSOM FESTIVAL

Every spring, thousands of cherry trees around the Jefferson Memorial and throughout all of Washington, D.C., are suddenly covered with delicate white blossoms. *(p. 213)*

STURGIS MOTORCYCLE RALLY

More than a half-million bikers roll into South Dakota's scenic Black Hills each August for rides, races, concerts, and camaraderie. Sturgis has been the site of this roaring spectacle since 1938. *(p. 448)*

The Best Family-Friendly Travel in the USA

DISNEYLAND
Florida's Walt Disney World has many times the acreage, but the original park in Anaheim, California, packs more fun into every square foot. Don't miss the Haunted Mansion. (*p. 484*)

CHILDREN'S MUSEUM OF INDIANAPOLIS
Dinosaurs literally burst through the walls at this beloved institution, the largest of its type in the world. It has five floors of exhibits, including fossils from an archaeological dig. (*p. 722*)

BEARIZONA WILDLIFE CENTER
There are plenty of bears on display at the drive-through nature preserve, including fearsome grizzlies, but you might find yourself enchanted by little guys like the beavers, badgers, and porcupines. Located in Williams, Arizona, it's 50 miles south of the Grand Canyon's South Rim entrance. (*p. 566*)

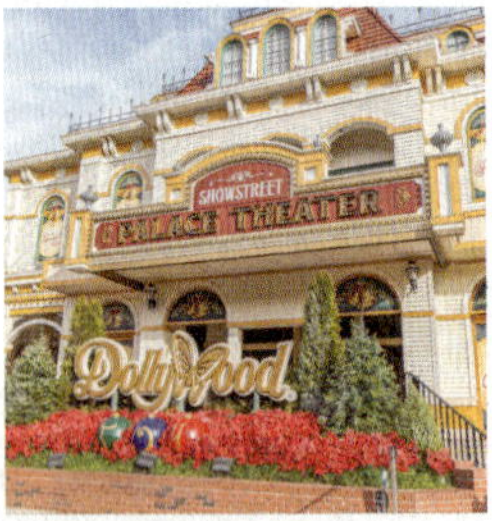

DOLLYWOOD
In the bustling town of Pigeon Forge, Tennessee, this country-music theme park is named for legendary singer and songwriter, Dolly Parton. Favorite attractions include Klondike Katie, a coal-fired steam engine, and the Lightning Rod roller coaster. (*p. 359*)

CEDAR POINT
Thrill-seekers flock to this venerable Ohio theme park, where the Steel Vengeance is the world's fastest and tallest hybrid roller coaster. It also has the steepest and longest drop and four inversions. *(p. 770)*

COLONIAL WILLIAMSBURG
You can walk the same streets as George Washington and Thomas Jefferson at Virginia's Colonial Williamsburg, where 18th-century structures have been lovingly restored. *(p. 201)*

KENNEDY SPACE CENTER
A thrill for young scientists, Florida's Kennedy Space Center lets you gaze in awe at the Space Shuttle *Atlantis*, relive the thrilling launch of *Apollo 8*, or talk with a real astronaut. *(p. 265)*

GEORGIA AQUARIUM
The largest of its type in the world, the Georgia Aquarium is home to more than 500 species of underwater creatures. It's one of the only facilities with massive whale sharks, and the playful beluga whales are adorable. *(p. 282)*

SAN DIEGO ZOO
With nearly 700 species of animals, the world's most celebrated wildlife park delights visitors of all ages. Highlights for kids include the Elephant Play Yard and the interactive Wildlife Explorers Basecamp. *(p. 479)*

THE AMERICAN MUSEUM OF NATURAL HISTORY
The 43-foot-long *T. rex* may be the signature attraction of this famed museum on Manhattan's Upper West Side, but hundreds of other amazing exhibits await, including the Hall of African Animals and the touch-friendly Gilder Center. Scenes in the *Night at the Museum* film trilogy were filmed here. *(p. 164)*

The Best Roadside Attractions in the USA

CADILLAC RANCH
Outside the Texas town of Amarillo—mentioned prominently in the song "Route 66"—is this way-out art project. The brainchild of several San Francisco hippies, it's a series of 10 spray-painted Cadillacs buried grill-first on the prairie. (*p. 626*)

LUCY THE ELEPHANT
Built in 1881 just outside Atlantic City, New Jersey, to promote real estate sales and tourism, this six-story structure is now America's oldest-surviving roadside attraction; Lucy is now even a popular overnight rental on Airbnb. (*p. 157*)

THE ENCHANTED HIGHWAY
If you're near Regent, North Dakota, locals will steer you to this 32-mile stretch of road north of town lined with metal sculptures. Massive pheasants dash across the plain, huge grasshoppers nibble on leaves, and trout leap from imaginary streams. The gift shop in Regent sells miniature versions of the larger-than-life sculptures. (*p. 422*)

JIMMY CARTER PEANUT
Inspired by the toothy grin of the country's 39th president, this giant smiling peanut is on display in his hometown of Plains, Georgia. Made from chicken wire covered with polyurethane foam, it's proved to be a remarkably durable attraction in the middle of peanut country. (*p. 287*)

PRADA MARFA

Way out in the West Texas high desert, 26 miles northwest of the funky art town of Marfa, you'll find this art installation that captures a Prada storefront stuck in time in 2005. (*p. 617*)

CARHENGE

England's prehistoric circle of standing stones is faithfully re-created in Alliance, Nebraska, except for the fact that here it's made from vintage automobiles. Just as at the original, thousands of believers congregate here whenever there's a solar eclipse. (*p. 405*)

BLUE WHALE OF CATOOSA

Rising out of its own little lake on Route 66 in Catoosa, Oklahoma, the Blue Whale is one of the region's most whimsical sights. Built in the 1970s as an anniversary present, it's taken on a life of its own as a tourist attraction. (*p. 435*)

PAUL BUNYUN AND BABE THE BLUE OX

In the middle of the 20th century, huge statues popped up all over the Midwest to catch the eye of passing motorists. Bemidji, Minnesota, is home to the larger-than-life lumberjack and his oddly colored animal companion, built to attract tourists to the logging town. (*p. 756*)

COCAINE BEAR

We swear this is a true story: back in 1985, a black bear in the Chattahoochee National Forest became a local hero after ingesting $20 million of cocaine that a drug dealer had jettisoned from an airplane. It died, but it was stuffed and put on display at Lexington's Kentucky Fun Mall. (*p. 303*)

CORN PALACE

Completed in 1921 in South Dakota, this massive, ornate structure with Russian and Moorish architectural flourishes is famed for its imaginative murals, which are redesigned each year and made entirely with corn and local natural grasses. (*p. 452*)

The Best Local Souvenirs in the USA

SWEETGRASS BASKETS
A centuries-old tradition started by the Gullah Geechee people of the Carolinas, descendants of enslaved people from Africa, these intricately woven baskets are the most popular gift item in South Carolina. Charleston City Market is a great place to shop for them.

ROSEBUD LIP BALM
You can still sample soothing salves and ointments at the century-old Rosebud Perfume Company shop in Woodsboro, Maryland. If you can't make it for a visit, pick up a tube of the luscious lip balm at any pharmacy. It's a must to avoid dry or cracked lips in wintertime.

CRYSTAL HOT SAUCE
Louisiana residents have strong opinions about the best hot sauce in the state, and there are many. Some swear by Tabasco, even though it cheats a bit by not using aged red cayenne peppers (though its factory earns points for its location on a lush salt dome called Avery Island). However, Crystal is the best seller, and simply the best.

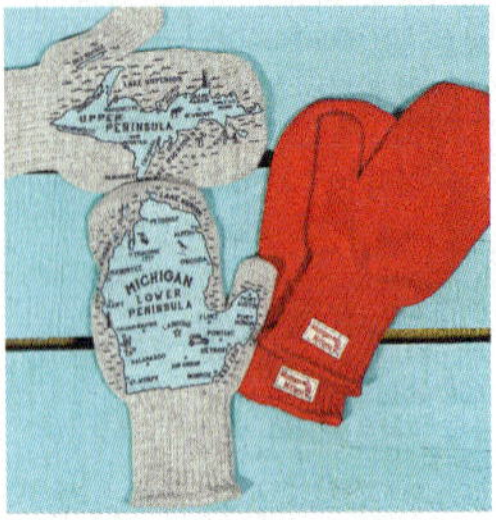

STATE-SHAPED MITTENS
Michigan and Wisconsin are locked in a bruising battle over who has the most adorable mittens. Get some emblazoned with a map of either state, and they'll surely keep you warm in a Great Lakes winter.

SHRIVER'S SALT WATER TAFFY
The oldest business (it dates to 1898) on the boardwalk in Ocean City, New Jersey, is this confectionary. The best flavors to try are banana (look for the yellow with an orange stripe) and watermelon (green with a red center).

PETERBORO PICNIC HAMPER
Made in New Hampshire, these baskets made of sturdy Appalachian white ash are perfect for packing a picnic lunch for your hike in the White Mountains of the Granite State.

Amana Woolen Mill wool throws

AMANA WOOLEN MILL WOOL THROW
Made in Iowa, these snuggly throws come in handsome plaids and stripes you'll want to keep on display. Find them at the showroom in Amana, or gift shops around the state.

HUCKLEBERRY LIQUEUR
On a visit to Montana, you can find huckleberries in everything from ice cream to barbecue sauce. Try (and take home) the huckleberry sweet cream liqueur made at Willie's Distillery in Ennis.

MINIATURE BASEBALL BAT
Kentucky's Louisville Slugger Museum and Factory boasts the world's biggest baseball bat. Pick up a much smaller version in the gift shop or at souvenir stands around the state.

MINNETONKA MOCCASINS
Named after nearby Lake Minnetonka, Minnesota's must-have footwear was first manufactured in 1946. The family-owned company proudly supports Native American organizations.

GOO GOO CLUSTERS
If you grew up in Tennessee, you grew up loving these sticky-sweet candy bars. Newcomers won't be able to resist tucking a few away in their bag for the trip back home.

CACTUS SEEDS
Arizona's giant saguaro cactus plants can grow to more than three stories tall. Grow a much smaller version at home with seeds from Desert Gatherings.

What to Watch, Read, and Listen To

Watch

THE BUCKET LIST

Even people who've never seen this 2007 film starring Jack Nicholson and Morgan Freeman have been inspired by this story of two not-so-lovable old codgers who decide to see and do everything they've been putting off for years. (The scene at California Motor Speedway will definitely make you want to watch a race, if not drive in a race car.)

FREE SOLO

If you have a fear of heights, then this 2019 documentary probably isn't for you. It follows legendary free climber Alex Honnold and his climbing partner Kevin Jorgeson as they decide to be the first to scale the 3,000-foot vertical rock face of El Capitan. It's a nail-biter, with cameraman Jimmy Chin often making the climb beside him and worried that he might distract his friend at a critical moment and watch him "fall out of frame." The cinematography is so beautiful that you'll soon be planning your own trip to Yosemite National Park. Another great documentary about rock climbing is 2017's *The Dawn Wall.*

GIRLS TRIP

Although filled with laughs, thanks in large part to the perfect comic timing and chemistry of leads Tiffany Haddish, Regina Hall, Queen Latifah, and Jada Pinkett Smith, there's real heart and plenty of travel inspiration in this 2017 romp about four friends from college reuniting years later for a vacation in New Orleans to attend the Essence Music Festival.

THE NATIONAL PARKS: AMERICA'S BEST IDEA

In addition to being beautifully filmed, this seminal six-part documentary from Ken Burns, one of the greatest filmmakers working in the genre, brings vividly to life the miracle that is the U.S. National Park system. Famous actors like Tom Hanks and John Lithgow narrate the mesmerizing account of the people, the landscapes, and the challenges behind some of America's most sacred places.

NOMADLAND

Moviegoers are fascinated with tales of people who leave everything behind and follow their dreams. This 2021 film features Oscar-winner Frances McDormand as Fern, a down-on-her-luck woman who buys a van and joins a community of nomadic people who gather in temporary communities. It just happens to be filmed in some gorgeous spots: Nevada's Black Rock Desert, California's San Bernardino National Forest, and the austerely beautiful Badlands of South Dakota.

ROUTE 66

Adjust your eyes for the gorgeous black-and-white cinematography of this beloved 116-episode series from the early 1960s that recounts the often melodramatic but entertaining exploits of hunky young buddies Buz Murdock and Ted Stiles. Available on a few free-with-ads streaming sites, the show was filmed on location at still recognizable places throughout the country (Glen Canyon Dam and Vermont's Green Mountains, for instance).

TASTE THE NATION

Longtime *Top Chef* host Padma Lakshmi sets out on her own to discover the culinary traditions of various parts of the country, especially those whose roots here go back a generation at the most. The series is part cooking show, part travelogue, and part exploration of the immigrant experience. Most memorable is her conversation with a Thai woman whose high-end food was initially rejected by Las Vegas diners used to cheap and greasy fare. She triumphs, and so does the series.

WILL & HARPER

Not long after her gender transition, former head writer at *Saturday Night Live* Harper Steele came out as trans to her good friend Will Ferrell. The two soon hatched a plan to make this poignant, courageous, and funny documentary that follows them on a cross-country road trip from New York City to Los Angeles. The parts of their journey that pass through several socially conservative communities are particularly absorbing, and yield both discouraging and uplifting moments.

Read

AMERICAN GUIDE SERIES BY THE WPA

In the late 1930s and early '40s, the WPA Federal Writers' Project produced comprehensive guides to every state as well as dozens of cities across the country. Many of these riveting, photo-filled books have been reprinted and are easily available, but it's also well worth seeking original editions at vintage bookstores or on eBay and online booksellers.

BLUE HIGHWAYS BY WILLIAM LEAST HEAT-MOON

After both his college teaching job and marriage came to unexpected ends in 1978, author William Least Heat-Moon set out in a beat-up van to explore every corner of the country, exclusively by way of non-interstates, those smaller state and federal roads—or "blue highways"—that pass directly through both big cities and small towns. The author explores his own Osage and European lineage as he meanders through the nation's diverse landscapes, meeting memorable characters along the way.

DEEP SOUTH: FOUR SEASONS ON BACK ROADS BY PAUL THEROUX

The renowned novelist and travel scribe Paul Theroux brought his compelling blend of keen (if sometimes judgmental) observation and candid conversations with strangers to this memorable account of crisscrossing America's history-rich Southern states. His route tends toward the off-the-beaten-path and includes a wide range of experiences, from college football games and gospel church services to blues festivals and barbecue joints.

DRIVE-THRU DREAMS: A JOURNEY THROUGH THE HEART OF AMERICA'S FAST-FOOD KINGDOM BY ADAM CHANDLER

In this tome, journalist Adam Chandler explores the country's complicated relationship with fast food. It starts at the industry's bootstrapping beginning, chronicling the rise of colorful characters like Kentucky Fried Chicken's Harlan Sanders, a "ham who served chicken." As he brings us up to the present, he touches on all the fast-food joints frequently stopped at during family road trips.

LASSOING THE SUN: A YEAR IN AMERICA'S NATIONAL PARKS BY MARK WOODS

The 100th anniversary of the national park system inspired writer Mark Woods to take a bucket list journey. He revisits many of the places he had first seen from the windows of the family station wagon when he was a child: Redwood, Yosemite, and the Grand Canyon, for starters. What starts out as a sentimental journey becomes something more when his travel-loving mother dies suddenly, and he's forced to confront bigger issues like love, loss, and the meaning of travel.

What to Watch, Read, and Listen To

ON THE TRAIL OF WOLVES BY PHILIPPA FORRESTER

When Philippa Forrester, her husband, and three young children relocated to the farthest reaches of Wyoming, she found that many of her neighbors were at odds with the wolves that had been reintroduced into the area. Forrester rediscovered her fascination with the creatures, and went on to learn how the contentious relationship began and what it meant for the future of the animals.

WILD HORSES OF CUMBERLAND ISLAND BY ANOUK MASSON KRANTZ

There's believed to have been a herd of horses on Cumberland Island, a remote spot off the Georgia coast, since they were brought over in the 16th century by Spanish conquistadors. In a project that was 10 years in the making, award-winning photographer Anouk Masson Krantz captures the majesty of these animals and the sandy dunes, sugar-white beaches, and old-growth forests of their habitat.

THE UNLIKELIEST BACKPACKER: FROM OFFICE DESK TO WILDERNESS BY KATHRYN BARNES

Author Kathryn Barnes and her husband decamp from their one-bedroom London apartment so that they can camp along the Pacific Crest Trail, making their way through California, Oregon, and Washington along the way. She might not be the unlikeliest of backpackers, but she was woefully unprepared. Finding her way is the book's through line, and it's inspiring for would-be hikers.

Listen

FAMILY TRIPS WITH THE MEYERS BROTHERS

On this engaging podcast, witty and good-natured comedians, actors, and siblings Seth and Josh Meyers share hilarious tales of their own travels and interview celebrity guests about their family vacations.

THE SPLENDID TABLE

This eclectic podcast helmed by the affable Francis Lam explores the rich culture of what we eat and drink, often shining a light on the foodways, recipes, and chefs of different parts of the United States. It's a must-listen if dining on regional specialties is on your bucket list.

THIS AMERICAN LIFE

With a catalog of compelling hour-long shows dating back to 1995, this venerable storytelling radio show and podcast hosted by Ira Glass explores thought-provoking and often quite surprising tales of the American experience. Some shows touch on travel explicitly, and in many the geographical setting is integral to the story.

WILD IDEAS WORTH LIVING

A lot of us want to hike the Appalachian Trail, but this podcast ups the ante by talking with a guy who ran the whole way and set a record. It's these kinds of interviews that make Wild Ideas Worth Living so inspiring. Host Shelby Stanger, who quit her job to pursue a more adventurous life, seems to really love talking with others who've done the same.

Chapter 2

NEW ENGLAND

Updated by Jordan Barry, Diane Bair, Adam H. Callahan, Andrew Collins, Bob Curley, and Alexandra Hall

WELCOME TO NEW ENGLAND

TOP REASONS TO GO

★ **Leaf-peeping:** Embrace autumn at Moosehead Lake in Maine, the Kancamagus Highway in New Hampshire, Scenic Route 100 in Vermont, and U.S. 7 in the Berkshires.

★ **American history:** Explore fascinating colonial historic sites, such as Plimoth Patuxet Museums, Salem, Boston's Freedom Trail, and Walden Pond.

★ **Coastal charm:** Sail, bike, and beachcomb on a beautiful island, maybe Nantucket or Martha's Vineyard in Massachusetts, Mount Desert Island in Maine, or Block Island in Rhode Island.

★ **Mountain majesty:** In Vermont's Green Mountains, New Hampshire's White Mountains, and interior Maine, some of the East Coast's tallest peaks beckon hikers in summer and skiers and snowboarders in winter.

★ **Seafood:** Eat your way through the region's many hubs of artisanal food and drink, including Burlington, New Haven, Portland, and Providence.

1 Connecticut. Vibrant small cities, alluring coastal towns, grand old inns, and a pair of famous casinos appeal to a wide range of visitors.

2 Maine. Classic villages, rocky shorelines, lobster shacks, and picturesque main streets abound along the coast, while the rugged interior attracts outdoors enthusiasts.

3 Massachusetts. Home to New England's largest city, this diverse state also offers beaches, a thriving arts scene, and elegant country inns.

4 New Hampshire. Portsmouth is the star of the state's 18-mile coastline, while the Lakes Region is a popular summertime escape and the White Mountains' dramatic vistas attract year-round visitors.

5 Rhode Island. The nation's smallest state has big draws: great sailing and glitzy mansions in Newport, beautiful beaches in South County and Block Island, and a hip scene in Providence.

6 Vermont. The peaceful Green Mountain State has farms, rural towns and lively small cities, quiet country lanes, and bustling ski resorts.

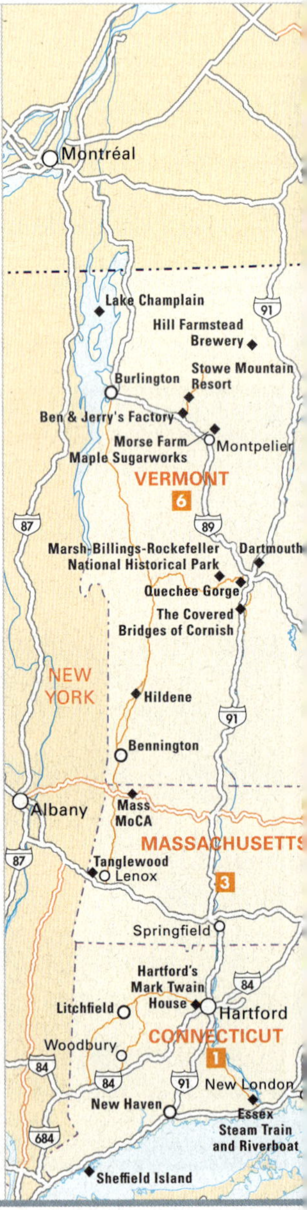

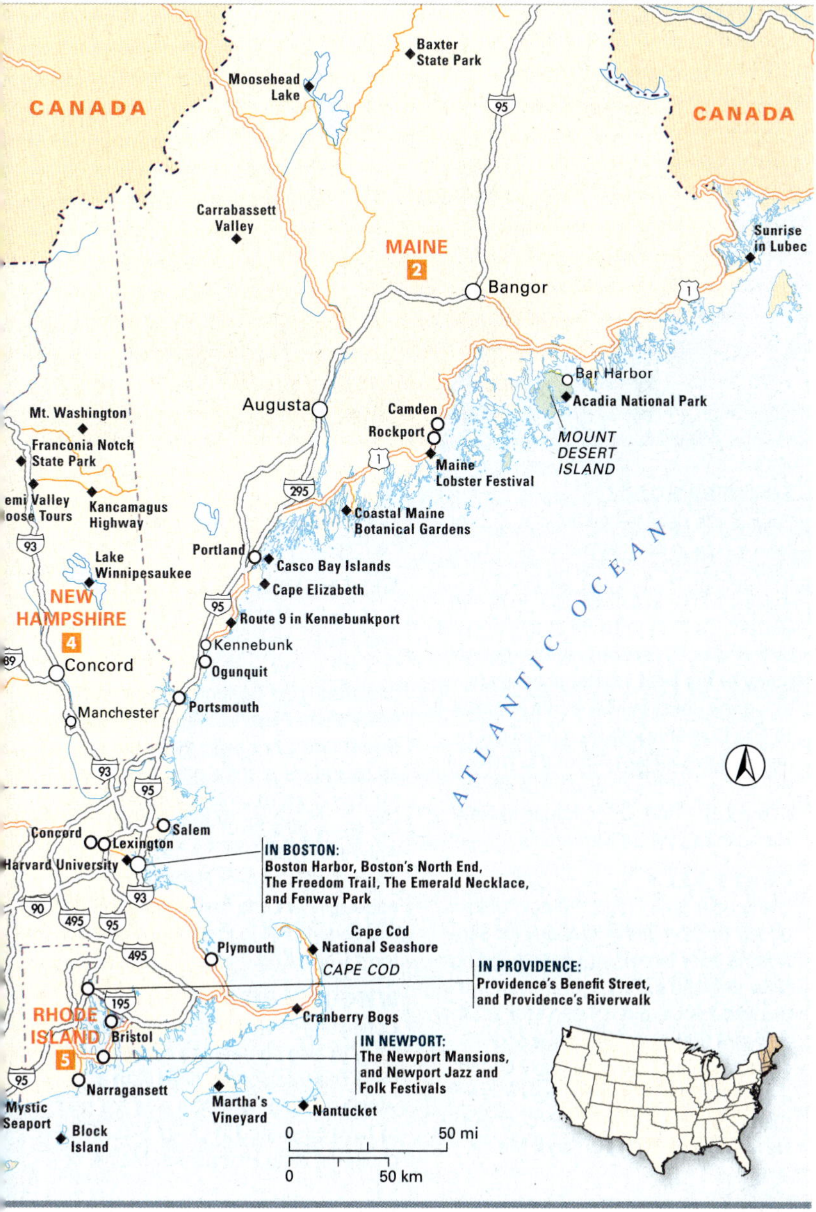
CANADA
CANADA
Baxter State Park
Moosehead Lake
Carrabassett Valley
MAINE 2
Bangor
Sunrise in Lubec
Bar Harbor
Acadia National Park
MOUNT DESERT ISLAND
Augusta
Camden
Rockport
Maine Lobster Festival
Coastal Maine Botanical Gardens
Portland
Casco Bay Islands
Cape Elizabeth
Route 9 in Kennebunkport
Kennebunk
Ogunquit
Portsmouth
Mt. Washington
Franconia Notch State Park
Kancamagus Highway
Lake Winnipesaukee
NEW HAMPSHIRE 4
Concord
Manchester
ATLANTIC OCEAN
Salem
Concord
Lexington
Harvard University
IN BOSTON:
Boston Harbor, Boston's North End, The Freedom Trail, The Emerald Necklace, and Fenway Park
Plymouth
Cape Cod National Seashore
CAPE COD
IN PROVIDENCE:
Providence's Benefit Street, and Providence's Riverwalk
RHODE ISLAND 5
Bristol
Cranberry Bogs
IN NEWPORT:
The Newport Mansions, and Newport Jazz and Folk Festivals
Narragansett
Martha's Vineyard
Nantucket
Mystic Seaport
Block Island
0 50 mi
0 50 km
95
1
1
295
95
93
95
93
90
495
95
495
195
95

WHAT TO EAT AND DRINK IN NEW ENGLAND

Lobster roll

LOBSTER ROLLS

Passionate debates take place all over New England each summer about how lobster rolls should be served: tossed with mayo or drizzled in drawn butter? It's best to arrive at this answer by trying both versions. And although many of the best lobster shacks are along the coast in Maine, it's possible to find heavenly lobster rolls all over New England, from Abbot's Lobster in the Rough on the Connecticut shore to the Little Red Schoolhouse in New Hampshire's White Mountains.

CRAFT BEER

Many beer fans credit the now ubiquitous Boston Beer Company (of Sam Adams beer fame) with spearheading New England's craft beer movement in the mid-1980s, but it wasn't for another 20 years that truly innovative and entrepreneurial brewers really began making waves. There are now more than 600 craft breweries throughout New England, with Portland, Maine, supporting more per capita than any city in America and Vermont with more per capita than any state.

NEW HAVEN-STYLE PIZZA

Among the first U.S. cities to popularize pizza, New Haven, Connecticut, first fell in love with coal-fired-oven, blistered-crust Neapolitan pies when Frank Pepe Pizzeria opened on Wooster Street (the city's tiny Little Italy) in 1925. Pepe's is still a go-to (especially for its signature white clam version), but many fans favor competitors Sally's Apizza and Modern Apizza. Exceptional pizza thrives all over New England, especially in Little Italy neighborhoods, like Federal Hill in Providence and Boston's North End.

WHOOPIE PIES

Consisting of two soft, round cakes (they're also sometimes called moon pies) and traditionally filled with a vanilla frosting, whoopie pies are said to have originated in either Massachusetts, New Hampshire, Maine, or (let's not even go there) Pennsylvania, but they're a favorite sweet all around New England today. Maine probably leads the way in whoopie pie adoration, and shops there now offer all kinds of imaginative flavors like salted caramel or gingerbread.

PANCAKES AND MAPLE SYRUP

The quintessential New England breakfast, fluffy pancakes topped with local maple syrup (with Vermont and New Hampshire being the region's top producers) are a year-round delight. Note that Rhode Island has its own variation, the silver-dollar-size johnnycake made with cornmeal batter. And throughout New England, pumpkin pancakes are a hit in autumn.

ARTISANAL CHEESE

From smaller dairies with cult followings—like Willow Hill Farm and Twig Farm in Vermont and Sandwich Creamery in New Hampshire—to bigger national players such as Cabot Creamery, Jasper Hill, and Vermont Creamery, New England abounds with exceptional cheese makers. To sample some of the best, attend the Vermont Cheesemakers Festival, typically held in July at Shelburne Farms.

Pancakes with maple syrup

Clam chowder

CLAMS

These smiling bivalves are a top delicacy up and down the coast but especially in Rhode Island, home of the fictional town of Quahog on TV's *Family Guy* (in honor of the state's most popular clam variety). Quahogs (like littlenecks and cherrystones) are hard-shell clams and are popular in famed creamy New England clam chowder (the Rhode Island version has a clear rather than creamy broth), pasta sauces, and eaten raw on the half shell. Soft-shell clams, known as steamers, are what you find fried (whole belly or in strips) at clam shacks all around the region.

APPLES

Prime apple-picking in New England starts in late summer and can last until the first week of November. It's at this time that numerous orchards and cider mills offer apple-picking and even weekend festivals featuring fresh cider, pies, and fritters, along with music, hayrides, and other family fun. Cider doughnuts are a big part of the tradition (there's cider in the batter), and New England also has a bevy of superb hard-cider makers.

Connecticut

"Connecticut Yankees" or "Nutmeggers" enjoy 253 miles of shoreline that blows salty sea air over beach communities like Old Lyme and Mystic, while patchwork hills and peaked mountains fill the state's northwestern corner and once-upon-a-time mill towns line rivers such as the Housatonic. Connecticut has seemingly endless farmland in the northeast, where cows might just outnumber people, as well as chic New York City bedroom communities such as Greenwich and New Canaan and increasingly hip cities like New Haven and West Hartford.

Capital: Hartford

Population: 3,675,069

Area: 5,018 square miles

Statehood Date: January 9, 1788

Major Airports: Bradley International Airport (BDL); Tweed New Haven Airport (HVN)

Travel and Tourism Information: 🌐 *www.ctvisit.com* 🌐 *www.ctinsider.com*

Famous Residents: Eli Whitney (inventor); Harriet Beecher Stowe (writer); Katharine Hepburn (actress); Paul Newman and Joanne Woodward (actors); Ocean Vuong (writer and poet)

Fun Fact: Connecticut is a state for readers, laying claim to the nation's first dictionary (published in 1806 by West Hartford native Noah Webster, whose house is now a museum), original publicly funded free library (welcoming patrons since 1803 in Salisbury), and oldest continuously published newspaper (the *Hartford Courant*, going strong since 1764).

Mystic Seaport

The Nation's Largest Maritime Museum

The largest maritime museum in the United States, Mystic Seaport encompasses 19 acres of indoor and outdoor exhibits, and includes a re-created New England coastal village, a working shipyard, and more than 2 million artifacts that provide a fascinating look at the area's rich shipbuilding and seafaring heritage. In narrow streets and historic homes and buildings, craftspeople give demonstrations of open-hearth cooking, weaving, and other skills. The museum's more than 500 vessels include the *Charles W. Morgan*, the last remaining wooden whaling ship afloat (which you can climb aboard to explore). Surrounding downtown Mystic has plenty of interesting boutiques and galleries, especially in **Olde Mistick Village**, a centrally located collection of charming shops and restaurants. ✉ 75 *Greenmanville Ave., Mystic, CT* 🌐 *www.mysticseaport.org*

Don't Miss

Just up the road, **Mystic Aquarium** is best known for its famous beluga whales, but you can also see African penguins, harbor seals, Steller sea lions, sea horses, and Pacific octopuses here. ✉ 55 *Coogan Blvd., Mystic, CT* 🌐 *www.mysticaquarium.org*

When to Go

The seaport and aquarium are open year-round, and there are a number of events held in every season. Keep in mind that summer gets very *very* crowded.

Getting Here and Around

Mystic is off Interstate 95 in coastal southeastern Connecticut, just east of the small city of New London, which has ferries to Long Island, New York. Some Amtrak trains stop a 10-minute walk from downtown Mystic.

New Haven

A Surprisingly Impressive Arts Hub

New Haven is best known as the home of **Yale University**, whose prestigious museums and highly respected theaters downtown help make New Haven one of New England's leading arts centers. Within easy walking distance of the stately 16-acre New Haven Green and the gracious Gothic architecture of Yale's campus, you can view original works by John Constable and Thomas Gainsborough in the sleek **Yale Center for British Art**, see everything from Etruscan vases to Picassos and van Goghs at the **Yale University Art Gallery** (both buildings designed by Louis I. Kahn), and admire Audubon prints and an original Gutenberg Bible at the Beinecke Rare Book & Manuscript Library.

Don't Miss

New Haven has a world-class theater scene, and tickets to shows are quite reasonable compared to New York City. Top venues include the **Shubert Performing Arts Center** (which also presents music and dance) and the **Yale Repertory Theatre**, where Yale drama students (including Lupita Nyong'o, Frances McDormand, Paul Newman, and Meryl Streep) have taken the stage. The highly regarded **Long Wharf Theatre**, once a venue, is now a roving troupe performing throughout the city and state.

Best Offbeat Attraction

One of the more peculiar stops is the Cushing Center at Yale's Whitney Medical Library, where you can examine over 400 jars containing human brains.

Getting Here and Around

New Haven's downtown core is easily reached from Interstates 95 and 91 and several train routes via Union Station (including Metro-North from Grand Central in New York City).

Hartford's Mark Twain House

Mark Twain's World

Built in 1874, this grand 25-room mansion was the home of Samuel Langhorne Clemens, better known as Mark Twain, until 1891. Twain wrote his most important works during the years he lived here, including *The Adventures of Tom Sawyer, Adventures of Huckleberry Finn*, and *A Connecticut Yankee in King Arthur's Court*. The house features interior decor designed by Louis Comfort Tiffany, including elaborate stenciling and carved woodwork. Visit the Billiard Room where Twain did his writing and see the bed carved with angels where he slept. A contemporary museum on the grounds presents a Ken Burns documentary, a café, and gift shop. The Nook Farm neighborhood also contains the Connecticut Science Center, the State Capitol, and Wadsworth Atheneum Museum of Art. ✉ *351 Farmington Ave., Hartford, CT* 🌐 *www.marktwainhouse.org*

Don't Miss

Next to Twain's house, you'll find the **Harriet Beecher Stowe Center**, the 1871 Victorian Gothic cottage where the abolitionist and author (1811–96) spent her final years. Stowe's personal writing table and effects are inside. ✉ *77 Forest St., Hartford, CT* 🌐 *www.harrietbeecherstowecenter.org*

When to Go

The Mark Twain House is decked out for the holidays in December, and the gorgeously landscaped historic gardens are at their peak from late spring through early fall.

Getting Here and Around

The museum and Nook Farm neighborhood are a five-minute drive west of downtown Hartford, just off Interstate 84, and a 25-minute walk from Hartford Union Station, with frequent Hartford Line trains running between New Haven and Springfield, Massachusetts.

Essex Steam Train and Riverboat

Connecticut's Most Scenic Ride

Offering some of the best views of the Connecticut River valley from 1920s-era coaches pulled by a vintage steam locomotive and an old-fashioned riverboat, the Essex Steam Train and Riverboat is the only steam train and riverboat connection in the country. Chug through archetypal New England landscapes, from the neatly preserved 19th-century shipbuilding town of Essex to equally charming Deep River, passing by genuinely quaint hamlets and tidal wetlands along the way. At Deep River Landing, passengers board the vintage *Becky Thatcher* riverboat for a serene cruise along the Connecticut River. ✉ *1 Railroad Ave., Essex, CT* 🌐 *www.essexsteamtrain.com*

Don't Miss

A magnificent 1876 Victorian-gingerbread "wedding cake" theater, East Haddam's **Goodspeed Opera House** played a vital role in the preservation and development of American musical theater and still offers performances April through early December. ✉ *6 Main St., East Haddam, CT* 🌐 *www.goodspeed.org*

When to Go

Essex Steam Train and Riverboat runs from May through October (though many train-only special events run beyond those months, including family-friendly holiday rides with Santa), but the scenery is especially stunning in prime leaf-peeping season in late October.

Getting Here and Around

Essex is near the coast on Route 9, just off Interstate 95. Bucolic Route 154 meanders up through the same charming towns as the steam train and riverboat. To get to Gillette Castle, take Route 148 and the historic Chester–Hadlyme Ferry.

Litchfield

The Quintessential New England Town

The northwestern Connecticut town founded in 1719 offers a combination of beautiful scenery (especially during leaf-peeping season), historic charm, great hiking, and critically acclaimed dining. The cultural hub of the surrounding Litchfield Hills, the town's impressive Litchfield Green and white Colonial and Greek Revival homes that line the broad, tree-shaded streets were once graced by the likes of Harriet Beecher Stowe, author of *Uncle Tom's Cabin*, and her brother, abolitionist preacher Henry Ward Beecher, both born and raised here, as well as many famous Americans who earned their law degrees at the Litchfield Law School, founding father Aaron Burr among them. These days, the village center abounds with lovely boutiques and art spaces, including Alofft Gallery, Jeffrey Tillou Antiques, and Hope and Honey.

Don't Miss

The 4,000-acre **White Memorial Conservation Center** houses top-notch natural-history exhibits, including 30 bird-watching platforms, two self-guided nature trails, several boardwalks, boating facilities, and 40 miles of hiking, cross-country skiing, and horseback-riding trails. ✉ *80 Whitehall Rd., Litchfield, CT* 🌐 *www.whitememorialcc.org*

Best Detour

Make the scenic 15-mile drive south to the colonial town of **Woodbury**, which is said to have more antiques shops than in the rest of the Litchfield Hills combined. Five magnificent colonial churches line Main Street, which is also home to one of the state's top farm-to-table eateries, Good News Restaurant and Bar.

Getting Here and Around

Litchfield's walkable downtown is at the junction of U.S. 202 and Route 63, about 30 miles west of Hartford.

Sheffield Island

Clambakes at a Historic Lighthouse

It doesn't get more enchanting New England than sea, sand, and a clambake feast beneath a picturesque lighthouse. Tuesday nights in summer, the Seaport ferry in South Norwalk takes passengers on a scenic boat ride to 3-acre Sheffield Island for a tour of the 10-room, four-story 1868 lighthouse and then serves a classic New England clambake—BYOB, so bring drinks and cups if you want them. Collect seashells on the beach, take in the Long Island Sound views, and then head to the tented pavilion on the lighthouse lawn for a sunset dinner that includes steamed clams and mussels—for an upcharge, you can splurge for steamed lobster or local oysters. Ferries leave from the SoNo District, which is adjacent to the outstanding Maritime Aquarium. ✉ *Washington and N. Water St., Norwalk, CT* 🌐 *www.seaport.org*

Don't Miss

Norwalk's SoNo business district is a hot spot for trendy shopping, culture, and dining, most of it along North Main and Water Streets.

When to Go

The clambakes take place on Tuesday evening from July through August, but you can visit the lighthouse sans clambake throughout the summer via ferry tours that take you around Norwalk Harbor and to the lighthouse.

Getting Here and Around

SoNo is just off Interstate 95 in the southwestern Connecticut city of Norwalk, and frequent Metro-North trains between New York City and New Haven stop at South Norwalk station.

When in Connecticut

CONNECTICUT ART TRAIL

With locations spanning from New London to Greenwich and north to Hartford, the Connecticut Art Trail connects 30 world-class museums and historic sites, with a focus on Connecticut's role as the cradle of the American Impressionist movement that thrived here from shortly after the Civil War until the 1910s. A must is the Weir Farm National Historic Park in Wilton, where you can tour the farmhouse and grounds that belonged to one of the icons of American Impressionism, J. Alden Weir.

Do This: The nation's oldest continuously operating public art museum, the stunning Wadsworth Atheneum Museum of Art in Hartford contains not only superb collections of American (and European) Impressionists, but also almost 50,000 works across 5,000 years, along with 7,000 items documenting African-American history and culture in partnership with the Amistad Foundation. ⊕ *600 Main St., Hartford, CT* ⊕ *www.thewadsworth.org*

FOXWOODS RESORT CASINO

Owned and operated by the Mashantucket Pequot Tribal Nation on reservation lands near Ledyard, Foxwoods is the largest resort casino in North America. The enormous compound, which opened in 1992, draws 40,000-plus visitors daily to its seven casinos with more than 3,400 slot machines, 300 gaming tables, and a 3,600-seat bingo parlor. There's also luxury hotels, spas, a retail concourse, numerous dining options, and several entertainment venues. ✉ *350 Trolley Line Blvd., Ledyard, CT* ⊕ *www.foxwoods.com*

Do This: About 15 minutes away from Foxwoods, the Mohegan Tribe of Connecticut, known as Wolf People, operates Mohegan Sun casino, with more than 300,000 square feet of gaming space in three casino areas, totaling nearly 5,000 slot machines and more than 300 gaming tables. The Mohegan Sun Arena is home to the WNBA's Connecticut Sun. ✉ *1 Mohegan Sun Blvd., Norwich, CT* ⊕ *mohegansun.com*

GROTON'S SUBMARINE HERITAGE

Home to the Naval Submarine Base New London (the U.S. Navy's first) and to the Electric Boat Division of General Dynamics, designer and manufacturer of nuclear submarines, Groton is often referred to as the "submarine capital of the world." Kids and adults love learning about these intriguing underwater vessels at the Submarine Force Museum, where you can tour the world's first nuclear-powered submarine, the *Nautilus*, which was launched and commissioned in Groton in 1954. It's permanently berthed here at the museum, a repository of artifacts, documents, photographs, and interactive exhibits detailing the history of the U.S. Submarine Force component of the U.S. Navy. ✉ *1 Crystal Lake Rd., Groton, CT* ⊕ *www.ussnautilus.org*

Do This: Across the Thames River in the historic seafaring city of New London, visit the 100-acre campus of redbrick buildings that's home to the prestigious U.S. Coast Guard Academy. A museum explores the Coast Guard's 200 years of maritime service and includes some 200 ship models, as well as figureheads, paintings, uniforms, and cannons. ✉ *15 Mohegan Ave. Pkwy., New London, CT* ⊕ *www.history.uscg.mil/museum*

LAKE COMPOUNCE

Opened in 1846, the country's oldest amusement park is a charming blend of old-fashioned family fun and modern thrills. Today's attractions include a lakefront beach and Connecticut's largest water park with a clipper ship that dumps a 300-gallon bucket of water on unsuspecting guests.

Do This: Roller coasters include the Wildcat (New England's oldest roller coaster), Boulder Dash (the "World's #1 wooden coaster"), and vertigo-inducing Zoomerang. ✉ *185 Enterprise Dr., Bristol, CT* 🌐 *www.lakecompounce.com*

NEW HAVEN PIZZA

Even more famous than Yale among foodies, New Haven's Wooster Street has been drawing pizza lovers since Frank Pepe's Pizzeria Napoletana opened in 1925. The city's unique "apizza" style is defined by its thin, chewy, blistered crusts, some still baked in coal-fired ovens. Many popular purveyors exist, but for everything from the original tomato pie to white clam, potato, and other specialties, start with the "Big Three": Pepe's, which serves a coveted fresh tomato pie seasonally; Sally's Apizza, Pepe's main rival since Frank's nephew opened it two blocks away in 1938; and Modern Apizza, which is a 20-minute walk away and has been going strong since 1934.

Do This: Connecticut's tourism board has really gone hard in advertising itself as the "Pizza Capitol of the United States" with New Haven's aforementioned apizza the favorite child. But Connecticut is also the originator of Greek-style pizza, with a pan-baked crust that results in a particularly bready, focaccia-like texture. It was invented by a Greek-Albanian immigrant in New London in 1955, but you can find it in pizza parlors around the state (if a spot isn't advertised as New Haven– or New York–style pizza, it's probably Greek-style).

PHILIP JOHNSON GLASS HOUSE

For nearly 60 years, right up until his death in 2005, the seminal modernist architect Philip Johnson lived with his partner in this modest but visually mesmerizing glass-walled house that he spent three years designing in the late 1940s. Per his bequest, ownership of the house passed on to the National Trust for Historic Preservation, which gives guided tours of this fascinating structure, which also includes other parts of the 49-acre estate in the affluent commuter town of New Canaan.

Do This: There are several tour options available from April through December, including a basic one-hour house tour, but for the most immersive experience, book the Extended Tour, which lasts 2½ hours and covers more of the estate, including Johnson's studio and painting and sculpture galleries, traversing a mile of pathways. ✉ *199 Elm St., New Canaan, CT* 🌐 *www.theglasshouse.org*

UCONN BASKETBALL

For professional sports, most Connecticut residents choose allegiance between Boston or NYC teams, but in terms of college basketball, everyone bleeds blue and roots for the Huskies. Both the men's and women's basketball teams of the University of Connecticut in Storrs are two of the most decorated in NCAA history: the men have won six national championships and 45 conference titles while the women are the most successful college basketball dynasty in the nation (men's or women's), with 12 national championships, and the two longest winning streaks in college basketball history, with an astounding

About Our Writers

Adam H. Callaghan currently lives in New Haven, Connecticut. He believes that the Connecticut coast has the Northeast's most scenic train line and he is constantly amazed that a city as small as New Haven has one of the world's best pizza styles. He is a freelance editor and writer specializing in food and drink, travel, and sustainability, and currently works as a Quality Team Developmental Editor for *Food & Wine*.

111, and then 90, straight wins. ✉ *2098 Hillside Rd., Storrs, CT* 🌐 *uconnhuskies.com*

Do This: Seeing a UCONN home game at Gampel Pavilion is a must, but while you're on campus, grab some ice cream at the UCONN Dairy Bar (the university is also well-known for its agricultural and animal science programs). ✉ *17 Manter Rd., Storrs, CT* 🌐 *dining.uconn.edu/uconn-dairy-bar*

Cool Places to Stay

Hotel Marcel. This Brutalist icon, designed by Bauhaus legend Marcel Breuer for Armstrong Rubber Company in the 1960s, is now the country's first Passive House–certified hotel, boasting a net-zero carbon footprint. All 165 stylish guest rooms are powered by renewable electricity generated on-site and potent insulation doubles as robust soundproofing. ✉ *500 Sargent Dr., New Haven, CT* 🌐 *www.hotelmarcel.com*

Mayflower Inn & Spa. Running streams, rambling stone walls, and rare-specimen trees fill this country manor–style inn's 28 manicured acres, which include a 20,000-square-foot spa and one of the state's most refined restaurants. Bonus: the inn and its charming town inspired the beloved *Gilmore Girls* TV series. ✉ *118 Woodbury Rd., Washington, CT* 🌐 *www.aubergeresorts.com/mayflower*

Winvian. This private 113-acre hideaway consists of 18 imaginative and luxuriously outfitted cottages, each with a distinct, often amusing, theme: the Stone Cottage is made with massive boulders with a wavy-slate roof and an enormous fireplace while the Helicopter Cottage contains—you guessed it—a genuine 17,000-pound U.S. Coast Guard helicopter (the fuselage has been refitted with a wet bar). ✉ *155 Alain White Rd., Morris, CT* 🌐 *www.winvian.com*

Essential Eats

Abbott's Lobster in the Rough. To feast on some of the state's best mussels, clams, and Connecticut-style lobster rolls—served warm and dripping with drawn butter—head to this seasonal stalwart in sleepy Noank, a few miles southwest of Mystic. Most seating is outdoors, overlooking the picturesque Mystic River. ✉ *117 Pearl St., Noank, CT* 🌐 *www.abbottslobster.com*

Coracora. This vibrant eatery is named for the small mountain town from which the founders emigrated. Their daughters, chefs Macarena and Grecia Ludena, are now stewards of family recipes and creative interpretations of Peruvian flavors, from the classic steak stir-fry lomo saltado to a vegan tiger's milk ceviche featuring avocado and quinoa. ✉ *162 Shield St., West Hartford, CT* 🌐 *www.coracoraeats.com*

Louis's Lunch. For another taste of New Haven history, visit this vintage luncheonette that opened in 1895 and, per the Library of Congress, is the birthplace of the "hamburger sandwich." Though evidence of earlier examples has since emerged, it's still an excellent place to get a quality, no-frills burger cooked on an old-fashioned cast-iron grill. ✉ *261 Crown St., New Haven, CT* 🌐 *louislunch.com*

The Port of Call. This world-class cocktail bar—upstairs distinguished, downstairs divey—has a kitchen to match and frequent live jazz and drag shows. Informed by her Puerto Rican heritage, chef Reneé Touponce artfully transforms the local bounty into "mofongo" made of fermented parsnips with Stonington red shrimp or empanadas stuffed with sweet corn. ✉ *15 Water St., Mystic, CT* 🌐 *www.theportofcallct.com*

Maine

Counting all its nooks, crannies, and crags, Maine's coast would stretch for thousands of miles if you could pull it straight. The southern coast is the most visited section, stretching north from Kittery to just outside Portland, but don't let that stop you from heading farther "Down East" (this nautical term is Maine-speak for "up the coast"), where you'll be rewarded with the majestic mountains and rugged coastline of popular Acadia National Park. Slow down to explore the museums, galleries, and shops in the larger towns and cities, like Portland.

Capital: Augusta

Population: 1,405,012

Area: 30,845 square miles

Statehood Date: March 15, 1820

Major Airports: Portland International Jetport (PWM); Bangor International Jetport (BGR); Augusta State Airport (KAUG)

Travel and Tourism Information: *www.visitmaine.com www.mainetourism.com www.maine.gov*

Famous Residents: Stephen King (horror author); Martha Stewart (lifestyle queen/entrepreneur); Henry Wadsworth Longfellow (poet); Anna Kendrick (actress); Andrew Wyeth (painter)

Fun Fact: It's always been highly debated where New England clam chowder was invented, and what the ingredients should be. But Mainers have historically felt so strongly about it that in 1938, the state legislature actually proposed a bill to outlaw any version containing tomatoes. The penalty for anyone found guilty? To dig up an entire barrel of clams during high tide.

Acadia National Park

The Highest Point on the North Atlantic Seaboard

At 1,530 feet, Cadillac Mountain dominates New England's only national park, Acadia, a rugged 49,000-acre tract of surf-pounded granite coastline and an interior graced by sculpted mountains, sheer cliffs, quiet ponds, and lush, deciduous forests. The park also has graceful stone bridges, miles of carriage roads, and a 27-mile Park Loop Road, which you can drive to Cadillac's summit. But the most memorable way to access the summit is to hike to the top via the 4-mile round-trip North Ridge Trail. ✉ *25 Visitor Center Rd., Bar Harbor, ME* 🌐 *www.nps.gov/acad*

Don't Miss

Bar Harbor is the artistic, culinary, and social center of Mount Desert Island, and the main entry point to Acadia National Park. Distinctive shops, excellent restaurants, and historic buildings are clustered along Main, Mount Desert, and Cottage Streets; take a stroll down West Street to admire Bar Harbor's many fine old houses.

Best Restaurant

This is how local history shines: the Asticou Hotel's restaurant was owned by the area's big-name families for eons, but has since been bought and come into its own. Renamed **Dahlia's**, the view, food, and setting now perfectly encapsulate Acadia's fusion of civilization and nature. ✉ *15 Peabody Dr., Northeast Harbor, ME* 🌐 *www.asticoumaine.com*

When to Go

The trails and inlets of Acadia National Park, as well as the village of Bar Harbor, are at their most stunning from June through October.

Getting Here and Around

The park and Bar Harbor are on Mount Desert Island, off Route 3, about 40 miles south of Interstate 95 in Bangor.

Portland

A Stellar Eating and Drinking City

Maine's largest city may be considered small by national standards—its population is just 69,000—but its character, spirit, and fantastic food and beverage scene make it feel much larger. It's well worth at least a day or two of exploration, even if all you do is spend the entire time eating and drinking at the many phenomenal restaurants, cocktail bars, and craft breweries scattered across its cobblestoned blocks. A good place to begin is in the historic Old Port district, at any of the town's award-winning eateries (Duck Fat, Fore Street, Scales, Eventide) before hitting some breweries in the nearby East Bayside neighborhood (such as Rising Tide and Austin Street).

Don't Miss

At the **Portland Museum of Art**, Maine's largest public art institution's collection includes fine seascapes and landscapes by Winslow Homer, John Marin, Andrew Wyeth, Edward Hopper, Marsden Hartley, and other American painters. ✉ *7 Congress Sq, Portland, ME* 🌐 *www.portlandmuseum.org*

Best Restaurants

Traditional Maine fare meets inventive and scrumptious fine dining in the artful kitchen of **Twelve** (🌐 *www.twelvemaine.com*), perched on the Portland Foreside waterfront. And don't pass up a chance to try Maine potato-based doughnuts at the **Holy Donut** (🌐 *www.theholydonut.com*), glazed in flavors such as dark chocolate–sea salt, maple, pomegranate, triple berry, and chai, or stuffed with delicious fillings like bacon and cheddar or ricotta.

Getting Here and Around

Portland is off Interstate 95 via Interstate 295 in southwestern Maine.

Cape Elizabeth

Iconic Lighthouses

Venture along scenic Highway 77 through South Portland to affluent Cape Elizabeth, where a detour along two-lane Shore Road shows off the famed **Portland Head Light,** which you may recognize from Edward Hopper's eponymous 1927 painting. The towering, white-stone lighthouse—commissioned by George Washington in 1790—stands over the keeper's quarters, a white home with a blazing red roof. It's now a museum that anchors the walking paths, beach, and picnic areas of 90-acre Fort Williams Park. Continue south to the dramatic 1828 **Cape Elizabeth Light,** which Winslow Homer depicted in numerous paintings. You can get a great photo of it from the end of Two Lights Road in the surrounding state park of the same name. ✉ *1000 Shore Rd., Cape Elizabeth, ME* 🌐 *www.portlandheadlight.com*

Don't Miss

At the tip of Cape Elizabeth's gorgeous Prout's Neck peninsula, the seaside **Winslow Homer Studio** was the great landscape painter's home between 1883 until his death in 1910. It's easy to see how this rocky, jagged peninsula might have been inspiring. The Portland Museum of Art leads 2½-hour strolls through the historic property; just note that those strolls can book up far in advance, so call ahead. ✉ *5 Winslow Homer Rd., Scarborough, ME* 🌐 *www.portlandmuseum.org/homer*

When to Go

Summer through mid-fall is the best time to visit Cape Elizabeth and the lighthouses, especially as Winslow Homer Studio is closed late fall through early spring.

Getting Here and Around

Cape Elizabeth is off Route 77, 5 miles southeast of Portland.

Baxter State Park

Hike the North End of the Appalachian Trail

Baxter State Park is the jewel in the crown of northern Maine: a 210,000-acre wilderness area that surrounds **Mt. Katahdin**, Maine's highest mountain and the terminus of the Appalachian Trail. Every year, the 5,267-foot peak draws thousands of hikers to make the daylong summit, rewarding them with stunning views of forests, mountains, and lakes. The crowds climbing Katahdin can be formidable on clear summer days and fall weekends, so if it's solitude you crave, tackle one of the park's many other mountains. 🌐 *www.baxterstatepark.org*

Don't Miss

A spectacular 92-mile corridor of lakes, ponds, streams, and rivers, the **Allagash Wilderness Waterway** cuts through vast commercial forests, beginning near the northwestern corner of Baxter State Park and running north to the town of Allagash, 10 miles from the Canadian border. From May to mid-October, the Allagash is prime canoeing and camping country.

Best Outfitter

Based in Millinocket, New England Outdoor Center offers guided hikes throughout Baxter State Park, including treks to Katahdin's summit. But these knowledgeable pros can also get you out canoeing and kayaking on the Allagash and St. John rivers and white-water rafting on the Penobscot River. 🌐 *www.neoc.com*

Getting Here and Around

Millinocket, on Route 157 about 10 miles west of Interstate 95, is the gateway to Baxter State Park and Allagash Wilderness Waterway. It's about a 15-mile drive to get to the park.

Route 9 in Kennebunkport

Maine's Prettiest Coastal Road

Begin the stunning Route 9 coastal drive at U.S. 1 south of Kennebunk, following the road east through the famous resort community of Kennebunkport, sometimes described as the Hamptons of the Pine Tree State. A resort area since the 19th century, its most recent residents—the dynastic Bush family—have made it even more famous. Follow Route 9 east to the fishing village of **Cape Porpoise**, and plan on some beach-combing along breathtaking 3-mile-long **Goose Rock Beach**. The route continues past the charming resort villages of Camp Ellis and Ocean Park to Saco Bay, where you might stop for a picnic at Ferry Beach State Park.

Don't Miss

Clothing boutiques, art galleries, and convivial restaurants line Kennebunkport's bustling Dock Square, spreading out along the nearby streets and alleys. Walk onto the drawbridge to admire the tidal Kennebunk River.

Best Family Activity

The incredibly family-friendly **Nonantum Resort** on the sparkling Kennebunk River, with its poolside kids club (next to civilized dining for parents), partners with the *Pineapple Ketch*—a three-mast sailboat offering 1½-hour cruises midday and again at sunset. 🌐 *www.nonantumresort.com*

When to Go

This scenic coastal town is at its prime in summer and fall, although hotels are far less expensive and crowded in winter. During the holidays, the area puts on a rolicking, multiweek Christmas festival called Prelude.

Getting Here and Around

Route 9 runs along the coast through Kennebunkport and Old Orchard Beach, connecting at both ends with U.S. 1, between Ogunquit and Portland.

Ogunquit

Not Your Average Seaside Resort

At first a small shipbuilding and fishing village, then an artists' colony in the late 19th century, Ogunquit has since become an explosively fun and synergic swirl of cultures. Some visitors come for the beaches while others are here for the extraordinary cultural creativity or perhaps the thriving gay community—and/or because they're families. The town has both a superb summer-stock theater (the **Ogunquit Playhouse**) and the excellent **Ogunquit Museum of American Art.** Art galleries galore line the streets, as do superb restaurants. The town's gay population swells in summer, and you'll find drag shows among the nightlife as well as trolleys shuttling you to the kid-friendly beaches, motels, and candy stores. And for nature lovers, there are beautiful nearby hikes and conservation lands as well.

Don't Miss

Perkins Cove, a neck of land off Shore Road in the lower part of Ogunquit village, has a jumble of sea-weathered fish houses and buildings that were once part of an art school, but have largely been transformed into inviting shops and restaurants. When you've had your fill of browsing, stroll out along Marginal Way, a mile-long, paved footpath that hugs the shore of a rocky promontory known as Israel's Head. In the other direction, it's a short stroll to the small but excellent Ogunquit Museum of American Art.

Getting Here and Around

Ogunquit is along both U.S. 1 and Interstate 95, about 35 miles southwest of Portland.

Camden/Rockport

Idyllic Coastal Charm

More than any other towns on Penobscot Bay, Camden and Rockport are postcard-perfect Maine coastal villages. The towns' compact sizes makes them ideal for exploring on foot: friendly boutiques, groundbreaking restaurants, and inventive galleries line the streets, and hikes in Camden Hills (with mesmerizing views) wait just a short drive away.

Don't Miss

Originally designed primarily to carry cargo, **Windjammers** are mostly wood-hulled vessels that were built all along the East Coast in the 19th and early 20th centuries. Today you can take an excursion on one, which typically lasts from one to eight days; passengers can often participate in the navigation, be it hoisting a sail or playing captain at the wheel. The Camden Windjammer Festival, held Labor Day weekend, is a great time to gather and watch the region's fleet sail into the harbor, and most boats are open for tours. 🌐 *www.mainewindjammercruises.com*

Best Restaurant

Even if you don't go for the over-the-top lobster tasting menu (and you probably should), a meal at **Natalie's** is one you'll remember for years. The romantic dining room's exquisite setting overlooking Camden has seen many a marriage proposal. ✉ *83 Bay View St., Camden, ME* 🌐 *www.camdenharbourinn.com*

When to Go

June to September is best for Windjammer cruising; however, the towns do get crowded then. Late spring and fall offer more breathing room, and it's still beautiful weather if you're staying on land.

Getting Here and Around

Camden and Rockport are along U.S. 1 on Maine's Mid-Coast, between Brunswick and Bar Harbor.

Carrabassett Valley

Head for the (Ski) Hills at Sugarloaf

Home to famed Sugarloaf Ski Resort, Maine's stunning western mountains are a magnet for skiers come winter. But there are plenty of things to pursue in this natural wonderland besides winter sports—from excellent golfing and fishing to world-class spas and art galleries.

Don't Miss

Twin brothers (and Kingfield, Maine natives) Francis and Freelan Stanley invented America's first steam-powered car, the famed "Stanley Steamer" automobile. And you can learn all about it at Kingfield's **Stanley Museum**, which celebrates the many types of genius exhibited by the Stanley family. ✉ *40 School St., Kingfield, ME* 🌐 *www.stanleymuseum.org*

Best Resort

Sugarloaf Resort is at the heart of the Valley's activities for good reason: it has endless groomed ski trails to explore and the largest Nordic Center in the state. Its offerings include Nordic skiing, snowshoeing, ice skating, snow-go ski biking, and fat-tire biking. Meanwhile, there's also a slew of summertime pursuits, including a golf course designed by Robert Trent Jones Jr., hiking and biking trails, axe-throwing, and disc golf. For all seasons, there's a terrific spa as well as an antigravity complex complete with trampolines, a climbing wall, and a skate park. ✉ *5092 Sugarloaf Access Rd., Carrabassett Valley, ME* 🌐 *www.sugarloaf.com*

Getting Here and Around

Carrabassett Valley is located 10 miles north of Kingfield on ME Routes 16 and 27.

Sunrise in Lubec

First Sunrise in the United States

The nation's easternmost point of land is marked by candy-striped **West Quoddy Head Light**, which dates to 1806, and is just a short drive south of tiny, charming downtown Lubec. You can't climb the tower, but the former lightkeeper's house has a great museum and the mystical 2-mile path along the bluffs in the surrounding 540-acre Quoddy Head State Park yields magnificent views of Canada's Grand Manan Island. You can often see whales and seals—as well as ubiquitous bald eagles—just offshore. It's the perfect place to watch the sunrise any time of year, but it's especially popular on New Year's Day.

Don't Miss

Don't forget to bring your passport: this area is a perfect base for day trips to New Brunswick's **Campobello Island**, reached by a bridge—the only one to the island—from downtown Lubec. There you can visit Roosevelt Campobello International Park, and tour the 34-room rustic summer cottage of the family of President Franklin Delano Roosevelt.

When to Go

Lubec is pretty quiet in winter, although a solid group always arrives on New Year's Eve to see the first sunrise of the new year. Summer is the most pleasant time to visit, and Roosevelt Campobello International Park is closed November through mid-May.

Getting Here and Around

Lubec is on Route 189 on the Maine coast, at the Canadian border, about 10 miles northeast of U.S. 1.

Moosehead Lake

Maine's Most Beautiful Body of Water

The Moosehead Marine Museum runs three- and seven-hour afternoon trips on Moosehead Lake, the largest mountain lake in the Northeast, and at nearly 250 feet, one of the deepest. Cruises are given aboard the 115-foot *Katahdin*, a National Historic Site and stately steamship (converted to diesel) that has been a fixture on this lake for over 100 years. The boat and the free shoreside museum have displays about these steamships, which transported people and cargo for a century starting in the 1830s. ✉ *12 Lily Bay Rd., Greenville, ME* 🌐 *www.katahdincruises.com*

Don't Miss

Mt. Kineo State Park occupies most of a 1,200-acre peninsula that's accessible only by boat and offers gorgeous hiking trails that summit its spectacular 700-foot cliffs. You can also play a round on the 9-hole Mt. Kineo Golf Course, one of the oldest courses in New England. The park preserves the former Mt. Kineo House resort, once a thriving upscale summer retreat.

Best Town

Tucked at the southern end of island-dotted, mostly forest-lined Moosehead Lake, **Greenville** is an outdoors lover's paradise. Boating, fishing, and hiking are popular in summer, while snowmobiling and ice-fishing are the rage in winter.

Getting Here and Around

The departure point for Katahdin Cruises and the best town for exploring Moosehead Lake, Greenville is on Route 6 in west-central Maine, about a three-hour drive north of Portland.

Casco Bay Islands

Experience Portland's Islands by Ferry

They're just a short boat ride away from Portland, but you'd never know it: the seven Casco Bay islands reachable by ferry (there are nearly 140 in total, but many are inhabitable) are a welcome step back in time. In some cases that means pristine natural beauty (like on Cliff Island); quiet fishing communities (as with Bailey Island); or old-school, unplugged activities like tennis, hiking, and camping (as on Chebeague and Peaks, among others). All come with a slower pace and a breath of fresh air.

Don't Miss

Nature lovers should set their sights on Long Island's **Andrews Beach** and **Fowler Beach**. Both are not only beautiful picnic spots, but are also prime territory for spying migratory birds and dolphins.

When to Go

Unlike many parts of Maine, the islands don't tend to get as crowded in the summertime (the only arguable exceptions to this are Peaks Island and parts of Chebeague, which are more populated). Therefore, visiting June through September will still allow you some peace and quiet. After that time, things get almost silent, and on some islands, the weather becomes downright inhospitable.

Getting Here and Around

Peaks Island, Long Island, Cliff Island, Bailey Island, Chebeague Island, and Little Diamond and Great Diamond Islands are serviced via Casco Bay Lines out of Old Port in Portland.
🌐 *www.cascobaylines.com*

Coastal Maine Botanical Gardens

New England's Prettiest Public Garden

Set aside at least two hours to amble among the roses, lupines, rhododendrons, and contemporary art installations at the 300-acre Coastal Maine Botanical Gardens. Highlights include the "children's garden," a wonderland of stone sculptures, rope bridges, small teahouse-like structures with grass roofs, and even a hedge maze. Pine-shaded, fern-lined trails curve down to several tranquil woodland gardens and a dock on Boothbay's scenic Back River. The on-site restaurant and café, as well as the bookshop and resource library, are also delightful. ✉ *132 Botanical Gardens Dr., Boothbay, ME* 🌐 *www.mainegardens.org*

Don't Miss

The shoreline of the surrounding Boothbay Peninsula is a craggy stretch of inlets, where pleasure crafts anchor alongside trawlers and lobster boats tied up in the snug village of Boothbay Harbor, which feels like a smaller version of Bar Harbor.

Best Hotel

The Adirondack chairs on the immense lawn of the **Topside Inn** have one of the best bay views on the Maine Coast. ✉ *60 McKown St., Boothbay Harbor, ME* 🌐 *www.topsideinn.com*

When to Go

The gardens are stunning when in full bloom in summer, but there's beautiful floral scenery in spring and fall colors from late September to late October.

Getting Here and Around

Boothbay is on Route 27, 14 miles south of U.S. 1 at Wiscasset, about 30 miles east of Freeport.

Maine Lobster Festival

The Best Lobster in the United States

This annual get-together that draws thousands of devotees of lobsters takes place in early August and is the popular coastal region's largest annual event. About 10 tons of lobsters are steamed in a huge lobster cooker—you have to see it to believe it. The festival, held in Harbor Park in Rockland, includes a parade, live entertainment, a lobster dinner, an all-you-can-eat blueberry-pancake breakfast, a "Steins and Vines" beer and wine tasting, and—of course—the crowning of the Maine Sea Goddess. 🌐 *www.mainelobsterfestival.com*

Don't Miss

Are your nerves strong enough to risk tumbling into the ocean in front of hundreds of onlookers? Then sign up for the International Great Crate Race, an annual tradition that's part of the Lobster Festival. It has participants run across floating wooden lobster crates precariously strung together, and drama and hilarity always ensue.

Best Restaurant

James Beard Award–winning chef Melissa Kelly's world-class restaurant **Primo**, which occupies a restored Victorian home, serves some of the finest farm-to-table fare in coastal New England. And although this is certainly no seafood shack, there is often a butter-poached 1½-pound lobster with risotto on the menu. ✉ 2 *Main St., Rockland, ME* 🌐 *www.primorestaurant.com*

When to Go

The lobster festival takes place in early August, which is perhaps the most enchanting time to explore this stretch of Maine's Mid-Coast.

Getting Here and Around

Rockland is on U.S. 1, about midway between Brunswick and Bar Harbor.

When in Maine

L.L. BEAN

Founded in 1912 as a mail-order merchandiser after its namesake invented a hunting boot, L.L.Bean's giant flagship store attracts more than 3 million shoppers annually and is open 24 hours a day, 365 days a year, right in the heart of Freeport's outlet shopping district. A massive 16½-foot-tall statue of its signature rubber boot greets you outside the front door and you can still find those original hunting boots, along with cotton and wool sweaters, outerwear of all kinds, and camping equipment, plus all kinds of fun gifts and goods. As you walk through the store, note the impressive display of taxidermied animals and the giant 3,500-gallon aquarium of freshwater Maine fish. ✉ *95 Main St., Freeport, ME* 🌐 www.llbean.com

Do This: After a dizzying day of shopping, enjoy some fresh air on the beautiful trails at Wolfe's Neck Woods State Park, with its fragrant pine and hemlock forests and pristine salt marsh estuaries.

MAINE MARITIME MUSEUM

For a compelling look at the state's rich seafaring heritage, spend at least a half day visiting this cluster of historic buildings in Bath that once made up the Percy & Small Shipyard. Tours show how New England's massive wooden ships were built, and in the boat shop, you can still watch boatbuilders wield their tools. Inside the main museum, you can view ship models, paintings, photographs, and other artifacts while a separate historic building houses a fascinating lobstering exhibit. There's also an excellent gift shop and bookstore, and you can grab a bite to eat in the café or bring a picnic to eat on the grounds. The town of Bath has been a shipbuilding center since 1607, and the result of its prosperity can be seen in its handsome mix of Federal, Greek Revival, and Italianate homes. ✉ *243 Washington St., Bath, ME* 🌐 *www.mainemaritimemuseum.org*

Do This: In summer, the museum offers a variety of nature and lighthouse cruises on the scenic Kennebec River—one takes in 10 lighthouses. The 142-foot Grand Banks fishing schooner *Sherman Zwicker* docks here during the same period.

OWLS HEAD TRANSPORTATION MUSEUM

In the rural coastal community of Owls Head, just south of bustling Rockland, you'll find one of the Northeast's most impressive collections of planes, vehicles, and other forms of transportation—even antique bicycles, nearly all of them in operational condition. These beautifully restored and maintained gems include a 1929 Rolls-Royce Tourer, a 1919 Harley-Davidson motorcycle, 1909 Bleriot monoplane, and a 1926 Ford Model T snowmobile (this is Maine, after all). Count on this museum for rotating exhibits that include the likes of "Women Who Dare." ✉ *117 Museum St., Owls Head, ME* 🌐 *www.owlshead.org*

About Our Writers

Alexandra Hall is a lifelong coastal New Englander—she grew up in Boston, fell in love with Maine over many years of writing about the region, and now lives on the water in the Portland area with her big, loud, fun family. Together they eat as much local, sustainable seafood as possible. She is an award-winning travel and food writer, and the co-author of more than a dozen travel guides and cookbooks.

Do This: It's a scenic 10-minute drive from the museum to one of Maine's older lighthouses, Owls Head, which sits at the tip of a rugged, 80-foot-high headland that guards the western entrance to Penobscot Bay. The old keeper's house has been turned into the American Lighthouse Foundation Interpretive Center, and in summer you can take a tour to the top of the light.

PENOBSCOT NARROWS BRIDGE AND OBSERVATORY

An "engineering marvel" is how experts describe the 2,120-foot-long Penobscot Narrows Bridge, which opened in 2006 and is taller than the Statue of Liberty. It's certainly beautiful to look at—from the surrounding countryside it pops up on the horizon like the towers of a fairy-tale castle. Spanning the Penobscot River across from Bucksport, the bridge's 437-foot observation tower is the tallest public bridge observatory in the world; an elevator shoots you to the top. In summer, the observatory often offers moonrise viewings. ✉ *711 Fort Knox Rd., Prospect, ME* 🌐 *www.maine.gov/mdot/pnbo*

Do This: On the mainland (west) side of the bridge, you can visit Fort Knox, the state's largest historic garrison. It was constructed between 1844 and 1869, when—despite a treaty with Britain settling boundary disputes—invasion was still a concern. The fort never saw any real action, but it was used for troop training and to keep guard during the Civil War and the Spanish-American War. Visitors can explore the many rooms and passageways, and guided tours are given during the warmer months.

Cool Places to Stay

The Dunes on The Waterfront. Ogunquit can be a bit like Disney World in the summer: lots of fun but very crowded. These seaside cottages are a civilized happy medium. They're beautifully decorated without feeling overdone or stuffy, and many are outfitted with fireplaces, flat-screen TVs, breezy screened-in porches, and lavishly landscaped patios. There are boat shuttles to a nearby beach and bus shuttles to town; there's also a private path to the lobster pound next door and a pool. ✉ *518 Main St., Ogunquit, ME* 🌐 *www.dunesonthewaterfront.com*

Norumbega Inn. With its stone-castle-like facade, this oft-photographed bed-and-breakfast built in 1886 looks like something out of a novel by Stephen King, but its beautifully designed interior abounds with creature comforts. ✉ *63 High St., Camden, ME* 🌐 *www.norumbegainn.com*

Press Hotel. Portland's sleekest hotel is a pared-down, mid-century-modern stunner with a fun typography and printing theme alluding to the building's past, stylish furnishings handcrafted by Maine artisans, and a sophisticated gallery featuring contemporary works by Maine artists. ✉ *119 Exchange St., Portland, ME* 🌐 *www.thepresshotel.com*

Quisisana. There's arguably no other place in the country like this family summer camp on pristine Lake Kezar, where guests stay in pretty cabins for a full week (stays begin and end on Saturday); evenings revolve around world-class (transportive, even) arts performances; and by day, those performing cast members are the people who run the camp. That's all part of the all-inclusive rate, as are the unusually superb meals and all of the lake activities (rowboats, paddleboards, volleyball, etc.). Guests are encouraged to unplug and engage with the natural environment—and one another. ✉ *Lake Kezar, Lovell, ME* 🌐 *www.quisisanaresort.com*

Salt Cottages. It's tough for any one property to capture everything Acadia has to offer, but this stylish little gem just about does. It's the closest resort to all the activities of the national park and minutes from Bar Harbor yet not so close that you're caught up in the downtown frenzy. And there's plenty to do on-property: play lawn games, hang at the firepits, or lounge at the pool and watch the skies over Frenchman Bay. ✉ *Frenchman Bay, Bar Harbor, ME* 🌐 *www.saltcottagesbar-harbor.com*

The Viewpoint. As the name suggests, views don't get much more iconic than this. The sleek, chic rooms and suites here—all discreetly built into the hill-side—directly overlook Nubble Light-house and its rocky coast. There's also a serene spa and bathhouse, a welcoming alfresco restaurant and bar (by way of a 1969 Airstream trailer), and a lively pool scene. ✉ *York Harbor, York, ME* 🌐 *www.viewpointhotel.com*

Essential Eats

Abel's Lobster. Mainers fight like crazy over who makes the best lobster roll and plenty of wonderful ones abound. But the one thing they agree on is that making people wait in line for hours isn't a cute tradition—it's rude. And charging upward of $35 without even offering a nice view is downright inhospitable. Abel's clearly got that memo: set on the banks of Mt. Desert Island's sparkling Somes Sound, they serve an exquisite, delicately buttered and toasted roll teeming with plump and ultrafresh, sweet lobster meat. It's lightly dressed in chive mayo and delivered to your table alongside feather-light fries. ✉ *13 Abels La., Mount Desert, ME* 🌐 *www.abelslob-stermdi.com*

The Alna Store. It may not look like much from the outside and it may be in the middle of nowhere, but devotees drive from all over to sample the inspired dishes here—all of them powered by ingredients from surrounding farms. The lively kitchen is devoted not only to sustainable foods, but to experiment-ing with big flavors and fermentation, resulting in gems like their famous sourdough chocolate chip cookie. And at the always-packed brunch, you'll discover orchestrations such as mushroom toast with jalapeño cilantro coconut labneh, pickled radish, and gochugaru peanuts. Consider this place your portal to Maine's freshest, most inventive foods. ✉ *2 Dock Rd., Alna, ME* 🌐 *www.thealnastore.com*

Duck Fat. This gastronomically hum-ble-yet-ambitious legend helped put Port-land on the national culinary map. Yes, you can still expect the addictively crisp Belgian-style fries made from Maine potatoes, sizzled in duck fat and dipped into creative sauces. But to *really* know why you're here, look for dishes like rabbit rillettes with apple jam and grainy mustard or the best pulled-pork cubano sandwich this side of Miami. ✉ *43 Middle St., Portland, ME* 🌐 *www.duckfat.com*

Fore Street. Portland's refined-but-unpre-tentious eatery is the O.G. of locavore dining, and it employs live-fire cooking to delicious effect. The open kitchen and welcoming service make diners feel essential to the experience, and the ever-changing menu keeps everyone guessing and returning again and again. Reservations can be tough to nab, but those in the know line up at the door at 5 pm for the walk-in seats. ✉ *288 Fore St., Portland, ME* 🌐 *www.forestreet.biz*

Massachusetts

Massachusetts is far more than just Boston, but the capital city is a great place to start. Sports, culture, and tourism come together here, where you can eat a Fenway frank while watching the Boston Red Sox or follow the red line of the Freedom Trail to Paul Revere's House. Step outside the city limits to see how the American Revolution began in nearby Lexington and Concord, head to the rolling hills of the Berkshires, or experience the nautical New England charms of Cape Cod. In every corner of the Bay State, you'll find exciting opportunities.

Capital: Boston

Population: 7,136,171

Area (square miles): 10,554 square miles

Statehood Date: February 6, 1788

Major Airports: Logan International Airport (BOS); Cape Cod Gateway Airport (HYA); Nantucket Memorial Airport (ACK); Martha's Vineyard Airport (MVY); Worcester Regional Airport (ORH)

Travel and Tourism Information: 🌐 *www.visitma.com*

Famous Residents: John Adams (president and Founding Father); Emily Dickinson (poet); Nathaniel Hawthorne (novelist); Dr. Seuss (children's author and illustrator); John F. Kennedy (president); Ben Affleck (actor); Ayo Edebiri (actress)

Fun Fact: Lake Chargoggagoggmanchauggagoggchaubunagungamaugg, in Webster, is the lake with the longest name in the United States.

The Freedom Trail

Follow the Founding Fathers

Walk in the footsteps of America's forefathers and pay tribute to renowned figures like Paul Revere, John Hancock, and Ben Franklin as you follow the red stripe marking the 2½-mile Freedom Trail through Boston's most historic neighborhoods. The pedestrian trail connects 16 of the city's most historic sites related to the American Revolution, laying out Boston's colonial history on the very streets where some of the country's most important events unfolded several hundred years ago. In one day, you can visit **Faneuil Hall**; the site of the incendiary Boston Massacre; and the **Old North Church**, where lanterns hung to signal Paul Revere on his thrilling midnight ride. Faneuil Hall adjoins **Quincy Market**, a good spot to grab a bite to eat, with its three block-long annexes filled with international food stalls and souvenirs. 🌐 *www.thefreedomtrail.org*

Don't Miss

The perfect ending to a walk along the trail? A walk to the top of the **Bunker Hill Monument**, in Charlestown, for its incomparable vistas. The hill was the site of one of the first battles of the Revolutionary War.

Best Bar

Sam Adams Downtown Boston Taproom has a roof-deck beer garden and serves both the classics and plenty of exclusive rotating taps, like the Strawberry Rhubarb IPA and Blueberry Lager. ✉ *60 State St., Boston, MA* 🌐 *www.samadamsbostontaproom.com*

Getting Here and Around

The trail's starting point, Boston Common, is in the center of the city, accessed by numerous bus and T lines.

Fenway Park

America's Most Historic Baseball Stadium

The home field for the Boston Red Sox, Fenway Park is considered hallowed ground to any Bostonian. Opened in 1912, the nation's oldest ballpark has some cherished quirks, including the 37-foot-tall left field wall, known as the Green Monster, and a short foul pole in right field known as Pesky's Pole. You don't have to be a serious baseball fan to appreciate the history that has played out here, like the crowning moment when the Sox overcame a famous 86-year-drought (the "Curse of the Bambino" aka revenge from Babe Ruth for his 1920 trade to the New York Yankees) to win a World Series Championship in 2004. ✉ *19 Yawkey Way, Boston, MA* 🌐 *www.mlb.com/redsox/ballpark*

Don't Miss

Hour-long Fenway Park tours are available daily, year-round and take you behind the scenes of the beloved ballpark. Take in the view from the Green Monster and walk in the footsteps of Yaz, Williams, Fisk, and other greats. 🌐 *www.mlb.com/redsox/ballpark/tours*

When to Go

Regular baseball season runs from early April to late September/early October. Postseason play continues into November. The Sox traditionally play a home game on Patriot's Day, the third Monday in April that also sees the Boston Marathon. That day (a Massachusetts state holiday) and the entire preceding weekend is a great time to come and soak up the sports fervor of Boston.

Getting Here and Around

Parking near Fenway Park on game day will cost you a small fortune. It's best to use public transportation. The MBTA's Green Line is a handy option; take the Green Line to Kenmore Station or Fenway Station and walk to the ballpark.

Boston Harbor

America's Most Historic Harbor

Revolutionaries famously dumped British tea into the Boston Harbor in protest during the Boston Tea Party of 1773, and today this waterfront part of town spanning the Seaport and Waterfront districts is packed with marine marvels and cultural gems. Take a walk along the **Boston Harborwalk** for stunning views of the water, learn about American history at the **Boston Tea Party Ships & Museum**, where you can catch reenactments and sip the tea that started it all, then visit the nearby **New England Aquarium.** Boston Harbor City Cruises offers excursions on the USS *Constitution*, whale-watching cruises, brunch trips, and sunset and fireworks adventures. ✉ *306 Congress St., Boston, MA* 🌐 *www.bostonteapartyship.com*

Don't Miss

The **New England Aquarium** is justly renowned for its four-story, 200,000-gallon Giant Ocean Tank—so big, the rest of the aquarium was built around it. ✉ *1 Central Wharf, Boston, MA* *www.neaq.org*

Best Waterfront Museum

A 15-minute walk along the waterfront, the **Institute of Contemporary Art** is housed in a breathtaking cantilevered edifice that juts out over the Boston waterfront. ✉ *25 Harbor Shore Dr., Boston MA* 🌐 *www.icaboston.org*

Getting Here and Around

The Boston Tea Party Ships & Museum can be accessed by South Station. The New England Aquarium is along the waterfront on Long Wharf, accessed by the T and just off Interstate 93.

The Emerald Necklace

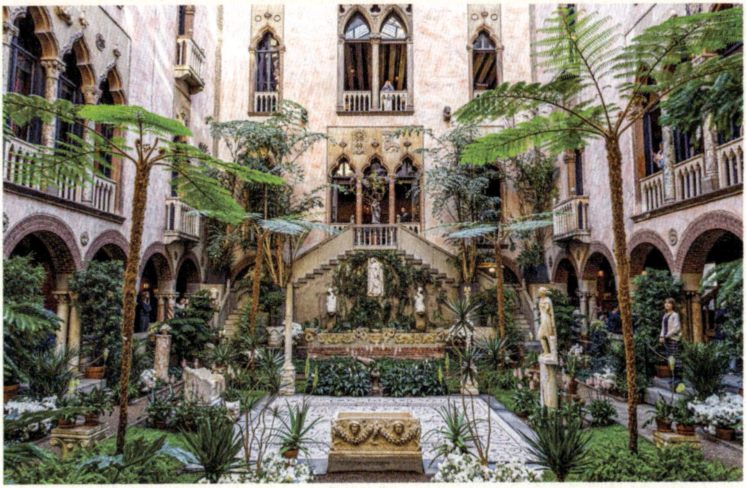

The Most Beautiful Urban Trail

Designed in the late 19th century by landscape architect Frederick Law Olmsted, this delightful string of green spaces and parks runs about 7 miles from one end of the city to the other and includes the Boston Common and Public Garden, Back Bay Fens, the Riverway, Olmsted Park, Jamaica Pond, Arnold Arboretum, and Franklin Park. You can walk along shady paths, row a boat on Jamaica Pond, visit the zoo at Franklin Park, or just laze away an afternoon sitting under a tree. The Emerald Necklace Conservancy provides bike and walking tours, maps, exhibits, and other info from its visitor center in the Back Bay Fens. 🌐 *www.emeraldnecklace.org*

Don't Miss

The stunning **Isabella Stewart Gardner Museum**—with its Gothic tapestries, Spanish leather panels, and majestic Venetian courtyard—contains such masterpieces as Titian's *Rape of Europa*, Rembrandt's *Self-Portrait, Age 23* , and John Singer Sargent's *El Jaleo*. The museum also saw an infamous art heist in 1990 that remains unsolved today; empty frames still hang in the museum as placeholders for the missing works. ✉ *25 Evans Way, Boston, MA* 🌐 *www.gardnermuseum.org*

When to Go

The gardens of the Emerald Necklace, and Arnold Arboretum in particular, burst with color from mid-April through mid-October.

Getting Here and Around

You can access the Emerald Necklace at numerous points, including the Back Bay Fens, Jamaica Pond, Arnold Arboretum, and Franklin Park.

Boston's North End

Glorious Italian Food

You can eat your way through one of America's most colorful and prolific Little Italy neighborhoods in Boston's North End. This is the city's haven not only for Italian restaurants but also for Italian groceries, bakeries, bocce courts, churches, social clubs, and street-corner debates over home-team soccer games. July and August are highlighted by a series of street festivals, or *feste*, honoring various saints and by local community events that draw people from all over the city. A statue of St. Agrippina di Mineo—which is covered with dollar bills when it's paraded through the streets—is a crowd favorite. Although gentrification has diluted the quarter's character some, linger for a moment along Salem or Hanover streets and you can still hear people speaking with Abruzzese accents.

Don't Miss

Take a stroll down Hanover Street, the North End's main thoroughfare, and you'll find all the cannoli and cappuccinos your heart could desire. Hanover's excellent and time-honored bakeries include **Modern Pastry Shop**, **Mike's Pastry**, or a block over on Salem Street, **Bova's Bakery**.

While You're Here

Walk off the calories in the **Paul Revere Mall**, a tree-lined corridor on Hanover Street, pausing on a bench in the greenery to admire Revere's statue.

Getting Here and Around

The North End is easily accessible; take the Orange or Green Line to the Haymarket T stop. Like most of Boston, the neighborhood is extremely walkable.

Harvard University

America's Oldest College

One of the world's most prestigious and storied educational bodies, Harvard University and its tree-studded, shady, and redbrick campus has weathered the footsteps of students since 1636, although the oldest buildings date from the 18th century and collectively chronicle American architecture from the colonial era to the present. Holden Chapel, completed in 1744, is a Georgian gem. The graceful University Hall was designed in 1815 by Charles Bulfinch. Sever Hall, completed in 1880 and designed by Henry Hobson Richardson, represents the Romanesque revival. The neoclassical Widener Library is a highlight of any campus visit. ✉ *1350 Massachusetts Ave., Cambridge, MA* 🌐 *www.harvard.edu*

Don't Miss

Tides of students, tourists, political activists, and street performers make up the nonstop pedestrian flow of Harvard Yard, the most celebrated of Cambridge crossroads.

Best Museum

In 2014, the combined collections of the Busch-Reisinger, Fogg, and Arthur M. Sackler museums were united under one glorious, mostly glass roof, in the six-level **Harvard Art Museums** designed by Renzo Piano. Highlights to the free museum include American and European paintings and works by German expressionists. ✉ *32 Quincy St, Cambridge, MA* 🌐 *www.harvardartmuseums.org*

Getting Here and Around

Harvard's campus is in the heart of Cambridge, just across the Charles River from Boston and easily reached by public transit or by car via Memorial Drive.

Cape Cod National Seashore

New England's Prettiest Beaches

Extending nearly 40 miles from Chatham to Provincetown and encompassing Cape Cod's outer "hook," this 43,000-acre swatch of superb beaches, undulating dunes, marshes and wetlands, and pitch-pine and scrub-oak forest is laced with walking, biking, and horseback trails. Even when the rest of Cape Cod feels packed with summer revelers, it's possible to find solitude here. Highlights include Fort Hill, with its pastoral hills that roll gently down to Nauset Marsh (popular with bird-watchers and nature photographers), and Marconi Station, where a lookout deck marks the spot where the first American wireless message to Europe was sent. Don't miss the boardwalk trail through a gorgeous Atlantic white cedar swamp.

Don't Miss

You'll find some of New England's prettiest beaches at Cape Cod National Seashore, with two of the most spectacular in Provincetown: **Race Point Beach** and **Herring Cove Beach.**

Best Dune Tour

Art's Dune Tours has been taking eager passengers into the dunes of Province Lands since 1946. Head out at sunset for a stunning ride, available with or without a clambake feast. 🌐 *www.artsdunetours.com*

When to Go

Cape Cod is warmest and most alluring—but also very crowded—in summer.

Getting Here and Around

The national seashore is located along U.S. 6 and has two visitor centers, one in Eastham and one in Provincetown.

Salem

The Witchiest Town in the Country

Long infamous for the witchcraft hysteria that resulted in the 1692 witch trials, which led to the executions of 20 innocent people, this historic city just north of Boston has quite a lot going for it year-round, including stunning examples of First Period architecture. In October, its streets, bars, restaurants, and attractions are a lively backdrop for **Haunted Happenings** (🌐 *www.hauntedhappenings.org*), the world's largest Halloween celebration. Take a walking tour, join a parade, and book a tarot reading, but also be sure to visit the **Salem Witch Museum,** which occupies a striking Gothic Revival church overlooking Salem Common (✉ *19½ Washington Sq. N, Salem, MA* 🌐 *www.salemwitchmuseum.com*). Another must-visit is the 1668 **House of the Seven Gables,** immortalized in Nathaniel Hawthorne's classic novel of the same name, and home to a secret staircase and some of the finest Georgian furnishings in the country (✉ *115 Derby St., Salem, MA* 🌐 *www.7gables.org*).

Don't Miss

The world-class **Peabody-Essex Museum** celebrates superlative works from around the globe and across time. ✉ *161 Essex St., Salem, MA* 🌐 *www.pem.org*

When to Go

As you might guess, Salem gets incredibly popular (and incredibly crowded) throughout the entire month of October. Most area museums are open year-round, however, and there's a spirit of spookiness no matter the month.

Getting Here and Around

Salem's pedestrian-friendly historic core is at the junction of Routes 1A, 114, and 107, about 15 miles northeast of Boston.

Lexington and Concord

The Ultimate Revolutionary Towns

Just northwest of Boston, Lexington and nearby Concord embody both the spirit of the American Revolution as well as Early American literature. These two quintessential New England towns were the sites of the first skirmishes of the Revolutionary War and where patriot leader Paul Revere warned that the British were coming. They were also home to the country's first notable writers, including Ralph Waldo Emerson, Nathaniel Hawthorne, Louisa May Alcott, and Henry David Thoreau.

Don't Miss

Minute Man National Historical Park preserves the key sites of the American Revolutionary War's opening battle on April 19, 1775. See the point where Revere's midnight ride ended with his capture by the British. 🌐 *www.nps.gov/mima*

While You're Here

For devotees of Early American literature, a trip to Concord isn't complete without a pilgrimage to Henry David Thoreau's most famous residence, **Walden Pond**. ✉ *915 Walden St., Concord, MA* 🌐 *www.mass.gov*

When to Go

Autumn lovers, take note: Concord is a great place to start a fall foliage tour. As lovely as it is in summer, Walden Pond can get crowded and visitors are sometimes turned away.

Getting Here and Around

Walden Pond is in Concord off Route 126 at Route 2. It's 5 miles west of Minute Man National Historical Park, which is off Interstate 95, about 20 miles northwest of Boston.

Martha's Vineyard

Bike New England's Most Beautiful Island

With more than 60 miles of gently (and steeply) undulating roads, relatively little car traffic, numerous cycling trails, and captivating views in every direction, Martha's Vineyard is the ultimate New England island to tour on a bike. Less developed than Cape Cod, Martha's Vineyard abounds with scenic and sophisticated diversions, including the charming villages of Vineyard Haven, Oak Bluffs, and Edgartown among its six towns. And then there's the quiet, simpler beauty: the ancient docks and weathered fishing boats of Menemsha Harbor, and the serene landscapes—especially if you make the short ferry ride to sleepy Chappaquiddick Island—of the Japanese-style gardens at Mytoi and the dunes, salt marshes, and tidal flats of Cape Poge Wildlife Refuge.

Don't Miss

At the southwestern tip of the island, the spectacular red-clay **Aquinnah Cliffs** and adjoining **Moshup Beach** are a must-stop on your bike tour. Native American crafts and food shops line the short approach to the overlook, and you can tour the 1856 Gay Head Lighthouse.

When to Go

Summer—though beautiful—is prime high season on Martha's Vineyard, and roads can be more crowded then, and rates steeper. Visiting during the quieter shoulder seasons can be more enjoyable.

Getting Here and Around

Most visitors get here by ferry—car and passenger boats connect with Falmouth, Hyannis, and a few other ports. You'll find bike rental shops by the ferry landings in Vineyard Haven and Oak Bluffs. You can also fly here from Boston, Hyannis, New Bedford, and Westchester County, NY.

Mass MoCA

Amazing Art in the Berkshires

Set in the handsome 1860s redbrick buildings that once housed the Sprague Electrical Company, Massachusetts Museum of Contemporary Art (Mass MoCA) is one of the nation's largest centers for contemporary visual and performing arts. In this 250,000-square-foot multi-building museum, you can admire wall drawings of Sol LeWitt, an immersive light-based exhibit by James Turrell, and sculptures from Louise Bourgeois. ✉ *1040 Mass MoCA Way, North Adams, MA* 🌐 *www.massmoca.org*

Don't Miss

Just 5 miles west, **Williamstown** is famous in summer for its renowned Williamstown Theatre Festival and year-round for prestigious Williams College, home to the fantastic Williams College Museum of Art and its excellent American and 20th-century collections. Within walking distance, you can tour one of the nation's notable small art museums, the Clark Institute.

Best Hotel

Across the street from Mass MoCA, the **Porches Inn** occupies a series of 1890s former workers' cottages that have been restored and connected with one long porch. ✉ *231 River St., North Adams, MA* 🌐 *www.porches.com*

When to Go

In October, the area offers some of the most spectacular fall foliage in the Berkshires, but the area's art museums are open and well worth a visit any time of year.

Getting Here and Around

Mass MoCA is in North Adams, just off Route 2, in the Berkshires—at the very northwestern corner of the state.

Plymouth

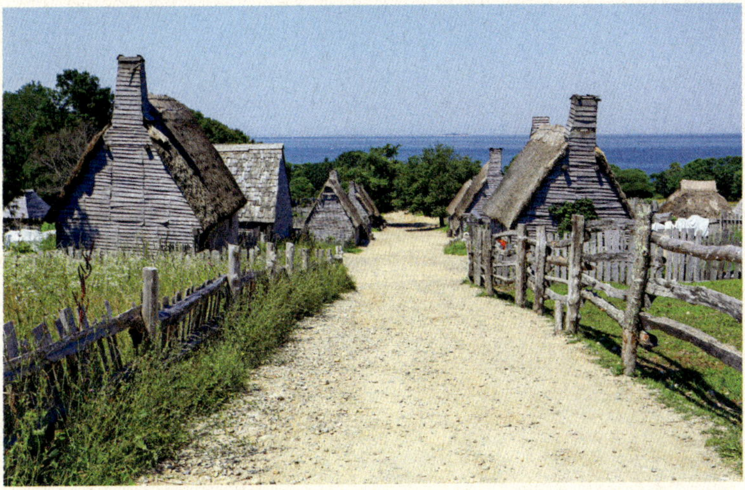

The Original Pilgrim Settlement

On December 26, 1620, 102 weary men, women, and children disembarked from the *Mayflower* to found the first permanent European settlement north of Virginia (they had found their earlier landing in Provincetown to be unsuitable). Today Plymouth is characterized by narrow streets, clapboard mansions, shops, antiques stores, and a scenic waterfront. To mark Thanksgiving, the town holds historic-house tours and a parade.

Don't Miss

Against the backdrop of the Atlantic Ocean, **Plimoth Patuxet Museums** (formerly known as Plimoth Plantation) is a fascinating living museum that shares the rich, interwoven stories of the Plymouth Colony and the indigenous Wampanoag homeland through engaging daily programs and interactive experiences. ✉ *137 Warren Ave., Plymouth, MA* 🌐 *www.plimoth.org*

Best Tour

Get a sense of what life was like for Pilgrims on the journey to Plymouth by climbing aboard the meticulous replica of the legendary *Mayflower*, the *Mayflower II*. Before or after, you may as well get a glimpse of nearby Plymouth Rock, the spot where the pilgrims allegedly first landed in America. It's downright disappointing (it's really just a small boulder) and the actual historical accuracy is dubious, but it's still inexplicably popular with visitors.

Getting Here and Around

The Plimoth Patuxet Museums are 3 miles south of downtown Plymouth, off Route 3A, about 40 miles southeast of Boston and 20 miles northwest of the bridge to Cape Cod.

Nantucket

The Whaling Capital of the World

At the height of its prosperity in the early 19th century, Nantucket's harbor bustled with whaling ships and merchant vessels and it was known as the whaling capital of the world—no small feat for an island that is a mere 14 miles long by 3½ miles wide. The entire town of Nantucket is now an official National Historic District, encompassing more than 800 pre-1850 structures within 1 square mile. Day-trippers usually take in the architecture and historical sites, go to the beach, dine at one of the many delightful restaurants, and browse in pricey boutiques.

Don't Miss

With exhibits that include a fully rigged whaleboat and a skeleton of a 46-foot sperm whale, the exceptional **Whaling Museum** offers a lively look at the island's colorful history. ✉ *13 Broad St., Nantucket, MA* 🌐 *www.nha.org*

When to Go

Nantucket is a prime summer destination, but the mellow and relatively mild spring and fall shoulder seasons are quite pleasant and far less expensive.

Getting Here and Around

You can most easily get to the island by car or passenger ferry and by plane from Hyannis. Seasonal ferries also run to several other ports around the East Coast and to Martha's Vineyard. Most attractions and businesses are in Nantucket Town, within walking distance of the ferry, and taxis and buses can get you farther afield.

Tanglewood

Summertime Symphonies

Set in the verdant landscape of the Berkshire hills, Tanglewood is the 529-acre summer home of the Boston Symphony Orchestra and since 1937, it has hosted world-famous musicians and attracts up to 350,000 music lovers every season. The 5,000-seat main shed hosts larger concerts; the more intimate Seiji Ozawa Hall seats around 1,200 and is used for chamber music and solo performances. Among the most rewarding ways to experience Tanglewood is to purchase lawn tickets, arrive early with blankets or lawn chairs, and enjoy a music-filled picnic under the stars. Except for the occasional big-name concert, lawn tickets are quite reasonable. ✉ *297 West St., Lenox, MA* 🌐 *www.bso.org*

Don't Miss

The sophisticated little town of **Lenox**—home to a number of posh inns and eateries—is also home to Shakespeare and Company, an acclaimed theater group that presents the works of the Bard and other writers. One of these, a tented outdoor stage called the Rose Footprint Theatre, reflects the dimensions of the Rose, Shakespeare's first performance space in London. 🌐 *www.shakespeare.org*

Best Preshow Dinner

Make a delectable feast of Mediterranean small plates and hand-tossed pizzas at **Brava**, a dapper downtown Lenox bistro. ✉ *65 Church St., Lenox, MA* 🌐 *www.bravalenox.com*

When to Go

Concerts at Tanglewood typically take place from late June through early September, while Shakespeare and Company performs year-round.

Getting Here and Around

Lenox is in the heart of the Berkshires, off U.S. 7 and 20.

Cranberry Bogs

All-American Harvest in Cape Cod

Cape Cod's famous cranberry industry took off in Harwich in 1844, when Alvin Cahoon was its principal grower. Today you'll still find working cranberry bogs throughout the Cape. The best way to see them, in all their scarlet glory, is on an autumn bike ride on the Shining Sea Bikeway in Falmouth or the Cape Cod Rail Trail, running from Yarmouth to Wellfleet. Or you can celebrate the Cape's favorite fruit with music, crafts, and food at the two-day **Harwich Cranberry Arts and Music Festival** (🌐 *www.harwichcranberryartsandmusicfestival.org*), held in mid-September. Also look for cranberry-infused treatments at local spas.

Don't Miss

In the Upper Cape village of Cataumet, in Bourne, family-owned **Somerset Creamery** has been producing rich, thick ice cream since 1937. It's the destination on Cape Cod for a refreshing scoop of Cranberry Bog ice cream, a beloved cranberry-based concoction studded with dark chocolate, craisins, and walnuts. ✉ *1268 Rte. 28A, Cataumet, MA* 🌐 *www.somersetcreamery.com*

When to Go

Cranberries have a surprisingly long growing season—April to November—but come in the fall to see them when they're red and ripe. They're harvested on the Cape from September to November.

Getting Here and Around

Harwich is 82 miles southeast of Boston via Route 3 and U.S. 6.

When in Massachusetts

THE BIG E

Also known as the Eastern States Exposition, this is the eastern seaboard's largest agricultural fair. While located just outside Springfield, Massachusetts, the event brings together purveyors from all across New England, with a dizzying amount of food vendors, farm stands, local crafts, Midway rides, live music, and agricultural competitions. ✉ *1305 Memorial Ave., West Springfield, MA* 🌐 *www.thebige.com*

Do This: On the Avenue of the States, you'll find six buildings, each one a replica of a New England state house and dedicated entirely to the local character of that state, with plenty of custom foods and local crafts.

CASTLE HILL ON CRANE ESTATE

This 59-room Stuart-style mansion, built in 1928 and depicted memorably as Jack Nicholson's love nest in *The Witches of Eastwick,* is part of the Crane Estate, a glorious patch of more than 2,100 acres along the Essex and Ipswich rivers, encompassing Castle Hill, Crane Beach, and the Crane Wildlife Refuge. Although the original furnishings were sold at auction, the mansion has been elaborately furnished in period style and is open for tours. There's also fishing, kayaking, and other activities on-site as well as accommodations in the opulent and exquisite Inn at Castle Hill. The estate is a lovely base for exploring Cape Anne, a rocky and scenic peninsula just 30 miles northeast of Boston that's home to picturesque fishing and boating towns like Essex, Rockport, Gloucester, and Manchester-by-the-Sea. ✉ *290 Argilla Rd., Ipswich, MA* 🌐 *www.thetrustees.org*

Do This: Luxuriously wide and inviting, Crane Beach is considered one of the best beaches in New England. On the right-hand side of the parking lot, a trailhead leads to hiking paths through dunes, along the ocean, and into a maritime scrub forest, revealing a true coastal wonderland.

MONTAGUE BOOKMILL

This incredibly picturesque 1840s mill complex along the Pioneer Valley's Saw Mill River—since converted into a row of businesses that includes a vintage music store and an outstanding art gallery—exudes old New England. The Bookmill is a quirky, well-stocked secondhand bookshop whose comfortable chairs make it easy to curl up with a book. The good-humored staffers at the adjoining Lady Killigrew Café serve craft beer, strong coffee, and delicious curry chicken and Brie–apple–apricot jam sandwiches. ✉ *440 Greenfield Rd., Montague, MA* 🌐 *www.montaguebookmill.com*

Do This: On a short drive south, explore the charming downtowns of Amherst and Northampton, with their lively college campuses and fervent creative—and especially literary—vibes. Book lovers should make a point of visiting the Emily Dickinson Museum, the Federal-style home in which the legendary poet lived and wrote for decades, and the light-filled Eric Carle Museum, which celebrates and preserves not only the works of renowned children's book author Eric Carle, who penned *The Very Hungry Caterpillar,* but also original picture-book art by Leo Lionni, Susanne Suba, William Steig, Ashley Bryan, and many others.

NAISMITH BASKETBALL HALL OF FAME

Located in Springfield, this 80,000-square-foot facility—named for Canadian phys-ed instructor Dr. James Naismith, who invented the game of basketball in 1891 during his five years at the city's YMCA Training Center—showcases plenty of jerseys, memorabilia, and video highlights. High-profile players such as Michael Jordan and Kareem Abdul-Jabbar of the NBA and Nancy Lieberman of the WNBA are among the nearly 300 enshrinees, but the hall celebrates the accomplishments of players, coaches, and others at all levels of the sport. The hall is easy to find: look for the 15-story spire with an illuminated basketball on top. ✉ *1000 Hall of Fame Ave., Springfield, MA* 🌐 *www.hoophall.com*

Do This: Also in Springfield is the Amazing World of Dr. Seuss Museum, which offers a look into the Springfield childhood of Theodor Geisel (aka Dr. Seuss) with a wide range of interactive exhibits and wall drawings, all among rooms so colorful that the museum is like walking into a Dr. Seuss book. ✉ *21 Edwards St., Springfield, MA* 🌐 *springfieldmuseums.org*

THE NORMAN ROCKWELL MUSEUM

The quintessence of small-town New England charm, Stockbridge is untainted by large-scale development. It is also the blueprint for small-town America as represented on the covers of the *Saturday Evening Post* by painter Norman Rockwell, the official state artist of Massachusetts. From 1953 until his death in 1978, Rockwell lived in Stockbridge and painted the simple charm of its buildings and residents.

Do This: The charming Norman Rockwell Museum traces the career of one of America's most beloved illustrators, beginning with his first *Saturday Evening Post* cover in 1916. The crown jewel of the 570 Rockwell illustrations is the famed Four Freedoms gallery, although various works—including his *Post* covers and self-portraits—are equally charming. Rockwell's studio was moved to the museum grounds and is complete in every detail. ✉ *9 Rte. 183, Stockbridge, MA* 🌐 *www.nrm.org*

PROVINCETOWN'S COMMERCIAL STREET

Stretching 2½ miles through Provincetown, with wonderful harbor views along the way, Commercial Street is one of the liveliest and most colorful main thoroughfares on the Eastern Seaboard. Here in the heart of what could be considered America's original LGBTQ+ summer resort, you'll find an astounding diversity of fun stops as you make your way from the East End to the West End, passing offbeat gift shops, prestigious art galleries, hip home-accent stores, sassy purveyors of club and swimwear, buzzy bars, campy cabarets, lively restaurant patios, and an impressive array of historic buildings in many architectural styles—Greek Revival, Victorian, Second Empire, and Gothic, to name a few. In summer, Commercial Street is practically a parade of people-watching, but it's a pleasant stroll even in the peaceful off-season months.

Do This: Founded in 1914 to collect and exhibit the works of artists with local connections, the impressive Provincetown Art Association and Museum holds more than 4,000 works by 900-plus artists, a mix up-and-comers and established 20th-century figures including Milton Avery, Helen Frankenthaler, Mark Rothko, Lee Krasner, Andy Warhol, and Agnes Weinrich. The museum store is fantastic. ✉ *460 Commercial St., Provincetown, MA* 🌐 *www.paam.org*

Cool Places to Stay

Lands End Inn. Built in 1904 on a sweeping bluff in Provincetown's historic West End, this wildly ornate and idiosyncratic former summer home is now a fascinating inn with 18 one-of-a-kind rooms—many with unusual architectural details like domed ceilings, cozy alcoves and lofts, stained-glass windows and Tiffany lamps, and huge decks overlooking the water. ✉ *22 Commercial St., Provincetown, MA* 🌐 *www.landsendinn.com*

Liberty Hotel Boston. This chic Luxury Collection hotel—formerly Boston's 1850s Charles Street Jail—is famous both as a place to rest in luxury and to revel in its swank Liberty Bar; rooms are either in the original granite building or an adjacent 16-story modern tower, and feature rich hardwood floors, herringbone-patterned walls, and artwork that focuses on the building's rich history. The hotel makes the most of its notorious history; a bar called Alibi is housed in the jail's old drunk tank and is adorned with celebrity mugshots. ✉ *215 Charles St., Boston, MA* 🌐 *www.libertyhotel.com*

Lizzie Borden House. In 1892, Lizzie Borden was accused of brutally murdering her father and stepmother in this very house. She was tried and acquitted for the murders, but they still remain unsolved and have become a morbid fascination for all true crime lovers. Much of the original furnishings and decor remain in the house and can be seen on daily house tours, but it's also a popular B&B where you can stay the night—if you dare (it's considered one of the most haunted properties in the United States). ✉ *230 2nd St., Fall River, MA* 🌐 *www.lizzie-borden.com*

Red Lion Inn. An inn since 1773, this imposing building in the Berkshires has hosted presidents, senators, and other celebrities; these days lodging is situated between a large main building and nine annexes, so if you want to experience a historic environment filled with antiques, request a room in the main building. Just keep in mind that many rooms are cozy and have thin walls, but the ambience is endearingly authentic. ✉ *30 Main St., Stockbridge, MA* 🌐 *www.redlioninn.com*

Winnetu Oceanside Resort. A departure from most properties on Martha's Vineyard, the contemporary Winnetu—styled after the grand multistory resorts of the Gilded Age—has successfully struck a fine balance in that it both encourages families and provides a contemporary seaside-resort experience for couples. Rooms have kitchenettes and decks or patios, and there's a huge pool. Guests can book add-on experiences like summer clambakes and oyster farm tours to enhance the "New England Vacation" vibe. ✉ *31 Dunes Rd., Edgartown, MA* 🌐 *www.winnetu.com*

About Our Writers

Diane Bair has lived in Massachusetts for most of her life, primarily on the North Shore (Marblehead and Beverly) and currently on Cape Cod. She bleeds green—a Boston Celtics fan to the bone—and believes that Massachusetts is home to the best fried clams and roast beef sandwiches (get the three-way at Kelly's!) on the planet. She writes for *The Boston Globe* and *Yankee* magazine, among others, and sometimes pops up on local radio shows.

Essential Eats

Clam Box of Ipswich. A landmark in the North Shore town of Ipswich, the Clam Box is hard to miss—the building is designed to look like a giant take-out box of clams. The fried native clams, with gooey bellies intact, are legendary, but you can also get fried scallops, shrimp, calamari, and oysters, served by the plate with fries, onion rings, and slaw (pick two) or by the box, along with haddock, clam strips, and chicken fingers. ✉ *246 High St., Ipswich, MA* 🌐 *www.clambox-ipswich.com*

Galleria Umberto. Among the many Italian options in Boston's North End, family-owned Galleria Umberto has been a local favorite for its crispy-edged squares of Sicilian-style pizza since 1974. The arancini and calzones also draw fans, but few can resist the pizza—so when they sell out, they close for the day. It's cash-only, too; you don't get more old-school than that. ✉ *289 Hanover St., Boston, MA* 🌐 *galleria-umberto.res-menu.com*

Skipper Chowder House. Since 1936, the Skipper crew has been serving award-winning clam chowder (they even do a fried clam version) in a sit-down space right across the street from Nantucket Sound. Go for a whole-belly clam roll or a hefty lobster roll, served hot with butter on brioche or lobster salad–style with lettuce on a toasted French bun. Save room for dessert—the on-site ice-cream shack serves loaded sundaes and a fabulous sea salt caramel ice cream. ✉ *152 S. Shore Dr., South Yarmouth, MA* 🌐 *www.skipperrestaurant.com*

Sullivan's Castle Island. Heading to Sully's for its opening day in the spring is a rite of passage for generations of Bostonians. The family-run concession stand and James Beard Award–winner opened in 1951 near Fort Independence; it's famous for hot dogs and crinkle-cut fries, but their lobster rolls and local seafood wraps are also worthy. Sully's generally stays open from late February/early March to late November/early December. ✉ *2080 William J. Day Blvd., South Boston, MA* 🌐 *www.sullivanscastleisland.com*

Union Oyster House. Eating at this circa-1826 establishment (the oldest continuously operating restaurant in the United States) puts you in esteemed company: Daniel Webster dined lavishly on oysters and brandy here, and JFK was such a regular, he had his own booth (yes, you can sit there today). The menu leans on seafood standards like broiled Boston scrod, crab cakes, and seafood platters with homey sides like Boston baked beans and cornbread. For dessert, there's warm apple cobbler and Boston cream pie for dessert. ✉ *41 Union St., Boston, MA* 🌐 *www.unionoysterhouse.com*

New Hampshire

New Hampshire's mountain peaks, clear air, and sparkling lakes have attracted trailblazers and artists (and untold numbers of tourists) for centuries. The state's varied geography is part of the attraction, but hospitality and friendliness are major factors, too: visitors tend to feel quickly at home in this place of beauty and history. Whether you're an outdoors enthusiast seeking adventure or just want to enjoy a good book on the porch swing of a century-old inn, you'll find plenty of opportunities to explore this breathtaking countryside.

Capital: Concord

Population: 1,415,860

Area: 9,349 square miles

Statehood Date: June 21, 1788

Major Airports: Manchester-Boston Regional Airport (MHT); Portsmouth International Airport at Pease (PSM)

Travel and Tourism Information: 🌐 *www.visitnh.gov* 🌐 *www.nhmagazine.com*

Famous Residents: Daniel Webster (early American lawyer and statesman); Franklin Pierce (president); John Irving (writer); J.D. Salinger (writer); Ken Burns (documentary filmmaker); Adam Sandler (comedian)

Fun Fact: Since 1960, the tiny northern White Mountains town of Dixville Notch has been the first town in the United States to vote during each U.S. presidential election. The polls open at midnight on election Tuesday and close moments later, once every registered voter has cast their ballot.

Mt. Washington

Ascend the Northeast's Highest Peak

At 6,288 feet, Mt. Washington is a land of superlatives. It's the tallest peak in the northeastern United States, and some of the world's strongest winds, 231 mph, were recorded here in 1934. You can take a guided van tour, a drive, or a hike to the summit—a number of challenging trails circle the mountain and access other peaks in the adjoining Presidential Range. The drive to the top, along narrow, curving Mt. Washington Auto Road—which climbs 4,600 feet in about 7 miles—is truly memorable. ✉ *Mt. Washington Auto Rd., off Rte. 16, Gorham, NH* 🌐 *www.mt-washington.com*

Don't Miss

Featuring a dramatic 28-mile network of both mild and wild cross-country ski and mountain-biking trails at the foot of Mt. Washington, **Great Glen Trails Outdoor Center** provides access to hundreds of acres of backcountry. ✉ *1 Mt. Washington Auto Rd., Gorham, NH* 🌐 *greatglentrails.com*

Best Train Ride

Since 1869, the **Mt. Washington Cog Railway** has chugged its way up to the summit along a 3-mile track on the mountain's west side. It's a beloved attraction, and a thrill in either direction. 🌐 *www.thecog.com*

When to Go

The cog railroad runs year-round (but to the summit only in early May through mid-October) and the auto road is open early May to late October.

Getting Here and Around

The Mt. Washington Auto Road is off Route 16, north of Jackson. The cog railroad station is on the opposite (west) side of the mountain, off U.S. 302 in Bretton Woods, by the historic Omni Mount Washington Resort.

Lake Winnipesaukee

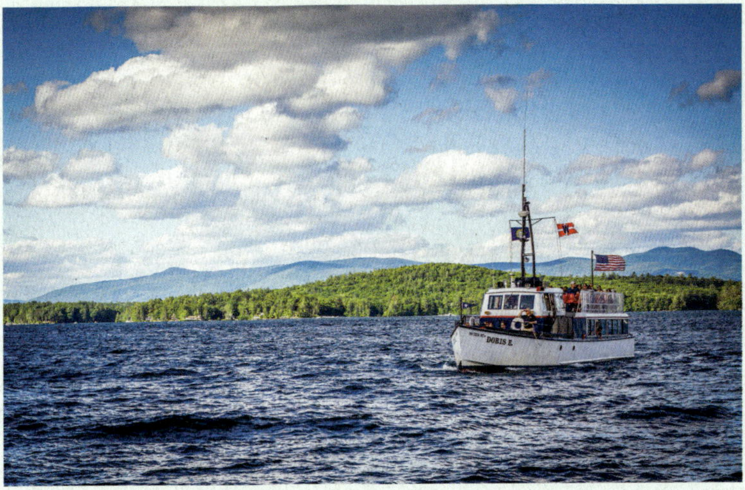

Beauty in a High Place

With about 240 miles of shoreline dotted with inlets and coves, Lake Winnipesaukee, which means "beautiful water in a high place," is the largest lake in New Hampshire and the state's big summer destination. The lake is encircled by well-preserved colonial and 19th-century villages, but Wolfeboro with its artsy boutiques, galleries, eateries, and summering celebrities is the original and best summer resort. The nostalgic sign on the outskirts of this quietly upscale town welcomes you to "The Oldest Summer Resort in America," thanks to a summer house built here in 1769.

Don't Miss

Less than 10 miles north of Lake Winnipesaukee, peaceful Holderness village straddles two of the state's most scenic lakes, Squam and Little Squam, both of which have been spared from excessive development but do offer some memorable inns perfect for a tranquil getaway. Don't miss the Squam Lakes Natural Science Center's nature trails, live-animal habitats, naturalist-led wildlife cruises, and lush Kirkwood Gardens. ✉ *23 Science Center Rd., Holderness, NH* 🌐 *www.nhnature.org*

Best Lake Views

Looking like a fairy-tale castle, Castle in the Clouds, a grand 1914 mountaintop estate, is anchored by an elaborate mansion with 16 rooms. ✉ *455 Old Mountain Rd., Moultonborough, NH* 🌐 *www.castleintheclouds.org*

When to Go

The entire Lakes Region is at its prime for beauty and bustle in summer.

Getting Here and Around

The region is easily accessed via U.S. 3, off Interstate 93 at Exit 20.

Franconia Notch State Park

Family Fun in the White Mountains

Traversed by the Appalachian Trail, this stunning 6,807-acre state park feels as epic as a national park and offers dozens of diversions, including myriad hiking trails, summer swimming at Echo Lake Beach, and winter downhill skiing at Cannon Mountain, whose 4,080-foot summit observation tower you can visit via the Aerial Tramway (just check ahead, as the Tramway will be closed through at least 2026 while cars are replaced with newer models). The dramatic, narrow, 800-foot-long **Flume Gorge** is reached from a modern visitor center via a picturesque 2-mile loop hike along wooden stairways. ✉ *260 Tramway Dr., Franconia, NH* 🌐 *www.nhstateparks.org*

Don't Miss

From 1915 to 1920, Robert Frost lived in a modest homestead on a peaceful unpaved road in Franconia. It's surrounded by well-tended gardens and offers sweeping mountain views. Out back, you can follow short trails marked with lines from his poetry. Poetry readings are scheduled some summer evenings. ✉ *158 Ridge Rd., Franconia, NH* 🌐 *www.frostplace.org*

Best Restaurant

In the Dexter family for generations, **Polly's Pancake Parlor** has been serving up pancakes and waffles (from its own original recipe, with several batter options available, including cornmeal and gingerbread) since 1938. ✉ *672 Rte. 117, Sugar Hill, NH* 🌐 *pollyspancakeparlor.com*

Getting Here and Around

The park is bisected by Interstate 93, between Lincoln and Franconia.

Kancamagus Highway

New Hampshire's Most Scenic Road

In 1937, two local roads were connected from Lincoln to Conway to create this remarkable 34½-mile designated National Scenic Byway through a breathtaking swath of the White Mountains. This section of Route 112 known as the Kancamagus—often called simply "the Kanc"—contains no businesses or billboards and is punctuated by overlooks, picnic areas, and memorable hiking trailheads. The road's highest point, at 2,855 feet, crosses the flank of Mt. Kancamagus, near Lincoln—the most perfect place to view the fiery displays of foliage each autumn.

Don't Miss

Connected to the Kanc via Bear Notch Road, scenic U.S. 302 winds northwest from the town of Bartlett through steep, wooded mountains on either side of spectacular **Crawford Notch State Park.** You can picnic and hike to Arethusa Falls, the longest drop in New England, or to the Silver and Flume cascades—they're among more than a dozen outstanding trails. ✉ *1464 U.S. 302, Hart's Location, NH* 🌐 *www.nhstateparks.org*

Best Hike

There are several excellent hikes along the Kancamagus Highway, but the most rewarding trek is the easy 6½-mile round-trip **Lincoln Woods** hike, which follows a picturesque railroad bed, crosses a dramatic suspension bridge over the Pemigewasset River, and ends at a swimming hole formed by dramatic Franconia Falls.

Getting Here and Around

The Kancamagus Highway is along the span of Route 112 between Lincoln and Conway.

Pemi Valley Moose Tours

Spy New England's Largest Land Mammal

Among the many majestic creatures that inhabit New Hampshire's rugged forests, moose—of which there are 3,500 to 4,000—are perhaps the most beguiling and mysterious. Weighing about 1,000 pounds on average and standing at about 6 feet at their shoulders, these powerful animals are the largest land mammals in the Northeast. You may just be lucky enough to see one through your car window—U.S. 3 and Routes 16 and 26 in the state's remote Great North Woods are a good bet, especially at dusk in summer. But you can greatly increase your odds by taking a three-hour guided excursion with Pemi Moose Tours—moose are seen on about 90% of these trips. ✉ *136 Main St., Lincoln, NH* 🌐 *www.moosetoursnh.com*

Don't Miss

The isolated and alluring **Great North Woods,** centered on the logging town of Pittsburg, occupies the 250-square-mile northern tip of the state. The 90-mile drive up U.S. 3 from Littleton to the Canadian border is a favorite for moose and other wildlife viewing.

Best Hotel

Old-world elegance and stunning views of the upper White Mountains define the **Mountain View Grand Resort and Spa.** ✉ *101 Mountain View Rd., Whitefield, NH* 🌐 *www.mountainviewgrand.com*

When to Go

Moose tours are offered early May through mid-October, which is also the best time to enjoy the area's scenery.

Getting Here and Around

Pemi Moose Tours operates out of Lincoln in the White Mountains, on Route 112, just off Interstate 93. The Great North Woods lies about 30 miles north via U.S. 3.

The Covered Bridges of Cornish

The Longest 19th-Century Covered Bridge

The 449-foot **Cornish–Windsor Bridge** connects New Hampshire to Vermont across the Connecticut River. Erected in 1866, it is the longest historic covered wooden bridge in the United States that carries automobile traffic. The notice on the bridge reads, "Walk your horses or pay two dollar fine." Serene and picturesque Cornish has two more scenic covered bridges and is also famous for having been home of the late reclusive author J.D. Salinger as well as a number of other acclaimed writers and artists, including Maxfield Parrish and Augustus Saint-Gaudens.

Don't Miss

The pastoral **Saint-Gaudens National Historic Site** celebrates the life and artistry of the leading 19th-century sculptor. In summer you can tour his house (with original furnishings), studio, and galleries, and it's a pleasure year-round to explore the 83 gorgeous acres of lawns, gardens, and woodlands dotted with casts of his works and laced with 2½ miles of hiking trails. ✉ *139 St. Gaudens Rd., Cornish, NH* 🌐 *www.nps.gov/saga*

Best Ice Cream

One of the Northeast's best purveyors of artisanal, small-batch ice cream, **Walpole Creamery** always features a long list of both regular and seasonal flavors, such as Fijian ginger, maple cream, wild blueberry, and mint–dark chocolate chip. ✉ *532 Main St., Walpole, NH* 🌐 *www.walpolecreamery.com*

Getting Here and Around

Just off Route 12A, about 20 miles south of Hanover, the Cornish–Windsor Bridge crosses the Connecticut River, leading to Interstate 91 in Vermont.

Dartmouth

The Stateliest Small-Town College Campus

The poet Robert Frost spent part of a brooding freshman semester at this Ivy League school before giving up college altogether, but Dartmouth counts politician Nelson Rockefeller, actor Mindy Kaling, TV producer Shonda Rhimes, and author Theodor ("Dr.") Seuss Geisel among its many illustrious grads. The buildings clustered around the picturesque green, which is lovely for strolling, include the **Baker Memorial Library**, which houses such literary treasures as 17th-century editions of William Shakespeare's works and Mexican artist José Clemente Orozco's 3,000-square-foot murals. ✉ *N. Main and Wentworth Sts., Hanover, NH* 🌐 *www.dartmouth.edu*

Don't Miss

The college's excellent (and free) **Hood Museum of Art** contains works by Picasso, Rothko, and Miró and is housed in a series of austere, copper-roof, redbrick buildings arranged around a courtyard. The Hopkins Center for the Arts bears a striking resemblance to Lincoln Center—architect Wallace K. Harrison designed both structures. ✉ *6 E. Wheelock St., Hanover, NH* 🌐 *hoodmuseum.dartmouth.edu*

Best Detour

From Hanover, make the beautiful 60-mile drive up Route 10 to **Littleton** for an enchantingly scenic tour of the upper Connecticut and lower Ammonoosuc river valleys.

Getting Here and Around

Hanover is just across the Connecticut River from Interstate 91 in Vermont and 10 miles up Route 120 from Interstate 89.

Portsmouth

New Hampshire's Coastal Jewel

More than a bustling and handsome harbor city with a storied history, Portsmouth is an unpretentiously upscale destination with trendy farm-to-table restaurants, contemporary art galleries, and cultural venues that host nationally recognized speakers and performers. Settled in 1623 as Strawbery Banke, Portsmouth grew into a prosperous port before the Revolutionary War. Today, swank cocktail bars, bumping live music, and late-night eateries create a convivial buzz in downtown's Market Square. And the pristine beaches of New Hampshire's short but scenic Atlantic shoreline, including Wallis Sands and Jenness, lie just a short drive away.

Don't Miss

On the site of Portsmouth's original seaport, known as Puddle Dock, the indoor-outdoor living history museum **Strawbery Banke** preserves local life from the late 1600s through the 1950s. English settlers named the area for the wild strawberries growing along the shores of the Piscataqua River, and the name lives on at this 10-acre campus with around 40 homes and other structures dating from 1695 to 1820. ✉ *14 Hancock St., Portsmouth, NH* 🌐 *www.strawberybanke.org*

Best Boat Tour

From May to early October, you can take a fascinating narrated cruise out to the rocky Isles of Shoals, located about 6 miles off the coast. A history of piracy, murder, and ghosts suffuses the archipelago. 🌐 *www.islesofshoals.com*

Getting Here and Around

Portsmouth is on the Atlantic coast, just south of the Maine border, off Interstate 95.

When in New Hampshire

CANTERBURY SHAKER VILLAGE

Established in 1792, this village 20 miles southwest of Lake Winnipesaukee flourished in the 1800s and practiced equality of the sexes and races, common ownership, celibacy, and pacifism. The last member of the religious community passed away in 1992. Shakers invented such household items as the clothespin and the flat broom and were known for the simplicity and integrity of their designs. Engaging guided tours—you can also explore on your own—pass through some of the 694-acre property's more than 25 restored buildings, many of them with original furnishings. Crafts demonstrations take place daily. ✉ *288 Shaker Rd., Canterbury, NH* 🌐 *www.shakers.org*

Do This: The on-site Creamery Café serves light lunch fare in a beautiful Shaker-designed dining room and sells seasonal vegetables and maple syrup. An excellent shop sells handcrafted wares, from handcrafted round boxes and soaps to lotions and home furnishings.

CURRIER MUSEUM OF ART

In a historic residential neighborhood in Manchester, the state's largest city, this superb museum maintains an astounding permanent collection of works by European and American masters, among them Claude Monet, Edward Hopper, Winslow Homer, John Marin, Andrew Wyeth, and Childe Hassam. It presents excellent rotating exhibits of contemporary art, too. Be sure to set aside some time to stroll a few blocks west to Manchester's bustling dining and nightlife strip, Elm Street, which has a number of excellent cafés, cocktail bars, and craft breweries. ✉ *150 Ash St., Manchester, NH* *www.currier.org*

Do This: The Currier also arranges guided tours of the only two Frank Lloyd Wright–designed residences in New England open to the public, the Zimmerman House and the Kalil House. Completed in the 1950s, both designs are in the architect's sparse and functional Usonian style and contain their original Wright-designed furnishings. Kalil House is one of only seven "Usonian Automatic" homes ever built—these were built with interlocking concrete blocks intended to make their construction quick and economical.

LAKE SUNAPEE

Greater Lake Sunapee's pristine 6-square-miles of water—one of the highest and cleanest in New Hampshire—is the perfect peaceful retreat for families, artists, nature lovers, and anyone seeking lakeside tranquility. On the west shore you'll find Sunapee Harbor, an old-fashioned summer resort community with a large marina, a small museum, a few restaurants and shops on the water, and a tidy village green with a gazebo. Mt. Sunapee State Park has a pretty beach and a 3,000-foot mountain with excellent skiing and hiking. The beloved League of New Hampshire Craftsmen's Fair, the oldest crafts fair in the nation, takes place in early August.

Do This: A buffet dinner is included on the two-hour sunset cruises aboard Sunapee Cruises' MV *Kearsarge,* a vintage-style steamship. 🌐 *www.sunapeecruises.com*

PETERBOROUGH

While summering in the famed MacDowell artists' colony in this longtime hub of creativity in the lush Monadnock Mountains, Thornton Wilder wrote the classic play *Our Town,* basing it on Peterborough itself. This is also where Aaron Copland and Leonard Bernstein composed works, and James Baldwin, Willa Cather, and Alice Walker wrote novels. The town draws crowds in summer for its Monadnock Music and Peterborough Folk Music Society concerts, and performances by the Peterborough Players. You can play instruments or try on costumes from around the world at the nonprofit Mariposa Museum, which is dedicated to hands-on exploration of international folk art.

Do This: Said to be America's most climbed mountain, nearby Mt. Monadnock rises to 3,165 feet, and on clear days you can see the Boston skyline. Five trailheads branch out into more than two dozen trails of varying difficulty. ✉ *580 Mountain Rd., Jaffrey, NH* 🌐 *www.nhstateparks.org*

PICKITY PLACE

Set down a remote wooded lane near the Massachusetts border, this endearing 1786 cottage looks right out of a fairy tale, and indeed, it served as the model for artist Elizabeth Orton Jones for her illustrations of the popular 1948 edition of the children's tale, *Little Red Riding Hood*. These days it's the centerpiece of a hilltop estate surrounded by fragrant gardens patrolled by a friendly team of cats and consisting of a nursery, a gift shop that sells herbs and gourmet goods, and an inviting restaurant that serves delicious locally sourced prix-fixe lunches that feature produce grown on the property. ✉ *248 Nutting Hill Rd., Mason, NH* 🌐 *www.pickityplace.com*

Do This: Walk off your meal with a ramble among the more than 105 contemporary sculptures set throughout the 140-acre Andres Institute of Art, which is 10 miles away in Brookfield. The hilly property that used to occupy a small ski area is laced with peaceful trails. ✉ *106 Rte. 13, Brookline, NH* 🌐 *andresinstitute.org*

TAMWORTH

President Grover Cleveland summered in what remains a place of almost unreal quaintness: the town of Tamworth, convenient both to Lake Winnipesaukee and the White Mountains. Today it is equally photogenic in verdant summer, during the fall foliage season, or under a blanket of winter snow. Cleveland's son, Francis, returned and founded the acclaimed Barnstormers Theatre in 1931. One of America's first summer theaters, it continues to this day. Tamworth has a clutch of villages within its borders and six historic churches. In the hamlet of Chocorua, the view through the birches of Chocorua Lake has been so often photographed that you may experience déjà vu. Rising above the lake is Mt. Chocorua (3,490 feet), which has many good hiking trails.

Do This: Using a 250-gallon copper constructed in Kentucky, artisanal Tamworth Distilling is set in a stately barn just a short stroll from famed Barnstormers Theatre. It produces exceptional craft spirits, including 9-Year-Aged Bourbon, Strawberry Rhubarb Cordial, Tamworth Garden Watermelon Gin, and several flavorful cordials. If you're lucky, your stop will include a chance to sample Eau de Musc, a limited-release whiskey infused with an oil extracted from the castor glands of beavers. ✉ *Rtes. 113 and 113A, Tamworth, NH* 🌐 *www.tamworthdistilling.com*

About Our Writers

Andrew Collins resides part-time near Lake Sunapee in a small lake cottage that's been in his family for three decades. His favorite part of just about every spring-through-fall evening is paddling around the lake, visiting with its two loons and occasional heron, eagles, and barred owls, and watching the sun set gently over the surrounding foothills. A regular contributor to numerous Fodor's guidebooks, he also writes for *Yankee Magazine* and the Points Guy.

Cool Places to Stay

Inn at East Hill Farm. For those with animal-obsessed kids, East Hill Farm is heaven: a family resort (rates include all meals) with daylong children's programs on a 160-acre farm overlooking Mt. Monadnock that include milking cows; collecting eggs; feeding the sheep, donkeys, cows, rabbits, horses, chickens, goats, and ducks; horseback and pony rides; hiking and hayrides in summer; and sledding and sleigh rides in winter. ✉ *460 Monadnock St., Troy, NH* 🌐 *www.east-hill-farm.com*

Omni Mount Washington Resort. The two most memorable sights in the White Mountains might just be Mt. Washington and this dramatic 1902 resort with a 900-foot veranda, glimmering public rooms, astonishing views of the Presidential Range, and dozens of recreational activities like tubing, sleigh rides, horseback riding, and fly-fishing. ✉ *310 Mt. Washington Hotel Rd., Bretton Woods, NH* 🌐 *www.mountwashingtonresort.com*

Pickering House Inn. This striking yellow 1813 Federal mansion within walking distance of Lake Winnipesaukee ranks among New Hampshire's most luxurious small inns, with its luxe rooms and superb adjacent restaurant, Pavilion. ✉ *116 S. Main St., Wolfeboro, NH* 🌐 *www.pickeringhousewolfeboro.com*

Squam Lake Inn. Graceful Victorian furnishings fill this peaceful farmhouse inn a short stroll from Squam Lake, the setting of the 1981 film *On Golden Pond*. Each of its 10 rooms are richly outfitted with comfortable beds, organic toiletries, and soft bathrobes; rates include a sumptuous gourmet breakfast. ✉ *28 Shepard Hill Rd., Holderness, NH* 🌐 *www.squamlakeinn.com*

Sugar Hill Inn. Although this upscale inn surrounded by neatly manicured gardens dates to 1789, it has a decidedly current vibe, thanks to its sumptuous rooms with modern perks like whirlpool tubs, gas fireplaces, and Bose sound systems as well as the superb prix-fixe restaurant serving contemporary American fare. ✉ *116 NH 117, Sugar Hill Rd., Sugar Hill, NH* 🌐 *www.sugarhillinn.com*

Essential Eats

Hungry Diner. This festive, family-friendly gastropub near the Connecticut River serves delicious, globally inspired comfort food that relies heavily on seasonal ingredients, including pasture-raised meats. Have a seat at a picnic table on the sprawling lawn. ✉ *9 Edwards La., Walpole, NH* 🌐 *www.hungrydinerwalpole.com*

Little Red Schoolhouse. Although miles inland, this counter-service eatery inside a funky converted schoolhouse with screened-in seating high above the Pemigewasset River serves some of the tastiest lobster rolls in New England, plus garlic fries, craft beer, and homemade ice cream sandwiches. ✉ *1994 Daniel Webster Hwy., Campton, NH* 🌐 *www.littleredschoolhousenh.com*

Stages at One Washington. The exquisite multicourse dinners presented here in the intimate dining room in a converted redbrick mill building showcase New Hampshire's freshest bounty, from succulent shellfish to locally foraged mushrooms. ✉ *1 Washington St., Dover, NH* 🌐 *www.stages-dining.com*

Super Secret Ice Cream. Savor unimaginably luscious frozen desserts at this cheerful artisan parlor in the quaint White Mountains village of Bethlehem. The flavors rotate regularly to feature local ingredients but might include honeycomb, raspberry lemon balm, or malted milk and fudge. ✉ *2213 Main St., Bethlehem, NH* 🌐 *www.supersecreticecream.com*

Rhode Island

"Rhode Island: 3% Bigger at Low Tide" reads a locally made T-shirt—an exaggeration, of course: the state geologist calculates it's actually more like 0.5%. But the smallest state's size is a source of pride, given all there is to do within its 1,545 square miles. You may find it hard to choose among so many experiences: historic walks, fine dining, and the WaterFire display in Providence; apple picking and riverboat cruises in the Blackstone Valley; fishing trips and beach excursions in South County and on Block Island; pedaling along the East Bay Bike Path; and taking sunset sails in Newport and touring the Gilded Age mansions.

Capital: Providence

Population: 1,112,308

Area: 1,045 square miles

Statehood Date: May 29, 1790

Major Airports: Rhode Island T.F. Green International Airport (PVD)

Travel and Tourism Information: 🌐 *www.visitrhodeisland.com*

Famous Residents: Roger Williams (minister and state founder); H.P. Lovecraft (writer); Meredith Vieira (television personality); Viola Davis (actress); Taylor Swift (singer)

Fun Fact: Rhode Island is the smallest state, but for centuries it had the longest name: the State of Rhode Island and Providence Plantations. In 2020, however, the "plantations" reference was removed due to its association with slavery.

Newport Mansions

The USA's Most Opulent Homes

The Gilded Age mansions of Bellevue Avenue are the go-to attraction for many Newport visitors. These ornately detailed late 19th-century homes, designed with a determined one-upmanship by the very wealthy, are almost obscenely grand. Their owners—Vanderbilts, Astors, Belmonts, and other budding aristocrats who made the city their playground for a mere six to eight summer weeks each year—helped establish the best young American architects and precipitated the arrival of the New York Yacht Club, which turned Newport into one of the sailing capitals of the world. ✉ *424 Bellevue Ave., Newport, RI* 🌐 *www.newportmansions.org*

Don't Miss

A visit to the 70-room "summer cottage" owned by Cornelius Vanderbilt II, **the Breakers**, offers a peek into the private lives of the one-percenters of the Gilded Age.

Best Stroll

See the backyards of Newport's Gilded Age mansions as well as dramatic views of Easton's Beach and Narragansett Bay while strolling along the 3½-mile **Cliff Walk**. 🌐 *cliffwalk.com*

When to Go

Many, but not all, of the most prominent mansions on Bellevue Avenue close from January through mid-April; The Breakers, Marble House, and The Elms are known for their winter holiday displays. Check the website of the Preservation Society of Newport County for seasonal schedules.

Getting Here and Around

Most of Newport's Gilded Age mansions are on Bellevue Avenue, a short drive southeast of downtown Newport or a leisurely half-hour to hour-long walk.

Providence's Benefit Street

An Architectural Showplace

Stretching just over a mile on Providence's East Side, this cobblestone street is a walkable museum comprising some of the country's best-preserved concentrations of colonial architecture and including parts of the campuses of Brown University and the Rhode Island School of Design. The city's wealthiest families lived along the "mile of history" during the 18th and early 19th centuries. Take a tour of the city's most famous 18th-century home, the three-story **John Brown House Museum**, which now serves as the Rhode Island history museum.

Don't Miss

The gorgeous **Rhode Island School of Design (RISD) Museum of Art** houses more than 86,000 objects ranging from ancient art to work by contemporary artists, from Cézanne and Picasso to Warhol and Hockney. Works by RISD graduates, such as glass artist Dale Chihuly, are among the collection. ✉ *20 N. Main St., Providence, RI* 🌐 *risdmuseum.org*

Best Historic Site

Philadelphia architect William Strickland designed the 1838 **Providence Athenaeum** in which Edgar Allan Poe courted the poet Sarah Helen Whitman. An 1870s Manet print that illustrated Poe's "The Raven" hangs in the rare book room. Admission is free, but only members can check out books. ✉ *251 Benefit St., Providence, RI* 🌐 *providenceathenaeum.org*

Getting Here and Around

Benefit Street is just east of and a short walk across the Providence River from downtown, set on the slope of College Hill.

Providence's Riverwalk

Rhode Island's Most Dynamic Promenade

Venetian-style footbridges, seasonal gondola rides, art installations, cobblestone walkways, historic monuments, quaint shops, excellent restaurants, and an amphitheater encircling a tidal basin make this 4-acre park along the Woonasquatucket River the place to take in the views and activity in downtown Providence. In summer, Waterplace Park is a gathering place for free concerts and for **WaterFire**, an award-winning fire sculpture installation on downtown's three rivers featuring music and nearly 100 burning braziers that rise from the water between dusk and midnight. Public parks edge both banks of the Providence River as it flows toward Narragansett Bay, connected by a pedestrian bridge.

Don't Miss

Curving across the lower end of the Providence River, the sleek and contemporary **Providence Pedestrian Bridge** is decked with artful wooden benches and is a lovely spot for a walk or a bike ride, especially at sunset. Pause mid-span for memorable views of the downtown skyline. The bridge connects the up-and-coming Jewelry District and Innovation District to East Side attractions like Wickenden Street and Fox Point, home to international restaurants and quirky cafés.

Best Restaurant

In a city where culinary newcomers tend to garner all the attention, **Hemenway's** continues to stand out for serving absolutely stellar seafood. ✉ *121 S. Main St., Providence, RI* 🌐 *www.hemenwaysrestaurant.com*

Getting Here and Around

The Providence riverfront is in the heart of the city's walkable downtown, just off Interstates 95 and 195.

Block Island

New England's Most Dramatic Sea Cliffs

With a rugged, windswept beauty that's reminiscent of the coast of Scotland, laid-back Block Island lies about 12 miles off the state's southern coast. The Nature Conservancy designated the island one of the "Last Great Places on Earth" (one of only 12 in the Western Hemisphere) in 1991, commending its efforts to preserve the island's precious ecosystem. You'll find the most awe-inspiring terrain atop the 200-foot cliffs traversed by the Mohegan Trail, from which you can see all the way to eastern Long Island on a clear day. A steep, 141-step staircase leads to a picturesque beach at the bottom (although the lower section of the stairs is currently closed due to erosion damage). More dramatic views can be had at the Southeast Lighthouse, where a museum is housed inside an 1875 redbrick lighthouse with gingerbread detail.

Among the island's prettiest stretches of white sand, 3-mile **Crescent Beach** runs north from the main village, Old Harbor.

Don't Miss

Animal lovers will want to stop at the **1661 Inn Animal Farm** located on the property of Block Island Resorts to spot black swans, yaks, fainting goats, and a famed ZeDonk—zebra-donkey hybrid. ✉ *43 Spring St., New Shoreham, RI* 🌐 *www.blockislandresorts.com*

Getting Here and Around

You can reach Block Island by car ferry from Point Judith, at the south tip of Narragansett, and by seasonal passenger ferry from Newport, Fall River, New London, and Montauk. There are also daily 12-minute flights from the town of Westerly. The island is best explored by bike but taxis and rental mopeds also are available. 🌐 *www.blockislandferry.com*

Narragansett

Rhode Island's Prettiest Beaches

A lively summer-long resort destination since the Victorian era, "'Gansett" still has as its main landmark The Towers, the last remaining section of the 1886 Narragansett Pier Casino designed by McKim, Mead & White. The town is much quieter these days, but its historic charm, rocky coastline hikes, and pretty beaches still draw day-trippers, beach lovers, and hikers. Take a scenic drive down Route 1A to see the ocean and grand old shingle-style homes. Favorite spots for enjoying the sand include **Narragansett Town Beach** and **Roger W. Wheeler State Beach**.

Don't Miss

A little corner of Narragansett with a lively working fishing village, the **Port of Galilee** is where you can eat at a fish shack, go for a swim at Salty Brine State Beach, or just watch fishermen unload their catch. From the Galilee, it's a short drive to **Point Judith Lighthouse**, an 1857 tower with a beautiful ocean view.

Best Restaurant

Aunt Carrie's has been a must for locals every summer since it opened in 1920. Try the Indian pudding, a traditional dessert made with cornmeal, molasses, and spices. ✉ *1240 Ocean Rd., Narragansett, RI* 🌐 *www.auntcarriesri.com*

When to Go

Summer is the prime season to experience Narragansett's beaches. Late spring and early autumn are far less crowded.

Getting Here and Around

Narragansett is along the coast in southern Rhode Island, just off U.S. 1 via Route 108 and Route 1A, about 15 miles west of Newport and 30 miles south of Providence.

Newport Jazz and Folk Festivals

New England's Most Respected Music Festivals

Held at Fort Adams State Park, on a scenic peninsula that abuts the city's yacht-filled harbor, the Newport Jazz and Newport Folk festivals are among the country's most respected music showcases. Launched in 1959 and held each summer on the last weekend in July, the **Newport Folk Festival** (🌐 *newportfolk.org*) books acts spanning folk, blues, country, bluegrass, folk rock, alt-country, indie folk, and folk punk. It's where, controversially, Bob Dylan went electric in 1965, most recently documented in the 2024 film*A Complete Unknown*. The grandfather of all jazz festivals, **Newport Jazz** (🌐 *newportjazz.org*) has been held the first weekend in August since 1954 and featured Miles Davis and Frank Sinatra back in the day and Terence Blanchard, Ravi Coltrane, Jon Batiste, and Corinne Bailey Rae more recently.

Don't Miss

Home of the largest coastal fortification in the United States, **Fort Adams State Park** hosts not only music festivals but also sailing events like the Volvo Ocean Race. The views of Newport Harbor are exquisite. Guided and self-guided tours of the fort, which dates to 1841, are available most of the year, including hard-hat tours that take visitors into tunnels beneath the massive outer walls. ✉ *80 Fort Adams Dr., Newport, RI* 🌐 *fortadams.org*

Getting Here and Around

Fort Adams State Park forms the southwestern edge of Newport Harbor; the Harrison Avenue entrance to the park is a little over 3½ miles south of the Newport Visitor Information Center that serves as the main gateway to the city's waterfront district.

Bristol

The Nation's Oldest Fourth of July Party

America's longest-running July 4 celebration, which features a 2½-mile parade, has been taking place in Bristol since 1785. The town celebrates this heritage with a red-white-and-blue center stripe down Hope Street, which bisects its charming business district. Bristol sits on a 10-square-mile peninsula between Narragansett Bay and Mount Hope Bay and was once a boatbuilding center. The southern end of the East Bay Bike Path, which crosses the access road for Colt State Park, is a great spot for picnicking and kite-flying.

Don't Miss

A beautifully situated museum on Bristol Harbor that's devoted to the sport of yachting, the **Herreshoff Marine Museum** honors the Herreshoff Manufacturing Company—maker of yachts for eight consecutive America's Cup defenses. It has several dozen boats ranging from an 8½-foot dinghy to the *Defiant*, a 75-foot successful America's Cup defender. ✉ *1 Burnside St., Bristol, RI* 🌐 *herreshoff.org*

Best Restaurant

Family-owned **Quito's** has been serving fresh seafood—including Rhode Island's distinctive take on clam chowder—to Bristol residents and visitors since 1956 from its modest waterfront dining room and patio. ✉ *411 Thames St., Bristol, RI* 🌐 *www.quitosrestaurant.com*

Getting Here and Around

Bristol is in southeastern Rhode Island's East Bay region, midway between Providence and Newport on Route 114. The Mount Hope Bridge connects the town to Aquidneck Island, where Newport, Portsmouth, and Middletown are located.

When in Rhode Island

INTERNATIONAL TENNIS HALL OF FAME

Tennis fans —but really any lovers of history, art, and architecture—shouldn't miss visiting the birthplace of American tournament tennis. The beautifully designed museum contains interactive exhibits, a holographic theater that offers an "almost live" conversation with Roger Federer, displays of tennis attire worn by the sport's biggest stars, video highlights of great matches, and memorabilia that includes the 1874 patent from England's Queen Victoria for the game of lawn tennis. The 6-acre site just up the street from Newport's famous mansions is home to a grandstand, the shingle-style Newport Casino, which opened in 1880 and was designed by architects McKim, Mead & White, and the opulent Casino Theatre. ✉ *194 Bellevue Ave., Newport, RI* 🌐 *www.tennisfame.com*

Do This: Anybody can play on the 13 grass tennis courts, one clay court, and in the indoor tennis facility—just try to book a few days in advance, especially on weekends. And in mid-July, you can attend the prestigious Hall of Fame Open, which also features a Hall of Fame induction ceremony.

OLD SLATER MILL

Concord and Lexington may legitimately lay claim to what Ralph Waldo Emerson called "the shot heard round the world" in 1776, but Pawtucket's Slater Mill provided the necessary economic shot in the arm. Built in 1793, this focal point of the Blackstone River Valley National Historical Park was the first successful water-powered spinning mill in America; it touched off the industrial revolution that helped secure America's sovereign independence in the early days of the republic. The museum complex explores this second revolution with expert interpretive guides dressed in period clothing, who demonstrate fiber-to-yarn and yarn-to-fabric processes and discuss how industrialization forever changed this nation. ✉ *67 Roosevelt Ave., Pawtucket, RI* 🌐 *www.nps.gov/blrv*

Do This: Drive about 15 miles up the Blackstone River from Pawtucket to visit the cleverly designed Museum of Work & Culture in Woonsocket, which occupies another prominent former mill. This interactive museum examines the lives of American factory workers and owners during the Industrial Revolution, with a focus on the many French Canadian immigrants who toiled in the city's textile mills. ✉ *42 S. Main St., Woonsocket, RI* 🌐 *www.rihs.org*

PROVIDENCE'S FEDERAL HILL

Federal Hill has been the heart of the city's Italian community for generations. Around colorful DePasquale Plaza and along the main drag, Atwells Avenue, you'll find a slew of inviting, old-world Italian restaurants. Favorites include Angelo's Civita Farnese (✉ *141 Atwells Ave., Providence, RI* 🌐 *www.angelosri.com*), with its flavorful eggplant Parmesan and braciola like grandma used to make, and romantic, warmly lighted Pane e Vino (✉ *365 Atwells Ave., Providence, RI* 🌐 *www.panevino.net*), which stands out for its exceptional wine list and sophisticated fare like imported burrata with prosciutto di Parma and bone-in veal chops with a mushroom demi-glace.

Do This: After dinner, walk a few blocks south into the hip and increasingly trendy foodie neighborhood of West Broadway for dessert at Tricycle Ice Cream, whose delicious small-batch ice cream sandwiches come in imaginative flavors. Consider the toasted-coconut cookies with Thai tea ice cream or a banana pudding ice cream sandwich. ✉ *70 Battey St., Providence, RI* 🌐 *www.tricycleicecream.com*

SAILING NARRAGANSETT BAY

For a small state, Rhode Island has a huge amount of coastline—400 miles—much of which is accounted for by Narragansett Bay. Among the best ways to experience the state's most vital and beautiful natural resource is to take a sunset tour from Newport Harbor on boats like the schooners *Madeline* and *Adirondack II* or the classic motor yacht *Rum Runner II*. During summer, the Seastreak Providence Newport Ferry delivers a one-hour tour of the length of Narragansett Bay along with transportation between Rhode Island's two most prominent cities. Conservation group Save the Bay operates lighthouse tours in the summer and seal watch tours from November to April, which is the best way to encounter Narragansett Bay's marine mammals in their natural habitat.

Do This: Sail Newport's Public Sailing Center offers sailing lessons and J/22 and Rhodes 19 sailboat rentals in Newport Harbor. Three-hour rentals start at $114. ✉ *72 Fort Adams Dr., Newport, RI* 🌐 *www.sailnewport.org*

TOURO SYNAGOGUE

In 1658, more than a dozen Jewish families from Barbados, whose ancestors had fled Spain and Portugal during the Inquisition, founded a congregation in Newport. A century later, Peter Harrison designed this two-story, Palladian-style house of worship for the community. The oldest surviving synagogue in the United States, Touro was dedicated in 1763 and its simple exterior and elegant interior remain virtually unchanged. ✉ *85 Touro St., Newport, RI* 🌐 *www.tourosynagogue.org*

Do This: The John L. Loeb Visitors Center has two floors of state-of-the-art exhibits on early American Jewish life and Newport's Colonial history.

WATCH HILL LIGHTHOUSE

For generations, the seaside village of Watch Hill has attracted movers and shakers looking for a low-key getaway. Its nearly 2 miles of gorgeous beaches—including Napatree Point Conservation Area—are a great spot to see shorebirds and raptors and take in the sunset. A highlight of any visit is touring the tiny museum at the often-photographed 1808 Watch Hill Lighthouse, which contains the original Fresnel light, letters and journals from lighthouse keepers, and photos of the hurricane of 1938 (✉ *14 Lighthouse Rd., Westerly, RI* 🌐 *www.watchhilllighthousekeepers.org*). Nearby on Bay Street, you can go for a ride on the Flying Horse Carousel, one of the oldest in America—it dates to the 1870s. This is also the town where Taylor Swift has a summer home (you can spot its location by the cheeky "I Knew You Were Trouble When You Walked In" no trespassing sign).

Do This: Overlooking Watch Hill Cove since it first opened as an ice-cream parlor in 1916, the Olympia Tea Room is now one of South County's most sophisticated and charming bistros. Varnished wood booths and a long marble counter echo the restaurant's rich history. The kitchen focuses on local and artisanal ingredients served with simple elegance, including Portuguese baked haddock and Milanese style roast chicken. The sommelier has curated a wine list with more than 100 selections, a number of which are available by the glass. ✉ *74 Bay St., Westerly, RI* 🌐 *www.olympiatearoom.com*

Cool Places to Stay

Hotel Manisses. One of the several stately Victorian hotels on relaxing Block Island, this elegant 1870 inn is a short stroll from the ferry dock and stands out with its distinctive mansard roof and central tower. ✉ *251 Spring St., New Shoreham, RI* 🌐 *www.hotelmanisses.com*

Ocean House. High on bluffs overlooking Block Island Sound stands this extraordinary replica of the Victorian grande dame of the same name built here in 1868. After the dilapidated original was torn down in 2004, Ocean House was rebuilt with the same warm yellow exterior, lobby fireplace stonework, and front desk mail slots. This new version has a third of the original's rooms, however, and more than twice the windows—the better to appreciate the stunning views. ✉ *1 Bluff Ave., Westerly, RI* 🌐 *www.oceanhouseri.com*

Renaissance Providence Downtown Hotel. This posh hotel occupies one of Providence's most mysterious addresses, a stately nine-story Neoclassical Revival building constructed as a Masonic temple between 1926 and 1928 but unoccupied for an inconceivable 75 years—the decor pays tribute to the building's history with photos of vintage graffiti found in the long-empty corridors during its restoration. ✉ *5 Ave. of the Arts, Providence, RI* 🌐 *www.marriott.com*

Rose Island Lighthouse. Visible at the mouth of Narragansett Bay from the soaring Claiborne Pell bridge and reached via seasonal Jamestown Newport Ferry, this 1870 lighthouse beside colonial Fort Hamilton offers overnight accommodations from April to October in several different buildings, including the keeper's apartment, the museum, the 1912 Foghorn Building, and the dramatically high-ceilinged Fort Hamilton Barracks. ✉ *Rose Island, Newport, RI* 🌐 *www.roseisland.org*

Essential Eats

Gracie's. This Providence landmark has consistently delivered a top fine-dining experience for more than 25 years; the five- and seven-course tasting menus are the quintessential special occasion splurge in the state. ✉ *194 Washington St., Providence, RI* 🌐 *www.graciesprov.com*

Los Andes. Chef Cesin Curi is widely credited with bringing Peruvian and Bolivian cuisine to the mainstream of the Rhode Island food scene; enjoy the ceviches, churrascos, and paellas here in a charming courtyard. ✉ *903 Chalkstone Ave., Providence, RI* 🌐 *www.losandesri.com*

Matunuck Oyster Bar. Only a restaurant this good could survive a devastating fire, reopen in a tent, and still attract droves of guests for fresh seafood, including shellfish from owner Perry Raso's own aquaculture operation. ✉ *629 Succotash Rd., Wakefield, RI* 🌐 *www.rhodyoysters.com*

Pasquale's Pizzeria Napoletana. The Neapolitan-style pizzas referenced in the eatery's name are chef Pasquale Illiano's calling card, but this Wakefield pizzeria also serves the best New York–style pie in Rhode Island—plus a square "Grandma" pizza that's worthy of Nonna's kitchen. ✉ *59 S. County Commons Way, Wakefield, RI* 🌐 *www.pasqualespizzeriari.com*

About Our Writers

Bob Curley grew up in New York but has spent more years in the Ocean State than the Empire State. A resident of North Kingstown for more than three decades, he discovered the charms of Little Rhody early on by wandering the back roads of his adopted state, researching stories and travel books. Bob continues to work as a freelance travel, lifestyle, and health writer as well as working in communications for Bryant University in Smithfield, RI.

Vermont

Vermont is a land of hidden treasures and unspoiled scenery. Wander anywhere in the state—over 70% is forest—and you'll find pristine countryside dotted with farms and framed by mountains. Tiny towns with picturesque church steeples, village greens, and clapboard colonial-era houses are perfect for exploring. In fall the leaves have their last hurrah, painting the mountainsides in yellow, gold, red, and orange. But almost anywhere you go, no matter what time of year, the Vermont countryside will make you reach for your camera.

Capital: Montpelier

Population: 648,493

Area: 9,217 square miles

Statehood Date: March 4, 1791

Major Airports: Patrick Leahy Burlington International Airport (BTV); Rutland–Southern Vermont Regional Airport (RUT)

Travel and Tourism Information: ⊕ *www.vermontvacation.com* ⊕

Famous Residents: Ethan Allen (military officer and politician); Calvin Coolidge (president); Robert Frost (poet); Jamaica Kincaid (writer); Noah Kahan (singer/songwriter)

Fun Fact: Vermont's state fruit is the apple, and if you're serving it in pie form, be sure to offer cheddar cheese, ice cream, or milk along with each slice—it's literally a state law.

Stowe Mountain Resort

Ski Vermont's Tallest Mountain

The name of the village is Stowe and the name of the 4,393-foot mountain is Mt. Mansfield—but to generations of winter sports enthusiasts, it's all just plain "Stowe." The area's mystique attracts as many serious skiers as social ones. Stowe is a giant among eastern ski mountains thanks to its intimidating expert runs, but riders of all abilities enjoy the long, satisfying runs from the summit. Improved snowmaking capacity, new lifts, and free shuttle buses that gather skiers along Mountain Road have made it all much more convenient. Yet the traditions remain, like the Winter Carnival in January and the Sugar Slalom in April. ✉ *5781 Mountain Rd., Stowe, VT* 🌐 *www.stowe.com*

Don't Miss

Stowe village is tiny but charming—just a few blocks of shops and restaurants clustered around a picture-perfect white church with a lofty steeple. At **Cold Hollow Cider Mill**, you can watch apples pressed into possibly the world's best cider and sample it right from the tank. Its store sells all the apple butter, jams and jellies, and Vermont-made handicrafts you could want, plus legendary cider doughnuts. ✉ *3600 Waterbury–Stowe Rd., Stowe, VT* 🌐 *www.coldhollow.com*

When to Go

Ski season runs from late November through April, but events like Music in the Meadow, Stowe Jazz Festival, Stowe Hot Air Balloon Festival, and Race to the Top of Vermont take place in summer and fall.

Getting Here and Around

The ski area is 8 miles northwest of downtown Stowe on Route 108, and a 50-minute drive east of Burlington.

Burlington and Lake Champlain

New England's Largest Lake

As you drive along Main Street toward downtown Burlington, it's easy to see why this city is often called one of the most livable small cities in the United States—locals Bernie Sanders and Ben & Jerry certainly think so. Stroll downtown Burlington for cool bars and galleries; just beyond, Lake Champlain shimmers beneath the towering Adirondacks on the New York shore. The revitalized Burlington waterfront teems with outdoors enthusiasts who bike or stroll along its 8-mile recreation path, picnic on the grass, laze in the sand at North Beach, and ply the waters in sailboats and motor craft in summer. Narrated dinner and sunset sails are offered by Lake Champlain Shoreline Cruises on the 363-passenger Ethan Allen III (🌐 *www.soea.com*).

Don't Miss

Pedestrian-only Church Street Marketplace is Burlington's center of commerce and activity, with boutiques, cafés, restaurants, and street vendors by day, and a lively bar scene at night.

Best Breweries

Craft beers are huge in Vermont, and Burlington is home to quite a few gems that offer taprooms, including **Foam Brewers** (🌐 *www.foambrewers.com*) and **Zero Gravity** (🌐 *www.zerogravitybeer.com*).

Getting Here and Around

Burlington is in northwestern Vermont just off Interstate 89, and the Lake Champlain waterfront is at the end of College Street, a short walk down the hill from downtown.

Morse Farm Maple Sugarworks

Vermont's Most Celebrated Syrup

With eight generations sugaring over the past 200 years, the Morses may be the oldest maple family in existence, so you're sure to find an authentic experience at their farm. More than 5,000 trees produce the sap used for syrup (you can sample all the grades), candy, cream, and sugar—all sold in the gift shop. Grab a creemee (soft-serve ice cream available year-round), take a seat on a swing, and stay awhile. ✉ *1168 County Rd., Montpelier, VT* 🌐 *www.morsefarm.com*

Don't Miss

Here in the nation's smallest capital city, the regal **Vermont State House** building features a gleaming dome topped by the goddess of agriculture and columns of Barre granite measuring 6 feet in diameter. A free half-hour tour (guided July through October, self-guided the rest of the year) takes you through the governor's office and the house and senate chambers. Interior paintings and exhibits make much of Vermont's sterling Civil War record. ✉ *115 State St., Montpelier, VT* 🌐 *www.statehouse.vermont.gov*

Best Distillery

On the aptly named Gin Lane, Vermont's top distillery **Barr Hill** crafts award-winning spirits from raw honey. Stop in for a tasting and tour, but be sure to hang around for a classic Bee's Knees or G&T. ✉ *116 Gin La., Montpelier, VT* 🌐 *barrhill.com*

When to Go

The farm and shop are open year-round, and sell fresh seasonal veggies in summer. But for the sweetest experience, visit during the sugaring season, February through April.

Getting Here and Around

The farm is just 3 miles north of downtown Montpelier, which is off Interstate 89 in central Vermont.

Hill Farmstead Brewery

America's Best Craft Beer

It is difficult to quantify owner and master brewer Shaun Hill's contribution to the international explosion of craft beer. Hill Farmstead has won Best Brewery in the World eight times since 2012, and it's a key player in Vermont tourism, where beer contributes as much to the state economy as skiing and hiking. Since opening in 2010, Hill's eighth-generation family farmstead off a rural mountain pass, miles from cell service, has drawn millions of local and international travelers pilgrimaging for a coveted pint and a growler to-go. A beautiful bar is surrounded by acres of woods and lawn space, and a small pond sits at the bottom of a sloping field—a nice spot for pondering over a pint. ✉ *403 Hill Rd., Greensboro Bend, VT* 🌐 *www.hillfarmstead.com*

Don't Miss

The staple brews at Hill Farmstead are named for Hill's ancestors who once occupied the farm. Grab a pour of Edward, Dorothy, or Arthur from the taproom and enjoy it—and the unspoiled view—on the wraparound porch.

Good to Know

Restaurants around here are scarce, but Hill Farmstead often hosts food trucks. For more provisions, head to the sprawling Willey's Store near Caspian Lake's public beach to find a treasure trove of Greensboro's award-winning Jasper Hill Farm cheese, with the best prices around. ✉ *7 Breezy Ave, Greensboro, VT* 🌐 *www.facebook.com/willeys.store*

Getting Here and Around

Hill Farmstead is 4 miles from the tiny town of Greensboro in Vermont's Northeast Kingdom. Greensboro is 30 miles northwest of Interstate 91 in St. Johnsbury, 30 miles northeast of Stowe, and 40 miles south of the Canadian border. Cell phone service is limited to nonexistent in the area.

Marsh-Billings-Rockefeller National Historical Park

Vermont's Only National Historical Park

The nation's first national historical park focused on conserving natural resources, this pristine 555-acre spread includes the mansion, gardens, and carriage roads of Frederick H. Billings, a financier and the president of the Northern Pacific Railway. You can learn about its history at the visitor center, take a ranger-led or self-guided tour of the residential complex, and explore the 20 miles of trails and old carriage roads that climb Mt. Tom. The surrounding town of Woodstock is a Currier & Ives print come to life, with well-maintained Federal-style houses surrounding the village green. ✉ *69 Old River Rd., Woodstock, VT* 🌐 *www.nps.gov/mabi*

Don't Miss

Also founded by Frederick H. Billings, **Billings Farm and Museum** is one of the oldest operating dairy farms in the country. Pick up some raw-milk cheddar while you're here. ✉ *69 Old River Rd., Woodstock, VT* 🌐 *www.billingsfarm.org*

Best Restaurant

With the table literally on the farm, **Cloudland Farm** delivers a unique farm-to-table experience. ✉ *1101 Cloudland Rd., Woodstock, VT* 🌐 *www.cloudlandfarm.com*

When to Go

With more limited hours in winter at Billings Farm and Museum and Woodstock looking particularly splendid when flowers are in bloom or leaves are turning, summer and fall are ideal times to visit.

Getting Here and Around

The national historic park and Billings Farm are just a short drive northwest of Woodstock's cute downtown, which lies at the junction of U.S. 4 and Route 12, a 20-minute drive west of the junction of Interstates 89 and 91.

Quechee Gorge

Vermont's Deepest Chasm

An impressive 165-foot-deep canyon cut over thousands of years by glacial activity and the Ottauquechee River, the stunning Quechee Gorge sits just downriver from the small, historic mill town of Quechee. Most people view the gorge from U.S. 4. To escape the crowds, visit the adjacent state park, where you can hike several trails down to the river. There's camping, too—perfect for a moonlight view of this natural wonder. Just a half-mile away, hundreds of dealers sell their wares at Quechee Gorge Village's Vermont Antique Mall, which is set in a reconstructed barn that also houses a country store, an old-fashioned candy shop, and a craft brewery's tasting room. ✉ *5800 Woodstock Rd., Hartford, VT* 🌐 *www.vtstateparks.com*

Don't Miss

Next to Quechee Gorge, the **Vermont Institute of Natural Science Nature Center** has more than 15 raptor and nature exhibits, including a forest canopy walk, bald eagles, peregrine falcons, and owls. All caged birds have been found injured and are unable to survive in the wild. ✉ *149 Natures Way, Quechee, VT* 🌐 *www.vinsweb.org*

Best Shop

A restored woolen mill by a waterfall holds the region's most interesting attraction, **Simon Pearce**, a marvelous glassblowing factory, store, and restaurant. ✉ *1760 Quechee Main St., Quechee, VT* 🌐 *www.simonpearce.com*

Getting Here and Around

Quechee is on U.S. 4, just a few miles west of the junction of Interstates 89 and 91, 7 miles east of Woodstock and 12 miles west of Hanover, NH.

Ben & Jerry's Factory

America's Most Famous Ice Cream

The closest thing you'll get to a Willy Wonka experience in New England, the 30-minute tours at the first factory of this legendary brand famous for supporting progressive social causes are unabashedly corny and only skim the surface of the behind-the-scenes goings-on. But this flaw is forgiven when the samples are dished out. To see the machines at work, visit on a weekday (but call ahead to confirm if they will indeed be in operation). ✉ *1281 Waterbury-Stowe Rd., Waterbury, VT* 🌐 *www.benjerry.com*

Don't Miss

Arguably even more fun than visiting the factory floor itself is strolling through the "Flavor Graveyard," where flavors of yore (remember Wavy Gravy and Holy Cannoli?) are given a tribute with tombstones inscribed with cheeky poetry.

Other Great Ice Cream

Less than an hour's drive southwest of Ben & Jerry's in the charming town of Vergennes, you can sample the delicious small-batch ice cream and sorbet at **lu-lu**. Tantalizing flavors include garden basil and honey-lavender. ✉ *185 Main St., Vergennes, VT* 🌐 *www.luluvt.com*

When to Go

There's really no bad time to stop by for some ice cream, even in winter. But the outdoor picnic areas with Green Mountains views are best enjoyed in summer.

Getting Here and Around

Ben & Jerry's is on Route 100, just a mile north of Interstate 89 in Waterbury, and 9 miles south of Stowe.

Bennington

Home to Vermont's Highest Observation Deck

From miles away you can spy the striking **Bennington Battle Monument**, a stone obelisk that rises 306 feet over stately Old Bennington historic district. It commemorates General John Stark's Revolutionary War victory over the British, and the observation deck, at 200 feet up, serves views as far as the Berkshires in Massachusetts to the south and the Adirondacks in New York to the west. Afterwards, make your way into Bennington's Victorian downtown, home to Vermont's oldest indie bookstore, the Bennington Bookshop. Be sure to tour the exceptional Bennington Museum, which contains the world's largest collection of works by Grandma Moses. ✉ *15 Monument Cir., Bennington, VT* 🌐 *www.benningtonbattlemonument.com*

Don't Miss

A short drive northwest of downtown, visit the verdant grounds of prestigious **Bennington College**, where you can walk in the footsteps of such esteemed alumni as actor Peter Dinklage and novelist Donna Tartt. ✉ *1 College Dr., Bennington, VT* 🌐 *www.bennington.edu*

Best Restaurant

Finish your day of exploring Bennington's old-world charms with a Wanderlust cocktail and Bennington flatbread—topped with maple chicken, bacon, cheddar, and bourbon-caramelized apples—at the **Miller's Toll**. ✉ *716 Main St., Bennington, VT* 🌐 *www.millerstoll.space*

Getting Here and Around

Bennington lies at the junction of U.S. 7 and Route 9, about 25 miles south of Manchester.

Hildene

The Lincoln Family's Summer Home

On the outskirts of one of Vermont's stateliest resort towns, the summer home of Abraham Lincoln's son Robert provides fascinating insight into the lives of this fabled family. Robert Todd Lincoln enjoyed his own illustrious career, serving as secretary of war, U.S. ambassador to Great Britain, and later president of the Pullman Palace Car Company. He built this lavish 24-room Georgian Revival mansion in 1905, and it's now the centerpiece of a beautifully preserved 412-acre estate that holds many of the family's prized possessions. Be sure to step aboard the restored 1903 Pullman car, hike the miles of trails and the wetland boardwalk, view the elaborate formal gardens, and stroll around the farm. ✉ *1005 Hildene Rd., Manchester, VT* 🌐 *www.hildene.org*

Don't Miss

The home is in **Manchester**, a town at the base of 3,848-foot Mt. Equinox (you can drive or hike to the top), which has a beautiful village center and the unique American Museum of Fly Fishing.

Best Hotel

The **Equinox Golf Resort & Spa** in quaint Manchester Village has been the fancy hotel in town since the 18th century. ✉ *3567 Main St., Manchester, VT* 🌐 *www.equinoxresort.com*

When to Go

Hildene is prettiest in late June when the gardens bloom with more than 1,000 peonies.

Getting Here and Around

The estate is just off Route 7A, 2 miles south of bustling Manchester, which is in the southwest corner of the state, at the junction of U.S. 7 and Route 30.

When in Vermont

AMERICAN PRECISION MUSEUM

A stone's throw from the famous covered bridge that crosses the Connecticut River between New Hampshire and Vermont, this stately four-story 1846 former armaments factory is packed with fascinating exhibits that shine a light on the ingenuity behind how all sorts of things are made, from sewing machines to automobiles. A curator from the Smithsonian saved the building from demolition in 1966 and turned it into this imaginative museum where docents demonstrate how many tools and machines work. ✉ *196 Main St., Windsor, VT* 🌐 *www.americanprecision.org*

Do This: After visiting the museum, you can embark on one of the state's prettiest and most popular hikes, the 2.9-mile Weathersfield Trail up to the fire tower atop 3,144-foot Mt. Ascutney, from which you can take in marvelous views of the upper Connecticut River valley. Afterward, head to Harpoon Brewery taproom and beer garden, where you can sample classic New England–style IPAs and tasty sandwiches on the patio or stroll through the adjacent riverside sculpture garden. ✉ *336 Ruth Carney Dr., Windsor, VT* *www.harpoonbrewery.com*

DOG MOUNTAIN

Set on an idyllic 150-acre mountaintop in Vermont's sparsely populated and picturesque Northeast Kingdom, Dog Mountain is pooch paradise, complete with swimming ponds, hiking trails, an art gallery full of dog-related artwork, and even a Dog Chapel. The sign outside says "Welcome all creeds, all breeds, no dogmas allowed." And on any given day, you will find all breeds and creeds here. Originally an art studio for the late Stephen Huneck, Dog Mountain was conceived when Huneck recovered from a near-death experience and was moved to create a place for pet-lovers to celebrate the spiritual bond they have with their dogs. ✉ *143 Parks Rd., St. Johnsbury, VT* 🌐 *www.dogmt.com*

Do This: Thousands of pet owners visit Dog Mountain annually to post messages and photos in the chapel and to gain closure for lost canine companions, but Dog Mountain is also a place for pups and their people to play and run off-leash and roll in the grass.

SHELBURNE FARMS

Founded in the 1880s as a private estate for two very rich New Yorkers, this 1,400-acre farm is much more than an exquisite landscape: it's an educational and cultural resource center with a working dairy farm, an award-winning cheese producer (the venue hosts the renowned Vermont Cheesemakers Festival each August), an organic market garden, and a bakery whose aroma of fresh bread and pastries is an olfactory treat. Children and adults alike get a kick out of hunting for eggs in the oversize coop, milking a cow, and meeting baby lambs in spring. If you fall in love with the scenery, arrange a romantic dinner at the lakefront inn or spend the night. ✉ *1611 Harbor Rd., Shelburne, VT* 🌐 *www.shelburnefarms.org*

Do This: While in the area, visit the Shelburne Museum. You can trace much of New England's history simply by wandering through its 45 acres and 39 buildings, which have an outstanding 100,000-plus-object collection of art, design, and Americana consisting of antique furniture, fine and folk art, quilts, trade signs, and weather vanes; there are also nearly 200 carriages and sleighs. ✉ *6000 Shelburne Rd., Shelburne, VT* 🌐 *www.shelburnemuseum.org*

VERMONT COUNTRY STORE

This venerable shop in a quiet village northeast of Manchester opened in 1946 and is still run by the Orton family, though these days it has become something of an empire, with a large catalog and online business. One room is set aside for Vermont Common Crackers and bins of fudge and copious candy. In others you'll find nearly forgotten items such as stove polish and old-timey toys, as well as practical items like sturdy outdoor clothing. Nostalgia-evoking implements dangle from the rafters. ⊠ *657 Main St., Weston, VT* ⊕ *www.vermontcountry-store.com*

Do This: The village's Greek Revival playhouse sits empty after flood damage, but the Weston Theater Company's summer season goes on at nearby Walker Farm—it's the oldest professional theater in Vermont. ⊠ *705 Main St., Weston, VT* ⊕ *www.westontheater.org*

About Our Writers

Jordan Barry grew up in Arlington, VA, went to college in Burlington, and currently lives in Vergennes, the state's smallest city (population: 2,600). She's well on her way to joining the 251 Club—an elite group of Vermonters who have visited all *252* of the state's towns, cities, and gores—and plans to arrive at them all via dirt road. She is currently a food and drink writer at *Seven Days*, Vermont's alt-weekly newspaper.

Cool Places to Stay

Hotel Vermont. This cool, stylish boutique hotel just steps from Waterfront Park has the sort of spacious, comfy lobby that you actually want to hang out in, ideally while sipping a craft cocktail from the adjacent Juniper restaurant. You'll also find gorgeously appointed rooms with local artwork. ⊠ *41 Cherry St., Burlington, VT* *www.hotelvt.com*

Moose Meadow Lodge & Treehouse. Sleep in your very own two-story, 31-window tree house or in one of the rustic-chic rooms decorated with sleigh beds, steam showers for two, handmade twig furniture, or a private screened porch at this magical alpine hideaway set on 86 wooded, tranquil acres surrounded by the Green Mountains. ⊠ *607 Crossett Hill Rd., Duxbury, VT* ⊕ *www.moosemead-owlodge.net*

Trapp Family Lodge & Resort. Built by the Von Trapp family (of *The Sound of Music* fame), this Tyrolean-style lodge offers thrilling mountain vistas, a cozy beer hall that's perfect for après-ski relaxation, and a concert series and several festivals during the warmer months. ⊠ *700 Trapp Hill Rd., Stowe, VT* ⊕ *www.vontrappre-sort.com*

Twin Farms. Let's just get it out there: Twin Farms is the best lodging in Vermont, and the most expensive, but it's worth it. Rates include all meals (some of Vermont's best), alcohol, and activities, and each incredible space is furnished with a blend of high art (Jasper Johns, Milton Avery, Cy Twombly), gorgeous folk art, and furniture that goes beyond comfortable sophistication. ⊠ *452 Royalton Tpke., Barnard, VT* ⊕ *www.twinfarms.com*

The Weston. For one of the few true luxury lodging experiences in small-town Vermont, head to this stunning boutique hotel in a white clapboard building just down the road from Weston's town center. Each of the exquisitely designed guest rooms is unique, but all come with lush fabrics, hand-carved four-poster beds, and antique furniture. ⊠ *630 Main St., Weston, VT* ⊕ *www.thewestonvt.com*

Woodstock Inn & Resort. This romantic 1890s inn, one of northern New England's most memorable accommodations, is steps from Woodstock's fine eateries and inviting shops and features plenty of great amenities on property, including an impressive full-service spa, an acclaimed golf course, and several exceptional restaurants. ✉ *14 The Green, Woodstock, VT* 🌐 *www.woodstockinn.com*

Essential Eats

Cheese. Vermont is the artisanal cheese capital of the country, with several dozen creameries open to the public churning out hundreds of different cheeses. Many creameries are "farmstead" operations, meaning that the animals whose milk is made into cheese are kept on-site. The Vermont Cheese Trail map, which you can view or download on the website of the Vermont Cheese Council (🌐 *www.vtcheese.com*), has a comprehensive list of dairies, many of which you can visit. Waitsfield's 5th Quarter Butcher + Provisions (✉ *89 Mad River Green, Waitsfield, VT* 🌐 *www.madrivertaste.com*), a Vermont-centric specialty grocer, stocks the best cheese counter in the state, with knowledgeable staff to match.

Hen of the Wood. Ask Vermont's great chefs where they go for a tremendous meal, and Hen of the Wood inevitably tops the list. Both locations, in downtown Burlington and Waterbury, are as farm-to-table as it gets, from the restaurant's namesake mushroom toast to seasonal vegetables hand-delivered by growers. Grab a walk-in seat at either spot's open kitchen counter to watch the action. ✉ *55 Cherry St., Burlington, VT* and ✉ *14 S. Main St., Waterbury, VT* 🌐 *www.henofthewood.com*

Honey Road. Anchoring the corner of Main Street and the pedestrian-only Church Street Marketplace in Burlington, Honey Road has garnered James Beard Award nominations for its highly creative takes on eastern Mediterranean cuisine—including one for co-owners Cara Tobin and Allison Gibson in the Outstanding Restaurateur category. At the Grey Jay on the other end of Church Street, they put that same mezze spin on brunch. ✉ *156 Church St., Burlington, VT* 🌐 *www.honeyroadrestaurant.com*

Maple Creemees. They may have a weird name, but the state's unique take on soft-serve ice cream is a perfect summer treat, especially swirled with coffee and topped with maple sprinkles. Vermonters are fiercely loyal to their creemee spot of choice: Vermont Cookie Love's Route 7 pitstop (✉ *6915 Rte. 7 N, Ferrisburgh, VT* 🌐 *www.vermontcookielove.com*) is one of the best, and chef-owned Canteen Creemee Company (✉ *5123 Main St., Waitsfield, VT* 🌐 *www.canteen-creemee.com*) is the most creative—so much so that it earned a James Beard Award semifinalist nod.

Philo Ridge Farm. Take a 20-minute drive south of Burlington and it's undoubtedly farm country, with pick-your-own berry operations, produce stands, orchards, and vineyards stretching from the Green Mountains to Lake Champlain. The jewel in the area's table-on-a-farm crown is nonprofit Philo Ridge, a 500-plus-acre regenerative farm. Its sustainably raised meat and produce is put to delicious use in the market and on-farm restaurant. ✉ *2766 Mt. Philo Rd., Charlotte, VT* *www.philoridgefarm.org*

Chapter 3

THE MID-ATLANTIC

Updated by Carly Fisher,
Constance Jones, Melissa Klurman,
Barbara Noe Kennedy, Laura Rodini,
Daniel Scheffler, Emma Way,
and Taryn White

WELCOME TO THE MID-ATLANTIC

TOP REASONS TO GO

★ **The Big Apple:** From its 840-plus-acre Central Park to world-class museums and stunning skyline views, New York City tops many a bucket list.

★ **The Appalachian Trail:** Virginia is home to more miles of the famous trail than any other state. There are many access points throughout the state, but the most popular, and most scenic, is Shenandoah National Park.

★ **The nation's capital:** Washington, D.C., is a sight every American should see, from the National Mall and Tidal Basin to the White House and the Smithsonian's 19 galleries and museums.

★ **Coastal charm:** Dine at a Maryland crab shack, take a water taxi in Lewes, Delaware, soak up the sun on Virginia Beach, and sail in Annapolis to take in the region's waterfront beauty.

★ **American foundations:** In Philadelphia, walk in the footsteps of America's founding fathers at Independence National Historical Park, where the Declaration of Independence forged a new democracy.

1 Delaware. Enjoy the beautiful beaches, marvelous mansions, and craft beer scene in this small wonder.

2 Maryland. Eat crabs at a seafood shack on Chesapeake Bay, then drive to Baltimore to visit the Inner Harbor.

3 New Jersey. Spend some time at the Jersey Shore enjoying the beach and the boardwalk.

4 New York. From bustling Manhattan to the serene Catskills to the famous Finger Lakes, there is a lot to love.

5 Pennsylvania. Explore the birthplace of America at Independence Hall, then take in the impressive Valley Forge.

6 Virginia. Hike the mountain trails of Shenandoah National Park, enjoy the Monticello-area wineries, and stroll Virginia Beach.

7 Washington, D.C. The White House, the Lincoln Memorial, the Washington Monument—landmarks are found in every corner of the nation's capital.

8 West Virginia. Drive along the winding country roads and hear traditional mountain music.

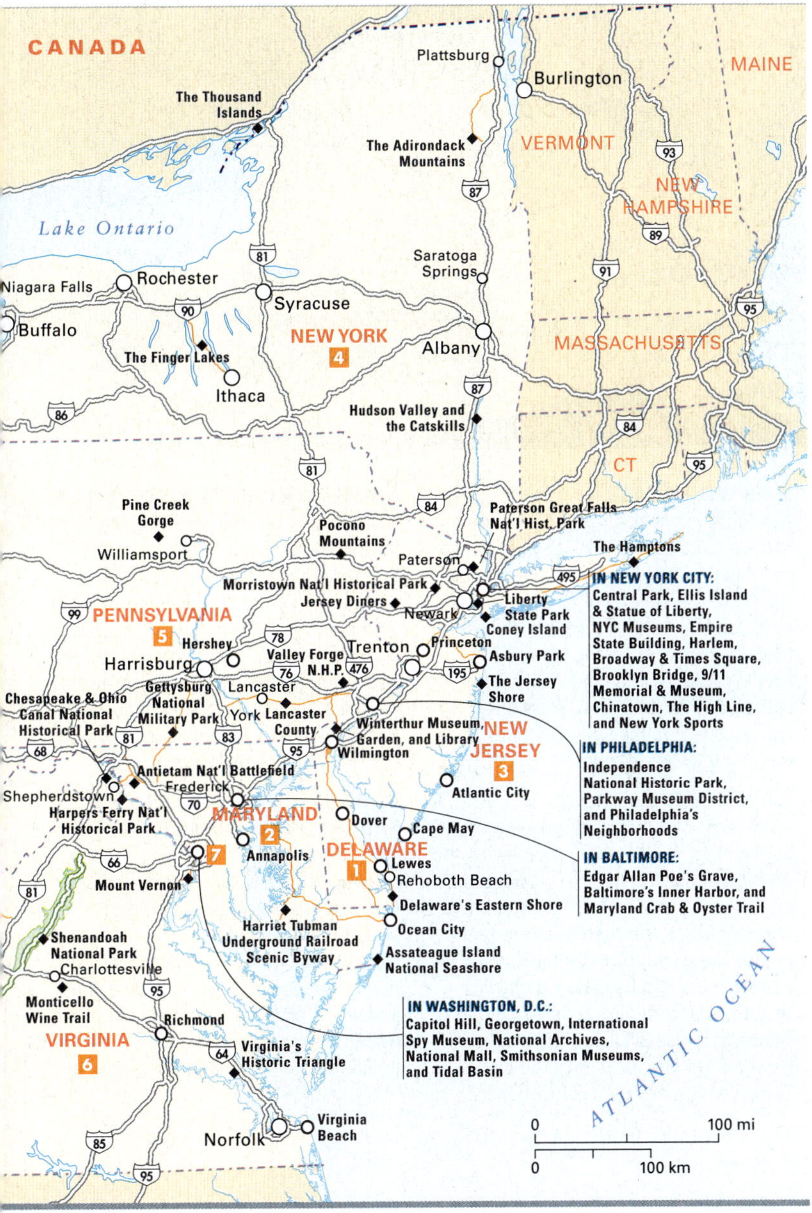
CANADA
Plattsburg
Burlington
MAINE
The Thousand Islands
The Adirondack Mountains
VERMONT
NEW HAMPSHIRE
Lake Ontario
Saratoga Springs
Niagara Falls
Rochester
Syracuse
Buffalo
NEW YORK
4
Albany
MASSACHUSETTS
The Finger Lakes
Ithaca
Hudson Valley and the Catskills
CT
Pine Creek Gorge
Williamsport
Pocono Mountains
Paterson Great Falls Nat'l Hist. Park
The Hamptons
Paterson
Morristown Nat'l Historical Park
Jersey Diners
Newark
Liberty State Park
Coney Island
IN NEW YORK CITY:
Central Park, Ellis Island & Statue of Liberty, NYC Museums, Empire State Building, Harlem, Broadway & Times Square, Brooklyn Bridge, 9/11 Memorial & Museum, Chinatown, The High Line, and New York Sports
PENNSYLVANIA
5
Hershey
Harrisburg
Valley Forge N.H.P.
Trenton
Princeton
Asbury Park
The Jersey Shore
Lancaster
Gettysburg National Military Park
Chesapeake & Ohio Canal National Historical Park
York
Lancaster County
Winterthur Museum, Garden, and Library
Wilmington
NEW JERSEY
3
IN PHILADELPHIA:
Independence National Historic Park, Parkway Museum District, and Philadelphia's Neighborhoods
Antietam Nat'l Battlefield
Frederick
Shepherdstown
Harpers Ferry Nat'l Historical Park
Atlantic City
MARYLAND
2
Dover
Cape May
Annapolis
DELAWARE
1
7
Lewes
Rehoboth Beach
IN BALTIMORE:
Edgar Allan Poe's Grave, Baltimore's Inner Harbor, and Maryland Crab & Oyster Trail
Mount Vernon
Delaware's Eastern Shore
Ocean City
Harriet Tubman Underground Railroad Scenic Byway
Shenandoah National Park
Charlottesville
Assateague Island National Seashore
Monticello Wine Trail
Richmond
VIRGINIA
6
IN WASHINGTON, D.C.:
Capitol Hill, Georgetown, International Spy Museum, National Archives, National Mall, Smithsonian Museums, and Tidal Basin
Virginia's Historic Triangle
ATLANTIC OCEAN
Norfolk
Virginia Beach
0
100 mi
0
100 km
93
87
89
81
91
90
95
87
86
84
81
95
84
495
99
78
76
476
195
81
83
95
68
70
66
81
95
64
85
95

WHAT TO EAT AND DRINK IN THE MID-ATLANTIC

New York pizza

NEW YORK PIZZA

New York is one of the few cities that has a distinct pizza style. Expect a thick crust that gradually gets thinner toward the center. A ladleful of tomato sauce and a sprinkling of mozzarella cheese traditionally serve as the base, and toppings like pepperoni, mushrooms, sausage, or onions are loaded on. Locals love Rubirosa in Nolita and Joe's Pizza in the West Village.

NEW YORK BAGELS

There are many reasons why New York bagels reign supreme: some say it's the water that contributes to the bagel's chewy, but not too chewy, texture. Others say it's the tried-and-true techniques that were brought by Jewish immigrants from Eastern Europe. Try Bo's Bagels in Harlem, Ess-a-Bagel in Midtown, Russ & Daughters on the Lower East Side, or one of the city's Tompkins Square Bagels locations.

MARYLAND STEAMED CRABS

Maryland's Chesapeake Bay is known for its blue crabs, a small, tasty crustacean that residents learn how to catch, steam, and devour at a young age. There are family-run crab houses throughout the state that have been serving them by the bushel for decades. Try Schultz's Crab House in Essex, Cantler's Riverside Inn in Annapolis, or Captain Billy's in Newburg.

FROZEN CUSTARD ON THE JERSEY BOARDWALK

New Jersey's miles and miles of beach boardwalks are home to many things that scream Americana, including a scoop of frozen custard. The most popular is Kohr Brothers, which has locations from Beach Haven to Cape May and is known for its creamy scoops of frozen custard available in a two-flavor twist and served in a cone or in a cup.

CLASSIC NEW YORK COCKTAILS

Perhaps the city's most famous cocktail is its namesake, the whisky- or rye-based Manhattan, which is said to have been created by a bartender at the Manhattan Club in the late 19th century. Times Square's Knickerbocker Hotel is where the gin and vermouth martini was first served. Many other cocktail bars, including Attaboy, Death & Company, and Harry's, also serve exemplary versions.

PHILLY CHEESESTEAK

People travel far and wide to try this sandwich made of chopped beef, onions, and cheese and served on a long roll. There is much debate about who created the first and where to find the best today. The ultimate cheesesteak rivalry is between Pat's King of Steaks and Geno's Steaks, located across the street from each other in the city's Italian Market.

PORK ROLL VS. TAYLOR HAM

John Taylor created this pork-based meat product in New Jersey in 1856. In the years since, it has become a favorite on eggy breakfast sandwiches at diners and bagel shops throughout the state. It's been the subject of much debate between North Jersey (which calls it by its brand name, Taylor Ham) and South Jersey (which prefers the plain-and-simple pork roll). But wherever you are, it tastes the same.

Amish whoopie pies

Philly cheesesteak

AMISH WHOOPIE PIES

Many believe that whoopie pies—two round cake patties sandwiched with frosting—were created by the Amish community in Lancaster County, Pennsylvania. Whether or not the Amish first created this dessert, farm stands throughout Lancaster serve them in classic flavors like chocolate, spiced pumpkin, and red velvet.

BUFFALO WINGS

The exact origins of Buffalo wings are hotly contested, but it is largely agreed that the tangy wings were made famous by the city's Anchor Bar, which now has locations across the country. There are many places throughout the Buffalo area—including Gabriel's Gate and Duff's Famous Wings—to get an order of the saucy staple.

PEPPERONI ROLL

For West Virginia's classic pepperoni roll, the meat is baked into a soft white-bread roll. The snack food was created as a no-refrigeration-necessary meal for coal miners throughout the region. Today, the snack is available throughout Appalachia in convenience stores and in casual restaurants.

Delaware

Delaware's founding fathers ratified the U.S. Constitution before others, earning Delaware the nickname "the First State." Although rich in colonial political history, today the state is a business leader—67% of Fortune 500 companies are incorporated here. Shoppers love Delaware, too, thanks to its zero sales tax. Varied landscapes keep Delaware from feeling like America's second-smallest state. Rolling hills and hardwood forests lay north. Vast tidal marshes and dunescapes line the shore. Gleaming corporate center Wilmington is a short train ride to New York, Philadelphia, and Washington, D.C.

Capital: Dover

Population: 1,051,917

Area: 1,982 square miles

Statehood Date: December 7, 1787

Major Airports: Wilmington Airport (ILG)

Travel and Tourism Information:
🌐 *www.visitdelaware.com*

Famous Residents: Joe Biden (president); Ryan Phillippe (actor); Aubrey Plaza (actress); Sarah McBride (politician)

Fun Fact: Delaware Bay is home to the world's largest gathering of spawning horseshoe crabs—ancient, helmet-headed creatures that crawl ashore by the millions each spring. At peak season, they outnumber humans in the entire state.

Delaware's Eastern Shore

Miles of Gorgeous Beaches

The Atlantic Ocean gently laps against Delaware's eastern coast, making way for miles and miles of beautiful seashore. Full-time residents and weekenders visit the beaches in the summer months for sunbathing, swimming, boating, and shoreline biking. The different beaches that make up the area each have distinct vibes. Party animals often head to **Dewey Beach**, while **Bethany Beach** is quieter.

Don't Miss

With its mile-long boardwalk featuring family-friendly attractions like the Funland Amusement Park, **Rehoboth Beach** is a beloved destination for families. It's also been a gay getaway for years, drawing members of the LGBTQ+ community from Baltimore and Washington, D.C. The popular Dogfish Head Brewery has a brewpub here, and there are plenty of other food and drink options facing the beach and on nearby streets.

Best Activity

In the late 17th century, William Penn opened Cape Henlopen to residents of the area, making **Cape Henlopen State Park** one the country's oldest public parks. Today, the historic waterfront continues to be a popular destination for Delaware residents. It's a draw for its hiking and biking trails, swimmable shores, kayaking opportunities, and fishing and clamming areas. ✉ *15099 Cape Henlopen Dr., Lewes, DE* 🌐 *www.destateparks.com/beaches/capehenlopen*

Getting Here and Around

A car is the best way to reach Delaware's Eastern Shore. The area is almost equidistant from Philadelphia International Airport and Baltimore/Washington International Thurgood Marshall Airport.

Lewes

First Town in the First State

The oldest town in Delaware is Lewes, a coastal community that was founded in 1631. Today, the area is visited for its historic sites, its beach access, and its small-town feel. The area is easily explored by foot. Within the half-mile historic area, visitors can find museums, restaurants, shops, and more, and plenty of waterfront areas for sunning, swimming, fishing, and boating are close by.

Don't Miss

The fastest, and most scenic, way to get to New Jersey from Delaware is aboard the **Cape May-Lewes Ferry**, which transports guests between Lewes, Delaware, and Cape May, New Jersey, located directly across the Delaware Bay. The ferry ride takes 85 minutes and passes lovely lighthouses and picturesque harbors. 🌐 *www.cmlf.com*

Best Activity

Make plans to visit the **Zwaanendael Museum**, named for the first European settlement in the area. A variety of special exhibits tell the story of the region, including the shipwrecks that dot the coast and the area's involvement in the War of 1812. ✉ *102 Kings Hwy., Lewes, DE* 🌐 *history.delaware.gov/zwaanendael-museum*

Best Tour

Cape Water Tours offers a wide range of on-the-water tours in the Lewes area. The evening cruises are perfect for taking in the sunset, but you might also want to sail off in search of dolphins or hear about the region's spooky lighthouses. 🌐 *www.capewatertaxi.com*

Getting Here and Around

It's easiest to drive to Lewes, but once you're here most attractions are accessible by foot or bike.

Wilmington

Big City with Small-Town Appeal

You know from the gleaming glass office buildings that Wilmington is a big city, but its walkable thoroughfares, charming neighborhoods, and waterfront promenade give it plenty of small-town appeal. There are excellent places downtown for dining and drinking, with the good spirits often spilling out into the streets. Riverfront Wilmington, the delightful walkway along the Christiana River, is home to an array of attractions, including the **Delaware Children's Museum**, the **Delaware Theatre Company**, **Tubman-Garrett Riverfront Park**, and **Frawley Stadium**.

Don't Miss

In recent years, the **Delaware Art Museum** has grown to encompass a large collection of American art, British Pre-Raphaelite art, and contemporary art, making it a favorite for art enthusiasts from all over. ✉ *2301 Kentmere Pkwy., Wilmington, DE* 🌐 *www.delart.org*

Best Restaurants

Bardea has grown into a small empire of stand-out eateries, earning chef Antimo DiMeo multiple James Beard Award nominations and helping cement Wilmington's status as a burgeoning food city. For upscale Italian in an elegant setting, the original **Bardea Food & Drink** (✉ *620 N. Market St., Wilmington, DE*) is a must, or check out **DE.CO** (✉ *111 W. 10th St., Wilmington, DE*), a stylish downtown food hall with an ever-expanding roster of stalls. 🌐 *www.bardeafoodanddrink.com/restaurants*

Getting Here and Around

Philadelphia International Airport is a 20-mile drive down Interstate 95. Once you're here, enjoy the miles of walking and biking trails connected to downtown.

Winterthur Museum, Garden, and Library

Delaware's Most Historic Mansion

One of America's richest families, the du Ponts lived on sweeping estates in the Delaware countryside that are now open to the public. Winterthur Museum, Garden, and Library is the largest and most opulent of the properties, and it draws history lovers from around the region. The mansion, which was the childhood home of Henry Francis du Pont, is surrounded by 1,000 acres of rolling hills and manicured gardens. In addition to rotating exhibitions, the home features a nearly 90,000-object collection of American-made or American-used items from 1630 to 1860.

Don't Miss

The nearby **Hagley Museum and Library**, located at the site of E.I. du Pont's gunpowder works, includes a historic home, some restored mills, and worker communities (✉ *200 Hagley Creek Rd., Wilmington, DE* 🌐 *www.hagley.org*). The French-inspired **Nemours Estate** features a beautiful mansion surrounded by the country's largest formal French gardens, a vintage car collection within the stately garage, and hundreds of acres of woodlands and meadows (✉ *1600 Rockland Rd., Wilmington, DE* 🌐 *www.nemoursestate.org*).

When to Go

Winterthur is lovely to visit at any time of the year, but yearly events include the Point-to-Point steeplechase races in May, the Artisan Market in July, and the Delaware Antiques Show in November.

Getting Here and Around

The three mansions are within a 15-minute drive to one another, about 15 minutes north of downtown Wilmington.

Dover

Car Racing in a Historic City

Racing fans often head to Delaware's Dover International Speedway to watch some of the sport's top names make their way around the 1-mile oval track, but the state's capital city has plenty more to see. Walk through Dover's **First State Heritage Park** area, which connects the city's parks with cultural and government buildings full of history and colonial charm. Then visit some of Dover's well-maintained museums like the **Biggs Museum of American Art** or the **Johnson Victrola Museum**, a celebration of Dover's own Eldridge Reeves Johnson, an inventor and recording industry pioneer.

Don't Miss

Dover International Speedway—aka the Monster Mile—hosts races throughout the year and has been a NASCAR mainstay since 1969. Miles the Monster is the speedway's mascot, and is a favorite with kids. If you're in for a thrill, book a NASCAR ride-along for a few high-speed laps around the track or take control of the wheel yourself. ✉ *1131 N. Dupont Hwy., Dover, DE* 🌐 *www.dovermotorspeedway.com*

Best Beer

Dover's lively **Rail Haus** beer garden is a local favorite for its rotating taps of Delaware craft beers and German classics as well as its German-inspired pub food menu and recurring events, including outdoor movies and night markets. ✉ *92 N. West St., Dover, DE* 🌐 *www.railhaus.com*

Getting Here and Around

Located in the center of the state, Dover is about a one-hour drive from both Wilmington and the Delaware beaches. True to its NASCAR roots, having a car is essential for a Dover visit.

When in Delaware

DOGFISH HEAD BREWERY

Beer fans nationwide know about Dogfish Head Brewery, a craft beer pioneer famous for its 60-minute IPA and 90-minute IPA. Since the brewery was founded, it has rapidly expanded its offerings to include tasting rooms, brewpubs, and even a hotel. The main brewery and tasting room are located in the town of Milton. ✉ *6 Cannery Village Center, Milton, DE* 🌐 *www.dogfish.com/brewery/tasting-room*

Do This: Pose for a picture in front of the unmissable Steampunk Treehouse, a functional sculpture made of recycled materials. The tree house weighs 8 tons and is a towering 40 feet tall.

BOMBAY HOOK NATIONAL WILDLIFE REFUGE

This 16,251-acre wildlife refuge in Kent County is a marshy goldmine for birders and nature photographers. Delaware is the only state without a national park, but you'll question why Bombay Hook doesn't hold the title after a visit here. ✉ *2591 Whitehall Neck Rd., Smyrna, DE* 🌐 *www.fws.gov/refuge/bombay-hook*

Do This: Walk or drive through the unspoiled park during spring to see flocks of migratory shorebirds. In the summer, you might be able to see eagle eggs hatch.

NEW CASTLE

Located just 6 miles outside Wilmington is New Castle, a small but lively town on the Delaware River. You'll find cobblestone streets and colonial buildings that have barely been touched by time, in addition to a number of great restaurants, bars, and shops. The town dates back to 1640, and its history is celebrated at the many museums throughout the area.

Do This: Have a proper pilgrim's feast at Jessop's Tavern, a colonial-style pub in the center of town. From the decor to the menu, Jessop's commits to the bit and feels like a restaurant happily stuck in time. One sign of the times, though, is its extensive beer list with over 300 varieties, including many rare finds. ✉ *114 Delaware St., New Castle, DE* 🌐 *www.jessops-tavern.com*

Cool Places to Stay

Bellmoor Inn and Spa. Two blocks from Rehoboth Beach's top dining and shopping spots, the Bellmoor Inn and Spa pampers you with soothing spa treatments and two sparkling pools. The beach is a 10-minute walk, but those who don't feel like walking can hop aboard a beach shuttle. ✉ *6 Christian St., Rehoboth Beach, DE* 🌐 *www.thebellmoor.com*

Dogfish Inn. Delaware residents love their Dogfish Head Brewery, so much so that the team behind the craft brewery opened the Dogfish Inn in Lewes. The 16 rooms are minimalist but carefully crafted to emit an outdoorsy vibe. ✉ *105 Savannah Rd., Lewes, DE* 🌐 *www.dogfish.com/inn*

Hotel DuPont. The Italian Renaissance–inspired Hotel DuPont has graced downtown Wilmington for nearly 100 years. The 217 European-style rooms are spacious and chic, and the hotel restaurant,

About Our Writers

Emma Way spent the first 20 years of her life, and every holiday since, in Newark, Delaware. She'll forever order Dogfish Head over any other craft beer. Now based in Charlotte, North Carolina, she's a newsroom leader for Axios Local and a freelance writer.

Le Cavalier, is beloved by locals. ✉ *42 W. 11th St., Wilmington, DE* 🌐 *www.hoteldupont.com*

Inn at Montchanin Village and Spa. Once a part of the du Pont family's estate at Winterthur, the Inn at Montchanin Village and Spa has been restored to honor its history and to add all modern amenities. There's an on-site spa and restaurant. ✉ *528 Montchanin Rd., Montchanin, DE* 🌐 *www.montchanin.com*

Massey's Landing. For beachgoers and boating enthusiasts, Massey's Landing is the ideal place to spend a few days. The waterfront campground has safari-style tents and beachfront cottages for overnight stays. ✉ *20628 Long Beach Dr., Millsboro, DE* 🌐 *www.masseyslanding.com*

Quion Hotel. This bank turned sleek boutique hotel is also home to three hot Wilmington establishments: a rooftop bar, a well-rated Italian restaurant, and an underground cocktail lounge in an old vault. ✉ *519 N. Market St., Wilmington, DE* 🌐 *www.thequoinhotel.com*

Essential Eats

Capriotti's Bobbie Sandwich. Thanksgiving is a year-round celebration at this sandwich chain, which first opened in Wilmington in 1976. The famous Bobbie sub features layers of slow-roasted turkey, cranberry sauce, stuffing, and mayo on a pillow-y roll. Like Thanksgiving itself, the Bobbie makes great leftovers, so order extra. 🌐 *www.capriottis.com*

Crab Cakes. Maryland gets all the credit for its blue crabs, but Delaware pulls from the same bays and serves up some of the best crab cakes around. For a no-frills, straight-from-the-sea experience, head to Woody's in Dewey Beach for their legendary crab cakes. ✉ *1904 Coastal Hwy., Dewey Beach, DE* 🌐 *www.deweybeachbar.com*

Grotto Pizza. Sauce on top of a pizza? It's a Delaware thing. Each pie from this classic Delaware restaurant with multiple locations comes topped with a spiral drizzle of its signature sweet sauce. It's not for everyone, but everyone should try it once. 🌐 *www.grottopizza.com*

One Coastal. Delaware's first-ever James Beard Awards finalist, One Coastal is a celebration of the splendor of the state, featuring local produce and fresh seafood straight from the boats of area fishermen. Reservations go fast, so locals and visitors alike often line up outside the intimate and unpretentious Fenwick Island restaurant before it opens. ✉ *101 Coastal Hwy., Fenwick Island, DE* 🌐 *www.one-coastal.com*

Scrapple. Delaware's favorite mystery meat is made with pork scraps and served sliced and fried in decades-old diners. The best way to try this weird delicacy, though, is at the Bridgeville Apple-Scrapple Festival in Bridgeville every October. 🌐 *www.applescrapple.com*

Maryland

Maryland's mythic hero is the waterman who prowls the Chesapeake in his skipjack, dredging oysters. Today the waterman is a symbol of contemporary Maryland: not in the manner in which he works, but in the variety of his catch. Maryland has always been a land of diversity, and from its rich Civil War history to the contemporary appeal of cities like Baltimore and Annapolis, Maryland casts a wide net.

Capital: Annapolis

Population: 6,263,220

Area: 12,407 square miles

Statehood Date: April 28, 1788

Major Airports: Baltimore/Washington International Thurgood Marshall Airport (BWI); Hagerstown Regional Airport (HGR); Salisbury Regional Airport (SBY)

Travel and Tourism Information: 🌐 *www.visitmaryland.org*

Famous Residents: Harriet Tubman (abolitionist); Frederick Douglass (civil rights leader); Edgar Allen Poe (writer); Thurgood Marshall (Supreme Court Justice); Gayle King (TV personality); Cal Ripken Jr. (baseball player); Ta-Nehisi Coates (writer); Jada Pinkett Smith (actress)

Fun Fact: Maryland is often referred to as "America in Miniature" because of its diverse geography: from the Eastern Shore's coastal plains and wetlands, to its central farmlands and rolling hills, to the steep ridges and forests that make up its westernmost Appalachian Mountain region.

Baltimore's Inner Harbor

One of the Country's Best Urban Waterfronts

One of Baltimore's most-visited destinations is the Inner Harbor, a waterfront neighborhood that's just as popular with locals as it is with out-of-towners. The area was once known for its steel mills and shipyards, and today you can learn about its seafaring past while you board some of the centuries-old vessels, including a three-masted beauty called the **USS** *Constellation*. There are also world-class museums, waterfront restaurants, and spectacular views.

Don't Miss

A can't-miss attraction at the Inner Harbor, the sprawling **National Aquarium** is home to more than 750 species of underwater creatures. The permanent exhibits include a thriving coral reef, a 225,000-gallon tank called Shark Alley, and six gregarious bottlenose dolphins at Dolphin Discovery. ✉ *501 E. Pratt St., Baltimore, MD* 🌐 *www.aqua.org*

Best Restaurant

The **Rusty Scupper** is an Inner Harbor institution that has been serving the tastiest catches from the sea alongside views of the water for decades. ✉ *402 Key Hwy., Inner Harbor Marina, Baltimore, MD* 🌐 *www.rusty-scupper.com*

Getting Here and Around

While most of the attractions of the Inner Harbor are reachable by foot, visiting the city's other charming neighborhoods is as easy as hopping aboard a water taxi. Stops include Harborplace in the Inner Harbor, Harbor East, Federal Hill, Fells Point, and Fort McHenry National Monument and Historic Shrine. Service runs April through October. 🌐 *www.baltimorewatertaxi.com*

Maryland Crab and Oyster Trail

The Best Crabs in the World

Thousands of seafood lovers head to the state every year to get their hands on some Chesapeake blue crabs at one of the state's famous crab shacks. Also a draw are the freshly caught oysters that are shucked throughout seafront restaurants. The official Maryland Crab and Oyster Trail starts on the Eastern Shore, heads to the Annapolis area, and then fans out across the rest of state. 🌐 *www.visitmaryland.org/article/maryland-crab-oyster-trail*

Don't Miss

Ask any local and they will have their favorite crab shack or oyster spot. If you don't get a personal recommendation, head to standbys like the **Crab Claw** in St. Michaels, **Nick's Fish House** in Baltimore, or **Woody's Crab House** in North East.

Best Activity

Marylanders love to celebrate the state's maritime history and the season's bounty at seafood festivals held annually all across the state, including the Maryland Seafood Festival in Annapolis, the J. Millard Tawes Crab & Clam Bake in Crisfield, and the Saint Mary's County Crab Festival.

When to Go

Blue crab season runs from spring to late fall. Many of the best seafood restaurants are outdoor establishments, making Maryland the ideal summertime destination.

Getting Here and Around

Baltimore/Washington International Thurgood Marshall Airport is the place to fly to, and a car is pretty much required to get to the stops on the trail.

Harriet Tubman Underground Railroad Scenic Byway

Remembering the Long Road to Freedom

This 125-mile trail, running from Cambridge to Goldsboro, takes you past sites where the influential abolitionist led enslaved people to freedom. Stops along the way include hidden waterways, safe houses, churches, and other places that served as way stations. 🌐 *www.visitmaryland.org/scenic-byways/harriet-tubman-underground-railroad*

Don't Miss

Start your day at the **Harriet Tubman Underground Railroad Visitor Center**, which is home to permanent exhibits on Tubman, the Underground Railroad, and those who escaped slavery. ✉ *4068 Golden Hill Rd., Church Creek, MD* 🌐 *www.nps.gov/hatu*

Best Activities

Some of the major sites along the trail include the **Harriet Tubman Museum and Educational Center** (which has a powerful mural of Tubman), the **Tuckahoe Neck Meeting House** (a Quaker meetinghouse that was a prominent stop on the Railroad), and the **Jacob and Hannah Leverton House** (the region's main stopping place on the Railroad).

Before You Go

For a more enriching experience and better understanding of the challenges faced on the road to freedom, watch Amazon's drama series *The Underground Railroad* by award-winning director Barry Jenkins.

Getting Here and Around

Since the trail spans more than 120 miles, it's best accessed by car. The tour runs through much of Maryland, making it accessible from many points throughout the state. The driving tour takes about three to four hours.

Assateague Island National Seashore

Where Wild Horses Run Along the Beach

Assateague Island National Seashore draws animal lovers from all over who want to catch a glimpse of the wild horses that make their home on this barrier island surrounded by Chincoteague Bay to the west and the Atlantic Ocean to the east. The horses—originally brought here by farmers during the 17th century—roam freely, but spend any amount of time here and they are sure to gallop by. Many visitors also enjoy hiking or camping on the sandy shores, while others find the open water ideal for kayaking, fishing, crabbing, and swimming. ✉ *7206 National Seashore La., Berlin, MD* 🌐 *www.nps.gov/asis*

Don't Miss

The wild horses are a must-see for anyone visiting the island. Rangers at the visitor center will be able to tell you the best places to spot them. Remember not to feed or touch the animals, as doing so increases the chance they will beg for food and get hit by a car. Also use caution on the road, as wild horses have tragically gotten hit by careless drivers.

Best Tour

Park rangers lead tours of the island during the spring and summer. Book one at the Assateague Island Visitor Center.

When to Go

April through October is the best time to visit, with the last Wednesday in July being especially significant, as that's the date the Chincoteague herd is rounded up and swum across the island.

Getting Here and Around

This fairly remote area is best accessed by car.

Ocean City

Maryland's Seaside Party Town

Stretching some 10 miles along a narrow barrier island off Maryland's Atlantic coast, action-packed Ocean City draws millions from neighboring states (New Jersey, Pennsylvania, Virginia, and Delaware) and the District of Columbia virtually year-round to its broad beaches and the innumerable activities and amenities that cling to them, as well as to the quiet bay side between the island and the mainland. "O.C." is a premier Mid-Atlantic leisure-travel destination, at once big and small, sprawling and congested, old and new, historic and hip, noisy and quiet, sophisticated and tacky, expensive and cheap, and everything in between. The oceanfront boardwalk is a big draw, with arcades and amusement parks that make it a hit with families.

Don't Miss

Make plans to stroll at least part of the 3-mile-long boardwalk, a favorite activity in Ocean City. Kids love the towering Ferris wheel and the carousel dating back to 1902. For food, stop for fresh fish at **Harrison's Harbor Watch** (🌐 *harborwatchrestaurant.com*) or **Bull on the Beach** (🌐 *www.bullonthebeachoc.com*) for a classic pit beef sandwich.

Best Tour

Ocean City Food Tours has seafood-focused tours that show you how to crack open a hard-shelled crab. 🌐 *www.ocfoodietour.com*

Getting Here and Around

Traffic can be heavy, so many people choose to explore Ocean City by bike. For travel along the boardwalk, the Boardwalk Tram is an affordable and quick way to get from place to place.

Annapolis

America's Sailing Capital

The grandeur and pageantry of the **United States Naval Academy** draw visitors to the state capital of Annapolis, but so do the cobblestone streets dating back four centuries and its lovely location on the Chesapeake Bay. A slice of Americana, the must-visit Annapolis Historic District has stately homes dating to the colonial era. Annapolis is renowned as one of the country's sailing capitals, so you can take in an exciting race, rent a sailboat, or hop aboard a leisurely cruise around the port.

Don't Miss

Watch the boats come and go at **Ego Alley**, where boaters are known to show off their yachts and sailing vessels to those strolling the downtown area.

Best Tour

Learn about the ghostly side of the city's history on a tour of the downtown district. **Annapolis Ghost Tours** runs 90-minute walks and pub crawls around the city, and guides share lots of creepy tales. 🌐 *www.annapolisghosts.com*

Best Activity

Spend a day on the shores of **Sandy Point State Park**, a beachfront public park located on the Chesapeake Bay. It's a family-friendly spot for swimming, sunbathing, crabbing, and picnicking, and is home to two short walking trails, too. ✉ *1100 E. College Pkwy., Annapolis, MD* 🌐 *dnr.maryland.gov*

Getting Here and Around

On the Chesapeake Bay, Annapolis is 45 minutes south of Baltimore and just under an hour east of Washington, D.C.

Antietam National Battlefield

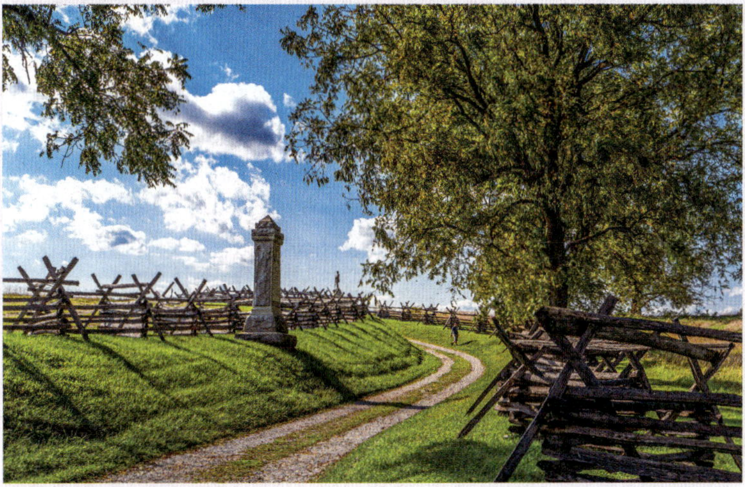

A Somber Reminder of "America's Bloodiest Day"

Antietam National Battlefield was the scene of one of the worst clashes during the Civil War. During the battle on September 17, 1862, more than 23,000 soldiers were killed or injured; the battle led to President Abraham Lincoln's issuing of the Emancipation Proclamation. Today, Antietam is a national military park that draws visitors from around the country and the world. It's a chance to learn about the history of the battle, see some of the original cannons and other military equipment, and duck into a church, field hospital, and other historic buildings. ✉ *5831 Dunker Church Rd., Sharpsburg, MD* 🌐 *www.nps.gov/anti*

Don't Miss

Following the battle, a mill property owned by Joshua Newcomer, now known as the **Newcomer House**, was used to care for those who were injured. It is now home to the Heart of the Civil War Heritage Area Exhibit. ✉ *18422 Shepherdstown Pike, Keedysville, MD* 🌐 *www.heartofthe-civilwar.org/newcomer-house*

Best Hikes

There are several self-guided hiking tours of the key battlefields. Most are easy to moderate and range from a quick stroll around a scenic loop to a longer hike taking you 2 miles. The short Tidball Trail brings you to one of the best overlooks of the battlefield, while the Snavely Ford Trail follows the banks of Antietam Creek.

Getting Here and Around

The battlefield is best reached by car; parking is available in lots surrounding the military park.

Edgar Allan Poe's Grave

Baltimore's Spookiest Unsolved Mystery

One of the spookiest spots in America is the grave of Edgar Allan Poe, the Gothic writer and poet whose life—and afterlife—are shrouded with mystery. For 75 years, a shadowy stranger dressed in a dark coat and hat pulled low over his face appeared at the graveside at Westminster Hall and Burial Grounds every January 19, raising a glass of cognac in Poe's honor and leaving behind three roses. While the original Poe Toaster is believed to have died, in 2015, the public elected a new Poe Toaster who now makes a daylight appearance in honor of Poe's birthday. Be sure to check out the other Poe haunts in Baltimore, where he lived and died. 🌐 *www.poeinbaltimore.org/poe-places*

Don't Miss

Start your tour at the **Edgar Allan Poe House and Museum,** his home during the 1830s, where you'll see artifacts like his chair and desk and a collection of works that he wrote in Baltimore. ✉ *203 N. Amity St., Baltimore, MD* 🌐 *www.poeinbaltimore.org*

Best Tour

A stop at Westminster Hall and Burial Grounds, where both of Poe's graves (yes, there are two) are located, is a must. ✉ *515 W. Fayette St., Baltimore, MD* 🌐 *www.westminsterhall.org*

Best Ghostly Stop

The **Horse You Came In On Saloon** in Fells Point is believed to be the place where Poe had his final drink. Some say his spirit can be seen wandering the historic bar. ✉ *1626 Thames St., Baltimore, MD* 🌐 *www.thehorsebaltimore.com*

Getting Here and Around

The attractions linked to Edgar Allan Poe are scattered throughout the city. Some are within walking distance from one another while others require short drives or cab rides.

Chesapeake & Ohio Canal National Historical Park

A Mule Boat Ride Back in Time

A waterway that allowed for coal to be transported from western Maryland to Washington, D.C., the Chesapeake & Ohio Canal was operational for nearly 100 years. Canal boats full of coal were pulled by mules, who navigated a towpath on the shore. At night they'd actually sleep in a stable aboard the boats. Today you can follow these same paths for nearly the entire length of the 184-mile canal. A scenic place to start is the Great Falls Tavern Visitor Center, northwest of Washington, D.C. ✉ *11710 Macarthur Blvd., Potomac, MD* 🌐 *www.nps.gov/choh*

Don't Miss

The **Billy Goat Trail** is a popular hiking and biking spot along the C&O Canal. It's actually three different trails that offer challenging hiking and even some rock climbing. The trails are accessible at the towpath entrance at Great Falls Tavern.

Good to Know

There are visitor centers located along the route, including in popular spots like Cumberland and Williamsport. The visitor centers are a great place to pick up brochures and maps, learn helpful information about the route, and start a hike. 🌐 *www.canaltrust.org/plan/highlights-and-amenities/co-canal-visitor-centers*

Getting Here and Around

There are many entrances to the C&O Canal, but the one at the Great Falls Tavern Visitor Center in Potomac is among the most accessible.

When in Maryland

FREDERICK

The city of Frederick is the kind of place where you can visit a historic site in the morning, an interesting museum in the afternoon, and then join the locals at a hip cocktail bar. At the National Museum of Civil War Medicine, you can learn about the critical role that early medicine played in the Civil War; housed in a former funeral home that prepped the bodies of soldiers who died at Antietam, it's said that ghostly footsteps sometimes echo in the night. The Monocacy National Battlefield is also nearby, as is Wye Oak Tavern, the buzzy restaurant from celebrity chef Bryan Voltaggio.

Do This: AARCH Society offers guided African-American History walking tours of downtown Frederick between April and October. Tours last between 60 and 90 minutes and cost $10. ✉ *125 E. All Saints St., Frederick, MD* 🌐 *www.aarchsociety.org/walking-tours*

MERRIWEATHER POST PAVILION

Set within 40 acres of woodlands is the Merriweather Post Pavilion, a treasured outdoor performance venue in Columbia, Maryland. Designed by renowned architect Frank Gehry, the venue was the summer home for the National Symphony Orchestra in 1967. In recent years, it has changed to accommodate mosh pits, massive crowds, and modern-day technology. The venue has hosted everyone from Jimi Hendrix, who first performed his now-famous version of the "Star-Spangled Banner" here, to Phish, Pitbull, and Sabrina Carpenter.

Do This: Sure, you could reserve a seat, but locals prefer to bring a blanket and enjoy a picnic on the expansive lawn. ✉ *10475 Little Patuxent Pkwy., Columbia, MD* 🌐 *www.merriweathermusic.com*

About Our Writers

Laura Rodini grew up in Valley Forge, PA and Columbia, MD and has lived in Baltimore for 15 years. She counts herself lucky to have been among the hushed crowd at Westminster Burying Ground when the new Poe Toaster made his first appearance. She has traveled the world while working on more than 100 destination and luxury hotel guides for Fodor's Travel, ApartmentAdvisor, and Northstar Travel Media; she currently teaches at Johns Hopkins University.

ORIOLE PARK AT CAMDEN YARDS

With a name that calls to mind Maryland's brilliantly colored state bird, the Baltimore Orioles are the city's hometown baseball team. They play at the eye-catching Oriole Park at Camden Yards in downtown Baltimore, known as one of the most beautiful stadiums in baseball. ✉ *333 W. Camden St., Baltimore, MD* 🌐 *www.mlb.com/orioles*

Do This: If you're a big-time baseball fan, head to the nearby Babe Ruth Birthplace and Museum. ✉ *216 Emory St., Baltimore, MD* 🌐 *www.baberuthmuseum.org*

ST. MICHAELS

Waterfront St. Michaels is named for an Episcopal church established in the town in 1677. The Chesapeake Bay town is a favorite with boating enthusiasts and seafood fans, as well as architecture buffs who come to see its streets lined with late-18th- and early-19th-century structures. Enjoy Maryland crabs at The Crab Claw and take in views of the Inn at Perry Cabin, a hotel made famous by the film *Wedding Crashers*.

Do This: Learn about the area's vast maritime history at the Chesapeake Bay Maritime Museum, which is also home to a working shipyard where shipwrights can be seen working on oceangoing vessels. ✉ *213 N. Talbot St., St. Michaels, MD* 🌐 *www.cbmm.org*

Cool Places to Stay

Governor Calvert House. In the heart of Annapolis, this historic inn has a timeless feel and a downtown setting. The guest rooms are decorated to reflect its proud past. In the sitting room, a glass floor gives you a view of the building's original foundation. ✉ *58 State Circle, Annapolis, MD* 🌐 *www.historicinnsofannapolis.com/stay/governor-calvert-house*

The Inn at Perry Cabin. Most famously known as the setting for the film *Wedding Crashers*, the Inn at Perry Cabin has a waterfront setting on Maryland's Eastern Shore. Relaxing and serene, the hotel grounds have restaurants, bars, a pool, a fleet of sailboats for scenic cruising, and plenty of space for outdoor lounging. ✉ *308 Watkins La., St. Michaels, MD* 🌐 *www.innatperrycabin.com*

Jacob Rohrbach Inn at Antietam. Dating back to 1804, the Jacob Rohrbach Inn has a historic setting just a few steps away from Antietam National Battlefield. The five-room inn is in the heart of downtown Sharpsburg, putting you within walking distance of the restaurants, taverns, and shops that line the main street. ✉ *138 W. Main St., Sharpsburg, MD* 🌐 *www.jacob-rohrbach-inn.com*

Sagamore Pendry Hotel. Located in Baltimore's trendy Fells Point neighborhood, the beautiful Sagamore Pendry Hotel combines reclaimed history with plenty of luxury—all in a waterfront setting. The pool offers prime harbor views, as do many of the refined guest rooms and suites. ✉ *1715 Thames St., Baltimore, MD* 🌐 *www.pendry.com*

Essential Eats

Baltimore Snowballs. During the Great Depression, many of Baltimore's working class families couldn't afford ice cream; instead, they cooled off with snowballs, or finely shaved ice drizzled with flavored syrups and topped with marshmallow cream. The tradition continues today. Ice Queens, by Fort McHenry National Monument and Historic Shrine, adds "smiles and sprinkles" for no extra charge. ✉ *1648 E. Fort Ave., Baltimore, MD* 🌐 *www.instagram.com/_icequeens*

Blue Crabs. The Chesapeake Bay's brackish waters are home to several species of crab; *Callinectes sapidus*, or blue crabs, are the most famous, as they are prized for their delicate, buttery meat, which comes from the extra fat they store when they hibernate. While buzzy crab shacks seem to pop up whenever the weather turns warm, long-standing favorites include The Crab Claw (✉ *304 Burns St., St. Michaels, MD* *www.thecrabclaw.com*), Nick's Fish House (✉ *2600 Insulator Dr., Baltimore, MD* 🌐 *www.nicksfishhouse.com*), and Woody's Crab House (✉ *29 S. Main St., North East, MD* 🌐 *www.woodyscrabhouse.com*), all of which serve prime waterfront views along with their seafood.

Pit Beef. You may be familiar with Carolina- and Memphis-style BBQ—Maryland's answer is pit beef. Top round steak is grilled over charcoals, then sliced thin; it's crusty on the outside while the inside is rare—we're talking *really* red—and served with a horseradish sauce on a kaiser roll or rye bread. Chaps Pit Beef has several locations around the state as well as in Baltimore (✉ *720 Mapleton Ave.* 🌐 *www.chapspitbeef.com*); sports fans can also enjoy a sandwich when the Os are in town at the Boog's BBQ stand at Oriole Park at Camden Yards.

New Jersey

The "Garden State" offers an exciting mix of cities and greenery. It has the third-largest state park system in the country and is almost entirely bordered by water—the Atlantic Ocean (and the famous Jersey Shore) to the east, the Delaware River to the west, and Delaware Bay to the south. Along the Hudson River, you'll find the urban centers of Jersey City and Hoboken as well as the famous Palisades, all of which offer heart-stopping views of the Manhattan skyline. And locals pride themselves on a unique "only in Jersey" culture marked by diners and shore life that are epic in their own right.

Capital: Trenton

Population: 9,500,851

Area: 7,355 square miles

Statehood Date: December 18, 1787

Major Airport: Newark Liberty International Airport (EWR); Atlantic City International Airport (ACY); Trenton–Mercer Airport (TTN)

Travel and Tourism Information: *www.visitnj.org*

Famous Residents: Thomas Edison (inventor); Frank Sinatra (singer and actor); Bruce Springsteen (musician); James Gandolfini (actor); Whitney Houston (singer)

Fun Fact: The game Monopoly was created in Atlantic City and used its streets as inspiration. Driving around the beachside city can feel like you're playing the game in real life.

Liberty State Park

Epic Views of the Manhattan Skyline

The 1,212-acre Liberty State Park has one of the most spectacular views anywhere. Located along the mouth of the Hudson River in Jersey City, it offers unobstructed views of the Manhattan skyline, the Statue of Liberty, and Ellis Island. The waterfront walking paths through the park wind through the picnic areas, playgrounds, and moving memorials. ✉ *200 Morris Pesin Dr., Jersey City, NJ* 🌐 *www.nj.gov/dep/parksandforests/parks/liberty.html*

Don't Miss

One of the most moving memorials to the September 11, 2001, attacks on the World Trade Center is the **Empty Sky Memorial** at Liberty State Park. It features two stainless-steel walls printed with the names of the 749 New Jersey residents who lost their lives that day. It sits on the waterfront facing Manhattan.

If You Have Kids

On the western edge of the park is **Liberty Science Center**, which has plenty of hands-on exhibits that will keep kids occupied for hours. ✉ *222 Jersey City Blvd., Jersey City, NJ* 🌐 *www.lsc.org*

Best Tour

Any real NJ-er will tell you that the Statue of Liberty is *technically* in New Jersey. To get there or Ellis Island, take a ferry operated by Statue Cruises. They depart from Jersey City's Liberty State Park and usually are less crowded than their counterparts in New York City. 🌐 *www.statuecruises.com/cruises/new-jersey-reserve*

Getting Here and Around

Newark Liberty International Airport is a little over 10 miles away. PATH trains from Manhattan stop in downtown Jersey City and you can take the city's light-rail to the Liberty State Park station.

Asbury Park

New Jersey's Coolest Beach Town

It's easy to see why Asbury Park is considered one of the Jersey Shore's coolest beach towns. **The Stone Pony** music venue made Asbury a household name decades ago when musicians like Bruce Springsteen, the Ramones, and Blondie graced its stage, and it's still going strong today. The town is also known for its exciting arts, culture, and dining scenes. The **Asbury Park Boardwalk** is a prime spot for people-watching, shopping, and eating. The downtown streets are filled with favorites like the **Asbury Hotel**—check out the rooftop bar—the **Asbury Brewing Company**, and **Asbury Park Distilling**.

Don't Miss

Take advantage of the varied offerings at the majestic landmark known as the **Asbury Park Convention Hall**—part music venue, part dining and drinking destination. Within the Convention Hall, the Asbury Oyster Bar is particularly popular for its namesake bivalve. ✉ *1300 Ocean Ave. N, Asbury Park, NJ*

Hip Street Art

Asbury is known for its outdoor murals, the brainchild of a local gallery owner. Both local and national artists were commissioned to create murals along the boardwalk and throughout downtown. 🌐 *www.woodenwallsproject.com*

When to Go

Asbury Park in the summer means plenty of outdoor dining and drinking as well as beachside concerts, but crowds and prices can get high.

Getting Here and Around

Asbury Park is about 45 miles from Newark Liberty International Airport and about 57 miles from Manhattan, off the Garden State Parkway. The town is accessible by New Jersey Transit trains as well.

Cape May

America's Original Seaside Getaway

The southernmost point in New Jersey is Cape May, a seaside town with a year-round population just shy of 4,000 people. At the height of summer, though, that number jumps to 40,000 or even 50,000 people. Known for its picturesque beaches, Victorian mansions, quaint bed-and-breakfasts, and historic hotels, Cape May is also popular for its **Washington Street Mall**, an outdoor street filled with quaint shops and restaurants. Beyond the downtown area, **Cape May Lighthouse**, the adjacent **Cape May Point State Park**, and **Cape May County Park and Zoo** are big draws.

Don't Miss

Cape May has quite the impressive winery, distillery, and brewery scene. **Nauti Spirits Distilling** produces vodkas, gins, and whiskeys all made from ingredients grown on the on-site farm while breweries like **Cape May Brewery**, **Behr Brewing**, and **Cold Spring Brewery** (located on the same site as the Cold Spring Village living history museum) offer quality brews in tasting rooms with plenty of games and outdoor seating. New Jersey wines are slowly but surely making an impression on the wine scene, too, which you can see for yourself at **Hawk Haven Winery**, **Cape May Winery**, and **Willow Creek Winery**.

Best Tour

Cape May Whale Watcher offers an array of tours, including an excellent whale and dolphin watch. If you don't spot one, you'll receive a free pass for a future date. 🌐 *www.capemaywhalewatcher.com*

Getting Here and Around

Best reached by car, Cape May is the last exit on the Garden State Parkway. For a more special trip, the Cape May–Lewes ferry takes you on an 80-minute ride across Delaware Bay from Lewes, Delaware.

The Jersey Shore

Experience Going Down the Shore

The coastal beach region of New Jersey, fondly known as the Jersey Shore, extends for 330 miles from Sandy Hook National Seashore in the north to Cape May in the south. Any New Jersey resident will have an opinion about the best beach town, which they have likely been visiting for decades. Among the most popular are **Ocean City**, a family-friendly destination with a food- and ride-filled boardwalk; **Seaside Heights**, made famous by MTV's *Jersey Shore;* the barrier island beaches of **Long Beach Island**; and **Wildwood**, which offers 2 miles of boardwalk attractions.

Don't Miss

Island Beach State Park is one of the largest undeveloped barrier islands in the country. Visitors love the relaxed atmosphere and the opportunity for swimming, kayaking, or fishing at different parts of the 10-mile-long island. ✉ *2401 Central Ave., Seaside Park, NJ* 🌐 *www.state.nj.us/dep/parksandforests/parks/island.html*

Best Tour

Hop aboard **Salt Marsh Safari's** 40-foot pontoon boats and tour the salt marshes along the coast. Tours depart from Stone Harbor and last for two hours. 🌐 *www.skimmer.com*

Getting Here and Around

The Jersey Shore is best reached by car via the Garden State Parkway, but many beach towns such as Long Branch, Asbury Park, Belmar, and Point Pleasant Beach are accessible via New Jersey Transit trains and buses. Seastreak ferries take you from Manhattan to Sandy Hook.

Atlantic City

The All-American Boardwalk

The weathered wooden boards seem to go on forever along the wide beaches of Atlantic City, and for good reason: this is the longest boardwalk in the country, measuring more than 4 miles long. It was also the nation's first boardwalk, created in 1870 and known for its unique entertainment, including a diving horse and the Miss America Pageant. Casinos didn't open for another century, but now their high-adrenaline gaming, all-star entertainment, and top-tier restaurants are what most people picture when they think of AC. And today there are some pretty chic hotel rooms steps away from one of New Jersey's only admission-free beaches, not to mention the world's largest indoor/beachfront waterpark, **Island Waterpark** at the Showboat Resort; the tallest lighthouse in New Jersey, **Absecon Lighthouse**; and even the largest musical instrument in the world, the pipe organ at Art Deco **Boardwalk Hall**.

Don't Miss

Steel Pier is where to find rides for all ages, ranging from a classic carousel to the Sling Shot, which rockets riders 225 feet in 15 seconds. Ride the modern Ferris wheel at night for neon-lit views across the boardwalk. 🌐 *steelpier.com*

Getting Here and Around

Atlantic City is part of a barrier island in the southern part of the Jersey Shore, about 60 miles from Philadelphia and 120 miles from New York City. It's accessible by NJ Transit buses and trains as well as by Greyhound. Both Spirit and American Airlines fly into the small Atlantic City International Airport (ACY).

Morristown National Historical Park

Follow In George Washington's Footsteps

George Washington and his Continental Army spent two bitterly cold winters in New Jersey. Morristown National Historical Park memorializes their struggle at several different sites, including two Continental Army encampments and a fortified hilltop nicknamed Fort Nonsense. The Ford Mansion, home to Theodosia Ford and her children, became headquarters for Washington and a close group of advisors, including Alexander Hamilton. ✉ *30 Washington Pl., Morristown, NJ* 🌐 *www.nps.gov/morr/index.htm*

Don't Miss

Be sure to visit the soldier huts at Jockey Hollow. The rebuilt structures resemble the wood cabins where the soldiers lived during the cold winters in Morristown.

Best Tour

Grab a map and head off on a self-guided tour of the 27 miles of trails throughout the park. Trails are marked by their difficulty level.

When to Go

To best enjoy the park's hiking trails, the fall, spring, and summer are great times to visit.

Getting Here and Around

Since the main sites are spread around the Morristown area, it's best to have a car when visiting. The attraction is off Interstate 287 in Morristown, New Jersey.

Princeton

Ivy League Attractions

Princeton may be best known for its resident Ivy League university, and the Gothic Revival architecture in buildings like Blair Hall, Holder Hall, and Cleveland Tower make it well worth exploring. But the town itself is also a gem, and Nassau Street and the surrounding thoroughfares are popular among locals and visitors for their variety of shops, restaurants, and taverns. Residents take pride in **Princeton Battlefield State Park**, a 681-acre historic park where, on January 3, 1777, General George Washington and his troops defeated a group of British foot soldiers. Today, the expansive park is home to the **Clark House Museum**.

Don't Miss

The 5-acre **Morven Museum and Garden** was built by Richard Stockton, a signer of the Declaration of Independence, in the 1750s. Many New Jersey governors lived at the property before it was opened to the public. ✉ *55 Stockton St., Princeton, NJ* 🌐 *www.morven.org* 🎫 *$12*

Best Tour

The impressive **Princeton University Art Museum** is home to more than 97,000 works of art. Self-guided tours of the museum are available, but guided tours at 2 on weekends include an interesting commentary on the collection. ✉ *Elm Dr., Princeton, NJ* 🌐 *artmuseum.princeton.edu*

Getting Here and Around

Princeton is located halfway between New York City and Philadelphia. It's about 40 miles from Newark Liberty International Airport and is accessible by NJ Transit and Amtrak.

Paterson Great Falls National Historical Park

New Jersey's Niagara Falls

A 77-foot-high waterfall is the centerpiece of Paterson Great Falls National Historical Park. During the Industrial Revolution, Paterson was the country's first planned industrial community, which Alexander Hamilton helped to create. The hydro power from the falls was used to power the town. Visit for sweeping waterfall views, and set out on one of the many walking trails through the park. ✉ *72 McBride Ave., Paterson, NJ* 🌐 *www.nps.gov/pagr*

Don't Miss

Walk along the Great Falls footbridge for uninterrupted aerial views for the waterfall.

Best Tour

There are several ranger-led tour options if you book in advance, and a kids' junior ranger program. You can also download a free self-guided walking tour app.

Dining and Drinking Detour

Head 10 minutes south to the small city of Clifton, where you can enjoy the famous deep-fried hot dog ("the Ripper") at **Rutt's Hut** (🌐 *www.ruttshut.com*). Across the street, you can wash them down with local brews from **Ghost Hawk Brewing Company** (🌐 *www.ghosthawkbrewing.com*) or craft cocktails from **Silk City Distillers** (🌐 *silkcitydistillers.com*).

When to Go

The park is open year-round. Spring, summer, and fall are the best times to visit since the footbridge closes when the weather gets icy.

Getting Here and Around

A few minutes off I–80, the state park is less than a 30-minute drive from Newark Airport. Parking is available at Overlook Park and along Maple Street.

Jersey Diners

Diner Capital of the World

New Jersey is fondly known as the "diner capital of the world" with an estimated 500 diners populating the state. Each undeniably has its own personality and go-to menu items, but all share the same approachable vibes. Many have retro details, remaining almost untouched since the 1950s, like the **Summit Diner**. Most are open late, and some even operate 24 hours a day. The menus are usually laughably long, offering everything from Greek and Italian dishes to classic American options (hello, burgers and shakes), plus breakfast all day. At the **Ritz Diner** in Livingston, there are Asian offerings alongside Jewish blintzes and bagels, plus their famous sky-high apple pie.

Don't Miss

Clinton Station Diner, a 24-hour operation in Clinton, stands out with its partially converted dining car. The menu features classics like salads, fries, deli sandwiches, Reubens, breakfast combos and more, in addition to a full bar, but what it's really known for are its burger-eating challenges, which result in free meals for winners. ✉ *2 Bank St., Clinton, NJ* 🌐 *www.clintonstationdiner.com*

Good to Know

East Newark's **Tops Diner** has received numerous accolades for its excellent food and fun vibes, so it's no wonder it's been called one of the best diners in the country. Tops has been serving classic American fare since 1942 with options like egg platters, breakfast sandwiches, and pancakes. Don't miss the Disco Fries, a Jersey diner classic, smothered in a rich brown gravy and melted mozzarella cheese. ✉ *500 Passaic Ave., East Newark, NJ* 🌐 *www.thetopsdiner.com*

Getting Here and Around

There are diners in every county and most towns throughout the state.

When in New Jersey

BRANCH BROOK PARK

Every spring, the tidal basin of this park is filled with thousands of cotton candy–hued Japanese cherry blossoms. But, no, this isn't D.C.; instead, you've arrived at Branch Brook Park, 360 acres of water and greenery in big-city Newark, NJ. The park is home to 5,300 Japanese cherry trees (that's 1,500 more trees than the nation's capital) that burst into a pink wave starting in early April. And fun fact: Branch Brook was designed by Frederick Law Olmsted, who also famously created New York City's Central Park. ✉ *Branch Brook Park Dr., Newark, NJ* 🌐 *branchbrookpark.org*

Do This: Plan a visit to see the blooms during the annual Essex County Cherry Blossom Festival, which is held at the beginning of April. Activities include a 10K run, live music, food, cultural demonstrations, and special children's entertainment.

DELAWARE WATER GAP NATIONAL RECREATION AREA

Located on the New Jersey and Pennsylvania border, the 70,000-acre Delaware Water Gap National Recreation Area is the picturesque point where the Delaware River meets the Appalachian Mountain Range. There are miles of hiking trails of varying skill levels that bring explorers past waterfalls, to mountaintop overlooks, and along riverfront walks. Rafting and tubing on the Delaware River are a popular summer activity, so much so, in fact, there's a hot dog vendor that sets up a floating outpost. ✉ *Old Mine Rd., Hardwick, NJ* 🌐 *www.nps.gov/dewa*

Do This: Journey back in history at Millbrook Village, which shows what life was like here in the mid-1800s. On many weekends throughout the year, costumed volunteers bring the town to life with woodworking, weaving, spinning, blacksmithing, and gardening demonstrations.

GROUNDS FOR SCULPTURE

There are nearly 300 outdoor sculptures—some towering more than 30 feet—on display across 42 acres of land at this expansive outdoor art park. Many of the sculptures that you'll find tucked into the wooded setting are hyperrealistic re-creations of famous paintings (think *The Boating Party,* come to life) by Seward Johnson, who created the sculpture park. The landscape itself is reason enough to visit, with walking paths that meander past ponds and meadows. Inside the museum, six galleries welcome a rotating lineup of up-and-coming artists. ✉ *80 Sculptors Way, Hamilton Township, NJ* 🌐 *www.groundsforsculpture.org*

Do This: Plan to have lunch at one of the facility's on-site restaurants. Visit Rat's Restaurant, named for *The Wind in the Willows* character, to be transported to the French town of Giverny. For a more casual meal, the Van Gogh Cafe sells picnic lunches that come complete with a bottle of wine.

HOLLAND RIDGE FARMS

A slice of the Netherlands in the heart of New Jersey, this tulip company was founded by Casey Jansen six decades ago after immigrating from Holland. Today, Holland Ridge Farms is a pick-your-own flower farm spanning 153 acres in Central New Jersey. People from throughout the region visit in the spring to pick tulips and in the fall to pick sunflowers as well as to sample Dutch bakery treats, take tractor rides, and pet the farm animals. ✉ *86 Rues Rd., Cream Ridge, NJ* 🌐 *www.hollandridgefarms.com*

Do This: The tens of thousands of flowers make for an ideal backdrop for family photos. Bring your camera—or your own photographer—for an unforgettable shot.

LUCY THE ELEPHANT

The country's oldest roadside attraction, six-story-tall Lucy the Elephant is a towering wood and tin elephant located by the beach in Margate, New Jersey. The giant structure was created by James V. Lafferty in 1881 as a way to draw tourists to the beachfront community. More than 130 years later, the towering elephant is still a draw for visitors of all ages. ✉ *9200 Atlantic Ave., Margate City, NJ* 🌐 *www.lucytheelephant.org*

Do This: The only way to explore the inside of the towering elephant is on a 25-minute guided tour. From the howdah (the bed-like structure at the top of the elephant's back), you can take in great views of Margate.

MOUNTAIN CREEK RESORT

Swoosh down the slopes at Mountain Creek, New Jersey's ski mountain in the state's northern border town of Vernon. Although the 1,400-foot elevation is much lower than ski spots like Vermont and Colorado, the 46 ski trails and a 1,000-foot vertical still provide plenty of thrills. And when summer arrives, a water park takes over the mountain terrain, taking full advantage of the natural setting with Tarzan swings into cold springs and speedy downhill waterslides. Fall and spring offer opportunities for mountain bikers to try out the trails, too. ✉ *200 Rte. 94, Vernon, NJ* 🌐 *www.mountaincreek.com*

Do This: Visit Vernon in the autumn for apple-picking and fabulous foliage views. Stop at the Dairy Swirl for homemade ice cream in flavors such as pumpkin and apple pie. ✉ *71 Rte. 94, Vernon Township, NJ* 🌐 *www.facebook.com/dairyswirl*

NEW JERSEY PINELANDS NATIONAL RESERVE

The country's first national reserve, the New Jersey Pinelands comprises 1.1 million acres in seven counties across the southern part of New Jersey. It's home to a wide array of wildlife, farms, and wetlands. The sheer size can be overwhelming, but the Edwin B. Forsythe National Wildlife Refuge and Cape May National Wildlife Refuge both offer easy-to-follow trails and are a good place to start to learn about the region. ✉ *15 Springfield Rd., New Lisbon, NJ* 🌐 *www.nj.gov/pinelands*

Do This: The Historic Village of Allaire, once a bustling community that was home to 400 people, has been preserved to show off a way of life that no longer exists. You can explore 13 of the original buildings, including a bakery, a boardinghouse, and a blast furnace where iron was once smelted. ✉ *4263 Atlantic Ave., Farmingdale, NJ* 🌐 *www.allairevillage.org*

STERLING HILL MINING MUSEUM

New Jersey may not be famous for its mining, but the history of Sterling Hill Mine might just make up for that. Without taking a stance on mining, the museum discusses the history of the industry, its effects on the community, and its long-term consequences. Located at the site of a former zinc mine, the museum includes a 1,300-foot tunnel through the actual mine (bring a jacket, as it's chilly underground). It's accessible via two-hour-long guided tours. ✉ *30 Plant St., Ogdensburg, NJ* 🌐 *www.sterlinghillminingmuseum.org*

Do This: Inside the mine, keep an eye out for the Rainbow Tunnel, a colorful exhibition that highlights the fluorescent zinc ore. Then visit the Warren Museum of Fluorescence, with four rooms full of glow-in-the-dark minerals.

THOMAS EDISON NATIONAL HISTORICAL PARK

Thomas Edison called West Orange, New Jersey home for close to 50 years, and the site of his former home and laboratory are now known as Thomas Edison National Historical Park. The laboratory is where Edison invented devices like the phonograph and the motion picture camera. There are more than 300,000 items in the museum's collection, making this one of the National Park Service's most expansive museums. The house explores the Edison family's daily life. ✉ *211 Main St., West Orange, NJ* ⊕ *www.nps.gov/edis*

Do This: Embark on the self-guided tour of the home, which shares stories about Edison and his family.

About Our Writers

Melissa Klurman is a born-and-raised Jersey Girl (the kind Bruce Springsteen sings about), currently living in Montclair with her husband, son, and rescue dog Babka. She strongly believes that NJ bagels are the best in the world (and yes, she will fight a New Yorker about that). A former Fodor's staff editor, she is a frequent contributor to *Reader's Digest*, The Points Guy, Tripadvisor, and *Parents*, among other publications.

Cool Places to Stay

Asbury Hotel. Located in the heart of hip Asbury Park, this lively hotel was once a Salvation Army, but now offers up a cool pool scene, tasty drinks and tacos, and laid-back vibes. The comfortable guest rooms are sleek, minimalist, and dog-friendly. There are even rooms with multiple bunk beds for groups. The rooftop bar, Salvation, is a draw for its ocean views, craft cocktails, and DJs spinning the hottest tunes. ✉ *210 5th Ave., Asbury Park, NJ* ⊕ *www.theasburyhotel.com*

Congress Hall. When driving through Cape May, it's impossible to miss iconic Congress Hall, America's oldest seaside resort and one of the most charming places to stay in New Jersey. While there is a ton to do in Cape May, guests never have to leave hotel grounds with its stellar dining, luxe spa, chair-side beach service, and swimming pool. ✉ *200 Congress Pl., Cape May, NJ* ⊕ *www.caperesorts.com/congress-hall*

Lambertville House Hotel. This historic hotel first opened its doors in 1812, and since then has hosted notables like President Andrew Johnson and General Ulysses S. Grant. The rooms are all classically decorated to match the hotel's history and offer modern amenities like gas fireplaces and whirlpool tubs. ✉ *32 Bridge St., Lambertville, NJ* ⊕ *www.lambertville-house.com*

The MC Hotel. The town of Montclair, 14 miles west of Manhattan, is popular for its diverse and exciting arts scene, including annual film and jazz festivals, and this hotel encapsulates the area's cool aesthetic. The hotel has a sleek rooftop bar and lounge with stunning views of the New York City skyline, an indoor-outdoor Mediterranean restaurant, and art created by up-and-coming artists. ✉ *690 Bloomfield Ave., Montclair, NJ* ⊕ *www.themchotel.com*

Pendry Natirar. In the quiet, rolling hills of Somerset County, this British estate–like getaway is centered around an elegantly restored 1912 Tudor mansion that boasts luxurious rooms, 500 acres of greenery, a working farm, and a special-occasion-worthy restaurant, Niney Acres, that also has a cooking school. The fall foliage surrounding the property is especially impressive, as is the fabulous spa. ✉ *400 Natirar Dr., Peapack, NJ* ⊕ *www.pendry.com/natirar*

Essential Eats

Belmont Tavern. This old-school Italian institution is the only spot that knows, and serves, the secret recipe for the legendary Stretch's chicken savoy, although that hasn't stopped other spots from trying to re-create it. The original is baked with vinegar, grated cheese, and oregano (that's as much as people know) until the bone-in chicken pieces form a crunchy exterior and a fragrant sauce, an addictive combo that's kept a loyal following despite the eatery's no-reservations policy. ✉ *12 Bloomfield Ave., Belleville, NJ* 🌐 *www.instagram.com/belmont_tavern_nj*

Milburn Deli. A sloppy Joe in northern New Jersey is not what you're thinking. Instead of a pile of saucy meat on a bun, it's a delicately layered cold cut masterpiece comprising several deli meats such as corned beef, turkey, or pastrami; coleslaw; Russian dressing; and Swiss cheese stacked between three thin slices of rye bread. It was invented here at the Milburn Deli, where it's still a popular menu item. It can be ordered around Essex County, but leave this region and it's back to saucy meat. ✉ *328 Millburn Ave., Millburn, NJ* 🌐 *www.millburndeli.com*

Razza. The unofficial New Jersey motto toward food might just be that anything New York can do, New Jersey can do better (and with less crowds). And once you try the pizza at this Jersey City hot spot, you'll see what they mean. The wood-fired pizzas are true works of art, with perfectly crispy crusts and a creative variety of local ingredients from New Jersey farms, like the zucchini with summer squash and ricotta or the Project Hazelnut with Rutgers hazelnuts and honey. ✉ *275 Grove St., Jersey City, NJ* 🌐 *www.razzanj.com*

Taylor Ham/Pork Roll. A pork product sold in large tubes, then sliced and grilled, it's part of the state's quintessential breakfast sandwich—a bagel, egg, cheese, and a slice of, well, it depends what end of the state you're in. Although New Jersey is the fourth-smallest U.S. state, there's a fierce north/south Jersey divide on this issue. The north is firmly in the "Taylor ham" camp while the south adamantly adheres to "pork roll." Try it for yourself at Johnny's Pork Roll and Coffee Too (✉ *8A Monmouth St., Red Bank, NJ* 🌐 *www.johnnyporkroll.com*), Bagel Nosh (✉ *24 E. Prospect St., Waldwick, NJ* 🌐 *bagelnoshofwaldwick.com*), or at various deli counters and bagel stores throughout the state.

Tomato Pie. When is a pizza not a pizza? When you put a sauce of crushed tomatoes on top of the cheese (instead of tomato sauce like most pizzas) supported by a cracker-thin crust, as they famously do in the southern part of New Jersey near Trenton; then you call it a tomato pie. Try it near where it was invented at Delorenzo's (✉ *2350 Rte. 33, Robbinsville, NJ* 🌐 *www.delorenzostomatopies.com*) or with a side of sea breezes on the Ocean City boardwalk at Manco & Manco (✉ *9th and Boardwalk, Ocean City, NJ* 🌐 *www.mancospizza.com*).

New York

Say the words "New York" and icons like Times Square and the Statue of Liberty may be the first things that come to mind. But the state is also very much a destination for appreciating the outdoors, in every season. Across New York State, from Niagara Falls to the tip of Long Island, there are breathtaking hiking trails, lakes and rivers for fishing and boating, mountains for skiing, and lovely ocean beaches for relaxing. More still, charming towns in the Catskills and Hudson Valley offer art and culture amid quiet solitude.

Capital: Albany

Population: 19,867,248

Area: 47,124 square miles

Statehood Date: April 20, 1777

Major Airports: John F. Kennedy International (JFK); LaGuardia Airport (LGA); Albany International Airport (ALB); Buffalo Niagara International Airport (BUF); Ithaca Tompkins International Airport (ITH); New York Stewart International Airport (SWF); Syracuse Hancock International Aiport (SYR)

Travel and Tourism Information: 🌐 *www.iloveny.com* 🌐 *www.visitnyc.com*

Famous Residents: Alexander Hamilton (founding father); Franklin and Eleanor Roosevelt (president and first lady); Lucille Ball (comedian); Spike Lee (director); Notorious B.I.G. (rapper)

Fun Fact: Think you've heard it all? In New York City, you just might. With over 800 languages spoken (including many that are endangered), it's the most linguistically diverse city on the planet.

Central Park

New York's Big Backyard

Upward of 42 million people visit New York City's iconic Central Park every year, but with its 843 acres of wide-open spaces, you can usually find a spot all to yourself. Designed by Frederick Law Olmsted and Calvert Vaux in 1858, Central Park was created to give city dwellers lots of fresh air. The park is now home to major attractions including the **Central Park Zoo**, with more than 130 species of animals; **Sheep Meadow** and its sunbathers; and **Conservatory Water** and its regatta of model boats. **Wollman Rink** is a wintertime destination for ice-skaters while the open-air **Delacorte Theater** is the summertime home to Shakespeare in the Park. 🌐 *www.centralparknyc.org*

Don't Miss

Paddleboats are available for rent at the **Loeb Boathouse** on Central Park Lake, one of the park's largest bodies of water. Visit the restaurant at the boathouse for a post-paddle treat. 🌐 *www.centralparkboathouse.com*

Best Tour

The sheer size of Central Park can make it overwhelming. Guides for **Central Park Bike Tours** can take you to the best spots and point out filming locations for New York City–based shows like *Sex and the City* and *Friends*. 🌐 *www.centralpark.com/tours/bike*

Good to Know

The park starts at 59th Street in Midtown Manhattan and continues up for more than 50 blocks to 110th Street in South Harlem. In other words, the park is huge, measuring 3 miles long.

Getting Here and Around

Central Park is located in the heart of Manhattan, making it easily accessible via public transit. Penn Station is less than 2 miles away.

Ellis Island and the Statue of Liberty

The Gateway to America

In the late 19th century and early 20th century, more than 12 million immigrants came to America by way of Ellis Island, which is located at the mouth of the Hudson River. You're likely to have at least one ancestor who passed through the grand doorways of this French Renaissance–style structure, and that's why a visit here is so moving. On nearby Liberty Island stands the Statue of Liberty, a symbol of hope for anyone whose first sight of America was from New York Harbor. ⊕ *www.statueofliberty.org*

Don't Miss

On Ellis Island, visit the **National Museum of Immigration**, located within the ornate main building. Many people visit the museum to scour the easily searchable historic records for family members' names. Others visit to learn about the important role that Ellis Island played through artifacts and heirlooms.

Good to Know

A short ferry ride away from Ellis Island is the Statue of Liberty, a towering structure that was a gift from the French. The Statue of Liberty Museum explores the history of the statue and exhibits artifacts like the original torch. It also offers prime views of Lady Liberty. While the statue's torch is closed to the public, you can buy special tickets to access her pedestal and crown.

Getting Here and Around

Both Ellis Island and the Statue of Liberty are only reachable by ferries from Battery Park in Manhattan and Liberty State Park in Jersey City. Ferry tickets grant you access to both destinations.

Niagara Falls State Park

Three Spectacular Waterfalls

There isn't just one spectacular waterfall in Niagara Falls State Park. In the country's oldest state park are three separate sights: Horseshoe Falls (this is the U-shape one that most people think of when they hear "Niagara Falls"), American Falls, and Bridal Veil Falls. At its highest points, the falls tumble 176 feet. Beyond the falls, the state park features includes several islands: Goat Island—with great views and several attractions of its own—Luna Island, and Three Sisters Islands. ✉ *332 Prospect St., Niagara Falls, NY* 🌐 *www.niagarafallsstatepark.com*

Don't Miss

Catch a glimpse of the falls from above at Niagara Falls Observation Tower, which has the only panoramic view of all three waterfalls. It sits between American Falls and Bridal Veil Falls.

Best Tour

On the *Maid of the Mist* boat tour, visitors get to view Horseshoe Falls from below on a 20-minute boat tour. The boat gets so close that guests get waterproof ponchos to protect them from the mist. 🌐 *www.maidofthemist.com*

When to Go

Niagara Falls is most enjoyable in warmer weather when there is no snow or ice to worry about.

Getting Here and Around

Buffalo-Niagara International Airport is about 30 miles away.

NYC Museums

The Best of the Best

It's no secret that New York City has some of the best museums in the world. There are upward of 100 museums in New York City, ranging from massive institutions (the Whitney Museum of Art) to smaller, topic-specific attractions (the Museum of Sex). While most of the city's museums are well worth a visit, the five that are most deserving are fondly known as the Big Five: the **Metropolitan Museum of Art** (✉ *1000 5th Ave., New York, NY* 🌐 *www.metmuseum.org*), the **American Museum of Natural History** (✉ *200 Central Park W, New York, NY* 🌐 *www.amnh.org*), the **Museum of Modern Art** (✉ *11 W. 53rd St., New York, NY* 🌐 *www.moma.org*), the **Solomon R. Guggenheim Museum** (✉ *1071 5th Ave., New York, NY* 🌐 *www.guggenheim.org*), and the **Intrepid Sea, Air, and Space Museum** (✉ *Pier 86, W. 46th St., New York, NY* 🌐 *intrepidmuseum.org*).

Don't Miss

The Metropolitan Museum of Art has been a destination for art fans for generations. The Met is the largest art museum in the country and features everything from a complete Egyptian temple to a Frank Lloyd Wright house.

Best for Kids

The Hayden Planetarium at the American Museum of Natural History takes you to infinity and beyond. 🌐 *www.amnh.org/exhibitions/space-show*

Getting Here and Around

The Met and the Guggenheim are located on the Upper East Side, right next to Central Park. Across the park, you'll find the Natural History Museum on the Upper West Side. The MoMa is located in midtown Manhattan while the Intrepid is at Pier 86 on the Hudson River at West 46th Street. All are easily accessible via the subway.

The Empire State Building

The Spectacular NYC Skyline

With a legendary silhouette recognizable virtually worldwide, the Empire State Building is an Art Deco monument to progress, a symbol of NYC, and a star in many romantic scenes—on- and off-screen. Built in 1931 at the peak of the skyscraper craze, this 103-floor limestone giant opened after 13 months of construction. The framework rose at a rate of 4½ stories per week, making the Empire State Building the fastest-rising skyscraper ever built, to date. ✉ *20 W. 34th St., New York, NY* 🌐 *www.esbnyc.com*

Don't Miss

Rise from Floor 2 to reach Floor 80's enclosed observatory, with interactive kiosks to create custom NYC itineraries and an impressive NYC skyline drawing by memory artist Steven Wiltshire. Then head to the 86th-floor observatory (1,050 feet high) to find another enclosed area and the spectacular wraparound outdoor deck, offering 360-degree views of the city and way beyond.

Best Tip

The views at the top of the Empire State Building are amazing, but those skyline views are missing one thing: the Empire State Building. To get a glimpse of the city skyline that includes this iconic building, head to the **Top of the Rock Observation Deck** in Rockefeller Center. ✉ *30 Rockefeller Plaza, New York, NY* 🌐 *www.rockefellercenter.com/attractions/top-of-the-rock-observation-deck*

Getting Here and Around

The Empire State Building is located in the center of Manhattan; it's walking distance to several subway lines as well as Grand Central and Penn Station.

Broadway and Times Square

The Country's Most Iconic Theater District

Only a handful of theaters actually face the avenue that gave New York City's theater district its name—most of the 40 or so theaters are on side streets, from the Nederlander way down on 41st to the Vivian Beaumont up on 65th. The oldest ones, like the New Amsterdam, are Beaux-Arts gems from the days of the Ziegfeld Follies. All together they are known for producing the best of American theater, from Disney musicals to classic play revivals. If you can't see a show at the Shubert or the Booth, at least stroll by to see a couple of architectural masterpieces. Nearby, Shubert Alley is filled with starry-eyed theater fans waiting to enjoy a post-performance slice of cheesecake at Junior's. 🌐 *www.broadway.com*

Don't Miss

New Yorkers hate **Times Square**, and will do anything they can to avoid it, but it's a must for first-timers. The billboards are dazzling, and the illuminated red stairs above the TKTS booth are a great place to see the ball that drops every New Year's Eve.

Good to Know

While shows often sell out months in advance, the TKTS booth in Times Square sells heavily discounted same-day Broadway tickets. 🌐 *www.tdf.org*

When to Go

The busiest seasons are around the holidays and in the summer months. You're more likely to get tickets (at better prices) in January or February.

Getting Here and Around

Broadway is located in the middle of Manhattan, making it accessible from all over. Both of the city's major train stations, New York Penn Station and Grand Central Station, deposit you blocks from the district.

Brooklyn Bridge

The City's Most Gorgeous Bridge

Perhaps more than any other activity, New Yorkers send their out-of-town visitors for a stroll across the Brooklyn Bridge. The wide walking and biking paths are a big draw for those who want to take in panoramic views of the Manhattan skyline—and, of course, pose for pictures. The bridge opened in 1883 after more than 10 years of construction, and the engineering marvel is still the most beautiful of the city's bridges. On the Brooklyn side, Brooklyn Bridge Park is well worth the walk. 🌐 *www.brooklynbridgepark.org*

Don't Miss

Go for a walk through **DUMBO**, a Brooklyn neighborhood whose name is short for Down Under the Manhattan Bridge Overpass. It's full of converted warehouses, cobblestone streets, and prime Manhattan views, and is known for its excellent independently owned eateries.

Best Activity

Dating back to 1922, **Jane's Carousel** is a wooden merry-go-round that was moved to Brooklyn Bridge Park from Youngstown, Ohio. The painstakingly detailed carousel is enclosed in a glass pavilion, making it an all-year attraction. 🌐 *www.janescarousel.com*

When to Go

The bridge is busiest in the summer months, so if you're looking to avoid crowds, visit before Memorial Day or after Labor Day.

Getting Here and Around

The Brooklyn Bridge and the DUMBO neighborhood are easily accessible via the subway.

9/11 Memorial and Museum

New York's Most Moving Memorial

It's impossible not to be moved by Memorial Plaza, the centerpiece of the 9/11 Memorial and Museum. A pair of 30-foot-tall waterfalls occupy the giant, square footprints where the Twin Towers once stood. Edging the pools are bronze panels inscribed with the names of the nearly 3,000 people who were killed in the 1993 and 2001 terrorist attacks. In the museum, interactive exhibitions tell the story of the attacks and honor the lives lost. ✉ *180 Greenwich St., New York, NY* 🌐 *www.911memorial.org*

Don't Miss

Built on the site of One World Trade Center is the Freedom Tower, otherwise known as **One World Observatory**, rising to 1,776 feet tall. After a truly thrilling elevator ride to the top, see the city from above the clouds. ✉ *117 West St., New York, NY* 🌐 *www.oneworldobservatory.com*

Best Tour

Embark on a self-guided tour of the 110,000-square-foot 9/11 Memorial and Museum. The permanent collection consists of 70,000 items that were either found at the site or donated by survivors, their friends and family, or first responders.

Getting Here and Around

New Jersey's PATH trains travel directly to the World Trade Center station. The subway gets you here as well.

Chinatown

The Best of Chinese Culture

Manhattan's Chinatown, a bustling area filled with restaurants, grocery stores, and specialty stores, is regularly regarded as one of the best in the country. Although Chinese is the dominant culture here, it's not hard to find other Asian fare, such as Thai and Malaysian. Want to learn more about the neighborhood? Head to the **Museum of Chinese in America** (✉ *215 Centre St., New York, NY* 🌐 *www.mocanyc.org*). **Nom Wah Tea Parlor**, the **Hong Kong Supermarket**, and the **Original Chinatown Ice Cream Factory** are other delicious diversions.

Don't Miss

There are also Chinatowns in the Sunset Park neighborhood of Brooklyn and the Flushing neighborhood of Queens. They are less flashy, but New Yorkers swear the food is more authentic.

Best Restaurants

New Yorkers love **Joe's Shanghai** (✉ *46 Bowery, New York, NY* 🌐 *joesshanghai.online*) and **Nom Wah Tea Parlor** (✉ *13 Doyers St., New York, NY* 🌐 *www.nomwah.com*) and will regularly wait in line for their delicious (and inexpensive) pork buns, dumplings, and dim sum, but you can't go wrong with any restaurant that's filled with locals.

When to Go

Chinatown is great to visit at any time of year, but it is especially vibrant during the Lunar New Year in February or March, when the neighborhood puts on a colorful parade filled with dragon floats, firecrackers, and more.

Getting Here and Around

The subway runs to nearly all the neighborhoods mentioned here.

Harlem

Celebrate Black Music, Culture, and Food

One of Upper Manhattan's most famous neighborhoods, Harlem has long been known as a haven for Black culture: jazz, poetry, art, and more. During the Great Migration, millions of African-Americans from the South moved here in search of a better life. During the Harlem Renaissance, the neighborhood produced some of America's best works of literature, poetry, and jazz from the likes of Langston Hughes, Zora Neale Hurston, and Duke Ellington. Today, the area continues to be a draw, with attractions like the **Langston Hughes House**, **El Museo del Barrio**, and soul food standouts like **Sylvia's**.

Don't Miss

The historic **Apollo Theater** was a haven for Black performers starting in 1934, when musicians like Louis Armstrong, Duke Ellington, Ella Fitzgerald, and Sam Cooke graced the stage. The 1,500-seat theater still welcomes performers throughout the year, including for the legendary Amateur Night at the Apollo. It's a tough crowd, so success here means you're going places. ✉ *253 W. 125th St., New York, NY* 🌐 *www.apollotheater.org*

Best Tour

Discover the rich heritage of Harlem through the eyes of born-and-raised locals who know and love their community. **Harlem Heritage Tours** offers several multimedia-driven walking tours that explore the music, art, theater, and film that cemented the neighborhood as an icon of Black American history. 🌐 *www.harlemheritage.com*

Getting Here and Around

The Harlem-125th station is a Metro-North commuter rail stop in Harlem. The 125th Street subway station also drops you here.

Coney Island

Seaside Fun in NYC

More than a century ago, Coney Island ranked among the country's preeminent seaside resorts, and even though its heyday has passed, an aura of faded glory endures. Decades-old concessions line the boardwalk and plenty of local characters keep Coney Island weird, especially during the annual **Mermaid Parade**. Minor-league baseball team the Brooklyn Cyclones plays at Coney Island's **Maimonides Park**, and the **New York Aquarium** sits right near the boardwalk. 🌐 *www.coneyisland.com*

Don't Miss

Luna Park is home to the Cyclone, a wooden roller coaster that has been in operation since 1927. It's the second steepest in the world and always has a line of excited thrill-seekers waiting in line. ✉ *1000 Surf Ave., Brooklyn, NY* 🌐 *www.lunaparknyc.com*

Good to Know

The first **Nathan's Hot Dogs** opened here in 1916. The hot dogs are still a staple here, and a world-famous hot dog–eating contest takes place every year on July 4. ✉ *1205 Riegelmann Boardwalk, Brooklyn, NY* 🌐 *www.nathansfamous.com*

When to Go

Coney Island is open from Easter to Halloween. The summer months are ideal if you're looking to swim or sunbathe, but come in spring or fall if you're looking to avoid the crowds. The Mermaid Parade takes place on the Saturday closest to the summer solstice, usually late June.

Getting Here and Around

Located at the bottom of Brooklyn, Coney Island is easily accessible by car. From Manhattan, it's about an hour away by subway.

The High Line

New York's "Park in the Sky"

The High Line almost didn't happen. The 1½-mile-long "park in the sky," once an elevated train line, was originally scheduled for demolition. It was residents who demanded it be transformed into a public space complete with swaths of greenery, meandering pathways, and areas for lounging about on the grass or under the trees. It was so popular that it was extended to Hudson Yards, an upscale shopping arcade built on top of what used to be the rail yards outside Penn Station. Its most notable structures are the Vessel, a beehive-like building filled with standout shops, and the Edge, a nail-biting glass floor observation deck and bar perched on the 100th floor. 🌐 *www.thehighline.org*

Don't Miss

At the southern end of the High Line is the **Whitney Museum of Art,** which occupies a sleek building facing the Hudson River. Its collections of modern masterpieces make it well worth a visit before or after your High Line journey. ✉ *99 Gansevoort St., New York, NY* 🌐 *www.whitney.org*

Best Eating Experience

Directly below the High Line between 15th and 16th streets, **Chelsea Market** is a great stop when you're looking to fuel up during your exploration of the area. There are numerous eateries, but the Mexican street food at Los Tacos No. 1 is unbeatable. ✉ *75 9th Ave., New York, NY* 🌐 *www.chelseamarket.com*

When to Go

Summer can be hot and crowded, but fall is a great time to stroll along the High Line.

Getting Here and Around

Penn Station is about 1 mile away, making it easy to get here on foot, by cab, or on the subway. The 34 Street–Hudson Yards station is the closest subway stop.

New York Sports

Cheer on the Yankees (or the Mets)

There's nothing like sitting in the stands and cheering on the Yankees—that is, unless you're a fan of the Mets. Or the Nets. Or the Knicks. Or the Liberty. Everyone knows that New York City is filled with sports fans. The main venues are spread around the city: the Bronx is home to **Yankee Stadium** while Queens is where the Mets play at **Citi Field**. **Madison Square Garden**, New York City's top entertainment venue, hosts the NHL's Rangers and basketball's Knicks and **Brooklyn's Barclays Center** is home to the NBA's Nets and the WNBA's Liberty.

Don't Miss

Yankee Stadium is the best place to watch America's favorite pastime while chowing down on a ballpark hot dog. The stadium was completely rebuilt in 2009 but still reflects the original 1923 design. Within the stadium is the New York Yankees Museum, home to a variety of artifacts. ✉ *1 E. 161st St., Bronx, NY* 🌐 *www.mlb.com/yankees/ballpark*

For Tennis Fans

Tennis fans flock to New York each August to watch the U.S. Open, the fourth and final of tennis's global Grand Slam events. It takes place at the **USTA Billie Jean King National Tennis Center** in Flushing, Queens. 🌐 *www.ntc.usta.com*

When to Go

Regular baseball season runs from early April to late September/early October. Postseason play continues into November (and since 2009, the Yankees have reached the postseason in all but 4 seasons; they have won 27 World Series championships in total, the most in the major leagues).

Hudson Valley and the Catskills

Marvelous Mountain Getaways

Known for their hiking trails, gushing waterfalls, and forest-topped mountains, the Hudson Valley and the adjacent Catskill Mountains have been an escape for New Yorkers for decades. These all-year destinations are popular for their resorts like **Hunter** and **Windham** mountains in the winter, colorful foliage in and around Catskill Park in autumn, and shopping in quaint villages like **Woodstock** and **Hudson** all year long. You'll find plenty of chic bars, restaurants, and hotels throughout the area, especially in small cities like **Beacon** and **Kingston**.

Don't Miss

Near the town of Hudson, **Olana State Historic Site** is the former estate of Frederic Edwin Church, a renowned painter. His lofty estate is now a state park and museum. The 250 acres of grounds are open for tours. ✉ *5720 Rte. 9G, Hudson, NY* 🌐 *www.olana.org*

Hudson Valley's Art Scene

A wide range of galleries and museums beckon in this creative region that has long attracted artists. Visitors love **Dia: Beacon** (✉ *3 Beekman St., Beacon, NY* 🌐 *www.diaart.org*), **Opus 40** (✉ *356 George Sickle Rd., Saugerties, NY* 🌐 *www.opus40.org*), **Storm King Art Center** (✉ *1 Museum Rd., New Windsor, NY* 🌐 *stormking.org*), and **Hudson Valley MOCA** (✉ *1701 Main St., Peekskill, NY* 🌐 *www.hudsonvalleymoca.org*).

Getting Here and Around

Albany International and Stewart International are the closest airports, but a car is necessary to get around. Metro North and Amtrak trains stop at multiple towns along the Hudson River.

The Finger Lakes

The Northeast's Largest Wine-Making Region

More than 550 million years ago, huge sheets of ice carved out the V-shape valleys that make up New York's Finger Lakes region. Today these long, narrow lakes are known for their on-the-water activities, quaint towns, and more than 140 wineries. There's also a thriving restaurant scene and an ever-growing number of craft beer breweries. In between, set aside some time for hiking, biking, swimming, and sailing.

Don't Miss

At the northern end of the region's largest body of water—lovely Seneca Lake—sits the town of **Geneva**, a historic hamlet that attracts many visitors each year. Downtown Geneva is home to boutiques, breweries, eateries, and views of the water from **Seneca Lake State Park**. Nearby are sprawling wineries, including the must-visit **Belhurst Castle and Winery** (✉ *4069 W. Lake Rd., Geneva, NY* 🌐 *www.belhurst.com*).

Best Tour

Since the region's vineyards are spread out, it's a good idea to see the area on a guided tour. **Crush Beer and Wine Tours** offers a wide variety of excursions, taking in the Canandaigua Lake Wine Trail, the Keuka Lake Wine Trail, and the Seneca Lake Wine Trail. 🌐 *crushbeerwinetours.com*

When to Go

This is definitely a warm-weather destination.

Getting Here and Around

Frederick Douglass Greater Rochester International Airport is the closest airport to the Finger Lakes.

The Adirondack Mountains

Stunning Mountains and Lakes in Upstate New York

More than 6 million acres make up northern New York's Adirondacks, an area known for its brilliant blue lakes, towering evergreen forests, and picturesque villages. The vast expanse is made up of 12 smaller regions, with the most well-known being Lake Placid, **Lake George**, **Lake Champlain**, and **Saranac Lake**. Visit for skiing, snowshoeing, and sledding in the winter and for boating, swimming, and hiking in the summer.

Don't Miss

Known by some as the "Grand Canyon of the Adirondacks," **Ausable Chasm** is an outdoor adventure park offering activities ranging from hiking to river rafting to rock climbing. The sandstone gorge is a lovely place for picnics. ✉ *2144 U.S. 9, Ausable Chasm, NY* 🌐 *www.ausablechasm.com*

Best Activity

Thousands and thousands of people head to **Gore Mountain** every year for its winter sports, especially skiing and snowboarding. In the warmer months, the attraction offers hiking and biking. 🌐 *www.goremountain.com*

When to Go

This is a year-round destination, and it's one part of the state that's hopping all winter.

Getting Here and Around

Amtrak's Adirondack service offers a scenic ride from New York's Penn Station. Plattsburgh International Airport serves the wider region.

The Hamptons

A Glittering Summer Playground

On the eastern end of Long Island, the Hamptons are the summertime destination for New Yorkers who have plenty of money (or want to give the impression that they do). If the gossip columns report on a lavish fundraiser or a celebrity behaving badly, it's likely to be in the Hamptons. Towns like **Sag Harbor**, **Southampton**, and **Montauk** sit along miles of sandy beaches and have a wide assortment of high-end bars, restaurants, and boutiques. Come for the quintessential summer activities: swimming, boating, and lounging in the sun (usually behind a privacy fence).

Don't Miss

At the easternmost point on Long Island, **Montauk Lighthouse** is the ideal place for sweeping ocean views. Dating back to the late 18th century, the lighthouse has beautiful grounds and an on-site museum. ✉ *2000 Montauk Hwy., Montauk, NY* 🌐 *www.montaukhistoricalsociety.org*

Best Beach

Southampton's **Coopers Beach** is often rated one of the best beaches in the country—and for good reason. Open to the public (unlike a number of beaches in the area), it's beloved for its white sand, picturesque dunes, and many beachfront mansions in the distance.

When to Go

The Hamptons are hopping in the summer. If you're weary of crowds and some truly mind-boggling prices, visit before Memorial Day or after Labor Day.

Getting Here and Around

The Hampton Jitney arrives from New York City, making stops in towns like East Hampton, Southampton, and Montauk. A car is the easiest way to get around, but Uber is always available.

The Thousand Islands

Castles and Cruises Galore

Located along the St. Lawrence River is Thousand Islands, an archipelago that consists of more than 1,864 individual islands. Some are home to cottages and castles, while others are uninhabited areas ideal for outdoor exploration. If you get tired of exploring communities like **Alexandria Bay, Sackets Harbor**, and **Cape Vincent**, head across the border to find other quaint villages in Canada. Visit the area for boating, fishing, swimming, and small-town exploration.

Don't Miss

Castles built by wealthy industrialists dot the islands near Alexandria Bay. The 120-room **Boldt Castle** (✉ *1 Heart Island, Alexandria Bay, NY* 🌐 *www.boldtcastle.com*) was begun in 1900, left unfinished for more than 70 years, then finished in spectacular fashion. Modest in comparison is the 28-room **Singer Castle** (✉ *1136 County Rte. 6, Chippewa Bay, NY* 🌐 *www.singercastle.com*).

Best Tour

Clayton Island Tours is the best way to see the Thousand Islands. Head to Rock Island Lighthouse aboard a glass-bottomed boat or take a sunset cruise on the St. Lawrence River. 🌐 *www.claytonislandtours.com/boat-tours*

When to Go

Because so much here is weather-dependent, summer is the best time to visit the Thousands Islands.

Getting Here and Around

Watertown International Airport is about 30 miles from most Thousand Islands destinations. The islands also run parallel to New York's Seaway Trail (Route 12), one of the state's most scenic drives.

When in New York

COOPERSTOWN

On the shores of Otsego Lake—James Fenimore Cooper's beloved Glimmerglass—Cooperstown provides the backdrop for a number of museums and attractions. Fans of the great American pastime make pilgrimages to the National Baseball Hall of Fame.

Do This: At the National Baseball Hall of Fame, you'll find Lou Gehrig's Yankee Stadium locker and Jackie Robinson's World Series cap, among many other memorabilia that help to make this shrine to America's favorite pastime so beloved. Plaques bearing the pictures and biographies of major-league notables line the walls in the actual hall of fame. ✉ *25 Main St., Cooperstown, NY* 🌐 *baseballhall.org*

THE CLOISTERS AND FORT TRYON PARK

Located in Fort Tyron Park in Upper Manhattan's Washington Heights neighborhood, this unforgettable museum is made up of four authentic cloisters brought over brick by brick from France and Spain. There's also a French Romanesque chapel, a 12th-century chapter house, and a Romanesque apse. One room is devoted to the 15th- and 16th-century Unicorn Tapestries, which date to 1500—a must-see masterpiece of medieval mythology. ✉ *99 Margaret Corbin Dr., New York, NY* 🌐 *www.metmuseum.org/visit/plan-your-visit/met-cloisters*

Do This: Listen to one of the audio tours as you stroll the grounds. You'll hear interviews with curators, conservators, and educators about the art and architecture of medieval Europe.

HOME OF FRANKLIN D. ROOSEVELT NATIONAL HISTORIC SITE

In Hyde Park is Springwood, the stately home of the Roosevelt family. Franklin Delano Roosevelt—the country's longest-serving president—returned here often even when his governmental duties were wearing on him. When he was gravely ill during his fourth term, it functioned as a remote White House. This site is also where you'll find the Franklin D. Roosevelt Presidential Library and Museum. ✉ *4097 Albany Post Rd., Hyde Park, NY* 🌐 *www.nps.gov/hofr*

Do This: The comparatively modest Eleanor Roosevelt National Historic Site preserves a house called Val-Kill where the First Lady spent time away from her official duties at nearby Springwood. She gathered around her an always-changing group of intellectuals and activists, many of them women. ✉ *106 Valkill Park Rd., Hyde Park, NY* 🌐 *www.nps.gov/elro*

HOWE CAVERNS

A true natural wonder, Howe Caverns takes you 16 stories belowground into another world. Following an elevator ride straight down, the 90-minute tours are both on foot and in a boat that floats along the cave's mirrorlike large lake. Geologists estimate that Howe Caverns are millions of years old, and they are continuously changing. ✉ *255 Discovery Dr., Howes Cave, NY* 🌐 *www.howecaverns.com*

Do This: For more adventurous types, Howe Caverns offers two-hour spelunking adventures. All caving supplies are provided, and you'll crawl through tight spaces and explore areas of the caverns most people never see.

ROOSEVELT ISLAND

Located in the middle of New York's East River is 2-mile-long Roosevelt Island, a historic spot that was once home to psychiatric hospitals and prisons. Today it's a largely residential retreat with pretty parks, waterfront walks, and sweeping views of Manhattan. Accessible via the superscenic Roosevelt Island Tramway, the island is a great place to visit for outdoor spaces like Franklin D. Roosevelt Four Freedoms Park and Roosevelt Island Lighthouse.

Do This: Roosevelt Island Lighthouse is by the same architect who designed St. Patrick's Cathedral and Grace Church. The tower was built with stone mined by inmates from the island's penitentiary. Views from here are jaw-dropping.

SARATOGA SPRINGS

Mineral-water springs first brought Indigenous tribes and, later, American settlers to this area just south of the Adirondack foothills. By the 1870s, Victorian society had turned Saratoga Springs into one of the country's principal vacation resorts, and the city became known as the "Queen of Spas." Today, in Saratoga Spa State Park, you can sample the naturally carbonated waters of a dozen active springs, which were created by complex geological conditions centuries ago. ✉ *19 Roosevelt Dr., Saratoga Springs, NY* 🌐 *parks.ny.gov/parks/saratogaspa*

Do This: In 1977, the Battles of Saratoga were fought 12 miles southeast of Saratoga Springs, and is today recognized as the turning point in the American Revolution that convinced the French to join the Americans in the conflict. Check out Saratoga National Historical Park to learn about the pivotal battle and its significance. ✉ *648 Rte. 32, Stillwater, NY* 🌐 *www.nps.gov/sara*

THE STATEN ISLAND FERRY

One of the best ways to take in the New York City skyline is from one of the boats that circle the island. The free Staten Island Ferry takes passengers to and from Staten Island, passing by some jaw-dropping sights on the way. 🌐 *siferry.com*

Do This: Circle Line Cruises also offers an array of tours, including a "Best of New York" tour that takes you past the Statue of Liberty and other monumental attractions. A sunset cruise shows off the Williamsburg Bridge and the Empire State Building. 🌐 *www.circleline.com*

STORM KING ART CENTER

This Hudson Valley standout has dozens of large-scale sculptures tumbling across its 500 acres of grounds. The works on view include masterpieces by Alexander Calder, Sarah Sze, and Isamu Noguchi. Take the free shuttle, or walk through the grounds and find the perfect spot for a picnic lunch. ✉ *1 Museum Rd., New Windsor, NY* 🌐 *www.stormking.org*

Do This: There are four main areas to explore: Museum Hill, North Woods, Meadows, and South Fields. Each has its own unique landscape, so be sure to visit them all.

WOMEN'S RIGHTS NATIONAL HISTORICAL PARK

Elizabeth Cady Stanton, Lucretia Mott, and a handful of other pioneers in the women's rights movement organized the first Women's Rights Convention in Seneca Falls in 1848. Today, the park incorporates the site of the convention (the Wesleyan Chapel), a visitor center, and several off-site historic homes of key convention participants. Exhibits explore the development of the women's rights movement in the United States. ✉ *136 Fall St., Seneca Falls, NY* 🌐 *www.nps.gov/wori*

Do This: The meticulously restored Elizabeth Cady Stanton House is where one of American feminism's most important leaders shaped social reform as she raised seven children. Stanton's feminist colleague, Susan B. Anthony of Rochester, was a guest in the house. ✉ *32 Washington St., Seneca Falls, NY*

Cool Places to Stay

Belhurst Castle and Winery. Resembling one of the grand "cottages" once built as country retreats for famous families like the Astors and Vanderbilts, Belhurst Castle is stunningly beautiful. Overlooking Seneca Lake, it's one of the most lavish places to stay in the Finger Lakes. ✉ *4069 W. Lake Rd., Geneva, NY* 🌐 *www.belhurst.com*

The Box House Hotel. With a hip vibe, Brooklyn's Box House Hotel is filled with original artwork and one-of-a-kind furnishings. The 10,000-square-foot rooftop space has a retractable cover and unobstructed views of Manhattan, Brooklyn, and Long Island City. ✉ *77 Box St., Brooklyn, NY* 🌐 *www.theboxhousehotel.com*

Camp Orenda. If you like the idea of camping more than the reality, then head to this upscale retreat in Adirondack State Park. The tents are actually canvas-walled cabins furnished with all the usual creature comforts. Bathrooms and showers are communal. ✉ *90 Armstrong Rd., Johnsburg, NY* 🌐 *www.camporenda.com*

Mohonk Mountain House. Its jumble of towers, turrets, and chimneys make Mohonk Mountain House a delight. It looks like a cliff-side castle with its large stone facade and towering structures. The rate includes meals, activities, guided hikes, and amenities like an indoor pool. ✉ *1000 Mountain Rest Rd., New Paltz, NY* 🌐 *www.mohonk.com*

The Plaza. The Plaza is definitely ready for its closeup, having added its unmistakable allure to films like *Home Alone 2, North by Northwest, The Great Gatsby,* and more. Located along the southern edge of Central Park, the French Renaissance–style masterpiece opened in 1907 as a lavish getaway for well-to-do travelers. ✉ *768 5th Ave., New York, NY* 🌐 *www.theplazany.com*

About Our Writers

Like many New Yorkers, **Carly Fisher** is a transplant (by way of Chicago, with a few stops along the way) who adopted New York City as her forever home a decade ago. Her second greatest ambition: owning a writer's cottage somewhere between Hudson Valley and the Catskills. She is a James Beard Award–nominated journalist, author, and longtime contributing editor at Fodor's Travel.

Scribner's Catskill Lodge. Tucked within the Catskill Mountains, Scribner's Catskill Lodge has a cachet that draws in-the-know weekenders from Manhattan and Brooklyn. There are sleek, modern rooms with balcony views of the valley below, an on-site restaurant, and indoor and outdoor spaces for hanging out with fellow guests. ✉ *13 Scribner Hollow Rd., Hunter, NY* 🌐 *www.scribnerslodge.com*

The William Vale. The sleek, 23-story tower of glass and steel dazzles with stylish rooms—each of which has its own balcony. While the hotel has big spaces for weddings and events, the city's longest outdoor pool, Little Fino (an all-day bar and café), and its flagship Italian restaurant Leuca under the helm of a James Beard Award–winning chef Andrew Carmellini, its biggest selling point is its outstanding view of the Manhattan skyline. ✉ *111 N. 12th St., Brooklyn, NY* 🌐 *thewilliamvale.com*

Essential Eats

Bagels. Around the turn of the 20th century, Jewish immigrants introduced New York City to the beloved bagel, kickstarting a cultural phenomenon spurring countless variations, toppings, and "schmears" (spreads). Don't miss Russ & Daughter, Tompkins Square Bagel, Ess-a-Bagel, Popup Bagels, Leon's, Black Seed, and Kossar's.

Buffalo Wings. Like any good food story, Buffalo wings were created by a happy accident. In 1964, Anchor Bar Restaurant owner Teressa Bellissimo was asked to make a late-night snack for her son and his friends. Frying up some spare chicken wings, she tossed them with a splash of hot sauce, butter, and vinegar—a recipe so good, they became world-famous. You can still order Buffalo wings at Anchor Bar in Buffalo, but locals will argue that New York Bar Bill Tavern in East Aurora and Duff's Famous Wings in Amherst give them a run for their money.

The Culinary Institute of America. One of the country's most prestigious culinary schools, the CIA offers several student-led eateries that outside guests are welcome to experience, including the Bocuse, which uses modern techniques pioneered by the late, great French chef Paul Bocuse, and American Bounty, which highlights the produce of the Hudson Valley in various traditional American dishes. ✉ *1946 Campus Dr., Hyde Park, NY* 🌐 *www.ciachef.edu*

Hot Dogs. It wouldn't quite be New York City without hog dogs. Whether you're grabbing a dog on the way to the Met, walking around Central Park, at a baseball game, or down at Coney Island, New York City hot dogs make the best snack beloved by locals and tourists alike. Among the most notable names in hot dogs are Nathan's, Sabrett's, Crif Dogs, Grey's Papaya, and Glizzy's.

Katz's Delicatessen. Everything and nothing has changed at Katz's since it first opened in 1888, when the Lower East Side was dominated by Jewish immigrants: lines still form for the giant, hand-carved corned beef and pastrami sandwiches, soul-warming soups, juicy hot dogs, and crisp half-sour pickles. ✉ *205 E. Houston St., New York, NY* 🌐 *www.katzsdelicatessen.com*

Pizza. If New York City wasn't known as the Big Apple, it would probably be the Big Slice. Pizza has become an iconic NYC symbol over the past century, with hundreds of pizzerias scattered across the five boroughs. While you could live here your whole life and still not try all of them, put Patsy's Pizzeria, Di Fara Pizza, Joe's Pizza, John's on Bleecker, Lombardi's, Rubirosa, and Roberta's on your bucket list for a pizza crawl.

Smorgasburg. Called the Woodstock of Eating, the country's largest weekly open-air food festival is a favorite among both locals and visitors. Food trucks and vendors line up at different parks throughout New York City; depending on the day of the week, the food-fueled event can be found in Williamsburg, Prospect Park, or the World Trade Center. The event regularly sees crowds of 20,000 to 30,000 enjoying everything from loaded lobster rolls to sweet waffles topped with ice cream. 🌐 *www.smorgasburg.com*

Thousand Islands Dressing. The special sauce best known for salads, Reuben sandwiches, and McDonald's hamburgers was invented at Boldt Castle in Alexandria Bay in 1900, named after the Thousand Islands–Seaway region before being brought back to the Waldorf Astoria where it gained its notoriety. Today, you can buy the dressing while taking a tour at Boldt Castle. 🌐 *www.boldtcastle.com*

Pennsylvania

From the dramatic hills of Pittsburgh across rolling farmland and majestic forest to the narrow streets of colonial-era Philadelphia, Pennsylvania provides a wide range of experiences. The state reflects a rich history—from halcyon days as the seat of the American Revolution and a fledgling nation's first capital through its role in the country's transformation into an industrial powerhouse. Today it's a leader in the health-care and pharmaceutical industries, a center for the arts, and a burgeoning tourist destination.

Capital: Harrisburg

Population: 13,080,000

Area: 46,055 square miles

Statehood Date: December 12, 1787

Major Airports: Philadelphia International Airport (PHL); Harrisburg International Airport (MDT); Pittsburgh International Airport (PIT)

Travel and Tourism Information: *www.visitpa.com*

Famous Residents: Benjamin Franklin (founding father and inventor); Andrew Carnegie (industrialist); Kobe Bryant (basketball player); Will Smith (actor and rapper); Bradley Cooper (actor); Taylor Swift (pop star)

Fun Fact: The official state dog of Pennsylvania is the Great Dane.

Independence National Historical Park

The Cradle of America

Much of America's origin story can be traced back to a few blocks in downtown Philadelphia now known as Independence National Historical Park, home to **Independence Hall** and the **Liberty Bell**. They may not have the same instant name recognition, but other attractions like the **Second Bank of the United States**, **Congress Hall**, and the **National Constitution Center** are all well worth a visit. Throughout the area you'll find actors dressed in 18th-century garb, horse-drawn carriages, and cobblestone streets—the pull of history is undeniable. 🌐 *www.nps.gov/inde*

Don't Miss

Independence National Historical Park can be overwhelming. Visit the Independence Visitors Center to pick up detailed maps and to find out about any special events going on that day. ✉ *599 Market St., Philadelphia, PA* 🌐 *www.phlvisitorcenter.com*

Best Tour

Join a guided tour to see Independence Hall. Tours are first come, first served and depart every 20 minutes. A highlight is the Assembly Room, where the signing of the Declaration of Independence and the U.S. Constitution took place.

When to Go

This part of town is busy almost all year round, especially in summer and whenever kids are out of school. Visit in the fall for smaller crowds and shorter lines.

Getting Here and Around

Philadelphia International Airport is about a 20-minute drive from Independence National Historical Park, which is located in the Old City neighborhood of downtown Philly. All the sites are within walking distance of one another.

Parkway Museums District

A Mile of Masterpieces

Some of the country's leading museums line Philadelphia's Benjamin Franklin Parkway, which runs from City Hall to the Philadelphia Museum of Art. The roughly mile-long stretch is lined with flags from all of the world's nations, picturesque parks, and educational institutions. Put these on your must-see list: the **Barnes Foundation**, the **Franklin Institute**, the **Academy of Natural Sciences at Drexel University**, and the **Rodin Museum**. 🌐 *www.parkwaymuseums-districtphiladelphia.org*

Don't Miss

Pretend that you're Rocky Balboa and run up the famous steps of the **Philadelphia Museum of Art**. There's a sculpture of the world's most famous fictional boxer in front of the museum. ✉ *2600 Benjamin Franklin Pkwy., Philadelphia, PA* 🌐 *www.philamuseum.org*

Best Tour

Explore the outdoor art installations along Benjamin Franklin Parkway on the Association for Public Art's free self-guided tours. The 1.3-mile stroll features major works like Robert Indiana's *Love* sculpture, Rodin's *The Thinker*, and Alexander Calder's Swann Memorial Fountain. 🌐 *www.associationforpublicart.org/tours/along-the-benjamin-franklin-parkway*

When to Go

There are exciting exhibitions throughout the year, but spring, summer, and fall are best for walking from location to location.

Getting Here and Around

The Parkway Museums District is located in the center of the city, making it easily accessible from Amtrak's 30th Street Station. All of the District's major attractions are a short walk apart.

Philadelphia's Neighborhoods

That Unique Philly Culture

Ask any local and they'll quickly name their favorite neighborhood in Philadelphia. The heart of the city is **Rittenhouse Square,** an upscale neighborhood known for its town houses, brand-name shopping, cool bars, and award-winning restaurants. Next to Rittenhouse Square, **Midtown Village** is home to the city's Gayborhood, an area with bustling bars and rainbow-painted crosswalks, in addition to some of the city's most popular restaurants. **Old City** is loved for its history—Independence National Historical Park is the big draw—along with its boutiques, galleries, and monthly First Friday open houses.

Don't Miss

Fishtown is loved for its one-of-a-kind bars and restaurants. It's also a center of Philly's beer culture; breweries like Evil Genius Brewing, Tired Hands Brewing Company, and Philadelphia Brewing Company all have Fishtown outposts, while bars like Martha, Johnny Brenda's, and Frankford Hall pour a curated selection of brews.

Best Tour

Philadelphia is known as the "City of Murals" for good reason. The Mural Arts organization enriches neighborhoods with colorful murals on otherwise drab walls. Tours might cover a particular neighborhood or a theme like Black History Month. 🌐 *www.muralarts.org*

Getting Here and Around

Philadelphia International Airport is about a 20-minute drive from most parts of the city. Philadelphia's subway system (SEPTA) runs regular trains throughout the day. Its geographic reach is somewhat limited to an east–west line and north–south lines, but it takes you close to major spots quickly.

Gettysburg National Military Park

The Country's Biggest Battle

History buffs should allow about two days to explore the vast Gettysburg National Military Park, downtown Gettysburg, and the surrounding attractions. The sprawling park covers much of the ground where the 1863 Battle of Gettysburg was fought over three days during the Civil War. Engaging more than 165,000 Union and Confederate soldiers, it was the largest battle ever fought in North America. Today, the national park includes the battlefield and other important sites like the 17-acre Gettysburg National Cemetery. ✉ *1195 Baltimore Pike, Gettysburg, PA* 🌐 *www.nps.gov/gett*

Don't Miss

Begin your day at the Gettysburg National Military Park Museum and Visitor Center to get your bearings. A short film, *A New Birth of Freedom*, narrates the history of the Battle of Gettysburg and its importance in history. The cyclorama, a huge 360-degree painting of Pickett's Charge, is a must-see.

Best Tour

Gettysburg Battlefield Bus Tours offers a number of tours led by guides who know an incredible amount about the area. 🌐 *www.gettysburgbattlefield-tours.com*

When to Go

Spring, summer, and fall are the best times to visit. In winter, snow and ice can make it hard to get around the sprawling park, and certain areas sometimes close for weather.

Getting Here and Around

Gettysburg, about 145 miles west of Philadelphia via I–76 and U.S. 15, is best reached by car. Parking is available in municipal lots throughout the town. The closest airport is Harrisburg International Airport, about 45 miles away.

Pittsburgh

Urban Renewal in Action

Once an industrial powerhouse, Pittsburgh became a notch in the Rust Belt when manufacturing tanked in the early 1980s. But now it's making a comeback as an eminently walkable city of universities, parks, and creative businesses. The coolest neighborhood in town, the historic **Strip District** of once-crumbling mills and warehouses, is now home to independent eateries, shops, art galleries, and even an opera house.

Don't Miss

The **Andy Warhol Museum**, dedicated to the pop art legend, houses nearly half a million objects. Its collection of Warhol paintings, prints, sculptures, and videos includes 1960s screen prints of celebrities like Marilyn Monroe and the iconic Campbell's Soup Cans series. ✉ *117 Sandusky St., Pittsburgh, PA* 🌐 *www.warhol.org*

Best Family-Friendly Experience

Mt. Washington is basically a large hill rising about 450 feet above the city, but riding up and down in an 1800s wooden cable car is fun. The Duquesne Incline takes you up the mountainside to an observation deck with excellent views of Pittsburgh. ✉ *1197 W. Carson St., Pittsburgh, PA* 🌐 *www.duquesneincline.org*

Best Sandwich

Have a hunger-busting bite on 18th Street at the famous **Primanti Brothers**, where sandwiches are piled high with meat, coleslaw, and French fries. ✉ *46 18th St., Pittsburgh, PA* 🌐 *www.primantibros.com*

Getting Here and Around

Pittsburgh is 32 miles east of Pennsylvania's western border via U.S. 22 and 300 miles west of Philadelphia via I–76. Public transit is fairly good within the city, but a car can come in handy.

Frank Lloyd Wright's Fallingwater

An Architectural Masterpiece

About 1½ hours southeast of Pittsburgh is architect Frank Lloyd Wright's undisputed masterwork—a stone, concrete, and glass house dramatically cantilevered over a waterfall. Instantly recognizable to architecture fans, Fallingwater was designed in 1935 for Edgar J. Kaufmann, who owned the largest department store in Pittsburgh. Using native sandstone, Wright's design incorporated much of what was already on the site, including rocks, trees, and a rushing creek. While a number of Wright-designed properties are open for tours, Fallingwater is the only one that became a public space with its original furniture and artwork. ✉ *1491 Mill Run Rd., Mill Run, PA* 🌐 *www.fallingwater.org*

Don't Miss

Self-guided tours of the grounds and walks through the surrounding 5,100-acre Bear Run Nature Reserve are great ways to take in the natural beauty of Pennsylvania's Laurel Highlands.

Best Tour

You can see the house's interior via guided tour only. Take the extended tour to venture into rooms not visited by the standard tour.

When to Go

While Fallingwater is beautiful all year round, in June and July blooming rhododendrons turn the grounds into a riot of blossoms.

Getting Here and Around

Fallingwater is about 65 miles from Pittsburgh. You'll need a car to get here.

Pocono Mountains

Pennsylvania's Relaxing Retreat

The Pocono Mountains—known as the Poconos—are a range of thickly forested peaks running along the Delaware Water Gap, a pass in the mountains created by the Delaware River. Quaint towns are sprinkled around four mostly rural counties: Carbon, Monroe, Pike, and Wayne. Dozens of resorts offer a wide range of outdoor pursuits. Visit for skiing and snowboarding in winter or swimming, biking, and hiking in summer.

Don't Miss

Small towns like **Honesdale**, **Stroudsburg**, **Jim Thorpe**, and **Milford** are known for their varied arts scenes, independent shops, and eclectic dining.

Best Family-Friendly Experience

Great Wolf Lodge offers plenty of activities for families. There's a huge indoor water park with waterslides, a wave pool, a lazy river, and pools for splashing and lounging. There are some tasty on-site dining options, too. ✉ *1 Great Wolf Dr., Scotrun, PA* 🌐 *www.greatwolf.com*

Best Tour

Leaving from Jim Thorpe, the vintage **Lehigh Gorge Scenic Railway** makes a 16-mile, 70-minute round-trip along the Lehigh River and through breathtaking Lehigh Gorge State Park. A special leaf-peeping train runs in October. ✉ *1 Susquehanna St., Jim Thorpe, PA* 🌐 *www.lgsry.com* 🎫 *From $22*

Getting Here and Around

The Poconos encompasses a vast area that requires a car to get around. The closest large airport is Wilkes-Barre Scranton International Airport, within an hour's drive of most Poconos towns.

Lancaster County

America's Oldest Amish Settlement

You'd never know from the buggies traversing the quiet country lanes that Lancaster County is less than two hours away from the bustling streets of Philadelphia. Lancaster is synonymous with Amish Country, and the Amish population is crucial to the area's economy and culture. To learn more about Pennsylvania Dutch history, visit the 300-year-old **Amish Farm and House** (✉ *2395 Covered Bridge Dr., Lancaster, PA* 🌐 *amish-farmandhouse.com*). Change gears in downtown Lancaster, which has become a mini-urban hub in recent years, with plenty of interesting restaurants, craft breweries, shops, and art galleries. Northeastern Lancaster County is also known for its antiques and is home to hundreds of quaint shops.

Don't Miss

Established in 1832, the **Strasburg Railroad**, America's oldest continuously operating railroad, offers 45-minute narrated train rides through the farmland of Lancaster County. ✉ *301 Gap Rd., Ronks, PA* 🌐 *www.strasburgrailroad.com*

Eat This

Keep an eye out for farmers' markets and roadside stands that sell homemade Pennsylvania Dutch classics like shoofly pie and whoopie pies, along with pickles and preserves. Try **Bird-in-Hand Bake Shop** (in the town of the same name) and **Busy Bee's Farm Market** in Ronks.

Getting Here and Around

The closest major airports to Lancaster county are Philadelphia International Airport and Harrisburg International Airport. Downtown Lancaster is very walkable, but a car is necessary for exploring the rest of the county.

Hershey

Chocolate-Dipped Fun

If you're a chocolate fan (and/or have kids in tow), the town of Hershey makes a great stop. The municipality was created in 1903 by Milton S. Hershey as a model community for workers at his factory; it's now home to several entertaining chocolate-theme museums and Hersheypark, a major amusement park. Stop at **Hershey's Chocolatetown and Chocolate World** (✉ *101 Hersheypark Dr., Hershey, PA* 🌐 *www.chocolateworld.com*) to learn how cacao beans become Hershey's Kisses and Reese's Peanut Butter Cups. Chocolate World also contains the world's largest Hershey store. Trolley tours of the town depart from here to visit historical sites related to Hershey and his famous candy.

Don't Miss

Hersheypark is famous worldwide for its 15 roller coasters. Amid 70 other rides and attractions in the park, the coasters range in thrill level from the kid-friendly Cocoa Cruiser to the 1946 wooden Comet to the 75-mph SkyRush. Loops, inversions, barrel rolls, and zero-G drops are here in exhilarating abundance. ✉ *100 Hersheypark Dr., Hershey, PA* 🌐 *www.hersheypark.com*

Drink This

The **Hershey Story Museum**, in downtown Hershey, offers a comprehensive look at the life of Milton S. Hershey and the community he founded. In the café, sip a flight of hot chocolate for a tasting tour of different chocolates from around the world. ✉ *63 W. Chocolate Ave., Hershey, PA* 🌐 *hersheystory.org*

Getting Here and Around

Hershey is 30 miles northwest of Lancaster via Routes 283 and 743. Harrisburg International Airport is 11 miles away. You'll need a car to explore the area.

Pine Creek Gorge

Pennsylvania's Vast Natural Wonder

The stunningly beautiful Pine Creek Gorge, in Tioga State Forest in north-central Pennsylvania, is often referred to as the Grand Canyon of Pennsylvania. The gorge is nearly a mile wide, descends nearly 1,500 feet, and offers breathtaking views: overlooks at Colton Point State Park and Leonard Harrison State Park are two of the best places to take in the majesty of the place. The natural wonder runs for more than 45 miles along Pine Creek, a scenic river that is perfect for kayaking, canoeing, and white-water rafting. ✉ *4797 Rte. 660, Wellsboro, PA* 🌐 *www.pacanyon.com*

Don't Miss

The 65-mile **Pine Creek Rail Trail**, a former section of the New York Central Railroad, is beloved by walkers, runners, hikers, cyclists, and cross-country skiers. The trail meanders through the bottom of Pine Creek Gorge and winds past small towns and quiet green spaces.

Best Tour

For an on-the-water tour of the Grand Canyon of Pennsylvania, seek out **Pine Creek Outfitters'** guided rafting or kayaking tours. Guides share information on the history of the region and the wildlife that calls it home. 🌐 *www.pinecrk.com*

When to Go

The ideal time to visit Pine Creek Gorge is April to October. In August, the **Little League World Series** takes place 25 miles to the east in Williamsport. Come October, the gorge is a great location to take in the autumn colors.

Getting Here and Around

There are multiple entry points to Pine Creek Gorge, and all of them are most easily reached by car. Park at Leonard Harrison State Park or Colton Point State Park.

Presque Isle State Park

Pennsylvania's Only "Seashore"

In the port town of Erie, on the shore of Lake Erie, Presque Isle State Park is a picturesque 3,200-acre peninsula that is home to more than a dozen beaches and prime waterfront views. Visitors head to Presque Isle—the name translates to "almost an island" in French—for on-the-water or in-the-water activities like swimming, fishing, and boating, in addition to land-based activities like hiking, cycling, and birding. ✉ *301 Peninsula Dr., Erie, PA* 🌐 *www.dcnr.pa.gov*

Don't Miss

At the entrance to Presque Isle State Park is **Tom Ridge Environmental Center**, dedicated to Presque Isle's history, wildlife, and outdoor attractions. The best view of the state park is from the 75-foot-tall observation tower.

Best Tour

Presque Isle Boat Tours offers 90-minute narrated floats on Lake Erie. Guides point out sights like Presque Isle Lighthouse. 🌐 *www.piboattours.com*

When to Go

Presque Isle State Park is open year-round. Winter is best for cross-country skiing and ice-skating, while summer is ideal for paddling and picknicking.

Getting Here and Around

Two hours north of Pittsburg, Presque Isle State Park is 4 miles from downtown Erie, making it easily accessible from the city. The entrance to the park is less than 4 miles from Erie International Airport.

Valley Forge National Historical Park

In Washington's Footsteps: America's Coldest Winter

Valley Forge National Historical Park presents the story of the harsh winter endured by General George Washington and the Continental Army in 1777–78. A 10-mile driving tour hits reconstructed soldiers' huts and other sights, including monuments to the troops who helped win the American Revolution. The vast national historical park occupies 3,452 acres of rolling hills, open fields, and tree-covered valleys. ✉ *1400 N. Outer Line Dr., King of Prussia, PA* 🌐 *www.nps.gov/vafo*

Don't Miss

See the **Isaac Potts House**, the historic home that Washington made his headquarters. The home was built in 1768, and much of the original structure remains. ✉ *1400 N. Outer Line Dr., King of Prussia, PA*

Best Tour

Drive the nine-stop encampment tour to visit **Artillery Park**, **National Memorial Arch**, **Muhlenberg's Brigade**, and other sites.

When to Go

The huge park is beautiful all year, though a trip during winter gives an appreciation for the harsh conditions the soliders faced here. The 20-plus miles of walking and biking trails are always accessible.

Getting Here and Around

Located in King of Prussia—about 45 minutes outside Philadelphia—the park is readily accessible via I–76. Philadelphia International Airport is 33 miles from the park via I–476 and I–76.

When in Pennsylvania

BUSHKILL FALLS

The most impressive of this park's eight waterfalls—and the one for which it's named—is more than 100 feet tall. Wooden boardwalks and bridges along the walking and hiking trails of varying difficulty take you through sun-dappled woods past other waterfalls. Exhibits explore the area's flora and fauna and the history of the falls and the Native Americans that once called the area home. ✉ *138 Bushkill Falls Trail, Bushkill, PA* 🌐 *www.visitbushkillfalls.com*

Do This: If you're up for it, hike the Red Trail to Bridal Veil Falls. The 2-mile trail passes all eight falls; it's a hike of at least two hours.

EASTERN STATE PENITENTIARY HISTORIC SITE

Designed by John Haviland, Eastern State was the most expensive building in America when it opened in 1829; the massive, crumbling structure was built in a hub-and-spoke design that became the model for 300 prisons from China to South America. Before it closed in 1971, the atmospheric prison was home to Al Capone, Willie Sutton, and Pep the Dog, who allegedly killed the cat that belonged to a governor's wife. The prison's excellent audio tour is included with admission, and thoughtful permanent and changing exhibits examine contemporary issues relating to criminal justice and needed reforms. ✉ *2027 Fairmount Ave., Philadelphia, PA* 🌐 *easternstate.org*

Do This: The site hosts many events including Halloween Nights, a crowd-favorite selection of haunted house experiences (the penitentiary is reportedly quite haunted).

GRITTY

Perhaps an embodiment of Philly itself (weird and off-kilter yet incredibly beloved), Gritty is a 7-foot-tall, orange monster with googly eyes and an unhinged but hilarious social media presence; naturally, he is the mascot of the NHL's Philadelphia Flyers. He was introduced in 2018 and has since become a nationwide sensation for his game antics and his unabashed love for all things Philadelphia.

Do This: See the Flyers play at the Xfinity Mobile Stadium; NHL's regular season runs from October through April. ✉ *3601 S. Broad St., Philadelphia, PA* 🌐 *www.nhl.com/flyers*

MCGILLIN'S OLDE ALE HOUSE

On Philadelphia's Drury Street you'll find McGillin's Olde Ale House, the oldest continuously operating pub in the city. Irish immigrants Catherine and William McGillin opened the bar in 1860, living upstairs with their 13 children. Today, McGillin's is known for its quirks, including signs from now-shuttered Philadelphia establishments, old liquor licenses, and kitschy figurines. The bar has 30 taps, many pouring southeastern Pennsylvania draft beers, including McGillin's three namesake brews. ✉ *1310 Drury St., Philadelphia, PA* 🌐 *www.mcgillins.com*

Do This: Around the holidays, the pub is transformed into a winter wonderland.

MERCER MILE

If you're anywhere near Doylestown in Bucks County, don't miss Fonthill Castle, the Mercer Museum, and the Moravian Pottery and Tile Works, together known as the Mercer Mile. Henry Chapman Mercer, a gentleman scientist and ceramist, designed the buildings, which once served as his home and workshops. Today the trio of museums draws tens of thousands of visitors every year. Funky Fonthill Castle, where Mercer once lived, is studded throughout with Arts and Crafts tiles, while the adjacent Mercer Museum showcases tools and other objects from before the Industrial Revolution. ✉ *84 S. Pine St., Doylestown, PA* 🌐 *www.mercermuseum.org*

Do This: At the Moravian Pottery and Tile Works, artists create new ceramic works the old-fashioned way. You can buy these unique items in the gift shop. ✉ *130 E. Swamp Rd., Doylestown, PA* 🌐 *www.thetileworks.org*

THE MÜTTER MUSEUM

You haven't really experienced "weird" until you've visited Philadelphia's Mütter Museum, a collection of medical oddities. The items in the collection date back to the 7th century BCE and include an impressive array of medical devices, wax models, skeletons, and more. In the main room upstairs are more than 139 human skulls in a towering display case, part of the famous Hyrtl Skull Collection. The museum is one of only two places in the world that displays pieces of Albert Einstein's brain. ✉ *19 S. 22nd St., Philadelphia, PA* 🌐 *www.muttermuseum.org*

Do This: One of the museum's most famous permanent exhibits is The Soap Lady, whose body is encased in adipocere, a fatty substance that preserves the body. Her body was exhumed from a Philadelphia-area cemetery in 1875 and now lies in a glass case.

PHILADELPHIA'S MAGIC GARDENS

Artist Isaiah Zagar has been creating mosaics throughout Philadelphia's South Street area for decades. When some works he created on vacant lots were almost destroyed, the community opened a museum dedicated to his work. Magic Gardens showcases Zagar's immersive mosaic murals, made up of found objects like mirrors, glass bottles, and bicycle tires. There's a two-level outdoor sculpture garden and two indoor galleries. ✉ *1020 South St., Philadelphia, PA* 🌐 *www.phillymagicgardens.org*

Do This: While the sculpture garden is covered top to bottom with tiles, the streets around the museum are great spots for a photo op.

RINGING ROCKS COUNTY PARK

In Bucks County, these noisy boulders are jokingly called "the world's first rock concert." Visitors are encouraged to bring a hammer to tap the rocks and hear the ringing for themselves. Aside from the boulders, the 128-acre park is perfect for picnicking, biking, and hiking. ✉ *Ringing Rocks Rd., Upper Black Eddy, PA* 🌐 *www.buckscounty.gov*

Do This: Ringing Rocks County Park is also home to High Falls, Bucks County's largest waterfall.

About Our Writers

Constance Jones has been exploring Pennsylvania for 20-odd years. Among her favorite places are the Magic Gardens in Philadelphia, the Hotel Hershey in Hershey, and Frank Lloyd Wright's Fallingwater. A former senior editor at Fodor's, Constance has contributed to publications such as the *New York Times* and *National Geographic Traveler* and has authored 15 books on topics ranging from cooking to history.

Cool Places to Stay

Four Seasons Hotel Philadelphia. At the top of Philadelphia's tallest skyscraper is the luxurious Four Seasons Hotel Philadelphia, which complements its gorgeous guest rooms with multiple bars and restaurants and a world-class spa. On the 59th floor, you can dine at Jean-Georges Philadelphia. ✉ *1 N. 19th St., Philadelphia, PA* 🌐 *www.fourseasons.com/philadelphia*

Hotel Hershey. Like a grand Mediterranean villa, Hotel Hershey sprawls atop a hill with a panoramic view over forested countryside. Milton S. Hershey built the hotel during the Great Depression to accommodate the well-heeled in elaborate splendor. Now, there's a chocolate-theme spa, a pool complex, fitness trails, and even falconry lessons. Don't miss dinner at The Circular dining room followed by drinks in the Iberian Lounge. ✉ *100 Hotel Rd., Hershey, PA* 🌐 *www.thehotelhershey.com*

The Inn at Jim Thorpe. In the heart of a National Register Historic District, the Inn at Jim Thorpe in the Pocono Mountains has charm to spare. Its cast-iron balcony has a wonderful view of the town's old brick storefronts. ✉ *24 Broadway, Jim Thorpe, PA* 🌐 *www.innjt.com*

Polymath Park. This architectural gem, designed by Frank Lloyd Wright, is available for overnight stays near Frank Lloyd Wright's Fallingwater. TreeTops Restaurant, a fine dining spot, has indoor tables and an outdoor TreeHouse with private dining pods. The grounds span 125 acres in the Laurel Highlands. ✉ *187 Evergreen La., Acme, PA* 🌐 *www.franklloydwrightovernight.net*

Skytop Lodge. One of the most popular lodgings in the Pocono Mountains, Skytop Lodge offers a bevy of outdoor activities, including kayaking, fishing, golfing, and hiking. In addition to rooms in the handsome main building, there are cottages throughout the property and an inn overlooking the golf course. ✉ *1 Skytop Lodge Rd., Skytop, PA* 🌐 *www.skytop.com*

Essential Eats

Dobbin House Tavern. Immerse yourself in Gettysburg history at this 1776 house that was once a stop on the Underground Railroad. Guests dine in six creaky-floored, low-ceilinged, candlelit rooms on traditional dishes including King's onion soup, Maryland crab cakes, and warm gingerbread. If you're in a more casual mood, try the lighter fare downstairs in the Springhouse Tavern. ✉ *89 Steinwehr Ave., Gettysburg, PA* 🌐 *www.dobbinhouse.com*

Philly Cheesesteaks. You can find them all over Pennsylvania and beyond, but you haven't really had a cheesesteak until you've had one in Philly. Juicy rib eye is sliced onto a long roll atop gooey cheese ("wiz," provolone, or American) and topped, if you like, with sautéed onions (order "wit" or "witout" depending on your taste). You may have heard of the long-time rivalry between Pat's and Geno's, but there are better choices, such as Joe's Steak and Soda Shop in Fishtown, Jim's South Street near the Magic Gardens, and Campo's Deli in Old Town. Some might argue that this is Philly cuisine at its finest.

Reading Terminal Market. Opened in 1893, this 80-vendor market offers up everything from fresh Amish produce and meat to soft pretzels and cannoli. Other merchants hawk craft items, international foods, and Pennsylvania-made spirits. Grab yourself a hot pork sandwich and have a seat in the food court. ✉ *N. 12th St. between Filbert and Arch Sts., Philadelphia, PA* 🌐 *www.readingterminalmarket.org*

Vetri Cucina. One of the hardest weekend dinner reservations to get in Philadelphia, Vetri is one of Pennsylvania's best restaurants. Lucky diners in the elegant, intimate dining room enjoy a set tasting menu of Italian classics touched with world influences. The ever-changing four-course menu might include a sweet onion crepe, garganelli with duck ragù, or smoked short rib. Wine pairings are supported by a 2,500-bottle cellar. ✉ *1312 Spruce St., Philadelphia, PA* 🌐 *www.vetricucina.com*

Virginia

From its mountains to its beaches, Virginia offers a little bit of everything. Within a few short hours, it's possible to visit the historic homes of founding fathers, explore Shenandoah National Park and the Blue Ridge Parkway, relax on the sunny shores of Virginia Beach, relive colonial times in Colonial Williamsburg and Jamestown, and sip local wines at charming wineries nestled in rolling hills.

Capital: Richmond

Population Area: 8,811,195

Statehood Date: June 25, 1788

Major Airports: Washington-Dulles International Airport (IAD); Washington-Reagan Airport (DCA); Richmond International Airport (RIC); Norfolk International Airport (ORF); Roanoke-Blacksburg Airport (ROA)

Travel and Tourism Information: 🌐 *www.virginia.org*

Famous Residents: George Washington (president); Thomas Jefferson (president); Katie Couric (journalist); Sandra Bullock (actress); Dave Matthews (musician); Pharrell Williams (music mogul); Missy Elliott (rapper)

Fun Facts: Virginia is the birthplace of eight U.S. presidents, Virginia Beach is the world's longest continuous pleasure beach, and the Barter Theatre in Abingdon is the nation's oldest continuously operating theater.

Shenandoah National Park

Virginia's Ribbon of Green

Shenandoah National Park may look like just a narrow stretch on the map, winding for 70 miles through the Blue Ridge Mountains, but it's one of Virginia's most stunning natural treasures. The park spans over 200,000 acres and is split down the middle by **Skyline Drive**, a 105-mile scenic route that's often ranked among the most beautiful road trips in the United States. Along the way, you might spot bears, deer, and other wildlife crossing the road, so it's worth taking it slow and soaking in the views. For hikers, adventure is never far, as some of the park's 500 miles of trails (many part of the Appalachian Trail) are just steps from the road, leading to breathtaking overlooks and peaceful forest paths. ✉ *3655 U.S. 211, Luray, VA* 🌐 *www.nps.gov/shen* 🎟 *$30 per car*

Don't Miss

Nearby **Luray Caverns**, the largest cave system in the eastern United States, features 64 acres of geological formations, including stalactites, stalagmites, and mirrored pools. The caverns also contain rare attractions like the world's only stalacpipe organ and historic signatures left by Union and Confederate soldiers who once took shelter there. ✉ *101 Cave Hill Rd., Luray, VA* 🌐 *luraycaverns.com*

Good to Know

The three main visitor centers—Mobile Visitor Center, Harry F. Byrd Sr. Visitor Center, and Dickey Ridge Visitor Center—are great places to start your exploration.

Getting Here and Around

Shenandoah is about 90 minutes from both Washington, D.C. and Richmond, Virginia.

Virginia's Historic Triangle

A Journey Through History

Virginia's Historic Triangle, comprised of Williamsburg, Jamestown, and Yorktown, offers a fascinating journey into America's colonial roots. These three cities played key roles in shaping the early history of the nation, and visiting them is like stepping back in time. Start in **Colonial Williamsburg** (✉ *101 Visitor Center Dr., Williamsburg, VA* 🌐 *www.colonialwilliamsburg.org*), the largest living-history museum in the country, where costumed interpreters, historic buildings, and immersive reenactments bring 18th-century America to life. Just a short drive away, the **Jamestown Settlement** (✉ *2110 Jamestown Rd., Williamsburg, VA* 🌐 *www.jyfmuseums.org*), established in 1607, tells the story of the first permanent English colony in America, while **Yorktown** (✉ *1000 Colonial Pkwy., Yorktown, VA* 🌐 *www.nps.gov/york*) is most famous for its pivotal battlefield victory that ended the Revolutionary War; the American Revolutionary Museum here highlights the story of America's fight for independence.

Don't Miss

Historic Jamestowne, the original site of the 1607 settlement, is where visitors can walk in the footsteps of America's first English colonists. ✉ *1368 Colonial Pkwy., Jamestown, VA* 🌐 *www.historicjamestowne.org*

Best Shops

At the heart of Williamsburg is **Merchants Square**, which was built in the 1920s as one of the first planned shopping districts in the country.

Getting Here and Around

Colonial Williamsburg is located off Route 60 in Virginia, making it easy to reach by car. Jamestown is 7 miles southwest of Williamsburg on Route 31 while Yorktown is 16 miles southeast of Williamsburg via Route 199.

Mount Vernon

George Washington's Riverfront Home

Set on a hillside overlooking the Potomac River, George Washington's estate is one of the most visited sites in Northern Virginia. You can stroll around the estate's 500 acres and three gardens, visiting the kitchen, carriage house, and—down the hill toward the boat landing—the tomb of George and Martha Washington. There's also a 4-acre farm with a reconstruction of George Washington's 16-sided barn as its centerpiece. Two on-site museums contain hundreds of artifacts. ✉ *3200 Mount Vernon Memorial Hwy., Mount Vernon, VA* 🌐 *www.mountvernon.org*

Don't Miss

Some of the most memorable experiences at Mount Vernon, particularly for kids, are in the Museum and Education Center. Interactive displays, movies with special effects straight out of Hollywood, life-size models, and revolutionary artifacts illustrate Washington's life and contributions.

Essential Tour

Throughout Mount Vernon, you can learn about the more than 300 enslaved people who lived here, and whose labor you see all around you. "The Enslaved People of Mount Vernon Tour" explores their lives and experiences and the role slavery had in the life of Washington and how he built and ran this estate.

When to Go

Mount Vernon is open throughout the year, but you'll want to visit in warmer months when you can stroll around the grounds.

Getting Here and Around

Mount Vernon is a 30-minute drive from Washington, D.C. It's also possible to visit by taking a 20-minute bus ride from the Huntington Station of Metrorail.

Monticello Wine Trail

Birthplace of American Vintages

Wine making has been a strong tradition throughout Virginia since colonial times, and this wine trail, inspired by Thomas Jefferson's vision of grape growing at his Monticello home, connects the best vineyards in the region. In 2023, Charlottesville and the Monticello American Viticultural Area (AVA) was named Wine Enthusiast's Wine Region of the Year. The Monticello Wine Trail extends throughout the Blue Ridge Mountains and includes dozens of wineries producing excellent reds, whites, and rosés. Many offer vineyard walks, cellar tours, and tastings throughout the year. Some have on-site eateries with delicious dishes chosen to complement the latest vintages. 🌐 *www.monticellowinetrail.com*

Don't Miss

Break up the adventure with a stop at the place that started it all, **Monticello**, just outside Charlottesville. Monticello (which means "little mountain") is the most famous of Jefferson's homes, constructed from 1769 to 1809. Allow at least three hours to explore Jefferson's life as exemplified by the architecture, inventions, and exhibits throughout the grand hilltop estate. ✉ *1050 Monticello Loop, Charlottesville, VA* 🌐 *www.monticello.org*

Best Winery

Family-owned **Veritas Vineyard and Winery** is beloved for its delicious wines made on the premises. It also has some of the most beautiful views of the mountains. ✉ *151 Veritas La., Afton, VA* 🌐 *veritaswines.com*

Getting Here and Around

The wineries are spread out, but all are within about 30 miles of Charlottesville.

Richmond

Virginia's Capital of Cool

Richmond's cool factor has increased exponentially in recent years. Neighborhoods throughout the city are now home to renowned restaurants, quaint bakeries, and one-of-a-kind shops, many of which are outposts of famous establishments in New York or Washington, D.C. In fast-growing **Scott's Addition**, you'll find more than a dozen breweries, cideries, and distilleries, many of which are housed within converted warehouses. Favorites include the **Veil Brewing Company**, **Blue Bee Cider**, and **Reservoir Distillery**. For food, try **Boulevard Burger and Brew**, **Fat Dragon Chinese Kitchen and Bar**, or **Mama J's Kitchen**.

Don't Miss

The **Virginia Museum of History and Culture** provides an excellent overview of the state's compelling history and diverse communities. Long-term exhibits include the *Story of Virginia* and *History Matters*. ✉ *428 N. Arthur Ashe Blvd., Richmond, VA* 🌐 *virginiahistory.org*

While You're Here

The **Belle Isle Pedestrian Bridge** lets you walk right over the James River with awesome views of downtown Richmond and the rushing rapids below. It's a fun, easy way to reach Belle Isle, a 54-acre riverside park with walking trails, large rocks, and riverfront hangout spots.

Best Walk

Stroll down colorful Cary Street in Richmond's **Carytown** neighborhood. The thoroughfare is home to a mix of locally owned shops, restaurants, and ice-cream parlors.

Getting Here and Around

Richmond International Airport is a short drive away. For those arriving by train, Richmond's Main Street Station welcomes multiple Amtrak trains each day.

Virginia Beach

Virginia's Best Beach Destination

While the sun and sand is definitely the main draw in Virginia Beach, the 3-mile-long boardwalk, which runs for almost 40 blocks, is where everyone ends up sooner or later. There's an old-fashioned fishing pier, a waterfront park, and lots of family-friendly fun. You can also commune with nature on a bike trail.

Don't Miss

Virginia Beach's **First Landing State Park**—Virginia's most popular state park—is where English colonists first touched dry land in the early 17th century. Native American canoes were already navigating these waters long before that. Today, there are 20 miles of hiking trails and a mile and a half of beachfront access. ✉ *2500 Shore Dr., Virginia Beach, VA* 🌐 *www.dcr.virginia.gov*

Best Tour

A must for nature loves, **Rudee Tours** offers whale-watching excursions and dolphin-watching trips. 🌐 *www.rudeetours.com*

When to Go

Summer is prime time for visiting Virginia Beach, with numerous festivals along the oceanfront. But it can get noisy and crowded so make reservations well ahead of time. Alternatively, you can visit during fall and winter to enjoy the area's lesser known arts, culture, and food scenes with fewer crowds.

Getting Here and Around

Norfolk International Airport is a 25-minute drive from Virginia Beach. Once you're in Virginia Beach, much of the area is accessible by foot or by bike.

The Appalachian Trail

500 Miles of Forests and Farmland

The Appalachian Trail runs from Georgia to Maine, but almost a quarter of the world-famous hiking trail can be found in Virginia. There are 555 miles waiting to be explored, and sections are appropriate for everyone from first-timers to seasoned experts. It's a combination of forests and farmland, and can be accessed at many points throughout the state. More than 100 miles of the trail run through breathtaking Shenandoah National Park, and the fairly level terrain makes it a popular starting place for newer hikers.

Don't Miss

McAfee Knob is arguably the most iconic spot on the Appalachian Trail in Virginia. Begin your journey at the VA 311 trailhead and follow the Appalachian Trail northbound along Catawba Mountain. The moderate route passes two trail shelters before ascending to the summit of McAfee Knob. ✉ *Catawba Valley Dr., Catawba, VA*

Best Hikes

The Appalachian Tour Conservancy has a great list of hiking routes that can be completed in a day. In Virginia, popular short hikes include the 4-mile-long **Apple Orchard Falls Trail** from Bedford to Lynchburg, the 2.6-mile **Chestnut Knob Trail** in Tazewell and Wytheville, and the 4-mile hike to the summit of **Mary's Rock** near Luray.

Getting Here and Around

The Virginia portion of the Appalachian Trail can be accessed at many points, including Shenandoah National Park and George Washington and Jefferson National Forests.

When in Virginia

ARLINGTON NATIONAL CEMETERY

One of the most serene spots near the nation's capital, this 639-acre military cemetery draws tourists from all over the world. The welcome center at Memorial Drive is a great first stop for those who are seeking out the graves of the monumental figures buried here, including Supreme Court justices (Thurgood Marshall), presidents (John F. Kennedy), and civil rights heroes (Medgar Evers). Located on a hill overlooking the Potomac River, the Tomb of the Unknowns honors the fallen soldiers who remained unidentified. ✉ *Memorial Ave., Arlington, VA* 🌐 *www.arlingtoncemetery.mil*

Do This: The changing of the guard ceremony at the Tomb of the Unknowns is a moving, must-see Army tradition that takes place at different times throughout the day depending on the season.

NATURAL BRIDGE

This stunning limestone arch has been gradually carved out by Cedar Creek, which flows past more than 200 feet below. It was a sacred site for the Monacan Native American tribe, who called it the "Bridge of God." The arch is part of the larger Natural Bridge State Park, which has miles of hiking trails.

Do This: Start your day at the Natural Bridge State Park Visitor Center, where you can learn about the area's history. ✉ *6477 S. Lee Hwy., Natural Bridge, VA* 🌐 *www.dcr.virginia.gov/state-parks/natural-bridge*

OLD TOWN ALEXANDRIA

One of the quaintest communities in northern Virginia is Old Town Alexandria, not far from Washington, D.C. Located on the Potomac River, the historic area has cobblestone streets lined with handsome brick buildings that hold exquisite restaurants, interesting bars, and unique shops. On the waterfront is the Torpedo Factory Art Center (✉ *105 N. Union St., Alexandria, VA* 🌐 *torpedofactory.org*), a former munitions factory that has been transformed into the largest collection of publicly accessible working artist studios in the United States.

Do This: Stroll along King Street, peeking down narrow alleys and into pretty gardens along the way. Grab a coffee from renowned Misha's Coffee to fuel your walk, and then take a guided tour with Manumission Tour Company to learn about the city's compelling African American history. 🌐 *www.manumission-tours.com*

ROANOKE

Known as the "East Coast Mountain Biking Capital," Roanoke is Virginia's premier destination for outdoor adventure. Visitors can hike or bike the well-maintained trails (or drive) at Mill Mountain to reach the iconic Roanoke Star and take in sweeping panoramic views of the Roanoke Valley below.

Do This: Visit the Taubman Museum of Art, the historic City Market, and the Virginia Museum of Transportation. And be sure to take a drive along a stretch of the scenic Blue Ridge Parkway, which has convenient access just outside the city.

Favorite Places

Taryn White is a Virginia-based freelance travel and food writer and founder of The Trip Wish List. She has journeyed to all corners of Virginia, whether it's savoring farm-to-table food and wine in Central Virginia or exploring the state's historical and cultural roots. Her work has appeared in *Travel + Leisure, Forbes, Condé Nast Traveler, National Geographic,* and other outlets.

Cool Places to Stay

The Historic Cavalier Hotel and Beach Club. This beachfront hotel opened during the Roaring '20s and has hosted presidents, movie stars, and famous writers during its 100-plus-year history. Because of its hilltop location, most of the gorgeous guest rooms have views of the ocean. ✉ *4200 Atlantic Ave., Virginia Beach, VA* 🌐 *www.marriott.com*

Keswick Hall. Located on a 600-acre estate near Charlottesville, Keswick Hall offers 80 elegantly styled rooms, the upscale Marigold by Jean-Georges restaurant, and the luxurious Keswick Spa. Guests can also enjoy an outdoor infinity pool, a Pete Dye–designed golf course, red-clay tennis courts, walking trails, and a refined atmosphere that reflects the best of Southern hospitality. ✉ *701 Club Dr., Keswick, VA* 🌐 *www.keswick.com*

Lewis Mountain Cabins. In Shenandoah National Park, the rustic Lewis Mountain Cabins have fans who return year after year. They aren't luxurious, but they couldn't be more homey. Cabins have one or two bedrooms and outdoor spaces ranging from breezy porches to covered picnic areas. ✉ *Skyline Dr., Elkton, VA* 🌐 *www.goshenandoah.com*

Primland Resort. This stunning mountain getaway is situated on 12,000 private acres in Virginia's Blue Ridge Mountains, with accommodations ranging from cozy lodges to tree houses overlooking the gorge. Whether you're into golf, fly-fishing, horseback riding, spa days, or stargazing through a real observatory, there's something for everyone to enjoy here. ✉ *2000 Busted Rock Rd., Meadows of Dan, VA* 🌐 *www.aubergeresorts.com/primland*

Quirk Hotel Richmond. A welcome fixture along Richmond's West Broad Street, the Quirk Hotel gives you easy access to coffee shops, vegan restaurants, and one-of-a-kind boutiques. With a sleek, minimalist lobby, it's easy to see why this downtown hotel is a go-to for many trendy travelers. ✉ *201 W. Broad St., Richmond, VA* 🌐 *www.quirkhotels.com*

Salamander Middleburg. This Black-owned luxury resort is set on 340 acres of Virginia horse and wine country, about one hour outside of Washington, D.C. It offers fine dining, a luxury spa, and outdoor activities ranging from ziplining to horseback riding. ✉ *500 N. Pendleton St., Middleburg, VA* 🌐 *www.salamander-resort.com*

Essential Eats

The Dining Room at the Inn at Little Washington. Established in 1978 by Chef Patrick O'Connell in a former gas station, this three-Michelin-starred gem sits in a quaint village surveyed by George Washington. It's renowned for its theatrical fine dining, 14,000-bottle cellar, and lavish lodging, and has become an iconic spot for food lovers and celebrities alike. ✉ *Middle and Main Sts., Washington, VA* 🌐 *www.theinnatlittlewashington.com*

Fat Canary. What began as a family-run cheese shop in 1971 has expanded into an award-winning restaurant serving upscale American fare, with dishes like fricassee of rabbit and gingered barbecue pork chops. The restaurant also has an extensive wine list that includes local and international wines. ✉ *410 W. Duke of Gloucester, Williamsburg, VA* 🌐 *www.fatcanarywilliamsburg.com*

Gadsby's Tavern. This 18th-century tavern is a National Historic Landmark, beloved by George Washington, Thomas Jefferson, and the Marquis de Lafayette. It offers period-inspired fine dining in original colonial-era rooms lit by candlelight. Dishes include Surrey County peanut soup and "George Washington's Favorite" roasted half duck. ✉ *138 N. Royal St., Alexandria, VA* 🌐 *www.gadsbystavernrestaurant.com*

Washington, D.C.

With its neoclassical government buildings and grand avenues, Washington, D.C. looks its part as America's capital, where majestic monuments and memorials pay tribute to notable leaders and historic triumphs. But the city is far from stuck in the past. Beyond the marble and history, D.C. pulses with contemporary energy. Once-sleepy enclaves like Shaw, Navy Yard, and NoMa now thrive with acclaimed restaurants, indie boutiques, rooftop bars, and live music venues, joining long-established hot spots like Georgetown, U Street, and Adams Morgan in defining a vibrant, ever-evolving cultural landscape.

Population: 678,972

Area: 68.3 square miles

Major Airports: Ronald Reagan Washington National Airport (DCA); Dulles International Airport (IAD)

Travel and Tourism Information: *www.washington.org*

Famous Residents: Clara Barton (founder of the American Red Cross); Frederick Douglass (abolitionist and writer); Marvin Gaye (singer); Wolf Blitzer (journalist); Samira Wiley (actress)

Fun Fact: While the streets here follow an alphabetical pattern, there's no J Street. City planners felt "I" and "J" looked too similar, so "J" was omitted.

National Mall

America's Front Yard

Fondly known as "America's front yard," Washington, D.C.'s National Mall is a 2-mile-long green expanse in the heart of the city. Bordered by the U.S. Capitol to the east and the Lincoln Memorial to the west, it's home to the country's most iconic monuments and memorials, including the **Washington Monument**, **Vietnam Veterans Memorial**, **Korean War Veterans Memorial**, **World War I Memorial**, and **World War II Memorial**. Park rangers are often on hand to share insights, and many of the Smithsonian museums line its edges east of 14th Street. 🌐 *www.nps.gov/nama*

Don't Miss

The top of the Washington Monument is perhaps the best, most breathtaking place to see the city and get a good idea of its layout. Up to six tickets can be requested in advance for just $1 per person at 🌐 *recreation.gov*. Free same-day tickets are available, but space is not guaranteed.

Best Tour

Want the inside scoop on Washington? Pay-what-you-like **Tours by Foot** offers little-known facts about the attractions surrounding the National Mall. Reservations are required. 🌐 *www.freetoursbyfoot.com/national-mall-tour*

Getting Here and Around

The National Mall is located in the heart of Washington, making it easy to access by foot, by bike, or by public transportation. The Smithsonian Metro station stop deposits you in the center of the National Mall.

The Smithsonian Museums

America's Shared Story

The Smithsonian Institution, known around the world simply as the Smithsonian, has 17 galleries and museums, including the National Zoological Park, in Washington, D.C. All of them are free to visit. Many of the museums rate among the world's most visited, including Smithsonian's **National Air and Space Museum** (✉ *601 Independence Ave. SW, Washington, DC* 🌐 *www.airandspace.si.edu*), where you'll find the 1903 Wright Flyer, Neil Armstrong's Apollo 11 spacesuit, and other fan favorites; the **National Museum of Natural History** (✉ *1000 Madison Dr. NW, Washington, D.C.* 🌐 *www.naturalhistory.si.edu*), with highlights including the Hope Diamond, the Wildlife Hall, and the Insect Zoo; and the **National Museum of American History** (✉ *1300 Constitution Ave. NW, Washington, DC* 🌐 *americanhistory.si.edu*), home to the original Star-Spangled Banner, Dorothy's ruby slippers, and Julia Child's kitchen.

Don't Miss

Opened in 2016, the **National Museum of African American History and Culture** remains one of the Smithsonian's most popular and impactful museums. Its expansive collection traces centuries of Black history and culture, with powerful artifacts like Harriet Tubman's shawl, Nat Turner's Bible, and a campaign banner from President Barack Obama's 2008 campaign headquarters. ✉ *1400 Constitution Ave. NW, Washington, DC* 🌐 *nmaahc.si.edu*

Getting Here and Around

The museums are spread out throughout Washington, D.C., with the bulk of the Smithsonian attractions located at the National Mall. All are easily accessible by car and public transit.

Capitol Hill

The Government's Neighborhood

Crowned by the iconic U.S. Capitol building, Capitol Hill is home to some of the nation's most important landmarks. Tour the **Library of Congress**—the largest library in the world, with more than 170 million items and a stunning, mural-filled interior—or visit the **Supreme Court** to hear oral arguments and explore educational exhibits. Beyond the grandeur, Capitol Hill is also a welcoming neighborhood with tree-lined streets, historic row houses, indie boutiques, and local restaurants. Leafy parks like Stanton Park and Lincoln Park add to its walkable, village-like charm. 🌐 *www.visitthe-capitol.gov*

Don't Miss

The handsome brick **Eastern Market** has been providing the community with fresh meat, fish, cheese, and produce for more than 100 years. Drop by the indoor-outdoor market on Sunday, when the covered walkway and adjacent lot are filled with arts and crafts vendors. Its casual restaurant, Market Lunch has promised "great food, no frills" since 1978; it delivers with North Carolina barbecue and Chesapeake Bay crab cakes. ✉ *225 7th St. SE, Washington, DC* 🌐 *www.easternmarket-dc.org*

Best Tour

Washington Tours provides the inside scoop on Capitol Hill, including local favorites such as Mr. Henry's, a watering hole famous for jazz singers; Barracks Row, the neighborhood's commercial heart; and the remains of a 1795 estate called The Maples. 🌐 *www.washingtonwalks.com*

Getting Here and Around

Capitol Hill is easily accessible by Metro, including Capitol South and Union Station for the monumental sights and Eastern Market for the eponymous market.

The Tidal Basin

Cherry Blossom Central

Just steps from the National Mall, the Tidal Basin is a serene, man-made reservoir within West Potomac Park that offers one of Washington, D.C.'s most emblematic landscapes. Spanning 107 acres, it's framed by the famous Yoshino and Kwanzan cherry trees—gifts from Japan in 1912 that have become a symbol of friendship between the two nations. Each spring, they erupt in clouds of pink and white, drawing visitors from around the world during the city's famed **National Cherry Blossom Festival.** Gently curving pathways circle the basin, inviting leisurely strolls and bike rides while providing views of the Jefferson Memorial in one direction and the Washington Monument in the other. 🌐 *nationalcherryblossomfestival.org*

Don't Miss

Three major memorials ring the Tidal Basin: the **Franklin Delano Memorial**, honoring the 32nd president; the **Martin Luther King Jr., Memorial**, commemorating the civil rights leader's enduring memory; and the **Thomas Jefferson Memorial**, celebrating the third president and principal author of the Declaration of Independence.

When to Go

To see the cherry blossoms in all their glory, visit in late March or early April (though the exact dates for peak bloom can vary). Even if you miss the blooms, you can enjoy the four-week National Cherry Blossom Festival from mid-March to mid-April, featuring a parade, free concerts, a kite festival, and more.

Getting Here and Around

The Tidal Basin is close to many of D.C.'s other must-see attractions, including the National Mall. The Smithsonian Metro station is about a 15-minute walk from the area.

The National Archives

America's History Vault

The nation's most treasured documents reside in this hallowed neoclassical landmark in downtown D.C. At its heart lies the hushed, marble-lined Rotunda, where the Declaration of Independence, the U.S. Constitution, and the Bill of Rights—together known as the Charters of Freedom—are enshrined for all to see. But the National Archives is far more than a monument to founding ideals. Its reimagined, state-of-the-art museum "The American Story" spans 250 years of U.S. history through original documents, rare artifacts, films, and immersive exhibits that bring the American journey vividly to life. Interactive digital stations help visitors explore millions of records customized to their interests. Among the fascinating items you might see on display: George Washington's draft of the U.S. Constitution, annotated in his own handwriting; a set of horseshoes gifted to President George H. W. Bush by the Queen of England; and the original patent for the Barbie doll. ✉ *701 Pennsylvania Ave. NW, Washington, DC* 🌐 *www.archives.gov*

Don't Miss

Discover your own family's history firsthand at the National Archives, where you can explore everything from census and military records to immigration documents (including ship passenger lists), naturalization papers, and land records. Just be sure to plan your visit in advance. Can't make it in person? Research assistance is also available by phone, mail, or email.

Getting Here and Around

The closest Metro station is Archives–Navy Memorial–Penn Quarter.

Georgetown

D.C.'s Most Charming Neighborhood

There's much more to this neighborhood than its namesake university. Located on the Potomac River, quaint Georgetown radiates outward from the busy intersection of Wisconsin Avenue and M Street. On the surrounding blocks are cobblestone streets, elegant homes, buzzy restaurants, and upscale boutiques. Follow the towpath along the **Chesapeake and Ohio Canal** for a completely different look at Washington's oldest neighborhood.

Don't Miss

Often called the "Secret Garden," the 53-acre **Dumbarton Oaks** sits on the highest hill above Georgetown. Locals love the meandering trails through manicured gardens and classical fountains. The on-site museum is a treasure trove of Byzantine and Pre-Columbian art. ✉ *R St. NW, Washington, DC* 🌐 *www.doaks.org*

Best Restaurant

The 10-acre **Georgetown Waterfront Park** has plenty of interesting eateries, including the very popular **Founding Farmers Fishers & Bakers**. There are sweeping views of the Potomac River and access to kayaking, canoeing, and paddleboarding, and even a labyrinth. ✉ *3000 K St. NW, Washington, DC* 🌐 *www.farmersfishersbakers.com*

Getting Here and Around

Georgetown is one of the few downtown neighborhoods that isn't served by Metrorail. It's a 20-minute walk from the Foggy Bottom/GWU station.

International Spy Museum

Become an Undercover Spy

The moment you step into this 140,000-square-foot, state-of-the-art museum at L'Enfant Plaza, you're assigned a secret identity—complete with codename and undercover mission—that guides your journey. The International Spy Museum pulls back the curtain on the high-stakes world of intelligence gathering through immersive exhibits and interactive experiences. Test your skills in missions like tracking Osama bin Laden or confronting future cyber threats. Explore the history of spying from the ancient Greeks and the Roman Empire to today. You'll also hear firsthand stories from top intelligence officers and get an up-close look at real gadgets, weapons, and disguises used in the field. ✉ *700 L'Enfant Plaza SW, Washington, DC* 🌐 *www.spymuseum.org*

Don't Miss

At the "Disguise" stop on your Undercover Mission, RFID-enabled technology snaps your photo and instantly transforms you into a master of disguise. Watch yourself morph with digital overlays of your choosing—scarves, hats, facial hair, and more—revealing how you'd blend in as a real-world spy on assignment.

Best Shopping

The Spy Museum store is a destination in itself, packed with some of the coolest take-home treasures. Think real-deal gadgets like HD pen cameras with built-in DVRs, invisible ink pens, and secret decoder cypher wheels.

Getting Here and Around

The museum is easily accessible from the L'Enfant Plaza Metro Station.

When in Washington, D.C.

ADAMS MORGAN

Named for two elementary schools that were desegregated in the 1950s—Adams had been for white students, while nearby Morgan had been for black students—this vibrant neighborhood is a multicultural celebration. Bars, coffee shops, and restaurants line 18th Street and spill out onto many of the adjacent blocks, making this a good place to start your explorations. Be sure to visit Tryst for coffee, the casual Julia's Empanadas for food, and Madam's Organ for nightly live music and quirky cocktails.

Do This: One of the spots that helped establish this neighborhood as a foodie destination is Perry's, a Japanese restaurant with a wonderful rooftop dining area and popular Sunday drag brunch. ✉ *1811 Columbia Rd. NW, Washington, DC* 🌐 *www.perrysam.com*

BLUES ALLEY

For the past five decades, Blues Alley in the upscale Georgetown neighborhood has been hosting up-and-coming and big-name jazz and blues musicians. Over the years, the venue has welcomed storied performers including Ella Fitzgerald, Tony Bennett, and Stan Getz. Wynton Marsalis, Pat Martino, and others have recorded live albums here. ✉ *1073 Wisconsin Ave. NW, Washington, DC* 🌐 *www.bluesalley.com*

Do This: The club is also a popular bar and restaurant, so come before a show and enjoy delicious Southern fare.

DISTRICT WHARF

Southwest D.C., the smallest of the city's quadrants, has become a destination of its own thanks to the Wharf, the mile-long complex next to the boat-filled Washington Channel, an offshoot of the Potomac River. It's an exciting place for locals and visitors to enjoy diverse cuisines, try out kayaking and stand-up paddleboarding, or listen to live music at places like The Anthem. 🌐 *www.wharfdc.com*

Do This: The Municipal Fish Market—America's oldest continuously operating seafood market—has served fresh catch from the same spot since 1805. Once part of a working waterfront, it now adds old-school flavor to the modern wharf. ✉ *1100 Maine Ave. SW, Washington, DC* 🌐 *www.wharfdc.com/fish-market*

FREDERICK DOUGLASS NATIONAL HISTORIC SITE

Abolitionist, orator, and statesman Frederick Douglass lived in the nation's capital for the last 17 years of his life. Today, his handsome Anacostia home, called Cedar Hill, has been painstakingly restored to reflect its appearance in 1895. You can also explore the Growlery, the reconstruction of a small stone cabin where he wrote his third autobiography, *The Life and Times of Frederick Douglass*. ✉ *1411 W St. SE, Washington, DC* 🌐 *www.nps.gov/frdo*

Do This: At the visitor center, don't pass up a chance to watch the 19-minute film called *Fighter for Freedom: The Frederick Douglass Story*.

NATIONAL GALLERY OF ART

This two-building art museum on the National Mall—often mistaken for part of the Smithsonian, though it isn't—showcases a world-class collection of Western masterpieces. In the West Building, explore European paintings and sculptures from the 13th to 19th centuries, including French Impressionists, Rembrandt, Vermeer, and the only Leonardo da Vinci in the Americas, *Ginevra de' Benci*. Across the way, the striking I.M. Pei–designed East Building focuses on modern and contemporary art, featuring works by Rothko, Newman, and a soaring Calder mobile. ✉ *West Bldg.: 6th St. and Constitution Ave. NW; East Bldg.: 4th St. and Constitution Ave., Washington, DC* 🌐 *www.nga.gov*

Do This: The Sculpture Garden, just across from the West Building, features larger-than-life contemporary works by artists like Oldenburg and Miró, set amid landscaped paths and a relaxed garden café.

THE NATIONAL ZOO

The Smithsonian's National Zoo and Conservation Biology Institute features more than 2,200 animals representing more than 400 species, as close as you can get to their native surroundings (and for free!). The multigenerational herd of elephants—part of the zoo's conservation campaign to save this endangered species from extinction—is a perennial favorite. ✉ *3001 Connecticut Ave. NW, Washington, DC* 🌐 *nationalzoo.si.edu*

Do This: While you're sure to be charmed by many animals in the zoo, the zoo's giant pandas have been a massive hit since the Chinese government donated two pandas in 1972 following President Richard Nixon's historic visit to China. Other pandas have followed, including cubs; Bao Li and Qing Bao have been the current panda residents since 2024.

UNITED STATES HOLOCAUST MEMORIAL MUSEUM

This museum asks you to consider how the Holocaust was made possible by the choices of individuals, institutions, and governments and what lessons they hold for us today. The permanent exhibition, *The Holocaust,* tells the stories of the millions of Jews, Romani, Jehovah's Witnesses, homosexuals, political prisoners, the mentally ill, and others killed by the Nazis between 1933 and 1945. The exhibitions are detailed and sometimes graphic but powerful. Rotating exhibitions highlight how genocide is still a real worldwide issue, featuring the stories of current survivors. ✉ *100 Raoul Wallenberg Pl. SW, Washington, DC* 🌐 *www.ushmm.org*

Do This: After this powerful experience, the *Hall of Remembrance,* filled with candles, provides a much-needed space for quiet reflection.

U STREET

In the early 20th century, U Street became known as "Black Broadway," a thriving center of African American life and creativity. Jazz greats like Duke Ellington, Louis Armstrong, Cab Calloway, and Sarah Vaughan performed at its legendary clubs and theaters—including the historic Lincoln Theater, which has been beautifully restored. After periods of upheaval and change, the neighborhood has reemerged as a dynamic hub of culture and community. Today, Ethiopian cuisine, independent boutiques, and a rich music scene continue to draw people—just as they did a century ago.

Do This: For more than 20 years, Dukem has been a favorite of those seeking authentic Ethiopian food. Guests come for the injera, a spongy flatbread topped with tibs, a dish with cubed tender lamb or beef fried with onion, rosemary, jalapeño pepper served with injera, and salad and spicy awazie sauce. ✉ *1114–1118 U St. NW, Washington, DC* 🌐 *www.dukemrestaurant.com/US*

WASHINGTON NATIONAL CATHEDRAL

Its official name is the Cathedral Church of St. Peter and St. Paul, but the world knows it as Washington National Cathedral. Inspired by 14th-century English Gothic architecture, this stunning cathedral features a soaring nave, flying buttresses, transepts, and vaulted ceilings—all built painstakingly, stone by stone. It's also home to 112 gargoyles and over 3,000 other grotesques, including one shaped like Darth Vader. After 83 years of construction, the cathedral was completed in 1990, and has since hosted major national moments, including including the state funerals for Presidents George H. W. Bush and Jimmy Carter. ✉ *3101 Wisconsin Ave. NW, Washington, DC* 🌐 *www.cathedral.org*

Do This: The 57-acre Washington National Cathedral gardens, also known as Cathedral Close, are well worth a visit. The expanse is meticulously maintained and features a wide range of colorful flowers and plants.

THE WHITE HOUSE

Designed in 1792 by Irish architect James Hoban, the country's most famous residence was known officially as the Executive Mansion until 1901, when President Theodore Roosevelt renamed it the White House. It was opened in 1800, but was partly destroyed in 1814 when British forces set fire to many government buildings throughout the city. Hoban himself led the restoration efforts. Tours are hard to come by, as they must be requested through a member of Congress (and tours are currently suspended indefinitely due to White House renovations), but the view from the outside is still iconic. ✉ *1600 Pennsylvania Ave. NW, Washington, DC* 🌐 *www.whitehouse.gov/visit*

Do This: If you want to do more than just take a picture of the exterior, The People's House: A White House Experience, a block away, is an excellent option. This immersive museum delves into the history and inner workings of the White House, including a full-scale replica of the Oval Office where you can sit behind the Resolute Desk; an immersive theater that transforms into various State Floor rooms; and a 1:5 scale model of the White House's South Façade. ✉ *1700 Pennsylvania Ave. NW, Washington, DC* 🌐 *www.thepeopleshouse.org*

Cool Places to Stay

The Line Hotel. A true institution in the vibrant Adams Morgan neighborhood, the Line Hotel is part luxury lodging, part hip bar and restaurant. Located in a 1900s church, the space has soaring vaulted ceilings, stained-glass windows, and a rooftop space with eye-popping views. ✉ *1770 Euclid St. NW, Washington, DC* 🌐 *www.thelinehotel.com/dc*

The Mansion on O Street. Each of the more than 100 rooms within the Mansion on O Street is individually decorated to provide a one-of-a-kind experience. The hotel is a favorite among celebrities and political figures because of the hotel's code of silence: information on guests is never shared. ✉ *2020 O St. NW, Washington, DC* 🌐 *www.omansion.com*

Tabard Inn. For a glimpse of 1920s Washington, step inside Tabard Inn, a rambling retreat tucked in a row of Victorian town houses near Dupont Circle. Opened in 1922 by Marie Willoughby Rogers, it's the city's oldest continuously operating hotel, known for its creaky floors, antique-filled parlors, and a fireplace that invites lingering. With no TVs, spotty Wi-Fi, and an acclaimed farm-to-table restaurant, the Tabard offers a delightfully unplugged stay steeped in old-world charm. ✉ *1739 N St. NW, Washington, DC* 🌐 *www.tabardinn.com*

The Watergate Hotel. The Watergate—the name might sound familiar because it lent its name to a scandal that brought down a president—blends a mid-century

About Our Writers

Barbara Noe Kennedy has called the Washington, D.C. area home for three decades. Her quest to bike to all 40 boundary stones—the oldest federal monuments, marking the capital's original boundaries—with her then-boyfriend ended in an unexpected twist: a marriage proposal. Today, she is a freelance journalist exploring the intersections of travel with history, culture, and social justice.

modern aesthetic with luxurious touches that are very 21st century. Room 214, used during the infamous break-in, has tongue-in-cheek touches like binoculars and a reel-to-reel tape recorder. The views of the Potomac River are stunning. ✉ *2650 Virginia Ave. NW, Washington, DC* 🌐 *www.thewatergatehotel.com*

Yours Truly. Many think of Washington, D.C. as a town of buttoned-up government officials and policy wonks. But those who call the nation's capital home know that it's actually is a vibrant city full of personality. Yours Truly embraces the playful side of the city with colorful, bohemian decor sprinkled throughout the hotel. Luxe amenities include bathrooms stocked with ecological Karl Lagerfeld products and gourmet dog biscuits for four-legged guests. ✉ *1143 New Hampshire Ave. NW, Washington, DC* 🌐 *www.ihg.com*

Essential Eats

Ben's Chili Bowl. A U Street fixture for decades, Ben's serves chili—on hot dogs, on Polish-style sausages, on burgers, and on its own—to Washingtonians and visitors alike. The shiny, red-vinyl stools give the impression that little has changed since the 1950s (the original location still doesn't accept credit cards), but don't be fooled: this favorite has rocketed into the 21st century. Its tasty half-smoke—a sausage topped with spicy chili, mustard, and onions—is the reason to visit. ✉ *1213 U St. NW, Washington, DC* 🌐 *www.benschilibowl.com*

José Andrés's Culinary Empire. World-renowned chef, humanitarian, and restaurateur, José Andrés launched his U.S. career in Washington, D.C. with the opening of Jaleo in 1993—one of the nation's first tapas bars. Since then, the Spanish-born chef has built a six-restaurant empire in the city, earning Michelin recognition along the way. Highlights include Oyamel, a lively Mexican spot; Zaytinya, known for eastern Mediterranean small plates; the exclusive minibar and barmini, both offering avant-garde tasting menus and cocktails; and the Bazaar, serving Americana-inspired cuisine. 🌐 *www.joseandres.com*

Old Ebbitt Grill. Established in 1856, Old Ebbitt is Washington's oldest saloon and boarding house, a longtime favorite of political insiders and power players. Originally located in Chinatown, it moved to its current address in 1983, yet its rich character endures through antique gas chandeliers, vintage fixtures, and mounted animal heads (the walrus was reportedly shot by Theodore Roosevelt). Known for its raw oysters, Old Ebbitt remains a go-to happy hour destination just steps from the White House. ✉ *675 15th St., Washington, DC* 🌐 *www.ebbitt.com*

Rose's Luxury. This award-winning restaurant on Capitol Hill, set in a cozy town house, is beloved for its inventive New American small plates. Its playful five-course "choose your own adventure" tasting menu invites diners to select their own appetizer and pasta courses, along with three to share—including famously over-the-top desserts like baklava sundaes. The pork and lychee salad has been on the menu since the restaurant's opening in 2013. ✉ *717 8th St. SE, Washington, DC* 🌐 *www.rosesluxury.com*

Union Market District. One of D.C.'s hottest hubs for food and fun, the Union Market District is anchored by its namesake food hall that's home to 40 culinary artisans. Here, sample such inventive bites as Fishwife's Hawaiian poke bowls; TaKorean's Korean-fusion tacos; and DC Dosa's South Indian lentil crepes. Around the district, you'll find the grilled meat haven of St. Anselm; award-winning Italian fare at Masseria; and down-home classics with a twist at Bidwell. And don't miss A. Litteri, a no-frills Italian market and deli dating from 1926, where shelves brim with olive oil, garlic, and old-world charm. 🌐 *www.unionmarketdc.com*

West Virginia

With more than 226,500 acres of state parks, forests, and recreation areas, and more than a million acres of federal lands, West Virginia offers a quick escape from the urban centers of Baltimore, Philadelphia, Pittsburgh, and Washington, D.C. Historic towns, ski resorts, caverns, and unparalleled natural scenery draw visitors to the Mountain State.

Capital: Charleston

Population: 1,769,979

Area: 24,230 square miles

Statehood Date: June 20, 1863

Major Airports: Yeager Airport (CRW); Tri-State Airport (HTS); North Central West Virginia Airport (CKB)

Travel and Tourism Information: *www.wvtourism.com*

Famous Residents: Mahlon Loomis (inventor of the wireless telegraph); Steve Harvey (television personality); Brad Paisley (country singer); Jennifer Garner (actress)

Fun Fact: Grafton, West Virginia, is the birthplace of Mother's Day. The first official Mother's Day service was held there in 1908.

New River Gorge National Park and Preserve

America's Newest National Park

One of the country's newest national parks, West Virginia's New River Gorge runs through a particularly gorgeous stretch of the Appalachian Mountains. The park includes 70,000 acres of land along the New River, which, contrary to its name, is one of the country's oldest rivers. To take it all in, be sure to visit Grandview Visitor Center, situated 1,400 feet above the river. Already one of the most popular climbing areas in the country, New River Gorge has sheer sandstone cliffs that provide a challenge for even pro climbers. ✉ *Grandview Rd., Beaver, WV* 🌐 *www.nps.gov/neri*

Don't Miss

Marvel at the **New River Gorge Bridge**, which towers 876 feet above the river. The graceful structure is the longest steel span in the western hemisphere, and among the most photographed sights in all of West Virginia. Daredevil BASE jumpers leap from the structure every October to celebrate Bridge Day. ✉ *U.S. 19, Victor, WV*

Best Tour

The 17-stop **African American Heritage Auto Tour** is a self-guided tour of the New River Gorge area. Learn about the African American people who worked in the mines, on the railroads, and lived in the communities.

Best Activity

Adventures on the Gorge is one of the best outfitters offering rafting trips through the national park. 🌐 *www.adventuresonthegorge.com*

Getting Here and Around

Raleigh County Memorial Airport in Beaver is the closest airport to the national park. A car is necessary for touring this area.

Gauley River National Recreation Area

America's Best Rapids

For many white-water rafting fans, there's nothing better than an exciting and exhilarating ride down the 25-mile-long Gauley River. The free-flowing river's rocky sections make for a challenging trip, as do its stretches of Class V-plus rapids. It's one of the wildest trips on the East Coast. Some gentler sections are perfect for kids. As you're traveling through spectacular gorges, keep an eye out for songbirds like the cerulean warbler. ✉ *104 Main St., Glen Jean, WV* 🌐 *www.nps.gov/gari*

Don't Miss

Ace Adventure Resort has two options for rafters: the Fall Upper Gauley (for more experienced rafters) and the Fall Lower Gauley (open to those of all levels, including those who have never tried white-water rafting before). 🌐 *www.aceraft.com/white-water-rafting/gauley-river-rafting*

Be On the Lookout

Colorful small fish known as candy darters are native to the upper Kanawha River Basin, which includes the Gauley River. Due to habitat loss and other factors, the fish are considered endangered. They're fun to spot (they're about 4 inches long and have bright red stripes on their blue/green bodies), but be sure to leave no trace behind to ensure their continued survival.

When to Go

White-water rafting is a summertime activity, but hiking and other activities are pleasant in spring and fall.

Getting Here and Around

Roanoke–Blacksburg Regional Airport in Virginia is about 2½ hours away.

Harpers Ferry National Historical Park

The Precursor to the Civil War

Located at the confluence of the Potomac and Shenandoah rivers, Harpers Ferry is West Virginia's easternmost point. It comes up in history books surprisingly often, most notably in 1859 when abolitionist John Brown led a failed revolt that he hoped would bring an end to slavery. There's plenty here to keep you occupied today, including Civil War battlefields, museums, and hiking trails. Start at the Harpers Ferry Visitor Center, which provides guests with maps, trail information, and helpful history. ✉ *171 Shoreline Dr., Harpers Ferry, WV* 🌐 *www.nps.gov/hafe*

Don't Miss

The downtown area of Harpers Ferry, known as Lower Town, is a popular destination for visitors. Look for beautifully restored businesses from the period, including **Mrs. Stipes' Boarding House** and **Frankel's Clothing Store**.

Best Tour

The Harpers Ferry area has 22 miles of hiking trails through historic sites. Take a self-guided walking tour of the **Chesapeake and Ohio Canal National Historical Park**, which goes through the town.

When to Go

Summer can be hot in Harpers Ferry, making fall and spring ideal times to visit. In fall, the foliage is a true must-see.

Getting Here and Around

Harpers Ferry is a little over an hour away from both Washington, D.C. and Baltimore.

Monongahela National Forest

West Virginia's Mountain Paradise

The views of the Allegheny Mountains from the 919,000-acre Monongahela National Forest are breathtaking. The sheer size of the park is hard to comprehend at first, because it spans 10 counties. This is one of the most biologically diverse areas of the country, which you'll notice as you pass through stands of white and chestnut oak, maple, sycamore, birch, and mountain ash trees. The area is beloved for its hiking (there are literally hundreds of miles of trails), mountain biking, and boating. ✉ *200 Sycamore St., Elkins, WV* 🌐 *www.fs.usda.gov*

Don't Miss

The **Seneca Rocks** are one of the most popular attractions at Monongahela National Forest. Gaze up at the breathtaking rock formations, or grab some gear and climb them.

Best Tour

Embark on a self-guided tour of the **Cranberry Mountain Nature Center** to learn about the plants and animals that call the national forest home. There's an easy-to-conquer nature trail that surrounds the center, too. ✉ *Intersection of Rtes. 39/55 and Rte. 150, Hillsboro, WV*

Good to Know

The winding **Highland Scenic Highway** takes you past four beautiful overlooks with views as far as the eye can see.

Getting Here and Around

Monongahela National Forest is remote, which is why many people love it, and getting here is a bit of a trek. A car is a necessity.

Cass Scenic Railroad State Park

Train Ride Through Spectacular Scenery

History comes alive at Cass Scenic Railroad State Park, home to a working steam locomotive that can take you on an 11-mile trip to Bald Knob, a breathtaking mountain peak. The railroad was built in 1901 to transport lumber from the nearby forests to the mill in the town of Cass. Many of the open-sided passenger cars in use today are converted logging cars. ✉ *242 Main St., Cass, WV* 🌐 *www.wvstateparks.com/park/cass-scenic-railroad-state-park*

Don't Miss

The train is the draw at Cass Scenic Railroad State Park, but be sure to visit the community of **Cass**, a company town built for workers at nearby Cheat Mountain. There's a soda fountain, a sit-down restaurant, a gift shop, and a museum dedicated to railroading history.

Stay Overnight

To get the full experience, stay overnight in one of the **Cass Company Houses**, which used to house workers. Set behind picket fences, they have lots of character. 🌐 *www.wvstateparks.com/places-to-stay/cabins/cass-scenic-railroad-cabins*

When to Go

Visit in the fall for views of the colorful foliage on the mountain range.

Getting Here and Around

The state park is just a short drive over the border from Virginia. Roanoke is 130 miles away, while Charlottesville is 125 miles away.

Traditional Mountain Music

Country Roads, Take You Home

The music of West Virginia is a major part of the state's culture and history. Known as Appalachian music, the genre combines elements of bluegrass, folk, and country. You can enjoy it at outdoor festivals, music halls, backyard barbecues, and lots of other places. Performers traditionally play stringed instruments like the banjo, fiddle, and guitar while vocalists sing about the things that make the region special.

Don't Miss

Along Route 219 are plenty of destinations that make up the **Traditional Mountain Music Trail**. The first stop on the trail is **Davis & Elkins College**, home to summertime's Augusta Heritage Festival (🌐 *augustaartsandculture.org*) and many concerts throughout the year. Additional stops include **Big Timber Brewing Company** in Elkins, the **Purple Fiddle** in Thomas, and **Carnegie Hall** in Lewisburg. 🌐 *www.wvtourism.com/heart-of-mountain-music*

Good to Know

Some of the biggest annual events celebrating traditional mountain music include the five-day Appalachian String Band Festival in late July/early August and the West Virginia State Folk Festival in June.

Getting Here and Around

Music venues can be found all over the state, making a car pretty much necessary.

When in West Virginia

ABOLITIONIST ALE WORKS

Inspired by the abolitionists and insurrectionists who are major figures in West Virginia's history, Abolitionist Ale Works doesn't make beer like anyone else. Located in the historic community of Charles Town, West Virginia, the brewery is known for its one-of-a-kind drafts like its Notorious FIG Stout, Elderberry Saison, and Labor Haze IPA. ✉ *129 W. Washington St., Charles Town, WV* 🌐 *www.abolitionistaleworks.com*

Do This: While you're downtown, look for the green cupola that marks the Jefferson County Courthouse. It's the spot where abolitionist John Brown was tried for treason for inciting a slave rebellion in 1859. ✉ *100 E. Washington St., Charles Town, WV*

SHEPHERDSTOWN

Along the Potomac River you'll find Shepherdstown, a community that played a crucial role in our nation's history. The town was established in 1762, making it one of the oldest in West Virginia. Many of the buildings here were built before the Revolutionary War (at the Sheetz House, the family made muskets for George Washington's troops), and Civil War–era history can be found at nearly every corner (the Chapline-Shenton House was used as a hospital for Confederate soldiers during the Battle of Antietam). Union troops soon occupied the town to preserve the Baltimore and Ohio Railroad route.

Do This: Explore by bike or boat at Shepherdstown Pedal and Paddle (🌐 *www.thepedalpaddle.com*). There's no better way to travel to nearby Antietam Battlefield. The town is also said to be one of America's most haunted, and Shepherdstown Mystery Walks leads you on 90-minute walking tours that include lots of ghostly stories (🌐 *www.shepherdstownmysterywalks.com*).

THE WASHINGTON HERITAGE TRAIL

The 136-mile George Washington Heritage Trail winds through three West Virginia counties: Morgan, Berkeley, and Jefferson. There are more than 40 stops along the way—including Berkeley Springs, a colonial-era spa town our first president helped to found. 🌐 *www.washingtonheritagetrail.com*

Do This: According to historians, Washington bathed in a tublike rock formation during his teen years when he'd visit Berkeley Springs as a surveyor's assistant. You can see the spot in Berkeley Springs State Park. ✉ *2 S. Washington St., Berkeley Springs, WV* 🌐 *www.wvstateparks.com/parks/berkeley-springs-state-park*

WEST VIRGINIA CAPITOL COMPLEX

Sitting next to the Kanawha River is Charlestown's opulent West Virginia Capitol Complex, an 18-acre area that is home to the gold-domed capitol building and the stately governor's mansion. Both are open for tours and surrounded by monuments, historical markers, and the beloved West Virginia State Museum. ✉ *Kanawah Blvd. E, Charleston, WV* 🌐 *www.state.wv.us*

Do This: Mere steps from the capitol building, the dazzling West Virginia State Museum has a theatrical take on the state's history. Step through the door of a log cabin, duck your head as you enter a coal mine, and walk along a street lined with storefronts. ✉ *1900 Kanawha Blvd. E, Charleston, WV* 🌐 *wvculture.org*

WEST VIRGINIA PENITENTIARY

The Gothic-style West Virginia Penitentiary is an eerie-looking place, crowned with turrets and battlements. It held some of the state's most hardened criminals between 1876 and 1995, but now it's a destination for those who are intrigued by its reputation as one of the most haunted places in America. The

90-minute guided tours take you through a cell block nicknamed "the Alamo" that was reserved for the most dangerous prisoners. ✉ *818 Jefferson Ave., Moundsville, WV* 🌐 *www.wvpentours.com*

Do This: Three-hour-long Twilight Tours are creepy, but by far the creepiest are the six-hour "Ghost Hunts" where you roam the empty corridors on your own.

Cool Places to Stay

Ace Adventure Resort. If you want to get your adrenaline pumping, head to this resort a few miles from New River Gorge. Ziplining and white-water rafting are both available right on the property, and the 1,500 acres put plenty of other activities at your doorstep. The cabins are rustic but have tons of amenities. ✉ *1 Concho Rd., Oak Hill, WV* 🌐 *www.aceraft.com*

Blackwater Falls State Park Lodge. Dozens of fully furnished cabins are available for overnight stays within Blackwater Falls State Park. The comfortable cabins have plenty of privacy, but are close to great outdoor adventures. You can also stay in the main lodge, which has the usual creature comforts plus a pool. ✉ *1584 Blackwater Lodge Rd., Davis, WV* 🌐 *wvstateparks.com/places-to-stay/lodges/blackwater-falls-state-park-lodges*

Capon Springs and Farms. Year after year, folks head back to the gracious Capon Springs and Farms, an all-inclusive resort on 4,700 acres in the mountains of West Virginia. Rates include three meals per day and access to the resort's many amenities, including hiking trails and a fishing pond. Spring water fills the swimming pool and the soaking baths in the spa. There's a large main house and 14 other individually decorated cottages. ✉ *3818 Capon Springs Rd., High View, WV* 🌐 *www.caponsprings.net*

General Lewis Inn. Right in the town of Lewisburg is the historic General Lewis Inn dating back to 1929 but fully modernized. The boutique property with just 24 rooms and suites is also known for its ghost stories, with one of the most prominent being the "Lady in White" who is said to haunt room 208. ✉ *1236 Washington St. E, Lewisburg, WV* 🌐 *www.generallewisinn.com*

The Greenbrier. West Virginia's most famous hotel is The Greenbrier, a sprawling resort that has hosted presidents, diplomats, and celebrities of all stripes. On 11,000 acres, the luxurious lodging has more than a dozen restaurants, four golf courses, a casino, and spa. Beneath the Greenbrier is a bunker that was intended for use by Congress during the Cold War. ✉ *101 W. Main St., White Sulphur Springs, WV* 🌐 *www.greenbrier.com*

Essential Eats

Country Club Bakery. If you want to eat the unofficial signature dish of the state, then make sure you make a stop at Country Club Bakery in Fairmont. This is where the state's iconic pepperoni roll originated in 1927. It is a soft white yeast bread roll with pepperoni baked inside—it was once quite popular with area coal miners. ✉ *1211 Country Club Rd., Fairmont, WV* 🌐 *www.countryclubbakery.net*

About Our Writers

Daniel Scheffler was born in South Africa and raised all over Europe, but now lives in California and owns a vacation home in West Virginia. He believes it would be wise to let go of West Virginia prejudice, and that Lewisburg is a gem worth discovering. He is a writer, producer, and podcaster at 🌐 *www.withoutmaps.com.*

Hillbilly Hot Dogs. This restaurant occupies a converted bus and is surrounded by items that are normally found in junkyards. There are more than a dozen West Virginia–style sausages on the menu, but start off with the namesake hot dog, which comes loaded with chili sauce, mustard, and onions. If you really want to go for it, the Homewrecker comes in two unbelievable sizes—15 inches and 30 inches—and is loaded with jalapeño slices, sautéed peppers and onions, chili sauce, slaw, and shredded cheese. This is a popular spot for road-trippers, so expect a lunchtime rush, particularly on weekends. ✉ *6951 Ohio River Rd., Lesage, WV* 🌐 *www.hillbillyhotdogs.com*

1010 Bridge. For an Appalachian "new Americana" dining delight, try 1010 Bridge in Charleston, whose chef Paul Smith is the first James Beard winner from the state. It showcases the best of the region, and really highlights local culinary traditions while adding a modern and sophisticated twist. Think fried green tomatoes to start, chicken and waffles for a main, and Bananas Foster bread pudding for dessert. ✉ *1010 Bridge Rd., Charleston, WV* 🌐 *www.1010bridge.com*

Thunderbird Taco. For Tex-Mex with a West Virginia twist, this little establishment inside the Wild Bean Coffee shop works with local farms for most of their ingredients, including chicken that comes from Rainbow Farms in Sandstone, beef from Caring Acres Farms on Muddy Creek Mountain, and produce from Sprouting Farms in Pence Springs when in season. Try the black bean burritos with homemade buttermilk crema, and order a side of the housemade slaw. ✉ *1058 E. Washington St., Lewisburg, WV* 🌐 *www.thewildbrew.com*

Chapter 4

THE SOUTHEAST

4

Updated by Allyson Alford, Kayla Becker,
Chris Chamberlain, Cherith Fluker,
Taylor Killough, Stratton Lawrence,
Rachel Roberts Quartarone,
Jill Rohrbach, and Cameron Todd

WELCOME TO THE SOUTHEAST

TOP REASONS TO GO

★ **Listen to the music:** The blues, country, and jazz clubs of Memphis, New Orleans, Nashville, and the Mississippi Delta are reason enough to visit the region.

★ **Trace the civil rights movement:** From Alabama to Atlanta, see how brave African American activists fought hard to change America for the better.

★ **Hit the beaches:** The southeastern coast stretches from North Carolina's Outer Banks to the Florida Keys, and is home to some of the best beaches in the country.

★ **Explore charming cities:** The South has a unique and often complicated past that's well preserved in the historical squares, buildings, homes, and museums in cities like New Orleans, Savannah, and Charleston.

★ **Get a taste of the South:** Whether you dive into a Lowcountry boil, find the best fried chicken in Atlanta, or stop at roadside stands for casual delicacies like boiled peanuts, eating is a main activity in the South.

1 Alabama. Experience civil rights history and hip culture in Montgomery and Birmingham.

2 Arkansas. Don't miss Hot Springs, the Ozark Mountains, and Ouachita National Forest.

3 Florida. White sand beaches, theme parks, and unique wetlands make the largest state in the Southeast popular.

4 Georgia. Savannah and Atlanta paint a pretty picture of history, culture, and the arts.

5 Kentucky. Bourbon, horses, and music are draws to the Bluegrass State.

6 Louisiana. New Orleans is the star, but Cajun Country and its wetlands make it varied.

7 Mississippi. Home to the rich blues history of the Delta region, the literary grace of Oxford, and a coastline of beaches.

8 North Carolina. Go from majestic mountains to lovely beaches in a matter of hours.

9 South Carolina. Historic Charleston and the Lowcountry are big draws.

10 Tennessee. From the bright lights of Nashville to the trails of the Great Smokies, this state has it all.

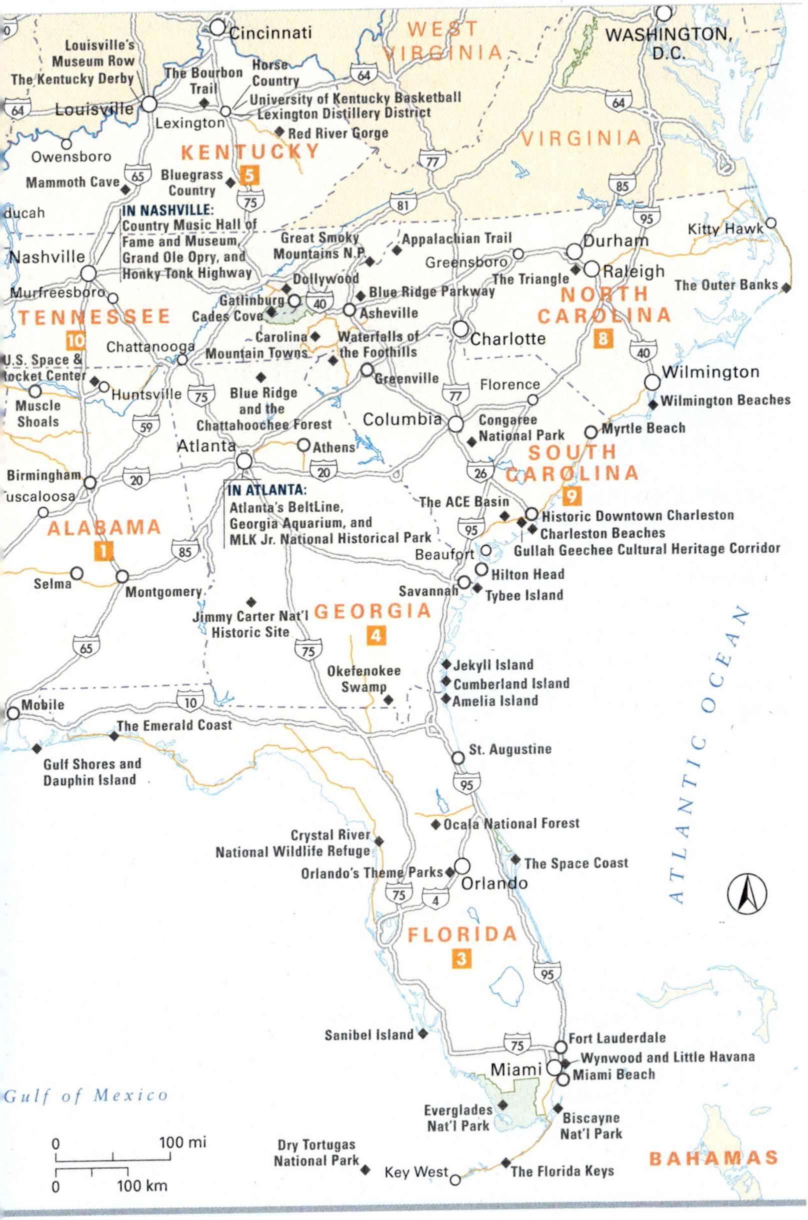
Cincinnati
WEST VIRGINIA
WASHINGTON, D.C.
Louisville's Museum Row
The Kentucky Derby
The Bourbon Trail
Horse Country
University of Kentucky Basketball
Lexington Distillery District
Louisville
Lexington
Red River Gorge
VIRGINIA
Owensboro
KENTUCKY
5
Mammoth Cave
Bluegrass Country
ducah
IN NASHVILLE:
Country Music Hall of Fame and Museum,
Grand Ole Opry, and
Honky-Tonk Highway
Great Smoky Mountains N.P.
Appalachian Trail
Durham
Kitty Hawk
Nashville
Greensboro
Raleigh
Dollywood
The Triangle
The Outer Banks
Murfreesboro
Blue Ridge Parkway
NORTH CAROLINA
Gatlinburg
TENNESSEE
Cades Cove
Asheville
10
Carolina Mountain Towns
Waterfalls of the Foothills
Charlotte
8
Chattanooga
U.S. Space & Rocket Center
Greenville
Wilmington
Huntsville
Florence
Wilmington Beaches
Muscle Shoals
Blue Ridge and the Chattahoochee Forest
Columbia
Congaree National Park
Myrtle Beach
Atlanta
Athens
SOUTH CAROLINA
Birmingham
uscaloosa
IN ATLANTA:
Atlanta's BeltLine,
Georgia Aquarium, and
MLK Jr. National Historical Park
The ACE Basin
9
Historic Downtown Charleston
Charleston Beaches
ALABAMA
1
Beaufort
Gullah Geechee Cultural Heritage Corridor
Selma
Montgomery
Hilton Head
Savannah
Tybee Island
Jimmy Carter Nat'l Historic Site
GEORGIA
4
Okefenokee Swamp
Jekyll Island
Cumberland Island
Amelia Island
Mobile
The Emerald Coast
Gulf Shores and Dauphin Island
St. Augustine
ATLANTIC OCEAN
Ocala National Forest
Crystal River National Wildlife Refuge
The Space Coast
Orlando's Theme Parks
Orlando
FLORIDA
3
Sanibel Island
Fort Lauderdale
Wynwood and Little Havana
Miami
Miami Beach
Gulf of Mexico
Everglades Nat'l Park
Biscayne Nat'l Park
0
100 mi
0
100 km
Dry Tortugas National Park
Key West
The Florida Keys
BAHAMAS
64
64
64
65
75
77
81
85
95
95
40
40
77
26
75
59
20
20
85
95
65
75
10
95
75
4
95
75

WHAT TO EAT AND DRINK

Shrimp and grits

SHRIMP AND GRITS

An iconic dish that several states claim (and compete over), shrimp is paired with flavored, usually cheesy grits, often topped with green onions and cooked with bacon. It's on menus everywhere in the Southeast—coastal Carolinas and New Orleans being hot spots. Fresh shrimp is plentiful throughout the region, with Gulf Coast and Atlantic varieties each having their own unique texture and flavor profile.

BARBECUE

You could craft an itinerary based on barbecue alone in the Southeast, where cooking styles vary from state to state. There's a whole world of sauce to explore: vinegar-based concoctions in the Carolinas, hundreds of ketchup- and mustard-based variations, plus the mayonnaise-heavy Alabama sauce and dry rubs in Memphis. Slow-cooked pulled pork is on any worthwhile menu, but chicken, brisket, and ribs are finger-licking good, too.

BOURBON

The best bourbon—sweet and strong brown liquor, barrel-aged and made from corn mash—has been produced in the American South since the 18th century. True enthusiasts should visit the distilleries of Kentucky, where 95% of the world's bourbon is made, including big names like Jim Beam, Evan Williams, and Maker's Mark.

FRIED CHICKEN

You haven't had fried chicken until you've tasted it crisped to perfection in the Southeast. You'll see it on menus everywhere, but you're missing out if you don't order it from a gas station or hole-in-the-wall counter shop at least once on your trip. Nashville hot chicken—with a spicy sauce and coating—is the dish to order in its namesake city.

CATFISH

These large, endearingly ugly bottom-feeders are abundant in all types of waterways in the Southeast. The best catfish fillets are thin, lightly fried, and stuffed into a po' boy, roll, or served on a plate with slaw and other Southern sides. Seek out fried catfish in the no-frills roadside stops of rural Mississippi and Louisiana.

LOWCOUNTRY BOIL

This celebratory dining experience abounds in the backyards and casual restaurants of the South Carolina coast, where shrimp and other fresh crustaceans, sausage, corn, and potatoes are boiled in a large pot with plenty of spices, then poured over a newspaper or checkered cloth–covered table. Louisiana's traditional crawfish boil is similar.

CUBANO

Aside from freshly caught seafood, the biggest influence on South Florida food is its Cuban population, with *ropa vieja, arroz con pollo, croquetas,* and more found in the Miami area, Tampa, and other Florida cities. The Cubano (Cuban sandwich)—pressed bread with pickles, cheese, roast pork, and a slice of ham—is a must-try.

Key lime pie

Barbecue

BRUNSWICK STEW

There's a debate over Brunswick stew's origin—Georgia, Virginia, and North Carolina all claim it—and each state's iteration has its slight differences (Kentucky's burgoo is also similar). Regardless of its origin, the stew of slow-simmered pulled pork, tomato, beans, and corn is simply delicious anywhere in the South.

PIE

You can't get more Southern than a slice of pie perfected with generations of family recipes. The delectable desserts vary from state to state, such as key lime pie, pecan pie, sweet potato pie, Kentucky Derby pie (chocolate and pecan or walnut), Mississippi mud pie (chocolate and whipped topping), and peach cobbler.

SAZERAC

One of the world's original cocktails is a source of pride in New Orleans. A proper one is made from rye whiskey, sugar, Peychaud's bitters, and an absinthe rinse; it's served chilled in a rocks glass with a lemon twist. Drink one in New Orleans's French Quarter, where it was invented by the Creole apothecary Antoine Peychaud in the 1800s.

Alabama

A blend of thought-provoking history, modern cities, and natural beauty earns Alabama the nickname "Sweet Home Alabama." Elaborate homes dot Huntsville, known for engineering the Saturn V rocket and shaping America's space legacy while Montgomery, the state capital, balances government buildings with powerful landmarks along the Civil Rights Trail. Birmingham, a hub for medical research and innovation, is home to 99 historic neighborhoods that reflect its complex and compelling past.

Capital: Montgomery

Population: 5,157,699

Area: 52,420 square miles

Statehood Date: December 14, 1819

Major Airports: Birmingham-Shuttlesworth International Airport (BHM); Huntsville International Airport (HSV)

Travel and Tourism Information: 🌐 *www.tourism.alabama.gov*

Famous Residents: Harper Lee (author); Hank Williams (musician); Charles Barkley (former NBA player and basketball analyst); Tim Cook (Apple founder); Octavia Spencer (actress)

Fun Fact: In the city of Enterprise, you will find the Boll Weevil Monument, a tribute to the little beetle that devastated cotton crops in the early 1900s. But instead of destroying the town, the boll weevil actually helped the local economy by forcing farmers to diversify their crops. It's the only monument in the country dedicated to an agricultural pest.

Montgomery

The Birthplace of the Civil Rights Movement

Few places in the United States have done a better job of laying out the stakes of the civil rights movement than Montgomery, the city where the movement was born and a place that is still reckoning with its role in the slave trade and the era of slavery that followed. The Legacy Museum and the National Memorial for Peace and Justice, the must-see attractions here, have been driving forces in Montgomery's growth as a tourist destination.

Don't Miss

The **Legacy Museum** (✉ *400 N. Court St., Montgomery, AL*) explores the Atlantic slave trade and enduring damage wrought by slavery, with exhibits focusing on lynching, racial segregation ("Jim Crow") laws, and mass incarceration. The **National Memorial for Peace and Justice** (✉ *417 Caroline St., Montgomery, AL*) documents and memorializes the thousands of lynchings that occurred since the Civil War through 1950. Each county where the Equal Justice Initiative has documented a lynching gets a steel plaque, where names and dates are recorded. Finally, the **Freedom Monument Sculpture Park** honors the resilience and contributions of Black Americans through powerful sculptures and public art. It provides a space for reflection and inspiration, making it the perfect place to round out your civil rights journey through Montgomery. 🌐 *legacysites.eji.org*

Getting Here and Around

Atlanta is 160 miles northeast of Montgomery, a 2½-hour drive via Interstate 85 south. Downtown is walkable, though it's nice to have a car or take a ride share for further exploration. The Legacy Museum and the National Memorial for Peace and Justice are three-quarters of a mile apart. A shuttle runs between them every 10 minutes.

Gulf Shores and Dauphin Island

The Land of Sunsets

Thirty-two miles of white-sand beaches lie just south of Mobile, across the bay, at Gulf Shores, where over 6,500 acres of reserves and state parks protect much of the area. It's where locals in the know kick back and relax as they watch the sun dip into the Gulf. On the shore of Mobile Bay in Fairhope and Point Clear, incredible sunsets are not-to-be-missed events, especially over fresh seafood at waterfront restaurants. At the picturesque western peninsula past Gulf Shores, tour **Fort Morgan**, the star-shape, haunted grounds of an early 1800s fort used through several wars.

Don't Miss

Dauphin Island is known as the sunset capital of the state as the Gulf beach receives more than its fair share of unobstructed, colorful evening shows. From Fort Morgan, visitors can take the car ferry to the barrier island, which is surrounded by Mobile Bay, Mississippi Sound, and Gulf waters. It has quieter beaches than Gulf Shores and great bird-watching.

Best Detour

Gulf State Park sits along Alabama's Gulf Coast between Gulf Shores and Orange Beach. It is home to the Hugh S. Branyon Backcountry Trail, a nationally recognized 28-mile system that winds through dunes, marshes, and maritime forests. In addition to its trails, Gulf State Park features white-sand beaches, freshwater lakes, a fishing pier, and eco-educational experiences. 🌐 *www.alapark.com/parks/gulf-state-park*

Getting Here and Around

Gulf Shores is 55 miles from Mobile and 34 miles from Pensacola, Florida, making it easily accessible by car. For a convenient connection across the bay, the Mobile Bay Ferry travels between Fort Morgan and Dauphin Island (a scenic 40 minutes).

Birmingham

Hip Southern City

Birmingham is widely considered Alabama's hippest city. Downtown blends the old and new, with historic buildings transformed into coworking spaces and hotels, alongside restaurants, museums, a dozen local breweries, and one of the country's most unique bars: the **House of Found Objects**. In Avondale, converted warehouses have become coffee shops, music venues, and breweries like **Cahaba Brewing Company**. There's also great food throughout Birmingham, ranging from taco trucks and barbecue to cozy cafés and fine dining. The city is home to multiple James Beard–nominated restaurants and chefs that have helped Birmingham's culinary scene earn national recognition. The city also played an essential role in the civil rights movement.

Don't Miss

The **Birmingham Civil Rights Institute** traces African Americans' struggle for equality back to the 1800s. The Movement Gallery focuses on dramatic episodes of the 1955–63 civil rights movement. Located in the Civil Rights District, the museum can be part of a larger tour including Kelly Ingram Park, where large civil rights demonstrations were staged, and the 16th Street Baptist Church, the site of the 1960s bombing that killed four young girls. ✉ *520 16th St. N, Birmingham, AL* 🌐 *www.bcri.org*

Getting Here and Around

Downtown and Avondale are within walking distance to major attractions, but it's best to have a car to explore. Fly into the Birmingham-Shuttlesworth International Airport (BHM) or drive; Montgomery is approximately 87 miles away.

U.S. Space & Rocket Center

Huntsville, America's Rocket City

In the early 1950s, the Redstone rocket was developed in Huntsville, marking the launch of America's space program. Space, technology, and defense industries remain key economic sectors here. Today, you can experience missions to the moon and beyond at the U.S. Space & Rocket Center, which has a collection of rockets, space memorabilia, and simulators that mimic rocket launches and gravity forces. Go for a guided Sea TREK in the Underwater Astronaut Trainer or act like a military jet pilot at Aviation Challenge. The center runs a bus tour of NASA labs and shuttle test sites. ✉ *1 Tranquility Base, Huntsville, AL* 🌐 *www.rocketcenter.com*

Don't Miss

Train like an astronaut at the U.S. Space & Rocket Center's Space Camp and Space Academy. There's a weeklong camp for kids, but adults and families can join the fun, too. 🌐 *www.spacecamp.com*

While You're Here

Visit the **Von Braun Astronomical Society** if you're interested in the cosmos. Clear night skies over the city's plateaus come to life during astronomy programs presented by society members and guest speakers. The facility, located on a mountain in Monte Sno State Park, includes two telescope-equipped observatories, an astronomical library, and a solar telescope. ✉ *100 Observatory Dr. SE, Huntsville, AL* 🌐 *www.vbas.org*

Getting Here and Around

Huntsville is located 100 miles north of Birmingham and approximately 100 miles southwest of Chattanooga, TN. Both cities have airports. You can also reach Huntsville from Nashville International Airport, a two-hour drive away.

Selma

Walk the Road of Civil Rights Heroes

The Selma to Montgomery March of 1965 marked a pivotal moment in U.S. history, just a few months before the passage of the federal Voting Rights Act (which was partially invalidated by a 2013 U.S. Supreme Court decision). To understand the protest, you must visit the small Alabama city, and travel its 54-mile National Historic Trail spanning from Selma to Montgomery along U.S. 80. Before you begin, tour the **Old Depot Museum's Civil Rights room** to see scrawled hospital records preserving names of the injured brought in after the bridge attack. You can also visit the **National Voting Rights Museum**, which showcases official state police photos taken on Bloody Sunday.

Don't Miss

Walking across Selma's **Edmund Pettus Bridge** to honor those who marched in support of the Voting Rights Act is a must.

Then and Now

When John Lewis and the Rev. Hosea Williams of the Southern Christian Leadership Conference led 500 marchers across the Edmund Pettus Bridge on Sunday, March 7, 1965, they were met by a crowd of police. The brutality of the attack shocked the nation. Two weeks later, when the march was finally allowed to proceed, Lewis joined Martin Luther King Jr. and other clergies, leading the way across the bridge and to Montgomery. As of January 2021, a name change for the bridge is in the works (Pettus was a Confederate general and KKK member), with many calling for the name John Lewis Bridge.

Getting Here and Around

Selma is a good day trip from Montgomery, which is 54 miles away. It's just under two hours to Birmingham from Selma.

Muscle Shoals

A Low-Key Music Capital

Real fans of rock and R&B know that Alabama has made (and continues to make) an indelible impact on American music. Called the small town with big sound, Muscle Shoals (plus neighboring Sheffield, Tuscumbia, and Florence) has drawn many major international artists to create excellent music over the decades, especially from the 1950s to the 1970s. W.C. Handy, known as the "Father of the Blues," was the first artist to come out of the region, and you can still visit the one-room cabin where he grew up. Muscle Shoals is still home to many recording studios, including **FAME**, which hosted acts like Etta James and Aretha Franklin, in addition to contemporary artists like Alicia Keys and Demi Lovato. After exploring, enjoy casual small restaurants and hip, divey bars or visit the **Alabama Music Hall of Fame**, which highlights the state's notable musicians.

Don't Miss

Muscle Shoals Sound Studios is more than just a humble building on the highway. The music studio was created in 1969, when local musicians broke off from FAME to draw big national performers like the Rolling Stones. In 2009, The Black Keys recorded the first album here in 30 years, *Brothers*. The studio and museum are now run by the Muscle Shoals Music Foundation. ✉ *3614 N. Jackson Hwy., Sheffield, AL* 🌐 *muscleshoalssoundstudio.org*

Getting Here and Around

This area along the Tennessee River is 80 miles from Huntsville and a two-hour drive to Birmingham. You will need a car or a rideshare to explore the area.

Mobile

The Original Home of Mardi Gras

Long before beads flew through the streets of New Orleans, Mobile was celebrating Mardi Gras. In fact, Mobile wears the crown as the oldest annual Carnival celebration in the United States. Dating back to 1703, Mobile's Mardi Gras is a deeply rooted tradition filled with mystic societies, colorful parades, moon pies, and masked balls. This version is more family-friendly than NOLA's but just as lively, with ornate floats, live music, and a festive spirit that takes over the historic downtown. It's a proud part of Mobile's identity, blending French, Spanish, and African influences into one unforgettable party.

Don't Miss

Tour the USS *Alabama*battleship, a World War II warship permanently docked as the main attraction at **USS Alabama Battleship Memorial Park.** This iconic vessel earned nine battle stars and is nicknamed The Mighty "A." It has been featured in films and attracts impressive crowds each year. ✉ *2703 Battleship Pkwy., Mobile, AL* 🌐 *www.ussalabama.com*

Best Museum

If you're interested in Mobile's connection to a solemn yet powerful part of American history, visit the Africatown Heritage House. There, you can experience the legacy of *Clotilda*, America's last-known slave ship. *Clotilda: The Exhibition* showcases fragments of the ship and houses stories of the 110 survivors who founded the community of Africatown. ✉ *2465 Wimbush St., Mobile, AL* 🌐 *clotilda.com*

Getting Here and Around

Mobile is located on Alabama's Gulf Coast, about 60 miles west of Pensacola, FL and 140 miles south of Montgomery. Downtown Mobile is walkable, but a car is needed to explore other areas.

When in Alabama

F. SCOTT AND ZELDA FITZGERALD HOUSE

Literary fans will be jazzed to see the world's only museum dedicated to Scott and Zelda Fitzgerald in Zelda's hometown of Montgomery, where she was born in 1900. The power couple came back to Montgomery to live for about six months from 1931 to 1932 in this house, while Scott was writing *Tender Is the Night*, and Zelda began work on her only published novel, *Save Me the Waltz.* ✉ *919 Felder Ave., Montgomery, AL* 🌐 *www.thefitzgeraldmuseum.org*

Do This: Plan an hour to explore the museum, and check out Zelda's paintings, Scott's books, and various possessions, including their clothing.

NATURAL BRIDGE

In Northern Alabama, at the intersection of U.S. 278, Route 13, and Route 5, Natural Bridge is the name of this small town and its biggest sight. You'll find few formations like this towering sandstone and rock bridge—60 feet tall, and 148 feet long—on this side of the Rocky Mountains. The area surrounding the bridge is forested and nice for a short hike or picnic. ✉ *U.S. 278 W, Natural Bridge, AL*

Do This: Combine Natural Bridge with a trip to the waterfalls of the Sipsey Wilderness, in nearby Bankhead National Forest.

NEVERSINK PIT

In Jackson County, Alabama, near Huntsville, is a rare geological wonder you never knew you needed to see—a cavernous limestone sinkhole that's more than 150 feet deep. The ambitious hike up to the pit, on a rocky uphill trail, only makes the natural wonder feel more like a magical discovery. The bottom can only be reached with professional spelunking equipment, so you'll need to do a bit of planning to get here—it's a project only dedicated bucket listers should tackle, but perhaps that's what makes it so special. 🌐 *www.saveyourcaves.org*

Do This: You'll need a (free) permit from Southeastern Caves Conservancy to hike around or enter the cave, and you will need to be outfitted with proper spelunking equipment and training.

ROLL TIDE OR WAR EAGLE

In Alabama, it's not unusual to be asked two things when you meet someone: your name and whether you're Roll Tide or War Eagle. The rivalry between the University of Alabama in Tuscaloosa and Auburn University in Auburn is more than a football feud—it's a way of life. In these college towns, football is a cultural cornerstone, and on game days, the energy is unmatched. Streets are filled with the sounds of raucous cheers and neighborhoods transform into tailgating villages. The electric atmosphere can be felt for miles, even if you never step inside the stadium.

Do this: To experience firsthand how Alabama turns game day into a full-blown celebration, plan to stop in either Tuscaloosa or Auburn on game weekend, even if you don't have a game ticket. Walk around campus, soak in the tailgating scene, and grab a bite from a local food truck. (You'll likely be offered food from tailgaters.)

TALLADEGA SUPERSPEEDWAY

Nascar's longest track, Talladega Superspeedway, is known for thrilling speeds exceeding 200 mph and some of the most exciting racing in the sport. The track hosts several major NASCAR events each year. The surrounding land is beautifully wooded, perfect for RV camping near the speedway. A short drive from the speedway leads you to Cheaha State Park and Cheaha Mountain, where rugged trails and panoramic vistas invite visitors to explore Alabama's beauty. ✉ *3366 Speedway Blvd., Lincoln, AL* 🌐 *www.talladegasuperspeedway.com*

Do This: Whether or not you're at a race, be sure to visit the adjacent International Motorsports Hall of Fame. The Hall of Fame offers a fascinating self-guided tour through three exhibit rooms featuring the history of NASCAR, its legendary drivers, and an impressive collection of race cars and memorabilia. ✉ *3198 Speedway Blvd., Lincoln, AL* 🌐 *www.motorsportshalloffame.com*

Cool Places to Stay

Elyton Hotel Birmingham. This skyscraper was built in the early 1900s. It once served as a bank and stood vacant for years before reopening as a Marriott Autograph Collection hotel in 2017. The location can't be beat as it sits at the corner of 1st Avenue, near bars, restaurants, and the Civil Rights Institute. Vaulted ceilings and expansive windows in the guest rooms highlight the original architecture and create a sophisticated atmosphere. ✉ *1928 1st Ave. N, Birmingham, AL* 🌐 *www.marriott.com*

Grand Hotel in Point Clear. Laze in the sun or get active at one of the Gulf Coast's greatest treasures, from circa 1847. The Grand's 550 acres feature contemporary suites, seven restaurants, a 20,000-square-foot European-style spa, two golf courses, and 10 tennis courts. The pool area has a water park, fountains, geysers, and waterfalls. You can rent sailboats or kayaks at the man-made beach. ✉ *1 Grand Blvd., Point Clear, AL* 🌐 *www.marriott.com*

The GunRunner Boutique Hotel. This stylish hotel is located above a former car dealership not too far from Muscle Shoals. It features 10 uniquely themed suites that celebrate local culture and history, combing Southern charm with modern conveniences. ✉ *310 E. Tennessee St., Florence, AL* 🌐 *www.gunrunnerhotel.com*

About Our Writers

Cherith Fluker was born and raised in Talladega, Alabama, and now calls Pell City home. She believes Alabama's beaches are among the most beautiful in the country and visits them as often as she can. Author of *Secret Birmingham*, Cherith is passionate about uncovering hidden stories and sharing them to inspire others to explore, reflect, and embrace the joy of travel, especially in her home state.

Seven Springs Lodge and Rattlesnake Saloon. Come to the foothills of Northern Alabama to sleep in a silo, ride horses, and dine and drink in a cave. Aside from the pretty scenery and miles of hiking and riding trails, the epic Rattlesnake Saloon, sheltered directly beneath a dramatic bluff on the property, is the main draw here. Built right into the rock, and often welcoming live music, this is a kitschy (and historic) good time. ✉ *1292 Mt. Mills Rd., Tuscumbia, AL* 🌐 *www.rattlesnakesaloon.net/lodge*

Essential Eats

The Bright Star. Established in 1907 in Bessemer, the Bright Star is Alabama's oldest restaurant and a classic example of Southern hospitality and cuisine. It serves a blend of Greek and Southern dishes, including their famous snapper throats and delicious Greek-style beef tenderloin, in a charming historic setting. ✉ *304 Alabama Ave., Bessemer, AL* 🌐 *www.thebrightstar.com*

Chez Fonfon. Located in Birmingham's historic Five Points South neighborhood, Chez Fonfon is beloved for its authentic French cuisine and lively atmosphere. This charming bistro opened in 2000 by James Beard Award–winning chef Frank Stitt and his wife, Pardis. It offers a cozy, casually upscale atmosphere reminiscent of a Parisian neighborhood café. ✉ *2007 11th Ave. S, Birmingham, AL* 🌐 *www.chezfonfon.com*

Chris' Hot Dogs. A Montgomery institution since 1917, Chris' Hot Dogs serves classic, no-frills hot dogs piled high with chili, onions, mustard, and slaw. It's a true taste of South Alabama history, and the kind of place where generations gather for a quick, satisfying meal that's pure comfort food. ✉ *138 Dexter Ave., Montgomery, AL* 🌐 *www.chrishotdogs.com*

Dreamland BBQ. Known statewide for its legendary ribs, Dreamland BBQ is a must-visit for anyone craving authentic Southern barbecue. The ribs are smoky, tender, and slathered in their signature tangy red sauce. The atmosphere is casual and welcoming, perfect for families and groups. ✉ *12 4th Ave. NW, Tuscaloosa, AL* 🌐 *www.dreamlandbbq.com*

Top O' the River. A family-owned chain that started in Anniston in 1982, Top O' the River is a North Alabama favorite known for its fried catfish and Southern soul food classics. The Gadsden location's catfish and greens were even named one of Alabama's "100 Dishes to Eat" by the Alabama Tourism Department. With fresh seafood delivered twice weekly, hearty portions, and down-home hospitality, it's a must-visit for those craving authentic regional flavors. ✉ *2701 S. 3rd St., Gadsden, AL* 🌐 *www.topotheriverrestaurant.com*

Arkansas

The Natural State rolls out a welcome mat of lush terrain. The Ozark and Ouachita mountain ranges cradle the northern and western regions, draping 10 scenic byways in a tapestry of brilliant fall colors. Seven national park sites, 2.5 million acres of national forests, hundreds of miles of hiking and mountain biking trails, and 52 state parks preserve and interpret the state's diverse heritage, traditions, and natural resources.

Capital: Little Rock

Population: 3,088,354

Area: 53,179 square miles

Statehood Date: June 15, 1836

Major Airports: Bill and Hillary Clinton National Airport (LIT); Northwest Arkansas National Airport (XNA)

Travel and Tourism Information: *www.arkansas.com*

Famous Residents: Bass Reeves (Old West lawman); Daisy Bates (civil rights leader); Johnny Cash (singer); Sam Walton (Walmart founder); Bill Clinton (president); Mary Steenburgen (actress)

Fun Fact: Arkansas proudly claims to be the birthplace of cheese dip, thanks to Blackie Donnelly's creation in 1935 at Mexico Chiquito, a restaurant originally in Hot Springs. This creamy, spicy dip quickly captured the hearts and taste buds of Arkansans, sparking a statewide obsession that eventually created a good-natured rivalry with Texas over cheese dip versus queso, culminating in a blind taste test held at the U.S. Capitol and judged by senators from both states. Arkansas emerged victorious, solidifying cheese dip's status as more than just a favorite food.

Hot Springs National Park

America's Most Historic Hot Springs

You haven't really lived life to the fullest until you've soaked in thermal waters of Hot Springs, melting your muscle aches away with soothing heat. The water here has been reputed to have medicinal properties for thousands of years, when Indigenous peoples came to the springs. Congress created what is now Hot Springs National Park in 1832, setting aside land for the first time as a recreation area. Nine historic bathhouses dating from the early 20th century recall the days when high-society types—and, during Prohibition, gangsters and other shady figures—strolled down these streets. ✉ *369 Central Ave., Hot Springs, AR* 🌐 *www.nps.gov/hosp*

Don't Miss

There are two places in the park where you can watch the water bubbling out of the rock. (You can even reach out and touch it—it comes out of the ground at a steamy 147°F but quickly cools.) The **Display Spring** behind the Maurice Bathhouse flows into a shallow pool, a great place to relax and listen to the trickling water. **Hot Water Cascade**, at Arlington Lawn, is the largest visible spring in the park. It flows right beneath the Grand Promenade.

Places to Soak

There aren't any places to soak within the national park, but there are two bathhouses in town that pipe in thermal springs water: the stately **Buckstaff Bathhouse** (✉ *509 Central Ave., Hot Springs, AR* 🌐 *www.buckstaffbaths.com*) and the domed **Quapaw Bathhouse** (✉ *413 Central Ave., Hot Springs, AR* 🌐 *www.quapawbaths.com*).

Getting Here and Around

Hot Springs is an hour's drive southwest of Little Rock, Arkansas.

Little Rock

A City with Layers of History and Miles of Trails

True to Arkansas style, Little Rock blends urban energy with easy access to the outdoors. The Arkansas River Trail loops through the city, linking 15-plus miles of biking and walking paths with downtown attractions, historic neighborhoods, parks, and landmarks. Iconic sites include the **Big Dam Bridge**, the longest pedestrian and bike bridge in North America, and the **ESSE Purse Museum**, one of only two museums in the world focusing on handbags. The **Clinton Presidential Library**, the **River Market District**, the **Historic Arkansas Museum**, and the **Old State House** sit just minutes apart for easy exploration. Or head just west of town to gorgeous **Pinnacle Mountain State Park**.

Don't Miss

A pivotal site in American civil rights history, **Little Rock Central High School National Historic Site** brings the events of the 1957 desegregation crisis into sharp, human focus. The immersive visitor center and option for keen ranger-led tours make it a deep, historic experience. ✉ *2120 W. Daisy L Gatson Bates Dr., Little Rock, AR* 🌐 *www.nps.gov/chsc*

Best Neighborhoods

SoMa (South Main) stands out for its eclectic charm, trendy boutiques, bakeries, and lively galleries. **The Heights**, atop scenic bluffs, features tree-lined avenues, boutiques, upscale restaurants, and cafés along bustling Kavanaugh Boulevard. **Hillcrest** exudes a vibrant spirit with a variety of local shops, vintage stores, and eateries.

Getting Here and Around

Fly into Bill and Hillary Clinton National Airport (LIT), just minutes from downtown. You can hop on a vintage-style streetcar that runs through downtown and the River Market District.

The Ozark Mountain Region

The Country's First Designated National River

Outdoor enthusiasts flock to the Ozark Mountain region, which covers much of northern Arkansas, for its river and lake adventures, hiking and biking trails, and quaint mountain towns filled with the sounds of folk music. There are several areas to base yourself to experience the spectacular region, including the **Buffalo National River**, **Norfork Lake**, the **White River**, and **Bull Shoals Lake**. The country's first designated national river, Buffalo National River runs for 135 miles through these parts, passing majestic waterfalls and sheer limestone bluffs before it flows into the White River near Buffalo City. A canoe trip down the river, perhaps within sight of a tremendous herd of elk, is one of the best ways to experience the Ozark Mountains.

Don't Miss

Experience the scenic Buffalo National River with the help of NPS-authorized concessionaires, like **Buffalo River Outfitters**, who rent equipment for one or multiday kayaking, canoeing, and rafting trips. 🌐 *www.buffaloriver-outfitters.com*

Best Detour

About an hour northwest of the Buffalo National River is one of the most visited attractions in the Ozarks: the **Christ of the Ozarks**. Even nonbelievers will appreciate the sheer size of the seven-story statue, which vaguely resembles the similarly shaped Christ the Redeemer statue that rises above Rio de Janeiro, Brazil. ✉ *935 Passion Play Rd., Eureka Springs, AR* 🌐 *www.christoftheozarks.org*

Getting Here and Around

The Ozark Mountain Region of Arkansas covers much of the northwest part of the state north of Interstate 40. You'll need a car to reach it.

Crystal Bridges Museum of American Art

Where Art Meets Nature

An excellent collection of art anchors Crystal Bridges Museum of American Art, but the stunning architecture set within 134 acres of Ozark landscape frames the experience with equal impact. Spanning from the colonial era to today, the art collection illuminates the story of America's people, places, and its place in the world. New acquisitions, rotating works from the vault, and traveling exhibitions mean the art is always changing, just like the surrounding display gardens and arboretum, which shift with the seasons. ✉ *600 Museum Way, Bentonville, AR* 🌐 *www.crystalbridges.org*

Don't Miss

The museum houses iconic masterpieces such as Asher B. Durand's *Kindred Spirits*, Norman Rockwell's *Rosie the Rivete r*, Yayoi Kusama's *Infinity Mirrored Room*, and Frank Lloyd Wright's Bachman-Wilson House, moved from New Jersey and reconstructed on the museum grounds.

Best Activity

Several miles of hard-surface and soft-surface trails run through the museum campus, leading walkers and bikers past woodlands, natural springs, streams, quartz-covered boulders, and sculptures, all meant to connect visitors to the land and outdoor artworks. Connector trails lead to more than 140 miles of world-class mountain biking and downtown **Bentonville's** thriving restaurant, music, brewery, and art scene.

Getting Here and Around

The museum is 15 miles from Northwest Arkansas National Airport (XNA). Metropolitan areas such as Tulsa, Little Rock, Kansas City, St. Louis, Memphis, and Dallas are within a half-day's drive. Parking and shuttle service to the museum's main entrance are free.

Mount Magazine State Park

Arkansas's Highest Point

Rock climbing doesn't get much better in the Natural State than at Mount Magazine, home to Arkansas's highest point at 2,753 feet. The mountain's south bluff has a 1,500-foot-wide section with more than 100 routes reaching up to 80 feet high, a perfect playground for sport climbing and rappelling. Extreme-sports enthusiasts also love the chance to hang glide, ride ATVs, mountain bike, and hike on the rugged trails. All activities provide enchanting views of Petit Jean River Valley and Blue Mountain Lake. On a clear day, you can see about one-fourth of the state from the peak. ✉ *16878 Rte. 309, Paris, AR* 🌐 *www.arkansasstateparks.com/parks/mount-magazine-state-park*

Don't Miss

Snap a photo next to the signpost at **Signal Hill**, which marks the state's highest point. Or, take an epic hike to spot **Mount Magazine Falls**, a waterfall on the difficult North Rim Trail.

By Car

If you prefer driving through the park instead of hiking, you can still access fantastic views. Take the **Cameron Bluff Overlook Drive** and park along the route to see dramatic valleys and ridges and the Petit Jean River.

Where to Stay

There are about 18 campsites within the state park, but for a more comfortable experience, stay at the **Lodge at Mount Magazine** or one of the park cabins.

Getting Here and Around

Mount Magazine State Park is 16 miles south of Paris, Arkansas, on Scenic Highway 309. It's about a two-hour drive from Little Rock via Interstate 40 East or Route 10 East. The visitor center is open year-round from 8 am to 5 pm.

Ouachita National Recreation Trail

The State's Best Back-Country Hiking Challenge

The oldest national forest in the southern United States, Ouachita National Forest covers 1.8 million acres in central Arkansas and southeastern Oklahoma, and it has some serious treks. The best way to experience this swath of wilderness is the **Ouachita National Recreation Trail**, which runs for 223 miles across the national forest from near Talihina, Oklahoma to Pinnacle Mountain State Park in Little Rock. The unpaved trail is a popular byway for mountain bikers, hikers, and backpackers. There are huge elevation changes—from 300 to 2,600 feet—as the trail passes through forested mountains, across sweeping valleys, and near crystal clear streams. Parts of the trail are definitely challenging, even for experts, but there's no need to hike the entire distance. Numerous access points provide opportunities for hikers of all skill levels. 🌐 *www.ouachitamaps.com/ot.html*

Don't Miss

Take a short side trail to **Flatside Pinnacle** for 360-degree views of the Ouachita Mountain range. Day hikers and thru-hikers consider the scenic vista to be a highlight of their overall experience.

Good to Know

Water is hard to find on much of Ouachita National Recreation Trail, especially during dry periods, so bring plenty with you.

Getting Here and Around

Start at the eastern trailhead at the Pinnacle Mountain State Park Visitor Center, just west of downtown Little Rock on Highway 10. ✉ *9600 Rte. 300, Roland, AR* 🌐 *www.arkansasstateparks.com/parks/pinnacle-mountain-state-park*

Garvan Woodland Gardens

Arkansas's Best Gardens

Covering 210 acres in the Ouachita Mountains of southwest Arkansas and with nearly 5 miles of wooded shoreline along Lake Hamilton, Garvan Woodland Gardens sees a stunning profusion of color in the spring, when 160 different types of azaleas line the trails. Dozens of species of native plants are on display from spring to fall at the Perry Wildflower Overlook, where a flagstone terrace has views of the lake and Mt. Riante beyond. The gardens also feature some surreal architecture that brings the outdoors inside, including a "floating" tree house and a light-filled timber-and-glass chapel that have captured many an Instagrammer's eye. ✉ *550 Arkridge Rd., Hot Springs, AR* 🌐 *www.garvangardens.org*

Don't Miss

Get your cameras out for **Bob and Sunny Evans Tree House**, a showstopping spectacle of angles that brings you level with the forest canopy of the garden.

Good to Know

The **Evans Children's Adventure Garden** has 1½ acres of interactive activities with a waterfall and cave, an iron bridge that resembles woven tree branches, and rocks weighing more than 3,200 tons.

When to Go

Spring is obviously the best time for blooms, but winter has the annual Holiday Light display featuring 5 million twinkling lights.

Getting Here and Around

Garvan Woodland Gardens is located just south of Hot Springs, Arkansas, about an hour from Little Rock.

When in Arkansas

CRATER OF DIAMONDS STATE PARK

Park visitors have uncovered—and taken home—more than 35,000 diamonds since the Crater of Diamonds became a state park in 1972. It's one of the only places on earth where the public can search for real diamonds and keep what they find, so people from all over the world make the trek to Murfreesboro, Arkansas. Visitors can bring their own mining tools or rent them from the park to search the 37-acre volcanic crater for a variety of rocks, minerals, and gemstones. Notable diamonds found at the crater include the 40-carat Uncle Sam (the largest diamond ever unearthed in the United States), the 16-carat Amarillo Starlight, the 15-carat Star of Arkansas, and the nearly 9-carat Esperanza. ✉ *209 State Park Rd., Murfreesboro, AR* 🌐 *www.arkansasstateparks.com/parks/crater-diamonds-state-park*

Do This: Before heading out to the crater, spend some time in the visitor center to learn about diamonds and why so many of them are found on this site. You can also view a selection of real, uncut diamonds.

FAYETTEVILLE

This city in Northwest Arkansas is the home of the Razorbacks (aka the University of Arkansas), so the college town is full of youthful energy. Thanks to its location on the outskirts of the Boston Mountains, it's also a popular spot for hikers, mountain bikers, and cyclists. While you're here, check out the Clinton House Museum, where Bill and Hillary Clinton made their first home.

Do This: Beer lovers, this one is for you. The Fayetteville Ale Trail, Arkansas's first craft beer tasting experience, features more than 20 local breweries. The trail is self-guided, so you can go at your own pace and take the time to sample all the beer you want. Breweries on the trail include Crisis Brewing Company, Fossil Cove Brewing Company, Goat Lab Brewery, Ozark Beer Company, and more. Pick up a passport at participating locations and collect stamps at each brewery location. 🌐 *www.fayettevillealetrail.com*

GANGSTER MUSEUM OF AMERICA

This popular museum gives an entertaining account of how some of the country's most notorious criminals vacationed in the quaint small town of Hot Springs in the mountains of central Arkansas. It takes you back to the early 20th century when mineral water from the nearby thermal springs was not the only elixir that attracted visitors from all over the world. It was also a bootlegger's paradise during Prohibition, so the alcohol flowed freely, at least behind closed doors. ✉ *510 Central Ave., Hot Springs, AR* 🌐 *www.thegangstermuseum.com*

Do This: There are a couple of exhibits here you shouldn't miss. The Casino Gallery, the museum's most popular attraction, explains how the small town of Hot Springs ran the largest illegal gambling operation in the country between 1927 and 1967. The illegal activity here even extended to the country's favorite pastime; the Baseball Gallery documents the game's longtime connection to organized crime.

PRESIDENT WILLIAM JEFFERSON CLINTON'S BIRTHPLACE HOME

President Bill Clinton often talked about "believing in a place called Hope." He was referring to the Arkansas town where he lived for the first four years of his life with his mother and maternal grandparents. His childhood home is now maintained by the National Park Service. ✉ *117 S. Hervey St., Hope, AR* 🌐 *www.nps.gov/wicl*

Do This: Make sure to explore the second floor of the 1917 American Foursquare house, where the flooring and the beadboard in the hallway and nursery are among the original touches. Clinton's bedroom includes a desk and twin bed with a Hopalong Cassidy bedspread from that era.

Cool Places to Stay

Beckham Creek Cave Lodge. No caveman ever had it this good. This luxury escape is in a natural cavern that overlooks a valley in the Ozark Mountains. It has four bedrooms, four bathrooms, a large living room with a waterfall, and a firepit. The upper floor has a round bed surrounded by hanging stalactites. ✉ *Beckham Creek Cave, Parthenon, AR* 🌐 *www.beckham-cave.com*

1886 Crescent Hotel & Spa. Famous for being one of the most haunted hotels in the country, this historic hotel has nightly ghost tours guaranteed to give you goose bumps. Don't let that scare you off if you love Victorian elegance and being pampered in a spa. The Crescent also has a resort feel with its Frisco Sporting Club, an outdoor space with yard games, hatchet throwing, a pool, and live music. Daily programming ranges from yoga and hiking tours to craft beer and wine tastings. ✉ *75 Prospect Ave., Eureka Springs, AR* 🌐 *www.crescent-hotel.com*

The Empress of Little Rock. Immerse yourself in the Gilded Age opulence of this stunning gothic Queen Anne–style mansion that's now a grand inn. It's on the National Register of Historic Places and boasts unique architectural features such as octagonal-shape rooms. A block from Main Street, the Empress is a majestic stay with convenient city access. ✉ *2120 Louisiana St., Little Rock, AR* 🌐 *www.theempress.com*

Favorite Places

Jill Rohrbach is an Arkansas native who has called the college town of Fayetteville home for more than 30 years (go Hogs!). She believes the perfect Arkansas hike is Lost Valley Trail near the Buffalo National River, where the path winds along a stream through the Ozark forest to the mouth of a dark cave worth crawling through to reach the waterfall inside. She writes for Arkansas Tourism and freelances for regional and national media.

Planetarium Treehouse. Perched above Beaver Lake, this epic escape not only provides scenic lake views but also amazing stargazing. Its highlight is the observatory tower featuring a transparent dome ceiling, high-powered telescopes for stargazing, and atmospheric LED lighting. The main living area sits under a soaring geodesic dome, a hexagonal loft window, and a dazzling ceiling star projector for at-home celestial shows. Outdoors, there's a spacious deck and upper balcony. ✉ *22457 E. War Eagle Rd., Springdale, AR* 🌐 *www.mysticozark-adventures.com*

Turpentine Creek Wildlife Refuge. This wildlife refuge is a sanctuary for nearly 100 animals, including tigers, lions, leopards, cougars, bobcats, bears, ligers, servals, a coatimundi, and a macaw. Enjoy the roars and chuffing of the lions from the Zulu Safari lodging, tree house, and glamping tents. ✉ *239 Turpentine Creek La., Eureka Springs, AR* 🌐 *www.turpentinecreek.org*

Essential Eats

Hugo's. The basement location, juicy burgers, and heaping baskets of homemade French fries have made Hugo's a favorite eatery in Fayetteville since 1977. The beer cheese soup, grasshopper crepes, and Derek's Special chicken sandwich also keep folks coming back for more. You'll enjoy the fully stocked bar, neon signage, and historical decor lining the walls. ✉ *25½ N. Block Ave., Fayetteville, AR* 🌐 *www.hugosfayetteville.com*

Jones Bar-B-Q Diner. There are numerous reasons to eat at this iconic and nationally known eatery in Marianna: it's Arkansas's first recipient of a James Beard Award; it's thought to be the oldest continuously operating restaurant in Arkansas; and it's the oldest continuously operating restaurant in the South owned by a Black family. The menu is chopped pork (by the pound or in a sandwich) with a sweet and tangy vinegar-based sauce served with or without mustard-based slaw on white bread. Get there early or you might be disappointed. They close when the meat runs out, which can be as early as 11 am. ✉ *219 W. Louisiana St., Marianna, AR* 🌐 *www.facebook.com/jonesbarbqdiner*

Onyx Coffee Lab. Using solar energy from its roof, this spot roasts and ships coffee every weekday and is frequently named to Best Of lists for coffee shops and baristas. They also serve pastries, breakfast sandwiches, and other light fare in several locations. Their headquarters in Rogers is as beautiful and refined as their coffee. ✉ *101 E. Walnut Ave., Rogers, AR* 🌐 *www.onyxcoffeelab.com*

Taylor's Steakhouse. What started out as a Taylor's Grocery in 1954 has morphed into a renowned family-run steak house that regularly draws people from beyond Arkansas's borders. It's not only the flavor of the steaks, but also their size: 25–28 ounces for Kansas bone-in rib eyes and T-bone steaks, and an even larger porterhouse steak for two. Other favorites are the crawfish enchilada plate and the bread pudding. ✉ *14201 Rte. 54, Dumas, AR* 🌐 *www.taylorssteakhouse-dumas.com*

Florida

Talk about a vacation powerhouse. From Miami's world-famous beach to family-friendly theme parks to the quiet expanse of the Everglades, the Sunshine State has more than its fair share of bucket list–worthy stops. Whether you visit the powdery white beaches of the Northwest or the vibrant coral reefs of the Florida Keys, the ocean is always calling—for sailing, fishing, diving, swimming, and other water sports. Stray off the path a few miles, and you might glimpse a bit of the Florida of old, including cigar makers and mermaids.

Capital: Tallahassee

Population: 23,372,215

Area: 65,758 square miles

Statehood Date: March 3, 1845

Major Airports: Fort Lauderdale–Hollywood International Airport (FLL); Jacksonville International Airport (JAX); Miami International Airport (MIA); Orlando International Airport (MCO); Tampa International Airport (TPA)

Travel and Tourism Information: 🌐 *www.visitflorida.com* 🌐 *www.visitflorida.org*

Famous Residents: Zora Neale Hurston (writer); Ernest Hemingway (writer); Maya Rudolph (actress and comedian); Pitbull (rapper); Ariana Grande (singer)

Fun Fact: Florida is the only place in the world where alligators and crocodiles coexist.

Orlando's Theme Parks

Where Magic Happens

Walt Disney World (✉ *1180 Seven Seas Dr., Lake Buena Vista, FL* 🌐 *www.disneyworld.disney.go.com*) and **Universal Studios** (✉ *6000 Universal Blvd., Orlando, FL* 🌐 *www.universalorlando.com*) are both bucket list destinations in their own right. The beloved characters of Magic Kingdom, the countries of EPCOT, the out-of-this-world*Star Wars* adventures at Hollywood Studios, and the live animals of Animal Kingdom make Disney World a favorite. Universal Studios and Islands of Adventure have loud, fast, high-energy attractions, including the incredible Wizarding World of Harry Potter where muggles can explore a full-scale version of Diagon Alley before boarding a magical train at Platform 9¾.

Don't Miss

A magical evening in Orlando should include Butterbeer at the Leaky Cauldron in Universal Studios or fireworks at the Magic Kingdom after dinner in Cinderella's Castle.

Best Ride

Space Mountain is one of the world's most imaginative roller coasters, taking you on a trip into the depths of outer space—in the dark.

When to Go

Visit in the fall for the EPCOT Food and Wine Festival.

Getting Here and Around

Orlando International Airport is about a 20-minute drive to Universal Studios and a 25-minute drive to Magic Kingdom. The parks themselves are about 10 miles apart, but it's best to have two to three days to explore each park.

Miami Beach

Party in the Magic City

The hub of Miami Beach is South Beach and its energetic Ocean Drive, lined with neon-lit hotel lounges and sidewalk cafés, bronzed cyclists zooming past palm trees, and visitors flocking to see the action. Daylight should be spent on the beach itself, whether Jet Skiing, snapping a picture with the colorful lifeguard towers, or lounging at renowned resorts like Soho Beach House. At dusk, Miami Beach is a hotbed of nightlife with bars and lounges.

Don't Miss

Drag brunch at **the Palace** (✉ *1052 Ocean Dr., Miami Beach, FL* 🌐 *palacesouthbeach.com*) is a great way to embrace the glitz of Ocean Drive. If you're looking for a quieter spot, head inland to **Sweet Liberty** (✉ *237 20th St., Miami Beach, FL* 🌐 *www.mysweetliberty.com*).

Best Tour

Take an **Art Deco Tour** to spot the beach's iconic pastel 1930s–50s architecture, the biggest collection in the world. Be sure to snap a pic of the iconic **Breakwater** or the **Colony Hotel** on Ocean Drive. 🌐 *www.mdpl.org/tours*

Best Nightlife

There's nightlife for every mood and budget in Miami Beach, whether you want to sip craft cocktails by a pool lined in twinkle lights (**Broken Shaker**) or party till dawn at a packed club **(LIV).**

Getting Here and Around

Cross over Biscayne Bay via Interstates 395 or 195 to get to Miami Beach from mainland Miami (which is technically a separate city), about a 25-minute drive from Miami International Airport (MIA).

Everglades National Park

One of the Most Unique Ecosystems in America

More than 1½ million acres of South Florida's subtropical, watery wilderness were given national park status and protection in 1947, making it one of the country's largest national parks. A visit means a chance to see Florida's unique ecology up close, including sawgrass marshes, hardwood hammocks, and mangroves, in addition to wildlife like alligators and herons. The park is also recognized by the world community as a Wetland of International Importance, an International Biosphere Reserve, and a World Heritage site. ✉ *40001 Rte. 9336, Homestead, FL* 🌐 *www.nps.gov/ever*

Don't Miss

To spot swamp wildlife, walk the self-guided **Anhinga Trail** or take a ranger-led tram tour to **Shark Valley**.

Best Tour

Coopertown is the oldest airboat operator in the Everglades and one of the only allowed in national park boundaries. Operating since 1945, the business offers 35- to 40-minute tours. 🌐 *www.coopertownairboats.com*

When to Go

Winter is the best, and busiest, time to visit the Everglades. Temperatures and mosquito activity are more tolerable, while low water levels let you see the resident wildlife more easily and migratory birds settle in for the season.

Getting Here and Around

Miami International Airport (MIA) is 34 miles from Homestead and 47 miles from the eastern access to Everglades National Park. Southwest Florida International Airport (RSW), in Fort Myers, a little over an hour's drive from Everglades City, is the closest major airport to the Everglades' western entrance.

The Florida Keys

The Perfect Laid-Back Vacation Destination

The southernmost string of islands in the contiguous United States, where "no shoes, no shirt, no problem" is a way of life, the Keys are like no other place in America. Take an epic road trip from the tippity top (**Key Largo**) to the tippity bottom (**Key West**) along Florida Keys Scenic Highway and appreciate the Keys' overflowing bursts of bougainvillea, shimmering waters, and mangrove-lined islands. Whether you snorkel at **John Pennekamp Coral Reef State Park** in Key Largo or bar crawl in Key West, you're in for major R&R.

Don't Miss

Key West is the most popular of the Keys. Snap a selfie at the "Southernmost Point of the Continental U.S." buoy before catching the sunset on Mallory Square.

Best Tour

Amusing anecdotes spice up the guided tours of **Ernest Hemingway's home**. While living here between 1931 and 1942, the author wrote about 70% of his life's work, including classics like *For Whom the Bell Tolls*. ✉ *907 Whitehead St., Key West, FL* 🌐 *www.hemingwayhome.com*

Good to Know

The Keys provide plenty of boating and snorkeling opportunities, but there are few beaches. The exception is **Bahia Honda State Park** in Big Pine Key, which has three superb beaches.

Getting Here and Around

Head south out of Miami towards Highway 1, the only road to the Keys and one that's prone to standstill traffic. It's 60 miles to Key Largo from Miami's airport.

St. Augustine

America's Oldest City

Along the banks of the shining Matanzas River in the northeastern corner of Florida lies St. Augustine, the nation's oldest city. (Spanish explorers established it in 1565, long before the earliest English colony, Jamestown, in 1607.) The supposed site of the fabled Fountain of Youth, it shows its age with charm, its history revealed in the narrow cobblestone streets, the horse-drawn carriages festooned with flowers, and the coquina bastions of the Spanish fort that guard the bay like sentinels. Travelers find additional treasures in the Historic District, where terra-cotta roofs and narrow balconies overhang a wonderful hodgepodge of shops and eateries that can be happily explored for weeks before venturing to the idyllic beaches of Anastasia State Park.

Don't Miss

Castillo de San Marco is the focal point of St. Augustine. This massive and commanding fort was completed by the Spanish in 1695, and it looks every day of its three-plus centuries. ✉ *11 S. Castillo Dr., St. Augustine, FL* 🌐 *www.nps.gov/casa*

While You're Here

Saint Augustine Distillery is easily the best spirit maker in Florida, and a fun, popular place to take a tour—and get a taste of Florida-made bourbon and cane vodka. ✉ *112 Riberia St., St. Augustine, FL* 🌐 *www.staugustinedistillery.com*

Getting Here and Around

Jacksonville International Airport (JAX) is the region's air hub (55 miles north of St. Augustine).

Miami's Little Havana

The Heart of Cuban Culture

First settled en masse by Cubans in the early 1960s after Cuba's Communist revolution, Little Havana is the core of Miami's Hispanic community. Lined with cigar factories, cafés selling guava pastries and rose-petal flan, botanicas brimming with candles, and Cuban clothes and crafts stores, the area's sights and sounds transport you to Old Havana, an authentic slice of the vibrant culture in the United States. Giant hand-painted roosters span the neighborhood, an artistic nod to real-life counterparts that roam the streets.

Don't Miss

Your "Welcome to Little Havana" photo op shines on 27th Avenue and 8th Street. Afterward, watch a slice of Old Havana unfold in **Domino Park**, where the community gathers to play.

Best Nightlife

Salsa dance with a Cuba libre in hand at **Ball & Chain**, a legendary bar circa 1935 that nods to Old Havana (✉ *1513 S.W. 8th St., Miami, FL* 🌐 *ballandchainmiami.com*). Afterward, order ice cream next door at **Azucar Ice Cream Company** (✉ *1503 S.W. 8th St., Miami, FL* 🌐 *www.azucaricecream.com*), known for its guava-flavored Abuela Maria.

Good to Know

If you come to Little Havana expecting the Latino version of New Orleans's French Quarter, you're apt to be disappointed—it's not about the architecture here, but rather the atmosphere.

Getting Here and Around

Located in mainland Miami, Little Havana's semiofficial boundaries are 27th Avenue to 4th Avenue on the west, Miami River to the north, and Southwest 13th Street to the south. You'll need to drive (or Uber/Lyft) into Little Havana, since public transportation here is limited, but once on the main drag, Calle Ocho, it's best to explore on foot.

The Space Coast

NASA's Launch Site

America's space program—past, present, and future—is the star of a visit to Florida's Space Coast that extends from Titusville to Melbourne. The region is humming and rockets are once again flying, thanks to a revitalization of the nation's space program by companies such as SpaceX and Blue Origin. **Cape Canaveral** is where the rockets launch, and in Titusville, you can see the space shuttle *Atlantis* up close. The **Kennedy Space Center Visitor Complex** is a must-see for anyone interested in America's space program, and **Merritt Island National Wildlife Refuge** has arguably Florida's best bird-watching. The area is also home to a popular cruise ship port, **Port Canaveral**, and the laid-back town of **Cocoa Beach**, where surfing champion Kelly Slater caught his first wave.

Don't Miss

Within Canaveral National Seashore, **Playalinda Beach**—the longest stretch of undeveloped coast on Florida's Atlantic seaboard—provides one of the best views for rocket launches.

Best Activity

No trip to Florida would be complete without a visit to the Kennedy Space Center's Space Shuttle *Atlantis* exhibit, where a full day can be spent experiencing the life and history of the American space shuttle program. ✉ *Space Commerce Way, Merritt Island, FL* 🌐 *www.kennedyspacecenter.com*

Getting Here and Around

The region's location just 50 miles east of Orlando makes it a popular destination for side trips from Walt Disney World.

Crystal River National Wildlife Refuge

The Manatee Capital of the World

Situated along Florida's peaceful Nature Coast, Crystal River National Wildlife Refuge is a sanctuary for the manatee, and its natural-spring area is a low-key getaway spot in one of the most pristine and beautiful areas in the state. It's also one of the few places on the planet where you can legally swim with manatees (while abiding by the manatee sanctuary's strict interaction guidelines). Kings Bay, around which hundreds of manatees congregate in winter, feeds crystal clear water into the river at 72°F year-round. ✉ *1502 S.E. Kings Bay Dr., Crystal River, FL* 🌐 *www.fws.gov/refuge/crystal_river*

Don't Miss

Book a tour at Crystal River National Wildlife Preserve from November to March for the best chance to see manatees. Several companies, such as **River Ventures**, offer swimming tours. Or, book a 2½-hour tour in a crystal clear, glasslike kayak. 🌐 *www.riverventures.com*

Good to Know

Sometimes called "sea cows," manatees are aquatic relatives of elephants. They can weigh more than 1,500 pounds and live 50-plus years but move very slowly, making them subject to frequent boat accidents. While they were once endangered, there are now more than 6,000 in Florida's coastal waters. Do your part to ensure their safety by respecting them. Never touch or chase a manatee, and abide by all interaction rules.

Getting Here and Around

The closest and biggest airport near Crystal River is Tampa International Airport (75 miles).

Biscayne National Park

The USA's Largest Underwater National Park

Much of Biscayne National Park's treasures lie below the surface—95%, in fact. The water-covered wonder protects the continental U.S.'s only living coral reef, the Florida Reef Tract just off the coast of Miami. A boating, snorkeling, or kayaking outing here will bring you close to marine life galore (including 500 species of fish), plus tangles of mangroves that are unique to this Florida ecosystem and 10,000 years of history along the way, with shipwrecks to prove it. 🌐 *www.nps.gov/bisc*

Don't Miss

Explore six of the park's many shipwrecks dating back to the 1870s along the **Maritime Heritage Trail**, accessible by boat and marked with buoys. The *Mandalay* wreck can be explored by snorkeling while others are deeper and require scuba gear.

Best Tour

A half- or full-day guided boat tour with Biscayne National Park Institute is a must for snorkeling, paddleboarding, and sailing. Boats leave from Dante Fascell Visitor Center in Homestead. 🌐 *www.biscaynenational-parkinstitute.org*

Good to Know

Once you leave the visitor center, there's nowhere to buy food, so be sure to pack a lunch. The largest island in the park, **Elliott Key**, is a good stop for a picnic.

Getting Here and Around

Take U.S. Highway 1 or the Florida Turnpike to Homestead to reach the Dante Fascell Visitor Center. ✉ *9700 S.W. 328th St., Sir Lancelot Jones Way, Homestead, FL*

Dry Tortugas National Park

A Remote Island Paradise

Accessed only by boat or seaplane, this far-from-it-all national park with a 19th-century fort as its centerpiece makes for an epic day trip from Key West. Ninety-nine percent of its 100 square miles is under water, where a coral reef teeming with fish and sea turtles makes it a swimming, snorkeling, and diving paradise. The views are just as grand from the islands on the surface, where beaches with clear water reflect a mesmerizing shade of aquamarine. 🌐 *www.nps.gov/drto*

Don't Miss

Of the park's seven islands, **Garden Key** is home to park headquarters, a gradually sloped beach that makes swimming easy, and **Fort Jefferson**.

Best Tours

The trip to Dry Tortugas is half the fun. The *Yankee Freedom Ferry* (🌐 *www.drytortugas.com*) or **Key West Seaplane Charters** (🌐 *keywestseaplanecharters.com*) both depart from Key West.

Good to Know

Camping is possible on Garden Key, where the stargazing is a once-in-a-lifetime opportunity. But it's not for the faint of heart: campers must bring all the water, food, and shelter they'll need.

Getting Here and Around

Seventy miles west of Key West, Dry Tortugas is accessible only by boat or seaplane.

Wynwood, Miami

America's Coolest Street Art

Miami Beach may win the popularity contest, but Wynwood is undoubtedly the Magic City's coolest neighborhood—one that's become an international hot spot for street artists. With an impressive mix of colorful murals, one-of-a-kind shops and art galleries, public art displays, see-and-be-seen bars, breweries, slick restaurants, and plenty of eye-popping graffiti, it's the grungy artistic side of Miami you don't see on the beach.

Don't Miss

Check out the **Wynwood Walls**, a cutting-edge enclave of modern urban murals, reflecting diversity in graffiti and street art. More than 100 artists, including Shepard Fairey, have transformed 35,000 square feet of warehouse walls into an outdoor museum of colorful, spray-painted art. ✉ *2520 N.W. 2nd Ave., Miami, FL* 🌐 *www.thewynwoodwalls.com*

Best Nightlife

The neighborhood is known for its nightlife scene, whether you prefer a come-as-you-are bar (**Gramps**), a festive brewery (**Casa La Rubia**), a sports bar (**Grails**), or the many late-night clubs in between.

When to Go

Every second Saturday of the month, the neighborhood hosts **Wynwood Art Walk**, an evening block party with live music, food trucks, and immersive art. 🌐 *wynwoodmiami.com/experience/art-walk*

Getting Here and Around

Wynwood is located north of Downtown Miami, between Interstate 95 and Northeast 1st Avenue from 29th to 22nd Streets (it's a 30-minute drive from Miami Beach). Parking is a pain, so it's best to take a rideshare and explore the district on foot.

Amelia Island

A Florida Beach With a Southern Accent

At the northeasternmost reach of Florida, Amelia Island has beautiful beaches with enormous sand dunes along its eastern flank, a state park with a Civil War fort, sophisticated restaurants, interesting shops, and accommodations that range from bed-and-breakfasts to luxury resorts. The town of **Fernandina Beach** on the island's northern end beckons with an old-timey historic district, a wide beach where sea turtles nest, and its Isle of Eight Flags Shrimp Festival, held during the first weekend of May, which celebrates its history as the birthplace of the shrimping industry.

Don't Miss

Fernandina Historic District is home to Florida's oldest lighthouse, oldest bar, oldest hotel, and more than 50 blocks of buildings on the National Register of Historic Places.

Best Activity

Horseback riding on the beach of Amelia Island is a can't-miss activity. Arrange a ride with **Amelia Island Horseback Riding**, which has been in business since 1993. Rides follow along miles of untouched Atlantic shore. 🌐 *www.ameliaislandhorseback-riding.com*

Good to Know

Amelia Island gets its nickname, Isle of the Eight Flags, because it is the only place in the United States where eight different flags have flown: French, Spanish, British, Patriots, Green Cross, Mexican Revolutionary, the Confederacy, and finally the United States.

Getting Here and Around

Airlines fly nonstop to Jacksonville from major U.S. cities. From Jacksonville, the drive to Amelia Island is about 30 to 45 minutes.

Ocala National Forest

Dive Into Florida's Natural Springs

This breathtaking 387,000-acre national forest off Route 40 is a playground for outdoor lovers and Florida at its most natural. Among its more than 600 freshwater springs, lakes, swamps, and forests are some of the area's most popular hiking trails and campgrounds, plus rivers for canoeing. There are four springs with recreational areas, including **Alexander Springs**, with crystal clear water and a consistent temperature around 70°F that makes it great for swimming. At **Juniper Springs**, you'll find a stone waterwheel house, a campground, a natural-spring swimming pool, and hiking trails. Known as the Horse Capital of the World, Ocala also offers plenty of horseback riding trails within the forest. ✉ *17147 E. Rte. 40, Silver Springs, FL* 🌐 *www.ocalamarion.com*

Don't Miss

The **Black Bear Scenic Byway** is a picturesque drive from Silver Springs to the Atlantic Coast at Ormond Beach—and through the heart of Ocala National Forest.

Best Stop

Silver Springs State Park, at the Forest's western edge, has the world's largest collection of artesian springs, the last uninhabited spring run in Florida. Visitors can canoe, kayak, ride in a glass-bottom boat, hike, camp, and picnic. The park, inhabited by hundreds of rhesus monkeys, was the setting for many Tarzan movies. 🌐 *www.silversprings.com*

Getting Here and Around

Ocala National Forest is an hour south of Gainesville and a little over an hour north of Orlando.

Sanibel Island

America's Best Shelling Beach

Sanibel Island is so famous for being the world's best shelling ground that there's a term for the stance shell-seekers take when bending over to pick them up: the telltale "Sanibel stoop." Why's the shelling so great here? It's a function of the unusual east–west orientation of the island's south end. Just as the tide is going out and after storms, the pickings can be superb, and you can carry out bags of conchs, whelks, cockles, and other bivalves and gastropods. (Remember, it's unlawful to pick up live shells.) Away from the beach, flowery vegetation decorates small shopping complexes, pleasant resorts and condo complexes, mom-and-pop motels, and casual restaurants.

Don't Miss

Shelling is great anywhere along Sanibel's Gulf front. Remote **Bowman's Beach** (off Sanibel-Captiva Road at Bowman's Beach Road) offers the best shell selection.

Best Museum

Make **Bailey-Matthews National Shell Museum & Aquarium** your first stop to learn about the fascinating ecosystem in this part of the state. ✉ *3075 Sanibel Captiva Rd., Sanibel, FL* 🌐 *www.shellmuseum.org*

While You're Here

More than half of Sanibel is occupied by **J.N. "Ding" Darling National Wildlife Refuge**, 6,300 acres of wetlands and jungly mangrove forests home to roseate spoonbills, egrets, alligators, and more, named after a conservation-minded Pulitzer Prize–winning political cartoonist. 🌐 *www.fws.gov/refuge/jn-ding-darling*

Getting Here and Around

Southwest Florida International Airport, in Fort Myers, is the closest to Sanibel (28 miles); it's about 150 miles from the Miami area.

The Emerald Coast

Florida's Best-Kept Secret

Beaches along the Gulf Coast from **Destin** to **Panama City** have the whitest powdery sand and sparkliest emerald waters in all of Florida. Many of the smaller beaches along the stretch, namely the 16 neighborhoods (including **Seaside**, **WaterColor**, and **Grayton Beach**) strung together along Scenic Highway 30A in South Walton, don't see the same influx of tourists as the rest of the Sunshine State, giving them the quieter feel of a true local treasure. The area offers a unique mix of Southern charm, unspoiled nature, and small communities where you can walk or bike everywhere.

Don't Miss

At **Grayton Beach State Park**, you can climb sandy trails or paddleboard on lakes that show how Florida once was before it was developed. Or take a day trip to Seaside, the all-American small town planned to be picture-perfect—so perfect it was the setting for the film *The Truman Show*.

Best Activity

In WaterColor, try stand-up paddleboarding at **the Boathouse**—you'll paddle past lily pads and pine trees before you see something very rare: coastal dune lakes. They're only found in a few other places in the world, including New Zealand. 🌐 *www.boathousepaddleclub30a.com*

Good to Know

These beaches don't have your typical sand—it's pure Appalachian quartz that was dropped off by a glacier a few thousand years back, and it's so powder-soft, it squeaks.

Getting Here and Around

Destin–Fort Walton Beach Airport (VPS) serves Florida's Gulf Coast, about 15 miles from Destin. From there it's an easy drive to 30A beach towns like Seaside.

Fort Lauderdale

The Venice of America

More than 165 miles of canals and waterways earned Fort Lauderdale the nickname "the Venice of America," but it's also been dubbed the Yachting Capital of the World. Take to the waterways to appreciate this coastal beauty, one of the best places to boat right up to a restaurant in South Florida. Explore expansive beaches, showstopping resort hotels, and a food scene that's really heating up.

Don't Miss

What Lincoln Road is to South Beach, **Las Olas Boulevard** is to Fort Lauderdale. The street is home to the city's best shops and restaurants.

Best Tour

At once a sightseeing tour and a mode of transportation, the **water taxi** is a smart way to experience most of Fort Lauderdale and Hollywood's waterways. There are 15 scheduled stops and on-demand whistle stops. It's possible to cruise all day while taking in the sights. 🌐 *www.watertaxi.com*

Best Restaurants

Boat right up to **Casa Sensei**, a waterfront restaurant along the Himmarshee Canal (✉ *1200 E. Las Olas Blvd., Fort Lauderdale, FL* 🌐 *casasensei.com*). If it's fine dining you're after, **Maass** has the city's only Michelin star (✉ *525 N. Fort Lauderdale Beach Blvd., Fort Lauderdale, FL* 🌐 *www.maassftl.com*).

When to Go

Time your visit for the **Fort Lauderdale International Boat Show** in October, when the Yachting Capital of the World displays more than 1,000 types of boats and superyachts. 🌐 *www.flibs.com*

Getting Here and Around

Fly into Miami (MIA) or Fort Lauderdale (FLL). While you can use the water taxi to get around, you can also order Uber/Lyft.

When in Florida

ART BASEL

The most prestigious art show in the United States is held every December, with plenty of fabulous parties to go along with the pricey art. This is a who's who of the art world where collectors, emerging artists, renowned artists, curators, gallerists, and art aficionados convene alongside novices, trendsetters, and glitterati. ✉ *www.artbasel.com*

Do This: Although the main exhibition is held at the Miami Beach Convention Center, dozens of smaller exhibitions are set up on the beach, Downtown, and in the Wynwood District at galleries and in event spaces and hotel lobbies.

THE DALÍ MUSEUM

Inside and out, St. Petersburg's waterfront Dalí Museum is almost as remarkable as the Spanish surrealist's work. The state-of-the-art building has a surreal geodesic-like glass structure called the Dalí Enigma, as well as an outdoor labyrinth and a DNA-inspired spiral staircase leading up to the collection. The mind-expanding paintings in this downtown headliner include *Eggs on a Plate Without a Plate, The Hallucinogenic Toreador,* and more than 90 other oils. You'll also discover more than 2,000 additional works including watercolors, drawings, sculptures, photographs, and objets d'art. The museum also hosts temporary collections from the likes of Pablo Picasso and Andy Warhol. Hour-long tours are led by well-informed docents. ✉ *1 Dali Blvd., St. Petersburg, FL* 🌐 *www.thedali.org*

Do This: The Tampa–St. Pete's region has its share of boutique districts, spotted with shops and sidewalk cafés; Tampa's Hyde Park Village and downtown St. Petersburg's Beach Drive are among the top picks if you're looking to check out some upscale shops and dine alfresco while getting the most of the area's pleasant climate.

FLORA-BAMA MULLET TOSS

You may exclaim, "now I've seen everything" after witnessing this event at the world-famous Flora-Bama Lounge in Perdido Key, which sits atop a beautiful beach on the state line between—you guessed it—Florida and Alabama. The beach lounge is home to the annual "Mullet Toss," in which lively locals compete to see who can throw a fish farthest across the state line drawn in the sand (and drink the most beer). ✉ *17401 Perdido Key Dr., Perdido Key, FL* 🌐 *www.florabama.com/mullet-toss*

Do This: Drive, boat, or paddleboard in to the Flora-Bama Yacht Club, a waterfront open-air eatery that serves fresh Gulf seafood. Stay for the live music on the beach, or head over to the Flora-Bama bar if you're in the mood for a wild night out. ✉ *17350 Perdido Key Dr., Perdido Key, FL* 🌐 *www.florabamayachtclub.com*

MANSIONS OF PALM BEACH

Long reigning as the place where the crème de la crème go to shake off winter's chill, Palm Beach continues to be a seasonal hotbed of platinum-grade consumption. It's been the winter address for heirs of the iconic Rockefeller, Vanderbilt, Colgate, Post, Kellogg, and Kennedy families. Strict laws govern everything from building to landscaping, and not so much as a pool awning gets added without a town council nod.

Do This: Whether you aspire to be a former president or a rock legend (Kennedy, John Lennon, Rod Stewart, Jimmy Buffett—all onetime or current Palm Beach residents), no trip to the island is complete without gawking at the megamansions lining its perfectly manicured streets. Start at Casa de Leoni on 450 Worth Avenue before heading to Il Palmetto on 1500 South Ocean Boulevard.

SIESTA KEY

Across the water from Sarasota lies the barrier island of Siesta Key, which is home to what's often dubbed America's whitest, softest sand beach. The fine, powdery quartz sand squeaks under your feet because it comes from tiny particles that form the rocks of the Appalachian Mountains. This quality gives it a superpower: it doesn't get hot like other sand. With 40 acres of nature trails, Siesta Key is exceptionally wide and long, providing ample space for all types of activities.

Do This: Siesta Key really comes to life an hour before sunset on Sunday, with the weekly, festival-like gathering for the Siesta Key Drum Circle. Music, dancing, and oddball entertainment attract a lively crowd of festive spectators and beachgoers; bring a blanket or beach chair and get there early to snag a good spot in the parking lot.

WEEKI WACHEE MERMAID SHOW

At Weeki Wachee Springs, the spring flows at the remarkable rate of 170 million gallons a day with a constant temperature of 74°F. The spring has long been famous for something only Florida would think up: live "mermaids." Clearly not the work of Mother Nature, they wear bright costumes and put on an *Little Mermaid*–like underwater choreography show that's been virtually unchanged since the park opened in 1947. The park is considered a classic piece of Florida history and culture. In summer, Buccaneer Bay water park opens for swimming, beaching, and riding its thrilling slides and flumes. ✉ *6131 Commercial Way, Spring Hill, FL* 🌐 *www.weekiwachee.com*

Do This: Take a snorkel tour of the river, paddle a canoe, or board a wilderness boat ride for an up-close look at raccoons, otters, egrets, and other semitropical Florida wetlands wildlife.

About Our Writers

Kayla Becker was raised in Tallahassee, Florida, and has also lived in Gainesville and Miami. Her favorite beaches in the world are along Scenic Highway 30A, and she thinks there's nothing more refreshing than a dip in a Florida spring. Kayla was formerly a staff editor at Fodor's Travel, ShermansTravel, and *Travel + Leisure* and is currently a freelance travel writer and editor.

Cool Places to Stay

The Breakers. You can declare that you vacationed like a Vanderbilt or a Rockefeller at this historic 1926 beachfront property on Palm Beach that feels more like an Italianate palace than a hotel. The 200-foot-long lobby with soaring painted ceilings is a must-see itself: it took 75 artists from Italy to complete. ✉ *1 S. County Rd., Palm Beach, FL* 🌐 *www.thebreakers.com*

Disney's Animal Kingdom Lodge. It's not every day you wake up to giraffes, zebras, kudu, and flamingos roaming just outside your room, but that's exactly what's in store at Disney's sprawling safari-themed lodge meets wildlife park. African-theme restaurants and a "watering hole" for swimming round out the memorable experience. ✉ *2901 Osceola Pkwy, Lake Buena Vista, FL* 🌐 *disneyworld.disney.go.com*

Faena Hotel. This towering beachfront property on Miami Beach is a stunning reinvention of the art deco 1948 Saxony Hotel, with dramatic common areas and prolific art installations, including a $15 million gilded woolly mammoth sculpture by Damien Hirst. Gawk at the details throughout the "Cathedral" lobby, which glitters with gold-leafed columns, or scope out nirvana at the 22,000-square-foot, high-design Tierra Santa Spa, which is rooted in South America's rich Indigenous culture. Enjoy some burlesque in the 220-seat dinner theater and later retreat to your glamorous room, decked out in art deco–style interiors. ✉ *3201 Collins Ave., Miami Beach, FL* 🌐 *www.faena.com/miami-beach*

Grayton Beach Camping. One of the most scenic spots along the Gulf Coast, this 2,220-acre park has salt marshes, rolling dunes covered with sea oats, crystal-white sand, and contrasting blue-green waters. There's swimming, fishing, and snorkeling here, as well as hiking on many trails around the marsh and woods and an elevated boardwalk that winds over the dunes to the beach. Thirty fully equipped cabins and a campground provide overnight options; cabins sleep up to six, and the beach is a leisurely five-minute walk away via a private boardwalk. ✉ *8300 Main Park Rd., Santa Rosa Beach, FL* 🌐 *www.floridastateparks.org/graytonbeach*

Jules' Undersea Lodge. Dive 30 feet below the surface to sleep with the fishes at the only undersea hotel in the United States, located in Florida's snorkeling and diving capital, Key Largo. Aquatic life swims past a glass dome over the bedroom, but there are still some comforts of land, including a microwave, TV, and refrigerator. ✉ *51 Shoreland Dr., Key Largo, FL* 🌐 *www.jul.com*

Essential Eats

Cuban Classics. Musts for any bucket list include *bistec de palomilla*, *lechon asado*, *croquetas*, a mojito, and a cafecito to rev up your afternoon, but you absolutely have to try *ropa vieja* (a shredded beef dish with a name that translates to "old clothes"). You'll find hearty portions in Miami's Little Havana neighborhood at the iconic Versailles, a no-frills Cuban joint that's operated since 1971 (✉ *3555 S.W. 8th St., Miami, FL* 🌐 *versaillesrestaurant.com*). Those looking for a more creative, modern take should head to the lauded Cafe La Trova (✉ *971 S.W. 8th St., Miami, FL* 🌐 *www.cafelatrova.com*).

Fresh Grouper. The mild, flaky white fish is a Gulf Coast favorite. Try it grilled at Bud & Alley's (✉ *2236 E. County Rd. 30A, Santa Rosa Beach, FL* 🌐 *www.budandalleys.com*), a locally loved rooftop bar and restaurant on 30A overlooking the emerald water of the Gulf.

Joe's Stone Crab. An institution that you should visit at least once, this classic South Beach restaurant opened in 1913 and is *the* place to try that South Florida favorite, stone crab claws. ✉ *11 Washington Ave., Miami Beach, FL* 🌐 *joesstonecrab.com*

Key Lime Pie. If you visit the Keys without trying this Florida staple and its many iterations (think: Key lime Popsicles, frozen drinks, ice cream, etc.) you haven't really visited the Keys. The best place to sample it is Blue Heaven (✉ *729 Thomas St., Key West, FL* 🌐 *blueheavenkw.com*), where live music, outdoor dining, and a heavenly slice piled high with fluffy meringue await.

Victoria & Albert's. If you have only one meal at Walt Disney World, make it this Michelin-starred fine dining restaurant at Disney's Grand Floridian Resort & Spa, where the Victorian-era elegance is fit for royalty, or maybe a grown-up Cinderella. ✉ *4401 Floridian Way, Lake Buena Vista, FL* 🌐 *disneyworld.disney.go.com*

Georgia

Georgia encompasses two Souths—the Old South of Savannah with its elegant homes, planned squares, and Spanish moss–draped live oaks, and the New South of Atlanta, a bustling high-rise metropolis with enough to keep visitors busy for weeks. For white-columned mansions and a slower way of life, look no further than central Georgia. There's coastline here, too, with lush barrier islands stretching all the way to Florida.

Capital: Atlanta

Population: 11,180,878

Area: 57,717 square miles

Statehood Date: January 2, 1788

Major Airports: Hartsfield-Jackson Atlanta International Airport (ATL); Savannah/Hilton Head International Airport (SAV)

Travel and Tourism Information: 🌐 *www.exploregeorgia.org* 🌐 *www.discoveratlanta.com* 🌐 *www.visitsavannah.com*

Famous Residents: Jimmy Carter (president); Martin Luther King Jr. (civil rights icon); Jackie Robinson (baseball player), Julia Roberts (actress); Tyler Perry (director); André 3000 (rapper)

Fun Fact: Georgia has long been known as the "Peach State," although California and neighboring South Carolina now produce more of the famed Southern fruit. Given Georgia's rich agricultural history, you'll still find great affection for the peach and it still produces over 130 million pounds of peaches each year.

Savannah

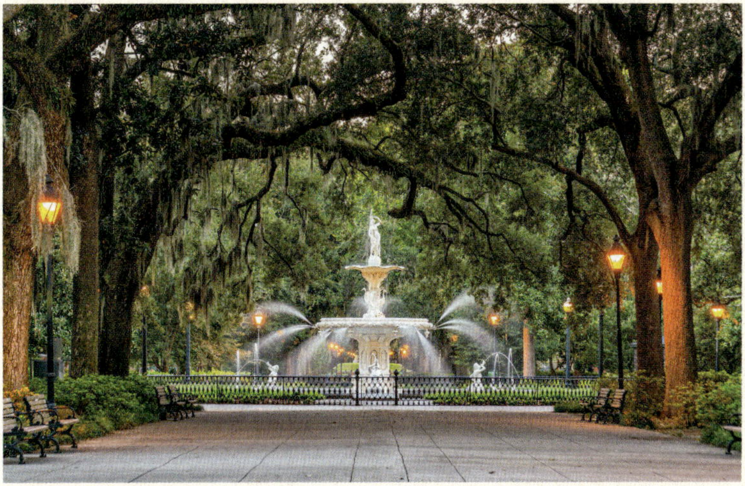

Historic Squares and Southern Charm

Dripping with Southern charm, Savannah beckons with stately architecture, rich history, and a culinary scene that spans classic down-home cooking to James Beard Award nominees. This is the place to appreciate art in lauded museums, people-watch in flower-filled squares, and imagine the past as you walk under canopies of live oaks draped in Spanish moss in **Forsyth Park**.

Don't Miss

As America's first planned city, Savannah is perhaps most recognized for its 22 squares, the diverse group of parks that dot the Historic District. **Telfair** (home to the Owens-Thomas House), **Franklin** (site of the historic First African Baptist Church), and **Monterey** (full of history and pretty views) are just some of the best squares to visit.

While You're Here

Check out hot restaurants like **The Grey** or **Husk** and head to the rooftop bar at **Peregrin** on Perry Street, where gorgeous views include the Cathedral Basilica of St. John the Baptist.

Best Museum

SCAD Museum of Art, an architectural marvel that rose from the ruins of one of the oldest surviving railroad buildings in the United States, covers fashion and African American arts and culture. ✉ *601 Turner Blvd., Savannah, GA* 🌐 *www.scadmoa.org*

Getting Here and Around

Savannah/Hilton Head International Airport (SAV) is about a 20-minute drive from downtown. Savannah is 100 miles from Charleston.

Martin Luther King, Jr. National Historical Park

Walk in MLK's Footsteps

Dr. Martin Luther King Jr. grew up in a home off of Auburn Avenue in Atlanta. His former home is now a National Historic Site that's part of 35 acres dedicated to the civil rights leader. A very short walk from his childhood home are blocks full of significant monuments and museums related to Dr. King, including the **King Center** and Ebenezer Baptist Church. At the King Center, you'll see the crypt of Dr. King and Coretta Scott King, and the Eternal Flame. Nearby is the **International Civil Rights Walk of Fame.** ✉ *450 Auburn Ave. NE, Atlanta, GA* 🌐 *www.nps.gov/malu*

Don't Miss

The historic **Ebenezer Baptist Church**, the district's Gothic revival–style church, came to be known as the spiritual center of the civil rights movement. Members of the King family preached at the church for three generations. Sitting in the sanctuary on a quiet day when light is shining through the stained-glass windows can be a powerful experience. ✉ *101 Jackson St. NE, Atlanta, GA* 🌐 *ebenezeratl.org*

Planning Your Time

Set aside at least an hour or two to walk around Auburn Avenue and its many surrounding monuments, historical buildings, and the World Peace Rose Garden.

Getting Here and Around

The historical park is located in the Sweet Auburn neighborhood of Atlanta, about a mile east of downtown. King Memorial Transit station is the Marta stop here, and there is an even more convenient Atlanta Streetcar (tram) stop across from the Ebenezer Baptist Church.

Atlanta's BeltLine

The Great Connector of a Thriving City

A 33-mile railway turned greenway, the BeltLine is an outdoor oasis of trails and parks that encircles Atlanta's urban metropolis, connecting more than 40 neighborhoods (and continuously expanding). During the warmer months, you can expect to find a consistent stream of people biking, jogging, or walking as they make their way around Old Fourth Ward, West End, and Virginia-Highland. On any given day, you can take a yoga class or attend a festival in one of the green spaces that run along the loop.

Don't Miss

The Eastside Trail section of the BeltLine links to great dining and hangout options, like **Krog Street Market**, **Kevin Rathbun Steak**, and **Ladybird Grove & Mess Hall**. **Ponce City Market** is a great place to stop off for some refreshments.

Good to Know

Visit the Atlanta BeltLine webpage before you go for the latest news on events and to book a bike or arboretum tour. You can also view an interactive map highlighting key access points, public transit, art, and parks along each trail. 🌐 *www.beltline.org*

While You're Here

Piedmont Park runs just off the northeast section of the BeltLine and is the perfect place to escape the frenetic energy of the city for a picnic with smashing views of the Midtown skyline. 🌐 *piedmontpark.org*

Getting Here and Around

Walkable stretches of the BeltLine can be found on the east (Old Fourth Ward and Virginia-Highland) and west (West End) sides of the city, but there are ambitious plans to expand. To bike the trail, rent from Atlanta Bicycle Barn or pick up a bike from several Bike Share stations nearby.

Georgia Aquarium

America's Largest Aquarium

With more than 10 million gallons of water, Atlanta's wildly popular Georgia Aquarium is the nation's largest. The 604,000-square-foot building, an architectural marvel resembling the bow of a ship, has tanks of various sizes filled with more than 80,000 animals, representing 500 species. You'll spot beluga whales, dolphins, stingrays, and more floating past. But not everything has gills: there are also penguins, sea lions, sea otters, river otters, sea turtles, and giant octopuses. ✉ *225 Baker St. NW, Atlanta, GA* 🌐 *www.georgiaaquarium.org*

Don't Miss

The aquarium's 6.3-million-gallon Ocean Voyager Gallery is the world's largest indoor marine exhibit, with 4,574 square feet of viewing windows that bring you face to face with whale sharks, the largest fish in the world.

Best Tour

The aquarium offers 45-minute behind-the-scenes tours every half-hour and daily dolphin shows, but to go further, you can swim with sea creatures on a diving adventure through the Ocean Voyager exhibit—or even cage dive with sharks.

While You're Here

Within walking distance, you'll find the moving **National Center for Civil and Human Rights**, which offers visitors a multisensory immersion into both the U.S. civil rights movement and global human rights efforts. ✉ *100 Ivan Allen Jr. Blvd., Atlanta, GA* 🌐 *www.civilandhumanrights.org*

Getting Here and Around

The aquarium is located in downtown Atlanta. There are two nearby Marta stations, at Civic Center and Peachtree Center.

Tybee Island

The Best Place to Kayak With Dolphins

This barrier island east of Savannah, formerly known as Savannah Beach, has been a destination since the 1920s, when a train connected downtown to the beach pavilion where jazz bands played. These days the island is a mix of kitschy shops and interesting restaurants, making a wonderfully quirky beach town. Whether you're looking to work on your tan, spend a day on a fishing charter, or paddle around in a kayak, this is a must-see during the summer months. Best of all, Tybee Island's myriad water activities, including stand-up paddleboarding and cruises, can help you catch a glimpse of the island's dolphins.

Don't Miss

Kayaking off Tybee Island via **Sea Kayak Georgia** or **AquaDawg** outfitters is an unforgettable experience, and you just might get close to schools of dolphins. For those really wanting to ditch the world, the paddle from Tybee Island to the uninhabited barrier island of Little Tybee is the perfect remedy. The only beings you'll see are egrets, ibis, osprey, Atlantic bottlenose dolphins, and maybe a manatee or two along the way.

Need a Break?

For lunch on Tybee, It's hard to beat the huge patio overlooking bird-filled marshlands at the casual **Crab Shack**, with a diverse menu featuring seafood platters, barbecue, and sandwiches. ✉ *40 Estill Hammock Rd., Tybee Island, GA* 🌐 *www.thecrabshack.com*

Getting Here and Around

Tybee is a short (15- to 20-minute drive) from Savannah and its airport (SAV).

Cumberland Island

Georgia's Most Unspoiled Island

This 18-mile spit of land off the coast of St. Marys is a national treasure, with an impressive collection of nearly unspoiled marshes, dunes, beaches, forests, lakes, and ponds. Although it has a long history of human habitation, including formerly enslaved African Americans following the Civil War, it remains much as nature created it: a dense, lacework canopy of live oak shades, sand roads, and foot trails through a thick undergrowth of palmetto. Wild horses roam freely on the pristine beaches and waterways are home to gators, sea turtles, otters, and more than 300 species of birds. During the 1880s, the family of Thomas Carnegie (brother of Andrew) built several lavish homes here.

Don't Miss

The 36,415-acre **Cumberland Island National Seashore** has pristine forests and marshes marbled with wooded nature trails, 18 miles of beaches, and opportunities for fishing, bird-watching, and viewing the ruins of Thomas Carnegie's great estate, **Dungeness.** 🌐 *www.nps.gov/cuis*

Where to Stay

Hike to one of the island's pretty campsites or book a night at the famed **Greyfield Inn**, the 1900 Carnegie home turned resort, sitting on 1,000 private acres on the island's south side. Note that reservations for both fill up months in advance, so plan ahead. ✉ *4 N. 2nd St., Cumberland Island, GA* 🌐 *greyfieldinn.com*

Getting Here and Around

The only way to access the island is by private boat or via the *Cumberland Queen II* ferry from St. Marys (45 minutes). The passenger ferry allows no cars, so prepare to explore the island on foot. St. Marys is about two hours south of Savannah by car.

Okefenokee Swamp

Land of the Trembling Earth

Larger than all of Georgia's barrier islands combined, the **Okefenokee National Wildlife Refuge** covers 700 square miles of southeastern Georgia and northeastern Florida, and is the largest intact freshwater wetlands in the contiguous United States. The term "swamp" hardly does the Okefenokee justice; the refuge contains numerous and varied landscapes, including aquatic prairies, towering virgin cypress, sandy pine islands, and lush subtropical hammocks. Alligators, otters, bobcats, white-tailed deer, turtles, bald eagles, red-tailed hawks, herons, cranes, and black bears all make their home here. 🌐 *www.fws.gov/refuge/okefenokee*

Don't Miss

At Okefenokee's southwestern entrance, **Stephen C. Foster State Park** is a 120-acre park offering trips to the headwaters of the Suwannee River, Billy's Island. The park is home to hundreds of species of birds and a large cypress-and-black-gum forest, a majestic backdrop for one of the thickest growths of vegetation in the southeastern United States. ✉ *17515 Rte. 177 Fargo, GA* 🌐 *www.gastateparks.org/StephenCFoster*

When to Go

Visit between September and April to avoid the biting insects that emerge in May, especially in the dense interior.

Getting Here and Around

Located about two hours south of Savannah, there are three main entrances to Okefenokee: the main entrance is outside of Folkston, GA; the western entrance (Stephen C. Foster Park) is just east of Fargo, GA; and the northern entrance (Okefenokee Swamp Park) is outside the town of Waycross, GA.

Athens

An Indie Rock Powerhouse

An artistic jewel of the American South, Athens is known as a breeding ground for famed rock groups such as the B-52s and R.E.M. It's no wonder creative types from all over the country flock to its trendy streets in hopes of becoming, or catching a glimpse of, the next big act to take the world by storm. At the center of this musical whirlwind is the University of Georgia (UGA), giving the quaint but compact city a distinct flavor that falls somewhere between a misty Southern enclave, a rollicking college town, and a smoky, jazz club–studded alleyway. Of course, it all goes "to the Dawgs" if the home team is playing, with students taking over the bars, but even then, Athens remains a blend of Mayberry and MTV. The effect is as irresistible as it is authentic.

Don't Miss

You must make a pilgrimage to **40 Watt Club**, a famed indie-rock club known for helping to launch the careers of R.E.M., the B-52s, and other local bands that grew out of the college scene. Nirvana, the Flaming Lips, and Sonic Youth all played here back in the day. Today, you'll see a mix of local and national acts gracing the stage—from country to punk to pop. ✉ *285 W. Washington St., Athens, GA* 🌐 *www.40watt.com*

While You're Here

As you hop through town, find funky dive bars like **Sister Louisa's Church**, try craft beers at **Creature Comfort Brewery**, and eat killer cuisine at **Five & Ten** and **Seabear Oyster Bar**.

Getting Here and Around

Athens is about 70 miles east of Atlanta on Interstate 20. The downtown and campus area are very walkable.

Jimmy Carter National Historic Site

Georgia's Presidential Pride

Jimmy Carter, the 39th President of the United States, grew up in Plains, a tiny southwest Georgia farming town that has become a destination for visitors from around the world. Plains was deeply important to the peanut farmer turned politician. When the president and his wife, Rosalynn Carter, weren't working around the globe, the Carters continued to come home to Plains and were an integral part of the community. Today, the Jimmy Carter National Historic Site encompasses Carter's boyhood home and farm, the former Plains Train Depot, and the former Plains High School which now serves as a visitor center and museum. Visitors may also pay tribute to the president and first lady by visiting their gravesites and the surrounding garden. ✉ *300 N. Bond St., Plains, GA* 🌐 *www.nps.gov/jica*

Don't Miss

For a fun and quirky photo op, stop by the smiling **giant peanut** on the northern edge of Plains. The 13-foot sculpture, created for a 1976 campaign event, pays tribute to the humble peanut and Jimmy Carter's trademark toothy grin. Look for it along Route 45. ✉ *120 Buena Vista Rd., Plains, GA*

Good to Know

Start your visit with a stop at the **Plains High School Visitor Center** where you can pick up a map and get a quick overview. While most of the sites are in walking distance, the boyhood home is a 2-mile drive. It's definitely a highlight, so be sure to save time to visit. ✉ *300 N. Bond St., Plains, GA*

Getting Here and Around

Plains is located about 150 miles south of Atlanta and 50 miles southeast of Columbus. It's best reached by car as there are no public transit options.

Jekyll Island

Vacation Like a Rockefeller

From the Gilded Age to the Great Depression, the Vanderbilts and Rockefellers, Morgans and Astors, Macys, Pulitzers, and Goodyears all shuttered their 5th Avenue castles in the winter and retreated to elegant cottages on the wild coastal island of Jekyll Island. It's been said that when the island's distinguished winter residents were all "in," a sixth of the world's wealth was represented. Jekyll Island is still a 7½-mile playground, but it's no longer restricted to the rich and famous. A water park, picnic grounds, and facilities for golf, tennis, fishing, biking, and jogging are all open to the public. One side of the island is lined by nearly 10 miles of hard-packed Atlantic beaches; the other by the intracoastal waterway and picturesque salt marshes. Deer and wild turkey inhabit interior forests of pine, magnolia, and moss-veiled live oaks while egrets, pelicans, herons, and sandpipers skim the gentle surf.

Don't Miss

Jekyll Island's clean, mostly uncommercialized public beaches are free and open year-round.

A Closer Look

Head to **Jekyll Island Club Resort** for a glimpse of the island's glorious heyday. The sprawling 1888 resort was once described as "the richest, the most exclusive, the most inaccessible club in the world," and its old-world charm persists. ✉ *371 Riverview Dr., Jekyll Island, GA* 🌐 *www.jekyllclub.com*

Getting Here and Around

Jacksonville International Airport (JAX) is 65 miles south, Savannah/Hilton Head International Airport (SAV) is 90 miles north, and Atlanta is about a five-hour drive. By car, travel through Brunswick and take the Jekyll Island Causeway.

Blue Ridge and the Chattahoochee Forest

A Breath of Fresh Mountain Air

North Georgia, home to the 750,000-acre Chattahoochee National Forest, is known for its abundant natural wonders and its cool mountain air. **Blue Ridge** is one of the most pleasant small mountain towns here. After you've eaten breakfast or lunch and shopped for antiques, gifts, or crafts at Blue Ridge's many small shops, you can explore the scenic surroundings; Fannin County (of which Blue Ridge is the county seat) is known as the "Trout Capital of Georgia" and the beautiful Toccoa River is a popular destination for fly-fishing, hiking, canoeing, and more. Just 15 miles southwest of Blue Ridge is the scenic town of **Ellijay.** Billed as "Georgia's Apple Capital," Ellijay is popular for its orchards and antiques shops.

Don't Miss

Brasstown Bald, about 40 miles east of Blue Ridge, is the highest peak in Georgia and home to fun, rigorous hikes; south of Blue Ridge is **Springer Mountain**, the southern endpoint of the Appalachian Trail.

Best Tour

Ride the rails on **Blue Ridge Scenic Railway's** four-hour, 26-mile round-trip excursion along the Toccoa River. The trip includes a stop in McCaysville, smack on the Georgia–Tennessee state line. 🌐 *www.brscenic.com*

When to Go

Visit in fall, when roadside stands brimming with ripe apples dot the landscape. The annual **Georgia Apple Festival** takes place on the second and third weekends of October. 🌐 *www.georgiaapplefestival.org*

Getting Here and Around

It's an easy 1½-hour drive from Atlanta to the Georgia foothills and the town of Blue Ridge.

When in Georgia

ATLANTA UNITED FC SOCCER CLUB

Atlanta United home games at Mercedes-Benz Stadium (shared with the Atlanta Falcons) have broken attendance records in recent years, carrying with them a welcome air of excitement about soccer that feels international. The team has one of the largest fan bases in all of U.S. soccer, and won the MLS Cup in 2018 and the U.S. Open and Campeones Cups in 2019. ✉ *1 AMB Dr. NW, Atlanta, GA* 🌐 *www.atlutd.com*

Do This: The Brewhouse Cafe, Der Biergarten, and Midway are some of Atlanta's best soccer pubs.

BONAVENTURE CEMETERY

The largest and most famous of Savannah's municipal cemeteries, Bonaventure spreads over 100 acres and sits on a bluff above the Wilmington River. An emblematic destination for visitors, the evocative landscape is one of lush natural beauty transposed against an elegant, eerie backdrop of lavish marble headstones, monuments, and mausoleums as well as sweeping oaks and blooming camellia trees. ✉ *330 Bonaventure Rd., Savannah, GA* 🌐 *bonaventurehistorical.org*

Do This: As you might learn at a visit to the cemetery, Savannah is considered one of America's most haunted cities. The Ghost Talk Ghost Walk Tour will send chills down your spine during an easygoing 1-mile jaunt through the downtown, the city's oldest area. 🌐 *www.ghosttalk-ghostwalk.com*

ETOWAH INDIAN MOUNDS

Dating back to AD 1000, this prominent site of Mississippian culture is the place to see and learn about the way of life of the Southeast's early peoples. Aside from the six mounds here (large earthen hills with flat tops, used as foundations to important buildings, the largest being the temple mound), there is a plaza, a river trail, and a museum with artifacts and art on display. ✉ *Cartersville, GA* 🌐 *www.gastateparks.org/etowahindianmounds*

Do This: Walk the 1.1-mile interpretive trail (marked with educational and historic signposts) along the Etowah River.

PROVIDENCE CANYON

Dubbed Georgia's "Little Grand Canyon" for its stunning red rocks, Providence Canyon is within driving distance from many Southern cities and well worth a day of hiking. The 1,000-acre park has 16 canyons layered in red rock of at least 43 shades, from deep ruby to peach. Ten miles of hiking loops in the park allow access to the canyons, many of which you can walk through. The formations were created not by natural forces but poor farming practices in the 1800s, which destroyed and eroded the land, and these staggering canyons are also a sobering reminder of the toll human interference can take on our environment. ✉ *Lumpkin, GA* 🌐 *www.gastateparks.org/providencecanyon*

Do This: Hike the Canyon Loop Trail, blazed with white markers and a 2½-mile loop starting at the visitor center. The easy hike allows access to Canyons 1 through 9, which are marked with signposts. Note that the climb up the canyons is steep and rough.

TALLULAH GORGE STATE PARK

The 1,000-foot-deep Tallulah Gorge is one of the most impressive in the country. In the late 1800s this area was one of the most visited destinations in the Southeast, drawing tourists who came to see the roaring falls on the Tallulah River. Then, in 1912, to provide electric power, the "Niagara of the South" was dammed, and the falls and tourism dried up. Today the State of Georgia has designated more than 20 miles of the state park as walking and mountain-biking trails. There's also a 16,000-square-foot interpretive center, a 63-acre lake with a beach, a picnic shelter, and 52 tent and RV sites. ✉ *Tallulah Falls, GA* 🌐 *www.gastateparks.org/tallulahgorge*

Do This: Take to the 80-foot-high suspension bridge (part of the Hurricane Falls Loop Trail) and imagine the tightrope walkers that twice braved such heights at the gorge.

WORLD OF COCA-COLA

This shrine to the brown soda's image, products, and marketing features more than 1,200 artifacts never before displayed to the public. You can sip samples of 100 different Coca-Cola products from around the world and peruse more than a century's worth of memorabilia from the corporate archives. ✉ *121 Baker St. NW, Atlanta, GA* 🌐 *www.worldofcoca-cola.com*

Do This: Across from the World of Coca-Cola is the Centennial Olympic Park that hosted the 1996 Olympics. At night, eight 65-foot-tall lighting towers highlight the beauty of the park. They represent the markers that led ancient Greeks to public events. ✉ *265 Park Ave. W, Atlanta, GA* 🌐 *www.gwcca.org*

About Our Writers

Rachel Roberts Quartarone is a lifelong Georgian with family roots deeply planted in the Peach State. Her favorite things to do in Georgia are eating her way through Atlanta's many restaurants, strolling the historic streets of Savannah, sunning on the coast, and antiquing in the North Georgia Mountains. When she isn't exploring, Rachel works as a writer, history consultant, and professional singer.

Cool Places to Stay

Amethyst Garden Inn. With plenty of historical appeal of its own, this tall, purple Victorian is within walking distance to Savannah's Historic District and Forsyth Park. The inn stands out for its bright jewel tones and ornate decor in its interior, where you'll be graciously served decadent Southern breakfasts with fluffy biscuits and cheesy grits. Alongside the antiques, canopy beds, and crystal chandeliers, modern comforts include high-quality linens, private bathrooms, and a lovely courtyard. ✉ *402 E. Gaston St., Savannah, GA* 🌐 *www.amethystgardensavannah.com*

Barnsley Resort. A respite for couples and families alike that's both luxurious and accessible, this northwest Georgia retreat is a 3,000-acre haven offering picturesque cottages, a 55-room modern inn, a world-class golf course, a saltwater pool, and a full-service spa. There's also biking, clay shooting, archery, disc golf, horseback riding, and pickleball long with casual and fine dining options. Warm Southern hospitably, gorgeous landscapes, and a historic setting make this a truly special place. ✉ *9862 Rte. 193 Chickamauga, GA* 🌐 *www.barnsleyresort.com*

Hotel Abacus. Centered on a former ironworks facility, this hip boutique hotel offers fresh, modern rooms, an outdoor pool, a coffee shop, and a restaurant and live-music venue (aptly named the Foundry). The atmosphere is historic but modern and playful with an old-school motor lodge appeal. With the inn's great amenities and villagelike setting, there's little need to leave the property, but if you do, you'll find the Classic Center Theater, the university campus, and historic downtown within easy walking distance. ✉ *295 Dougherty St., Athens, GA* 🌐 *www.hotelabacusathens.com*

Hotel Clermont. There's no better stay within walking distance of Ponce City Market and the BeltLine, and for a cool factor combined with modern conveniences and vintage touches, there may be no better stay in Atlanta. Lush foliage and wicker and rattan seating welcome you in the lobby, as does an ice-cold PBR in honor of legendary stripper Blondie, whom you may be lucky enough to catch at the downstairs lounge. The building itself dates to 1924, but with spacious rooms, a celebrated on-site French bistro, and dazzling rooftop bar, the experience is far from old-school. ✉ *789 Ponce De Leon Ave. NE, Atlanta, GA* 🌐 *www.hotelclermont.com*

Essential Eats

Mary Mac's Tea Room. Local celebrities and ordinary folks have lined up for the country-fried steak and fried chicken here since 1945. There's no better place in Atlanta to try Southern favorites like fried chicken, collard greens, fried okra, mac and cheese, and sweet tea. In the Southern tradition, the servers will call you "honey" and pat your arm to assure you that everything's all right. It's a great way to experience Southern food and hospitality all at once. ✉ *224 Ponce de Leon Ave., Atlanta, GA* 🌐 *www.marymacs.com*

The Olde Pink House. This time-tested Savannah classic is known for its sophisticated take on Southern and Lowcountry classics like crab cakes, shrimp and grits, fried chicken, and mac and cheese. The storied restaurant is housed in a historic 1771 mansion on Reynolds Square that is also a frequent point of interest on Savannah ghost tours. There's also a downstairs tavern that's more informal and perfect for a quick bite or late-night stop. ✉ *23 Abercorn St., Savannah, GA* 🌐 *www.theoldepinkhouserestaurant.com*

Southern Soul Barbeque. Housed in a former gas station on St. Simon's Island, Southern Soul offers some of the best barbecue in the state, with a touch of coastal flair. A favorite of tourists and locals alike, this classic BBQ joint has plenty of outside seating and easy to-go options for beachfront picnics. Favorites include pulled pork, whole smoked chicken, brisket, turkey, and sausage alongside soulful sides like collard greens, fried okra, Hoppin' John, and, of course, Brunswick stew. There's also a fun bar and gift shop on-site. ✉ *2020 Demere Rd., St. Simons Island, GA* 🌐 *www.southernsoulbbq.com*

Kentucky

From bourbon distilleries and horse races to Mammoth Cave (the longest cave system in the world), there's plenty to check off your to-do list in the "Bluegrass State." If you happen to be in the horse-farm region around Lexington early in spring, notice the sea of tiny buds in the fields of Kentucky: bluegrass does indeed have a bluish-purple color. This lush carpet of bluegrass grows in limestone-based soil, rich in calcium and phosphates, making it ideal feed for the Thoroughbred racehorses that are raised in the region.

Capital: Frankfort

Population: 4,505,836

Area: 40,408 square miles

Statehood Date: June 1, 1792

Major Airports: Louisville Muhammad Ali International Airport (SDF); Cincinnati/Northern Kentucky International Airport (CVG); Blue Grass Airport (LEX)

Travel and Tourism Information: *www.kentuckytourism.com*; *www.kentucky-monthly.com/magazine*

Famous Residents: Daniel Boone (frontiersman); Abraham Lincoln (president); Bill Monroe (musician considered the father of bluegrass); Muhammad Ali (boxer); Loretta Lynn (singer); Jennifer Lawrence (actress)

Fun Fact: The high five is said to have potentially originated in Kentucky. Some say Wiley Brown and Derek Smith of the Louisville Cardinals men's college basketball team first performed the gesture during the 1978–79 season.

Kentucky Bourbon Trail

America's Best Booze

Kentucky, where bourbon was first commercially produced, still makes close to 95% of the world's bourbon (and more than 2 million barrels a year!), making it the definitive home of the spirit. Visit the country's top distilleries in Central Kentucky, a picturesque area full of rolling hills of the lush bluish grass that earns the state its nickname. There's a storied history to whiskey here (you'll get a mouthful of it while touring), but the bourbon country of today is a decade or two into a great resurgence, with an entire map of distilleries that have detailed tours and tastings. 🌐 *www.kybourbontrail.com*

Don't Miss

Big-name distilleries include **Maker's Mark**, **Jim Beam**, and **Evan Williams**, but just as worthy are exciting newcomers like **Castle & Key**, on gorgeous historical grounds, and Black-owned distillery **Fresh Bourbon Distillery**.

Best Tour

A great introduction to the history, traditions, and continual refinement of Kentucky bourbon making is **Buffalo Trace**, located in the state capital of Frankfort. Some of the country's finest brands—from Pappy Van Winkle to W. L. Weller—pour from the charred oak barrels here. ✉ *113 Great Buffalo Trace, Frankfort, KY* 🌐 *www.buffalotracedistillery.com*

Getting Here and Around

Lexington and Louisville are good bases to kick off your Bourbon Trail experience, with dozens of distilleries in between and across the state.

Mammoth Cave

The World's Longest Cave System

Spanning a distance of more than 400 miles, Mammoth Cave is the world's longest cave system, with its own unique ecosystem and miles of underground that still have yet to be mapped or fully explored. The best place to experience a little stretch of this massive system is Mammoth Cave National Park. The National Park Service offers a range of themed tours throughout the year to different sections of the cave, ranging from an easy quarter-mile to a physically demanding six-hour exploration. In the aboveground sections of the park, there are also campgrounds and hiking, biking, and kayaking trails (the Green River runs through here). 🌐 *www.nps.gov/maca*

Don't Miss

It's tradition to go for lunch at the **Porky Pig Diner** in nearby Smith's Grove before or after spelunking.

✉ *125 National Park Boundary Rd., Smiths Grove, KY*

Best Tour

The ranger-led **Cleaveland Avenue Tour** is the best choice for active visitors who care just as much about the fascinating geology of the cave as about its history. The Accessible Tour allows guests to visit part of Cleveland Avenue without stairs (enter via elevator).

Good to Know

Research ahead of time for special tours for those with limited mobility or who are claustrophobic. It can also be chilly inside the caves (around 55°F), so dress appropriately.

Getting Here and Around

Mammoth Cave National Park is in Kentucky "Cave Country," 85 miles southeast of Louisville International Airport and close to the city of Bowling Green, Kentucky (30 minutes).

The Kentucky Derby

America's Most Famous Horse Race

It's known as "the most exciting two minutes in sports" for a reason. The stakes are high as Thoroughbreds race to win the first leg of the Triple Crown and their jockeys a big purse prize. Big hats and bow ties fill the stands of **Churchill Downs** betting on greats like Authentic and American Pharoah while sipping mint juleps. Of course, there's more to Churchill Downs than Derby Day (though that is certainly its crowning event). On other race days during the season, you'll encounter fewer people, and there are choice activities from sun up to sundown, like **Downs After Dark**, an event combining racing under the lights with live, local art. ✉ *700 Central Ave., Louisville, KY* 🌐 *www.churchilldowns.com*

Don't Miss

The **Kentucky Derby Museum** is an on-site museum dedicated to Churchill Downs and the Derby (check out the jockey jerseys), and hosts events, tours, visitor packages, and the Derby Cafe and Bourbon Bar. ✉ *704 Central Ave., Louisville, KY* 🌐 *www.derbymuseum.org*

Good to Know

While there's no strict dress code for general admission, dressing to impress—in your biggest hat or loudest bow tie—is the name of the game, whether you're in the stands or a private suite.

When to Go

The Kentucky Derby always takes place, rain or shine, on the first Saturday of May; book far in advance.

Getting Here and Around

Louisville Muhammad Ali International Airport (SDF) is a convenient 4 miles from Churchill Downs. Plan to use a rideshare or bring cash for parking in the neighborhoods just outside the track.

Lexington Distillery District

A Whiskey Wonderland

Lexington's trendy Distillery District is where history meets hipsterdom. The 25-acre drinking and entertainment area includes the grounds of one of Lexington's oldest distilleries, **James E. Pepper**, which began making bourbon in 1879. After sitting in ruins for 50 years, the historic distillery underwent massive renovation and began making whiskey again in 2017, and is largely responsible for the revitalization of the Distillery District. Today's revamped James E. Pepper and the rest of the historic area feature some of the most fun dining and entertainment options in Lexington. ✉ *1228 Manchester St., Lexington, KY* 🌐 *www.lexingtondistillerydistrict.com*

Don't Miss

The historic roots and architecture of the place, along with its Town Branch creek location, add a scenic, cool vibe to the area, with **Elkhorn Tavern** all the rage for dining and **Ethereal Brewing** the favorite spot for craft beer. Save room for desert at **Crank & Boom**, which sources milk, blackberries, strawberries, and other ingredients from local farms. There is often live music outdoors as well as firepits and games like bocce.

Best Distillery Tour

A tour of James E. Pepper Distillery focuses both on the history of the legendary spot (Colonel Pepper is the most famous and colorful figure here) and the art of making whiskey—both the traditions and the new distillers' modern touches. 🌐 *www.jamesepepper.com*

Getting Here and Around

Lexington's Blue Grass Airport (LEX) is about a 10-minute drive from the Distillery District. The district is a short cab ride from downtown. It's a little over an hour's drive from Louisville to Lexington.

Louisville's Museum Row

Culture in Kentucky's Biggest City

Downtown Louisville's Museum Row has a little bit of everything the small city is known for—its famous figures and moments in history, arts and science, plus good food and bourbon. Great stops include the Louisville Slugger Museum, the interactive **Kentucky Science Center**, the **Frazier History Museum**, the **Muhammad Ali Center**, and the **Kentucky Center for the Performing Arts**, which houses small- and large-scale plays and musicals. **Evan Williams**, **Angel's Envy**, and **Old Forester** distilleries are also along Main Street. 🌐 *www.museumrowonmain.com*

Don't Miss

The **Louisville Slugger Museum** is a home run of a museum, where a seven-story baseball bat leans against the building housing the museum and bat factory. (An appropriately sized baseball is embedded in one window of the plate-glass factory next door, too.) Autographed bats of virtually every baseball great are on display. 🌐 *800 W. Main St., Louisville, KY* 🌐 *www.sluggermuseum.com*

Need a Break?

When you've worked up an appetite after exploring, stop in to **Royals Hot Chicken**, **Bar Vetti**, or **Mussel & Burger Bar**.

Getting Here and Around

Downtown and the East Market District (also called NuLu) are very walkable parts of Louisville; in general, getting around Louisville is quite manageable. Rideshares are available everywhere, and the airport is about a 10-minute drive from downtown.

Red River Gorge

World-Class Rock Climbing

A canyon system on the Red River, the gorge is perhaps best known as a world-class rock-climbing and hiking destination. Unique geological features such as natural stone arches, hidden caves, exposed rock faces, and giant sandstone cliffs ensure that every hike in the gorge's forested trail network is a beautiful wilderness experience. ✉ *Stanton, KY* 🌐 *www.redrivergorge.com*

Don't Miss

For the best day hike, take the 5½-mile **Bison Way Trail** to the Sheltowee Trace National Recreation Trail, the backbone of the forest's trail system. If you're feeling brave, scramble up the unmarked **Indian Staircase Trail**, a difficult 3½-mile trail offering a panoramic view of the gorge.

Where to Stay

Sleep among woodland creatures at tree houses nestled high into the forest or built into the cliffs. They vary in size and degree of luxury, from glamping in solar-powered domes to staying in large homes with hot tubs and Wi-Fi. All are unique, well designed, and an adventurous but relaxing way to experience the area. 🌐 *redrivergorge.com/listing/treehouses*

Getting Here and Around

The Red River Gorge is an hour's drive east of Lexington. Come for the natural wonders but stay for the restaurants (like customizable pizza spot Miguel's), campgrounds, cabins, and the skylift at Natural Bridge State Resort Park.

Bluegrass Country

The Soundtrack to Kentucky

Bluegrass country's happenin' string music takes its name from the Bluegrass State (after one of its early founders, Kentucky native Bill Monroe, formed a band with the "Blue Grass Boys"). Both the history of bluegrass music and its current musical iterations can be enjoyed in Kentucky, with festivals, museums, and active music venues around the state. The **Bluegrass Hall of Fame & Museum** is a good place to start, and they also have a calendar of live music. ✉ *311 W. 2nd St., Owensboro, KY* 🌐 *www.bluegrasshall.org*

Don't Miss

The **Kentucky Opry Theater** (✉ *88 Chilton La., Benton, KY* 🌐 *www.kentuckyopry.com*) is an excellent place to see a bluegrass, gospel, or country music show. The **Renfro Valley Entertainment Center** (✉ *2380 Richmond St., Mt. Vernon, KY* 🌐 *www.renfrovalley.com*) is surrounded by beautiful countryside and includes an amphitheater, shops, campground, and a music venue inside a historical barn. Gospel shows are particularly noteworthy.

When to Go

The **Jerusalem Ridge Bluegrass Celebration** is a four-day festival held in September at the childhood farm of Bill Monroe, the father of bluegrass, near Rosine, Kentucky. 🌐 *www.jerusalemridgefestival.com*

Getting Here and Around

Good nightclubs and large concert venues abound in Lexington and Louisville, but rural venues also have authentic bluegrass, gospel music, and festivals. You'll have to travel to these small towns to discover them, as many are south of Louisville and Lexington. Don't miss the Country Music Highway, in the far eastern part of the state, along the borders of Ohio, West Virginia, and Virginia.

University of Kentucky Basketball

Go Wild for the Wildcats

Claiming the title of best team in NCAA Division I history (in overall wins and most NCAA tournaments won), the University of Kentucky Wildcats are kind of a big deal. Even if you're not a die-hard fan, attending a UK game in at Lexington's **Rupp Arena** can be a chance to see the best of the best in college hoops. Current NBAers like Demarcus Cousins, Devin Booker, and Anthony Davis are among UK alumni. You can find fun, unofficial Cats and Kentucky gear at **The Kentucky Shop**, just up the street from Rupp. ✉ *430 W. Vine St., Lexington, KY* 🌐 *www.ukathletics.com*

Don't Miss

Aside from attending a game at Rupp Arena (where you can spend the night at the Hyatt Regency next door), visitors can buy gear, tour the pretty University of Kentucky campus, and get fanatic at a local bar.

Best UK Bar

Winchell's, a tried-and-true sports bar (with at least two dozen flat screens), also serves surprisingly good renditions of casual Kentucky specials like beer cheese, hot browns, and Kentucky Derby pie. It's worth a visit just for the hearty grub, but game days are especially fun. ✉ *348 Southland Dr., Lexington, KY* 🌐 *www.winchellsrestaurant.com*

Getting Here and Around

Lexington's Blue Grass Airport (LEX) is just 6 miles from the University of Kentucky. It's a little over an hour's drive from Lexington to Louisville.

Lexington Horse Country

The Horse Capital of the World

The hundreds of horse farms in the Lexington area (often referred to as the horse capital of the world) are often family-owned operations passed on for generations, and are largely responsible for the Derby and champion winners you see at the tracks today. Touring a horse farm adds history and context to the racing industry, giving visitors the opportunity to walk the picturesque grounds and interact with the animals themselves. **Heritage Farm**, located in Goshen, is home to an amazing restaurant and a variety of activities; **Spendthrift Farm**, in Lexington, is responsible for some big recent winners; and **Claiborne Farm**, in Paris, is the former pasture of Secretariat.

Don't Miss

Keeneland, while less well-known than Churchill Downs, is nevertheless at the heart of horse racing. Some of the best Thoroughbred racing in the world takes place here. You can tour the grounds, where the movie *Secretariat* was filmed, year-round. ✉ *4201 Versailles Rd., Lexington, KY* 🌐 *www.keeneland.com*

Best Horse Farm

At **Mill Ridge Nursery Farm** near Keeneland, there's a special dedication to the women behind horse racing, starting with Alice Chandler, the farm's founder, and a key figure in Kentucky racing history. The farm has sired a Kentucky Derby winner, nine Breeders' Cup winners, and three Horses of the Year. Most importantly, you get to pet foals. ✉ *2800 Bowman Mill Rd., Lexington, KY* 🌐 *www.millridge.com*

Getting Here and Around

Base yourself in Lexington for an easy drive to the horse farms in the surrounding countryside.

When in Kentucky

COCAINE BEAR

The legend of "Pablo Escobear" is full of bizarre details: it all starts in the 1980s, when a drug-smuggling Lexingtonian and party-boy lawyer named Andrew C. Thornton II fell to his death after getting tangled in his parachute and abandoning his small plane in the woods—and the pounds and pounds of cocaine that were on board for delivery. Months later, a black bear was found dead in the forest near the crash, having tragically overdosed on about $20 million worth of cocaine dropped by Thornton. After undergoing a long journey, changing hands from many improbable owners, the (alleged) original taxidermied cocaine bear is on display at the Kentucky for Kentucky store in Lexington.

Do This: The Kentucky for Kentucky store is a legendary place to visit for Kentucky clothing and memorabilia—and to hear more about the cocaine bear and other colorful stories about the Bluegrass State. ✉ *1315 Winchester Rd., Lexington, KY 40505* 🌐 *www.kyforky.com*

COUNTRY MUSIC HIGHWAY

U.S. Route 23 is a great way to explore eastern Kentucky or as part of a musical road trip of the greater South. Loretta Lynn, Chris Stapleton, Billy Ray Cyrus, and Ricky Skaggs are just some of the legends to emerge from these scenic hills and hollers. You can visit state parks, art centers, country music birthplaces, and several museums along the way—as well as the legendary feuding grounds of the Hatfields and McCoys. 🌐 *www.countrymusichighway.com*

Do This: Make a detour in Staffordsville, Kentucky, at the U.S. 23 Country Music Highway Museum, and then continue on through the town of Paintsville to visit the historic coal company store of Webb's Grocery and the birthplace of Loretta Lynn. ✉ *100 Stave Branch Rd., Staffordsville, KY* 🌐 *paintsvilletourism.com*

HARLAND SANDERS CAFE AND MUSEUM

The historic home of Kentucky Fried Chicken is in Corbin, Kentucky, and it's worth a visit if you're heading to Lexington or Louisville from the south. In the 1930s, Sanders began his humble restaurant here as a way to satisfy diners traveling Route 25. By the 1950s, when Interstate 75 was built and left the road and town in the dust, Sanders had begun selling franchises. This location (where he developed his secret recipe) is now a museum and restaurant. ✉ *688 Rte. 25, Corbin, KY* 🌐 *www.sanderscafe.com*

Do This: Driving through this area of Kentucky is picturesque, especially during fall when the leaves change and the backdrop of the bluffs looks especially dramatic. Head to nearby Cumberland Falls for more scenery.

About Our Writers

Though not a Kentuckian by birth, **Taylor Killough** has lived in Louisville for more than a dozen years, exploring communities from the mountains to the Mississippi. She'll never recommend that you eat a Hot Brown unless you can nap afterward, and you can catch her on Auxier Ridge, her favorite Red River Gorge trail. She's written for the *Washington Post*, the *Daily Beast*, and *Louisville Magazine*, and she currently produces media at a museum design-build firm.

Cool Places to Stay

The Brown. Opened in 1923, this grand but intimate hotel has a gilded second-floor lobby that gleams with marble and polished wood. Rooms are furnished with fine reproductions and luxurious bedding. A special Louisville dish, the Hot Brown, was invented here—you can order the turkey, bacon, and cheese sandwich–casserole hybrid from room service. It's worth a stop at the bar for an incredible bourbon selection even if you don't stay the night. ✉ *335 W. Broadway, Louisville, KY* 🌐 *www.brownhotel.com*

The Inn at Shaker Village of Pleasant Hill. At Pleasant Hill, traditional Shaker lodgings feel clean and chic. Spread out through the village, they range from boarding house–type rooms to private cottages. At the Historic Centre (an old Kentucky Shaker village) and the working farm, visitors learn and explore, with many options for tours and activities. The property, along the Kentucky River, is also home to a restaurant and riding stable. ✉ *3501 Lexington Rd., Harrodsburg, KY* 🌐 *www.shakervillageky.org/the-inn*

The Kentucky Castle. Only in a town called Versailles—though Kentuckians pronounce it Ver- *sails*—would you be able to stay in an honest-to-goodness castle. Nestled in the bluegrass hills outside of town, you'll find the pointy turrets, stone walls, and expansive grounds of the Kentucky Castle, originally the ambitious project of a real estate developer in 1969 after he and his wife returned from an inspirational tour of Europe. Now a high-end B&B, a fairy-tale stay comes with a ballroom, spa, and farm-to-table restaurant, where the property's "Bourbon Steward-in-Residence" prepares pairings with dinner. ✉ *230 Pisgah Pike, Versailles, KY* 🌐 *www.thekentuckycastle.com*

21C Museum Hotel Lexington. Rooms at this downtown boutique chain are home to gallery art—and not the placid, background stuff you might expect in a hotel lobby, but real, exciting installations and up-and-coming contemporary pieces. Aside from the nice amenities (spacious rooms, a good gym, nice breakfast options, and on-site fine dining), walking the gallery at night, with a cocktail from the bar in hand, makes this a special treat. There is another 21C property in downtown Louisville. ✉ *167 W. Main St., Lexington, KY* 🌐 *www.21cmuseumhotels.com/lexington*

Essential Eats

The Bar at Willet. Relax after a distillery tour at this intimate and modern full-service bar and restaurant. The drink menu features pages of Willett single-barrel selections, but the true stars here are the clever and thoughtfully presented cocktails like the Italian Julep, with bourbon, Fernet, and nicotine-free tobacco bitters, in a cold julep cup topped with crushed ice and a decorative cigarette (don't worry, it's fake). Order the egg salad sandwich, made with three types of eggs and smoked Duke's mayo on toasted brioche and topped with shredded aged Gouda (it has its own social media, it's that good). ✉ *1869 Loretto Rd., Bardstown, KY* 🌐 *www.thebaratwillett.com*🌐

Ferrell's Snappy Services. This gut-busting spot is the perfect time capsule of classic diners and burger joints gone by. Established in 1929, Ferrell's is a second-generation mom-and-pop eatery serving breakfast, burgers, and whatever else is listed on the chalkboard and dry erase menus behind the counter. There are three Western Kentucky locations (Madisonville, Cadiz, and Hopkinsville), but for the biggest nostalgia factor, follow the green neon sign to the original Ferrell's on Hopkinsville's Main Street. The prices are nostalgic, too—you can eat a whole meal here for under $10. ✉ *1001 S. Main St., Hopkinsville, KY*

Freight House. The small town of Paducah is worth the trip to the western edge of Kentucky, and Freight House is at the top of the list of reasons why. The two-time James Beard Award–nominated restaurant headed up by *Top Chef* runner-up Sarah Bradley features a menu that perfectly encapsulates the unique mix of Southern and Midwestern tastes found only in this region. Their specialty is hearty comfort food, like deviled eggs, pork rinds, pimento cheese, and shrimp and grits. Locally caught catfish are served up with couscous, tomato salad, and tahini caramel. ✉ *330 S. 3rd St., Paducah, KY* 🌐 *www.freighthousefood.com*

Kentucky Native Cafe. Part café, part bakery, and part garden, the path to the Native Cafe takes you through the stunning greenhouses of Michler's Florist, leading to a lush, green oasis that serves wine, craft beers, small plates, gelato, and more. The fare here matches the surroundings—light, airy, and mostly vegetarian. They always offer pretzels, hummus bowls, and a cheese plate for the table, but the rest of the menu rotates seasonally and sources ingredients locally. ✉ *417 E. Maxwell St., Lexington, KY* 🌐 *www.michlers.com/pages/cafe*

Louisiana

This former French (and Spanish) colony is divided into 64 parishes instead of counties, a mix of swampland and vibrant towns as well as a melting pot of the French, Creole, African, and American cultures that settled along its many waterways. The largest city, New Orleans, bursts with the jovial sounds of jazz, beckoning travelers to its French Quarter and festive Mardi Gras celebrations with a colorful parades, loud music, and larger-than-life floats. Don't you dare leave without tasting a beignet, a po'boy, and gumbo.

Capital: Baton Rouge

Population: 4,657,757

Area: 52,378 square miles

Statehood Date: April 30, 1812

Major Airports: Louis Armstrong International Airport (MSY); Baton Rouge Metropolitan Airport (BTR); Shreveport Regional Airport (SHV)

Travel and Tourism Information: 🌐 *www.explorelouisiana.com* 🌐 *www.64parishes.org*

Famous Residents: Tennessee Williams (playwright); Louis Armstrong (musician); Marie Laveau (voodoo queen); Lil Wayne (rapper); Britney Spears (singer); Peyton and Eli Manning (football players)

Fun Fact: Everything is a little different in Louisiana, so it's fitting that the state should have its very own werewolf. According to Cajun folklore, the *Rougarou*, a formidable creature with the body of a human and head of a wolf, haunts bayous and swamps, terrorizing children who misbehave.

The French Quarter

A Famous City's Historic Heart and Soul

New Orleans's oldest neighborhood is visually stunning, with Creole cottages, Spanish colonial architecture, and cobblestoned streets steeped in legends of brothels and pirates, ghosts and fires, and more packed with activity than anywhere else in the city. You must take a romp down rowdy **Bourbon Street** at least once (perhaps with a to-go drink in hand which is famously legal in the city); stroll the **French Market**; window-shop the galleries and antiques stores on **Royal Street**; get your fortune told at Jackson Square overlooking iconic **St. Louis Cathedral**; and eat a po'boy or two.

Don't Miss

It's practically a rite of passage to order beignets and a café au lait from **Café Du Monde**, New Orleans's mainstay coffee stand since 1862. It's cash only. ✉ *813 Decatur St., New Orleans, LA* 🌐 *shop.cafedumonde.com*

Best Bar

Lafitte's Blacksmith Shop, a ramshackle one-story building often called the oldest standing building in New Orleans, was once the workshop of infamous pirate Jean Lafitte. The front room is packed with tourists and rowdy locals drinking Abita beer and the shop's frozen "Purple Drink," a sugary, boozy specialty. ✉ *941 Bourbon St., New Orleans, LA* 🌐 *www.lafittes-blacksmithshop.com*

Getting Here and Around

It's fairly unpleasant to drive around the Quarter because of congestion, which is why you'll see streets filled with pedestrians and pedicabs. The St. Charles Avenue, Canal Street, and Rampart streetcar lines all go to the Quarter, and it's easy to walk around once you're here.

Mardi Gras

The Most Epic Carnival Season

Mardi Gras means so much more to New Orleans than beads, booze, and Bourbon Street; it's a historic and cultural event at the core of the city's identity. New Orleanians celebrate Fat Tuesday (traditionally one last day of indulging in rich foods before the start of Lent), with epic parades, balls, DIY costumes, concerts, and revelers lining the streets and balconies day and night. Carnival season begins long before Fat Tuesday (Krewe du Vieux and Chewbacchus are the parades to catch in earlier weeks) and appeals to costume-clad partygoers, music and art lovers, foodies, families, and more, from all over the world. 🌐 *www.mardigrasneworleans.com*

Don't Miss

The best places to catch a parade are along St. Charles Avenue in the Garden District and CBD, and along Canal Street in the French Quarter/CBD (many parades end here).

Best Stop

The **Backstreet Cultural Museum** is the Mardi Gras meeting place for tribes of Mardi Gras Indians, African American krewes clad in elaborate, painstakingly hand-sewn bead and feather getups. ✉ *1531 St. Philip St., New Orleans, LA* 🌐 *www.backstreet-museum.org*

When to Go

Major parades take place from the Thursday before Fat Tuesday through Mardi Gras evening; the exact dates change every year due to the Lenten calendar, but it's sometime between early February and early March.

Getting Here and Around

Parade routes block traffic for much of Mardi Gras week. Be prepared to walk, or plan far ahead for parking in the Garden District and Uptown.

Louisiana Swamps

Bewitching Bayous

Southeastern Louisiana's swamps and wetlands are known for their eerie beauty—with jutting cypress knees, swinging Spanish moss, and picturesque palmetto palms—and carry whole ecosystems in their submerged fields and forests. These are the places to spot alligators, especially on a sunny day with a boating guide who's expert at drawing them out. For a relatively quick trip to scenic swamplands, where you'll spot alligators and other fauna from a walking trail and boardwalk, head to **Jean Lafitte National Park and Preserve** about 20 miles outside New Orleans. Also close to New Orleans, you can board an airboat to explore the **Manchac** or **Honey Island Swamp**.

Don't Miss

Atchafalaya Basin, an 800,000-plus-acre swamp wilderness just northeast of Lafayette, is the largest wetland and swamp in the country—larger than the Florida Everglades—and home to bald eagles, alligators, black bears, and the tens of millions of pounds of crawfish that the country eats every year. Canoe, rent a boat, or walk the trails. 🌐 *www.atchafalaya.org/atchafalaya-basin*

Best Tour

You'll find boat rentals on the edge of the Atchafalaya Basin along Henderson Levee Road. **McGee's Louisiana Swamp & Airboat Tours** offers speedy airboat rides and slower-paced swamp boat rides, including a sunset weekend tour. More adventurous visitors can rent canoes from McGee's to peacefully explore the swamplands on their own. 🌐 *www.mcgeesswamptours.com*

Getting Here and Around

The Atchafalaya National Wildlife Refuge lies between Baton Rouge and Lafayette, Louisiana. The area welcome center is in the town of Breaux Bridge, just west of Lafayette.

The Tremé

The Birthplace of Jazz

The jubilant sounds of trumpets, trombones, and cornets fill the air every night of the year in the New Orleans neighborhood where jazz was born. Just above the French Quarter, the Tremé is the place it all began, the home of legends including Louis Armstrong, Jelly Roll Morton, and Trombone Shorty. **Congo Square**, a small cobblestone square off Rampart Street, was historically the Sunday meeting place (and the only meeting place allowed) for enslaved people to sing, dance, and celebrate African music and culture. A tradition born of oppression eventually formed the roots of contemporary jazz, and today musicians still gather here for percussion jams. Elsewhere in the city, **Frenchmen Street**, **Preservation Hall**, the **New Orleans Jazz Museum**, and the **Musical Legends Park** are good places to explore the sounds of the city.

Don't Miss

Catch live music in Congo Square in **Louis Armstrong Park** or in the excellent small music clubs like **Kermit's Tremé Mother-in-Law Lounge** or **Treme Hideaway**.

When to Go

Events like the famous **New Orleans Jazz Fest** (late April–early May) and **French Quarter Festival** (typically the third week of April) are the way to pack an entire weekend (or two) with the best local music acts. 🌐 *www.nojazzfest.com*

Getting Here and Around

You can walk to Congo Square and Frenchmen Street from the French Quarter or take a cab or rideshare. Once there, plan to walk the few blocks choosing clubs to enter at your leisure.

Bywater and Marigny

Epic NOLA Nightlife

The New Orleans neighborhoods of the Bywater and Faubourg Marigny are a mix of colorful shotgun houses, tropical plants and community gardens, small businesses, and muraled industrial spaces. They're at the core of the Crescent City's most innovative and creative areas, where newly arrived artists and entrepreneurs add to their historic legacy. **Frenchmen Street** is the place for packed-in live music, but you should also sip cocktails in the secret gardens of **Bacchanal** or **N7**, dance the night away at bars on **St. Claude Avenue**, or enter the magical, interactive world of the **Music Box Village**.

Don't Miss

Frenchmen Street in the Marigny, lined with popular cafés, clubs, and live-music joints like the **Spotted Cat Music Club** (✉ *623 Frenchmen St., New Orleans, LA* 🌐 *www.spottedcatmusicclub.com*) and **Blue Nile** (✉ *532 Frenchmen St., New Orleans, LA* 🌐 *www.bluenilelive.com*), is the ultimate night out for music lovers.

When to Go

For the most fun, visit a weekend in early Carnival season for Krewe of Chewbacchus, a sci-fi-theme parade through the Marigny and Bywater border, or early Mardi Gras morning for St. Anne's Parade, a magical, costume-clad march through the neighborhood's colorful streets.

Getting Here and Around

The Marigny is the smaller of the two neighborhoods and sits between the French Quarter and Bywater (also known as the Upper Ninth Ward) along the Mississippi River. There is a bus, and a short streetcar line (Rampart Street) that runs from the French Quarter to St. Claude in the Bywater.

The Whitney Plantation and Museum

A Sobering Memorial

Between New Orleans and Baton Rouge, many antebellum plantations along the Mississippi are open to visitors, filled with period antiques and evoking tales of Yankee gunboats and the ghosts of former residents. But the Whitney is the only antebellum mansion in this scenic stretch (and the only museum in all of Louisiana) that's exclusively dedicated to the history of slavery and the memory of those it harmed. The museum, opened by a retired lawyer in 2014, is on the grounds of a former indigo and sugarcane plantation dating back to 1752. Scenes from the movies *Django Unchained* and *12 Years a Slave* were filmed here. ✉ *5099 Hwy. 18, Wallace, LA* 🌐 *www.whitneyplantation.org*

Don't Miss

Seek out the original cabins and the commemorative "Children of Whitney" statues by Woodrow Nash.

Good to Know

To visit the Whitney, you must book a guided tour ahead of time (it lasts a little over an hour) but this experience is well worth it. An incredibly somber and emotional tour contains recorded personal accounts from formerly enslaved workers, and walks through the well-maintained grounds, including historical structures and former dwellings of enslaved peoples, museum exhibits, artifacts, and memorials.

Getting Here and Around

The museum, located on the west bank of the Mississippi River, is an hour's drive from both New Orleans and Baton Rouge. Avoid taking a rideshare since return service will be all but nonexistent. To get there, take Interstate 10 to Exit 194 and plan to spend the better part of a day taking it all in.

Haunted New Orleans

America's Most Haunted City

To truly know New Orleans is to understand its strong ties to the spiritual realm, including voodoo practices, legendary ghost and vampire stories, and eerily beautiful cemeteries where more than a few things have been said to go bump in the night. Ghost tours typically take visitors through the famous aboveground graves of **St. Louis Cemetery No. 1** (✉ *425 Basin St., New Orleans, LA* 🌐 *cemeterytourneworleans.com*), the oldest and most famous of New Orleans's cities of the dead. Tours will also walk the grounds and weave in the legends of the city's most haunted sites, like **Storyville**, the former red-light district, and the **LaLaurie Mansion**, the former home of the cruel and torturing slave owner dramatized in *American Horror Story*.

Don't Miss

The superstitious should not skip Marie Laveau's **House of Voodoo**, a place to learn about voodoo priestess Marie Laveau, who ruled over all things occult in the 19th century. She lived blocks from Congo Square, where she would lead chants, sell talismans, and gather useful information. Visit Laveau's grave in St. Louis Cemetery No. 1. ✉ *628 Bourbon St., New Orleans, LA* 🌐 *www.voodooneworleans.com*

Best Tour

To experience it all with a dose of extra drama, spend a couple of hours with **Ghost City Tours** or **French Quarter Phantoms**, and book a haunted hotel for extra frights.

Getting Here and Around

Most haunted history and ghost tours meet in the French Quarter near the St. Louis Cathedral and Jackson Square. While St. Louis Cemetery No. 1 is the most famous, you can easily hop a street car to arrive at No. 2 (✉ *300 N. Claiborne Ave.*) and No. 3 (🌐 *3421 Esplanade Ave.*).

Cajun Country

Culture and Crawfish Capital

When Acadians (French-Canadian colonists) migrated south to the bayous of Louisiana in the 18th century, they brought a way of life revolving around food, family, and music. After centuries of calling this area home, meeting with influences of African, Spanish, Italian, Creole, and Native American peoples, the Acadian corner of the world continues to flourish. Visit Lafayette and surrounding towns like **Breaux Bridge**, **St. Martinville**, **Abbeville**, and **New Iberia**, trying foods like boudin sausage, cracklins, and crawfish; "cutting a rug" at Cajun dance halls and music festivals; and touring cultural centers like **LARC's Acadian Village**.

Don't Miss

The crawfish capital of the world is **Breaux Bridge**, a small town full of personality, where there's a legendary crawfish festival every spring. There are also many antiques shops, nearby bayous, and great Cajun food. On Saturday, Zydeco Breakfast at **Buck and Johnny's** is the can't-miss event. ✉ *100 Berard St., Breaux Bridge, LA* 🌐 *www.buckandjohnnys.com*

While You're Here

It's essential to stop for boudin—a specialty sausage stuffed with rice and seasoning—at one of the humble stands around Interstate 10 and its backroads, such as **Poche's** or **Billy's**.

Getting Here and Around

Lafayette is the biggest city in Cajun Country, 135 miles west of New Orleans. From Lafayette, you can easily explore the Atchafalaya National Wildlife Refuge and the towns of Breaux Bridge, St. Martinville, Abbeville, and New Iberia.

Fishing Louisiana's Waters

An Angler's Paradise

Considering that almost half Louisiana is covered by water of some sort—over 3 million acres of wetlands, with 5,000 miles of navigable rivers, creeks, bayous, and canals—it's no wonder that hobbyists and professionals come from all over the world to fish for prize-winning tarpon, red fish, bowfin, and more. Among the intricate system of waterways that convene as the Mississippi River flows into the Gulf of Mexico, anglers can cast a line from the shore, sight-fish the marshes in a jon boat or kayak, or book a deepwater fishing expedition in the Gulf. Visiting the fishing towns southeast and southwest of New Orleans is also a chance to commune with nature, bird-watch, and get to know the communities and cultures that have built their lives along the water. Elsewhere in the state, Chicot State Park or **Lake Bistineau State Park** are great spots for catching bass and crappie.

Don't Miss

From New Orleans, drive southwest to **Grand Isle**, a coastal town with a popular fishing beach, where you'll see the land simply melt away as you approach the Gulf. In Grand Isle State Park, you can fish, camp, bird-watch, climb the observation tower, or take a walk along the interpretive nature trail. Fun fact: Grand Isle is the only inhabited barrier island in Louisiana, and the resort town is also the setting of Kate Chopin's novel *The Awakening*.

Good to Know

Offshore fishing trips in the Gulf leave from **Venice Marina**, southeast of New Orleans. Follow LA-23 all the way down to the southernmost piece of land in the state, and you'll soon understand why Venice is nicknamed "The End of The World."

When in Louisiana

ABITA MYSTERY HOUSE

Artist John Preble's strange vision—sort of a Louisiana version of the Watts Towers of Los Angeles—is an obsessive collection of found objects (combs, old musical instruments, paint-by-number art, and taxidermy experiments gone horribly awry) set in a series of ramshackle buildings, including one covered in mosaic tiles. The museum is truly odd and entertaining. ✉ *22275 Rte. 36, Abita Springs, LA* 🌐 *www.abitamysteryhouse.com*

Do This: Make a day out of a visit to this quaint town. Along with the Abita Brewing Company, there are small shops and restaurants. On the Tammany Trace, you can bike or walk along scenic stretches of the North Shore.

AVERY ISLAND

While Avery Island is best known as the headquarters of Tabasco hot sauce—it has been privately owned by the creators, the Avery-McIlhenny family, for almost 200 years—it's also home to a wildlife refuge for snowy egrets and more than 50 archaeological sites. A unique ecological treasure, the island is actually a solid salt dome that rises above its flat coastal marsh surroundings and covers more than 2,000 acres. Most geologists credit its creation to salt deposits left over from an ancient seabed. After a fun tour of the Tabasco factory, take time to appreciate the island's flora and fauna. 🌐 *www.tabasco.com/visit-avery-island*

Do This: Avery Island is about 45 minutes southeast of Lafayette, so it makes a good day trip when exploring Cajun Country. New Iberia, the closest town, has lodging and restaurants. While you're on the island, marvel at the natural wonderland of Bird City—a sanctuary created for the snowy egret—and walk through the island's beautiful botanical gardens with a serene Buddhist temple and live oaks draped in Spanish moss.

MANCHAC MANSION

There's nothing quite as eerie as a house rising up in the middle of a swamp. This site, the ruins of a submerged house surrounded by water and cypress forest, make Manchac Swamp a particularly intriguing—and haunting—place to paddle. Canoe in Trails Adventures leads excellent guided tours of the swamp, though you can also rent your own to paddle the area and continue up through Lake Maurepas. The swamp is northwest of New Orleans via Interstate 10 West and Interstate 55. ✉ *Ponchatoula, LA* 🌐 *www.canoeandtrail.com*

Do This: Local boaters know it's essential to stop at Middendorf's nearby for lunch after a paddle or for a picnic po'boy to go. The restaurant is famous for its paper-thin fried catfish. ✉ *30160 U.S. 51, Akers, LA* 🌐 *middendorfsrestaurant.com*

About Our Writers

Cameron Todd lived in New Orleans for 13 years, most recently in Algiers Point, which she considers the best neighborhood in the city. Some of her favorite things include fresh Gulf shrimp, camping trips in her Japanese van, and French Quarter staycations (an art she has perfected as a Fodor's hotel reviewer). She is a freelance writer and editor.

Cool Places to Stay

The Chloe. A hip local restaurant group revamped this historic mansion on Saint Charles Avenue, painting it a moody blue-green, and adding an art deco–style pool area, an excellent restaurant, and impeccable interior decor. The house was originally designed by architect Thomas Sully, responsible for many of the area's most impressive mansions, and there are unique architectural features honored throughout the public spaces in rooms, in tucked away dining areas, and in seemingly hidden passages and entryways. Rooms have touches of luxury with local boutique bath products. ✉ *4125 St. Charles Ave., New Orleans, LA* 🌐 *www.thechloenola.com*

Country Charm Bed and Breakfast. Stay along the water at a funky fishing cabin here, and you'll get the best of the natural world of Cajun Country—with nearby culture and fun in Lafayette and in the small town of Breaux Bridge. Even if fishing is not your thing, the outdoor area overlooking the lake is appealing. The suites decorated with antiques and the hospitality and friendly touches provided by hosts are all you would want and expect from a place touting "country charm." ✉ *1144 Lawless Tauzin Rd., Breaux Bridge, LA* 🌐 *www.country-charmbb.com*

Hotel Peter and Paul. A longtime resident of the Marigny neighborhood teamed with a boutique-hotel group to renovate this former church and rectory, creating this one-of-a-kind hotel, supremely rooted in place. The unique architectural touches, careful color schemes (a different one on every floor), and sparse but dramatic oversized European antiques are just some of the features that make it so aesthetically pleasing. Food and drink is brought to you by the team behind Bacchanal, a very popular local bar. ✉ *2317 Burgundy St., New Orleans, LA* 🌐 *www.hotelpeterandpaul.com*

St. Francisville Inn. Full of luxurious touches and ornate detail, this Victorian inn ticks the box for Southern charm. The surrounding town of St. Francisville, with antiques shops, restaurants, and hikes at nearby Tunica Falls, is just two hours from New Orleans and makes for a great side trip. There are 11 well-appointed rooms with marble bathrooms, a pool and lounge area, a great restaurant, and front-porch rocking chairs overlooking lush gardens. ✉ *5720 Commerce St., St. Francisville, LA* 🌐 *www.stfrancisvilleinn.com*

Essential Eats

Cajun vs. Creole Food. Cajun and Creole food dominate the Louisiana culinary world as well as its history: recipes are passed down from generation to generation, and even the fanciest restaurants seek to re-create Grandma's gumbo or Mamaw's étouffée. Cajun food has Acadian roots, is often more rustic yet spicier than Creole food, and rarely uses tomatoes. The best Cajun food—crawfish étouffée, boudin, and their version of gumbo—can be found around Lafayette and other rural areas. Creole flavors come from the melting pot of African, Native American, and European cultures that made up early New Orleans; Creole dishes, best tasted in New Orleans restaurants, use more ingredients, rich sauces, tomatoes, and seafood.

Commander's Palace. No restaurant captures New Orleans's gastronomic heritage and celebratory spirit as well as this grande dame of New Orleans fine dining. The menu's classics include a spicy and meaty turtle soup; shrimp and tasso Henican (shrimp stuffed with ham, with pickled okra); and a wonderful pecan-crusted Gulf fish. The bread-pudding soufflé might ruin you for other bread puddings. Upstairs, the Garden Room's glass walls have marvelous views of the giant oak trees on the patio below. The weekend brunch is a not-to-be-missed New Orleans tradition, complete with live jazz—the band takes requests, so come armed with tip money. Jackets are preferred at dinner; shorts and T-shirts are forbidden, ripped jeans are not allowed, and men must wear closed-toe shoes. ✉ *1403 Washington Ave., New Orleans, LA* 🌐 *www.commanderspalace.com*

Crawfish. During crawfish season, Louisianans use any occasion or get-together as an excuse for a boil, cooking the live mudbugs with plenty of spice, potatoes, celery, and other fixings. The small crustaceans—the size of shrimp, but more closely related to lobster—are sold by the sack or platter at bars and seafood shacks (and the supermarket Rouses) from early spring to mid-summer. Frozen crawfish tails are used year-round in delicious creations that go well beyond the classic étouffée.

Fried Chicken. Don't get us wrong: you will eat some of the best fried chicken of your life at New Orleans institutions like Dooky Chase Restaurant and Willie Mae's Scotch House. But there's something delightful about discovering just how many gas stations (yes, gas stations), corner stores, and holes-in-the-wall in Louisiana get that balance of spice, tender meat, and crispy crunch *just* right.

Po'boys. Poor boy sandwiches were allegedly invented during a 1929 streetcar strike, as a way to cheaply feed the striking masses. Domilise's and Parkway Bakery and Tavern in New Orleans serve the best versions of classic po'boys: crispy fried shrimp with all the fixings, and slow-cooked roast beef, dripping in gravy.

Saint-Germain. For an unforgettable evening in NOLA, make your way to this tiny, tasting menu–only restaurant inside a shotgun house on an unassuming section of St. Claude Avenue. Reservations open up a month in advance. The 10-course meal always includes impressive technique and fresh, local flavors, creating the feeling of eating at the chef's home table. In the garden out back, you can sip glasses of natural wine under the citrus trees and wish you never had to leave. ✉ *3054 St. Claude Ave., New Orleans, LA* 🌐 *saintgermainnola.com*

Mississippi

Mississippi is a multifaceted landscape of rich history, legendary musical heritage, culinary delights, and stunning outdoor adventures. From the natural splendor of the mighty Mississippi River to the sandy beaches of the Gulf Coast, Mississippi celebrates diversity and creativity through its people, geography, sights, and sounds. Journey along miles of hiking and biking trails, savor a plate full of mouthwatering comfort food, or dance to the authentic sounds of blues, country, and rock and roll in the birthplace of it all.

Capital: Jackson

Population: 2,961,279

Area: 46,925 square miles

Statehood Date: December 10, 1817

Major Airports: Jackson–Medgar Wiley Evers International Airport (JAN); Gulfport-Biloxi International Airport (GPT)

Travel and Tourism Information: www.visitmississippi.org 🌐 *www.mstourism.com*

Famous Residents: William Faulkner (writer); Medgar Evers (civil rights activist); Elvis Presley (singer); B.B. King (blues legend); Oprah Winfrey (lifestyle guru); Faith Hill (country singer); Brett Favre (football player)

Fun Fact: Did you know that one of the world's most popular beverages, Coca-Cola, was first bottled in Mississippi? In 1894, Joseph A. Biedenharn bottled Coca-Cola in Vicksburg, Mississippi.

Clarksdale and the Mississippi Blues Trail

Land of the Delta Blues

At an intersection of Highways 61 and 49, marked today by a blue pole affixed with electric guitars called the "Crossroads," musician Robert Johnson sold his soul to the devil so he could play guitar. It's no surprise then, that this Mississippi Delta town is home to several iconic blues landmarks commemorating area musicians like Ike Turner, Muddy Waters, and Sam Cooke. Today's Clarksdale is a mix of commemorative Blues Trail plaques, small museums, sleepy streets, "eat places" (casual traditional Delta restaurants), and a few still-active music joints. 🌐 *www.msbluestrail.org*

Don't Miss

The best way to feel the blues is to enter one of the town's historic juke joints (small music clubs that are still in operation), like **Ground Zero Blues Club** (✉ *387 Delta Ave., Clarksdale, MS* 🌐 *www.groundzerobluesclub.com*) and **Red's Lounge** (✉ *398 Sunflower Ave., Clarksdale, MS* 🌐 *www.facebook.com/redsblueslounge*).

Best Museum

The **Delta Blues Museum** provides a deep understanding of the blues and is home to some impressive pieces of music history, including the remnants of the cabin where Muddy Waters lived when he was a sharecropper at Stovall Farms. ✉ *1 Blues Alley, Clarksdale, MS* 🌐 *www.deltabluesmuseum.org*

Getting Here and Around

Clarksdale is about 70 miles southwest of Memphis International Airport, which is a 1½-hour drive.

Oxford

Home of Southern Gothic Literature

Oxford is a literary powerhouse and was home to one of literature's most prominent figures, William Faulkner, who had a major influence on the Southern Gothic genre. Among its other celebrated former residents are Barry Hannah and Larry Brown, who fully embraced living in Oxford until their passings. In addition to its prose-driven reputation, Oxford is home to one of the state's largest universities: the **University of Mississippi** (or "Ole Miss"). Known for its dedication to traditional Southern culture, academic excellence, and high-energy football games, Ole Miss encapsulates the full essence of Oxford.

Don't Miss

You can tour **Rowan Oak**, Faulkner's historic home, on a guided tour. A pleasant walk through Bailey's Woods, between Rowan Oak and the University of Mississippi Museum, provides real-life illustrations to familiar Faulkner scenes. ✉ *916 Old Taylor Rd., Oxford, MS* 🌐 *www.rowanoak.com*

Best Bookstore

A literary stroll through Oxford should end at **Square Books**, a renowned bookstore in Town Square. There are signed books from local and visiting authors, an expansive Faulkner collection, and an impressive selection of wider Southern and literary fiction. ✉ *160 Courthouse Sq., Oxford, MS* 🌐 *www.squarebooks.com*

Getting Here and Around

The university-owned Oxford-University Airport is for public use, but it's rare to find a flight into Oxford. The best way to get here is to fly into Memphis International Airport and drive 1½ hours south.

The Mississippi Freedom Trail in Jackson

A Capital City of Civil Rights

Civil rights history is one of the primary reasons why Mississippi's state capitol is worth visiting. The Mississippi Freedom Trail passes through here, with several landmarks and museums commemorating the city's civil rights leaders and the sobering acts of violence, and centuries of racism, that spurred the movement. Two noteworthy museums that carefully examine the state's role in the civil rights movement are the **Mississippi Civil Rights Museum** (✉ *222 North St., Jackson, MS* 🌐 *mscivilrightsmuseum.com*) and the **Smith Robertson Museum and Cultural Center** (✉ *528 Bloom St., Jackson, MS* 🌐 *jacksonms.gov/smith-robertson-museum*).

Don't Miss

The **Medgar and Myrlie Evers Home National Monument** is the home where the activist lived and was murdered in 1963; while visiting, you can also learn about the 1963 Woolworth sit-in. ✉ *2332 Margaret W. Alexander Dr., Jackson, MS* 🌐 *www.nps.gov/memy*

Best Neighborhood

Jackson's **Fondren District**—home to artists, shops, cafés, and a cocktail bar at Brent's Drugs—is a great neighborhood for walking and soaking up the sights and sounds of the city.

While You're Here

During college football season, score tickets to see Jackson State's Marching Band, the **Sonic Boom of the South**, who made a virtual cameo performance in the 2021 presidential inauguration.

Getting Here and Around

The Jackson–Medgar Wiley Evers International Airport is about 6 miles from downtown Jackson. The city is a 3½-hour drive from Memphis, and just under 3 hours from New Orleans.

Natchez Trace Parkway

A Scenic Drive Through History

Natchez Trace Parkway is a slow and scenic road following what was once the Natchez Trail, a 444-mile Native American footpath running from Natchez, Mississippi, to Nashville, Tennessee. Make a drive of it, stopping at a beautiful cypress swamp near Canton, plus two waterfalls (**Jackson Falls** and **Fall Hollow Waterfall**) as well as a natural spring (**Rock Spring**) and parts of the original path. There's also a visitor center at the trail's northern point in Tupelo, and a few landmarks highlighting the former "stands" (inns) of European and American traders, plus points of local American Indian history. 🌐 *www.nps.gov/natr*

Don't Miss

In **Port Gibson**, southwest of Jackson, visitors can walk part of the original, much-eroded "Sunken Trace," canopied by a beautiful ancient forest.

Best Stop

The southernmost destination on the trail is the town of Natchez. The **Natchez Museum of African American Culture** has free guided tours and is a worthwhile way to spend a couple of hours. Some Mississippi River cruises also dock in this city. ✉ *301 Main St., Natchez, MS* 🌐 *www.visitnapac.net*

Good to Know

Bear in mind that the speed limit on the trace is slow, and this scenic parkway is not the fastest way to reach anywhere. In Tupelo, pick up a map and talk to a ranger about what sections you'd like to see.

Getting Here and Around

Within Mississippi, the trace extends north to south, from Tupelo to Natchez. If you're up for more exploration, Madison and Kosciusko both make great stops for a road trip along the trace.

Ocean Springs

Small Town Funk

For a small town, Oceans Springs holds an incredibly concentrated amount of funk and personality that attracts artists and musicians—it's also home to the entrance and visitor center for the **Gulf Islands National Seashore**. The area's best-known artist is the late Walter Anderson, whose art was inspired by the eerie Gulf Shore landscapes and is still on display in shops throughout the town and in a local museum. Adding to the eclectic atmosphere of Ocean Springs is **the Shed**, a funky barbecue joint with live music and sprawling porches.

Don't Miss

Aunt Jenny's Catfish Restaurant isn't just the best spot for fried catfish fillets—it's full of colorful local history as well. After their meal, guests can request a tour (peppered with local lore) of the **Julep Room Lounge**, an underground music club where Elvis used to hang. ✉ *1217 Washington Ave., Ocean Springs, MS* 🌐 *www.facebook.com/auntjennyscatfish*

Best Museum

The **Walter Anderson Museum of Art** showcases the best of prolific painter and craftsman Walter Anderson. The New Orleans–born artist made a home in Ocean Springs, and his best works are ethereal landscapes and other media reflecting a spiritual and imaginative relationship with his Gulf Shores surroundings. The museum exhibits other local and up-and-coming artists as well. ✉ *510 Washington Ave., Ocean Springs, MS* 🌐 *www.walterandersonmuseum.org*

Getting Here and Around

Ocean Springs is located between Interstate 10 and U.S. 90, 22 miles east (30 minutes) of the Gulfport-Biloxi International Airport and 100 miles (1½ hours) from New Orleans International Airport.

Biloxi and the Gulf Coast Scenic Byway

The Great Coastal Road Trip

The stretch of U.S. 90 that runs along Mississippi's Gulf Coast is one of the most popular road trips in the state. **Pass Christian**, **Waveland**, and **Bay St. Louis** are popular beach towns here with relaxing scenery, Gulf-side restaurants, and interesting small shops. **Biloxi**, the last and largest town along the way, is known for its casinos and resorts. The annual **Frida Fest**, in the eclectic little town of Bay St. Louis, brings lovers of the Mexican artist together each July for fun activities and art. 🌐 *www.gulfcoast-scenicbyways.com*

Don't Miss

In Waveland, camp out in **Buccaneer State Park** surrounded by mossy oak and marsh. Take a hike through the 1.8-mile Pirate's Alley Nature Trail. Afterward, hit the water before driving to the next beach town.

Order This

Royal reds are a large and sweet species of shrimp (they've been compared to lobster) that are a unique delicacy in the area. They appear on Mississippi Gulf menus beginning in late summer.

Good to Know

Although there are many draws to the Gulf Shore, swimming isn't necessarily one of them. While beaches can be nice, the Gulf water can get almost unpleasantly warm (think a bathtub in a bad way) in summer, and it isn't the cleanest water, especially around Biloxi.

Getting Here and Around

Biloxi is about an hour's drive from Louis Armstrong New Orleans International Airport (MSY), though travelers can also fly directly into Gulfport-Biloxi International Airport, located nearby.

Tupelo

Birthplace of Elvis

This north Mississippi town's claim to fame is being the humble hometown of the King of Rock and Roll, Elvis Presley. There are plenty of Elvis-related activities available, including tours, landmarks, and a summer festival dedicated to the King as well as plenty of Elvis-inspired art. While Elvis's legacy is the main attraction, there are other small-town wonders to enjoy like quaint barbecue and burger shops, a summer concert series, and variety of shopping boutiques. The Natchez Trace Parkway also begins in Tupelo, and visitors can dive into the history of the trace and its inhabitants at the visitor center.

Don't Miss

Elvis Presley's two-room home on the outskirts of town is now a prominent landmark, along with his childhood church. ✉ *306 Elvis Presley Dr., Tupelo, MS* 🌐 *www.elvispresleybirthplace.com*

Best Tour

Elvis' Tupelo Self-Guided Bicycle Tour is the ultimate way to tour the King's hometown. Rent a bike at Trails and Treads before accessing the free bicycle tour map to explore 13 stops where the King grew into a legend. Aside from his house, there's **Tupelo Hardware**, where Elvis's mother bought him his first guitar, and a stop at Tupelo's oldest restaurant, **Johnnie's Drive-in**, where guests can sit at the same booth as Presley. 🌐 *www.tupelo.net/blog/elvis-tupelo-self-guided-bicycle-tour*

Getting Here and Around

Contour Airlines flies to Tupelo Regional Airport from Nashville. The closest major airport is Memphis International Airport (MEM), which is a little over a 1½-hour drive.

Red Bluff

Mississippi's Own Little Grand Canyon

Nestled in the small town of Foxworth is Red Bluff, a geographical wonder that mimics the appearance of the much more famous Grand Canyon. Red Bluff started as a small erosion on Route 587, and from there, it slowly grew into the deep valley you see today, one of the Magnolia State's most remarkable landmarks. With each and every drop of rain, Red Bluff gets larger and deeper than it was before. Make sure to visit with caution and wear nonslip shoes to prevent falls.

Don't Miss

To make the best of your Red Bluff experience, start with your attire. Wear comfortable clothing and shoes with good traction. After that, trek through the bluff itself. Don't miss hiking the loop trail, where beautiful canyon views and striking clay-red walls make this incredible, natural wonder a must-see.

Best Restaurants

Nothing quite says "Mississippi" like fried seafood and steak. Located in Foxworth, only 16 minutes from Red Bluff, **Kane's Catfish, Seafood, and Steakhouse** (✉ *3129 Rte. 35 S, Foxworth, MS* 🌐 *kanescatfish.com*) is a small-town favorite for their scrumptious catfish platter and mouthwatering hush puppies. Also in Foxworth, **Cha-Cha's Custard and More** (✉ *28 Rte. 587, Foxworth, MS*) is the perfect stop for a refreshing treat after spending time at Red Bluff. Here you can enjoy a snowball or a frozen custard with a variety of toppings.

Getting Here and Around

The closest large city is Hattiesburg, just under an hour away from Red Bluff. The Hattiesburg-Laurel Regional Airport is located right off of Interstate 59 between Hattiesburg and Laurel.

When in Mississippi

BIRTHPLACE OF KERMIT THE FROG

A shack along the river seems fitting for the birthplace of America's favorite amphibian, celebrated in this small museum in Jim Henson's hometown, where you can explore Henson's childhood and inspiration. It's hokey, but hey, it's not easy being green. ✉ *415 S. Deer Creek Dr. E, Leland, MS*

Do This: Take a look at the beautiful, colorful murals sprinkled throughout downtown Leland. These murals feature iconic blues legends who helped shape the culture of the state.

GULF ISLANDS NATIONAL SEASHORE

Sink your feet in the sand on one of the barrier islands found between Mississippi and Florida. This nationally protected seashore is paradise epitomized, with uninterrupted natural landscapes, beaches, flora, and fauna. With an entrance outside of Ocean Springs, the islands belonging to Mississippi offer a range of activities including bike trails, trekking adventures through Davis Bayou Trail's coastal forest, and exceptional fishing, snorkeling, and kayaking. The preserved wildness of this area, along with its unique ecosystem, are what makes this area so special. 🌐 *www.nps.gov/guis*

Do This: Ship Island, where dolphin sightings abound, is the most popular of the area's coastal barrier islands (the others are Cat Island, Horn Island, Petit Bois, and West Petit Bois). Take the Ship Island Ferry, which runs from March through October, to the island's swim beach and historic fort. 🌐 *msshipisland.com*

MCCARTY'S POTTERY

This shop is an unlikely hidden gem in the charming Delta town of Merigold. It's run by a ceramicist couple who opened their kiln in the 1950s and have since been showcased in museums and lauded with awards. Today the shop sells all sorts of fine goods made from Mississippi clay, from whimsical animal figurines to fine serving dishes and everything in between. Surrounded by slightly wild and equally whimsical gardens, this road stop is unassuming, but loaded with character and history. ✉ *101 St. Mary St., Merigold, MS* 🌐 *www.mccartyspottery.com*

Do This: The shop also delightedly serves lunch at the McCarty's Gallery. Make sure to reserve a table in advance to enjoy an afternoon of fine dining while being surrounded by beautiful, handmade ceramic pieces. ✉ *100 Sunflower St., Merigold, MS*

MISSISSIPPI PETRIFIED FOREST

This seemingly unexpected roadside attraction 26 miles northwest of Jackson makes for a peaceful stop on a road trip through Mississippi. Beginning in the gift shop, visitors make their way along a walking path through the only preserved petrified forest in this part of the country. Pamphlets and markers tell the ancient history of the trees. The visit ends in a small museum of natural artifacts, where you can gain insight about the geological history of this incredible area. ✉ *124 Forest Park Rd., Flora, MS* 🌐 *www.mspetrifiedforest.com*

About Our Writers

A proud Foxworth, Mississippi native, **Allyson Alford** currently resides in Hattiesburg. She has a knack for discovering hidden gems within the Magnolia State and believes the best gems are found within Mississippi's small towns. Allyson is a graduate of the University of Mississippi and a contributing writer for *Our Mississippi Home*.

Do This: Have lunch at the Flora Butcher on the nearby town of Flora's quaint main street. The old-school butcher shop sells quality cuts of local meat. ✉ *4843 E. Main St., Flora, MS* 🌐 *www.facebook.com/theflorabutcher*

Cool Places to Stay

The Graduate Oxford. Just a mile from University of Mississippi campus, this boutique hotel celebrates all things Ole Miss, with plaid and seersucker decor and a funky retro vibe throughout. The on-site restaurant serves up classic Southern comfort favorites while its four-floor cocktail bar offers excellent views of the city's main square. ✉ *400 N Lamar Blvd, Oxford, MS* 🌐 *www.hilton.com*

Shack Up Inn. Rough around the edges and steeped in history, with plenty of music along the way, it doesn't get more Delta than lodging in these old sharecropper cabins (with an on-site juke joint). This is weathered Americana at its best ("the Ritz we ain't," the Shack Up Inn boasts) with plenty of front-porch rocking chairs. ✉ *001 Commissary Cir. Rd., Clarksdale, MS* 🌐 *www.shackupinn.com*

Travelers Hotel Clarksdale. For decades, the Delta region has been a meeting place of creative minds, and this unique spot follows suit. The 20-room hotel is run by a cooperative of artists, and you're sure to meet some interesting people here. In the open-air lobby surrounded by local art, you'll find craft beer on tap and locally roasted coffee. There's a lot of natural light, historic industrial features, and handmade furniture in each room. ✉ *212 3rd St., Clarksdale, MS* 🌐 *www.stayattravelers.com*

Essential Eats

Ajax Diner. If you're looking for a taste of Cajun cuisine mixed with Mississippi-style cooking, Ajax is the perfect place. Tucked into the town square of Oxford since 1997, Ajax is known for its relaxed atmosphere, kind service, and exceptional food, including hearty po'boys and pot roast. ✉ *118 Courthouse Sq., Oxford, MS* 🌐 *www.ajaxdiner.com*

The Old Country Store. A quintessential Southern road trip stop, this old general store doesn't look like much from the outside, and to be honest, the inside isn't all that fancy either, but it's an excellent stop for all the down-home Southern favorites you can imagine, served buffet-style, with a special focus on fried chicken in all its glory (you'll find plenty of other fixins, including corn bread, collard greens, and berry cobbler). ✉ *18801 U.S. 61, Lorman, MS*

Shaggy's Biloxi Beach. With a two-story beachside structure, eclectic decor, and mouthwatering seafood and burgers, Shaggy's fully encapsulates the ambience of the Mississippi Gulf Coast. ✉ *1763 Beach Blvd., Biloxi, MS* 🌐 *www.shaggys.com*

North Carolina

From the Outer Banks' secluded barrier islands to the Smoky Mountains' majestic peaks, North Carolina is an outdoor enthusiast's dream. There are scenic drives along the Blue Ridge Parkway, quaint mountain towns, and numerous opportunities for hiking, biking, and fishing. Urban adventures include hip Asheville and university-centric cities like Raleigh, Durham, and Chapel Hill.

Capital: Raleigh

Population: 11,046,024

Area: 53,819 square miles

Statehood Date: November 21, 1789

Major Airports: Charlotte Douglas International Airport (CLT); Raleigh-Durham International Airport (RDU); Asheville Regional Airport (AVL)

Travel and Tourism Information: 🌐 *www.visitnc.com* 🌐 *www.ourstate.com*

Famous Residents: Andy Griffith (actor); Nina Simone (singer); James Taylor (musician); Michael Jordan (basketball player); Nicholas Sparks (writer); Amy Sedaris (comedian)

Fun Fact: North Carolina was once a major exporter of turpentine, tar, and rosin—products of the state's bountiful longleaf pine forests—used in shipbuilding. By 1840, North Carolina shipped out over 95% of the nation's naval stores, and those who worked with the sticky tar and pitch earned the nickname "Tar Heels." Today, the Tar Heel nickname is most often associated with UNC–Chapel Hill sports' teams.

Need to Know: September 2024 brought the storm of the century to Asheville and the surrounding mountain towns of Western NC. Heavy wind and rain from Hurricane Helene caused unprecedented, catastrophic damage to entire neighborhoods and towns, mostly in the form of deadly landslides and historic flooding of rivers and creeks. The region is strong in community and spirit, and ready to welcome back visitors, but check local information before planning your visit.

Great Smoky Mountains National Park

The USA's Most Popular Park

Great Smoky may be the most visited national park in the United States, but that doesn't mean there's no peace or wonder to be found. The park straddles the state line between North Carolina and Tennessee, and the Carolina side is far less visited than Gatlinburg and Pigeon Forge in Tennessee. The area provides boundless opportunities for off-the-beaten-path outdoor adventures such as hiking and fishing, and you will almost always spot elk in the evening and early morning, as well as wild turkeys, deer, and perhaps bears. The **Oconaluftee Visitor Center** is a helpful starting point for a trip here. ✉ *1194 Newfound Gap Rd., Cherokee, NC* 🌐 *www.nps.gov/grsm*

Don't Miss

Camping in Great Smoky is like having a backstage pass to the park's majesty; there are developed sites at Cataloochee, Balsam Mountain, and Smokemont. Secure a backcountry permit to plan an epic overnight hiking trip.

Best Stop

One of the most memorable and eerie sites in Great Smoky is the **Cataloochee Valley**, a community that was abandoned when taken over by the NPS in 1934. You can visit many of the original buildings that were left behind.

While You're Here

The **Mountain Farm Museum** next to the Oconaluftee Visitor Center is perhaps the best re-creation anywhere of an Appalachian mountain farmstead.

Getting Here and Around

The most popular park entrance on the North Carolina side is Oconaluftee in Cherokee. Asheville, about a 1½-hour drive from the Oconaluftee entrance, is a good base.

Asheville

The Hippest Mountain Town

A scenic mountain town that seems always to be growing, Asheville has a few personalities, but that's half the fun. It has an outdoorsy side, which beckons you to trek trails along the Blue Ridge Parkway and Catawba River; a tourist-driven downtown, with lots of shops, excellent restaurants, and breweries within walking distance of one another (craft brews from **DSSOLVR** are a must). West Asheville is edgier and artsy, with some of the town's best dining and small shops (try **Sunny Point Café** for brunch).

Don't Miss

The **River Arts District** is home to standout studios and galleries, plus breweries and bars along the river. The neighborhood was hit hard by Hurricane Helene, but remains the creative heart of Asheville as it continues to rebuild.

While You're Here

Tour the largest private home in America, the **Biltmore Estate,** to find the opulent yin to the laid-back yang of the town. ✉ *1 Lodge St., Asheville, NC* 🌐 *www.biltmore.com*

Good to Know

The **North Asheville Tailgate Market**, open Saturday in spring and summer on the UNC-A campus, is Asheville's best seasonal farmers' market. 🌐 *northashevilletailgatemarket.com*

Getting Here and Around

Asheville Airport (AVL) is about 15 miles from downtown. Downtown Asheville is easily walkable, and there's a bus system (ART), but you'll want a car if you plan to explore the surrounding mountains.

Blue Ridge Parkway

A True American Road Trip

Driving the Blue Ridge Parkway's winding roads, past mountain peaks as far as the eye can see, is an epic journey. Stopping to hike or swim in a waterfall along the way takes the trip to the next level. The parkway's 252 miles within North Carolina wind down the High Country through Asheville, ending near the entrance of Great Smoky Mountains National Park. Highlights include **Mt. Mitchell** (the highest mountain peak east of the Rockies), **Grandfather Mountain**, and **Mt. Pisgah**. Nearly all the towns and cities along the route offer accommodations, dining, and sightseeing. In particular, **Boone, Blowing Rock, Burnsville, Asheville, Waynesville, Brevard**, and **Cherokee** are all near popular entrances to the parkway.

Don't Miss

Linville Falls, one of North Carolina's most photographed waterfalls, is an easy ½-mile hike from the Linville Falls Visitor Center at milepost 316.4. The trail winds through evergreens and rhododendrons to overlooks with views of tumbling cascades. ✉ *Warrior La., Newland, NC*

Best Stay

If you love the parkway, stay at **Pisgah Inn**. At mile marker 408 in Canton, this tranquil motel on top of Mt. Pisgah comes with hiking trails of its own and an observation deck. The restaurant has great views and serves memorable mountain trout and fried chicken. There is also a large national park campground nearby. ✉ *408 Blue Ridge Pkwy., Canton, NC* 🌐 *www.pisgahinn.com*

Getting Here and Around

You can access the parkway from Route 70 east of Asheville, and south of town from Route 191, near Interstate 26 and Biltmore Park (about a 15-minute drive from Asheville Regional Airport).

The Outer Banks

The Country's Wildest Beaches

Home to mysterious shipwrecks, the Lost Colony of Roanoke, and the Wright Brothers' first flight, this scenic string of barrier islands and their small towns (from Corolla south through Ocracoke) has no shortage of fascinating history. The wild horses of **Corolla,** however, take the cake. These feral mustangs, allegedly stranded here in the 1500s by Spanish explorers, now roam free (and are protected) on the OBX's northern beaches. Pair the ethereal sight with historic lighthouses you can climb plus beautiful beaches with white sand and pristine water, and you can see why the Outer Banks continue to draw seasoned vacationers to its shores.

Don't Miss

Within **Cape Hatteras National Seashore**, a 60-mile geographical treasure great for shelling, surfing, birding, fishing, camping, and lighthouse exploring, the undeveloped Coquina Beach and Ocracoke Island beaches are some of the Outer Banks' loveliest shorelines. 🌐 *www.nps.gov/caha*

Best Tour

Race along 20 miles of beach with **Wild Horse Adventure Tours'** entertaining, informative guides in an open-air Hummer along Corolla's uninhabited beaches for some great photo ops of the wild horses. 🌐 *www.wildhorsetour.com*

Getting Here and Around

The closest large, commercial airports are Norfolk International Airport (ORF) in Virginia, a two-hour drive, and Raleigh-Durham International Airport (RDU), a four-hour drive. Route 12 is the only road connecting the Outer Banks. Ferry travel is also prevalent; Ocracoke Island, in the south, can be reached only by boat or ferry.

The Triangle

NC's Food and Culture Capital

The Triangle area—**Raleigh**, **Durham**, **Chapel Hill**, and surrounding towns—is the most concentrated area of culture in North Carolina, competing with places like Atlanta for international, on-trend food and drink as well as art and nightlife. Raleigh is biggest, Durham is hippest, and Chapel Hill has the "college town" feel. Visit the latter for a nostalgic night out on Franklin Street or downtown Durham for intimate shows at **Pinhook** and **Motorco**, tapas at **Mateo**, or craft beer at **Ponysaurus Brewing Company**. If the outdoors appeals, you'll be pleased to know many parts of the Triangle are tucked into the woods, such as Raleigh's **Capital Greenway** and **Duke Forest Trail**.

Don't Miss

The **North Carolina Museum of Art** (NCMA) on Raleigh's west side is a heavy hitter in Southern art with more than 5,000 years of artistic heritage, including one of the nation's largest collections of Jewish ceremonial art. The 164-acre park features nine monumental works of art, which visitors can view on foot or by bike. ✉ *2110 Blue Ridge Rd., Raleigh, NC* 🌐 *www.ncartmuseum.org*

While You're Here

While the NCMA is epic, Duke University's smaller **Nasher Museum of Art** also deserves a visit. It's incredibly well curated and manageable for an afternoon of Southern contemporary art—the photography is always fantastic—and there's a lovely little café. ✉ *2001 Campus Dr., Durham, NC* 🌐 *nasher.duke.edu*

Getting Here and Around

Raleigh-Durham International Airport (RDU) serves the Triangle area and is a major hub. Interstates 40, 85, and 77, as well as several state highways, offer easy access to most of the region's destinations.

Wilmington Beaches

North Carolina's Best Surf

The North Carolina coast doesn't lack beaches, but the ones around Wilmington are a little more activity-packed. The closest beach is at **Wrightsville**, which is its own laid-back surfing town very popular with locals, a long boardwalk, and the best waves in the area. Keep going south and there's an array of seaside restaurants at **Carolina Beach** and a large aquarium, historic fort, and a ferry at **Kure Beach**. In the other direction, north of Wrightsville, **Figure 8 Island** and **Topsail Beach**, up to **Emerald Isle**, are mostly quiet beach towns, with limited development, that make for great summer vacation spots.

Don't Miss

Take the **Southport–Fort Fisher Ferry** from Kure Beach and Fort Fisher via U.S. 421 out of Wilmington. This state-operated year-round car ferry provides a 35-minute Cape Fear River ride between Old Federal Point at the tip of the spit and the mainland. **Bald Head Island Lighthouse** on Bald Head Island is seen en route along with the Oak Island Lighthouse and the ruins of **Price's Creek Lighthouse**—in fact, this is the only point in the United States where you can see three lighthouses at the same time. It's best to arrive early (30 minutes before departure), as it's first come, first served. 🌐 *www.ncdot.gov*

While You're Here

Battleship *North Carolina* is permanently docked at the Cape Fear River; you can tour the ship itself, or take a river tour with Wilmington Water Tours. ✉ *1 Battleship Rd. NE, Wilmington, NC* 🌐 *battleshipnc.com*

Getting Here and Around

Wilmington is about a two-hour drive south of Raleigh on Interstate 40. The beach is 10 minutes from downtown Wilmington.

The Appalachian Trail

Highest Point of America's Ultimate Hike

The famous 2,000-mile-plus hiking trail from Maine to Georgia has beautiful elevated stretches in North Carolina—the most mountainous section of the whole trail. The Appalachian Trail (or A.T. if you want to sound like a local) runs through Great Smoky Mountains National Park, along the Carolina-Tennessee border and past the popular Kuwohi (formerly Clingman's Dome). The trail also runs through the historic town of Hot Springs: stand on Main Street and you're technically on the trail. This former railroad town is a stopover for many hikers, so there are adventure outfitters, campgrounds, and several restaurants with good local craft beer.

Don't Miss

Climbing the steep stairs of the observation tower at **Kuwohi**—the highest point of the entire A.T., and a sacred place for the Cherokee people—is an essential experience for panoramic views of the Great Smokies.

Best Day Hike

Max Patch, a trail near Hot Springs, will get you "I hiked the A.T." bragging rights. West of Asheville, it takes a winding drive to get to—but the views at the top of this bald are worth it. There's a 1.5-mile loop to the top, and a longer, strenuous hike (9.7 miles) from Lemon Gap to Max Patch.

Après Climb

The old resort at **Hot Springs** is still active, and you can book a soak in the private spring-fed tubs to soothe your muscles after your climb.

Getting Here and Around

Hot Springs is about 45 minutes northwest of Asheville. In Great Smoky, many hikers start in the southwest of the park and take the A.T. up to Kuwohi; there is also parking at the base of the observation tower.

Carolina Mountain Towns

Outdoor Adventures and Rustic Retreats

Folks head to the Carolina mountains for hiking and river rafting—the area's best activities. Even a short drive out of Asheville, northwest toward the Pisgah National Forest, south toward Great Smoky Mountains National Park, or northeast into High Country, promises jaw-dropping views from lookout points, seasonal roadside stands, and quaint mountain towns. Main streets of towns like **Marshall** have small breweries, vintage and ceramics shops, and restaurants that serve mountain cooking. South of Asheville, the towns of Hendersonville and **Brevard** (home of **Oskar Blues Brewery** and nearby trips to **Sliding Rock**, a natural slide that the adventurous zoom down in summer) are worth visiting.

Don't Miss

Banner Elk, surrounded by the lofty peaks of Grandfather, Hanging Rock, Beech, and Sugar Mountains, is the place for good dining. Experience the town's **Wooly Worm Festival** in October, when actual woolly worms race to predict the winter weather forecast for North Carolina's High Country. 🌐 *woollyworm.com*

Best Activity

White-water rafting at **Blue Heron** is a must. About 30 minutes northwest of Asheville, the French Broad River winds through mountains and becomes white water, with some Class II, III, and IV rapids that are safe for families with a professional raft guide, but splashy and exciting enough for everyone. 🌐 *www.blueheronwhitewater.com*

Getting Here and Around

U.S. 221 northeast from Asheville leads to High Country towns of Banner Elk, Boone, and Blowing Rock. U.S. 25/70 (northwest) is the road to rafting outfitters, and the towns of Marshall and Hot Springs.

When in North Carolina

GREAT DISMAL SWAMP

The forbidding name for this massive swamp—a uniquely large and wild ecosystem between northeastern North Carolina and Virginia—was possibly assigned to the area by William Byrd on one of his early 18th-century surveying expeditions. George Washington once hoped to drain it. Today the swamp is a 106,000-acre refuge and harbors bobcats, black bears, and more than 220 varieties of birds. Lake Drummond, a remarkably shallow lake that covers 3,000 acres and is only 6 feet deep, is surrounded by skinny cypress trees that lend the scene a primeval quality.

Do This: One hundred miles of hiking and biking trails, including a wheelchair-accessible boardwalk, cover the Dismal Swamp State Park; trails around Washington Ditch (Lake Drummond) and Jericho Lane are particularly nice (you'll cross into Virginia for most trails). There's also a self-guided auto tour, beginning at the Railroad Ditch entrance. ✉ *2294 U.S. 17 N, South Mills, NC* 🌐 *www.ncparks.gov/state-parks/dismal-swamp-state-park*

GREENSBORO

After you get past its outer ring of small-city sprawl, Greensboro quickly grows on you. There's a feeling of possibility here created by a constant influx of new residents, which include college students and immigrants from around the world. This mixture of new folks and natives makes this unassuming city surprisingly diverse. Like Winston-Salem with tobacco and High Point with furniture, Greensboro's historical claim to relevance lies in textiles. In the early 20th century, it was the country's largest producer of denim, and Wrangler jeans is still headquartered here. Greensboro is also known for its role in the fight for civil rights (the most well-known lunch counter sit-in of the mid-'60s occurred here). Today, the multifaceted city is creating a brand-new identity.

Do This: With an unflinching eye, the International Civil Rights Center and Museum documents the beauty and horror of America's civil rights movement of the 1960s. The star attraction is the actual Woolworth's lunch counter where countless African Americans staged sit-ins to protest segregation for more than six months in 1960. A guided tour shows viewers how this act of defiance spread to more than 50 cities throughout the South and helped finally bring segregation to an end. Other exhibits uncover the brutality of America's racism throughout the South. ✉ *134 S. Elm St., Greensboro, NC* 🌐 *www.sitinmovement.org*

KITTY HAWK AND KILL DEVIL HILLS

Kitty Hawk and contiguous Kill Devil Hills, with a combined population of about 11,000 residents, are synonymous with the first powered flight, but the towns' respective roles in that drama occasionally create some confusion. When arriving at the Outer Banks, the Wright brothers first stayed in the then-remote fishing village of Kitty Hawk, but their flight took place some 4 miles south at Kill Devil Hills, a gargantuan sand dune where the Wright Brothers National Memorial now stands.

Do This: One of the most popular photo sites on the Outer Banks is the 60-foot granite airplane's tail that pays tribute to Wilbur and Orville Wright, two bicycle mechanics from Ohio who took to the air here on December 17, 1903. A sculptured replica of their *Wright Flyer* and stone markers showing the exact points and distances soared help you experience the historic day humans first made powered flight—and the multiyear, trial-and-error process the perseverant brothers endured leading up to it. ✉ *1000 N. Croatan Hwy., Kill Devil Hills, NC* 🌐 *www.nps.gov/wrbr*

MOUNT AIRY

This pleasant small town is where Andy Griffith grew up and is believed to have been the inspiration for Mayberry on his famous show. Andy's home and its grounds are now a museum, where visitors can tour a large collection of props and memorabilia. There's even a festival dedicated to Griffith; the annual Mayberry Days, held in September, takes families on a nostalgic tour of Andy's time. It's also home to the grave site of Chang and Eng, the famous traveling Siamese twins, and there's an exhibit dedicated to them at the Andy Griffith Museum. Elsewhere, you can visit the Earl Theatre, inside a 1930s music hall, and Pilot Mountain State Park, where visitors can paddle in to a campsite along the Yadkin River or climb the knoblike peak of Big Pinnacle for panoramic views of the Piedmont.

Do This: Go for vintage, nostalgic comforts at the Snappy Lunch (Mount Airy's oldest restaurant, mentioned on the *Andy Griffith Show*). ✉ *125 N. Main St., Mt. Airy, NC* 🌐 *thesnappylunch.com*

SAXAPAHAW

Tiny Saxapahaw, a former cotton-mill town reinvented as an artsy farming community, makes for a good day trip from the Triangle area. The 25-minute drive takes you through acres of farmland; you can even get an overnight farm-stay experience at Terrastay Farms. Both the Saxapahaw General Store and the Eddy Pub next door are great for a meal. The deck at the Eddy overlooks Haw River, where you'll watch the herons soar, and (hopefully) spot some otters at play.

Do This: Explore the trails of the Saxapahaw Island Park, or rent a canoe or kayak and head out for a paddle on the river at Haw River Canoe & Kayak Co. ✉ *5550 Church Rd., Graham, NC*

About Our Writers

Cameron Todd fell in love with a North Carolinian 15 years ago and has been living in or visiting the state ever since—currently, she is fixing up a homestead on 10 acres outside of Chapel Hill. You can find her at a Durham Bulls Game, The Saxapahaw General Store, or any number of swimming holes and hiking trails from the Haw River to the French Broad. She is a freelance writer and editor.

VOLLIS SIMPSON WHIRLIGIG PARK

This towering display of outdoor art powered by wind, especially active on a breezy day, is a fun stop if you're traveling from the Triangle to the Carolina coast. Farm machine repairman Vollis Simpson began constructing his kinetic "whirligigs" out of scrap metal as an older man, soon attracting the national attention of curious visitors to the area—as well as big-time art galleries and museums. In Simpson's later years (he died in 2013 at age 94), his sculptures were moved from his family farm to their own park in downtown Wilson, becoming an official landmark of the town. ✉ *301 Goldsboro St. S, Wilson, NC* 🌐 *www.wilsonwhirligigpark.org*

Do This: Beyond its whirligigs, downtown Wilson is a nice place to wander for an hour or so. There are art galleries, shops, and many good restaurants, including burgers, cafés, a few soul food and Southern options, and great BBQ at Parker's.

Cool Places to Stay

Atlantis Lodge. This 1960s-style surf lodge, oceanfront on North Carolina's chill Crystal Coast, welcomes couples, families, and pets with style. It's all you'd want from a casual beach resort, and more: it has great outdoor hangout areas, bikes and ocean kayaks to rent, a saltwater swimming pool, a game room, and an on-site dog park. ✉ *123 Salter Path Rd., Atlantic Beach, NC* 🌐 *www.atlantislodge.com*

Cataloochee Campground. Camping in Great Smoky is a good way to get close to all the park's hiking, fishing, and best activities while avoiding the crowds. Cataloochee is secluded, with epic scenery and a nice climate when the campground is open from April through October. Hiking trails and fishing streams can be reached from the site. There are bathrooms (but no showers) and drinking water, plus a nearby horse camp for overnight riding trips. 🌐 *www.recreation.gov/camping/campgrounds/233284*

The Durham. Located in the heart of Durham, this boutique hotel with mid-century modern decor emphasizes everything local, from its overall design to the in-room snacks. The rooms are bright, service is friendly, and the hotel restaurant and bar are run by one of the best chefs in the state. The rooftop bar offers sweeping views of the city and is a favorite nightspot. ✉ *315 E. Chapel Hill St., Durham, NC* 🌐 *www.thedurham.com*

The Foundry Hotel Asheville. This boutique downtown lodging occupies a former steel foundry and several other industrial buildings around a central courtyard. In a historic former African American neighborhood called "The Block," The Foundry is within walking distance of many top bars and eateries. Adjacent to the lobby, the Workshop Lounge Bar is spacious and welcoming, with brick walls and gas fireplaces setting the mood. ✉ *51 S. Market St., Asheville, NC* 🌐 *foundryasheville.com*

Mother Earth Motor Lodge. Retro and colorful, this funky lodge pays homage to its past as a 1970s motor lodge, when Kinston was a popular stop for highway travelers. The lodge is a sister property to Mother Earth Brewing nearby, and, while Kinston may have quieted some over the years, there's still fun to be had in this small town along the Neuse River. On the property itself, you'll find local artwork and fun decor, a swimming pool, shuffleboard, and minigolf course. ✉ *501 N. Herritage St., Kinston, NC* 🌐 *www.motherearthmotorlodge.com*

Essential Eats

BBQ, Two Ways. In North Carolina, "barbecue" refers to pulled or chopped pork, cooked and sauced in one of two delicious ways, then served on a sandwich or platter with slaw, hush puppies, and other sides. "Eastern-style" purists eat a vinegar-based, peppery sauce over pork that has been roasted whole hog–style; Western (or Lexington/Piedmont)-style BBQ sauce is ketchup-based and often made from pork shoulder. Eat both, throughout the state, as often as possible. The best BBQ places have other specialties worth trying: the ribs at 12 Bones in Arden, brisket at Luella's in Asheville, and Brunswick stew at Smithfield's and Allen and Son's in the Piedmont.

Calabash Seafood. Decades ago, a small coastal town near the South Carolina border earned a name for itself by quickly frying the freshest delivered seafood right on the spot, resulting in simple, lightly battered shrimp, catfish, flounder, and other local catch, served with fries and coleslaw. You don't have to be in Calabash to try it (though head to Beck's if you are); Calabash-style seafood is served in seafood shacks and dockside restaurants everywhere, from Wilmington to the Outer Banks.

North Carolina Farmers' Markets. North Carolina has some of the longest and most plentiful growing seasons in the country, and the farmers' market scene is unrivaled. They're also the best places to find quality meat, cheese, bread, and numerous other items from small and carefully cultivated operations. Saturdays mornings at the Durham Farmers Market or the North Asheville Tailgate Market are lively and abundant, but look for one in any city or small town you visit.

St. Roch Fine Oysters + Bar. New Orleans and North Carolina exist at two very different ends of the Southern spectrum, yet their cuisines coexist quite peacefully thanks to chef Sunny Gerhart at this historic former-storefront space in the heart of downtown Raleigh. St. Roch doesn't rely on Creole clichés, as NC barbecued shrimp gets a coconut curry broth, the gnocchi delivers alligator Bolognese, and the dirty rice is enriched by duck confit. The cocktail list is equally elegant without taking itself too seriously, with butter-washed whiskey, pimento bitters, and a Creole trinity (onions, celery, and peppers) syrup among the ingredients. ✉ *223 S. Wilmington St., Raleigh, NC* 🌐 *www.strochraleigh.com*

Topsail Oysters. Oyster farmers take advantage of the unique combination of fresh and salt water in Stump Sound, just off of Topsail Beach near Wilmington, cultivating buttery, briny oysters that burst with umami. When in Wilmington, Tidewater Oyster Bar or Pinpoint restaurant are great places to try Topsail oysters, but don't be surprised to see them on menus at the best restaurants in the Triangle and Charlotte. Seafood purveyors make daily drives to these cities, bringing oysters, shrimp, and fresh local catch from the coast.

South Carolina

South Carolina's crown jewel is the port city of Charleston, one of the South's best-preserved cities, with beautifully restored homes and churches, cobblestone streets, hidden gardens, and a thriving culinary scene. But the state's coastal lowlands pack a punch too, featuring pretty landscapes of coastal forests and marshes, undisturbed beaches, and quaint fishing villages.

Capital: Columbia

Population: 5,478,831

Area: 32,020 square miles

Statehood Date: May 23, 1788

Major Airports: Charleston International Airport (CHS); Myrtle Beach International Airport (MYR) (Myrtle Beach); Greenville-Spartanburg International Airport (GSP)

Travel and Tourism Information: *www.discoversouthcarolina.com* *www.charlestoncvb.com* *charlestonmag.com*

Famous Residents: Dizzy Gillespie (jazz musician); Stephen Colbert (late night host); Bill Murray (comedian); Andie MacDowell (actress), Chadwick Boseman (actor)

Fun Fact: "BBQ" means pulled pork in South Carolina, but the debate over preparation is as fiery as Clemson versus South Carolina football. Expect a mustard-based sauce in the Midlands around Columbia and a tangy vinegar-based sauce along the coast.

Historic Downtown Charleston

America's Best-Preserved City

It's obvious why filmmakers look to Charleston as a backdrop for historic movies. Dozens of church steeples punctuate the low skyline, and horse-drawn carriages pass centuries-old mansions, their stately salons offering a crystal-laden and parquet-floored version of Southern comfort. Outside, magnolia-filled gardens overflow with carefully tended heirloom plants—in fact, you can take a trip outside the city to **Middleton Place**, the oldest landscaped garden in the country. The city may resemble a 19th-century etching come to life, but look closer and you'll see that block after block of old structures have been restored, making this one of the South's best-preserved cities.

Don't Miss

Get a great city introduction with a history, food, or ghost tour from **Bulldog Tours**. You'll learn about Charleston's layers, its Revolutionary and Civil War history, and get the lay of the land, including East Bay Street's famous **Rainbow Row**, with 13 pastel row houses built between 1748 and 1845. 🌐 *www.bulldogtours.com*

The Country's First Museum

Charleston Museum was America's first museum, founded in 1773. Exhibits include artifacts from the Revolutionary War and galleries of natural history and African American stories. You can also visit two historic houses maintained by the museum, and on the way, stroll some of downtown's hidden alleyways. ✉ *360 Meeting St., Charleston, SC* 🌐 *www.charlestonmuseum.org*

Getting Here and Around

While you might want a car to explore Charleston's beaches, it's best to park downtown and explore on foot, via the free DASH trolley, on a Lime rental bike, or in a pedicab bike taxi.

The ACE Basin

The Heart of the Lowcountry

The "Lowcountry" refers to the marshy territory and sea islands along the Atlantic Coast, just south of Charleston. A 1.6-million-acre reserve, the ACE Basin protects this primordial ecosystem and sets the tone for seafood-focused cuisine in nearby towns like **Beaufort** and **Bluffton.** Frogmore Stew (aka Lowcountry Boil) was born here on **St. Helena Island**, and enjoying seasoned shrimp and accoutrements in a casual outdoor setting is as Lowcountry as it gets.

Don't Miss

Water is more abundant than land in the ACE Basin. **Botany Bay Ecotours** (based on Edisto Beach) offers tours deep into the reserve. Observation towers and hiking trails at the **Ernest F. Hollings ACE Basin National Wildlife Refuge** also get you close to waterfowl, otters, and alligators. Boneyard beaches, where the ocean has overtaken maritime forest, create eerily beautiful scenes on **Hunting Island** and at **Botany Bay Heritage Preserve**.

Best Day Trip

Charming **Old Town Bluffton** has historic homes and churches on oak-lined streets dripping with Spanish moss and intermingled with newer businesses like **Bee-Town Mead and Cider**. The **Bluffton Oyster Company** (✉ *63 Wharf St., Bluffton, SC* 🌐 *blufftonoyster.com*) is the place to buy fresh raw local shrimp, fish, and oysters.

Getting Here and Around

Public transportation is limited south of Charleston, so you'll want a car to explore the Lowcountry. Beaufort and Bluffton each abound with charming hotels and B&Bs, or you can embrace resort life at the Montage Palmetto Bluff.

Gullah Geechee Cultural Heritage Corridor

The Cradle of South Carolina Culture

Learning about the heritage of the Gullah Geechee people, descendants of Western and Central Africans brought to the South Carolina coast as enslaved people, is essential to understanding the area. Now an official National Heritage Area aimed to protect and promote the natural environment, history, and culture of the people, the Gullah Geechee Cultural Heritage Corridor is full of events, special programs, and heritage sites including the **Sweetgrass Cultural Arts Pavilion** in Mt. Pleasant, **McLeod Plantation** in James Island, the **Gullah Museum and the Rice Museum** in Georgetown, **Caw Caw Interpretive Center** in Ravenel, and **Gullah Museum** of Hilton Head Island. 🌐 *gullahgeecheecorridor.org*

Don't Miss

About 9 miles southeast of Beaufort, **St. Helena Island** is a stronghold of the Gullah culture. The **Penn Center**, the first school for formerly enslaved West Africans in the South, is a National Historic Landmark. Several African American–owned businesses in the tight-knit nearby community of **Frogmore** make this a worthy day trip or stop en route to Fripp and Hunting Islands.

While You're Here

Visit the **Charleston City Market** to support resident artists practicing the 300-plus-year tradition of weaving the local sweetgrass into baskets (✉ *188 Meeting St., Charleston, SC* 🌐 *www.thecharlestoncitymarket.com*).

Getting Here and Around

The Charleston area and Lowcountry Sea Islands are home to these cultural sites. Charleston, Beaufort, or Hilton Head are good bases.

Charleston Beaches

The Edge of America

Many visitors think of Charleston only as its downtown peninsula, but the city actually occupies several islands across the Lowcountry's Atlantic coast. Exploring these beaches is half the fun in Charleston. **Folly Beach**—dubbed "The Edge of America" 40 years ago by still-operating Ocean Surf Shop—is the Lowcountry's most iconic summer playground, offering a chill, local's experience. The beach at **Sullivan's Island** is pristine, with 200 acres of walkable maritime forest adding to its beauty. Just north, the **Isle of Palms** is a family vacation paradise. Islands like **Kiawah** and **Seabrook** tend to be a mix of natural preserves and sophisticated beach clubs; riding horses on the beach at Seabrook is a special activity.

Don't Miss

Charlestonians have been eating oysters since pre-Columbian times and the love of the bivalve has only gotten stronger since then; for a real deal oyster experience, head to **Bowens Island** where the view over the tidal marshes is only matched by the taste of freshly shucked oysters.

Best Beach

Kiawah Beachwalker Park, about 28 miles southwest of Charleston, is the premier stretch of sand on one of the Southeast's largest barrier islands. The river-facing beach at Captain Sam's Spit offers a rare inland-facing sandy beach that's a favorite place to spot dolphins. You can walk for miles on Kiawah, shelling and beachcombing to your heart's content.

Getting Here and Around

Charleston is the obvious base for exploring the sea islands; aside from Sullivan's Island and Isle of Palms to the north, most are just south of the city. You'll need a car to reach the beaches. Once you choose a destination, biking and walking (or kayaking) are the best modes of transport.

Hilton Head

America's Best Seaside Golf

Hilton Head Island is known far and wide as a vacation destination that prides itself on its top-notch golf courses and tennis programs, world-class resorts, and beautiful beaches. But the island is also part of the storied American South and its rich, complicated history. The former plantation land was bought and developed in the 1950s, and contemporary Hilton Head was planned with environmental preservation in mind. Visitors today will see an island that values its history as well as its natural beauty. The full Hilton Head experience can involve a few nights at a stylish resort, where you'll hit the links, book a spa day, relax at a beach club, or bike through tree-covered trails.

Don't Miss

Climb Hilton Head's landmark candy-cane-stripe lighthouse to enjoy a view of Calibogue Sound. ✉ *149 Lighthouse Rd., Hilton Head Island, SC* 🌐 *harbourtownlighthouse.com*

Best Greens

On the south end of the island, **Sea Pines Resort** is home to three of the most celebrated golf courses in Hilton Head: Harbour Town, Heron Point, and Atlantic Dunes. ✉ *32 Greenwood Dr., Hilton Head Island, SC* 🌐 *www.seapines.com*

Getting Here and Around

The South Carolina coast is quite compact; Charleston is only two hours north of Hilton Head, and Savannah (the island shares its international airport) is less than an hour away. There's also a smaller airport on Hilton Head. With resort shuttles, a trolley, and bike trails, the island is easy to explore without a car.

Myrtle Beach

A Playground for Grown-Ups

It's no big city, but Myrtle Beach has bright lights aplenty. The Grand Strand boasts 60 miles of beaches, but just as many people visit for the golf and go-karts. Behind the glitz, there's deep culture and wild nature to explore. This is also where the state dance, the shag, began. Young couples and old-timers alike still twirl each other to "Under the Boardwalk" and "My Girl" at the clubs along Main Street in North Myrtle Beach. Several piers offer productive fishing, and **Huntington Beach State Park** is home to dozens of alligators that lie around lazily in the sun. The best approach? Relax and embrace this vacation-oriented stretch of coast in all its gaudy glory.

Don't Miss

The massive **SkyWheel** along Myrtle Beach's main strip forms a landmark you can see from a mile away—but the view is even better from 200 feet up. ✉ *1110 N. Ocean Blvd., Myrtle Beach, SC* 🌐 *skywheelmb.com*

Best Night Out

When the sun goes down, head to Main Street in North Myrtle Beach for a night of shag dancing and club hopping that's distinctly South Carolina. **Fat Harold's Beach Club** is home base, where the decor and dance floor feel like stepping back in time to a simpler age. Hop across the street to **Duck's Beach Club**, where live cover bands keep feet moving, before dropping into **OD Arcade & Lounge** for more shag dancing or a game of pool.

Getting Here and Around

Myrtle Beach has its own international airport (MYR) right on the edge of downtown. Uber/Lyft, taxis, and the Coast RTA bus system are available within Myrtle Beach.

Congaree National Park

The Redwoods of the East

This nearly 27,000-acre park (the only national park in South Carolina) contains many old-growth bottomland hardwoods, the oldest and largest trees east of the Mississippi River. Together, the water and trees are beautifully eerie. Self-guided canoe trails and 25 miles of hiking trails line the park, which is full of wildlife, including otters, deer, and woodpeckers, as well as plentiful (but invasive) wild boar. There's also a 2½-mile boardwalk through the swamp. Aside from the ancient trees, there's an abundance of human history to the park, dating as far back as prehistoric people. Notably, the dense swamp served as an important landscape for African Americans escaping slavery. ✉ *100 National Park Rd., Hopkins, SC* 🌐 *www.nps.gov/cong*

Don't Miss

Oakridge Trail (7 miles) is great for spotting wildlife, and **Sims and Bates Ferry Trails** trace some of the park's human history. For the adventurous, several outfitters offer kayak tours of **Cedar Creek**, the primary waterway through the park's heart.

Best Tour

The park's **Big Tree Hike**, a three-hour event covering 5 miles of swampland, takes you to the largest trees in the swamp, and is often led by one of the park's founders, John Cely.

When to Go

Visit Congaree from mid-May to June to see synchronous fireflies (and many human visitors from all over) grace the park for a sparkling evening show.

Getting Here and Around

Congaree is only 18 miles from the fun and sophisticated state capital of Columbia, South Carolina, which is also home to the closest regional airport. The big hub of Charlotte Douglas International Airport (CLT) is 110 miles north.

Greenville

A Hot Spot in the Foothills

Downtown Greenville's evolution during this century is striking—the 10-block corridor along Main Street is now one of the South's best walkable districts, filled with trendy shops, restaurants, and hotels. The city gives way to nature at the south end of downtown, where the Liberty Bridge crosses the Reedy River next to the impressive **Grand Bohemian Hotel**. People once moved here to work in textile plants, but today they come for creative cuisine, cultural arts anchored by two performance centers, and access to hiking and waterfalls just outside of town.

Don't Miss

The **Swamp Rabbit Trail** stretches 28 miles along a reclaimed railway, with ample options for dining and sightseeing along the way. Rent a bike from Reedy Rides and make a day out of pedaling to Traveler's Rest. Fill up on tacos or pizza and a microbrew before the scenic journey back to Greenville.

Best Restaurant

Warm lighting, wood-paneled walls, and wide windows that open to the sidewalk beckon passersby into **Jones Oyster Co.**, known for raw oysters and treats like a fried clam roll, a shrimp burger, and the Lowcountry Crab Rice. ✉ *22 E. Court St., Greenville, SC* 🌐 *thejonesoysterco.com*

Getting Here and Around

Greenville-Spartanburg International Airport (GSP) gains new connections each year, although Charlotte and Atlanta are each a two-hour drive away. Downtown Greenville is walkable, and Greenlink public trolleys can speed up the trip or take you farther afield.

Waterfalls of the Foothills

Land of Waterfalls

The Upstate of South Carolina is a land of waterfalls and wide vistas, cool pine forests, and fast rapids. Camping, hiking, white-water rafting, and kayaking are supreme in the **Jocassee Gorges Wilderness Area**, 50,000 acres of forest that take you past many gorges, waterfalls, and fantastic views. There's a vast network of trails here, but you can always start with a drive to get your bearings; pick up a guide at the visitor center to follow along for the best sights. **Sassafras Mountain**, the highest point in South Carolina, is reachable by car or hike, and the views of four states are rewarding. A few good hikes lead to waterfalls, or you can book a Waterfalls Tour with outfitters like Jocassee Lake Tours.

Don't Miss

The view from the top of **Caesars Head State Park** may be the state's best, and it's accessible via road. Then hike the park's **Raven Cliff Falls Trail** to see the state's highest waterfall. ✉ *8155 Geer Hwy., Cleveland, SC* 🌐 *southcarolinaparks.com/caesars-head*

Best Stop

Spend time at **Devils Fork State Park** on Lake Jocassee to get the most out of the water activities and natural beauty here. Lower Whitewater Falls plunges more than 200 feet over huge boulders to splash into the lake waters. You can view the falls from an overlook or from a boat on the lake. ✉ *161 Holcombe Circle, Salem, SC* 🌐 *www.southcarolinaparks.com/devils-fork*

Getting Here and Around

It's about a 50-minute drive from Greenville (home to the closest airport) to the Jocassee Gorge Visitor Center, Caesers Head, or Table Rock State Park, and the drive between each park is quite scenic.

When in South Carolina

SUMMERVILLE

In the 1700s, Puritans and colonists sought respite from the heavy Charleston heat and founded Summerville, a blooming paradise with a breeze. The "Official Birthplace of Sweet Tea" also prides itself on its flowers, and seeing the azaleas in bloom in spring is a joy. There's also a historic downtown full of antiques stores and small businesses.

Do This: One of the state's most overlooked but impressive landmarks, the Colonial Dorchester State Historic Site, is nearby, home to the best surviving example of 18th-century tabby (oyster shell) construction in the Lowcountry. ✉ *300 State Park Rd., Summerville, SC* 🌐 *southcarolinaparks.com/colonial-dorchester*

WORLD GRITS FESTIVAL

Each year the town of St. George's celebrates grits, a Lowcountry staple, in a pleasantly funky and fun small-town-Southern way. The festival began in 1985 when the community "discovered" (through some purchase orders) that they actually ate the most grits per capita of anywhere else in the world. The normally quiet town draws throngs of visitors for three days in April for a down-home celebration that features plenty of grits dishes, fundraising for their community, and fun activities like a grits-eating contest, rolling in the grits, a 5K, and a corn toss. 🌐 *www.worldgritsfestival.com*

Do This: If you dare, sign up for the rolling-in-the-grits contest. Contestants enter a large inflatable pool filled with—you guessed it—grits, and have 10 seconds to roll in the sloppy mixture before (hopefully) successfully exiting the pool.

About Our Writers

Stratton Lawrence moved to the South Carolina Pee Dee region 30 years ago, but it was Folly Beach that made him a permanent Carolinian. He's grown from bachelor beach bum to full-on family man on Folly's sandy shores, where he surfs, fishes, and still seeks out the saltiest watering holes. When he's not on Folly, he's cheering his kids to the tops of mountains and sharing family travel insight for savvy readers.

Cool Places to Stay

Edisto Treehouses. A 13-mile canoe trip on the Edisto River (about an hour inland of Charleston) ends with a stay at your own private (and rustic) oasis nestled among the trees. Small lounging decks among the branches come complete with grills; there are also screened-in sleeping lofts, hammocks, and a small outfitted kitchen. Visitors paddle in, stay the night, and continue on a leisurely 10 miles down river to the outpost in the morning. ✉ *1 Livery La., St. George, SC* 🌐 *www.canoesc.com*

Wentworth Mansion. Built as a private home in 1865, this hulking Historic Hotel of America property was carefully renovated and transformed into a B&B in 1998. With original Second Empire architecture—from inlaid floors and wainscoting to marble fireplaces, intricate crown molding, and Louis Comfort Tiffany stained glass windows—you'll feel like you're in another era (aside from the modern bathrooms, flat-screen TVs, and Wi-Fi, of course). ✉ *149 Wentworth St., Charleston, SC* 🌐 *www.wentworth-mansion.com*

Zero George. The impressively restored circa-1804 buildings offer the historic charm visitors seek from Charleston, while the guest rooms and common spaces are fresh, elegant, and comfortable, pleasing the pickiest of modern travelers. Rooms have a varied decor inspired by different elements of Charleston's past—tailored British trade, airy French Romantic, and nautical Yachting Design—and feature natural linens and fabrics, marble bathrooms, and custom furniture. One of the city's best fine dining restaurants (no small statement in Charleston) is on-site. ✉ *0 George St., Charleston, SC* 🌐 *www.zerogeorge.com*

Essential Eats

FIG. Of the three restaurants that earned Charleston chefs its first run of James Beard Awards two decades ago (the other two were McCrady's and Hominy Grill), only FIG remains, and Mike Lata still helms the kitchen. Expectations like sourcing from local farms, daily menus based on seasonal produce, and intense creativity that now feel commonplace were all spearheaded here, and that ethos remains. ✉ *232 Meeting St., Charleston, SC* 🌐 *www.eatatfig.com*

Rodney Scott's BBQ. Rodney Scott grew up stoking the fires in the pits where his family smoked whole hogs in Hemingway, SC before bringing his vinegar-soaked style (he applies the sauce with a mop) to downtown Charleston. He's expanded to three more states, but you have to experience the original in Charleston (or make a day trip to Hemingway, where his family still serves to-go sandwiches from their roadside market). ✉ *1011 King St., Charleston, SC* 🌐 *www.rodneyscottsbbq.com*

The Tomato Shed. What could be more perfect than local farmers preparing the week's harvest the way they like to eat it? This roadside market and café is the place to order all of the sides like tomato pie, squash casserole, butter beans, and savory collards that you'll dream about. ✉ *842 Main Rd., Johns Island, SC* 🌐 *www.stonofarmmarket.com*

Tennessee

Tennessee's music, scenic beauty, and history are top reasons the state continues to attract, entertain, and charm the masses. Several genres of American music have their roots and branches here: bluegrass and Appalachian music in the eastern parts of the state; country, Americana, and pop in Nashville; and blues, soul, gospel, and rock and roll in Memphis. Nashville's reputation as the "Music City," draws visitors to the Grand Ole Opry, Honky Tonk Highway along Lower Broad, and Country Music Hall of Fame & Museum.

Capital: Nashville

Population: 7,227,750

Area: 41,244 square miles

Statehood Date: June 1, 1796

Major Airports: Nashville International Airport (BNA); Memphis International Airport (MEM); McGhee Tyson Airport (TYS)

Travel and Tourism Information: 🌐 *www.tnvacation.com* 🌐 *www.tnmagazine.org* 🌐 *www.visitmusiccity.com*

Famous Residents: Andrew Jackson (president); Davy Crockett (frontiersman); Elvis Presley (singer); Johnny Cash (musician); Dolly Parton (musician); Miley Cyrus (singer)

Fun Fact: Although Jack Daniel's Tennessee Whiskey is the top-selling whiskey in the world, there are no liquor stores in Lynchburg where it is made because Moore County has been a dry county since Prohibition.

Nashville's Honky Tonk Highway

A Top American Nightlife Experience

The crown jewel of Nashville entertainment and a place that really embodies the city's soul is Lower Broadway, located right in the middle of downtown. This stretch of road is called the Honky Tonk Highway, where live country and rock music pour out of nearly every window while beer flows out of every tap. Surrounding Broadway is a growing fine-arts scene with multiple galleries and plenty of restaurants cooking up Southern food (including the city's must-try Nashville hot chicken). Just a few blocks away are world-class museums and the symphony.

Don't Miss

Robert's Western World is one of the best honky-tonks in town, with live music and dancing nightly. The two-level bar has been a local staple for decades and features some of the absolute best live bands on Broadway from before lunchtime until after midnight. ✉ *416 Broadway, Nashville, TN* 🌐 *www.robertswesternworld.com*

Best Nashville Hot Chicken

Prince's was the first, but Nashville chain **Hattie B's** does hot chicken especially well. Rumor goes that the Nashville specialty—a cayenne-spiced and battered fried chicken—first came to be when a woman served the dish to her cheating husband as a punishment. It backfired. At Hattie's, enjoy hot chicken of varying heat levels, wash it down with a sweet tea or craft brew, and complement your meal with a delicious Southern-inspired side or two. ✉ *5069 Broadway, Nashville, TN* 🌐 *www.hattieb.com*

Getting Here and Around

Downtown Nashville is located in the center of the circle that comprises the city. Take a cab or rideshare to go out on Lower Broadway.

Cades Cove

The Crown Jewel of the Smokies

A 6,800-acre valley surrounded by high mountains, Cades Cove has more historic buildings than any other area in Great Smoky Mountains National Park. Driving, hiking, or biking the 11-mile Cades Cove Loop Road, you can spot three old churches (Methodist, Primitive Baptist, and Missionary Baptist), a working gristmill (Cable Mill), a number of log cabins and houses in a variety of styles, and many outbuildings. The Cherokee, who hunted in Cades Cove for hundreds of years, called this valley *Tsiyahi* (place of otters), but today you're more likely to spot bears, deer, and wild turkeys. ✉ *Cades Cove Loop Rd., Townsend, TN* 🌐 *www.nps.gov/grsm*

Don't Miss

The **Cades Cove Loop** is the most popular route in the park and arguably the most scenic part of the entire Smokies. A highlight of the loop road is the Cable Mill area, with a visitor center, working water-powered gristmill, and a restored farmstead. On select days, the route is open for hikers and bicyclists only.

Good to Know

You can rent bikes at the Cades Cove Campground Store—also one of the only places to shop for provisions within the park.

Planning Your Time

The Loop Road gets 2 million visitors per year; at peak times traffic in and out of here can be extremely slow. Allow at least two to three hours just to drive the loop.

Getting Here and Around

The closest park entrance to Cades Cove is in Townsend, Tennessee, about 25 miles southwest of Pigeon Forge.

Grand Ole Opry

Country's Center Stage

The legendary country music stage and its enormously popular radio show, performed live in the Grand Ole Opry House, is an essential piece of American music history. The Opry has been broadcasting country music since 1925, making it the longest-running radio broadcast in America's history, and has packed in the crowds for live music just as long. You can see superstars, legends, and up-and-coming stars on this stage and at its sister property, the historic Ryman Auditorium. The Opry seats about 4,400 people and is broadcasted live on WSM AM 650 on Tuesday, Friday, and Saturday night, when you can join the audience. There's no better place to understand country music's past, present, and future. ✉ *2804 Opryland Dr., Nashville, TN* 🌐 *www.opry.com*

Don't Miss

Ryman Auditorium, the Opry's former home, opened for its first concert in 1892. You can tour both properties and catch country shows here as well. ✉ *116 5th Ave. N, Nashville, TN* 🌐 *www.ryman.com*

Best Souvenir

Hatch Show Print has been using the same letterpress printing techniques to create marketing materials since 1879. Artists like Patsy Cline and Kelsea Ballerini have advertised shows with posters from Hatch, and many reprints are available to purchase just outside the lobby of the Country Music Hall of Fame. ✉ *224 Rep. John Lewis Way S, Nashville, TN* 🌐 *www.hatchshowprint.com*

Getting Here and Around

The Opry is 8 miles from Nashville International Airport (BNA), and about 12 miles from downtown Nashville.

Dollywood

The Queen of Country's Theme Park

It's worth a trip to Dolly Parton's theme park just to honor this queen of country music—but Dollywood is also just a whole lot of fun. There's plenty of corny American fair attractions and actual thrills; Lightning Rod, once the world's fastest wooden roller coaster, is pretty terrifying. You can also ride a steam locomotive, catch a live show at the Back Porch Theater, visit old buildings, and ride the Smoky Mountain River Rampage—or head for the family-friendly FireChaser Express dual-launch coaster, which is a huge dollop of frosting on a tasty array of attractions, live shows, dining, shopping, and crafts displays. ✉ *2700 Dollywood Parks Blvd., Pigeon Forge, TN* 🌐 *www.dollywood.com*

Don't Miss

At the entrance to the park, find a replica of the humble cabin where Dolly was raised (two rooms with no running water, indoor plumbing, or electricity) in nearby Sevierville. This re-creation allows visitors to walk inside and explore her roots.

Where to Stay

Cabins at **Oak Haven Resort** provide a peaceful landing pad for Dollywood festivities, about a 20-minute drive from the park. Each have pool tables, foosball tables, hot tubs, and an arcade game, and there are some shared amenities on the property—including a series of walking trails, with great views of the Smokies. ✉ *1947 Old Knoxville Hwy., Sevierville, TN* 🌐 *www.oakhavenresort.com*

Getting Here and Around

Knoxville's McGhee Tyson Airport (TYS) is 37 miles away and the closest airport to Dollywood, but Tri-Cities Airport (TRI, near Johnson City) and Asheville Regional Airport (AVL) are each about a two-hour drive.

Memphis

Barbecue and Live Music

Music lovers flock to Memphis for its musical legends and their historic sights, and the still-happening beats of blues, soul, and rock at the clubs on **Beale Street.** At night, visitors can eat Memphis barbecue, stroll the lively blocks (adorned with historical markers commemorating music events) and pop in and out of clubs like **Rum Boogie Cafe** and **Tin Roof**, or catch a show at **B.B. King's Blues Club**.

Don't Miss

While in Memphis, visits to **Sun Studio** and to the Lorraine Motel—the location of MLK's tragic assassination, and now home to the moving **National Civil Rights Museum**—are essential pieces of Memphis, music, and greater American history. ✉ *450 Mulberry St., Memphis, TN* 🌐 *civilrightsmuseum.org*

Even More Live Music

Some good contemporary nightlife and live music can be found off the main stretch as well: **Wild Bill's Juke Joint**, in the Vollintine Evergreen District, is a local gem. ✉ *1580 Vollintine Ave., Memphis, TN* 🌐 *wildbillsmemphis.com*

Best Barbecue

Memphis is famous for its dry-rubbed ribs, and if you're looking for somewhere right off Beale Street, the basement dining room at **Charlie Vergos' Rendezvous** (✉ *52 S. 2nd St., Memphis, TN* 🌐 *hogsfly.com*) is an institution. It's worthwhile, though, to head farther uptown to the nondescript strip mall location of **Cozy Corner** (✉ *735 North Pkwy., Memphis, TN* 🌐 *www.cozycornerbbq.com*).

Getting Here and Around

Memphis International Airport (MEM) is 11 miles downtown Memphis. Memphis is relatively walkable and Lyft/Uber is widely available. MATA vintage trolleys travel between several important tourist sites, including Beale Street.

Graceland

The King's Castle
Even non-Elvis fanatics will appreciate the kitschy excess and ridiculous glamour of the King of Rock and Roll's estate (purchased for $100,000 in 1957, when Presley was 22). While touring, keep an eye out for decor details, particularly the carefully chosen wallpaper and upholstery. A recent over-the-top expansion packed in even more Elvis style, but his automobile museum is still a favorite feature, as are his famous pink Cadillac and "Jungle Room," with its green shag carpet and waterfall. ✉ *Elvis Presley Blvd., Memphis, TN* 🌐 *www.graceland.com*

Don't Miss
Elvis is buried outside the mansion, and tours conclude with many fans leaving tokens at his grave site.

While You're Here
Take a drive 10 minutes north to Soulsville for the **Stax Museum of Soul Music**. Look for the marquee reading "Soulsville U.S.A.," and listen for the sounds of soul icons like Otis Redding, Isaac Hayes, and Aretha Franklin as you approach the former home of Stax Records, rebuilt to look as it did during the label's heyday in the 1960s and early 1970s. Inside, it's wall-to-wall music along with a history of Stax, from its beginnings as a home base for local musicians to an international sensation. Nearby, **The Four Way** is Memphis's oldest soul food restaurant. ✉ *926 E. McLemore Ave., Memphis, TN* 🌐 *staxmuseum.org*

When to Go
The most popular (and busiest) time to visit Graceland is in August for "Elvis Week," when fans flock to Memphis to honor the King's life.

Getting Here and Around
Graceland is only 3 miles from Memphis International Airport (MEM), and 15 minutes from downtown Memphis.

Country Music Hall of Fame and Museum

A Tribute to Country Music

Often called "the Smithsonian of Country Music," the Country Music Hall of Fame and Museum is Nashville's tribute to the genre's finest artists and tunes. It's an impressive full city block long, filled with plaques and exhibits highlighting performers from the old-time favorites to the latest generation of stars, a theater, and a two-story wall with gold and platinum country records. Tours of the historic RCA Studio B recording studio are also run by the museum. The extensive collection of memorabilia and rotating exhibits make this an essential stop for any music fan or history buff. ✉ *222 Rep. John Lewis Way S, Nashville, TN* 🌐 *www.countrymusichalloffame.org*

Don't Miss

Elvis Presley's solid-gold 1960 Cadillac limo is a must-see. Circa, the museum store, is the place for Nashville-made goods and official musician merchandise.

While You're Here

Stop at the nearby **Johnny Cash Museum** between Broadway and the Country Music Hall of Fame and Museum. Performance costumes, handwritten lyrics, and a wall of gold and platinum records are among the items in this museum. ✉ *119 3rd Ave. S, Nashville, TN* 🌐 *www.johnnycashmuseum.com*

When to Go

The **Country Music Association (CMA) Music Festival** is typically held over four days in June; it's a festive time for country music fans to flock to Nashville. 🌐 *cmafest.com*

Getting Here and Around

The Hall of Fame is in downtown Nashville, off Broadway, and near many other attractions and hotels. Nashville's airport is about a 15-minute drive.

Gatlinburg

The Gateway to the Great Smokies

As a gateway to Great Smoky Mountains National Park, Gatlinburg hosts thousands of guests a night, who come to witness the wondrous mountains that attracted visitors a century ago and to take advantage of outdoor sports and recreation, including Tennessee's only ski resort. Dollywood might be the area's official theme park, but downtown Gatlinburg is just as entertaining, with many fun and cheesy attractions, go-karts, miniature golf, and an aerial tram.

Don't Miss

One of the longest aerial tramways in the country is at **Ober Gatlinburg**, and riding up the mountain provides great views of downtown Gatlinburg and surroundings. ✉ *1001 Parkway, Gatlinburg, TN* 🌐 *obermountain.com*

Best Tour

You don't have to whisper anymore to find moonshine in Gatlinburg—you can visit the state's first legal moonshine distillery, **Ole Smoky Distillery**. Take a tour to see the process in action, then sample magical mountain elixirs made with 200-year-old recipes and local corn. You can buy seasonal and special flavors—such as Blueberry Lavender and Lemon Drop—that aren't available in package stores. ✉ *903 Parkway, Gatlinburg, TN* 🌐 *www.olesmoky.com*

Getting Here and Around

Gatlinburg is the main entrance to Great Smoky Mountains National Park. Knoxville airport is about a one-hour drive to Gatlinburg; both Tri-Cities Airport (near Kingsport and Johnson City) and Asheville Regional Airport are about two hours away.

When in Tennessee

CHATTANOOGA

The outdoorsy coolness of this hip little mountain city have some calling Chattanooga the new Asheville. There's plenty of hiking and biking in the area, or just take in the scenic views while in town, where the Tennessee River flows (you can paddleboard or kayak). The Northshore neighborhood runs along the river, with parks and lots of food options (try Aretha Frankenstein's for breakfast). Hunter Museum of Art, in the Bluff View neighborhood also overlooking the river, is large and modern and definitely worth a couple of hours.

Do This: Craft beer and cocktails at small Chattanooga bars and eateries are especially good; there are several local breweries along with the Chattanooga Whiskey Experimental Distillery downtown. ✉ *1439 Market St., Chattanooga, TN* 🌐 *chattanoogawhiskey.com*

ELKMONT FIREFLIES

What began as a logging town in the early 20th century became a lively summer colony for families, and eventually—after the NPS took it over to create Great Smoky Mountains National Park—a ghost town. These days Elkmont is primarily a campground, but its true appeal is that it provides the ideal setting for synchronous fireflies to light up the wilderness in the summer, one of the few places this happens in the United States. From the campground, follow the Elkmont Nature Trail and then head to the Old Elkmont Cemetery to add a touch of spookiness—and historical relevance—to the eerily beautiful area. ✉ *504 Little River Rd., Gatlinburg, TN*

Do This: June is when the synchronous fireflies (hundreds of lightning bugs blinking in patterned responses) light up the Elkmont area in a truly magical show.

JACK DANIEL'S DISTILLERY

At the oldest registered distillery in the country, you can observe every step of the art of making sour-mash whiskey. Tours are lively and informative and involve a lot of walking throughout the beautiful grounds (including the spring that continues to source the whiskey) with stops at several buildings—among them Jack Daniel's office. Some tour options include sampling flights of different whiskeys. Note that even though Lynchburg is a dry town, you can buy a personalized bottle at the distillery's shop, and the whiskey inside it is considered "free," a loophole in the law. ✉ *182 Lynchburg Hwy., Lynchburg, TN* 🌐 *www.jackdaniels.com*

Do This: The town of Lynchburg is small and quaint, with a small town square playing host to shops and restaurants. If you're looking for souvenirs, head this way—the distillery itself offers little for sale.

THE LOST SEA AT CRAIGHEAD CAVERNS

Craighead Caverns is home to the second-largest underground lake in the world (and the largest in the United States), earning it the nickname "the Lost Sea." The very extensive cave system is located between Sweetwater and Madisonville, Tennessee. Former cave visitors include the Pleistocene jaguar, which left tracks in the cave about 20,000 years ago. The cave system was also extensively used by the Cherokee tribe. ✉ *140 Lost Sea Rd., Sweetwater, TN* 🌐 *www.thelostsea.com*

Do This: You can take a "boat adventure" through the lake, which will start with a guided walking tour of the caverns, followed by a boat tour of the Lost Sea itself.

RUBY FALLS

More than 80 years ago, Leo Lambert and a small crew spent 17 hours inside this cavern before discovering what is now the world's tallest and deepest underground waterfall (145 feet) open to the public. After your visit underground, head up the 70-foot-high Lookout Mountain tower for a spectacular panorama of the Tennessee River Valley, using either your own peepers or one of the coin-operated telescopes. ✉ *1720 S. Scenic Hwy., Chattanooga, TN* 🌐 *www.rubyfalls.com*

Do This: Friday (and select Saturday) evenings from February through November, visitors can book a guided night tour of the falls, lit only by handheld lanterns.

TITANTIC MUSEUM ATTRACTION

It's unclear why landlocked Pigeon Forge, Tennessee is the home of this doomed ship replica. Opened in 2010 at a cost of $25 million—plus, the acquisition of artifacts valued at more than $4.5 million—this half-scale replica of the RMS *Titanic* is designed to give an idea of what it may have felt like to be a passenger aboard the sinking ship on that fateful night during her maiden voyage. ✉ *2134 Parkway, Pigeon Forge, TN* 🌐 *www.titanicpigeonforge.com*

Do This: You'll have the opportunity to walk the grand staircase, touch an iceberg, try to stand on sloped decks, and plunge your hand into 28°F water. Most of all, throughout your self-guided tour, you'll learn more about the 2,208 passengers who perished and honor their memories. Allow about two hours to take it all in.

Cool Places to Stay

Blackberry Farm. If you're looking for luxury in the Great Smokies, this lauded farm and restaurant is the place to be. The setting is everything you can expect from the Tennessee mountains, but the amenities are what make it really decadent. Blackberry is particularly known for its excellent culinary endeavors that showcase local ingredients. There's also fly-fishing, horseback riding, cooking classes, and a wellness center and pool. ✉ *1471 W. Millers Cove Rd., Walland, TN* 🌐 *www.blackberryfarm.com*

Dive Motel & Swim Club. Blending the laid-back vibe of a retro motor lodge with a hip pool and bar scene, this 23-room motel is from the design masterminds behind the Urban Cowboy brand in Nashville, New York, and Denver. The mood is light and bright, with—unique to each room—yellow and pink shag bedspreads, nature-inspired cabin decor, vivid patterned wallpaper, and hand-painted wall murals. ✉ *1414 Dickerson Pike, Nashville, TN* 🌐 *www.thedivemotel.com*

LeConte Lodge. Set at 6,360 feet near the summit of Mt. LeConte in Great Smoky Mountains National Park, this hike-in lodge is remote, rustic, and remarkable (but not luxurious). Small, rough-hewn wood cabins and three group-sleeping cabins have bunk beds, propane heaters, and kerosene lamps, and there are privies with flush toilets, but no showers. The appeal of LeConte Lodge is in the mountaintop setting, where you can take in views from your deck rocking chair and stargaze at night. There is no road access to the lodge; the only way in is by hiking trail. 🌐 *www.lecontelodge.com*

About Our Writers

Chris Chamberlain has lived in Nashville, Tennessee his entire life, except for the four years he spent in California studying history at Stanford and learning how to use chopsticks. Although he respects the success of the Tennessee Vols football team, he feels being a lifelong Vanderbilt fan has built a lot of character. He has been a freelance food, drink, and travel writer since 2009.

The Peabody Memphis. Even if you're not staying here, it's worth a stop to see this 12-story downtown landmark, built in 1925. The lobby has the original stained glass skylights and the travertine-marble fountain that is home to the hotel's resident ducks. (The ducks parade to the fountain at 11 am, and they depart the fountain at 5 pm.) The rooms are decorated in a variety of period styles. ✉ *118 S. 2nd St., Memphis, TN* 🌐 *www.peabodymemphis.com*

Union Station Hotel. Set in a restored neo-Romanesque train station, Union Station is breathtaking with its 65-foot-high ceiling of 100-year-old Tiffany stained glass. Reflecting the city's style, each room displays a blend of curated artwork, cowhide headboards, or leather furnishings along with essential guest comforts like Wi-Fi and in-room coffee. Combining luxury of the past with nods to the present by way of local art, the hotel is a reminder to embrace the romance of slow travel. ✉ *1001 Broadway, Nashville, TN* 🌐 *www.unionstationhotelnashville.com*

Essential Eats

Dancing Bear Appalachian Bistro. Appalachian cuisine epitomizes the popular trend toward farm-to-table dining, utilizing unpretentious ingredients like beans, field peas, foraged mushrooms, and local trout to create seasonal menus that tell the story of the bounty of the region. Here the kitchen goes a step further to elevate these humble foods to fine dining status. ✉ *7140 E. Lamar Alexander Pkwy., Townsend, TN* 🌐 *www.dancingbearlodge.com/dining*

Hagy's Catfish Hotel. Golden, crispy fried catfish is a Tennessee delicacy, and the Hagy family has been serving whiskerfish and hush puppies from various iterations of their restaurants on this site near the Shiloh battlegrounds for almost a century. Enjoy whole fish, fried fillets, fish tacos, or Cajun-style broiled catfish along with a choice of delicious side dishes. ✉ *1140 Hagy La., Shiloh, TN* 🌐 *www.catfishhotel.com*

Memphis Barbecue. The Bluff City is known for its signature dry-rub ribs, and Charlie Vergos' Rendezvous is the original home of these smoky pork treats. However, Cozy Corner also serves great ribs along with several other unique Memphis barbecue specialties like smoked Cornish hen and BBQ spaghetti, where pulled pork and smoky sauce take the place of traditional ragù alla Bolognese in the pasta dish.

Nashville Meat-and-Three Restaurants. A proper "meat-and-three" restaurant is defined as a cafeteria-style spot where patrons slide a tray down a serving line, selecting a meat from a list of Southern classics like fried chicken, meatloaf, and roast beef along with three vegetable sides from a steam table. Don't be surprised if the definition of "vegetable" in Nashville extends to Jell-O, banana pudding, or macaroni and cheese. Among the best in town are Arnold's Country Kitchen, Silver Sands Cafe, and Swett's.

Chapter 5

THE GREAT PLAINS

Updated by Kristi Eaton, Lori Erickson, Debbie Harmsen, Jim Holland, Alicia Underlee Nelson, and Rebecca Toy

WELCOME TO THE GREAT PLAINS

TOP REASONS TO GO

★ **From the mountains:** South Dakota's Badlands National Park exudes the same awe-inspiring beauty of the Grand Canyon, but its rugged lunar landscape is more accessible.

★ **To the prairies:** Traverse the Dakota Prairie Grasslands in North Dakota, or get lost on a bucket-list-worthy trip in the Flint Hills of Kansas.

★ **And the cities, too:** Spend a day in St. Louis riding to the top of the Gateway Arch or in Kansas City's 18th and Vine district enjoying lip-smacking barbecue, visiting museums, and taking in a blues concert.

★ **Active adventures:** The best way to experience the Plains is the great outdoors, whether you're on the water in the Ozarks or hiking in Pike Peaks State Park in Iowa

★ **American history:** Landmark moments in U.S. history are commemorated at sights including Kansas's Brown v. Board of Education National Historic Site and the Oklahoma City Memorial in OKC.

1 Iowa. Spend a day at the Iowa State Fair and take a selfie in front of the American Gothic house in Eldon.

2 Kansas. Stand in the geographic center of the United States and get out on the prairie.

3 Missouri. Ride to the top of the Gateway Arch, then head west for Kansas City barbecue.

4 Nebraska. Cheer at a College World Series game, watch prairie chickens dance, and gaze at the unique geological site of Chimney Rock.

5 North Dakota. Extending westward from the broad, flat Red River Valley, the prairies and plateaus here make it worth a trip to the north.

6 Oklahoma. Drive part of Route 66, be wowed by bison, and take in the vast Wichita Mountains Wildlife Refuge.

7 South Dakota. From Falls Park to the Black Hills and Badlands, there's more natural beauty than you can pack into one trip.

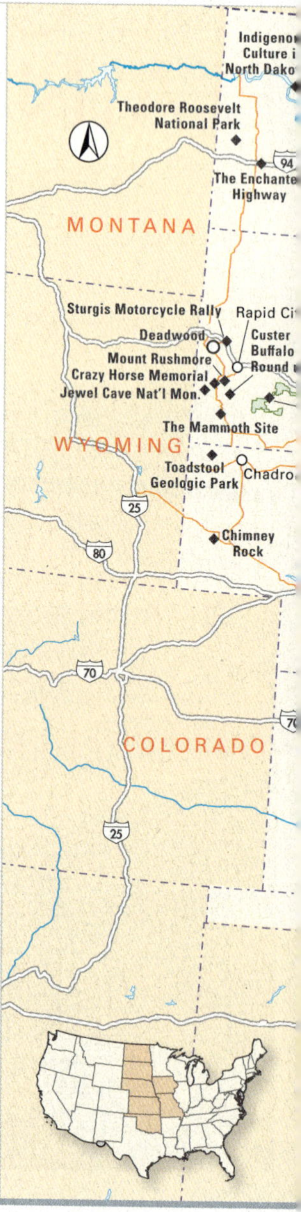

NORTH DAKOTA
5
Grand Forks
Lewis and Clark Trail
Cold War-Era Missile Bases
Dakota Prairie Grasslands
Fargo
Plains Art Museum
Downtown Fargo
Bismarck
94
83
29
MINNESOTA
35
0 100 mi
0 100 km
CANADA
U.S.
Lake Superior
SOUTH DAKOTA
7
The Oahe Dam
Pierre
WISCONSIN
Lake Michigan
43
Mitchell
Falls Park
90
Badlands National Park
Tanking Down a River
Sioux Falls
University of Okoboji Winter Games
Upper Iowa River
Pikes Peak S.P.
Fort Niobrara N.W.R.
Sioux City
Dubuque
IOWA
1
NEBRASKA
Norfolk
Loess Hills Nat'l Scenic Byway
Amana Colonies
Iowa City
Bike RAGBRAI
Mississippi Riverboat Cruise
Native American Pow Wows
4
The Henry Doorly Zoo and Aquarium
Des Moines
80
Davenport
College World Series
Iowa State Fair
Iowa City Literary Walk
North Platte
Omaha
Covered Bridges Scenic Byway
ILLINOIS
65
Sandhill Crane Migration
Lincoln
Willa Cather Sites
Big Red Football
55
McCook
35
IN KANSAS CITY:
18th and Vine District, and Kansas City Barbecue
Hannibal
St. Joseph
70
IN
Monument Rocks Natural Area
Topeka
St. Louis
Cheyenne Bottoms Wetland
KANSAS
2
Emporia
Jefferson City
Forest Park
The Gateway Arch
64
Brown v. Board of Education National Historic Site
Lake of the Ozarks
Dodge City
Kansas Cosmosphere
Wichita
Flint Hills National Scenic Byway
MISSOURI
3
KY
Gypsum Hills
44
OKLAHOMA
6
Branson
Natural Falls State Park
ARKANSAS
Tulsa
Tahlequah
40
Oklahoma's Route 66
TENNESSEE
Wichita Mountains Wildlife Refuge
IN TULSA:
Tulsa's Music Scene, and Tulsa's Historic Greenwood District
IN OKLAHOMA CITY:
Oklahoma City National Memorial & Museum, and Oklahoma City Museums
TEXAS
30
MISSISSIPPI

WHAT TO EAT AND DRINK IN THE GREAT PLAINS

Runza

RUNZA

You know you're in Nebraska if runza is on the menu. The state is considered the birthplace of the bread pocket filled with beef, onions, cabbage or sauerkraut, and seasonings. The Nebraska-based Runza restaurant chain has locations across the state, as well as a few in surrounding states. The sandwich is also big in Kansas, where it's known as bierock.

KANSAS CITY BARBECUE

Arthur Bryant's BBQ, located in the historic 18th and Vine District of Kansas City, might be the most famous barbecue joint in town, but there are now more than 100 others serving just about every kind of barbecued meat, including short- and long-end pork ribs, lamb ribs, brisket, pork shoulder, chicken, ham, and even mutton. No wonder Kansas City is known as the barbecue capital of the world.

KUCHEN

If you're in a part of the Great Plains with a large German-American population (that includes South Dakota, North Dakota, Nebraska, Kansas, and Iowa), chances are you can find a bakery or restaurant selling this pastry. Most recipes use fruit like apples, prunes, apricots, peaches, or rhubarb.

CHOKECHERRIES

Try the jellies and syrups made from chokecherries that grow wild across the Dakotas. The small, deep-red-to-purple berries are tart, really tart, so generations of local cooks have learned how to soften the tang and sweeten the flavor. Locally grown chokecherries provide the distinctive, tangy-sweet flavor to *wojapi* (pronounced *woe-jaw-pea*), which is the Lakota name for Native American berry sauce, most often spooned atop a freshly prepared piece of fry bread and served as a dessert treat. Try it at the Laughing Water Restaurant at the Crazy Horse Memorial.

CHISLIC

These bite-size cubes of meat served with toothpicks are the pride of South Dakota. The legislature named it the "official state nosh," although it's also served as a main dish. The traditional meat is mutton or lamb, but beef, venison, and occasionally some other red meats are used in chislic. The South Dakota Chislic Festival is held the last Saturday of July in the farming town of Freeman.

Chislic

BISON BURGER

More and more Great Plains restaurants are serving this healthier alternative to beef burgers. Bison has less fat, so it's a bit drier. It also has more of an earthy flavor because the animals munch on grass. Don't worry about what name to use—"buffalo burger" in cafés or "bison" at an upscale evening place—the terms are interchangeable. To ship a box of the lean, flavorful delicacy home, visit the Wild Idea Buffalo shop in Rapid City.

IOWA CHOP

Although it originated in Iowa, where hogs are said to outnumber people by roughly eight to one, this type of pork chop is popular around the Great Plains. The Iowa chop is a bone-in, center-cut loin chop that ranges from 1¼ to 1½ inches thick. The two most common ways of serving it are grilling and sautéeing.

Bison burger

TANKA BARS

Made in the region from a finely tuned recipe, Tanka is an energy bar that will really start your engine. Its principal ingredients include bison and berries.

MAID-RITE SANDWICH

Iowa butcher Fred Angell came up with the idea for this sandwich in the 1920s. Also known as a loose-meat sandwich, it's not pressed like a hamburger. It's more similar to a sloppy joe, but without the tomato-based sauce. Angell started the Maid-Rite restaurant chain that still operates today across parts of the Great Plains.

LEFSE

A Norwegian specialty, lefse is served at many holiday gatherings in North Dakota, as well as in other parts of the Great Plains. The traditional flatbread is cooked on a large griddle with potatoes, flour, butter, and milk or cream.

Iowa

There's more to Iowa than fields and farms. The state, which takes its name from a Native American word meaning "beautiful land," does indeed have among the most fertile, wisely managed, and lucrative soil on the planet. In fact, Iowa's 86,911 farms produce more corn, pigs, and eggs than any other state in the union. But it also has cultural riches, such as the Iowa State Fair and Iowa Literary Walk, which are not to be missed.

Capital: Des Moines

Population: 3,241,488

Area: 55,853 square miles

Statehood Date: December 28, 1846

Major Airports: Des Moines International Airport (DSM); Eastern Iowa Airport (CID)

Travel and Tourism Information:
www.traveliowa.com

Famous Residents: Laura Ingalls Wilder (writer); Herbert Hoover (president); John Wayne (actor); Grant Wood (painter); Ashton Kutcher (actor)

Fun Fact: Iowa will be the future birthplace of Captain James T. Kirk, who (according to *Star Trek* creator Gene Roddenberry) will arrive in Riverside, Iowa on March 22, 2228.

Iowa State Fair

The Midwest's Most Famous State Fair

The Iowa State Fair is the biggest annual event in the state and one of the oldest and largest agricultural and industrial expositions in the United States. The annual event held over 11 days each August attracts more than a million people. Besides serious exhibits, it's famous for serving more than 60 foods on a stick. There are the traditional favorites, like deep-fried desserts, corn dogs, and caramel apples, and more unusual options, including key lime pie, caprese salad, and peanut butter and jelly sandwiches. There are always great concerts in the grandstand, as well as tons of free entertainment. ✉ *3000 E. Grand Ave., Des Moines, IA* 🌐 *www.iowastatefair.org*

Don't Miss

Tipping the scales at around 600 pounds, the crowd-pleasing **Butter Cow** on display each year at the Iowa State Fair has enough rich, creamy butter to slather on more than 19,000 slices of toast. Inside a 40°F cooler, layers of pure butter are applied to a steel mesh frame until the shape of a cow emerges. It measures about 5½ feet high and 8 feet long.

Good to Know

Every four years, during presidential elections, the fair attracts politicians looking to sway the country's earliest voters. Regardless of your party affiliation, it's a great way to meet your favorite candidates.

Getting Here and Around

The Iowa State Fairgrounds is 5 miles east of downtown Des Moines, which is located in central Iowa.

Iowa City Literary Walk

The small towns of the strange middle of our lives
remain small
Streets wintry
even in summer...
- Robert Dana
"Summer in a Very Small Town"

The Writing Walk of Fame

The world-famous University of Iowa Writers' Workshop has drawn thousands of talented writers over the past few decades, so it's no wonder that Iowa City is designated a UNESCO City of Literature. One of the best ways to appreciate its connection to the written word is to stroll the Iowa Literary Walk, a Hollywood Walk of Fame of sorts for authors. Blocks of downtown celebrate the works of 89 writers who have ties to Iowa, from acclaimed poets and playwrights to accomplished novelists and journalists. The walk consists of bronze relief panels in sidewalks and book-theme sculptures. 🌐 *www.iowacityofliterature.org/lit-walk*

Don't Miss

Big-name authors including Kurt Vonnegut, Flannery O'Connor, and Rita Dove, who were all part of Iowa's creative writing program, are represented on the walk; the plaque of Tennessee Williams, who lived in Iowa as a student, reads: "We're all of us sentenced to solitary confinement inside our own skins, for life!"

While You're Here

The **University of Iowa** (UI) campus sits next to downtown. Take a stroll around campus and stop at the **Iowa Old Capitol Museum**, which has historical exhibits, and the **UI Museum of Natural History**.

Good to Know

Pick up Literary Walk booklets for a small fee at the city's famous **Prairie Lights Bookstore**. ✉ *15 S. Dubuque St., Iowa City, IA* 🌐 *www.prairielights.com*

Getting Here and Around

Located in Iowa City, the Walk's bronze markers are along both sides of Iowa Avenue between Clinton Street and Gilbert Street and on North Linn Street.

Mississippi Riverboat Cruise

Mark Twain for a Day

If you've never ridden on an old-fashioned riverboat, a trip on the *Twilight* is a great introduction to this traditional mode of travel. Standing on the deck as it chugs along, it's a great way to take in the majesty of the mighty Mississippi River, the second-longest river in the United States. This scenic, two-day cruise departs from and ends in LeClaire, Iowa. It includes a night of lodging at the riverfront Grand Harbor Resort in historic Dubuque. A continental breakfast will be ready when you board, and lunch and dinner will be served as you pass picturesque river towns that include Port Byron, Illinois; Princeton, Iowa; and Cordova, Illinois. There's also plenty of time to enjoy a glass of iced tea or lemonade and watch the world float by. ✉ *197 Front St., Le Claire, IA* 🌐 *www.riverboattwilight.com*

Don't Miss

Before or after your cruise, take in the thousands of one-of-a-kind objects at **Antique Archaeology**, where they filmed the series *American Pickers* on the History Channel. ✉ *115 Davenport St., Le Claire, IA* 🌐 *antiquearchaeology.com*

While You're Here

The **Buffalo Bill Museum** is a tribute to the man behind the famous "Buffalo Bill's Wild West" extravaganzas, and also includes history on the Mississippi River, the Civil War, and Native American heritage in the region. ✉ *199 Front St, Le Claire, IA* 🌐 *www.buffalobillmuseumleclaire.com*

Getting Here and Around

LeClaire is 15 miles northeast of Davenport, Iowa.

Pikes Peak State Park

Epic Climb, Epic Views

Situated on a spectacular 500-foot bluff overlooking the confluence of the Mississippi and Wisconsin rivers, Pikes Peak is one of Iowa's most photographed destinations. Eleven miles of trails run through its rugged landscape, including a 4-mile route to Point Ann that has views of the town of McGregor and the Mississippi River. Watch for fossil remains along the way, including brachiopods, gastropods, and cephalopods. ✉ *32264 Pikes Peak Rd., McGregor, IA* 🌐 *www.iowadnr.gov*

Don't Miss

Hike the half-mile boardwalk to **Bridal Veil Falls** and explore **Bear Mound**, an effigy built by Native Americans.

Good to Know

Mountain bikes are allowed on the Pikes Peak trail from Homestead Park to the McGregor parking lots. The park also has a campground with 62 sites.

While You're Here

Effigy Mounds National Monument, 7 miles north of the park, preserves more than 200 mounds built by Native Americans. Hike around the 2-mile Fire Point Loop Trail, where you can spot more than 20 mounds. ✉ *151 Rte. 76, Harpers Ferry, IA* 🌐 *www.nps.gov/efmo*

Getting Here and Around

Pikes Peak State Park is 56 miles north of Dubuque, Iowa. Take Route 3 west of Dubuque and then head north on U.S. 52. The park is just south of the town of McGregor.

The Covered Bridges Scenic Byway

A Charming Bridge-Centric Drive

If you've seen the 1995 film *The Bridges of Madison County* starring Meryl Streep and Clint Eastwood or read the best-selling book it was based on by Robert James Waller, these wooden structures have already made it to your bucket list, and driving the roughly 82-mile Covered Bridges Scenic Byway is a great way to see them. Five of the six wooden structures are originals built between 1870 and 1884. Other highlights along the way include a cidery, two wineries, and the **John Wayne Birthplace and Museum** in Winterset.

Don't Miss

At 122 feet long, the **Holliwell Covered Bridge** is the longest of the remaining bridges. The **Roseman Covered Bridge** is supposedly haunted by the ghost of an escapee from the county jail. The **Cedar Covered Bridge** was originally built in 1883 but has been twice destroyed by fire and rebuilt.

Good to Know

Contact the Madison County Chamber of Commerce for a detailed map of the bridges and an audio tour. ⊕ *www.exploremadisoncounty.com*

While You're Here

Save time to explore the **Iowa Quilt Museum** in the town of Winterset. This is where the television show *Fons & Porter's Love of Quilting* was created. If you want to bring home your own hand-stitched work of art, there are plenty of craft shops nearby. ✉ *68 E. Court Ave., Winterset, IA* ⊕ *www.iowaquiltmuseum.org*

Getting Here and Around

Winterset, the county seat of Madison County, is 37 miles southwest of Des Moines. Take Interstate 80 west to De Soto, Iowa, then head south on U.S. 169.

Loess Hills National Scenic Byway

Tour the Iowa Hills Built by Wind

Stretching along Iowa's western edge, the Loess Hills are a rare geological formation made of wind-blown silt. Rising from the Missouri River Valley like sculpted waves made of earth, they're a haven for rare plants and unique ecosystems. On the Loess Hills National Scenic Byway, you'll meander up and down hills and through charming small towns. Make time to stretch your legs in **Waubonsie, Stone,** or **Preparation Canyon state parks**, where the wild, windswept beauty of the Loess Hills is on full display.

Don't Miss

Near Crescent, visit the **Hitchcock Nature Center** (✉ *27792 Ski Hill Loop, Honey Creek, IA*) for sweeping views, hiking trails, and a nature center that explains how the Loess Hills were formed near the end of the last Ice Age. Be sure to climb its 45-foot observation tower, which in the fall is one of the best places in the Midwest to view migrating raptors. Another popular spot is the **Loess Hills Lavender Farm** (✉ *2278 Loess Hills Trail, Missouri Valley, IA* 🌐 *www.loesshillslavender.com*), especially lovely during the peak blooming season from mid-June through July. Savor the colors and fragrant air and shop for lavender-theme items in its store.

Good to Know

The Loess Hills are about 15 miles wide and 200 miles long. The best time to drive the Byway is late September through October, when the landscape blazes with fall colors. Throughout the growing season, you can find many farm stands along the way.

Getting Here and Around

The Byway includes roughly 220 miles of paved roads, with another 185 miles of optional detours. It's best explored by car, with plenty of scenic loops, overlooks, and small towns to tempt you off the main route.

Amana Colonies

Explore a Unique German Village

Indulge in uber German foods like Wiener schnitzel and brats while learning about a unique culture in the United States at the Amana Colonies in east-central Iowa. These seven villages were built by Germans who fled their homeland in the mid-1800s to establish a communal society based on their religion. Though they eventually gave up communal living, much of their traditional culture remains. The National Historic Landmark draws visitors far and wide for food, wine, and beers as well as quality handcrafted products, art, and quaint shops that line quiet streets. Notice the 19th-century buildings made of brick, sandstone, and wood, many of which date back to the communal era. 🌐 *www.amanacolonies.com*

Don't Miss

The Amana Colonies host a variety of annual festivals, including the **Wurst Festival**, which is held every year on the Saturday before Father's Day. Wurst (the German word for sausage) purveyors from around the region gather to celebrate their craft and compete for awards. Besides the classic bratwurst, there are local beers, live music, and a Dachshund Derby that picks the fastest wiener dog in Iowa.

Best Restaurants

The **Ox Yoke Inn** and **Ronneburg Restaurant** serve American fare, but also German favorites like sauerbraten, Wiener schnitzel, and brats while beer and pub grub are the features at the **Millstream Brau Haus**.

Getting Here and Around

To get to the town of Amana from Iowa City, drive 24 miles northwest on Interstate 80, U.S. 6, and U.S. 151.

Bike RAGBRAI

The World's Oldest, Largest, and Longest Bike Touring Event

Traveling through small towns, across rolling hills, and past seemingly endless fields of corn, the *Des Moines Register's* Annual Great Bike Ride Across Iowa will make you appreciate the camaraderie of the sport as you join thousands of cyclists for a challenging seven-day event. Held every July, RAGBRAI started in 1973 when a couple of newspaper columnists got together for a casual ride across Iowa. Over the years it's grown into the world's oldest, longest, and largest recreational bicycle touring event. Averaging a heart-pumping 67 miles a day, the event begins somewhere along the western border on the Missouri River and ends in the east at the Mississippi River. 🌐 *www.ragbrai.com*

Don't Miss

It may add a few miles to the route, but make sure to dip your tire in the Missouri River at the start and the Mississippi River at the end, a tradition for die-hards.

Good to Know

The route changes every year and is announced in late January. Sign up early, because RAGBRAI is limited to approximately 8,500 weeklong riders. And if a week seems like too much, don't worry. There are also spots for 1,500 daily riders.

Getting Here and Around

The starting point changes each year, but it's always in the western part of the state. If you're flying in, you'll likely head to the international airports in Des Moines or Omaha, Nebraska (just across the western Iowa border).

The Upper Iowa River

The Midwest's Most Scenic River

Steep, rocky cliffs are not something that comes to mind when you think of Iowa's rolling farmland. But the Upper Iowa River in the northeast corner of the state has spectacular scenery that make it one of the most picturesque rivers in the Midwest. Extending for 150 miles, the Upper Iowa was one of the first in the nation to be named a National Wild and Scenic River in the 1960s. Thanks largely to the conservation groups that care for it, the river has maintained its pristine beauty, passing by dramatic vertical limestone palisades and forested bluffs. It's not uncommon to see deer stopping for a drink or wild turkeys hurrying along the shore. The current is fairly gentle, so you'll share the waterway with anglers, bird-watchers, and other outdoors enthusiasts. The best way to experience it is from a canoe or kayak.

Don't Miss

On your trip, look for the **Bluffton Palisades**, limestone cliffs that soar hundreds of feet above the water.

While You're Here

There are three waterfalls within walking distance of the Upper Iowa River: **Dunnings Springs** and **Siewers Springs** in Decorah and **Malanaphy Spring Falls** in Bluffton.

Getting Here and Around

The stretch between Kendallville and Bluffton is among the most scenic parts of the river, with natural springs, bluffs, and enough riffles to add a little excitement to your paddling.

University of Okoboji Winter Games

Iowa's Oddball Olympics

You don't have to be Lindsey Vonn to participate in the University of Okoboji Winter Games, a variety of eccentric but always fun competitions held each January since the 1980s in the lakeside town of Arnolds Park. The games, which are named after an imaginary university started as a joke, include a chilling polar plunge, a keg toss, broomball, snowball fights, and human dogsled races in which teams of four people pull one rider on an inner tube along a 20-yard-long track. There are also ice auger races in which participants compete to be the first to drill a hole through the ice. Head indoors and there's axe throwing, a chili cook-off, pickleball, and even a stein-holding contest. It's great fun for both participants and spectators, who come from all over to take part and sometimes win prizes. ✉ *565 S. U.S. 71, Arnolds Park, IA* 🌐 *www.uofowinter-games.com*

Don't Miss

The polar plunge is the signature, bucket-list activity of the games, when the brave line up in their swimsuits in the snow and jump (extra points for creativity) into the icy cold water of West Lake Okoboji next to Arnolds Park. The $25 participation fee goes to support the local fire and rescue department.

While You're Here

Whether you participate in the games or not, make like a Midwesterner and ride downhill on an inner tube. The favorite local spot for this wintertime activity is **Horseshoe Bend Tubing Hill**, open every weekend in winter.

Getting Here and Around

Arnolds Park is located in northwest Iowa near the Minnesota border. The closest large airport is in Sioux Falls, South Dakota, about 100 miles west.

When in Iowa

AMERICAN GOTHIC HOUSE

Artist Grant Wood had arrived in Eldon, Iowa for an art exhibition in 1930 when he spotted a little white house with peaked windows on the second floor. He quickly sketched the unusual structure, and it eventually became the backdrop for his famous work, *American Gothic.* (Wood's two models were his sister, Nan Wood Graham, and his dentist, Dr. B.H. McKeeby, though they never posed in front of the house.) Today the house is owned by the State Historical Society of Iowa, while the adjacent museum is owned by the City of Eldon. The house is open on select days; the museum welcomes visitors Wednesday through Sunday. ✉ *300 American Gothic St., Eldon, IA* 🌐 *www.americangothichouse.org*

Do This: Obviously, you have to pose for a self-portrait in front of the house.

DO THE WAVE WITH THE HAWKEYES

Fans do "the wave" at University of Iowa football games at Kinnick Stadium, an event that's quickly become known as one of the best traditions in college football. The wave started with a simple idea from a fan. In 2017, at the end of the first quarter of the Hawkeyes season opener, more than 70,000 football fans in Kinnick Stadium were asked to turn toward the east and wave. Patients and their families gathered on the top floor of the nearby University of Iowa Stead Family Children's Hospital waved back. Ever since, those in the stadium and in the hospital have looked forward to it each week during home games. ✉ *University of Iowa, 886 Stadium Dr., Iowa City, IA* 🌐 *www.hawkeyesports.com*

Do This: Support the University of Iowa Stead Family Children's Hospital by buying an official Iowa Wave shirt.

About Our Writers

Lori Erickson grew up on a farm near Decorah, Iowa and now lives in Iowa City, happily surrounded by rolling hills and winding bike trails. She's smitten with Iowa's patchwork of farmland, rivers, and bluffs, and thinks Effigy Mounds National Monument is one of the most beautiful places on earth. A longtime travel writer, she's explored landscapes across the globe, but Iowa's quiet beauty keeps calling her back.

IOWA CORN MAZES

Each fall, corn mazes are a beloved Iowa tradition. These labyrinths of towering stalks and winding paths range from simple designs perfect for families to elaborate puzzles that can stump even seasoned navigators. After touring one, you'll see why Iowa is known as the Tall Corn State. Many farms pair their mazes with other offerings, from hayrides and kids' play areas to pumpkin patches and hot cider. Popular corn mazes include Bloomsbury Farm near Atkins and Harvestville Farm near Donnellson.

Do This: For a spooky, rustling adventure, try a corn maze by flashlight. Some farms offer this option on selected evenings.

Cool Places to Stay

Courtyard Waterloo Cedar Falls. Built in a renovated John Deere tractor factory, the Courtyard Waterloo Cedar Falls preserves many of the original architectural details. The original warehouse floors were raised, so guests can take in the views through the massive windows that once illuminated the manufacturing operation. ✉ *250 Westfield Ave., Waterloo, IA* 🌐 *www.marriott.com*

CR Station Train Caboose. In Decorah, this beautifully restored caboose comes with a lot of the original equipment, including the overhead handrails and the conductor's chairs, which are a great place to watch the sunset. 🌐 *www.airbnb.com/rooms/15408900*

Field of Dreams House. Kevin Costner won't get you coffee in the morning, but you can still enjoy a night in the three-bedroom farmhouse where the movie *Field of Dreams* was filmed near Dyersville, Iowa. You also have exclusive access to the adjacent baseball field that was used in the movie. ✉ *28995 Lansing Rd., Dyersville, IA* 🌐 *www.fieldofdreams-moviesite.com/the-house*

Historic Park Inn. In Mason City, the Historic Park Inn is the last remaining hotel designed by famed architect Frank Lloyd Wright. Its owners have taken pains to maintain its historic design while adding modern amenities. The Leadlight restaurant offers fine dining, or get a nightcap in its cellar-level bar the Draftsman. ✉ *15 W. State St., Mason City, IA* 🌐 *www.historicparkinn.com*

Hotel Grinnell. The quirky Hotel Grinnell is in a converted middle school. The granite structure was built in 1921 to serve as the local junior high, and now it's a modern, eco-conscious boutique hotel, eatery, and event destination. ✉ *925 Park St., Grinnell, IA* 🌐 *www.hotelgrinnell.com*

Essential Eats

Breaded Pork Tenderloin Sandwich. Made from center-cut pork loin and typically dwarfing the bun it's served on, the meat is tenderized, pounded thin, breaded, and deep-fried. Think of it as Iowa's answer to a Wiener schnitzel. As the nation's top pork producer, Iowa takes this sandwich seriously: the Iowa Pork Producers Association even crowns a yearly champion. Recent winners include Dairy Sweet in Dunlap and Ruby's Pub & Grill in Stuart.

Farm-to-Table Restaurants. Thanks to the state's rich soil, agricultural abundance, and creative chefs, farm-to-table restaurants are a vibrant part of Iowa's culinary landscape. A growing number of eateries specialize in seasonal, locally sourced products and produce, with menus that change throughout the year. Check out La Rana Bistro in Decorah, The Café in Ames, and Fresko in Des Moines for a taste of Iowa straight from the source.

Sweet Corn. Not to be confused with the state's abundant field corn, which is grown primarily for livestock, this is Iowa's favorite summer treat. With its high sugar content and quick maturity, sweet corn peaks in July and August. To enjoy it, the key is freshness: ideally it should be cooked and eaten the same day it's picked. Whether boiled or grilled, it's best served simply with butter and salt. You'll find the tastiest ears at local farmers' markets, which are typically held on Saturday in many small towns. Sweet corn isn't fancy, but it's pure Iowa deliciousness.

Wells Visitor Center & Ice Cream Parlor. Le Mars has good reason to call itself the Ice Cream Capital of the World. This small town in northwestern Iowa is home to Wells Enterprises, the makers of Blue Bunny ice cream and other dairy treats. Founded in 1913, the company produces so much ice cream that it requires a 12-story freezer to store it all. Stop by the Wells Visitor Center & Ice Cream Parlor for a tasty treat, information on how ice cream is made, and a dash of local and company history. Or plan your visit during the town's Ice Cream Days in June for extra festivities. ✉ *115 Central Ave. NW, Le Mars, IA* 🌐 *ilovewells.com*

Kansas

Kansas might not be the first state that comes to mind when planning a bucket list adventure, but there is far more to it than its oh-so-flat stereotypes. Experiences in awe-inspiring natural beauty, Native American history, and Wild West heritage beckon without the crowds. The state was home to legendary lawmen like Wyatt Earp and James Butler "Wild Bill" Hickok, who policed once-rowdy railroad and cattle towns like Abilene, Dodge City, and Ellsworth.

Capital: Topeka

Population: 2,970,606

Area: 82,278 square miles

Statehood Date: January 29, 1861

Major Airports: Kansas City International Airport (MCI); Wichita Dwight D. Eisenhower National Airport (ICT)

Travel and Tourism Information: *www.travelks.com*

Famous Residents: Wyatt Earp (Wild West lawman); Amelia Earhart (aviator); Dwight Eisenhower (president); Erin Brockovich (activist); Paul Rudd (actor); Jason Sudeikis (actor)

Fun Fact: Kansas may not only be the geographic center of the United States, but it's also allegedly the portal to hell. A tiny graveyard and its church ruins outside of Lawrence have conjured up stories of witchcraft, sudden storms, and the seventh gate to hell. In reality, teens have been the area's largest nuisance for generations.

Dodge City

Home to the O.K. Corral

Few towns evoke the Wild West like Dodge City, Kansas. Stroll along the wooden sidewalks of the **Boot Hill Museum**, a historic street that keeps the 1800s alive in the "Queen of Cowtowns." Learn about the town's unique characters like Wyatt Earp, Doc Holliday, and Bat Masterson. During summer, you can experience Dodge City's heyday through historical reenactments, including the famous gunfight at the **O.K. Corral**. You've seen shootouts in the movies, but this one makes you want to kick up your heels with Miss Kitty and the Can-Can Girls in the **Long Branch Saloon**.

Don't Miss

The **Dodge City Trail of Fame** commemorates the many famous and infamous people who walked these streets. Some of the markers are dedicated to notable movie and television stars who have portrayed some of the famous figures. A walking tour guide is available at the **Dodge City Visitor Information Center** (✉ *400 W. Wyatt Earp Blvd., Dodge City, KS*).

When to Go

Time your trip to coincide with the **Dodge City Days**, a 10-day festival that kicks off the last week of July. Events include a parade, an art show, feats of strength, concerts, BBQ competitions, and the Boot Hill Bull Fry. The celebration of the town's Western heritage culminates with the **Dodge City Roundup Rodeo**, a multiday competition of professional bull riding, bronc busting, and calf roping. 🌐 *www.dodgecitydays.org*

Getting Here and Around

Dodge City is 154 miles west of Wichita in southwest Kansas. When you arrive, stop at the Dodge City Visitor Information Center for a complete list of events.

Flint Hills National Scenic Byway

The Last of America's Tallgrass Prairie

Tallgrass prairie once covered 170 million acres of North America, but less than 4% remains intact. Almost 80% of the surviving ecosystem is in the Flint Hills. If you want to see what much of North America looked like before farming changed the landscape, this 47-mile drive is one of the few places left to experience it. The Flint Hills National Scenic Byway defies the state's flat stereotypes, with rolling views of the native grasses and flowers of the tallgrass prairie. 🌐 *nsbfoundation.com/nb/flint-hills-national-scenic-byway*

Don't Miss

One must-see stop along the way is the **Tallgrass Prairie National Preserve**, managed by the National Park Service. Established in 1996, it protects a nationally significant remnant of the once vast tallgrass prairie ecosystem. Start at the visitor center and then walk the trails of the 11,000-acre preserve where you might encounter a herd of bison. ✉ *2480B Rte. 177, Strong City, KS* 🌐 *www.nps.gov/tapr*

Good to Know

Much of the Flint Hills is unchanged since Native American like the Kanza and Osage nations were the original residents. Early European settlers passed by on the famous Santa Fe Trail through here, some stopping to settle the nearby towns of Council Grove, Cottonwood Falls, and Strong City.

Getting Here and Around

The 47-mile byway on Route 177 starts in Council Grove, Kansas, which is 77 miles southwest of Topeka and 98 miles northeast of Wichita. It ends in Cassoday.

Gypsum Hills

Spectacular Wildflower-Covered Red Soil

The Gypsum Hills belong on every nature lover's bucket list. Also known as the Medicine Hills, mesas, canyons, and buttes, much of it covered in wildflowers, jut up in the south-central region of the state. Yet this isn't standard Kansas soil. The earth contains large amounts of iron oxide—better known as rust—causing these hills to have an unforgettable reddish tint. That natural beauty draws artists, photographers, and outdoors lovers of all types who want to experience the unique landscape whose rivers drew Native American nations for centuries. ✉ *U.S. 160, Medicine Lodge, KS*

Don't Miss

The well-marked **Gypsum Hills Scenic Byway** is the best way to see the rugged hills, with several outlooks perfect for spotting antelope, coyotes, prairie dogs, and birds like pheasants and quail. While most of the region is private property, a stay at the Gyp Hills Ranch House gives you access to not only wildlife, but also a behind-the-scenes look at an active cattle ranch. Guests can camp in tents, hook up an RV, or reserve one of the lodge's five rooms. ✉ *3393 S.W. Woodward Rd., Medicine Lodge, KS* 🌐 *www.gyphills-guestranch.com*

Getting Here and Around

The Gypsum Hills are in south-central Kansas near the Oklahoma border. The state has designated a 42-mile scenic byway along U.S. 160 between Coldwater and Medicine Lodge, which is 86 miles southwest of Wichita. You can see the Gypsum Hills along the route, but there are few places to pull over to take photographs.

Brown v. Board of Education National Historic Site

A Civil Rights Milestone

The simplicity of this historic site in Topeka, Kansas belies its place in U.S. history. Congress established it in 1992 to commemorate the 1954 landmark decision of the U.S. Supreme Court that ended racial segregation in public schools. The national historic site consists of Monroe Elementary School, one of four elementary schools in the city that were designated for Black children. The parents of one of those pupils, Linda Brown, filed a lawsuit so that she could attend an all-white school in her neighborhood. In that case, Brown v. Board of Education, the justices unanimously declared that "separate educational facilities are inherently unequal." They ruled that segregated schools violated the 14th Amendment to the U.S. Constitution that guarantees all citizens "equal protection of the laws." ✉ *1515 S.E. Monroe St., Topeka, KS* 🌐 *www.nps.gov/brvb*

Don't Miss

Several galleries provide a stark look at segregation in America. The Road to Brown v. Board of Education gallery covers the barriers Black Americans faced while trying to receive an education. The Legacy gallery tells the story of the civil rights movement after the ruling, including its ongoing impact. The Hall of Courage is an evocative and powerful walk surrounded by immersive footage of real-life students integrating schools; it may not be suitable for younger children. The kindergarten still looks like it did in 1954, showing what it was like to attend the segregated school.

Getting Here and Around

The site is located in downtown Topeka.

Cheyenne Bottoms Wetland

Best Bird-Watching in the Plains

The largest inland marsh in the United States, Cheyenne Bottoms has 64 square miles of wetlands that draw an impressive array of birds throughout the year. Ornithologists have spotted at least 350 species in this rare prairie-marsh ecosystem, more than at any other place in the state. In the winter, rough-legged hawks and bald eagles are among the 148 species that spend the colder months here, joining the 63 species that make it their home year-round. In the spring, more than half a million ducks and geese and thousands of other birds like sandhill and whooping cranes pass through the region during their annual migrations. In early summer, thousands of shorebirds visit the marsh. And each autumn, 250,000 or more birds stop on their journey south. Together with **Quivira National Wildlife Refuge** just 40 miles southeast, the Cheyenne Bottoms is a delight for international bird lovers. ✉ *592 N.E. Rte. 156, Great Bend, KS* 🌐 *www.ksoutdoors.gov*

Don't Miss

No matter the season, the best place to spot the birds is the viewing platform not far from the entrance.

Good to Know

The **Kansas Wetlands Education Center** has plenty of information about birds, as well as the snakes, turtles, salamanders, and other creatures that are native to the surrounding area. The center also offers suggested driving tours and guided van tours of the wetlands. ✉ *592 Rte. 156, Ellinwood, KS* 🌐 *www.wetlandscenter.fhsu.edu*

Getting Here and Around

Cheyenne Bottoms is 119 miles northwest of Wichita, Kansas, and 11 miles northeast of Great Bend, Kansas. The Kansas Wetlands Education Center is on the southern end of the wetlands.

Monument Rocks Natural Area

One of the First National Natural Landmarks

Like stone fortresses rising out of the prairie, the Monument Rocks Natural Area features 50-foot-tall outcroppings of white chalk and sedimentary deposits that have eroded over time to form pinnacles, spires, and buttes. It takes some imagination to picture, but these prairies were once a great sea, stretching from Mexico up through Canada. As the waters receded in the Cretaceous period, they left behind these marine sediments full of the fossils of fish, turtles, and even mosasaurs. The National Park Service designated the formation as one of the first National Natural Landmarks in 1968 and it's considered one of the best regions in the country to examine the fossils of ancient sea life.

Don't Miss

The Cathedral and Arch monuments draw the most photographs, but wandering farther opens up wide panoramas. Get up early to see the monuments at sunrise, or stick around until sunset when the chalk glows gold and orange.

How to Visit

Monument Rocks Natural Area sits on private property, but the owners allow anyone to visit for free. They ask that you follow the rules: no climbing, fossil hunting, motorized vehicles, or overnight stays. One more thing: no taunting the cattle that roam in the area. The site is open sunrise to sunset.

Getting Here and Around

Monument Rocks Natural Area is on unpaved roads off U.S. 83, 20 miles south of Oakley and 268 miles northwest of Wichita.

Kansas Cosmosphere

Smithsonian-Level Planeterium and Space Museum

The state's motto, "Ad astra per aspera" (to the stars through difficulties), is never more literal than at the Kansas Cosmosphere. This Hutchinson museum is home to the world's largest combined collection of U.S. and Russian space artifacts. The Smithsonian affiliate features a world-class planetarium, an artifact preservation lab, and one of the nation's primary campus sites for "Space Camp," a week-long aerospace program complete with a space mission simulation that draws in high school students from around the country. ✉ *1100 N. Plum, Hutchinson, KS* 🌐 *www.cosmo.org*

Don't Miss

Here, the history of the Space Race unfolds before visitors. The gallery of Apollo 13 artifacts and the SR-71 Blackbird spy plane entrance history lovers. For those looking for more action, there are Gemini docking and rocket launching simulators, entry into shuttle replicas, and Dr. Goddard's Lab featuring the father of modern rocketry that leans more towards "mad science."

Good to Know

In another part of Hutchinson, visitors can turn away from the skies and go deep into the earth. **The Strataca**, a salt mine adventure experience for both geology and pop culture fans, is the perfect climate to store historical artifacts that would otherwise degrade. ✉ *3650 East Ave. G, Hutchinson, KS* 🌐 *www.underkansas.org*

Getting Here and Around

Hutchinson, in central Kansas, is 52 miles northwest of Wichita.

When in Kansas

GEOGRAPHIC CENTER OF THE UNITED STATES

A selfie taken here tells the world that you've been at the center of America. About 2 miles northwest of Lebanon, Kansas is a stone pedestal topped with a flagpole that marks the geographic center of the 48 contiguous U.S. states, according to the U.S. Geological Survey. (The actual center is a half-mile walk to the middle of a nearby field, but for most people this is close enough.) The marker is at the end of a paved road with not much else but rolling plains around it, but it's a good place to stretch your legs if you're traveling through Kansas on either U.S. 36 or 281. ✉ *Rte. 191, Lebanon, KS*

Do This: If it's open, duck into the tiny U.S. Center Chapel under the trees. If it looks oddly familiar, you probably remember it from a 2021 Superbowl ad featuring Bruce Springsteen. ✉ *130 Rd., Lebanon, KS*

EQUALITY HOUSE

The rainbow-color Equality House in Topeka, Kansas is the home base for the group Planting Peace. The group says the house stands as a visual reminder of its commitment to equality for everyone. It also serves as a contrast to its neighbor across the street, Westboro Baptist Church, whose members are known for protesting soldier funerals and fighting against marriage equality.

Do This: The group encourages visitors to take photos, show their pride, and "take some veggies or pull some weeds in our community garden." ✉ *1200 S.W. Orleans St., Topeka, KS* 🌐 *www.planting-peace.org/campaign/equality-house*

KEEPER OF THE PLAINS

The 44-foot-tall Keeper of the Plains, donated by Native American artist Blackbear Bosin, stands at the confluence of the Big and Little Arkansas rivers. Since the sculpture's installation in 1974, it has become a symbol for the city of Wichita and a tribute to the Indigenous tribes that continue to gather at the sacred site. You can access the display by way of two bow-and-arrow-inspired cable-stay bridges that span the two rivers. ✉ *650 N. Seneca St., Wichita, KS*

Do This: Come back at night to see the fire drums on the boulders at the base of the statue illuminate the night.

WAMEGO, THE CITY OF OZ

If you're a fan of *The Wizard of Oz*, you'll go over the rainbow at the Oz-themed town of Wamego, Kansas. In addition to the delightful Oz Museum, nearby businesses celebrate the Oz connection, such as Toto's Tacoz and Oz Winery, where you can sample wines like Ruby Slippers and Yellow Brick Road. Also check out the Columbian Theatre, a 19th-century opera house that has six massive oil paintings from the 1893 Chicago World's Fair that provided L. Frank Baum with the inspiration for the Emerald City.

Do This: Follow the yellow brick road to the Oz Museum, home to more than 2,000 artifacts from Baum's 1900 book

About Our Writers

Rebecca Toy was born and raised in Kansas City before attending college in Manhattan, Kansas, and then working throughout central Kansas as a rural community therapist. Her travel career started at the ripe age of three with road trips through her home state (when she lost her beloved Ziggy doll somewhere in Cottonwood Falls). Today she lives in Kansas City and is a freelance travel and history writer with Fodor's Travel and other publications.

The Wonderful Wizard of Oz and its 13 sequels, as well as the many film and television versions. Among the items on display: colorful posters from the various film productions, hand-painted character masks, miniatures of the flying monkeys that were used in the movie, and a reproduction of the Haunted Forest sign that warns Dorothy and her companions to "turn back." ✉ *511 Lincoln Ave., Wamego, KS* 🌐 *www.ozmuseum.com*

Cool Places to Stay

Dry Creek Post. Just 15 minutes west of the Tallgrass Prairie National Preserve, this glamping stay is perfect for those craving immersion into the Flint Hill prairies. For the adventurous, the family-owned business hosts guests in tents with furniture, bedding, an outdoor shower and restroom, and a clubhouse and kitchen. For those who want more comforts like air-conditioning, there are two "hippie" converted buses. ✉ *1763 Silver Creek Rd., Elmdale, KS* 🌐 *www.hipcamp.com/en-US/land/kansas-dry-creek-post-wz6hq2wp*

Hotel at Old Town. The century-old Hotel at Old Town was originally a warehouse for the Keen Kutter brand of tools. In 1999, Wichita hotelier Jack DeBoer reopened it as a luxury hotel with a vintage Keen Kutter collection and a Historic Aviation Floor whose museum-grade displays tell the story of why Wichita is the air capital of the world. ✉ *830 E. 1st, Wichita, KS* 🌐 *www.hotelatoldtown.com*

The Woodward Inn. No need to go to Europe to experience a chateau, because the Woodward in Topeka is a castlelike inn built in the early 1920s. The lofty library resembles King Henry VIII's Hampton Court Palace, and it's even built with imported timbers and stones from England.✉ *1272 S.W. Fillmore St., Topeka, KS* 🌐 *www.thewoodward.com*

Essential Eats

Chicken Mary's and Chicken Annie's. Locals draw definitive sides when it comes to the rivalry between these two "chicken joints" on the outside of Fort Scott. It's church picnic meets food feud, drawing in national networks and inspiring a novel. The difference is in the breading, but since they're right down the road from each other, bring stretchy pants and try both. Chicken Mary's: ✉ *1133 E. 600th Ave., Pittsburg, KS* 🌐 *www.chickenmarys1942.com*; Chicken Annie's: ✉ *1143 E. 600th Ave., Pittsburg, KS* 🌐 *www.chickenanniesoriginal.com*

Joe's Kansas City Bar-B-Que. Most of Kansas City's famous barbecue calls Missouri home, but one of the best in the country first started in a Kansas City, KS gas station. It has since expanded to several locations around the metro area, but wherever you go, don't miss the signature Z-Man sandwich—slow-smoked brisket, provolone, and onion rings on a kaiser bun. ✉ *3002 W. 47th Ave., Kansas City, KS* 🌐 *www.joeskc.com*

Old Mill Tasty Shop. This Wichita tradition has been slinging old-fashioned sodas since 1932. Blue-plate specials and creamy malts are at home on the marble counters. If you want to try something different, the peanut butter, banana, and honey sandwich is sticky goodness. ✉ *604 E. Douglas Ave., Wichita, KS* 🌐 *www.instagram.com/oldmilltasty*

Missouri

Missouri sits where the Midwest meets the South, and the state's central location—along with its great rivers—has made it an important hub for explorers and pioneers over the centuries. The Missouri River carried Lewis and Clark north as they began their great expedition; soon after, its banks saw the rise of the 19th-century wagon trains heading west. Today, St. Louis and Kansas City both reflect the diverse, enriching influences that came from when they were the country's crossroads.

Capital: Jefferson City

Population: 6,245,466

Area: 69,715 square miles

Statehood Date: August 10, 1821

Major Airports: St. Louis Lambert International Airport (STL); Kansas City International Airport (MCI)

Travel and Tourism Information: *www.visitmo.com* *www.showmemissouri.net*

Famous Residents: Mark Twain (writer); Harry Truman (president); Walt Disney (animator); Brad Pitt (actor); Nelly (rapper); Chappell Roan (singer)

Fun Fact: Geography trivia fans, stump your friends: no state has more border neighbors than Missouri (though Tennessee ties) with eight: Kansas, Nebraska, Iowa, Illinois, Tennessee, Kentucky, Arkansas, and Oklahoma.

The Gateway Arch

The Gateway to the West

The 630-foot-tall Gateway Arch broke several records the day it opened in 1965. The St. Louis landmark instantly became the world's biggest arch, easily beating the 220-foot-tall Monumento a la Revolución in Mexico City. It's the tallest monument in the Western Hemisphere, and the tallest building in Missouri. Once you reach the top via the four-minute tram ride, you're treated to views that stretch up to 30 miles to the east and west. The Gateway Arch was built to celebrate Thomas Jefferson and his idea of Manifest Destiny, since St. Louis was a major point of departure for settlers headed west. Since the arch's 50th anniversary, its story has broadened to include the Indigenous peoples who were displaced by westward expansion. ✉ *11 N. 4th St., St. Louis, MO* 🌐 *www.gatewayarch.com*

Don't Miss

Though the ride to the top of the arch is the star of the show, spend some time in the museum at its base. It does a great job covering the history of Native Americans, explorers, pioneers, and others who passed this way.

Good to Know

There are 1,076 steps to the top of the arch, but visitors aren't allowed to take them. On a windy day, be prepared for the most subtle sway up top—it's a design feature that allows it to withstand strong storms and even earthquakes.

Getting Here and Around

Gateway Arch National Park is located in downtown St. Louis. If you're driving, park in one of the downtown garages and walk to the arch complex.

Forest Park

America's Best City Park

One of the nation's greatest urban parks, the 1876 Forest Park in St. Louis lets you get back to nature without ever leaving the city. This 1,300-acre park is so vast it has entire ecosystems, and includes forests, lakes, and streams. It attracts more than 15 million people a year, more than Busch Stadium and the Gateway Arch combined. The park is also home to the **Missouri History Museum**, **St. Louis Science Center**, **St. Louis Zoo**, **St. Louis Art Museum**, and the **Municipal Theatre Association of St. Louis**. It's hosted everything from the 1904 Louisiana Purchase Exposition and the 1904 Summer Olympics to today's Great Forest Park Balloon Race, Shakespeare Festival of St. Louis, and Forest Park Cross Country Festival. ✉ *5595 Grand Dr. in Forest Park, St. Louis, MO* 🌐 *www.forestparkforever.org/visit*

Don't Miss

The **Anne O'C. Albrecht Nature Playscape** is the perfect spot for families. Nine distinct natural play areas spark adventure and imagination across the 17-acre play space. Visitors are encouraged to explore in activities like scrabbling up boulders, digging in the sand, crawling through willow tunnels, and more.

Best Activities

The grounds include an esteemed free city zoo, an art museum (also free), an outdoor ice-skating rink, an outdoor theater, a science museum, paddleboating, and ample picnic space. Waterways course the park, but the **Emerson Grand Basin** is a photogenic draw that's particularly alluring at sunset.

Getting Here and Around

Forest Park is located about 5 miles west of downtown St. Louis, not far from Washington University.

Kansas City Barbecue

The Midwest's Culinary Pride

Kansas City barbecue isn't just sauce and ribs, it's the city's identity, a way of life, and a source of delicious, delicious pride. No trip to the city would be complete without sampling the world-famous 'cue (some say it's the best in the country) marked by slowly smoked meat like chicken, pork, and beef smothered in a sweet, thick, molasses-based sauce. The city's real claim to fame is burnt ends, the fatty point of a brisket with a crispy, caramelized exterior.

Don't Miss

The world's first **Museum of BBQ** celebrates the historical flavors and pivotal pitmasters that make smoked meat a sensation. From the slab to the sauce to the sizzle, the museum breaks down styles around America. Don't skip the "secret" smoker entrance to the BBQ playground, complete with a "bean" ball pit that even adults can't resist. ✉ *2450 Grand Blvd., Kansas City, MO* 🌐 *museumofbbq.co*

Best Restaurant

Enter the door at **Arthur Bryant's** (aka the King of Ribs) at 18th and Brooklyn and get the boisterous greeting of this KC institution's famous line: "Hi, may I help you?" It's said original KC barbecue recipe was created here. Grab a tray and order away—the spot has gained the presidential seal of approval from Truman, Carter, and Obama. ✉ *1727 Brooklyn Ave., Kansas City, MO* 🌐 *www.arthurbryantsbbq.com*

Getting Here and Around

More than 100 barbecue restaurants are mapped all over Kansas City on the KC BBQ Experience app. Download it to put together an epic barbecue trail and check in to your favorite spots along the way. 🌐 *www.visitkc.com/bbq/app*

Kansas City's 18th and Vine District

The Home of Jazz, Baseball, and Barbecue

Just east of downtown Kansas City, this historic neighborhood at the intersection of 18th and Vine is known for its great barbecue and even better jazz. Its entertainment venues include the **Kansas City Juke House**, which features live blues, and **The Blue Room**, which highlights the countless musicians who crafted the Kansas City sound. No visit is complete with a visit to the immersive **American Jazz Museum**, a delight for music fans. The 18th and Vine is the historic heart of the city's vibrant Black community, and has 35 buildings listed on the National Register of Historic Places. The **Black Archives of Mid-America** documents Black experiences and contributions to Kansas City.

Don't Miss

The highlight of a visit to 18th and Vine is a stop at the **Negro League Baseball Museum**, an excellent museum that chronicles often-overlooked histories of the Black players who were prevented from playing in the Major League. The Field of Legends, with life-size bronze sculptures of Paige Satchel, Josh Gibson, Cool Papa Bell, and others, is a moving climax. ✉ *1616 E. 18th St., Kansas City, MO* 🌐 *www.nlbm.com*

While You're Here

Opened by jazz musicians and entrepreneurs, **Vine Street Brewery** is Missouri's first Black-owned brewery, known for innovative craft brews and deep community roots. Don't be surprised if your visit finds you joining a paint class, karaoke, live music, or bingo. ✉ *2010 Vine St., Kansas City, MO* 🌐 *vinestbrewing.com*

Getting Here and Around

The 18th and Vine neighborhood is just east of downtown Kansas City.

Lake of the Ozarks

A Top Midwest Waterfront Vacation

Central Missouri's Lake of the Ozarks, called the Magic Dragon for its twisting reptilian shape, is one of the top waterfront vacation destinations in the Midwest, drawing more than 5 million annual visitors. If you've seen the hit show *Ozark* you know the lake is a wonderland for swimming, boating, fishing, socializing, and relaxing (minus the dramatic storyline). Most of the shoreline is privately owned, so there are plenty of vacation homes for rent that give you spectacular views. ✉ *985 KK Dr., Osage Beach, MO* 🌐 *www.funlake.com*

Don't Miss

The big idea is to get on the water. Try out a pontoon boat, which is easiest for beginners, through the numerous companies in the Lake of the Ozarks region that rent watercraft. For those who want a break from motors, plenty of coves are perfect for kayaks and stand-up paddleboards.

While You're Here

Take a break from the summertime heat and join a guided tour of the 60°F **Bridal Cave** at Camdenton, Missouri. It features mineral deposits shaped like giant columns and massive draperies. Bridal Cave has more onyx formations than any other cavern. Lantern and black light tour options add an adventurous edge. ✉ *526 Bridal Cave Rd., Camdenton, MO* 🌐 *bridalcave.com*

Getting Here and Around

Lake of the Ozarks sits halfway between Springfield and Jefferson City, Missouri. It's 173 miles southeast of Kansas City and 180 miles southwest of St. Louis.

Hannibal

Mark Twain's Hometown

It's not hard to imagine Tom Sawyer, Huckleberry Finn, and Becky Thatcher getting into mischief in the streets of Hannibal, Missouri. This picturesque town, the childhood home of author Mark Twain, is fun to explore. A self-guided tour through the historic district is a good introduction to Twain—whose real name was Samuel Clemens—along with the friends, family members, and various townspeople that he eventually used as models for the characters in his stories. The **Mark Twain Boyhood Home & Museum** explores seven buildings related to Twain's life and work. ✉ *120 N. Main St., Hannibal, MO* 🌐 *marktwainmuseum.org*

Don't Miss

Stop at Twain's boyhood home at 208 Hill Street, where many of his real-life experiences between 1844 and 1853 influenced his creation of Tom Sawyer and other characters. Twain's friend Laura Hawkins lived at 211 Hill Street. He immortalized her in his books as Becky Thatcher, and the two close friends stayed in touch through the years. Adding to the nostalgic whimsy, the Museum Gallery includes the Norman Rockwell Room, with 15 original paintings that the renowned artist created for special editions of *Tom Sawyer* and *Huckleberry Finn*.

While You're Here

The **Mark Twain Cave Complex** is the oldest operating show cave in the state, a labyrinthine complex full of legends. Historic downtown has candy shops, antiques stores, and **Becky's Old-Fashioned Ice Cream Parlor**. Board the **Mark Twain Riverboat** on day or dinner cruises to get a sense of life on the Mississippi in Twain's days.

Getting Here and Around

Hannibal, Missouri lies along the Mississippi River in eastern Missouri, 114 miles northwest of St. Louis.

Branson

A Family-Friendly Live Music Mecca

Known for big-time entertainment for all ages, this southern Missouri city is the place to see live shows and music under bright lights, ride roller coasters, and stroll a landing lined with neon lights and spurting fountains. It's no wonder the town has been compared to Las Vegas—but one where no gambling is allowed and you can take the whole family. Branson bills itself as the "Live Music Capital of the World," and offers live shows in genres from country to bluegrass to good old-fashioned rock and roll. Are you a roller-coaster fanatic? **Silver Dollar City** has two unique thrill rides: Time Traveler reaches speeds of up to 50 miles per hour while you make a 10-story vertical drop, while Fire-In-The-Hole is an enclosed roller coaster that includes high-speed drops and surprises around every corner.

Don't Miss

Don't leave without seeing a live show on **76 Country Boulevard** or **Shepard of the Hills Expressway**, the town's busiest stretches. The number of theaters is truly impressive. When you're ready for a sensory break, head just south of town to **Table Rock Lake**, a world-class recreation reservoir with more than 800 miles of shoreline.

While You're Here

Simply put: the **Titanic Museum** is tons of fun. This massive re-creation of the ocean liner (the front half of it, anyway) that famously sank on its maiden voyage lets you wander the hallways, parlors, cabins, and grand staircase. ✉ *3235 W. 76 Country Blvd., Branson, MO* 🌐 *titanicattraction.com/branson*

Getting Here and Around

Branson is in southern Missouri, just north of the Arkansas border.

When in Missouri

GLORE PSYCHIATRIC MUSEUM

George Glore, who worked at the Missouri Department of Mental Health, started this collection of odd objects at an abandoned ward of the St. Joseph State Hospital in 1966. The museum includes historical psychiatric treatment devices (think surgical tools and other items) and artwork made by the patients of the hospital (pottery, paintings, and drawings that helped them express their pain, joy, and hopes). ✉ *3408 Frederick Ave., St. Joseph, MO* 🌐 *www.stjosephmuseum.org/glore-psychiatric-museum*

Do This: Check out the other museums in St. Joseph, including the Black Archives Museum, the Doll Museum, the Native American Galleries, and the Wyeth-Tootle Mansion.

HA HA TONKA CASTLE RUINS

Kansas City businessman Robert McClure Snyder Sr. bought this property and started building a castle in 1905. He was killed a year later in an auto accident, but his sons finished the project in the 1920s. The family used it as a weekend home for a while, and it was later converted into a hotel. A fire destroyed it in 1942. Missouri bought the castle and grounds in 1978 and created a state park. The castle walls aren't stable, so you have to keep your distance. ✉ *1491 State Rd. D, Camdenton, MO*

Do This: After gazing at the castle, spend some time in the park itself. Ha Ha Tonka State Park features sinkholes, caverns, sheer bluffs, and a huge natural bridge. A series of trails and boardwalks makes it easy to explore. 🌐 *www.mostateparks.com/park/ha-ha-tonka-state-park*

NATIONAL WORLD WAR I MUSEUM AND MEMORIAL

Located in the historic Crossroads District of downtown Kansas City, a monument tops one of the best World War I museums in the world. It opened as the Liberty Memorial in 1926 after Kansas City residents raised $2.5 million in 10 days. The memorial weathered the area's era of disrepair and is now restored and expanded. Exhibits include a tank used by the U.S. Army with a hole in the side from a German shell; a crater that shows the effects of a 17-inch howitzer shell on a French farmhouse; and life-size trenches featuring recordings of real-life soldiers. ✉ *2 Memorial Dr., Kansas City, MO* 🌐 *www.theworldwar.org*

Do This: The focal point of the memorial is a glass-floored walkway over a field of 9,000 poppies, each representing 1,000 people killed in battle, a reminder of the 9 million lives lost throughout the war.

About Our Writers

Rebecca Toy was born in Kansas City and raised on both sides of the state line, with regular trips to Springfield, Missouri to visit her grandparents. Her family comes from the part of the state that says "Missour-ah" and she thinks the rivers of the Ozarks are way more fun than the lakes. Today she lives in Kansas City and is a freelance travel and history writer with Fodor's and other publications.

Cool Places to Stay

Big Cedar Lodge. This remote and rustic getaway in Missouri's Ozark Mountains overlooks Table Rock Lake. Johnny Morris, founder of Bass Pro Shops, created Big Cedar Lodge as a luxe lodging for families and friends to connect in the great outdoors. It has inviting accommodations, great restaurants, two marinas, five golf courses, and a spa. ✉ *190 Top of the Rock Rd., Ridgedale, MO* 🌐 *www.bigcedar.com*

Elms Hotel and Spa. Considered one of the most haunted hotels in the country, the Elms is a historic luxury stay just northeast of Kansas City. The healing mineral waters here created a health spa popular with the region's politicians and glitterati, including the Midwest mob's kingpins. Al Capone, "Pretty Boy" Floyd, and Bugsy Moran hosted several bashes here. Whether you want a paranormal tour or a stellar spa treatment, the Elms has it. ✉ *401 Regent St., Excelsior Springs, MO* 🌐 *www.elmshotelandspa.com*

Fontaine Hotel. This luxury hotel features Renaissance-inspired artwork and Italian-glass chandeliers, evoking European luxuries in the heart of the Kansas City's Spanish-styled Country Club Plaza shopping district. ✉ *901 W. 48th Pl., Kansas City, MO* 🌐 *www.thefontainehotel.com*

Hotel Frederick. The historic Romanesque Revival–era Hotel Frederick is a free pedal away from the Katy Trail, which stretches for 237 miles across most of the state. The on-site bike shop rents by the hour or by the day. The boutique hotel's luxe touches create a welcoming retreat even for those who don't cycle. ✉ *501 High St., Boonville, MO* 🌐 *www.hotel-frederick.com*

Essential Eats

Booches Billiard Hall. This old-school pool hall has been around since 1884 and is beloved by University of Missouri students. The burgers are widely considered the best in the state and have garnered national attention multiple times. Just don't ask for fries—the tavern doesn't have a fryer. ✉ *110 S. 9th St., Columbia, MO* 🌐 *booches1884.com*

Cascone's. There are big feelings in Kansas City about which family-owned Italian restaurant is the best. All tell an underrated story of the prominence of the city's Italian communities, but you can't go wrong with Cascone's. Run by a Sicilian family since 1942, it's not hyperbole to have visions of *The Godfather* while dining. Just remember, *Sempre Famiglia* (forever family), and don't skip the chicken spiedini. ✉ *3733 N. Oak Trafficway, Kansas City, MO* 🌐 *www.cascones.com*

Lambert's Cafe. Since 1942, "The Home of the Throwed Rolls" has served up heaps of Southern comfort food like country ham and fried chicken with all the fixins. Think you're full? Servers with all-you-can-eat "pass arounds" of sides like fried okra will test you. Yes, they also lob fluffy dinner rolls across the room, but just pass that honey butter. ✉ *2305 E. Malone Ave., Sikeston, MO* 🌐 *www.throwedrolls.com*

Pappy's Smokehouse. St. Louis residents like to remind visitors that Kansas City isn't the only barbecue city in the state. The best-known contender in "the Lou" is Pappy's, popular with rib aficionados who prefer a dry rub over a saucy slather. It's first-come, first-served, with an eager crowd usually out the door. ✉ *3106 Olive St., St. Louis, MO* 🌐 *www.pappyssmokehouse.com*

Nebraska

The Cornhusker State is known for its corn and cattle, but this beautiful land yields more than just hearty crops and delectable steaks. The terrain varies from the Panhandle's bluffs and buttes that conjure images of the Old West frontier to the grass-stabilized sand dunes of the north-central Sandhills to the rolling hills of the tallgrass prairie along the Missouri River. The people here tend to be friendly and laid-back, even in the state's two largest cities, which offer great shops, restaurants, and cultural attractions.

Capital: Lincoln

Population: 2,005,465

Area: 77,358 square miles

Statehood Date: March 1, 1867

Major Airports: Omaha Eppley Airfield (OMA); Lincoln Airport (LNK)

Travel and Tourism Information: ⊕ *www.visitnebraska.com* ⊕ *www.nebraskalife.com*

Famous Residents: Johnny Carson (talk show host); Marlon Brando (actor); Willa Cather (writer); Warren Buffett (investor); Conor Oberst (musician)

Fun Fact: Hastings, Nebraska is the birthplace of Kool-Aid. The popular powdered drink mix was invented by Edwin Perkins in 1927. He later sold the product to General Foods, which created the smiling pitcher seen on the individual drink packets. You can view Kool-Aid memorabilia at the Hastings Museum, and the town also hosts annual Kool-Aid Days each August.

The Henry Doorly Zoo and Aquarium

America's Most Underrated Zoo

Winner of *USA Today*'s Readers' Choice award for the country's best zoo multiple years in a row, the 130-acre Henry Doorly Zoo showcases animals and ecosystems from around the globe. It includes the world's largest indoor desert representing vegetation and wildlife from deserts in the United States, Africa, and Australia, all contained within an 80,000-square-foot dome; America's largest indoor rain forest and the jungle creatures that inhabit them, from monkeys and macaws to gibbons and hippopotamuses; and an outdoor orangutan forest with a 20-foot waterfall. ✉ *3701 S. 10th St., Omaha, NE* 🌐 *www.omahazoo.com*

Don't Miss

There's so much to see in the zoo itself, but don't forget the aquarium. A 70-foot clear tunnel here takes you below the waters so you can view sea turtles and sharks up close. There are also sea lions, a coral reef, and many colorful fish. Best of all is the polar region with the always entertaining penguins. The aquarium is a great place to cool off on a hot day.

Best Ride

Riders on Henry Doorly's **Skyfari** enjoy an aerial perspective of the animals and habitats. This chairlift soars as high as the treetops and takes riders above the butterfly pavilion and African grasslands area.

For the Kiddos

When the little ones get bored and need to run around, the zoo has interactive areas with youngsters in mind. There's a splash park, a carousel, and even a tree house to climb.

Getting Here and Around

The zoo is about 5 miles from Omaha Eppley Airfield (OMA).

Sandhill Crane Migration

A World-Famous Flock

There's an 80-mile-long section of central Nebraska's Platte River that becomes the gathering central each spring and fall for about 80% of the world's population of sandhill cranes. Nearly 600,000 of the birds descend on the Platte River Valley as a stopping point on their spring migration back north to their nesting grounds in Canada and Alaska and on their fall migration south for the winter. When these large and beautiful birds spread their 6- to 7-foot-wide wings and take flight, it's a sight to behold. ✉ *44450 Elm Island Rd., Gibbon, NE* 🌐 *rowe.audubon.org/crane-season*

Don't Miss

The town of **Kearney**, billed as the "Sandhill Crane Capital of the World," is a prime spot to view the cranes from late February through mid-April. **Rowe Sanctuary**, located in Gibbons, just outside of Kearney, offers two-hour guided tours at sunrise and sunset as well as overnight visits. On the tours, bird-watchers view the cranes from discovery stations set up along the Platte River.

Other Viewing Spots

Grand Island, **North Platte**, and other Nebraska state parks around the Platte River offer decent viewing spots during the migration. 🌐 *www.visitnebraska.com/trip-idea/self-guided-crane-viewing*

When to Go

The cranes don't spend as much time in Nebraska in the fall, so the spring migration is the better time of the two to view them.

Getting Here and Around

Kearney, Nebraska is 180 miles west of Omaha. Rowe Sanctuary is 16 miles from Kearney Regional Airport (EAR).

Big Red Football

Cheer on the Cornhuskers

In the fall, Saturdays in Nebraska are abuzz with fervor for the state's most beloved sports team, the University of Nebraska Cornhuskers, or Huskers for short. Without a professional team in the state, sports-loving Nebraskans celebrate the main college football team with deep passion—and loyalty. Every home game at the 85,000-seat **Nebraska Memorial Stadium** in Lincoln has been a sellout since 1962. ✉ *1 Memorial Stadium Dr., Lincoln, NE* 🌐 *www.huskers.com*

Don't Miss

On a home game day, be a part of the sea of red, as the Memorial Stadium has been called. Before the game, stop by the **Husker Shop** in the Pinnacle Bank Arena to buy some team swag and take a tour of the stadium, which includes the Hall of Fame Plaza and a tribute to former coaches Bob Devaney and Tom Osborne. ✉ *321 N. 8th St., Lincoln, NE*

While You're Here

Former Nebraska football coach Tom Osborne continues to be a dearly loved and respected state hero. As the head Nebraska football coach, Osborne led the team to three national championships, with back-to-back victories in 1994 and 1995, and again in 1997. View two statues at the stadium erected in Osborne's honor.

Did You Know?

An earlier name for the Cornhusker football team was the Bugeaters, from 1892 through 1899. Clothed in scarlet and cream, the Bugeaters were part of the Western Interstate University Football Association. Other team names over the years were the Old Gold Knights, the Antelopes, and the Rattlesnake Boys. The team became known as the Cornhuskers beginning in 1900.

Getting Here and Around

The Lincoln Airport (LNK) is 5 miles from Memorial Stadium.

Native American Pow Wows

Experience the Indigenous Cultures of Nebraska

Native American tribes once roamed the Great Plains of Nebraska, hunting buffalo and living off the land. Today members of these tribal nations, including the Omaha, the Santee Sioux, the Winnebago, the Sac and Fox, the Iowa, and the Ponca, live primarily in reservations or on other designated federal land. Visitors can interact with these tribes during annual powwows.

Don't Miss

The energetic dancing, lively music, colorful costumes, and insightful stories at a powwow portray the culture and heritage of a people who were forced into a new way of life. Visitors can usually sample authentic dishes and peruse (and possibly purchase) native artwork. Something special can be had at any of the state's powwows, but two that are known to have a full slate of activities are the **Ponca Tribe Powwow** in Niobrara each August and the **North Platte Pow Wow** at Buffalo Bill Ranch State Historical Park each July.

Good to Know

A couple of powwows in Nebraska that bring multiple tribes together are the **Fort Omaha Intertribal Pow-Wow** at Metropolitan Community College's Fort Omaha Campus in Omaha and the **Intertribal Gathering** at Fort Robinson State Park in Crawford.

When to Go

Summer is the time to see the powwows. The website 🌐 *www.powwows.com* lists when and where powwows are taking place across North America.

Getting Here and Around

Several powwows are in the eastern part of the state, within driving distance from Omaha.

Fort Niobrara National Wildlife Refuge

Explore the Great Plains in Miniature

If you could condense the entire Great Plains into one small nature preserve, it would look like the breathtaking Fort Niobrara National Wildlife Refuge. This more-than-19,000-acre park was established in 1912 to protect native birds but soon after expanded to include large herds of elk and bison. Other wildlife includes deer, prairie dogs, bald and golden eagles, and wild turkeys. The Niobrara River, which winds through the refuge, defies people's impressions of Nebraska as a flat state as the peaceful waterway meanders past waterfalls and sandstone cliffs rising along the water's edge. ✉ *39983 Refuge Rd., Valentine, NE* 🌐 *www.fws.gov/refuge/fort_niobrara*

Don't Miss

The best way to explore the area is by canoe or kayak. Sign up for a four-hour kayak or canoe trip on the Niobrara with the outfitter **Little Outlaw**. Begin your trip at Fort Niobrara National Wildlife Refuge and go to Brewer Bridge, with a stop along the way to see **Smith Falls**, Nebraska's highest waterfall at 63 feet. 🌐 *www.outlawcanoe.com*

Best Hike

Be rewarded with views of the 45-foot-high Fort Falls Waterfall and the Niobrara River on the 1-mile round-trip hike on **Fort Falls Trail**.

Getting Here and Around

On Route 12, Fort Niobrara National Wildlife Refuge is 4 miles east of Valentine along the Niobrara River. A self-guided driving tour starts near the visitor center.

Tanking Down a River

Float Downstream the Nebraska Way

Nebraska's more than 79,000 miles of rivers attract ducks, geese, and Sandhill cranes as well as water sports enthusiasts. Many embark in canoes, tubes, or kayaks, but thanks to some enterprising locals many years back, a fourth vessel option is available: circular tanks used for watering livestock. Tanking, as it's called, has become a memorable way to spend a day on the water and a quintessential Nebraska activity.

Don't Miss

Tanking in the state began in the Sandhills, and it's an ideal place to experience Nebraska's peaceful, scenic vistas. The two popular Sandhill rivers for tanking are the **Middle Loup** and **Dismal rivers**. Glidden Canoe Rentals in Mullen can outfit you with a tank for your trip. 🌐 *www.gliddencanoerental.com*

Good to Know

A tank averages 8 feet in width and usually contains a bench or seats and enough room for four to six people, along with coolers, boom boxes, life jackets, paddles, and anything else you need for a float down a river. You can let the current take you downstream, but the paddles help to keep the tank from spinning in circles and to get you out of a jam. A trip typically lasts from two to six hours.

Other Places to Tank

To find tanking outfitters in the state, check out Visit Nebraska's list at 🌐 *www.visitnebraska.com/sports-adventure/tanking.*

Getting Here and Around

The Sandhills are in the central part of the state. About a five-hour drive from Omaha, Mullen is at the intersection of Routes 2 and 97. The nearest commercial airport is North Platte Regional Airport (LBF).

College World Series

Home Runs in Omaha

The men's College World Series has been in Omaha every June since 1950. The two-week event is the culmination of the National Collegiate Athletic Association Division I Baseball Championship, so the eight teams competing are the best of the best. Locals love going to the games at **Charles Schwab Field**, and fans come from all over the country to support their teams. ✉ *1200 Mike Fahey St., Omaha, NE* 🌐 *www.cwsomaha.com*

Don't Miss

Check out *The Road to Omaha*, designed in 1999 by artist John Lajba for the College World Series. Centered on the staircases at the Charles Schwab Field, the 1,500-pound bronze sculpture shows four baseball players celebrating a win at home plate. If you're with a group, reenact the scene in the sculpture for a fun photo op.

While You're Here

You're in downtown Omaha, so there's plenty to do nearby. Head to the **Old Market** for dining, shopping, and nightlife—try **Ted & Wally's** for ice cream. For something a little different, make your way to the history exhibits at the **Durham Museum** in the art deco building once used by the Union Pacific Railroad, or, alternatively, explore the riverfront at the **Heartland of America Park**.

Getting Here and Around

Omaha's Eppley Airfield (OMA) is only 2 miles from the stadium. Allow plenty of time for traffic and parking.

Chimney Rock

A Pioneer Passage Point

Nebraska was a major passageway for westward migration in the mid-1800s, and the California, Mormon, and Oregon trails all passed through the state. The intrepid individuals traveling those trails on horseback and in covered wagons used landmarks to help them navigate, and one of the most recognizable was Chimney Rock. Rising nearly 300 feet above the North Platte River Valley near Bayard in northwest Nebraska, the natural formation has a wide base and a narrow spire that makes it visible for miles. More than 90% of pioneer diaries mention Chimney Rock.

Don't Miss

You can view the rock from the historic site's visitor center or you can hike out to it. The visitor center has a theater, bookstore, and exhibits that detail the historical importance of the rock. If you want to learn more about the rock's place in history, Chimney Rock Museum has its own small assortment of artifacts and exhibits. To shop for souvenirs, stop by the Settlers Trading Post a mile away.

Making Their Mark

Explorers began trekking across Nebraska after the 1803 Louisiana Purchase, but it was after gold was discovered in 1848 that the covered wagons came en masse. More than 175 years later, remnants of these early homes on wheels passing through Nebraska remain: permanent ruts on the ground are still visible today. One terrific place to see this is at **Windlass Hill** in Ash Hollow near Lewellen. ✉ *4055 U.S. 26, Lewellen, NE*

Getting Here and Around

Chimney Rock is 4 miles south of Bayard. The nearest airport is Western Nebraska Regional Airport in Scottsbluff (BFF).

Toadstool Geologic Park

The Badlands of Nebraska

Part of Oglala National Grassland in far northwestern Nebraska, and operated by the U.S. Forest Service, Toadstool Geologic Park features unique formations that resemble toadstools. The rocky expanse looks like the surface of the moon, and the park is often called Nebraska's Badlands. The area is also known for its treasure trove of fossils, including the ancestors of modern dogs, horses, and even rhinoceroses. In one interesting discovery, you can clearly see where two hungry entelodonts (fearsome piglike creatures) were in pursuit for a meal along a small stream. ✉ *1811 Meng Dr., Crawford, NE* 🌐 *www.fs.usda.gov*

Don't Miss

Fossil hunting and hoodoo viewing are the things to do at the park. Before heading out on the 1-mile interpretative hike to look for fossils and spot the whimsical geological features, pick up an informative brochure at the interpretive kiosk.

Best Hike

Set aside some time to visit the **Hudson-Meng Education and Research Center**, which houses one of the most significant paleo-archaeological discoveries in North America: the fossilized remains of an extinct type of bison. The 3-mile **Bison Trail** connects the center with the park.

Getting Here and Around

Toadstool Geologic Park is about 15 miles from Crawford, Nebraska. The nearest airports are Western Nebraska Regional Airport in Scottsbluff (BFF), 97 miles away, and Rapid City Regional Airport (RAP), 110 miles away.

Willa Cather Sites

Stories of the Plains

The Pulitzer Prize–winning novelist Willa Cather was born in Red Cloud, Nebraska, and the small town is the basis for the fictional towns in her novels about life on the frontier, *My Antonia*, *The Song of the Lark*, and *O, Pioneers*. Between 1912 and 1940, she wrote nine additional novels, including *Death Comes for the Archbishop*, *A Lost Lady*, and *One of Ours*, set in World War I. She also wrote short stories and poetry collections, as well as speeches, letters, and journalistic works. ✉ *413 N. Webster St., Red Cloud, NE* 🌐 *www.willacather.org*

Don't Miss

The **National Willa Cather Museum** is a terrific place to learn about the author. After you've viewed the exhibits here, visit the Red Cloud Chamber of Commerce's website (🌐 *www.visitredcloud.com*) for a list of sites in town related to the author, including her childhood home and the J.L. Miner House, the home of Annie Pavelka, the woman who inspired the lead character in*My Antonia*.

More Nebraska Authors

Bess Streeter Aldrich (who also went by Margaret Dean Stevens) and Mari Sandoz both hail from Nebraska. Aldrich won an O. Henry Award for her debut novel, *A Lantern in Her Hand*. And her book *Miss Bishop* became a movie (*Cheers for Miss Bishop*). Sandoz wrote primarily about the Old West and is best known for her biography about Crazy Horse (*Crazy Horse: The Strange Man of the Oglalas*).

Getting Here and Around

The closest airport to Red Cloud is Central Nebraska Regional Airport in Grand Island (GRI), 70 miles away.

When in Nebraska

CARHENGE

England has Stonehenge, but Alliance, Nebraska has Carhenge. Designed and built by Jim Reinders as a memorial to his father, the quirky attraction along Route 87 consists of 39 vintage cars spray-painted gray and arranged in the same formation as the mystical Stonehenge, measuring roughly 96 feet in diameter. It's open year-round and there's no admission. ✉ *2151 CR 59, Alliance, NE* 🌐 *www.carhenge.com*

Do This: View the variety of cars, including a 1962 Cadillac, used in the sculpture, and then stop by the gift shop, where you can pick up kitschy items. With more time, explore the town of Alliance.

THE COWBOY TRAIL

At 321 miles, running from Norfolk to Chadron, the Cowboy Trail in Nebraska is one of the longest rails-to-trails projects ever in the works in the United States. About two-thirds of the distance—the 195 miles between Norfolk and Valentine—have a crushed limestone surface that's perfect for cycling. From Valentine to Chadron, the trail is mostly undeveloped except for an additional 15 miles between Gordon and Rushville.

Do This: Late-night television star Johnny Carson grew up in Norfolk, so for a fun stop before you begin your cycling journey, visit the Elkhorn Valley Museum. A special gallery holds his Emmy Awards, a replica of his famous stage, and artifacts that he personally chose to display. ✉ *515 Queen City Blvd,, Norfolk, NE* 🌐 *www.elkhornvalleymuseum.org*

NATIONAL MUSEUM OF ROLLER SKATING

It seems to be that there's a museum for everything, so why not roller skating? If you ever wanted to know everything there is to know about the sport of roller skating, this free Lincoln museum is the place for you. It has the largest collection of items and articles related to roller skating in the world, going back to 1819. ✉ *4730 South St., Lincoln, NE* 🌐 *www.rollerskatingmuseum.org*

Do This: After you've explored the museum's exhibits, head to the gift shop to pick up some fun items related to the sport.

NEBRASKA STAR PARTY

With plenty of wide-open spaces that are unobscured by light pollution from big cities, Merritt Reservoir's Snake Campground, near Valentine, Nebraska, has outstanding views. It's a terrific place for the annual Nebraska Star Party. ✉ *NE 97, Valentine, NE* 🌐 *www.nebraskastarparty.org*

Do This: If you're new to exploring the night sky, take part in the Beginner's Field School demonstrations. A three-day course teaches you the basics.

PRAIRIE CHICKEN DANCE

You may have thought chicken dances were just for weddings. Not in Nebraska. The Southwest Nebraska greater prairie chickens truly strut their stuff in the wild. During most of the year, these birds lead relatively quiet lives. But every spring during mating season, they let it all hang out in a spectacular fowl frenzy. There's a lot of emphatic stomping, jumping, and letting out its earsplitting cry. It's nature's most entertaining display.

Do This: Take an overnight chicken dance tour in McCook, Nebraska, organized by Red Willow County Visitors Bureau. The tour includes an orientation by a biologist and an early-morning viewing, followed by a hot breakfast. 🌐 *www.prairiechickendancetours.com*

ROBBER'S CAVE TOUR

Truly a den of thieves, Robber's Cave in Lincoln has been a place for social gatherings, both legal and illegal, for over 150 years. Legend has it that outlaw Jesse James hid out here, as did some of the enslaved people escaping along the Underground Railroad. There are 5,600 square feet of tunnels carved into this sandstone bluff. ✉ *925 Robbers Cave Rd., Lincoln, NE* 🌐 *www.robberscave-tours.com*

Do This: Take a tour of the cave with Joel Green, author of the book *Robber's Cave: Truths, Legends and Recollections*. He provides entertaining anecdotes along the way and answers questions.

Cool Places to Stay

Lied Lodge. Located on Arbor Day Farm, this lodging's 140 nature-inspired rooms were built by the Arbor Day Foundation to serve as a space for like-minded individuals to discuss trees, conservation, and environmental stewardship. ✉ *2700 Sylvan Rd., Nebraska City, NE* 🌐 *www.liedlodge.org*

Pawnee Teepee Village. Sleep in a teepee at the Platte River State Park between Omaha and Lincoln. The teepees are basic and have a platform floor. You will need to bring a sleeping bag, pillow, and blankets as well as a towel, soap, and cooking supplies—basically anything you'd bring if you were tent camping. At the park, you can enjoy the scenery and wildlife along the Platte River. There's also horseback riding, mountain biking, fishing, and boating. ✉ *14421 346th St., Louisville, NE* 🌐 *www.outdoornebraska.gov/location/platte-river*

River Inn Resort. A floating bed-and-breakfast on the Missouri River has a tranquil, romantic atmosphere. Activities include hiking, biking, and exploring local museums. A dinner cruise aboard the *Spirit of Brownsville* sets sail weekends in the summer. ✉ *72898 648A Ave., Brownville, NE* 🌐 *www.river-inn-resort.com*

Rowses 1+1 Ranch. This working cattle ranch in central Nebraska offers "the opportunity to not play cowboy, but to be one." Guests will learn how to ride, rope, brand, and sort cattle. And you do it all mounted on a trained quarter horse that's yours for the duration of your stay. There's a three-night minimum. ✉ *46849 833rd Rd., Burwell, NE* 🌐 *www.1plus-1ranch.com*

Spring Ranch Campground. This is your chance to stay overnight in a covered wagon—similar to one that an early pioneer would have stayed in, yet also completely different thanks to modern touches. Glamping at its best, each wagon has its own full bath as well as morning necessities like a coffee maker. During the day the campground has hiking, fishing, ziplining, and more. When it's time for dinner, no need to hunt: an uncooked meal will be brought directly to your door; you just need to cook it over your firepit. ✉ *30551 Rd. D, Fairfield, NE* 🌐 *www.springranchcampground.com*

Essential Eats

Gorat's Steak House. Nebraska has many wonderful steak houses, and among the best is one of billionaire Warren Buffett's favorites, Gorat's Steak House in Omaha. Opened since 1944, Gorat's pleases the palate with more than a dozen red meat options as well as chicken, Italian specialties, and seafood. Buffett prefers the 22-ounce T-bone steak. ✉ *4917 Center St., Omaha, NE* 🌐 *www.goratsomaha.com*

About Our Writers

Debbie Harmsen was born and raised in Omaha, Nebraska. She thinks the state's corn-fed cattle makes the absolute best steaks, and if you say Nebraska is flat, she dares you to drive in Omaha in the winter—and enjoy the city's great hills for sledding. She is currently a writer and editor based in Iowa.

Reuben Sandwich. In 1925, the Reuben sandwich was born in Omaha's Blackstone Hotel, with Reuben Kulakofsky piling corned beef, sauerkraut, Swiss cheese, and Russian dressing (similar to today's Thousand Island) onto rye bread for a group of poker players one night. Try one of these tasty sandwiches at the Orleans Room at the Cottonwood Hotel (formerly the Blackstone Hotel), which now substitutes Gruyère for Swiss. ✉ *302 S. 36th St., Omaha, NE* 🌐 *www.thecottonwoodhotel.com*

Runza. Beef, onion, and cabbage rolls, called bierocks by some and krautburgers by others, were a dish brought to the Great Plains states by Eastern European immigrants, specifically Volga Germans, those of German ethnicity who had been living in Russia. In 1949, Sally Everett and Alex Brening, a sister and brother in Lincoln, commercialized this dish when they created the popular fast-food Runza chain that now has restaurants throughout the state. The name is derived from the Russian word for "to wrap": *runtza.* 🌐 *www.runza.com*

North Dakota

In North Dakota, miles of prairie grasses sway beneath a brilliant blue sky. The rectangular state lies at the bottom of a glacial lake bed, with rich soil and farmland so flat, the horizon seems endless. The mighty Missouri River bisects the state and has influenced culture and commerce for hundreds of years. Craggy badlands buttes, striped in shades of rust, sand, and bone, rise up from the west. This harsh, dry landscape contains the nation's largest grassland as well as North Dakota's jewel, Theodore Roosevelt National Park.

Capital: Bismarck

Population: 796,568

Area: 68,995 square miles

Statehood Date: November 2, 1889

Major Airports: Hector International Airport (FAR); Bismarck Regional Airport (BIS); Minot International Airport (MOT)

Travel and Tourism Information: 🌐 *www.ndtourism.com* 🌐 *www.ndnta.com*

Famous Residents: Tatanka Iyotake, aka Sitting Bull (Indigenous resistance leader); Phil Jackson (basketball coach); Angie Dickinson (actress); Chuck Klosterman (writer); Josh Duhamel (actor)

Fun Fact: North Dakota became a state just seconds before (or after) South Dakota. No one knows which statehood papers President Harrison signed first, so North Dakota is either the 39th or the 40th state.

Theodore Roosevelt National Park

The Landscape That Inspired a President

Theodore Roosevelt first came to the Badlands in 1883 to hunt bison. He fell in love with the untamed landscape, and it inspired him to later create the U.S. Forest Service to protect wildlife on public lands. Today, part of Theodore Roosevelt National Park's allure is its utter lack of people. Its size (110 square miles) and remote location make it one of the least visited—but most spectacular—national parks. Composed of three parts (a North Unit, South Unit, and Elkhorn Ranch Unit, where Roosevelt lived), this tranquil park is perfect for birding, wildlife viewing, hiking, camping, stargazing, and scenic drives. 🌐 *www.nps.gov/thro*

Don't Miss

Hiking trails offer close-up views of wildflower-studded prairies, rugged ravines, unusual rock formations, craggy cliffs, and surprisingly steep plateaus. They include paved, flat, and accessible overlooks, as well as more challenging routes through coulees, canyons, coal veins, and an eerie petrified forest.

Good to Know

The South Unit of Theodore Roosevelt National Park abuts the small town of **Medora.** Stop here for cowboy and frontier history, engaging entertainment, Western-theme eateries, and lodging options that include the historic Rough Riders Hotel and covered wagon camping. The **Theodore Roosevelt Presidential Library** (completed in 2026) is also a must-see.

Getting Here and Around

The South Unit is located 30 miles west of Dickinson on Interstate 94. Find the North Unit 15 miles south of Watford City (which caters to park visitors) on U.S. 85. The Elkhorn Ranch Unit stands between the two on (often impassable) unpaved roads.

Indigenous Culture in North Dakota

America's First Nations, Then and Now

It's great to read about members of the tribal nations that share North Dakota's geography, and to visit the sites of former villages and riverside gardens. But it's even more interesting to meet them. Indigenous culture isn't frozen in amber: it's evolving and thriving—and Native American artists, storytellers, and historians guide the narrative. Follow the Missouri River to learn their stories and experience some of the landscapes that have inspired Indigenous communities for generations. 🌐 *www.ndnta.com*

Don't Miss

Dive deep into hundreds of years of Mandan, Hidatsa, and Arikara art, culture, and history at the **MHA Interpretive Center** in New Town. The space, which is inspired by a traditional earth lodge, includes an art gallery, historical artifacts, guided tours, a coffee shop, and a 500-seat amphitheater. ✉ *9386 Rte. 23, New Town, ND* 🌐 *www.mhainterpretivecenter.net*

Best Tour

Learn about family life, Indigenous trade networks, and riverside farming techniques during a tour of reconstructed Mandan earth lodges at **On-A-Slant-Village**. It's tucked inside Fort Abraham Lincoln State Park outside the city of Mandan. ✉ *4480 Ft. Lincoln Rd., Mandan, ND* 🌐 *www.parkrec.nd.gov/fort-abraham-lincoln-state-park*

When to Go

Try to time a visit to coincide with a powwow. The United Tribes Technical College International Powwow, held the second week of September in Bismarck, draws thousands of dancers, drummers, and spectators. Other communities host powwows throughout the summer. 🌐 *unitedtribespowwow.com*

The Enchanted Highway

Magic on the Prairie

This 32-mile stretch of roadway between Regent and Gladstone is a folk art fever dream. The Enchanted Highway is dotted with eight towering scrap metal sculpture installations. Self-taught artist Gary Greff crafted these whimsical creations from repurposed oil tanks, pipes, barbed wire, and discarded farm machinery. Huge grasshoppers frolic, a 70-foot trout leaps, and a family of pheasants weigh in at a combined 35,000 pounds. It's a strange and magical place, especially as the sun sinks low in the wide-open sky and the sculptures' long shadows stretch across the prairie. ✉ *I–94, Exit 72, Gladstone to Regent, ND*

Don't Miss

"Geese in Flight" (the World's Largest Scrap Metal Sculpture, according to *Guinness World Records*) is visible from Interstate 94. But it's well worth the drive to spot the rest. See "Deer Crossing" 3 miles down the road or snap a photo of the "World's Largest Tin Family." The newest installation, a knight and dragon, welcomes travelers to Regent on the opposite end of the Enchanted Highway.

Best Hotel

The **Enchanted Castle** entices travelers with large rooms, hot tub suites, and a medieval-theme tavern and steak house. Middle Ages decorative accents gleefully try to transform the former school building (although the gymnasium remains). It's the perfect place to end this quirky road trip. ✉ *607 Main St., Regent, ND* 🌐 *enchantedcastlend.com*

Getting Here and Around

To reach the Enchanted Highway, take Exit 72 off Interstate 94 near Gladstone and drive 32 miles south to Regent on Route 21. All sculptures except "Geese in Flight" have parking areas and information kiosks.

Downtown Fargo

The Place to Shop, Snack, and Socialize

Downtown Fargo shines in every season. This walkable neighborhood is packed with locally owned restaurants, shops, and galleries, with eye-catching public art spilling across the walls, alleys, and streets in between. The pool and lazy river inside shady **Island Park** (the city's oldest green space) define the district's southern border. But **Broadway Square** is the centerpiece. In warm weather, people picnic on bistro tables, kids streak through the splash pad, and the stage hosts a steady stream of free concerts, movies, classes, demos, and community celebrations. When snow blankets the city, ice skaters twirl across the square. 🌐 *www.fargoparks.com/broadway-square*

Don't Miss

Taking a photo by the **Fargo Theatre** marquee is practically a rite of passage. The art deco–inspired venue screens new and classic movies and presents concerts, comedians, and the Fargo Film Festival every March. 🌐 *314 Broadway N, Fargo, ND* 🌐 *www.fargo-theatre.org*

While You're Here

Just west of downtown, **Brewhalla,** Fargo's food and entertainment wonderland, punches way above its weight. The deliciously warped minds behind Drekker Brewing Company (their historic foundry-turned-taproom anchors the entire complex) ran wild in this 100,000-square-foot space. They dreamed up beers that taste like smoothies, pie, and funnel cake, plastered the place with trippy art by their beer label designer, and added a boutique hotel where guests literally check in at the bar (and get a free beer, naturally). ✉ *1702 1st Ave. N, Fargo, ND* 🌐 *www.brewhalla.co*

Getting Here and Around

Downtown is located in eastern Fargo along the Minnesota border.

Plains Art Museum

North Dakota's Largest Art Museum

Find a treasure trove of modern art displayed among the wooden beams and rough brick walls of a former 19th-century farm equipment warehouse in downtown Fargo. The permanent collection contains approximately 4,000 works by national and international artists from the 20th and 21st centuries, with an emphasis on Indigenous artists and creatives from the Great Plains. The Plains Art Museum hosts about a dozen large-scale special exhibitions each year, along with several smaller shows. Artist-led exhibit tours, art talks, and opening receptions invite guests to connect directly with artists. The annual Indigenous Art Festival in May introduces up-and-coming creators from around the region. ✉ *704 1st Ave. N, Fargo, ND* 🌐 *www.plainsart.org*

Don't Miss

The museum's only permanent work is a 13-by-24-foot oil painting called *The North Dakota Mural* by the late James Rosenquist, who was born in Grand Forks, North Dakota. This slightly surreal piece showcases symbols of the state against a colorful background. It's visible from all three levels, thanks to the airy atrium.

While You're Here

Sign up for a class at the **Katherine Kilbourne Burgum Center for Creativity** to try figure drawing, book binding, photography, or even make your own beer stein. Use the First Avenue entrance or follow a winding mosaic down a second-floor hallway and across the sky bridge.

Getting Here and Around

The Plains Art Museum is located in downtown Fargo. Numerous restaurants, locally owned shops, hotels, parks, and public gathering places are just a short walk away.

Dakota Prairie Grasslands

Solitude in a Sea of Grass

The Dakota Prairie Grasslands provide a peek into the past, when this entire region was a rippling expanse of grasses under an ocean of sky. Two of the most solitary and serene spots in this network of prairie landscapes are located in North Dakota. 🌐 *www.fs.usda.gov/main/dpg*

Don't Miss

Measuring over a million acres, the **Little Missouri National Grassland** is the largest grassland in the entire country. It hugs the rocky badlands buttes on the state's western edge and surrounds Theodore Roosevelt National Park. Intriguing hiking routes—including parts of the **Maah Daah Hey Trail**, a ruggedly beautiful single track hiking, biking, and equestrian trail—are located within its borders. So is the highest point in North Dakota, an ancient sedimentary rock formation called **White Butte** near Amidon.

Best Trails

The **Sheyenne National Grassland** is bordered by farmland in the southeast, so the hiking trails are flat and wide. They include a 30-mile section of the North Country National Scenic Trail. This is the longest national scenic trail in the nation (stretching 4,800 miles from Vermont to Lake Sakakawea State Park near Garrison, North Dakota) so even casual hikers can score major bragging rights. Paddlers glide down the Sheyenne River Water Trail, which meanders through the grassland.

Getting Here and Around

These two Dakota Prairie Grasslands are not contiguous, so be prepared to drive. The Sheyenne National Grassland is about an hour southwest of Fargo near Lisbon. Most visitors enter the Little Missouri Grassland from Dickinson, Watford City, or Medora.

The Lewis and Clark Trail

Follow In Famous Footsteps

North Dakota's **Fort Mandan** was an important stop on the journey west for the Lewis and Clark expedition, which had been dispatched by President Thomas Jefferson to survey the lands that became part of the United States after the Louisiana Purchase of 1803. The expedition spent the brutal winter of 1804–05 here and returned in 1806. This is where they met Sheheke-Shote, the chief of the Mandan people, as well as the Lemhi Shoshone woman called Bird Woman (or Sakakawea, as her name is spelled in North Dakota). She traveled with the expedition and introduced them to Native American people along the way to the Pacific Coast. ✉ *838 28th Ave. SW, Washburn, ND*

Don't Miss

The **Lewis and Clark Interpretive Center** in Washburn includes art, interactive exhibits, and historical artifacts that illuminate this era of exploration. **Fort Mandan State Historic Site** features a fully furnished replica of the fort, complete with bunks, games, and clothing. They're 5 miles apart and one admission fee covers both attractions.

Best Scenic Drive

The 23-mile **Sakakawea Scenic Byway** starts in Washburn and passes Fort Clark State Historic Site, home to the Mandan and Arikara people and two fur trade posts. Sakakawea lived in one of the Hidatsa communities within Knife River Indian Villages National Historic Site near present day Stanton.

Getting Here and Around

Washburn is about 40 miles from Bismarck. Go north along the Missouri River on Route 1804 (named for the expedition's time here) until it meets U.S. 83. Sakakawea Scenic Byway follows Route 200A from Washburn to Stanton.

Cold War-Era Missile Bases

Explore Top Secret Bunkers

Don't miss the chance to spot Cold War–era military installations tucked away on North Dakota's peaceful plains. They're the remnants of intercontinental ballistic missile launch sites spread across the state. Tour the buildings where the crews lived and worked, learn about their day-to-day routines, and discover why these sites were considered vital to national defense.

Don't Miss

The **Ronald Reagan Minuteman Missile State Historic Site** near Cooperstown actually consists of two attractions: the Oscar-Zero Missile Alert Facility (a command center) and the November-33 Launch Facility, where a missile was actually housed. A guided tour takes visitors behind the concrete blast door to see the launch control center, which looks straight out of a film like *WarGames*. The living quarters are frozen in time, right down to the 40-cent hamburgers in the dining hall. ✉ *555 113th Ave. NE, Cooperstown, ND* 🌐 *www.history.nd.gov/historicsites/minutemanmissile*

While You're Here

Remote **Sprint Launch Site No. 3** near Cavalier was part of a complex designed to shoot down incoming nuclear weapons. Tours explore the 16-silo missile field and a built-to-scale missile model, and descend through a 75-foot tunnel to reach the 12,500-square-foot underground bunker. ✉ *12329 Rte. 5, Cavalier, ND* 🌐 *www.rsl3.com*

Getting Here and Around

Oscar-Zero is 4 miles north of Cooperstown on Route 45. Find November-33 2 miles east of the city on Route 200. From there, the Remote Sprint Launch Site No. 3 is just over 125 miles north, mostly on Route 1.

When in North Dakota

BADLANDS DINOSAUR MUSEUM

North Dakota is a dinosaur fossil hot spot. Many of those finds (including a complete triceratops skull unearthed nearby) are on display at the Badlands Dinosaur Museum, inside the 12-acre Dickinson Museum Center. Check out full-scale dinosaur skeletons (including stegosaurus and allosaurus), observe current discoveries in the public viewing lab, and see gems, crystals, and minerals from around the world. The remains of mammals, Ice Age creatures, and dinosaur bones and teeth found in North Dakota and the surrounding region round out the largest collection of fossils in the state. ✉ *188 Museum Dr. E, Dickinson, ND* 🌐 *www.dickinsonmuseumcenter.com*

Do This: Experiment with an augmented reality sandbox that allows visitors to create mountains, coastlines, and volcanoes. Or touch petrified wood and bone casts in interactive exhibits.

THE WOODCHIPPER FROM *FARGO*

A prop from one of the most gruesome scenes in movie history has become a must-see tourist attraction. The actual wood chipper used in the 1996 movie *Fargo*, which was written, produced, and directed by brothers Joel and Ethan Coen, is on display inside the Fargo-Moorhead Visitors Center. Film fans don't seem to mind that not a single second of Fargo was actually filmed in North Dakota's largest city. ✉ *2001 44th St. S, Fargo, ND*

Do This: Don a trapper hat with ear flaps—the folks here are happy to loan you one—and shoot your own version of the famous scene. There's a replica wood chipper outside if you arrive after hours.

About Our Writers

Alicia Underlee Nelson was born in Fargo and has lived in Fargo and West Fargo for two decades. She loves how this community attracts artists, entrepreneurs, immigrants, and other outside-the-box thinkers, including the creators of Brewhalla, one of the most compelling food halls in the country. Alicia has written three books about North Dakota, co-authored two Midwestern anthologies, and covered destinations worldwide for numerous publications.

Cool Places to Stay

Coteau des Prairies Lodge. Perched high above the Coteau des Prairies plateau, this family-run lodge offers uninterrupted views of farm fields, grazing cattle, and the Tewaukon National Wildlife Refuge. Stays include continental breakfast. Additional meals, farm and ranch tours, machinery demos, and bird and wildlife excursions are available upon request. ✉ *9953 141st Ave. SE, Havana, ND* 🌐 *www.cdplodge.com*

Hotel Donaldson. Each room inside this stately brick hotel—known to locals as the HoDo—spotlights the work of a different regional artist. The complementary wine and cheese happy hour and chocolate truffle turndown service take indulgence to the next level. The seasonal rooftop bar and Blarney Stone Pub are open to all. ✉ *101 N. Broadway, Fargo, ND* 🌐 *www.hoteldonaldson.com*

Nome School House Inn and Event Center. Every room in this repurposed school and fiber arts retreat features homey quilts and rustic touches like reclaimed wood, barn doors, and exposed brick. On-site dining several days a week, a quiet prairie landscape, and meditative needle felting, basket weaving, and embroidery workshops make it easy to rest and unwind. ✉ *200 1st Ave., Nome, ND* 🌐 *nomeschoolhouse.com*

The Olive Ann Hotel. This downtown Grand Forks boutique hotel specializes in understated elegance. Sip a crème caramel in the lobby coffee shop or savor dinner, cocktails, or weekend brunch at Skies 322, the on-site restaurant. Nightly turndown service includes tomorrow's weather forecast and chocolate-covered potato chips from nearby Widman's Candy. ✉ *14 N. 4th St., Grand Forks, ND* 🌐 *www.theoliveannhotel.com*

Pipestem Creek Bed and Birding. Lush gardens and wide walking paths fill this family farm near Carrington with color and charm. It's located right in the heart of the prairie pothole region—a migration pit stop stop for over half of North America's waterfowl—so it's a prime spot for bird-watchers. ✉ *7060 Rte. 9, Carrington, ND* 🌐 *www.pipestemcreek.com*

Essential Eats

Anima Cucina. This downtown Bismarck fixture is a bustling counter service café and espresso bar by day and a pasta and wine bar by night. Favorites like house-made schiacciata, tender lobster paccheri, rotisserie chicken, and pork loin entrées, and almost impossibly photogenic charcuterie boards made the chef a James Beard Award semifinalist and keep the dining room buzzing. ✉ *101 N. 5th St., Bismarck, ND* 🌐 *www.animacucina.com*

Harry's Steakhouse. Ranching has shaped North Dakota for generations, so trying a perfectly cooked steak here is a must. Tufted booths and exposed brick imbue this Grand Forks restaurant with approachable elegance. A second location brings the classic steak-house atmosphere to West Fargo. Both entice diners with Midwest-raised steak, as well as bison, chops, and an expansive wine list. ✉ *915 19th Ave. E, West Fargo, ND* 🌐 *www.harryssteakhousend.com*

Red River Market. This Saturday market isn't just a great place to buy locally raised meat, eggs, mushrooms, and produce mid-July through October. It's also an easy way to sample Fargo's culinary diversity, from sambusas and spring rolls to naan tacos and fried plantains. Live music, cooking demos, and an ever-changing mix of shopping vendors mean the market's never the same twice. ✉ *201 Broadway N, Fargo, ND* 🌐 *www.redriver.market*

Rosewild. Located in Fargo's Jasper Hotel, Rosewild's seasonal menus showcase local ingredients in crisp salads, comforting desserts, and hearty entrées like pot pie and roasted vegetables. Weekend brunch is a vibe, and the flower-festooned sidewalk patio is the perfect spot to sip an artful, expertly mixed cocktail (or mocktail) and soak up the energy of downtown street life. ✉ *215 Broadway N, Fargo, ND* 🌐 *www.jasperfargo.com/rosewild*

Theodore's Dining Room. Named for President Roosevelt, Medora's casual fine-dining restaurant holds court just off the Rough Riders Hotel lobby. Pork belly Cobb salad, pan-seared walleye, duck leg confit with pimento cheese grits, and succulent braised bison shanks make it a favorite stop for foodies. Berry-studded porridge, corned beef hash, and avocado toast anchor the breakfast menu. ✉ *301 3rd Ave., Medora, ND* 🌐 *www.medora.com/theodoresdiningroom*

Oklahoma

The Sooner State is the geographical and cultural crossroads of America, where the green mountains of the East dissolve into the golden prairies of the West (and of course, where the wind blows sweeping down the plains). More than 10 ecosystems blanket the state, which cradles 200 man-made lakes, more than 1 million surface-acres of water, and more miles of shoreline than the Atlantic and Gulf coasts combined.

Capital: Oklahoma City

Population: 4,095,393

Area: 68,596 square miles

Statehood Date: November 16, 1907

Major Airports: OKC Will Rogers International Airport (OKC); Tulsa International Airport (TUL)

Travel and Tourism Information: *www.travelok.com* *www.oklahomatoday.com*

Famous Residents: Wilma Mankiller (first female chief of the Cherokee Nation); Will Rogers (humorist); Garth Brooks (country musician); Reba McEntire (country music singer and actress); Brad Pitt (actor)

Fun Fact: Bigfoot is believed to be alive and well by some in southeast Oklahoma. The Honobia Bigfoot Festival is held every year, bringing together enthusiasts from across the region and country.

Tulsa's Historic Greenwood District

Black History in Tulsa

Known as "Black Wall Street" for the wealth flowing through the community, Greenwood was created by the African-American community in Tulsa in the early 1900s. Home to restaurants, hotels, movie theaters, and more, Greenwood was the site of a deadly racially motivated attack in 1921, when up to 300 people were killed and a staggering amount of homes and businesses were destroyed. Today, Greenwood is undergoing a resurgence, with a focus on community initiatives. Though much smaller today, the area is home to restaurants, stores, and more. 🌐 *www.historicgreenwooddistrict.com*

Don't Miss

Vernon AME Church, located in Greenwood, was built in 1905. It survived the deadly and destructive Tulsa Race Massacre and today it is the only intact Black-owned structure that remains from the historic Black Wall Street era. ✉ *311 N. Greenwood Ave., Tulsa, OK* 🌐 *www.historicvernon-ame.church*

Best Museum

Greenwood Rising tells the story of the Tulsa Race Massacre through powerful and moving exhibits, storytelling, and artifacts. It honors the victims and survivors of the horrible incident. ✉ *23 N. Greenwood Ave., Tulsa, OK* 🌐 *www.greenwoodrising.org*

Getting Here and Around

The district is located in downtown Tulsa between I–244 to the north, Elgin Avenue to the west, Greenwood Avenue to the east, and the Frisco tracks to the south.

Oklahoma City National Memorial & Museum

A Moment of Remembrance

No trip to the state of Oklahoma would be complete without a stop at the Oklahoma City National Memorial and Museum, dedicated to "those who were killed, those who survived, and those changed forever" in the April 19, 1995, bombing at the Alfred P. Murrah Federal Building. The Outdoor Symbolic Memorial includes the land where the building once stood and the surrounding area that was devastated by the attack. The Field of Empty Chairs, which represents and memorializes all 168 people killed in the bombing, fills the foreground. The Reflecting Pool and memorial museum are just beyond. The interactive museum is located in the west end of the former Journal Record Building, which was built in 1923 and withstood the bombing. The museum takes you on self-guided tours through the events of the day and the world's immediate outpouring of support. The museum uses hundreds of hours of video footage to show the day's toll. ✉ *620 N. Harvey Ave., Oklahoma City, OK* 🌐 *www.memorialmuseum.com*

Don't Miss

The **Survivor Tree**, an American elm tree just yards away from the site of the explosion, survived the bomb's blast and stands tall as a symbol of hope and perseverance; its seedlings are available for purchase.

Good to Know

If you're a runner, consider taking part in the annual Oklahoma City Memorial Marathon, which supports the memorial and museum.

Getting Here and Around

The museum and memorial are located in downtown Oklahoma City; the memorial is open to the public 24 hours a day.

Tahlequah

Home of the Cherokee Nation

The headquarters of the Cherokee Nation, Tahlequah is a 90-minute drive from Tulsa. The Cherokee Nation is the largest tribal nation by population in the United States. Here you can learn more about its culture, people, and history through museums, interactive exhibits, and cultural performances. 🌐 *www.visitcherokeenation.com*

Don't Miss

The **Cherokee National Historic Museum** is housed in the original Cherokee National Capitol building. The museum, encompassing 7,000 square feet, includes tribal art, exhibits, and artifacts meant to educate the public about the Cherokee Nation past and present. Other museums of note include the **Cherokee National Prison Museum** and the **Cherokee National Supreme Court Museum**.

While You're Here

At **Sequoyah's Cabin Museum**, you can learn about the Cherokee man who was instrumental in developing the Cherokee language via his cabin on the reservation in Sallisaw. Built in 1829, the cabin is listed on the National Register of Historic Places and has been maintained to look like when Sequoyah lived there, so take a turn back in time and enjoy the beauty of the 10-acre park while learning about this historic figure. ✉ *470288 Rte. 101, Sallisaw, OK*

When to Go

Each Labor Day weekend, the Cherokee Nation hosts its annual holiday in Tahlequah, commemorating the signing of the 1939 Cherokee Nation Constitution. It features traditional Native American games, cultural performances, and a powwow.

Oklahoma City Museums

Funky Art and Fascinating History

As Oklahoma's capital and the 20th largest city in the country, Oklahoma City has a lot to offer in terms of museums. The **99s Museum of Women Pilots** has one of the largest collections of memorabilia about Amelia Earhart, one of the original 99s, who was the first woman to fly solo across the Atlantic Ocean. Also in Oklahoma City, the **National Cowboy and Western Heritage** Museum has a spectacular permanent exhibits with more than 28,000 pieces of Western and Native American art and artifacts.

Don't Miss

At **Factory Obscura: Mix-Tape,** a massive boom box where you can push the buttons on the tape player is just part of this 6,000-square-foot facility filled with audiovisual fun. The immersive art experience here is intended to recall the days when creative types used cassette tapes to record the soundtracks to their lives. Now, instead of just sounds, it's a whole sensory overload. Mix-Tape is located in the Factory Obscura art collective just north of downtown Oklahoma City. The team of around 30 artists from a wide variety of backgrounds is constantly changing the experience, so locals often come back again and again. ✉ *25 N.W. 9th St., Oklahoma City, OK* 🌐 *www.factoryobscura.com/mixtape*

While You're Here

Sure, it's a practical way for pedestrians to cross over busy Interstate 40 between downtown Oklahoma City and the Oklahoma River, but **SkyDance Bridge** is also much more. Inspired by Oklahoma's state bird, the scissor-tailed flycatcher, the 2012 structure is also a work of art. The bridge is 380 feet long, 197 feet tall, and is made of 412 tons of steel. It's illuminated nightly by lights that change color for holidays and other events.

Oklahoma's Route 66

Follow the Mother Road

Few other roadways conjure up images of America's past like Route 66, one of the first highways in the United States. It stretched nearly 2,500 miles from Chicago, Illinois, to Santa Monica, California, and was open between 1926 and 1985. Route 66 was the stuff of legend, with a song and a TV show named after it. It also figured prominently in John Steinbeck's novel *The Grapes of Wrath* about the westward migration during the Dust Bowl. Almost 400 miles of the road ran through the center of Oklahoma, cutting through both Oklahoma City and Tulsa and following small towns that once drew road-trippers with neon signs, diners, and motels. Today you can trace its history with top attractions including the **Oklahoma Route 66 Museum** in Clinton and the **National Route 66 & Transportation Museum** in Elk City.

Don't Miss

The **Oklahoma Route 66 Museum** in Clinton re-creates the heyday of the Mother Road, down to a 1957 Chevy and the counter from a diner. For some visitors, it's a trip down memory lane to a time when big band music dominated the airwaves. For younger generations, it's a great place to experience part of U.S. history that runs far deeper than a stretch of pavement. ✉ *2229 W. Gary Blvd., Clinton, OK* 🌐 *www.okhistory.org/sites/route66*

Good to Know

Show off to friends with a Route 66 Passport that you can get stamped at 66 spots along the way, including the famous **Blue Whale in Catoosa**. ✉ *2600 Rte. 66, Catoosa, OK*

Getting Here and Around

Clinton, where the Oklahoma Route 66 Museum is located, is about 90 miles west of Oklahoma City, which is served by major air carriers.

Natural Falls State Park

Where the Red Fern Grows

A dazzling 77-foot waterfall cascades through rock formations and into a beautiful pool at Natural Falls State Park. It may look familiar, because scenes for the 1974 classic film *Where the Red Fern Grows* were filmed at this park in the Ozark Highlands near the border of Arkansas. An observation platform with a picnic pavilion overlooks the falls. There's also a deck at the base of the falls, so it's possible to see the falls from above and below. ✉ *19225 E. 578 Rd., Colcord, OK* 🌐 *www.travelok.com/state-parks/natural-falls-state-park*

Don't Miss

There are more than 4 miles of hiking trails fanning out through the park. You'll see a variety of plants, including ferns, liverworts, mosses, flowering dogwood, sassafras, coral berry, spicebush, redbud, and pawpaw as well as numerous tree types such as maples, chinquapin, and white oaks.

Spend the Night

Book at least one night in one of the park's five yurts. You won't be exactly roughing it, as there's air-conditioning, microwaves, mini-refrigerators, and other amenities. Shower and restroom facilities are a short walk away.

Getting Here and Around

Natural Falls State Park is a 70-minute drive east of Tulsa.

Wichita Mountains Wildlife Refuge

A Real Home on the Range

One of the oldest wildlife refuges in the United States, Wichita Mountains was established in 1901. The 92-square-mile refuge gives you a rare opportunity to experience a mixed-grass prairie that's largely been untouched—mostly because the rocky soils made it difficult to plow. Besides protecting animals in danger of becoming extinct, the refuge's purpose was to rebuild populations that had already been wiped out from the area. Wildlife reintroduced over the years include American bison, Rocky Mountain elks, wild turkeys, prairie dogs, river otters, and burrowing owls. White-tailed deer and Texas longhorn cattle also graze the grasslands. Today, more than 240 species of birds, 64 reptiles and amphibians, 50 mammals, and 36 fish can be found on the refuge. ✉ *21088 State Hwy. 115, Cache, OK* 🌐 *www.fws.gov/refuge/Wichita_Mountains*

Don't Miss

There are 15 miles of designated hiking trails that wind through scrub oak forests, across rocky mountains, and over grass-covered prairies. The refuge preserves approximately 60,000 acres of mixed grass prairie, ancient granite mountains, and freshwater lakes and streams.

When To Go

The refuge is open year-round, but spring offers pleasant temperatures and blooming flowers. Fall is another option, when temperatures also drop a bit and the foliage is quite stunning.

Getting Here and Around

The wildlife refuge is located 4 miles north of Cache, Oklahoma. It's a two-hour drive southwest of Oklahoma City.

Tulsa's Music Scene

Music History in Tulsa

Tulsa, the second-largest city in Oklahoma, may be best known for its Art Deco architecture, but it also has a burgeoning music scene. From big acts showcasing their talent at the BOK Center to homegrown favorites playing in local dive bars, there's something for everyone here. The **Bob Dylan Center** and **Woody Guthrie Center** both shine a light on two of the most well-known artists of the 20th and 21st centuries. The museums, which are on the same street in downtown Tulsa, include artifacts, exhibits, and much more dedicated to the famed musicians. Nearby is the historic **Cain's Ballroom,** which played a role in the development of Western Swing in the 1930s and 1940s.

Don't Miss

A mix of blues, country, rock and roll, and more, the Tulsa Sound is a style of music created by music pioneers like J.J. Cale and Leon Russell. The **Church Studio** pays homage to this unique genre. Leon Russell bought the church in 1972 that would become his music studio and go on to host a number of well-known musicians, including Tom Petty and Eric Clapton. You can tour the studio today (it's still used for special recordings). ✉ *304 S. Trenton Ave., Tulsa, OK* 🌐 *www.thechurchstudio.com*

Best Live Music

Cain's Ballroom still regularly has live performances, or head to the SoBo (South of Boston) District's divey but legendary Mercury Lounge. ✉ *1747 S. Boston Ave., Tulsa, OK* 🌐 *www.mercuryloungetulsa.com*

Getting Here and Around

Many of the museums are located in downtown Tulsa. The Church Studio is located just outside of downtown.

When in Oklahoma

DEEP DEUCE DISTRICT

In Oklahoma City, the Deep Deuce district was the heart of black culture in the 1920s and 1930s. It was the hub for local blues and jazz musicians, including legends like Charlie Christian and Jimmy Rushing, who hailed from the district. Count Basie, Ma Rainey, Bessie Smith, and Mamie Smith were among the performers who played here. Deep Deuce also has a long history focusing on social justice. It was home to author Ralph Ellison, whose award-winning novel *Invisible Man* focused on issues faced by Black Americans in the middle of the 20th century. The neighborhood was also where Oklahoma students organized sit-ins at segregated lunch counters in 1957. ⊕ *www.deepdeucedistrict.com*

Do This: Soak up the live music and order a drink at Deep Deuce Bar and Grill. ✉ *307 N.E. 2nd St., Oklahoma City, OK* ⊕ *www.deepdeucebarandgrillokc.com*

HONEY SPRINGS BATTLEFIELD HISTORIC SITE

The Battle of Honey Springs was the last and largest engagement of the Civil War in the Great Plains, a decisive victory for Union troops in the effort to control what was then called Indian Territory. It took place on a rainy Friday, July 17, 1863. About 9,000 men took part, including Native American troops on both sides. Also on the scene were the First Kansas Colored Volunteers, the first African American regiment in the Union Army. ✉ *423159 E. 1030 Rd., Checotah, OK* ⊕ *www.okhistory.org/sites/honeysprings*

Do This: A reenactment of the Battle of Honey Springs allows you to experience military drills, demonstrations, and living history programs. Vendors sell books, clothing, and reproductions of 19th-century military equipment.

About Our Writers

Kristi Eaton was born and raised in Tulsa, Oklahoma, and also spent a few years living in Oklahoma City. She loves exploring by walking around neighborhoods—old and new—in her hometown. She is a freelance writer and public relations consultant currently living in Tulsa.

THE TOY AND ACTION FIGURE MUSEUM

In Paul's Valley, an hour south of Oklahoma City, you'll find the first museum in the world devoted to the art and sculpting of action figures. The museum displays more than 13,000 classic dolls dating back to the 1950s. The museum is also home to the Oklahoma Cartoonists Collection that features published comic artists and writers from Oklahoma, including Chester Gould of *Dick Tracy* and Jack and Carole Bender of *Alley Oop*. ✉ *111 S. Chickasaw St., Pauls Valley, OK* ⊕ *www.toyandactionfiguremuseum.com*

Do This: Check out the tribute to World War II veterans. The exhibit is filled with 12-inch G.I. Joes in lifelike representations of various military campaigns.

WILL ROGERS MEMORIAL MUSEUM

The Oklahoma community of Claremore, located just northeast of Tulsa, is best known as the hometown of Will Rogers, a homespun cowboy philosopher from the early 1900s. A century ago, he was considered to be one of the leading entertainers of the era. Rogers was a citizen of the Cherokee Nation, a vaudeville performer, a newspaper columnist, and a social commentator whose quotes are still widely repeated today. ("Even if you're on the right track," he once said, "you'll get run over if you just sit there.")

Do This: The Will Rogers Memorial Museum houses the world's largest collection of Will Rogers memorabilia and his entire collection of writings. ✉ *1720 W. Will Rogers Blvd., Claremore, OK* 🌐 *www.willrogers.com*

Cool Places to Stay

Eufaula Treehouse Tree-Sort. This unique getaway consists of a cluster of tree houses in a mature forest. There's a secluded picnic area for afternoon grilling and social gatherings. ✉ *120654 S. CR 4150, Eufaula, OK* 🌐 *eufaulatreesort.com*

Island Guest Ranch. First established in 1889, this working cattle ranch consists of several thousand acres of native grassland in northwest Oklahoma. You stay in rustic cabins or a bunkhouse near the lodge where meals are served. Activities include hiking, horseback riding, skeet shooting, and learning how to swing a rope. ✉ *267043 E. County Rd. 55, Ames, OK* 🌐 *theislandranch.com*

Lake Murray Floating Cabins. It's easier to enjoy the panoramic views of Lake Murray if you're actually on the water. These houseboats have knotty pine interiors, vaulted ceilings, circular stairways to a sleeping loft, and catwalks that stretch across the living room to the balcony. ✉ *3323 Lodge Rd., Ardmore, OK* 🌐 *www.lake-murray.org/floating-cabins*

The Mayo Hotel. In downtown Tulsa, the Mayo Hotel was instantly regarded as a place for high society when it opened in 1925. It stood vacant for more than 25 years until a $42 million renovation brought back its luster, keeping the original historic charm but adding the latest technology and amenities. ✉ *115 W. 5th St., Tulsa, OK* 🌐 *www.themayohotel.com*

Quartz Mountain State Park Lodge. After a day of boating, mountain biking, or rock climbing, relax in this handsome lodge on the shores of Lake Altus-Lugert. Done up in Native American, Western, and Southwestern decor, each room features four pieces of original art. ✉ *43393 Scissortail Rd., Lone Wolf, OK* 🌐 *www.travelok.com/state-parks/quartz-mountain-state-park*

Essential Eats

Country Bird Bakery. This James Beard Award–winning bakery uses regionally sourced grain and flour, meaning their baked goods are not only more nutritious but also have a more diverse flavor to them. The bakery is only open on Saturday, so be prepared to wait in a long line. ✉ *1644 E. 3rd St., Tulsa, OK* 🌐 *www.countrybirdbakery.com*

Ma Der Lao Kitchen. A finalist for the James Beard Awards, this Oklahoma City spot features the Laotian recipes of chef Jeff Chanchaleune's mother and grandmother, from sticky rice to Lao papaya salad. The food is served family-style at this popular eatery, which doesn't take reservations. ✉ *1634 N. Blackwelder Ave., Oklahoma City, OK* 🌐 *www.maderlaokitchen.com*

South Dakota

Marked by windswept prairies, rugged badlands, and an emerald oasis known as the Black Hills, South Dakota is a state of rugged beauty. The chiseled spires, ragged ridges, and steep-sided canyons of Badlands National Park are awe-inspiring, while the Black Hills, with its imposing peaks and the famed Mount Rushmore National Memorial, attracts sizable crowds in summer. At Custer State Park, don't miss the epic buffalo roundup.

Capital: Pierre

Population: 924,669

Area: 77,123 square miles

Statehood Date: Nov. 2, 1889

Major Airports: Sioux Falls Regional Airport (FSD); Rapid City Regional Airport (RAP)

Travel and Tourism Information: 🌐 *www.tourism.sd.gov* 🌐 *www.travelsouthdakota.com*

Famous Residents: Crazy Horse (Lakota Sioux leader and warrior); Wild Bill Hickok (Wild West lawman); Laura Ingalls Wilder (author); Bob Barker (game show host); Tom Brokaw (news anchor); January Jones (actress)

Fun Fact: South Dakota and neighboring North Dakota both joined the union on Nov. 2, 1889; North Dakota claims to be the 39th state, with South Dakota the 40th. But were they really admitted in that order? We'll never know. Legend has it President Benjamin Harrison shuffled the statehood documents and covered his hand as he affixed his signatures, meaning the actual order of statehood will remain a mystery.

Badlands National Park

A Moonlike Landscape Filled With Fossils

Until the moon opens up to tourism, a hike through the stunning landscape of Badlands National Park is about as close as you can get to taking "one small step for man, one giant leap for mankind." Because of the park's open hike policy, visitors are free to roam the entire 379 square miles of protected mixed-grass prairie. It's a great way to examine the rugged terrain that holds some of the best fossil beds anywhere in the world. Besides remnants of South Dakota's prehistoric past, the park's current residents include bighorn sheep, bison, prairie dogs, pronghorn antelope, and black-footed ferrets. 🌐 *www.nps.gov/badl*

Don't Miss

Badlands Loop Road has several stops along the way to take in the scenery and watch the wildlife without ever leaving your car. The best overlook is Pinnacles Overlook; with the highest elevation in the park's North Unit, it has the greatest sweeping views, and you can see the Black Hills on the horizon if conditions are clear.

Good to Know

Make sure you stop by the **Ben Reifel Visitor Center**, surrounded by towering rock formations. The center has a fossil preparation lab where you can see paleontologists at work and ask them questions. ✉ *25216 Ben Reifel Rd., Interior, SD*

Getting Here and Around

From Rapid City, drive 75 miles east on Interstate 90. Exit 110 connects to Wall (and famous Wall Drug) to the north and the Pinnacles Entrance and Badlands Loop Road to the south. Exit 131 leads to the Northeast Entrance and the Ben Reifel Visitor Center, which is a great place to get your bearings.

Custer Buffalo Roundup

Marvel at Hundreds of Bison

As recently as the 1500s, as many as 60 million bison roamed North America. By the early 1900s, their numbers had dwindled to just a few thousand. Thanks to preservation efforts, there are now herds of hundreds of thousands of these majestic animals. One of the largest herds roams the Black Hills of Custer State Park in southwest South Dakota. Every September, park rangers and volunteers gather the herd of roughly 1,300 in a roundup that's part tourist attraction, part park management. You can't get as close as Kevin Costner did in the hunting scene of *Dances With Wolves*, but you'll see and feel the thundering bison as they're corralled. Some are rounded up and sold, but most are released back into Custer State Park, where you can enjoy their rugged beauty throughout the year. ✉ *13329 U.S. 16A, Custer, SD* 🌐 *www.gfp.sd.gov/buffalo-roundup*

Don't Miss

When you're visiting Custer State Park, **Black Elk Peak**, **Sylvan Lake**, and **Needles Highway** offer amazing views of the Black Hills.

Good to Know

Get there early to secure a good spot, and dress for changing weather conditions. The roundup starts in mid-morning, and visitors have to remain in the viewing areas until all bison are corralled, which usually happens around noon. Breakfast and lunch are covered.

Getting Here and Around

To get to the north parking lot, head 31 miles south of Rapid City on Routes 79 and 36, then south on Wildlife Loop Road. To get to the south parking lot, head east on Wildlife Loop Road near Bluebell Campground.

Deadwood

An Iconic Wild West Town

More than 35 years after a devastating fire gutted nearly a full city block of Deadwood, the Black Hills boomtown is thriving again, 150 years after gold was first discovered in the area. In the wake of the fire, city voters approved limited-stakes gambling, with proceeds earmarked for the restoration of historic buildings. That commitment, along with attention garnered from the acclaimed HBO miniseries *Deadwood*, has helped bring this Old West town back. Now you'll find brick-paved streets, glittering casinos, top-rated restaurants, luxury hotels, and vibrant concert venues, all oozing with frontier ambience. 🌐 *www.deadwood.com*

Don't Miss

Mount Moriah Cemetery is the final resting place of many a Deadwood notable, including James Butler "Wild Bill" Hickok, a flamboyant gold seeker and feared gunfighter, who was shot in the back of the head while playing poker in a Main Street saloon on August 2, 1876. Interred in an adjacent grave is Martha Jane Canary, aka Calamity Jane, who preferred to dress like a man and was at least the equal of most men with a shot glass, spittoon, six-shooter, or swear word. ✉ *10 Mt. Moriah Dr., Deadwood, SD*

While You're Here

Tour the **Historic Adams House**, an 1892 Queen Anne–style mansion preserving the lavish lifestyle of Deadwood's founding families. Elsewhere, the **Adams Museum** and **Days of '76 Museum** house mementos of the town's cowboy, mining, and railroad heritage.

Getting Here and Around

From Rapid City, take I–90 and U.S. 14A 42 miles to Deadwood.

Crazy Horse Memorial

The World's Largest Mountain Carving

Henry Standing Bear, chief of the Lakota people, had long sought to have a memorial honoring Native Americans in the Black Hills. "My fellow chiefs and I would like the white man to know that the red man has great heroes also," he said. Standing Bear tapped sculptor Korczak Ziolkowski to take on the project of carving a monument to Crazy Horse, a Lakota warrior who was killed while being held by U.S. troops in 1877. It's taking several generations, but Standing Bear is achieving his goal. Still in progress, the Crazy Horse Memorial is considered the world's largest mountain carving. It will depict Crazy Horse on horseback and gesturing toward his people's land. ✉ *12151 Ave. of the Chiefs, Crazy Horse, SD* 🌐 *www.crazyhorsememorial.org*

Don't Miss

Though the mountain carving is the main attraction, the site is also home to museums featuring Native American art and artifacts from more than 300 tribes across North America.

Get Up Close

If you'd like to add a bucket-list hike to your visit, consider taking part in the spring or fall **Volksmarch**, a 6-mile trek to the top of the monument. You stand on Crazy Horse's outstretched arm and gaze at his nine-story-tall face.

Getting Here and Around

From Rapid City, head south on U.S. 16 for 37 miles. From Custer, go north 4 miles on U.S. 16.

Mount Rushmore

The Most Famous Presidential Sculpture

Sculptor Gutzon Borglum carved the likenesses of George Washington, Thomas Jefferson, Abraham Lincoln, and Theodore Roosevelt "to communicate the founding, expansion, preservation, and unification of the United States." Even if you've visited Mount Rushmore National Memorial before, it's worth checking out again because the visitor center and other facilities have been expanded to accommodate the 3 million people who visit each year. Other recent additions include more educational programs on Native American people who have lived in the Black Hills for centuries. ✉ *13000 Hwy. 244, Keystone, SD* 🌐 *www.nps.gov/moru*

Don't Miss

Want to get the perfect picture? The half-mile-long **Presidential Trail** is a great way to get closer to the sculpture and maybe even see some of the wildlife that roams the Black Hills. To get a photo of George Washington's profile, take a right on Route 244 when you leave the main parking lot and drive around to the side of the memorial.

When to Go

Mt. Rushmore is open year-round, but try to visit in May, September, or October when the crowds aren't as bad. Most other places in the Black Hills are open, so it's a great time to explore without the summertime rush.

Getting Here and Around

Mount Rushmore National Memorial is 24 miles south of Rapid City on U.S. 16. After visiting the memorial, check out the shops, restaurants, and other attractions in nearby Keystone and Hill City.

Jewel Cave National Monument

Stunning Caves of South Dakota

Even though its more than 200 miles of surveyed passages make this cave the world's third largest (Kentucky's Mammoth Cave is the longest), Jewel Cave isn't renowned for its size. Rather, it's the rare crystalline formations that abound in the cave's vast passages. Wander the dark passageways and you'll be rewarded with the sight of tiny crystal Christmas trees, hydromagnesite balloons that would pop if you touched them, and delicate calcite deposits dubbed "cave popcorn." ✉ *11149 U.S. 16 Custer, SD* 🌐 *www.nps.gov/jeca*

Don't Miss

Year-round, you can take ranger-led tours for a fee, from a simple half-hour walk to a lantern-light tour. Surface trails and facilities are free.

Best Tour

For those who are comfortable getting active on a moderately strenuous tour, book the **Scenic Tour**. The ½-mile tour led by NPS rangers involves climbing more than 700 stairs, but the paved trail leads the way to stunning chambers filled with calcite crystals and vibrant speleothems. Travelers with small children or those who have limited mobility can book the **Discovery Talk**, an accessible tour that dives into the cave's history.

While You're Here

About 30 minutes away is **Wind Cave National Park**. Wind Cave ranks as the sixth-longest cave in the world, but experts believe 95% of it has yet to be mapped. The park is also home to herds of bison and elk. 🌐 *www.nps.gov/wica*

Getting Here and Around

Jewel Cave National Monument is about 13 miles west of Custer in South Dakota's Black Hills, so it can easily be combined with a day or weekend trip to the Custer Buffalo Roundup.

Sturgis Motorcycle Rally

The World's Largest Motorcycle Rally

The largest motorcycle rally in the world is America's crowning event for all bike enthusiasts. Motorcycle racers started what is now known as the Sturgis Motorcycle Rally in the 1930s; today it's a 10-day-long marathon each August featuring live music, plenty of food and drink, people-watching, and, of course, motorcycles of all shapes and sizes. As many as 750,000 people from around the world have packed Sturgis and the Black Hills region for the annual event's races, rides, and communal love for Harleys. 🌐 *www.sturgismotorcyclerally.com*

Don't Miss

Motorcyle rides and races aren't the only reason to head to the rally. Performances from big-name artists like ZZ Top and Stone Temple Pilots cater to the biker crowd.

Good to Know

Downtown Sturgis is completely blocked off during the rally, so make sure you walk from one end of Main Street to the other to take it all in. Duck down the side streets as well.

Getting Here and Around

Sturgis is 29 miles northwest of Rapid City on Interstate 90. Be ready to find lodging miles away from Sturgis because of the overwhelming demand for hotel rooms.

The Mammoth Site

Dig Up Ice Age Fossils

The fossils of more than 60 mammoths, as well as 87 other animals from the Ice Age, have been recovered from a sinkhole at the Mammoth Site in southwestern South Dakota. The vast facility is the largest mammoth research facility in the world. In 1974, a worker clearing land for a housing project discovered the site when his blade struck what turned out to be a tusk. Today the museum displays full-sized replicas of mammoths, as well as the fossilized remains in the earth where they were discovered. There's a hands-on learning area for children and windows into the laboratory where scientists are still hard at work. ✉ *1800 U.S. 18 Bypass, Hot Springs, SD* 🌐 *www.mammothsite.org*

Don't Miss

See a working paleontological site, **the Bonebed**. There's even an excavation each summer, the Ice Age Explorers Program, where you can train with professionals, excavate and screen-wash sediments, and tour the lab.

While You're Here

If you're staying in Hot Springs, check out **Evans Plunge Mineral Springs**, the **Pioneer Museum**, and **Wind Cave National Park**.

Good to Know

Don't touch the bones; they are dry and fragile.

Getting Here and Around

From Rapid City, drive 57 miles south on Route 79 and U.S. 18 to Hot Springs.

Falls Park

South Dakota's Most Impressive Waterfalls

The churning waters of Falls Park—the namesake of Sioux Falls—have been attracting people for hundreds of years. Especially in years with heavy rainfall, the Big Sioux River rushes over the pink quartzite rocks and offers spectacular views from the walking trails that surround it. A five-story observation tower gives a bird's-eye view of the entire park and downtown skyline beyond. Other park attractions also include remnants of the Queen Bee Mill and the old Sioux Falls Light and Power Company Building, now home to Falls Overlook Cafe. ✉ *131 E. Falls Park Dr., Sioux Falls, SD* 🌐 *www.experiencesiouxfalls.com/falls-park*

Don't Miss

Falls Park lies along a 29-mile paved bicycle path following the Big Sioux River. There are dozens of great spots for photos, including a picturesque old iron bridge. The north end of the path is a perfect place to watch takeoffs and landings at the Sioux Falls Regional Airport. A 15-minute walk south brings you to the **Arc of Dreams**, a graceful 300-foot-long sculpture by South Dakota artist-in-residence Dale Claude Lamphere. A pair of stainless-steel arcs gently rise from each riverbank to a height of 70 feet, with an 18-foot gap representing, according to Lamphere, the leap of faith we must take to help our dreams come true.

When to Go

From November to January, Falls Park is decorated with more than 355,000 holiday lights, including some that illuminate the water and ice on the falls.

Getting Here and Around

The 128-acre city park is located just north of downtown Sioux Falls.

The Oahe Dam

Crossing the "Big Water"

Look at any map of the United States and in the middle of the Dakotas you'll notice a wider-than-usual strip of blue that extends from South Dakota's capital of Pierre to North Dakota's capital of Bismarck. That's Lake Oahe, created when engineers dammed the Missouri River in 1962. The ensuring dam, Oahe Dam, is one of the largest earth-rolled dams in the world. Located 6 miles north of Pierre, it was dedicated by President John F. Kennedy, who said the Oahe Dam would produce enough electricity "to light the entire city of Edinburgh, Scotland." On its 50th anniversary, experts hailed it as an "engineering marvel." Driving across it, or boating on the reservoir, is still a thrill today.

Don't Miss

The dam created **Lake Oahe**, the fourth-largest artificial reservoir in the United States. The lake is an impressive 231 miles long, so boating and fishing are popular activities. Along the shore are birds ranging from sharp-tailed grouse to Canadian geese. A good entry point for boats is Fort Yates Bay.

While You're Here

LaFramboise Island Nature Area, located downstream in Pierre, is covered in trees and meadows. Explorers Lewis and Clark recorded the beautiful island in their journals when they passed through in 1804.

Getting Here and Around

From Fort Pierre on the west side of the Missouri River, drive north on Route 1806 to Route 204, which crosses over Oahe Dam. After a stop at the visitor center, drive north on Route 1804, which runs along the east side of Lake Oahe.

When in South Dakota

BEAR BUTTE STATE PARK

The huge eruption of igneous rock rising above the plains in Bear Butte State Park is known as Mato Paha, or "Bear Mountain," in the Lakota language. Several indigenous tribes consider the mountain sacred and regularly hold religious ceremonies here. The trail to the top of the mountain, just under 2 miles in length, is a great way to see up close the colorful pieces of prayer cloth and small bundles of tobacco hanging from the trees. They represent the prayers offered by Native people during their worship and shouldn't be disturbed. ✉ *20250 Rte. 79, Sturgis, SD* 🌐 *www.gfp.sd.gov*

Do This: The top of the mountain has great views of the Black Hills to the southwest. If you have time, there's also a 2½-mile trail around Bear Butte Lake.

CORN PALACE

Built in 1892, the ornate Corn Palace was intended to show the world that South Dakota, then just three years old, had a thriving agriculture industry. More than a century later, farming is still a big part of the economy. So is tourism, which the World's Only Corn Palace helped build. Roughly 500,000 people visit this landmark each year. The exterior of the building is redecorated each year with colorful murals made with actual kernels of corn and other grains. ✉ *604 N. Main St., Mitchell, SD* 🌐 *www.cornpalace.com*

Do This: The annual Corn Palace Festival is held in late August each year.

DIGNITY OF EARTH AND SKY

This 50-foot stainless steel sculpture by South Dakota artist laureate Dale Claude Lamphere of Sturgis represents the indigenous Lakota and Dakota people of the Great Plains. The sculpture depicts a woman in Plains-style dress, wrapping herself in a star quilt. Multicolor patterns in the quilt flutter and dance with the wind. *Dignity* honors the past while looking toward the future, Lamphere has said. Motorists can see the sculpture from Interstate 90, overlooking the Missouri River from a tall bluff near Chamberlain.

Do This: Take the time to explore on your own at the Lewis & Clark Welcome Center, where *Dignity* stands. You'll find interpretive displays depicting life during the Lewis & Clark 1804–06 exploration of the Great Plains. Walking trails offer a panoramic view of the Missouri River. ✉ *Exit 264, I-90, Chamberlain, SD*

LAURA INGALLS WILDER HOMES

If you read the *Little House on the Prairie* books, or watched the 1970s/1980s NBC television series of the same name, this tour offers a major dose of nostalgia, bringing to life some of the places Laura Ingalls Wilder wrote about during her time in De Smet, South Dakota. The Discover Laura tour includes the Ingalls home built by Charles "Pa" Ingalls in 1889, the first school in De Smet that Wilder and her sister, Carrie, attended, and a replica of the Brewster School where Wilder taught when she was 15. ✉ *105 Olivet Ave., De Smet, SD* 🌐 *www.discoverlaura.org*

Do This: Visit the De Smet Cemetery, where members of the Ingalls Family are buried, and the Charles Ingalls homestead south of town.

PETRIFIED WOOD PARK

In the early 1930s, amateur geologist Ole S. Quammen oversaw construction of this display of petrified wood that takes up an entire block in the town of Lemmon. Besides petrified dinosaur and mammoth bones that were gathered from surrounding archaeological sites, Petrified Wood Park includes a castle and 20-foot-tall towers. ✉ *500 Main Ave., Lemmon, SD*

Do This: Make the trek during the holidays when the petrified trees are decorated with lights.

WALL DRUG

Hand-painted billboards offering free ice water brought weary travelers to Wall Drug during the Great Depression. Now 2 million people stop every year at this funky tourist attraction whose walls are adorned with kitschy signs and oddball items. There's also a serious side to Wall Drug, which has an art gallery with more than 300 original oil paintings of the Old West. Located near Badlands National Park, it's an easy, fun stop. ✉ *510 Main St., Wall, SD* 🌐 *www.walldrug.com*

Do This: Plan your visit to coincide with a meal. The restaurant is known for its doughnuts and coffee, but it also serves a variety of main dishes, including hot beef sandwiches and buffalo burgers. Top off your meal at the soda fountain, something that's been part of Wall Drug since the early days.

WOUNDED KNEE MASSACRE MONUMENT

Some monuments are spectacular. Some, like the one that marks the site of the 1890 Wounded Knee massacre, are moving because of their simplicity. On December 29, 1890, near Wounded Knee Creek in southwest South Dakota, the U.S. Army's 7th Cavalry killed as many as 300 Lakota men, women, and children. It was the last major confrontation between U.S. Cavalry and Northern Plains Indians.

Do This: The simple memorial, a National Historic Landmark, includes the mass grave where the victims were buried and a memorial listing many of their names. Wounded Knee is on the Pine Ridge Reservation, and the Oglala Sioux Tribe will occasionally limit travel. Visitors are asked to be respectful while at the memorial, which still elicits high emotion among descendants of those who lost their lives.

About Our Writers

Jim Holland was born and raised in the South Dakota Black Hills, and currently lives in Sturgis with his wife Debra. The Missouri River's split of the state has forged a good-natured East/West rivalry—cultural as well as geographical—among residents; Jim is strongly West River. Now retired, his 42-year journalism career included reporting and photography for newspapers in South Dakota and Nebraska.

Cool Places to Stay

Blue Bell Lodge. In Custer State Park, the log cabins at Blue Bell Lodge have stone fireplaces and hand-hewn timbers that lend them plenty of rustic charm. In the evenings there are hayrides and chuckwagon dinners. ✉ *25453 Rte. 87, Custer, SD* 🌐 *www.custerresorts.com/lodges-and-cabins/blue-bell-lodge*

Franklin Hotel. Teddy Roosevelt, Babe Ruth, and John Wayne are among the guests who have stayed at this historic hotel in the town of Deadwood. Take in the view of Main Street from the open patio on the ornate roof of the Victorian-era front porch. ✉ *700 Main St., Deadwood, SD* 🌐 *www.silveradofranklin.com/lodging*

Hotel on Phillips. When it was built in 1918, this nine-story building in downtown Sioux Falls was the tallest building in South Dakota. It was originally home to Sioux Falls National Bank, and it's since been transformed into an upscale boutique hotel with 90 elegant rooms and luxury suites. ✉ *100 N. Phillips Ave., Sioux Falls, SD* 🌐 *www.hotelonphillips.com*

Under Canvas Mount Rushmore. Camping under ponderosa pine and common juniper trees in the Black Hills would be a great experience, but add in spectacular views of Mt. Rushmore and it becomes a bucket-list experience. Between early May and late September, Under Canvas Mt. Rushmore offers upscale glamping accommodations that are hard to beat. There's a nature walk, firepit, and plenty of s'mores. ✉ *24342 Presidio Ranch Rd., Keystone, SD* 🌐 *www.undercanvas.com/camps/mount-rushmore*

Essential Eats

Alpine Inn Steakhouse. European charm abounds at the rustic Alpine Inn, nestled in the heart of downtown Hill City in a Victorian chalet dating back to 1886. The Inn is known for a lunch menu that changes frequently, but always highlights a healthy fare of sandwiches, wraps, and salads. The evening menu is even more streamlined: a signature filet mignon with baked potato Texas toast and wedge salad; and a Kaes Spaetzle Primavera, a German dumpling and Swiss cheese dish. ✉ *133 Main St., Hill City, SD* 🌐 *www.alpineinnhillcity.com*

Al's Oasis. This legendary landmark on I–90 at the Missouri River is an oasis in more ways than one. Providing a much-needed respite for travelers on a long journey across the state, Al's Oasis features a fuel stop, full-service grocery store, and clothing and gift shops featuring local crafts and souvenirs. The restaurant is known across the state and beyond for its small-town vibe, generous portions, and American-style menu selections, including steaks, buffalo burgers, a meal-in-itself salad bar, and specialty homemade pies. There is also a weekend breakfast buffet and a full-service bar, the Last Chance Saloon. ✉ *1000 E. U.S. 16, Oacoma, SD* 🌐 *www.alsoasissd.com*

Colonial House Restaurant & Bar. A must-stop for locals and travelers alike, Colonial House serves up hearty American food in a family-friendly atmosphere on busy Mt. Rushmore Road. The extensive menu features the full range of traditional favorites, including signature steaks, burgers (even ground buffalo), seafood, sandwiches, pasta, and salads. Topping a full bakery menu are the restaurant's mainstay caramel rolls, a favorite for more than 40 years. ✉ *2315 Mt. Rushmore Rd., Rapid City, SD* 🌐 *www.colonialhousernb.com*

Parker's Bistro. This spot offers eclectic dining in Sioux Falls's resurgent historic district, calling one of the city's last original native stone buildings its home. The Bistro offers regularly updated takes on classic American and European cuisine. Standouts include a rib-eye steak, a flown-in seafood-of-the-day, and house-made puttanesca pasta. Adventurous epicureans will note a grilled wild boar dinner selection. ✉ *210 S. Main Ave., Sioux Falls, SD* 🌐 *www.parkersbistro.net*

The Pheasant Restaurant & Lounge. This eatery's roots go back to 1949, when it was a roadhouse café and gas station on the then-outskirts of Brookings. Now a center of fine dining for more than six decades, the diverse American menu includes key South Dakota favorites. The namesake signature ring-necked pheasant salad forms the foundation for lunch and dinner choices. Another local favorite is the state's official nosh, chislic, deep-fried and lightly seasoned lamb cubes accompanied by crackers and bleu cheese dressing. ✉ *726 Main Ave. S, Brookings, SD* 🌐 *www.pheasantrestaurant.com*

Chapter 6

6

THE WEST COAST AND THE PACIFIC

Updated by Shelley Arenas, J. Besl, Margot Bigg, Shoshi Parks, and Anna Weaver

WELCOME TO THE WEST COAST AND THE PACIFIC

TOP REASONS TO GO

★ **Dramatic landscapes:** From Denali to Yosemite, see the West's iconic national parks, including desertscapes, towering snowcapped peaks, stunning coastline, active volcanoes, and the world's biggest trees.

★ **Wineries:** Sip your way through California, Oregon, and Washington's best vineyards and sample craft beer along the way.

★ **Wild things:** Spot grizzlies in Alaska, condors in California, and bald eagles, migrating whales, and seals up and down the Pacific Coast.

★ **Glaciers:** Get an up-close view of these fleeting ice formations, from trekking on Mendenhall glacier in Juneau to cruising past them in Kenai Fjords and Glacier Bay, to hiking beneath them in North Cascades National Park.

★ **Cool cities:** Los Angeles, Seattle, San Francisco, and Portland beckon with their trendy restaurants, bars, and cultural treasures, but you're never too far from wide open spaces.

1 Alaska. By far the largest state in the Union, the Last Frontier is a land of riveting contrasts, from the temperate rain forests and bays of the southeast to hulking snowcapped mountains and tundra to the north.

2 California. The nation's third-largest state is a land of incredible geographical diversity, from high peaks and boulder-strewn deserts in the interior to stunning beaches and temperate forests on the coast.

3 Hawaii. This tropical archipelago delights visitors with its sugary-sand beaches, lush canyons and rain forests, thrilling volcanic peaks, and beautiful islands each with a big personality.

4 Oregon. With a magnificent coast of headlands and sea stacks, lush valleys from Portland to the south, and soaring volcanic peaks, the views in Oregon change from point to point but are always stunning.

5 Washington. The Evergreen State comprises pristine coastal and Puget Sound waterways, the snowcapped Cascade Range, and winery-studded arid valleys and hills to the east.

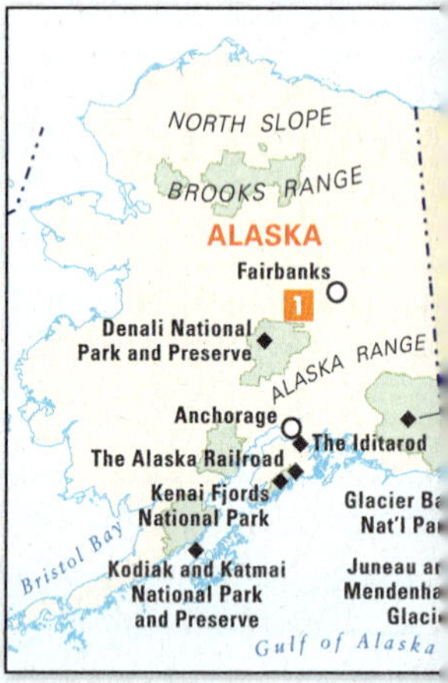

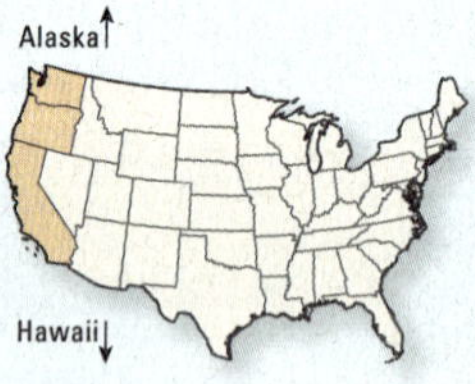

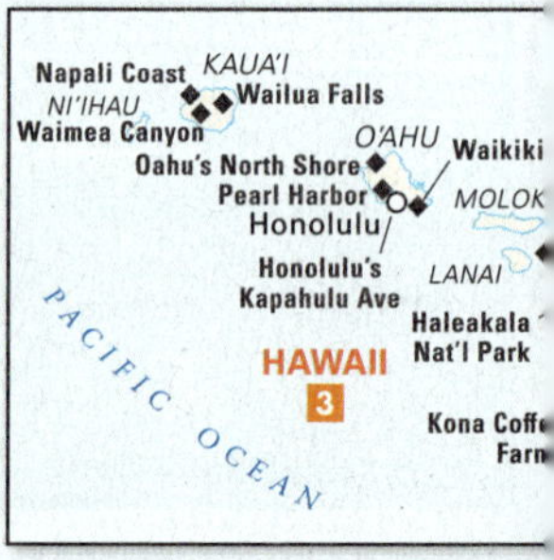

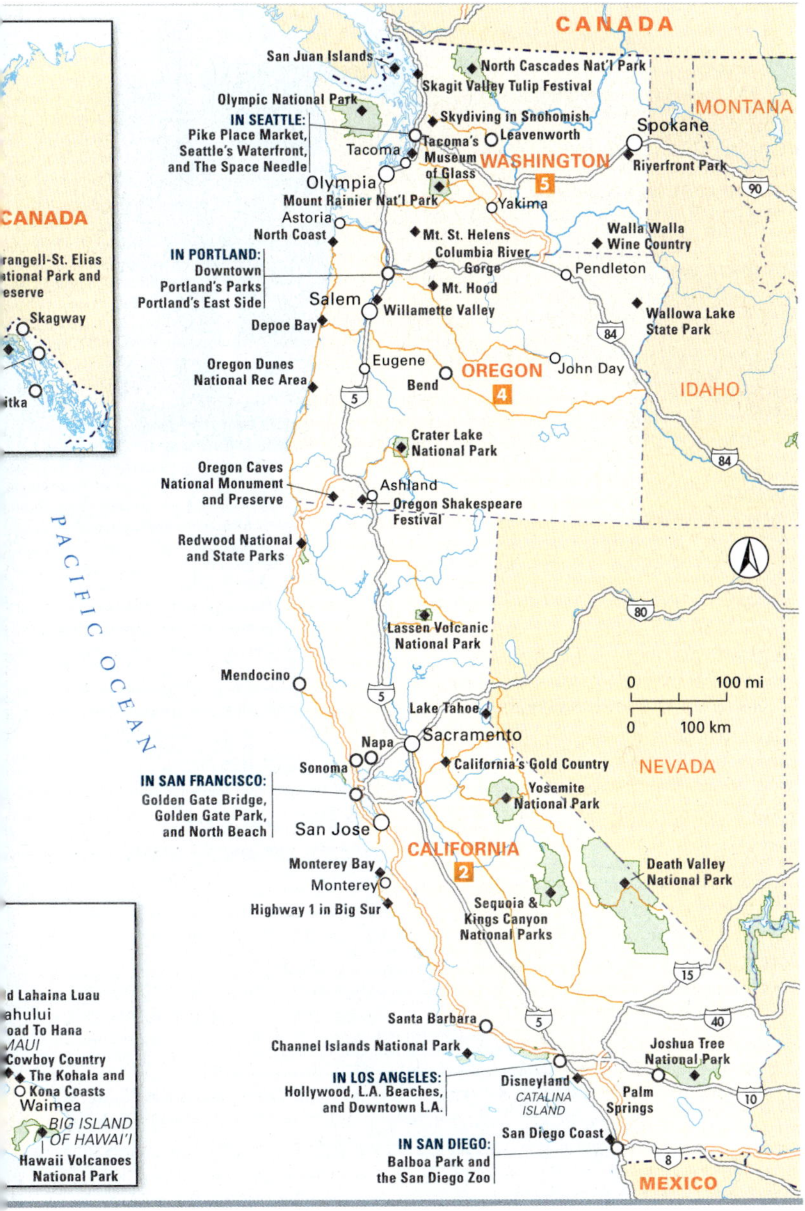
CANADA
San Juan Islands
North Cascades Nat'l Park
Skagit Valley Tulip Festival
Olympic National Park
IN SEATTLE:
Pike Place Market,
Seattle's Waterfront,
and The Space Needle
Skydiving in Snohomish
Tacoma's Museum of Glass
Leavenworth
Tacoma
Olympia
MONTANA
Spokane
WASHINGTON
5
Riverfront Park
90
Mount Rainier Nat'l Park
Yakima
Astoria
North Coast
Mt. St. Helens
Walla Walla Wine Country
IN PORTLAND:
Downtown
Portland's Parks
Portland's East Side
Columbia River Gorge
Pendleton
Mt. Hood
Salem
Willamette Valley
Wallowa Lake State Park
84
Depoe Bay
Oregon Dunes National Rec Area
Eugene
Bend
OREGON
4
John Day
IDAHO
5
Crater Lake National Park
84
Oregon Caves National Monument and Preserve
Ashland
Oregon Shakespeare Festival
PACIFIC OCEAN
Redwood National and State Parks
80
Lassen Volcanic National Park
Mendocino
5
0
100 mi
0
100 km
Lake Tahoe
Napa
Sacramento
Sonoma
California's Gold Country
NEVADA
IN SAN FRANCISCO:
Golden Gate Bridge,
Golden Gate Park,
and North Beach
Yosemite National Park
San Jose
CALIFORNIA
2
Monterey Bay
Monterey
Death Valley National Park
Highway 1 in Big Sur
Sequoia & Kings Canyon National Parks
15
Santa Barbara
5
40
Channel Islands National Park
Joshua Tree National Park
IN LOS ANGELES:
Hollywood, L.A. Beaches,
and Downtown L.A.
Disneyland
CATALINA ISLAND
Palm Springs
10
San Diego Coast
IN SAN DIEGO:
Balboa Park and
the San Diego Zoo
8
MEXICO
CANADA
rangell-St. Elias
ational Park and
eserve
Skagway
itka
d Lahaina Luau
ahului
oad To Hana
MAUI
Cowboy Country
The Kohala and
Kona Coasts
Waimea
BIG ISLAND
OF HAWAI'I
Hawaii Volcanoes
National Park

WHAT TO EAT AND DRINK ON THE WEST COAST AND THE PACIFIC

Napa Valley wine

WINE

Of the more than 250 official AVAs, or American Viticultural Areas, in the United States, about 175 are in California, Oregon, and Washington, which collectively form one of the world's most celebrated wine regions. Top destinations include Santa Barbara, Monterey, Napa, Sonoma, and Mendocino counties in California; the Rogue Valley, Willamette Valley, and Columbia Gorge in Oregon; and Walla Walla, Yakima Valley, and Woodinville in Washington.

SEAFOOD

Halibut, king crab, and salmon are must-eats in Alaska. Washington and Oregon specialize in Dungeness crab, razor clams, albacore, mussels, and oysters. As you venture south along the California coast, watch for local spot prawns, rockfish, spiny lobsters, and squid on menus. And in Hawaii, cubed, raw, marinated ahi is the basis for one of the state's great delicacies, poke, but menus also feature plenty of mahimahi, ono, and blue marlin.

COFFEE

Famous chains like Starbucks, Peet's, Stumptown, and Blue Bottle launched on the West Coast, but it's the smaller cult classics that thrill connoisseurs; try Coava in Portland, Sightglass in San Francisco, and Bird Rock in San Diego. The Kona Coast of Hawaii Island stands out as the one place in the United States famous for *growing* coffee. Roughly 600 coffee farms dot the west side of the island, each producing flavorful beans grown in the rich soil.

ICE CREAM AND SHAVE ICE

The West has gained a reputation for high-quality, often inventive, ice-cream ingredients—from pear–and–blue cheese at Portland's Salt & Straw to orange-cardamom at San Francisco's Bi-Rite. Other beloved shops include Molly Moon in Seattle, Sweet Rose in Santa Monica, and Wild Scoops in Anchorage. When in the Aloha State, you really want to try a dish of shave ice drizzled in Technicolor syrups and topped with mochi balls, azuki beans, and condensed milk.

TACOS
The Mexican influence on California accounts for the tremendous popularity of this delicious street food. For traditional street tacos, try Sonoratown in Downtown Los Angeles; for beer-battered fish tacos, head to Oscar's Mexican Seafood in San Diego; to experience what makes just about every Golden State "best taco" list, check out Nuestro Mexico in Bakersfield.

CRAFT BEER
Portland, San Diego, and Seattle are renowned hubs of innovative craft brewing, as are smaller metropolises like Bend and Yakima (the latter grows about 75% of the nation's hops)—crisp, hoppy IPAs are a regional favorite, as are sour beers that utilize West Coast's bounty of fresh fruit. Heady Scotch ales and aromatic sips brewed with spruce tips are popular in Alaska, while Hawaii incorporates local ingredients like lemongrass, tangerines, and passion fruit.

ASIAN FOOD
Many residents of these five states have strong ties to different parts of Asia and it's apparent in the food. Vibrant international districts thrive in Honolulu, Portland, Seattle, San Francisco, and Los Angeles. Quite a few regional Hawaiian dishes derive from a mix of Asian and European cultures, including the noodle dish saimin, the burger–fried egg dish loco moco, and the Spam-a-licious snack musubi.

Hawaiian shave ice

Baja fish tacos

BAKED GOODS
The history of sourdough is tied to both the Alaska and California gold rushes, when French bakers opened to feed the miners. Modern artisan bakeries excel with more interesting creations, from rich kouign-amann pastries to moist and robust potato bread. Portland and L.A. are famous for doughnuts, while Hawaii is known for malasadas, deep-fried Portuguese doughnuts filled with sweet creams.

WILD GAME
Many animals found in the wild appear on menus in this part of the world. Reindeer are often served in Anchorage at sausage stands and food trucks, while wild boar appears on many menus in Hawaii.

Alaska

Alaska is an outdoors extravaganza, with landscapes that stretch out seemingly to infinity. From the lush rain forests of Southeast to the vast, flat tundra in the North, you can stare in awe at calving glaciers, volcanic valleys, jagged sea cliffs, the northern lights, and more. Here you can kayak to icebergs, fly over the highest peak in North America, stay out all night celebrating the midnight sun, and spot wildlife from bears to belugas. For lovers of nature, few places exhilarate like Alaska.

Capital: Juneau

Population: 733,000

Area: 665,384 square miles

Statehood Date: January 3, 1959

Major Airports: Ted Stevens Anchorage International Airport (ANC); Fairbanks International Airport (FAI); Juneau International Airport (JNU)

Travel and Tourism Information: 🌐 *www.travelalaska.com* 🌐 *www.alaska.org* *www.alaskamagazine.com*

Famous Residents: Elizabeth Peratrovich (Tlingit civil rights activist); Jewel (singer); Irene Bedard (voice actress); Timothy Treadwell (bear enthusiast)

Fun Fact: An incredible 82% of Alaska's communities aren't connected to the road system, including the state capital of Juneau. Instead, residents rely on things like ferries, floatplanes, and seasonal ice roads. There's a reason 1 in 78 Alaskans has a pilot's license.

Denali National Park and Preserve

North America's Highest Mountain

America's third-largest national park is also Alaska's most visited attraction, and for good reason. The 6-million-acre park and preserve offers spectacular mountain views, amazing wildlife (including the "Big Five" of Alaska animals: the moose, grizzly bear, wolf, Dall sheep, and caribou), and unforgettable landscapes. The keystone is Denali itself (aka the Great One), whose peak measures in at 20,310 feet. It's often hidden behind clouds—your odds of viewing it increase the farther you travel along the 92-mile park road. Flightseeing tours are offered from Healy, Talkeetna, and Denali Park; they get you up close to the mountain, and many even include a glacier walk. 🌐 *www.nps.gov/dena*

Don't Miss

Famous for its views of Denali, the **Eielson Visitor Center** is at Mile 66 of the park road. Park rangers lead presentations and hikes from here.

Best Adventure

Don a drysuit and paddle down a park river with **Denali Raft Adventures**. For the past 50 years, this outfitter has guided trips both mild and wild down the glacial Nenana River that passes near the park gates. 🌐 *www.denaliraft.com*

When to Go

Denali is best visited mid-May through mid-September; many services are limited and businesses are closed the rest of the year.

Getting Here and Around

The park headquarters is just off the Parks Highway, the main road between Anchorage and Fairbanks. In summer, you can drive a private car the first 15 miles of the park road; beyond that, park transportation is by bus only.

Juneau and Mendenhall Glacier

Trek Alaska's Most Accessible Glacier

Glaciers are abundant in southeast Alaska, but only a very few are as accessible as Juneau's so-called drive-up glacier, Mendenhall, which extends 12 miles off the massive Juneau Icefield. You can view the glacier from the **Mendenhall Glacier Visitor Center**, which has interactive exhibits, but the most unforgettable way to experience it is by trekking across the glacier's striking blue surface. You can do this by helicopter tour—these trips offer astounding views of the icefield before landing on the ice for your walk. ✉ *6000 Glacier Spur Rd., Juneau, AK*

Don't Miss

Book a guided glacier hike—these roughly 4- to 8-mile adventures include the chance to tramp through the rain forest, venture on the ice, and possibly glimpse inside an electric-blue ice cave.

While You're Here

Get a bird's-eye view of Juneau's historic downtown and the beautiful Gastineau Channel by riding in the **Goldbelt Tram** some 1,800 feet up the side of Mt. Roberts. ✉ *490 S. Franklin St., Juneau, AK* 🌐 *www.goldbelttram.com*

Best Restaurant

Alaskan king crab—a not-to-be-missed Northern delicacy—is the specialty of popular **Tracy's King Crab Shack.** The waterfront wait is entirely worth it. ✉ *432 S. Franklin St., Juneau, AK* 🌐 *www.kingcrabshack.com*

Getting Here and Around

Mendenhall Glacier is a 12-mile drive from downtown Juneau, the only U.S. state capital that can't be reached by road: your options are ferry, cruise ship, or flight.

Kodiak and Katmai National Park and Preserve

Grizzly Bears in the Wild

Some 30,000 grizzly bears inhabit the wilds of Alaska, and two of the best places to see them are on 3,588-square-mile Kodiak Island and—on the mainland 30 miles across Shelikof Strait—Katmai National Park and Preserve. Visitors to Kodiak Island typically view bears by flying out to a remote lodge that also likely offers fishing, kayaking, and other activities, or by visiting Kodiak National Wildlife Refuge—home to some of the biggest bears in the world—with a tour operator. Accessible only by plane, Katmai features a dynamic combination of volcanic activity and coastal brown bears. Rangers offer daylong bus tours of the Valley of 10,000 Smokes, the site of last century's largest volcanic eruption. Float trips, hiking, and kayaking are also popular activities, all with a high chance of spotting bears. 🌐 *www.nps.gov/katm*

Don't Miss

At popular **Brook Falls**, viewing platforms overlook a 6-foot-high cascade where salmon leap to try to make it upstream to spawn while bears stand on the edge of the falls to catch them. The overlooks are a short walk from Brooks Lodge.

Best Lodge

Brooks Lodge is the prime location for overnighting in Katmai, but plan ahead. It's so popular they run a lottery for reservations. 🌐 *www.katmailand.com*

Getting Here and Around

Access Kodiak Island via the Alaska Marine Highway ferry (which makes several stops a week in summer) or by plane. Visitors to Katmai National Park and Preserve typically arrive by floatplane.

Kenai Fjords National Park

Alaska's Most Spectacular Waters

Ribboned with white waterfalls and tufted with deep-green spruce, Kenai Fjords National Park is a coastal parkland incised with sheer, dark, slate cliffs continuously carved by blue tidewater glaciers. Many outfitters offer tours of these pristine waters, and the best ones include a boat cruise around Resurrection Bay, followed by two or three hours of sea kayaking. You'll typically see frolicking sea otters, crowds of Steller sea lions lazing on the rocky shore, a porpoise or two, bald eagles, tens of thousands of seabirds, and hopefully even a humpback whale. 🌐 *www.nps.gov/kefj*

Don't Miss

Exit Glacier is the most accessible of the more than 40 glaciers descending from the national park's 1,100-square-mile Harding Icefield.

While You're Here

One of the best places to see the region's marine wildlife is Seward's **Alaska SeaLife Center,** an aquarium that rehabilitates stranded animals. You'll see fish, seabirds, and marine mammals, including harbor seals and a 2,000-pound sea lion. ✉ *301 Railway Ave., Seward, AK* 🌐 *www.alaskasealife.org*

When to Go

Kenai Fjords is best explored from May through September; in winter, the road to Exit Glacier isn't plowed, and rough seas make it impractical for boating and sea kayaking.

Getting Here and Around

Kenai Fjords National Park and Seward lie at the end of the Seward Highway, a staggeringly scenic 2½-hour drive south of Anchorage.

Anchorage

The Great Wilderness's Big City

By far Alaska's largest and most sophisticated city, Anchorage is situated in a truly spectacular location, with the permanently snow-covered peaks and volcanoes of the Alaska Range to the west of the city and part of the craggy Chugach Range within the eastern edge of the municipality. The Talkeetna and Kenai ranges are visible to the north and south. Two arms of Cook Inlet embrace the town's borders, and on clear days Denali looms on the horizon. Besides its natural beauty and opportunities for outdoor recreation, the city has an ever-growing range of restaurants, shops, and a great brewpub, plus excellent exhibits on Native Alaskan culture.

Don't Miss

It's a short drive from downtown to Alaska's most popularly hiked peak, **Flattop Mountain**, a 3-mile round-trip trek where you'll be treated to astounding views of the Anchorage Bowl, Cook Inlet, and the surrounding Chugach Mountains. Another option, **Tony Knowles Coastal Trail**, is a far flatter and equally popular choice for a stroll.

While You're Here

The **Alaska Native Heritage Center** is an active museum and cultural center featuring traditional homes circling a lake that represent the state's many Alaska Native cultures. Inside, the spacious Gathering Place hosts demonstrations, dances, storytelling, and films. ✉ *8800 Heritage Center Dr., Anchorage, AK* 🌐 *www.alaskanative.net*

Getting Here and Around

Alaska's biggest city is home to the state's largest airport. The People Mover bus connects most major neighborhoods, but the city itself is quite spread out and best explored by car.

Glacier Bay National Park

America's Most Breathtaking Glaciers

Tidewater glaciers in 5,150-square-mile Glacier Bay National Park and Preserve calve icebergs into the sea with loud blasts. Here humpback whales breach, spout, and slap their tails against the water. Coastal brown bears feed on sedge, salmon, and berries, and otters and harbor seals inhabit the rocky shorelines. Bald eagles soar overhead, and mountains in the Fairweather Range come in and out of view. This magical place rewards those who get out on the water—whether it be in a passing cruise ship, a day boat, or a kayak. 🌐 *www.nps.gov/glba*

Don't Miss

Kayak rentals can be arranged through **Glacier Bay Sea Kayaks** in Gustavus. One of the best opportunities to spot wildlife is a guided one-day paddle around Bartlett Cove, which includes a nature walk. 🌐 *www.glacierbayseakayaks.com*

Best Hotel

Glacier Bay Lodge is the only accommodation within the national park. The modern yet rustic lodge with a large porch overlooking the bay blends well into the thick rain forest surrounding it. ✉ *179 Barlett Cove Rd., Gustavus, AK* 🌐 *www.visitglacierbay.com*

Getting Here and Around

A popular way to see the park's most famous glaciers—such as Johns Hopkins and Margerie glaciers—is on a cruise ship. Many major cruise lines include the park on their Alaska itineraries, and park rangers often board the ships to answer questions. But you can also plan a DIY adventure by flying or taking the ferry to Gustavus.

Fairbanks

The Best Northern Lights Viewing in America

At 65 degrees north latitude, Fairbanks is renowned for the aurora borealis (northern lights), the midnight sun, and the most epic sunsets and sunrises. Roughly 245 nights a year, from late August to mid-April, you might experience nature's best light show. It often begins simply, as a pale yellow-green luminous band, but some evenings it can explode and fill the sky with curtains of celestial light that ripple wildly above the northern landscape. Visiting in early summer? You're still in for a different kind of show: Fairbanks experiences midnight sunshine for 70 straight days.

Don't Miss

Chena Hot Springs Resort is a great spot for sky-gazing. Located 60 miles northeast of Fairbanks, it experiences nearly 24 hours of darkness in mid-winter, making it ideal for viewing the aurora. The naturally occurring hot springs are also a welcome relief from air temperatures that reach -50°F. ✉ *17600 Chena Hot Springs Rd., Fairbanks, AK* 🌐 *www.chenahotsprings.com*

While You're Here

Fairbanks is home to a pair of museums: the free **Morris Thompson Cultural and Visitors Center** near Downtown on the Chena River, and the **University of Alaska Museum of the North**, which sits on a bluff overlooking the state's flagship campus.

Getting Here and Around

Fairbanks has one of the state's largest airports, and the Alaska Railroad offers daily service in the summer. The city sits at the junction of the Parks, Steese, and Richardson highways, and a car is ideal for exploring the town and getting to Chena Hot Springs.

Wrangell–St. Elias National Park and Preserve

America's Largest National Park

In a land of many grand and spectacularly beautiful mountains, those in the 13.2-million-acre Wrangell–St. Elias National Park and Preserve (America's largest national park) are perhaps the most spectacular of them all, with 18,009-foot Mt. St. Elias leading the way. This extraordinarily compact cluster of immense peaks also includes volcanoes, such as Mt. Wrangell, one of the largest active volcanoes in the world. The park is a largely undeveloped wilderness that's acclaimed for primitive hiking, mining history, glacier-walking, and fantastic rafting. 🌐 *www.nps.gov/wrst*

Don't Miss

Tramp over ancient ice at the foot of **Root Glacier**, mountain bike the **Nabesna Road**, or take a multiday, guided rafting tour down the Nizina, Chitina, and Copper rivers.

Best Tour Operator

St. Elias Alpine Guides, based in McCarthy, gives introductory mountaineering lessons, leads excursions ranging from half-day paddles to monthlong backpacking trips, and is the only authorized concessionaire that conducts guided tours of historic Kennecott buildings like the 14-story Concentration Mill. 🌐 *www.steliasguides.com*

While You're Here

The abandoned **Kennecott Mine** is one of the national park's most interesting attractions. The towering rust-red structures are as impressive as the mountains they stand against.

Getting Here and Around

The park is located in south-central Alaska, about a 3½-hour drive from Anchorage. Only two roads lead into the park: the Nabesna Road and the more popular McCarthy Road. Both are unpaved.

Sitka

A Cultural Crossroads

Friendly Sitka stands out for its remarkable blend of Alaska Native, Russian, and American history and its dramatic and beautiful open-ocean setting. This is one of the best Inside Passage towns to explore on foot, with St. Michael's Orthodox Cathedral, Sheldon Jackson Museum, Castle Hill, Sitka National Historical Park, and the Alaska Raptor Center topping the must-see list. The area was long home to the Tlingit people, and the 18th-century arrival of the Russians led to back-and-forth battles. Since 1821, both Tlingits and Russians have lived in Sitka and the town has prospered as a center of shipbuilding and commerce.

Don't Miss

A 20-minute walk from downtown, the **Alaska Raptor Center** rehabilitates roughly 200 birds each year. Guests can observe injured eagles relearning survival skills, including flying and catching salmon. ✉ *1000 Raptor Way, Sitka, AK* 🌐 *www.alaskaraptor.org*

Best History Lesson

The 113-acre **Sitka National Historical Park** houses a visitor center spotlighting Tlingit culture, plus a short trail past totem poles through the forest. The Russian Bishop's House near Downtown is also part of the park. ✉ *103 Monastery St., Sitka, AK* 🌐 *www.nps.gov/sitk*

When to Go

May through September is the best time to visit Sitka, when days are longest.

Getting Here and Around

Sitka is a common stop on cruise routes and a regular ferry stop along the Alaska Marine Highway System. Seaplanes connect Sitka to several Alaska cities. The best way to see the town's sights is on foot.

Skagway

Alaska's Most Storied Gold Rush Town

Located at the northern terminus of the Inside Passage, Skagway is an amazingly preserved artifact from North America's biggest, most famous gold rush. Many downtown buildings are part of the **Klondike Gold Rush National Historical Park**, which commemorates the frenzied stampede of 1897. Skagway still bustles in summers as visitors board round-trip trains to White Pass, drive the Klondike Highway into the Yukon Territory, or hike the Chilkoot National Historic Trail, the 33-mile route of the 1897–98 prospectors from Skagway into Canada.

Don't Miss

Travel the gold-rush route aboard the historic **White Pass & Yukon Route** narrow-gauge railroad. The diesel locomotives tow vintage-style viewing cars up steep inclines, hugging the walls of precipitous cliffs with views of craggy peaks, forests, and plummeting waterfalls. 🌐 *www.wpyr.com*

Best Food Truck

Known to attract repeat customers from as far away as Juneau, Thai restaurant **Starfire** earns kudos for its authentic, robustly seasoned Thai cuisine. The food truck operates from the corner of 2nd Avenue and State Street.

When to Go

The White Pass & Yukon Route runs only mid-May to late September, which is when Skagway is nicest.

Getting Here and Around

Most visitors arrive on cruise ships or catch a plane or ferry from Juneau. But Skagway also offers one of the few opportunities in southeast Alaska to arrive by car, by taking the Klondike Highway south from Whitehorse, the capital of Canada's Yukon Territory.

The Alaska Railroad

Take the Scenic Route

Mountains, glaciers, lakes, and streams fill the ever-changing panorama of your 360-degree dome windows on the historic Alaska Railroad, one of the most comfortable and picturesque ways to travel among Alaska's top sites. The railroad runs 470 miles between Seward and Fairbanks with stops in Anchorage, Denali, Talkeetna, and several other interesting stops along the way, and the best way to soak it all in is in a dome car. Popular routes include the Denali Star between Fairbanks and Anchorage with a stop in Denali; the Coastal Classic between Anchorage and Seward; and the Glacier Discovery running round-trip from Anchorage to Whittier and Grandview. The trip from Anchorage to Seward is especially scenic. *www.alaskarailroad.com*

Don't Miss

The railroad ends just short of Resurrection Bay in the seaside town of **Seward**. Here, passengers can continue their journey on kayaks, catamarans, sailboats, glacier tours, and fishing charters, then end the day in the busy bars and restaurants of 4th Avenue.

When to Go

The main season is mid-May to September, but a limited winter service runs once a week between Anchorage and Fairbanks.

Getting Here and Around

The railroad operates from a historic depot near Downtown Anchorage and stops in a number of key towns. Notably, the Hurricane Turn route north of Talkeetna is one the nation's last flag-stop services; off-the-grid Alaskans can stand by the tracks and flag down the passing train like a city bus.

The Iditarod

The Last Great Race

Alaska's most iconic and famous annual race, the Iditarod Trail Sled Dog Race, pulls in spectators (and mushers) from around the world to witness, assist, or even compete in a massive feat of endurance. The race, which runs in March, covers roughly 1,049 snowy, backcountry miles from the official start in Willow (70 miles up the road from Anchorage) to Nome, and usually takes from 8 to 15 days. Many visitors watch the dog teams take off from the ceremonial start in Anchorage, and then travel to Nome to celebrate as teams cross the finish line. 🌐 *www.iditarod.com*

Don't Miss

Iditarod mushers live all over Alaska. Visit a kennel to learn about managing a dog team and hop on the runners of a sled to try dogsledding. Dogsled rides take place year-round; in summer rides on wheels are available.

Best Coffee Break

Pingo is a bakery and chowder house near historic Old St. Joe's church in Nome. Stop in for a midday coffee, cookie, or croissant before watching Iditarod competitors complete their journey. ✉ *308 Bering St., Nome, AK* 🌐 *www.pingobakery-seafoodhouse.com*

When to Go

The Iditarod kicks off in Anchorage each year with a ceremonial start the first Saturday in March.

Getting Here and Around

To watch the ceremonial start of the race, head to 4th Avenue in downtown Anchorage. Not nearly as many spectators make it to Nome for the finish, but there are always a few hundred die-hard fans. Nome is on the Seward Peninsula just 170 miles from Siberia. If you're not planning to mush here, the only way to arrive is by plane.

When in Alaska

GATES OF THE ARCTIC NATIONAL PARK AND PRESERVE

Entirely north of the Arctic Circle, in the center of the Brooks Range, this nearly 8.5-million-acre park and preserve is the size of four Yellowstones and is the northernmost national park in the country. To the north lies a sampling of the Arctic foothills, where pale green tundra frames lovely, albeit buggy, lakes. There are no developed trails or campgrounds in the park, but the fly-in communities of Bettles and Anaktuvuk Pass host charter flights and seasonal ranger stations. 🌐 *www.nps.gov/gaar*

Do This: Many visitors who make it this far north combine their visit to Gates of the Arctic with 1.75-million-acre Kobuk Valley National Park, which is home to three sets of shifting sand dunes, remnants of retreating glaciers from the last ice age. Like most other remote Alaska parks, Kobuk Valley is undeveloped wilderness with no visitor facilities. In nearby Kotzebue, the National Park Service has a visitor center where staff can provide tips for travel into the park. 🌐 *www.nps.gov/kova*

GOLD DREDGE 8

From the comfort of a narrow-gauge railroad, take a two-hour tour of this impressive seasonal mining operation in Fox, about 10 miles north of Fairbanks. Miners demonstrate classic and modern techniques, after which visitors get to try their luck panning for gold. Many historic elements from the old El Dorado Gold Mine have been transported here, so a tour provides a fairly complete look at how Fairbanks got rich. ✉ *1803 Old Steese Hwy. N, Fairbanks, AK* 🌐 *www.golddredge8.com*

Do This: Beer lovers should definitely make the short drive to Silver Gulch for North America's northernmost brewery, Silver Gulch Brewing and Bottling Co. Check out the rotating specialty brews served at the restaurant, alongside hearty brick-oven pizzas, reindeer sausage, and beer-cheese soup. Relax in the beer garden if it's a nice day. ✉ *2195 Old Steese Hwy. N, Fairbanks, AK* 🌐 *www.silvergulch.com*

HOMER

Homer lies at the southwestern end of the Kenai Peninsula at the base of a narrow spit that juts 4½ miles into beautiful Kachemak Bay and offers some of the best fishing in the state. Glaciers and snowcapped mountains form a dramatic backdrop across the water. A commercial fishing and boat harbor at the end of Homer Spit has restaurants, hotels, sea-kayaking companies, art galleries, and numerous fishing outfitters and fishing-gear rental shops. On charter-fishing excursions, which can last from a half-day to several days, halibut, salmon, rockfish, and lingcod are the prize catches. You can also fish for trout, salmon, steelhead, and others in the area's prolific freshwater rivers.

Do This: Homer is home to the Alaska Maritime National Wildlife Refuge, one of the state's 16 U.S. Fish & Wildlife Service refuges. At the outstanding visitor center, naturalists provide an excellent overview to the history and biology of the refuge, which covers some 3½ million acres spread across some 2,500 islands. ✉ *95 Sterling Hwy., Homer, AK* 🌐 *www.fws.gov/refuge/alaska-maritime*

TALKEETNA

Said to be the inspiration for TV's *Northern Exposure,* Talkeetna lies at the end of a spur road near Mile 99 of the Parks Highway and is a must-visit if you're driving between Anchorage and Denali or Fairbanks. Talkeetna has a pebbly shore along the Susitna River with fantastic views of Denali on a clear day. Be sure to visit the West Rib Pub & Grill, on Main Street in the back of Nagley's Store. You're likely to hear tales of the former mayor of Talkeetna, Stubbs, an affable orange cat who served as the town's leader for nearly 20 years before he died in 2017. Grab a seat out back and wash down the French fries and reindeer hot dogs with a local microbrew.

Do This: Adventures in the sky is the name of the game at K2 Aviation, which has a long and esteemed history of Alaska flights. Among your options: get a bird's-eye view of Denali and its neighboring peaks, land on one of many surrounding glaciers, or pass over Kahiltna Base Camp, where ambitious adventurers gear up to summit the Great One. 🌐 *www.flyk2.com*

UNALASKA AND THE ALEUTIAN ISLANDS

Inhabited by Unangax⍰ people and their ancestors for thousands of years, the city of Unalaska overlooks Dutch Harbor and is by far the most popular destination in the Aleutians, a chain of volcanic islands that extends southwest from the Alaska mainland for about 1,200 miles (the westernmost island, Attu Island, is closer to Japan than Anchorage). Dutch Harbor, best known from the Discovery Channel's hit show *Deadliest Catch,* is one of the busiest fishing ports in the world, sometimes processing a billion—yes, billion—pounds of fish and crab each year.

Do This: The Aleutian World War II National Historic Area preserves bits of history from Alaska's role in World War II. The Aleutian Islands saw heavy fighting through much of the war; at its peak, more than 16,000 servicemen were stationed here in the farthest reaches of the United States. The National Park Service operates a seasonal visitor center from a historic World War II building to tell their story. 🌐 *www.nps.gov/aleu*

About Our Writers

J. Besl moved to Anchorage in 2014. He's been traveling the state's islands and outposts since then on a self-imposed and seemingly endless quest to visit all of Alaska's oldest bars and roadhouses. He currently works as a writer for the University of Alaska Anchorage.

Cool Places to Stay

Alyeska Resort. Most rooms in this resort 40 miles southeast of Anchorage have stunning views of the Chugach Mountains and the lush forests surrounding this large and luxurious hotel at the base of Alyeska Ski Resort. Even if you're not here to ski, take the aerial tram to the ski area to enjoy the sweeping vistas and dine at the high-end Seven Glaciers restaurant, or relax at the Nordic spa tucked into the trees. ✉ *1000 Arlberg Ave., Girdwood, AK* 🌐 *www.alyeskaresort.com*

Camp Denali and North Face Lodge. The legendary, family-owned and-operated Camp Denali and North Face Lodge both offer stunning views of Denali and active learning experiences deep within Denali National Park, at Mile 89 on the park road. Reservations require a minimum of three nights. 🌐 *www.campdenali.com*

Inn at Creek Street. This family-run inn offers rooms in seven historic buildings up and down Ketchikan's Creek Street boardwalk. Built on wooden pilings above the tides, these well-appointed accommodations are within easy walking distance to fishing charters, kayak guides, and the city's downtown core. ✉ *133 Stedman St., Ketchikan, AK* 🌐 *www.creekstreet.com*

Ma Johnson's Historical Hotel. A town with about 100 year-round residents, far away from urban comforts, seems an unlikely place to secure an attractive room and a five-star meal, but this fun little 1920s hotel in offbeat McCarthy is the perfect lodging for visits to the surrounding glaciers and mines of Wrangell–St. Elias National Park. ✉ *100 Kennicott Ave., McCarthy, AK* 🌐 *www.majohnsonshotel.com*

Essential Eats

King Crab. Plucked from the Bering Sea and delivered to tables across Alaska, king crabs are a Northern delicacy available in a range of restaurants, from the deluxe mountaintop restaurant Seven Glaciers in Girdwood to the Slammin' Salmon food cart, tucked inside a downtown alley in Sitka.

The Potato. Operating from end-of-the-road McCarthy (population 100), this seasonal restaurant has a big-time following, with Alaskans driving six or more hours for its steaks, salmon, and hand-cut curly fries. ✉ *Main St., McCarthy, AK* 🌐 *www.theroadsidepotatohead.com*

Reindeer Dogs. These umbrella-capped hot dog carts are a sure sign of summer in Anchorage. Look out for vendors any time of day along 4th Avenue. Most carts congregate near the Log Cabin Visitor Information Center at 4th Avenue and F Street.

Thai Food in Fairbanks. Fairbanks is known across Alaska for its Thai food. And like most of urban Alaska, the best restaurants are hiding inside unassuming strip malls. Check out local favorite Lemongrass for fresh seafood and Alaska-grown ingredients. ✉ *388 Old Chena Pump Rd., Fairbanks, AK* 🌐 *www.lemongrassalaska.com*

California

California's endless wonders, from Yosemite National Park to Disneyland, are both natural and man-made. Soul-satisfying wilderness often lies close to urbane civilization. With the iconic Big Sur coast, dramatic Mojave Desert, and majestic Sierra Nevada mountains, sunny California indulges those in search of great surfing, hiking, and more. Superb food, winery visits, and spas make it easy to live the California dream.

Capital: Sacramento

Population: 39,431,263

Area: 163,696 square miles

Statehood Date: September 9, 1850

Major Airports:
Los Angeles International Airport (LAX); San Francisco International Airport (SFO); San Diego International Airport (SAN); Sacramento International Airport (SMF); San Jose International Airport (SJC); John Wayne Airport (SNA); Oakland International Airport (OAK); Ontario International Airport (ONT); Palm Springs International Airport (PSP)

Travel and Tourism Information:
www.visitcalifornia.com

Famous Residents: John Steinbeck (writer); Marilyn Monroe (actress); Ronald Reagan (president); Maya Angelou (poet); Steve Jobs (Apple founder); Leonardo DiCaprio (actor); Snoop Dog (rapper); Serena and Venus Williams (tennis players)

Fun Fact: At a secret location in a remote area of Redwood National Park lives the world's tallest tree, a 379-foot coast redwood larger than the Statue of Liberty.

The Golden Gate Bridge

San Francisco's Iconic Drive

With its simple but powerful Art Deco design, the 1.7-mile suspension span that connects San Francisco to Marin County ranks among the world's most recognizable man-made structures. Drive or bike across to fulfill all your wildest California dreams, setting aside time to explore the many cool sites on both sides. That includes the 1,400-acre **Presidio** park and the wild hills of the Marin Headlands, which has several viewing areas with phenomenal skyline vistas. 🌐 *www.goldengate.org*

Don't Miss

Rent a bike and pedal across the bridge; good bets for picking up wheels include Golden Gate Bridge Bike Rentals and Bay Wheels.

While You're Here

Whether you drive or bike across the bridge, continue into **Sausalito**, with its bougainvillea-covered hillsides and yacht harbor. If you came by two wheels, take the half-hour ferry ride back to San Francisco.

Best Side Trip

A hilly 10-mile bike ride from Sausalito leads to **Muir Woods National Monument**, a 560-acre patch of old-growth redwoods. If you go by car, an advance parking reservation is required. 🌐 *www.nps.gov/muwo*

Good to Know

San Francisco's notoriously fickle weather can be especially—shall we say—exciting around the Golden Gate Bridge. Winds and fog are common, the latter especially on summer mornings. Pack extra layers.

Getting Here and Around

The U.S. 101 freeway crosses the Golden Gate Bridge, connecting San Francisco with Marin County.

Hollywood

The Heart of American Film

The Tinseltown mythology was born in Hollywood, still one of the largest and most vibrant neighborhoods in Los Angeles and the best place to discover the film industry's fascinating heritage. Key sights include the **Hollywood Walk of Fame**, **Grauman's (now TCL) Chinese Theater**, and the **Hollywood Museum**. Although just over the hills in the San Fernando Valley, **Universal Studios Hollywood** has a great amusement park along with a studio tour. Warner Bros. also has some fun backlots, while the venerable Paramount lot offers arguably the best glimpse of Hollywood's Golden Age, with authentic studio tours that provide an engaging look at the industry's long history. Many memorable movies and TV shows were shot here, from *Sunset Boulevard* and *Titanic* to TV's *Star Trek* and *I Love Lucy*.

Don't Miss

With letters 45 feet tall, the city's trademark **Hollywood Sign** can be spotted from miles away. The icon, which originally read "Hollywoodland," was erected in the Hollywood Hills in 1923. For a great view, visit **Griffith Park**, where several trails from the observatory parking lot lead to close-up vantage points.

Best Celebrity Spotting

A-listers are known to frequent **Runyon Canyon**, the city's most famous trail, but the 160-acre park in the middle of Hollywood is also a good place to hike, run, see the Hollywood Sign, and photograph the skyline.

Getting Here and Around

The heart of Hollywood is just off the U.S. 101 freeway, a short drive northwest of downtown; about 8 miles farther northwest, you'll reach the studios in the valley.

Balboa Park and the San Diego Zoo

The Smithsonian of the West

The 1,200-acre Balboa Park is filled with superb museums and cultural institutions. Often referred to as the "Smithsonian of the West," the park also contains a series of botanical gardens, performance spaces, and outdoor playrooms. Enchanting buildings and fountains dating from San Diego's 1915 Panama–California International Exposition are strung along the park's main east–west thoroughfare, El Prado. 🌐 *balboapark.org*

Don't Miss

San Diego's most famous attraction, the 100-acre **San Diego Zoo**, lies at the heart of beautiful Balboa Park. Nearly 4,000 animals of some 800 species roam in hospitable, expertly crafted habitats that replicate natural environments as closely as possible. The Skyfari Aerial Tram, which soars 170 feet above the ground, gives a good overview of the zoo's layout and, on clear days, a panorama of the park, downtown San Diego, the bay, and the ocean. ✉ *2920 Zoo Dr., San Diego, CA* 🌐 *www.sandiegozoo.org*

While You're Here

The **Old Globe** complex, comprising the Sheryl and Harvey White Theatre, the Lowell Davies Festival Theatre, and the Old Globe Theatre, offers some of the finest theatrical productions in Southern California. 🌐 *www.theoldglobe.org*

Getting Here and Around

Balboa Park is in the center of San Diego, just off Interstate 5 and directly north of downtown.

Yosemite National Park

California's Most Celebrated National Park

One of America's earliest-established and most storied national parks, Yosemite is renowned for countless iconic natural features, from the soaring granite monoliths of Half Dome and El Capitan to the shimmering cascades of Yosemite Falls and Bridalveil Fall to its towering sequoias. In fact, by merely standing in Yosemite Valley and turning in a circle, you can see more natural wonders in a minute than you could in a full day pretty much anywhere else. Historic buildings include the **Ahwahnee Hotel**, the **Mountain Room** restaurant, the **Ansel Adams Gallery**, and the **Yosemite Conservation Heritage Center.** 🌐 *www.nps.gov/yose*

Don't Miss

Made up of three powerful cascades, **Yosemite Falls** is the highest combined waterfall in North America and the fifth highest in the world. The water from the top descends a total of 2,425 feet, and when the falls run hard, you can hear them thunder across the valley. A ¼-mile trail leads from the parking lot to the base of the falls. For a more exciting but strenuous adventure, hike the 7.2-mile Upper Yosemite Fall Trail, a 2,700-foot climb to the top.

While You're Here

When it's open (from around late May through October), you can drive stunning **Tioga Road** (Route 120) across the park to the eastern Sierras.

Getting Here and Around

The heart of the park, Yosemite Valley, is 80 miles northeast of Merced via Route 140, and about 200 miles east of San Francisco.

Highway 1 in Big Sur

The Ultimate California Road Trip

One of the country's most spectacular drives, Highway 1 snakes down the coast south from Monterey over historic bridges, atop sheer sea cliffs, beside scenic state parks, and through fabled Big Sur, which instead of a conventional town is a loose string of coast-hugging properties that include some gorgeous boutique resorts. Numerous pullouts along the way offer tremendous views and photo ops. On some of the beaches, huge elephant seals lounge nonchalantly, seemingly oblivious to the attention of rubberneckers.

Don't Miss

Get a look at Big Sur's iconic **McWay Falls** from Highway 1, then hit the trail at **Julia Pfeiffer Burns State Park** or the water at Sand Dollar Beach or Andrew Molera State Park.

While You're Here

One of the most fantastic residences in the country, 115-room **Hearst Castle** sits in solitary splendor, crowning 127 acres of gardens high on a bluff 3 miles from Highway 1 as it curves south from Big Sur. ✉ *750 Hearst Castle Rd., San Simeon, CA* 🌐 *hearstcastle.org*

Best Restaurant

Cliff-top gem **Nepenthe** may just have the best coastal view of any restaurant between San Francisco and Los Angeles. ✉ *48510 Hwy. 1, Big Sur, CA* 🌐 *www.nepenthe.com*

Getting Here and Around

Scenic Highway 1 meanders along much of the state's coastline. The Big Sur stretch is especially dramatic if you drive it north to south, starting on the Monterey Peninsula and continuing about 100 miles to Cambria.

Napa and Sonoma

The Best Wine Regions in America

California has several incredible wine-making regions, all of them quite picturesque, but Napa and Sonoma stand out for their sheer variety of eye-popping landscapes. In Sonoma, walk beneath old-growth redwoods in the Russian River Valley, stroll atop windswept cliffs along the coast, and taste wine with views of sunny, undulating vineyards at more than 400 wineries. In Napa, too, it's easy to join in at famous wineries and rising newcomers off country roads or at trendy in-town tasting rooms.

Don't Miss

Wineries range from traditional grand estates with Old World vibes like **St. Francis Winery** in Santa Rosa, **Francis Ford Coppola Winery** in Sonoma, and **Opus One** in Napa to quirkier cult producers that can feel more personal, such as **Scribe** and **Zialena** in Sonoma and **Harlan Estate** in Napa.

Best Towns

Yountville, Healdsburg, and **St. Helena** have small-town charm as well as luxurious inns, hotels, and spas. In Sonoma County, **Guerneville** is one of the region's most inviting towns.

Best Food

The oft-photographed center of Sonoma's ritziest town, the tree-shaded **Healdsburg Plaza,** is lined on four sides with tony bistros, tasting rooms, and gourmet food shops.

Getting Here and Around

Most travelers to the Wine Country start their trip in San Francisco, about 50 miles away. Getting here takes less than an hour in normal traffic. In Napa Valley, base yourself in Napa, Yountville, or St. Helena. In Sonoma County, you can visit numerous tasting rooms on foot from Sonoma or Healdsburg.

Joshua Tree National Park

Experience the Magical Seuss-esque Trees

Named for the distinctive yucca trees that fill this massive desert park, Joshua Tree teems with fascinating landscapes and life-forms. It's a world-class destination for rock climbing, a mesmerizing landscape for spring wildflower viewing, and a magical destination for stargazing—Los Angeles is just two hours away, but in this park, especially the northern half, light pollution is minimal. 🌐 *www.nps.gov/jotr*

Don't Miss

Park Boulevard curves for nearly 40 miles through the park, offering countless photo ops and easy hikes—highlights include **Hidden Valley**, the **Barker Dam Nature Walk**, **Skull Rock**, and the **Key View** overlook.

Best Park Tour

On the NPS's engaging 90-minute **Keys Ranch Tour**, a guide takes you through the former home of a family that successfully homesteaded here deep in the heart of what is now Joshua Tree for 60 years. In addition to the 150-acre ranch, a workshop, store, and schoolhouse are still standing, and the grounds are strewn with vehicles and mining equipment.

When to Go

You can enjoy this 1,238-square-mile park any time of year, but the summer months—though less crowded—can be extremely hot, with average highs well over 100°F.

Getting Here and Around

Joshua Tree is in southeastern California, less than an hour east of Palm Springs, with entrances off of Interstate 10 and Route 62.

Disneyland

The Original Happiest Place on Earth

While Florida's Disney World may be larger, Disneyland in Anaheim, California, is the original. Opened in 1955 and the only one of the Disney parks to have been overseen by Walt himself, Disneyland has a genuine historic feel, and occupies a unique place in the Disney legend. Expertly run and perfectly maintained, with polite and helpful staff ("cast members" in the Disney lexicon), the park has plenty of signature draws, such as the Matterhorn roller coaster and Mr. Toad's Wild Ride as well as the newer Avengers Campus at the adjoining Disney California Adventure Park. ✉ *Disneyland Dr., Anaheim, CA* 🌐 *disneyland.disney.go.com*

Don't Miss

The park consists of several theme neighborhoods, including Main Street U.S.A., which was inspired by Walt's hometown of Marceline, Missouri; Fantasyland, with Sleeping Beauty castle as the photo-worthy showcase; and Adventureland, a tiny tropical paradise modeled after the lands of Africa, Polynesia, and Arabia.

While You're Here

The sprawling **Disney California Adventure**, adjacent to Disneyland, pays tribute to the Golden State with seven theme areas that re-create vintage architectural styles and embrace hit films including *Cars*, *Toy Story*, and *Guardians of the Galaxy* via engaging attractions.

Getting Here and Around

Disneyland is 30 miles southeast of Los Angeles via Interstate 5.

Redwood National and State Parks

The World's Tallest Trees

Home to the tallest trees in the world, this 172-square-mile tract of old-growth forest and spectacular Northern California coastline is a land of wonders—and not just for the redwoods. You can see herds of mighty Roosevelt elk in the park's prairies, and massive Pacific gray whales off the coast during their spring and fall migrations. You can drive the 8-mile-long, narrow, and mostly unpaved Coastal Drive loop, as well as the 10-mile **Newton B. Drury Scenic Parkway**, a scenic two-lane ribbon of pavement through soaring redwoods, with access to numerous trails. For a simple jaunt, you can hike the **Lady Bird Johnson Grove Nature Loop Trail.** 🌐 *www.nps.gov/redw*

Don't Miss

Visiting **Fern Canyon's** lush, other-worldly surroundings—which appeared in *Jurassic Park 2*—is like visiting another world. Allow an hour to explore the ¼-mile vertical garden. Permits are required May 15 through September 15.

Best Restaurant

Set in a two-story house on a quiet country road near the park, the charming **Larrupin' Cafe** has a romantic garden setting and candle-light. ✉ *1658 Patricks Point Dr., Trinidad, CA* 🌐 *www.larrupincafe.com*

When to Go

This is a great park to explore year-round, but it can be very rainy from October through April.

Getting Here and Around

Redwood stretches for about 50 miles up the coast, along U.S. 101, starting around 40 miles north of Eureka and extending to Crescent City, nearly to the Oregon border.

The San Diego Coast

Quintessential California Beaches

Friendly, laid-back, and blessed with year-round pleasant weather, San Diego is the ultimate West Coast beach destination, with a string of shoreline neighborhoods and villages that go north from downtown and its sheltered bay through lively surfing havens and along the base of dramatic sea cliffs. There's **Mission Beach**, near SeaWorld San Diego, with a bustling boardwalk that's frequented by walkers, cyclists, and people-watchers and is famous for myriad water sports. Farther north, you'll encounter the tony enclave of **La Jolla**, whose famously scenic cove is marked by towering palms that line a lovely promenade, and La Jolla Shores, which is known for its calm waves, sea caves, and underwater canyons. Perhaps most spectacular of all, **Torrey Pines State Beach** offers a long, narrow stretch of pristine beach framed by picturesque sea cliffs.

Don't Miss

The 166-acre **Cabrillo National Monument** sits atop rugged cliffs and shores with outstanding overlooks of both the ocean and downtown San Diego. Highlights of the preserve include the moderately difficult Bayside Trail, the Old Point Loma Lighthouse, and tide pools. ✉ *1800 Cabrillo Memorial Dr., San Diego, CA* 🌐 *www.nps.gov/cabr*

Best Quick Bite

A fun stop for a meal or picnic supplies, **Liberty Public Market** was a former naval training center and is now home to more than 30 vendors offering up a rich assortment of tasty fare. ✉ *2820 Historic Decatur Rd., San Diego, CA* 🌐 *www.libertypublicmarketsd.com*

Getting Here and Around

The city's beachfront parallels Interstate 5, running north from downtown San Diego.

Death Valley National Park

The Driest and Hottest Spot in the U.S.

America's driest and hottest spot has a name that captures the harshness of parts of its landscape, but Death Valley is a surprisingly varied and dynamic park. It's home to the lowest point in North America but also to riotously colorful explosions of greenery and wildflowers in the spring, bizarre boulders that appear to move on their own (scientists are baffled), fascinating ghost towns, and incredible geological features, from sweeping sand dunes to mountain peaks that soar over 11,000 feet. 🌐 *www.nps.gov/deva*

Don't Miss

At 282 feet below sea level, **Badwater** is the lowest spot on land in North America—and also one of the hottest. A wooden platform overlooks a sodium chloride pool, a reminder that the valley floor used to contain a lake, with a trail that continues beyond it.

Best Overlook

From **Dante's View**, a 5,450-foot lookout in the Black Mountains, you can see across most of 160-mile-long Death Valley in the dry desert air.

When to Go

Other than to satisfy your curiosity about how extreme heat feels, Death Valley is best avoided during the fiery months of May through September. Spring and October are still quite warm but enjoy cool nights, and winter sees lovely, temperate days. Make sure to pack plenty of water and know your limits.

Getting Here and Around

Death Valley is in eastern California (a small part of it crosses into Nevada) and is about 100 miles north of Interstate 40. From Las Vegas, NV, it's about a two-hour drive.

Los Angeles Beaches

West Coast's Legendary Beach Culture

When you're in the City of Angels, you must save a day or two to soak up the sunshine of L.A.'s legendary beach culture, from bohemian **Venice** to ultrarich and ultracasual **Malibu.** Santa Monica is popular, and adjacent **Santa Monica State Beach** is wide and sandy. For a memorable view, climb up the stairway over the Pacific Coast Highway (PCH) to Palisades Park at the top of the bluffs. Then stroll a few blocks to downtown's pedestrian-only Third Street Promenade, with its outdoor cafés, street vendors, movie theaters, and rich nightlife.

Don't Miss

Be sure to check out **Santa Monica Pier,** which has appeared in countless movies and is famous for its 1922 Looff Carousel. ✉ *200 Santa Monica Pier, Santa Monica, CA* 🌐 *www.santamonicapier.org*

Best People-Watching

At the **Venice Beach Boardwalk,** the surf and sand are fine, but the main attraction is eyeing the colorful collection of passersby, especially on weekends.

While You're Here

It's a quick hop to the **Getty Center,** which resembles a pristine fortified city of its own. The amazing Richard Meier design, unique gardens, and fascinating European art collections will keep you busy for hours (✉ *1200 Getty Center Dr., Los Angeles, CA* 🌐 *www.getty.edu*). Nearby in Malibu, **Getty Villa** is the center's much older progenitor (✉ *17985 Pacific Coast Hwy., Pacific Palisades, CA*).

Getting Here and Around

Santa Monica and Venice are reached via Interstate 10 and Venice Boulevard. The Getty Center is in Brentwood on L.A.'s west side, just off Interstate 405.

Golden Gate Park

Glorious Urban Green Space

Jogging, cycling, skating, picnicking, going to a museum, checking out a concert, dozing in the sunshine—San Francisco's most alluring green space has enough world-class diversions to keep you busy. A must on sunny days is the 55-acre **San Francisco Botanical Garden** at Strybing Arboretum, with its very own 4-acre redwood grove. The Conservatory of Flowers is a dream for horticulture lovers—don't miss the Aquatic Plants section, where lily pads float and carnivorous plants dine on bugs to the sounds of rushing water. At the **de Young Museum**, many adore the striking copper facade of this impressive repository of American, African, and Oceanic art, and there's no denying the impressive view from its 144-foot tower.

Don't Miss

With its native plant–covered living roof, retractable ceiling, three-story rain forest, gigantic planetarium, living coral reef, and frolicking penguins, the Renzo Piano–designed **California Academy of Sciences** is another of the park's treasures. ✉ *55 Music Concourse Dr., San Francisco, CA* 🌐 *www.calacademy.org*

Best Restaurant

A short walk north of Golden Gate Park, perennially crowded **Burma Superstar** earns kudos for its flavorful, well-prepared Burmese food, including the extraordinary signature tea leaf salad. ✉ *309 Clement St., San Francisco, CA* 🌐 *www.burmasuperstar.com*

Getting Here and Around

Golden Gate Park extends for 3 miles from Haight-Ashbury to the Pacific Ocean and is bisected by Highway 1.

Downtown Los Angeles

Taste the World in Downtown L.A.

With edgy and innovative chefs, access to a bounty of fresh ingredients, and breezy restaurant patios and terraces for miles, Los Angeles has become one of the nation's most deliciously exciting food cities. The best way to experience L.A.'s vast culinary riches is to tour its most dynamic international neighborhoods. Three of the biggies are in the heart of historic downtown: **Chinatown, Little Tokyo,** and **El Pueblo de Los Ángeles.** Fanning out a bit, you can discover the amazing eats and 24/7 energy of **Koreatown,** and smaller but no less vibrant districts like block-long Little Ethiopia, the El Salvador Community Corridor along Vermont Street, Filipinotown, Little Armenia, Thai Town, and several others.

Don't Miss

At **Grand Central Market**, handmade white-corn tamales, warm olive bread, dried figs, and Mexican fruit drinks are just the beginning. This mouth-watering gathering place is the city's largest and most active food market, home to various artisanal vendors representing a veritable United Nations of international cultures. (✉ *17 S. Broadway, Los Angeles, CA* 🌐 *www.grandcentralmarket.com*

Best Museum

The Broad in an intriguing, honey-comb-looking building wiith upward of 2,000 pieces by more than 200 artists, the collection has in-depth representations of the work of such prominent names as Jean Michel Basquiat, Jeff Koons, Cy Twombly, and Kara Walker. ✉ *221 S. Grand Ave., Los Angeles, CA* 🌐 *www.thebroad.org*

Getting Here and Around

The city's most historic food enclaves are in Downtown L.A., at the junction of the 110 and 101 freeways. It's one of the most walkable areas of L.A., and is also served by the subway.

San Francisco's North Beach

SF's Most Charming Hood

One of the older and most storied neighborhoods in a city with plenty of them, North Beach evokes everything from the Barbary Coast days to the no-less-rowdy Beatnik era, which centered on the still vibrant **City Lights Bookstore** (✉ *261 Columbus Ave., San Francisco, CA* 🌐 *citylights.com*), a great place to take in the city's rich literary history. A few blocks away, grassy **Washington Square** is surrounded by pizzerias and gelato shops and is still the social heart of Little Italy and an easy jumping-off point for visiting nearby **Chinatown** (the country's oldest)—a lively 17-block-quadrant always teeming with both locals and visitors.

Don't Miss

Among San Francisco's most distinctive skyline sights, 210-foot **Coit Tower** in nearby Telegraph Hill offers some of the best views in the city. You can ride the elevator to the top—the only thing you have to pay for here—to enjoy panoramas of the Bay and Golden Gate bridges, as well as Alcatraz Island. Surrounding Telegraph Hill is a warren of quirky, photogenic streets, secret gardens, and cypress trees full of wild parrots. ✉ *1 Telegraph Hill Blvd., San Francisco, CA*

While You're Here

Don't miss taking a ride on one of the city's famous cable cars; hilly North Beach is one of the best spots in the city to do so. The **Cable Car Terminus** at Powell and Market Streets is where conductors push the iconic cars on giant turntables.

Getting Here and Around

North Beach is a mile north of downtown's central Union Square and is easily reached by bus or on foot.

Sequoia and Kings Canyon National Parks

Towering Giants and Scenic Drives

You'll feel small—in a good way—walking among some of the world's largest living things in Sequoia's Giant Forest and Kings Canyon's Grant Grove. In these adjoining national parks, including the state's oldest (Sequoia was established in 1890), you can also explore the gleaming limestone formations of Crystal Cave and drive some of the most spectacular scenic roads in the West, including the 30-mile Kings Canyon Scenic Byway, which offers views into a gaping chasm that's deeper than even the Grand Canyon. 🌐 *www.nps.gov/seki*

Don't Miss

One of California's most scenic drives, 46-mile **Generals Highway** connects Sequoia and Kings Canyon and is named after the landmark Grant and Sherman trees that leave so many visitors awestruck. The road passes the turnoff to **Crystal Cave**, the **Giant Forest Museum**, **Lodgepole Village**, and several other key attractions.

Best Hike

At 14,494 feet, **Mt. Whitney** is the highest point in the contiguous United States and the crown jewel of Sequoia National Park's wild eastern side. The most popular route to the summit, the 20-mile round-trip Mt. Whitney Trail can be conquered by very fit and experienced hikers in a single day from May through October, but you must obtain a permit by lottery.

Getting Here and Around

These adjoining parks are about 90 miles east of Fresno via Routes 198 (entering from the south) and 180 (entering from the north).

Palm Springs

CA's Swankiest Desert Town

Sun-kissed and surrounded by dazzling mountain vistas, Palm Springs has been a playground for celebrities, artists, designers, the LGBTQ+ community, and fans of poolside relaxation for decades. Today, this oasis of about 50,000 is embracing its glory days. Owners of resorts, bed-and-breakfasts, and galleries have renovated the city's wealth of gorgeous mid-century modern buildings. Buzzy and festive Palm Canyon Drive is packed with alfresco restaurants, retro-chic design shops, and sceney bars. And just outside downtown, you'll find resorts and boutique hotels that host lively pool parties and house fabulous dining establishments.

Don't Miss

A trip on the **Palm Springs Aerial Tramway** provides a 360-degree view of the desert through the picture windows of rotating cars. The 2½-mile ascent through Chino Canyon, the steepest vertical cable ride in the United States, brings you to an elevation of 8,516 feet. Here you'll find an observation deck, restaurants, and a cocktail lounge. ✉ *1 Tramway Rd., Palm Springs, CA* 🌐 *pstramway.com*

Best Restaurant

Head to the Uptown Design District for the gorgeous interior design and eclectic Pacific Coast dishes made from scratch at **Eight4Nine**. Choose a table on the outdoor patio to soak up the mountain views. ✉ *849 N. Palm Canyon Dr., Palm Springs, CA* 🌐 *www.eight4nine.com*

Getting Here and Around

Palm Springs is 100 miles east of L.A. via Interstate 10 and is also a gateway to Joshua Tree National Park.

Lake Tahoe

North America's Largest Alpine Lake

Whether you swim, sail, or simply rest on its shores, you'll be wowed by the overwhelming beauty of Lake Tahoe, the largest alpine lake in North America. Famous for its cobalt-blue water and surrounding snowcapped peaks that draw skiers, Lake Tahoe straddles the state line between California and Nevada. The border gives this popular Sierra Nevada resort region a split personality: some visitors are intent on low-key sightseeing and outdoor fun, while the rest head to the casinos on the Nevada side. To get a feel for the lake's wealth of offerings, drive the 72-mile road that follows the shore through wooded flatlands and past beaches, climbing to vistas on the rugged southwest side of the lake.

Don't Miss

With a beach, marina, lodgings, and lots of activities, **Zephyr Cove** is a prime spot to book a cruise around the lake. One of the most interesting options is the Thunderbird Lodge Cruise & Tour.

Best Views

Whether you ski or not, you'll appreciate the impressive view of Lake Tahoe from the **Heavenly Gondola**. The eight-passenger cars travel from Heavenly Village 2.4 miles up the mountain. 🌐 *www.theshopsatheavenly.com*

When to Go

Famous for skiing in winter and all kinds of other outdoor fun the rest of the year, Tahoe is always in season, but snowy weather can bring road closures, so check conditions.

Getting Here and Around

Interstate 80 crosses just north of Lake Tahoe en route between San Francisco and Reno.

Monterey Bay

A Seaside Sanctuary

In Monterey Bay, life centers on the ocean. The bay itself is protected by the Monterey Bay National Marine Sanctuary, home to the nation's largest undersea canyon—bigger and deeper than the Grand Canyon. On-the-water activities abound, from whale-watching and kayaking to sailing and surfing. Bay cruises from Monterey and Moss Landing almost always encounter enchanting sea creatures, among them sea otters, sea lions, and porpoises. Quaint, walkable towns and villages such as Carmel-by-the-Sea and Carmel Valley Village lure with smart restaurants and galleries, while sunny Aptos, Capitola, Soquel, and Santa Cruz attract beach lovers with miles of sand and surf.

Don't Miss

The sea even takes center stage indoors at the world-famous **Monterey Bay Aquarium**, the best on the West Coast. The surrounding Cannery Row waterfront, immortalized in John Steinbeck's writing, is a fun place to explore afterward. ✉ *886 Cannery Row, Monterey, CA* 🌐 *www.montereybayaquarium.org*

While You're Here

Primordial nature resides in quiet harmony with palatial estates along **17-Mile Drive**, which winds through an 8,400-acre microcosm of the peninsula's Pebble Beach coastal landscape.

Most Charming Town

Even when its population quadruples with tourists on weekends and in summer, **Carmel-by-the-Sea** retains its identity as a quaint village. Charming upscale bistros, wine tasting rooms, and art galleries line the main commercial lane, Ocean Avenue.

Getting Here and Around

Scenic Highway 1 runs along the Monterey Peninsula between Santa Cruz and Big Sur.

Channel Islands National Park

The Galapagos of North America

Every day, tens of thousands of people gaze out at this mountainous archipelago about 11 miles off the coast from Ventura and Santa Barbara, but relatively few ever set foot on its uninhabited islands, five of which are part of the national park. For nature lovers, however, the trip here—it takes less than an hour via a high-speed cruise from the visitor center in Ventura—is an epic experience, and you may see dolphins, whales, sea lions, and myriad sea birds along the way. Activities on the islands themselves include hiking, primitive camping, and exploring some of the world's largest and deepest sea caves. 🌐 *www.nps.gov/chis*

Don't Miss

On **Santa Cruz Island**, you can hike amid the unspoiled landscape of 2,500-foot mountains and dramatic canyons.

Best Island Tour

Santa Barbara Adventure Company runs kayaking and snorkeling trips at Channel Islands National Park. It's a memorable way to explore the famous sea caves around the Scorpion Anchorage on Santa Cruz Island. 🌐 *www.sbadventureco.com*

While You're Here

Back on the mainland, it's a picturesque 20-mile drive to the **Ojai Valley**, which director Frank Capra used as the idyllic fantasy world of Shangri-La in his 1937 classic film *Lost Horizon*.

Getting Here and Around

Visiting the nautical park off the coast of Santa Barbara, Ventura, and Oxnard takes a little extra effort, as the only way to do it is via a boat excursion. The park's main visitor center in Ventura Harbor is just 3 miles off U.S. 101. ✉ *1901 Spinnaker Dr., Ventura, CA*

Lassen Volcanic National Park

CA's Geothermal Wonders

Boiling springs, steam vents, and mud pots are among the belching and steaming geothermal features that dot the eerie landscapes of this 165-square-mile Northern California park. The most famous feature inside this tract of peaceful forests and alpine meadows is the dormant plug dome, **Lassen Peak**. The volcano erupted dramatically in 1914 with a mudflow that destroyed vegetation for miles, and all sorts of evidence is still visible today, including fumaroles and bubbling hot springs. 🌐 *www.nps.gov/lavo*

Don't Miss

Lassen Peak may be the most popular hike, but don't skip **Bumpass Hell Trail**, a 3-mile round-trip hike with hot springs, mud pots, and steam vents plus a trailhead along the main park road.

While You're Here

An hour west of the park in Redding, **Turtle Bay Exploration Park** offers walking trails, an aquarium, an arboretum and botanical gardens, and the stunning Santiago Calatrava–designed Sundial Bridge, a metal and translucent glass pedestrian walkway spanning a broad bend in the Sacramento River. ✉ *844 Sundial Bridge Dr., Redding, CA* 🌐 *www.turtlebay.org*

When to Go

Summer is prime time for visiting this high-elevation park, but the quieter spring and fall shoulder seasons are still beautiful. In winter, the park is open, but most services as well as much of the park road are closed.

Getting Here and Around

Lassen Volcanic Park's two most prominent entrances are off Route 44 about 50 miles east of Interstate 5 in Redding, and Route 36, about 50 miles east of Red Bluff.

Santa Barbara

An Upscale Town Filled With History

Santa Barbara has long been an oasis for Los Angelenos seeking respite from big-city life. The attractions begin at the ocean and end in the foothills of the Santa Ynez Mountains. Perhaps the biggest hit is Old Mission Santa Barbara, widely referred to as the queen of the 21 missions that were established throughout the state during the late 18th-century Spanish colonial period. But Santa Barbara's downtown, too, is a stunner, considered one of the most architecturally striking on the West Coast. (After a 1925 earthquake demolished many buildings, the city seized a golden opportunity to assume a Spanish Mediterranean style.) Walk along the main drag, State Street, and also along the side streets a couple of blocks in either direction, and you'll discover beautiful buildings, inviting shops, and restaurants.

Don't Miss

Old Mission Santa Barbara is one of the most beautiful and frequently photographed buildings in coastal California. ✉ *2201 Laguna St., Santa Barbara, CA* 🌐 *www.santabarbaramission.org*

Coolest Neighborhood

A formerly industrial neighborhood near the waterfront and train station, the **Funk Zone** has evolved into a hip hangout filled with wine-tasting rooms, arts-and-crafts studios, murals, breweries, distilleries, restaurants, and small shops. 🌐 *www.funkzone.net*

Getting Here and Around

Santa Barbara is on the Central Coast, about a 90-minute drive up U.S. 101 from Los Angeles. The mission is just north of downtown in the city's striking foothills.

California's Gold Country

Relive the Quintessential Gold Rush

When James W. Marshall burst into John Sutter's Mill on January 24, 1848, carrying flecks of gold in his hat, the millwright unleashed the glittering California gold rush with these immortal words: "Boys, I believe I've found a gold mine!" California's coastal communities soon emptied as prospectors flocked to the hills. Today you can relive the era by journeying down the serpentine **Gold Country Highway**, a two-lane route appropriately numbered 49, to find rip-roaring mining camps, significant strike sites like **Empire Mine State Historic Park** in Grass Valley, and fascinating Mother Lode towns that now buzz with indie shops, coffeehouses, and wine bars, among them **Nevada City**, **Placerville**, and **Murphys**.

Don't Miss

Sprawling over three floors, the **California State Railroad Museum** in Old Sacramento celebrates the history of trains from their 19th-century English origins and the building of America's transcontinental railroad (Sacramento was its western terminus) to the glory days of rail travel and the high-speed trains in Europe and Asia today. ✉ *125 I St., Sacramento, CA* 🌐 *www.californiarailroad.museum*

Best Gold Rush Town

Once known as the Queen City of the Northern Mines, **Nevada City** is the most appealing of the northern Mother Lode towns. The iron-shutter brick buildings that line its downtown streets contain antiques shops, galleries, a winery, and more.

Getting Here and Around

Highway 49 stretches for about 180 miles through the heart of Gold Country, from Nevada City and Interstate 80 down through Placerville and Sonora.

Mendocino

Hollywood by the Sea

A flourishing logging town in the late 19th century, Mendocino seduces 21st-century travelers with windswept cliffs, phenomenal Pacific Ocean views, and boomtown-era New England–style architecture. Following the timber industry's mid-20th-century decline, artists and craftspeople began flocking here, and so did Hollywood: Elia Kazan chose Mendocino as a backdrop for his 1955 film adaptation of John Steinbeck's *East of Eden*, starring James Dean, and the town stood in for fictional Cabot Cove, Maine, in the long-running TV series *Murder, She Wrote*. Today, the small downtown area consists almost entirely of distinctive places to eat and shop.

Don't Miss

Something beautiful is always abloom in the marvelous **Mendocino Coast Botanical Gardens.** Along 3½ miles of trails, including pathways with ocean views and overlooks for whale-watching, lie a profusion of flowers. ✉ *18220 Hwy. 1, Fort Bragg, CA* 🌐 *www.gardenbythesea.org*

Best Restaurant

At **Trillium Cafe,** a block from the town's dramatic headlands, the seasonal menu emphasizes local produce and seafood and there's an exceptional list of Mendocino County wines. ✉ *10390 Kasten St., Mendocino, CA* 🌐 *www.trilliummendocino.com*

Getting Here and Around

Every road to Mendocino is windy, narrow, and stunning, whether you get here via beautiful ocean-hugging Highway 1 by driving north from coastal Sonoma County or south from California's redwood forests. It's every bit as beautiful driving here through the acclaimed wine country of Anderson Valley, taking Route 128 from northern Sonoma County.

When in California

ALCATRAZ ISLAND

Thousands of visitors to San Francisco come daily to walk in the footsteps of Alcatraz's notorious criminals (less than 2,000 inmates did time here). The stories of life and death on "the Rock" may sometimes be exaggerated, but it's almost impossible to resist the chance to wander the cell block that tamed the country's toughest gangsters and saw daring escape attempts of tremendous desperation. ✉ *Pier 33, Embarcadero, San Francisco, CA* 🌐 *www.nps.gov/alca*

Do This: The highly recommended audio tour includes observations by guards and prisoners about life in one of America's most notorious penal colonies. After you're back on the mainland, visit the jewel of the Embarcadero: the Ferry Building and its street-level marketplace, erected in 1896.

ANZA-BORREGO DESERT STATE PARK

One of the few parks in the California where you can follow a trail and pitch a tent wherever you like, Anza-Borrego Desert State Park comprises 1,000 square miles of spectacular desert and mountain wilderness. Route 78, which runs north and south through the park, has been designated the Juan Bautista de Anza National Historic Trail, marking portions of the Anza Colonizing Expedition of 1775–76 that went from northern Mexico to the San Francisco Bay area. ✉ *200 Palm Canyon Dr., Borrego Springs, CA* 🌐 *www.parks.ca.gov*

Do This: There are 110 miles of hiking and riding trails that allow you to explore canyons, capture scenic vistas, tiptoe through fields of wildflowers in spring, and possibly see wildlife—the park is home to rare Peninsular bighorn sheep, mountain lions, coyotes, black-tailed jackrabbits, and roadrunners.

CATALINA ISLAND

One of the only inhabited islands off America's West Coast, this 76-square-mile expanse of virtually unspoiled mountains, canyons, coves, and beaches gives visitors a glimpse of what undeveloped Southern California once looked like. A one-hour high-speed ferry from San Pedro, Long Beach, or Dana Point gets you to this rugged place popular for diving, kayaking, hiking, and biking. The nonprofit Catalina Island Conservancy owns nearly 90% of the island and helps preserve the area's natural flora and fauna, including the bald eagle and the Catalina Island fox.

Do This: The main town, Avalon, is a charming, old-fashioned beach community, where yachts and pleasure boats bob in the crescent bay. Wander beyond the main drag and find brightly painted little bungalows fronting the sidewalks. The circular white Casino structure is one of the finest examples of Art Deco architecture anywhere.

GRIFFITH PARK AND OBSERVATORY

Most visitors barely skim the surface of this gorgeous spot in L.A.'s Santa Monica Mountains, but those in the know will tell you there's more to Griffith Observatory than its sweeping views and stunning Greek Revival architecture. To start, this free-to-the-public mountaintop observatory is home to the Samuel Oschin Planetarium, a state-of-the-art theater with an aluminum dome and a Zeiss star projector that plays a number of ticketed shows. For a fantastic view, come and watch the dazzling sunset over the city skyline. ✉ *2800 E. Observatory Rd., Los Angeles, CA* 🌐 *www.griffithobservatory.org*

Do This: One of the country's largest municipal parks, 4,310-acre Griffith Park is a must for nature lovers and the perfect spot for respite from the hustle and bustle of the surrounding urban areas. Bronson Canyon (where the Batcave from the 1960s *Batman* TV series is located) and Crystal Springs are favorite picnic spots. You'll also find the Los Angeles Zoo and the Greek Theater.

HUNTINGTON LIBRARY

If you have time for just one stop in Pasadena, be sure to see this sprawling estate built for railroad tycoon Henry E. Huntington in the early 1900s. The library contains more than 700,000 books and 4 million manuscripts, but be sure to spend time in the Botanical Gardens, too, which include one of the world's largest groups of mature cacti and other succulents. ✉ *1151 Oxford Rd., San Marino, CA* 🌐 *www.huntington.org*

Do This: As seen in the New Year's Day Tournament of Roses Parade, the Norton Simon Museum has one of the finest collections of Western and Asian art on the West Coast. ✉ *411 W. Colorado Blvd., Pasadena, CA* 🌐 *www.nortonsimon.org*

LOS ANGLES COUNTY MUSEUM OF ART

Los Angeles has a truly fabulous museum culture and the ever-changing Los Angeles County Museum of Art (or LACMA, as its widely known) boasts the largest collection of art in the western United States. Highlights include the *Urban Light* sculpture by Chris Burden (an Instagram favorite), *Levitated Mass* by Michael Heizer, and prominent works by Frida Kahlo, Wassily Kandinsky, Henri Matisse, and Claude Monet. ✉ *5905 Wilshire Blvd., Los Angeles, CA* 🌐 *www.lacma.org*

Do This: Not too far from LACMA, the Academy Museum of Motion Pictures sits on the corner of Wilshire and Fairfax, with a giant spherical dome that features a 1,000-seat theater and stunning terrace with views of the Hollywood Hills. Inside, the museum has enlightening exhibitions that delve into the history of cinema with interactive exhibits, videos of award-winning storytellers, multiple theaters, and immersive experiences. ✉ *6067 Wilshire Blvd., Los Angeles, CA* 🌐 *www.academy-museum.org*

PINNACLES NATIONAL PARK

The many draws of this national park 50 miles east of Monterey include 30 miles of hiking trails, hundreds of rock-climbing routes, myriad wildlife species—including once-almost-extinct California condors—and most famous of all, distinctive caves set amid the parks craggy peaks and rocky spires. The caves found at Pinnacles are talus caves, meaning they were formed when huge boulders toppled into narrow canyons. 🌐 *www.nps.gov/pinn*

Do This: The two main cave areas are the Balconies Cave on the west side of the park, and the Bear Gulch Cave on the east side. Both are popular with hikers—flashlights or headlamps are required. The Bear Gulch Cave is home to a large colony of Townsend's big-eared bats, which rest there in winter and raise their young in the late spring and summer.

POINT REYES NATIONAL SEASHORE

One of the Bay Area's most spectacular treasures and the only national seashore on the West Coast, this 71,000-acre park encompasses hiking trails, secluded beaches, dramatic cliffs, and rugged grasslands, as well as Point Reyes itself, a triangular peninsula that juts into the Pacific. In late winter and spring, take the short walk at Chimney Rock, just before the park's oft-photographed lighthouse, to the Elephant Seal Overlook. Even from the cliff, the male seals look enormous as they spar, growling and bloodied, for resident females. 🌐 *www.nps.gov/pore*

Do This: The small gateway town of Point Reyes Station has several noteworthy galleries and boutiques, plus some excellent places to eat. Among these, don't miss the Palace Market, which occupies a former hay barn. Try the buffalo milk soft serve gelato. ✉ *11300 Hwy. 1, Point Reyes Station, CA* 🌐 *www.palacemarket.com*

SAN FRANCISCO'S CASTRO DISTRICT

The social, political, and cultural center of San Francisco's thriving LGBTQ+ community, the Castro stands at the western end of Market Street. This neighborhood is one of the city's liveliest and most welcoming, especially on weekends. It's well worth venturing a few blocks southeast to laze on the lawn at Dolores Park, a two-square-block microcosm of life in the adjacent—and famously eclectic—Mission District.

Do This: With the neighborhood's most famous landmark, the Art Deco–style Castro Theatre, temporarily closed for renovations, stop by another local fixture, the Twin Peaks Tavern instead. The historic gay bar first opened in 1935 and is a fun spot for people-watching with a cocktail in hand. ✉ *401 Castro St., San Francisco, CA*

SANTA CRUZ

In this lively and laid-back beach town known for its free-spirited surfing culture and liberal student vibe, visitors of all ages love to explore the small city's iconic old-fashioned beachfront, which includes a colorful municipal pier that juts out into a beautiful bay and—most famously—the old-fashioned Beach Boardwalk. Its Looff carousel and classic wooden Giant Dipper roller coaster, both dating from the early 1900s, are surrounded by high-tech thrill rides and easygoing kiddie rides with ocean views. ✉ *400 Beach St., Santa Cruz, CA* 🌐 *www.beachboardwalk.com*

Do This: The Santa Cruz Surfing Museum, inside the picturesque Mark Abbott Memorial Lighthouse, chronicles surfing history in one of America's most famous towns for this sport. It overlooks one of California's premier surfing locales, Steamer Lane. ✉ *701 W. Cliff Dr., Santa Cruz, CA*

About Our Writers

Shoshi Parks moved to the Bay Area at the age of nine and hasn't been able to quit the state since. She thinks Northern California is one of the most beautiful places on the planet, and is especially obsessed with the coasts of Sonoma and Mendocino. Shoshi is currently the executive editor at San Francisco-based *7x7 Magazine* and her writing has appeared in *Smithsonian Magazine, Atlas Obscura, Discover Magazine,* and a variety of other outlets.

WINCHESTER MYSTERY HOUSE

Even setting aside claims of haunting and a bizarre layout that includes stairs and doorways that lead to nowhere, this leviathan 160-room mansion with 52 skylights, 17 chimneys, and 6 kitchens ranks among one of the most strangely captivating homes in the country. Built over several decades by the widow of a Winchester firearms magnate, the palatial Queen Anne–style estate on the west side of San Jose is one of the Bay Area's most curious attractions. ✉ *525 S. Winchester Blvd., San Jose, CA* 🌐 *www.winchestermysteryhouse.com*

Do This: On guided tours, you can explore this fascinating home as well as the impressive gardens. (If you're visiting around Halloween, check out one of their nighttime haunted house extravaganzas.) Afterward, visit another amazing—if less idiosyncratic—654-acre estate, Filoli House and Garden, midway between San Jose and San Francisco.

Cool Places to Stay

The Ahwahnee. One of the most famous historic lodges in the U.S. national park system, this landmark hotel is constructed of sugar-pine logs and features Native American design motifs; public spaces are enlivened with Art Deco flourishes, Persian rugs, and elaborate iron- and woodwork. ✉ *1 Ahwahnee Dr., Yosemite Village, CA* 🌐 *www.travelyosemite.com*

Chateau de Vie. With its creeper-covered walls, gardens of lavender and roses, lap pool, and views of a vineyard that produces the inn's own first-rate Cabernet Sauvignon, this lovely five-room retreat in northern Napa Valley captures the elegance and sophistication of a world-class wine country. ✉ *3250 Rte. 128, Calistoga, CA* 🌐 *www.cdvnapavalley.com*

Elk Meadow Cabins. From the porches of these beautifully restored 1,200-square-foot former mill workers' cottages in the heart of Redwood National and State Parks, guests often see Roosevelt elk meandering in the meadows. ✉ *7 Green Valley Camp Rd., Orick, CA* 🌐 *www.elkmeadowcabins.com*

Hotel del Coronado. As much of a draw today as it was when it opened in 1888, the Victorian-style "Hotel Del" is always alive with activity, as guests—including U.S. presidents and celebrities—and tourists marvel at the fanciful architecture and ocean views. ✉ *1500 Orange Ave., San Diego, CA* 🌐 *www.hoteldel.com*

Inn at Death Valley. Built in 1927, this adobe brick–and–stone lodge in one of the park's greenest oases has been extensively renovated and offers Death Valley National Park's most luxurious accommodations, including 22 contemporary one- and two-bedroom casitas. ✉ *Rte. 190, Death Valley, CA* 🌐 *www.oasisatdeathvalley.com*

InterContinental Mark Hopkins San Francisco. The circular redbrick drive of this towering 1926 Nob Hill architectural landmark leads to an opulent lobby, and the legendary rooftop lounge, the Top of the Mark, offers a breathtaking near-360-degree view of San Francisco. ✉ *999 California St., San Francisco, CA* 🌐 *www.ihg.com/intercontinental*

Madonna Inn. From its rococo bathrooms to its pink-on-pink froufrou steak house, the Madonna Inn is a fabulous if incredibly kitschy getaway in the heart of the Central Coast wine country. It features some of the most playfully bizarre theme rooms in the state—the suites with rock-waterfall showers are especially fun. ✉ *100 Madonna Rd., San Luis Obispo, CA* 🌐 *www.madonnainn.com*

Orbit In. The fabulous mid-century modern architectural style of this hip inn on a quiet backstreet dates back to its 1955 opening—nearly flat roofs, wide overhangs, glass everywhere—and the period feel continues inside. ✉ *562 W. Arenas Rd., Palm Springs, CA* 🌐 *www.orbitin.com*

Palihotel. Catering to young and hip budget travelers who crave style over space, this design-centric boutique property on Melrose Avenue is in the heart of Hollywood's best shopping and dining. ✉ *7950 Melrose Ave., Los Angeles, CA* 🌐 *www.palisociety.com*

Queen Mary Hotel. Experience the golden age of transatlantic travel without the seasickness on the permanently docked *Queen Mary*, where a 1936 Art Deco style reigns, from the ship's mahogany paneling to its nickel-plated doors to the majestic Grand Salon. ✉ *1126 Queens Hwy., Long Beach, CA* 🌐 *www.queenmary.com*

Treebones Resort. Perched on a hilltop surrounded by national forest and stunning, unobstructed ocean views, this yurt resort provides a stellar back-to-nature experience along with creature comforts and the funky, tranquil vibe of Big Sur. ✉ *71895 Hwy. 1, South Big Sur, CA* 🌐 *www.treebonesresort.com*

Essential Eats

Animal-Style Fries. One of the most popular menu items on California fast food chain In-N-Out Burger's not-so-secret secret menu, animal-style fries began as a request from some rowdy customers at an outpost in L.A. The French fries, which are topped with melted cheese, grilled onions, and a spread similar to Thousand Island dressing are available on request at any In-N-Out restaurants in the state (281 of them at last count). ✉ *www.in-n-out.com*

Artichokes. Around 70% of the country's artichokes come from Monterey County, located between Big Sur and the Silicon Valley, with the town of Castroville at the heart (get it?) of the state's agricultural operation. There, you'll find crowd-pleasing deep-fried artichokes and cream of artichoke soup along with acquired tastes like artichoke ice cream and cupcakes. Try the Giant Artichoke Restaurant for both or stop by the shop at Pezzini Farms to see what's in stock.

California Burritos. While San Francisco lays claim to the burrito's origin, it's in San Diego that the tortilla-wrapped handheld got an upgrade. Sometime in the 1980s, taquerias began trading out the burrito's typical rice for french fries, creating a regional specialty that's somehow more addictive than the original. Give it a try at Rigoberto's Taco Shop, JV's Mexican Food, or one of dozens of other Southern California spots (they can sometimes be found at taquerias elsewhere in the state, too).

Chez Panisse. Alice Waters's legendary eatery Chez Panisse is known for its locally sourced ingredients, formal prix-fixe menus, and personal service, while its upstairs café offers simpler fare in a more casual setting. Both menus change daily and legions of loyal fans insist that Chez Panisse lives up to its reputation. ✉ *1517 Shattuck Ave., Berkeley, CA* 🌐 *www.chezpanisse.com*

Cioppino. This hearty seafood stew with a tomato-based broth came out of San Francisco's North Beach, where Italian fishermen are said to have once donated portions of their catch to feed those who came back from a day of work empty-handed. It's since become a staple of Northern California seafood, with excellent versions available at Sotto Mare in its neighborhood of origin, as well as at Anchor Oyster Bar in the Castro and Scoma's in Fisherman's Wharf.

Liguria Bakery. The Soracco family has been baking focaccia in San Francisco's North Beach since 1911, and many consider their fresh-from-the-oven bread—which you can order studded with olives, topped with cheese and jalapeños, or pizza-style—the city's best. Arrive before noon: when the focaccia is gone, the bakery closes. ✉ *1700 Stockton St., San Francisco, CA*

San Francisco-Style Garlic Noodles. Chef Helene An invented these savory noodles in the 1970s, combining flavors from her Vietnam homeland with those of her adopted home in San Francisco. The buttery, umami-rich dish at her Outer Sunset restaurant Thanh Long was an instant hit and has since become an icon of the Bay Area's complex cultural food scene. Excellent garlic noodles can be found at many Vietnamese and South Asian restaurants in Northern California (often served with sweet Dungeness crab), but Thanh Long's original recipe is still the one to beat. ✉ *4101 Judah St., San Francisco, CA* 🌐 *www.thanhlongsf.com*

Hawaii

Hawaii overflows with natural beauty. Piercing the surface of the Pacific from the ocean floor, the Hawaiian Islands are garlanded with soft sand beaches and dramatic volcanic cliffs. Long days of sunshine and fairly mild year-round temperatures make this an all-season destination, and the islands' offerings—from urban Honolulu on Oahu to the luxury resorts of Maui to the natural wonders of Kauai and the Big Island—appeal to all kinds of visitors.

Capital: Honolulu

Population: 1,446,146

Area: 6,423 square miles

Statehood Date: August 21, 1959

Major Airports: Daniel K. Inouye International Airport (HNL) on Oahu; Kahului Airport (OGG) on Maui; Ellison Onizuka Kona International Airport at Keahole (KOA) and Hilo International Airport (ITO) on the Big Island; Lihue Airport (LIH) on Kauai

Travel and Tourism Information: *www.gohawaii.com* *www.hawaii.com* *www.hawaiimagazine.com*

Famous Residents: Queen Lili'uokalani (last reigning Hawaiian monarch); Duke Kahanamoku (Olympian and father of modern surfing); Barack Obama (president); Bette Midler (actress and singer); Dwayne "The Rock" Johnson (actor and wrestler); Jason Momoa (actor)

Fun Fact: If you're driving on Oahu's Pali highway, don't take pork with you. That's based on a legend about the volcano goddess Pele and the pig god Kamapua'a. The onetime lovers battled it out until they decided to split the island of Oahu into two sides. Any pork brought from Pele's territory into Kamapua'a's can cause a car to break down.

Waikiki, Oahu

Hawaii's Most Famous Beach

Hawaii's most famous 2-mile stretch of sand has an undeniable appeal, and it's a must when you visit Oahu. Waikiki's beach, capped at one end by the volcanic peak of Diamond Head, is gorgeous. You can visit historic palaces like the Moana Surfrider and the Royal Hawaiian, sip mai tais and nosh on pupu platters at a slew of waterfront restaurants, take surfing lessons or ride in an outrigger canoe, or curl up on a beach blanket with that someone special (and thousands of others) while you enjoy the sunshine and soft ocean breezes. Waikiki is known for its wealth of nightspots, including the majority of Hawaii's LGBTQ+ hangouts.

Don't Miss

The views from **Diamond Head State Monument**, a 760-foot extinct volcano, extend from Honolulu in one direction and Koko Head in the other, and even as far as Maui and Molokai on a clear day. Surfers and windsurfers are scattered like confetti on the cresting waves below. For this awesome view, drive to the crater and hike the ¾-mile trail to the top.

While You're Here

An easy stroll from Waikiki's main drag, **Fort DeRussy Beach Park** is one of the finest beaches on the south side of Oahu. The soft, white sand and gently lapping waves make it a family favorite. 🌐 *www.fortderussyhawaii.com*

When to Go

Waikiki is sunny and beautiful year-round, but is most crowded from mid-December to April.

Getting Here and Around

On the southeastern side of Honolulu, Waikiki is easily reached from everywhere in town.

Hawaii Volcanoes National Park, Big Island

See an Active Volcano

Sprawling over 520 square miles and encompassing Kilauea and Mauna Loa, two of the five volcanoes that formed the Big Island nearly half a million years ago, this fascinating national park is one of the world's best places to see an active volcano. Kilauea, youngest and most rambunctious of the Hawaiian volcanoes, has been flowing lava off and on over the past several decades. More than 150 miles of trail traverse the park's wide expanses of a'a (rough) and pahoehoe (smooth) lava. The best way to explore the summit of Kilauea is to cruise along Crater Rim Drive to Kilauea Overlook, from which you can see all of Kilauea Caldera and Halemaumau Crater, an awesome depression in Kilauea Caldera measuring 3,000 feet across and nearly 300 feet deep. 🌐 *www.nps.gov/havo*

Don't Miss

One of the park's star attractions, the **Thurston Lava Tube** spans 600 feet underground. The massive tube, discovered in 1913, was formed by hot molten lava traveling through the channel. To reach the entrance of the tube, descend a series of stairs surrounded by lush foliage and the sounds of native birds.

Best Drive

The park's coastal region is accessed via **Chain of Craters Road**, which descends 19 miles to sea level. The scenic road winds past ancient craters and modern eruption sites.

When to Go

The island's weather makes this park perfect for a visit any time of year.

Getting Here and Around

The park is on the southeast side of the island, off Route 11, 30 miles from Hilo.

The Road to Hana, Maui

Hawaii's Most Thrilling Drive

The 55-mile Road to Hana is one of Hawaii's most exciting experiences—and arguably one of the most beautiful drives on the planet. It begins in the port town of Kahului and ends in the rustic village of Hana on the island's rain-gouged windward side. Many travelers venture further to Ohe'o Gulch, where you can cool off in basalt-lined pools and waterfalls. You'll want to slow the passage of time to take in foliage-hugged ribbons of road and roadside banana-bread stands, to swim beneath a waterfall, and to absorb the lush Maui tropics in all their glory.

Don't Miss

A black-sand beach fringed with palms, Hana's gorgeous **Wai'anapanapa State Park** will remain in your memory long after your visit. Stairs lead through a tunnel of interlocking Polynesian hau (a native tree) branches to a cave pool. In the other direction, a dramatic 3-mile coastal path continues past sea arches and blowholes all the way to Hana.

Best Restaurant

Hana Farms supplies produce and other items to its stand and restaurant, where you can buy them fresh or incorporated into pizza, banana bread, and more. ✉ *2910 Hana Hwy., Hana, HI* 🌐 *www.hanafarms.com*

Getting Here and Around

Without stops, Route 360 takes a couple of hours, but give yourself at least twice that time to enjoy the diversions along the way. A return option is to follow Route 360 completely around the rugged southeast side of the island. This is a rough road in places, so allow at least three hours, but the stunning scenery as you climb through Maui's Upcountry makes this option very appealing, especially if you break up the trip with an overnight in Hana.

Haleakala National Park, Maui

The Most Beautiful Sunrise

Nowhere else on Earth can you drive from sea level to 10,023 feet in only 38 miles. And what's more shocking: in that short vertical ascent to the summit of the volcano Haleakala you'll journey from lush, tropical foliage to the stark, moonlike basin of the volcano's enormous crater. Established in 1916, Haleakala National Park covers an astonishing 33,222 acres, with the Haleakala Crater as its centerpiece. There's terrific hiking, but the most remarkable activity is viewing the sunrise or—if you're unable to secure a coveted reservation—the similarly stunning sunset. ✉ *Haleakala Hwy., Kula, HI* 🌐 *www.nps.gov/hale*

Don't Miss

The west-facing upper slope of Haleakala is Maui's Upcountry, and this picturesque region is responsible for most of the island's produce. Cowboys still work the fields of the historic 18,000-acre **Ulupalakua Ranch** and the 30,000-acre **Haleakala Ranch**, and the charming town of **Makawao** is famous for its *paniolo* (Hawaiian cowboy) culture.

Best Farm Experience

Surfing Goat Dairy makes more than two dozen kinds of goat cheese, from the plain, creamy variety to more exotic flavors like lilikoi (passion fruit). Several types of farm tours are offered. ✉ *3651 Omaopio Rd., Kula, HI* 🌐 *www.surfinggoatdairy.com*

When to Go

Haleakala can have dramatic weather, and it's typically 30 degrees cooler up there than on the coast. Winter can be especially chilly, so call for the latest conditions before driving up.

Getting Here and Around

The summit of Haleakala is reached via Routes 378, 377, and 37 from the island's largest town, Kahului. The drive takes about 45 minutes.

Old Lahaina Luau, Maui

Immerse Yourself in Hawaiian Culture

Considered the best luau on Maui, Old Lahaina is certainly among the most traditional. Before the show starts, immerse yourself in Hawaiian culture by watching a traditional *imu* (underground oven) being unearthed. Sitting either at a table or on a *lauhala* (mat made of leaves), you feast on such traditional Hawaiian cuisine as pork *laulau* (wrapped with taro sprouts in ti leaves), ahi poke (raw tuna salad), diced *lomilomi* salmon (a traditional Hawaiian side dish), and *haupia* (coconut-milk pudding). Talented performers will charm you with beautiful music, powerful chanting, and a variety of dances, from *kahiko* (the ancient way of communicating with the gods) to *auana* (the modern hula). ✉ *1251 Front St., Lahaina, HI* 🌐 *www.oldlahainaluau.com*

Don't Miss

Lahaina was the capital of Hawaii from 1820 to 1845, when it was one of the world's top whaling ports. Since then, it has become a bustling waterfront town that, while filled with more than a few souvenir sellers, stands out for its historic architecture, excellent art galleries, and pretty harbor. But recent history hasn't been kind: in August 2023, wildfires devastated the area and killed 102 people. While many businesses and attractions have reopened, much rebuilding remains.

When to Go

Old Lahaina Luau takes place daily, and this dry and pretty side of Maui enjoys pleasant weather year-round.

Getting Here and Around

Lahaina is on Maui's northwest coast, off Route 30, just south of the popular Kaanapali resort area.

Pearl Harbor, Oahu

America's Most Poignant WWII Memorial

Just west of Honolulu, the World War II Valor in the Pacific National Monument preserves four different World War II sites at Pearl Harbor, including the USS *Arizona* Memorial. On December 7, 1941, the Japanese bombed Pearl Harbor, bringing the United States into World War II. The starting point for visitors is the **Pearl Harbor Visitor Center**, which contains moving exhibits featuring photographs and personal memorabilia from veterans. This is also where you start your tour of the USS *Arizona* Memorial, which was destroyed by a Japanese bomber and lies precisely where it sank. The USS *Bowfin* claimed to have sunk 44 enemy ships during World War II and now serves as the centerpiece of a museum honoring all submariners. Another key site is the Battleship *Missouri* Memorial, where the Japanese signed their Terms of Surrender after World War II. ✉ *1 Arizona Memorial Pl., Honolulu, HI* 🌐 *www.nps.gov/perl*

Don't Miss

The excellent **Pearl Harbor Aviation Museum** documents the history of aviation in the Pacific during World War II. It's in two hangars that survived the Japanese attack on Pearl Harbor, and there's an add-on tour of the Ford Island Control Tower that offers a panoramic view of the area. ✉ *319 Lexington Blvd., Honolulu, HI* 🌐 *www.pearlharboraviationmuseum.org*

When to Go

Pearl Harbor's memorials are a must-see anytime of year. Many make a point of visiting on the anniversary of the attack, December 7.

Getting Here and Around

Pearl Harbor is 3 miles northwest of the airport in Honolulu.

The Napali Coast, Kauai

The Most Gorgeous Sea Cliffs in the State

After seeing the overwhelming beauty of the Napali Coast, many are at a loss for words. Kauai's northwestern coastline is cut by a series of small valleys, like fault lines, running to the interior, with the resulting cliffs seeming to bend back on themselves like an accordion-folded fan made of green velvet. More than 5 million years old, these sea cliffs rise thousands of feet above the Pacific. There are three ways to experience this coastline—by air, by water, or on foot. A helicopter tour is your best bet if you're strapped for time. Boat tours are great for family fun; and hiking is the most budget-friendly and potentially invigorating option. Hiking just the first 2 miles of the famed 11-mile **Kalalau Trail** offers a tremendous sense of the Napali Coast's grandeur, though non-Hawaii residents now need a day-use reservation or camping permit to access the trail.

Don't Miss

A must-stop on the road to the Napali Coast, **Hanalei** offers a look at old-world Hawaii, including working taro farms, poi making, and evenings of throwing horseshoes at Black Pot Beach Park. The beach and river offer snorkeling, surfing, and kayaking.

Best Sunset Sail

Offering several catamaran sails out of Port Allen, Capt. Andy's Sailing Adventures offers a wonderful four-hour sunset tour that curves up along the Napali Coast. 🌐 *www.napali.com*

Getting Here and Around

The Napali Coast's Kalalau Trail starts at the end of Route 560; the well-marked trailhead is at the west end of Kee Beach. Paid parking passes, day-use reservations, or a park-and-ride shuttle spot are required for non-Hawaii residents.

Wailua Falls, Kauai

Splash Into Fantasy Island

Kauai's mighty Wailua River produces many dramatic waterfalls. Tucked away in the lush landscape near Lihue on the island's East Side, Wailua Falls is an impressive, cascading double-tiered waterfall best known from appearing in the opening sequences of the *Fantasy Island* television series. Kauai has plenty of other noteworthy waterfalls, but this one is especially gorgeous, easy to find, and easy to photograph.

Don't Miss

Opaeka'a Falls is just a short walk away. It plunges hundreds of feet to the pool below and can be easily viewed from scenic overlook **Opaeka'a Falls Lookout**, with ample parking. Fun fact: Opaeka'a means "rolling shrimp," which refers to tasty native crustaceans that were once so abundant they could be seen tumbling in the falls.

Falls On Other Islands

While the Garden Island is home to many beautiful waterfalls, it's not the only place in Hawaii to find them. The Big Island is home to cascades like **Manoa Falls**, and on Molokai, **Olo'upena Falls** is Hawaii's tallest waterfall at more than 3,000 feet.

While You're Here

It's a 40-minute drive to the South Shore from Wailua Falls. But near Poipu lies one of Kauai's other spectacular water features: Spouting Horn. The Old Faithful of Hawaii, this geyser, created from a lava tube under the surface, shoots water as high as 50 feet. Legend has it that it was once guarded by a lizard.

Getting Here and Around

To reach Wailua Falls, drive north from Lihue (Kauai's capital) following Maalo Road in Hanamaulu, then travel uphill for 3 miles.

Waimea Canyon, Kauai

The Grand Canyon of the Pacific

Carved over countless centuries by the Waimea River and the forces of wind and rain, this dramatic gorge on Kauai's southwest side is one of the state's most remarkable sites. Trails wind through the canyon, which is 3,567 feet deep, 2 miles wide, and 10 miles long. Over the eons, the cliff sides have sharply eroded, exposing swatches of colorful soil. The deep red, brown, and green hues are constantly changing in the sun, and frequent rainbows and waterfalls enhance the natural beauty. A favorite hike is the **Awaawapuhi Trail**, with 1,600 feet of elevation gain, that ends with a dramatic descent along a spiny ridge to a perch overlooking the ocean. ✉ *Rte. 550, Waimea, HI* 🌐 *www.dlnr.hawaii.gov*

Don't Miss

Adjacent Koke'e State Park is a 4,345-acre wilderness park, featuring large tracts of native ohia and koa forest, as well as many varieties of native plants.

Best Tour

Kauai Hiking Tours offers a variety of options for hiking in Waimea Canyon, from easy two-hour trail hikes to challenging full-day treks. 🌐 *www.kauaihikingtours.com*

When to Go

The parks' higher elevation can translate to cool and wet weather, especially in winter and on the Koke'e side, but even then it's pleasant.

Getting Here and Around

Waimea Canyon lies at the southwest end of the island, on Route 550, about 11 scenic miles north of the town of Waimea.

Oahu's North Shore

The Best Surfing Beaches in Hawaii

A relaxing respite from Honolulu's hustle and bustle, Oahu's North Shore is about roadside fruit stands and shrimp shacks, pretty parks, sandy shores, and endearing tourist traps. Lush, historic Waimea Valley, the nature reserve at Kaena Point, the plantation town of Kahuku, and the surf meccas of Pupukea, Waimea Bay, and Haleiwa are among the many reasons to visit. Don't miss the sugary sands of **Pupukea Beach Park**, one of the best places in the state to watch world-class surfers.

Don't Miss

As you make your way up the coast from Kaneohe, stop at **Byodo-In Temple**, where a meditation pavilion is set dramatically against the sheer, green cliffs of the Koolau Mountains. Tucked away in the back of the Valley of the Temples cemetery is a replica of the 11th-century Temple at Uji. ✉ *47–200 Kahekili Hwy., Kaneohe, HI* 🌐 *byodo-in.com*

Best Shrimp Truck

If you're looking to try a favorite North Shore treat, you can't go wrong with either of the long-running garlic shrimp establishments, Giovanni's (✉ *66–472 Kamehameha Hwy., Haleiwa, HI* 🌐 *giovannisshrimptruck.com*) or Romy's (✉ *56–1030 Kamehameha Hwy., Kahuku, HI* 🌐 *instagram.com/romys-kahukuprawnsandshrimp*). You may have to wait in a long line, but all is forgiven when you're handed a platter of spicy or garlicky shrimp.

Getting Here and Around

The most enjoyable way to make this trip from Honolulu is via scenic Kamehameha Highway. Allow 90 minutes without stops. If time is short, it's a more direct 45-minute drive taking the H-1 and H-2 and then Kamehameha Highway (Route 99) to Waialua.

Honolulu's Kapahulu Avenue, Oahu

The Best Old-School Hawaiian Food

Snaking northward from Waikiki Beach, Kapahulu Avenue isn't ready for its closeup and it's not at all trendy. But if you're looking to sample Hawaii's most famous treats, this is your go-to place. Sample plate lunches of loco moco or roast pork with gravy and generous sides at the **Rainbow Drive-In**, and ahi tuna poke bowls at **Ono Seafood**. And don't miss **Leonard's Bakery** for guava-filled Portuguese-style malasada doughnuts. At the **Side Street Inn**, you might spy some of Honolulu's most celebrated chefs getting their fix of lilikoi-glazed barbecue ribs.

Don't Miss

Hope you saved room for dessert. Longtime local favorite **Waiola Shave Ice** specializes in the state's cherished frozen treat: powdery shave ice drizzled with syrup in flavors like lychee or haupia (coconut cream), and crowned with toppings like condensed milk and azuki beans. ✉ *3113 Mokihana St., Honolulu, HI* 🌐 *www.waiolashaveice.co*

Best Detour

Diamond Head Market & Grill serves tantalizing, creative Hawaii fare all day long, including a rotation of cream cheese scone flavors. ✉ *3158 Monsarrat Ave., Honolulu, HI* 🌐 *www.diamondheadmarket.com*

When to Go

Many of the restaurants along this strip keep very late hours, making Kapahulu Avenue lively and fun for either an early breakfast or a post-clubbing feast.

Getting Here and Around

Most of the restaurants along Kapahulu are within a safe and easy walk or a short drive from Waikiki hotels.

Kona Coffee Farms, Big Island

Hawaii's Richest Crop

Roughly 650 coffee farms dot the western Kona Coast of Hawaii's Big Island, each producing flavorful coffee grown in the rich, volcanic soil. You can learn about this storied industry at the **Kona Coffee Living History Farm** (✉ *82–6199 Hawai i Belt Rd., Captain Cook, HI* 🌐 *konahistorical.org*), a meticulously preserved farm that includes a 1913 farmhouse surrounded by coffee trees, a Japanese bathhouse, a *kuriba* (coffee-processing mill), and a *hoshidana* (traditional drying platform). Among the excellent coffee plantations open to visitors, **Lions Gate Farms** (✉ *84–5085 Mamalahoa Hwy., Captain Cook, HI* 🌐 *www.coffeeofkona.com*) stands out for its spectacular ocean views. The coffee is processed in a mill that dates from 1942. Tours given by the friendly proprietors proudly show visitors how coffee beans and macadamia nuts are cultivated and harvested.

Don't Miss

Much of the coffee scene is centered on the artsy village of **Holualoa,** which hugs the hillside along the Kona Coast, 3 miles up winding Hualalai Road from Kailua-Kona. Galleries here feature all types of artists—painters, woodworkers, jewelers, and potters.

Best Coffeehouse

A fantastic stop before or after a morning of snorkeling at Kealakekua Bay, the **Coffee Shack** offers amazing views of the Honaunau Coast. ✉ *83–5799 Mamalahoa Hwy., Honaunau-Napoopoo, HI* 🌐 *www.coffeeshack.com*

Getting Here and Around

Kona's coffee country is easily reached via Route 11 just south of Kailua-Kona.

The Kohala and Kona Coasts, Big Island

The Big Island's Sunniest Beaches

The Big Island's—and some of the archipelago's—most beautiful beaches flank the lava-sculpted shores of the Kohala Coast. One of the best spots to explore is **Kealakekua Bay State Historical Park**, an underwater marine reserve with dramatic cliffs that surround super-deep turquoise water chock-full of stunning coral pinnacles and tropical fish. The Captain James Cook Monument, marking where the explorer died, stands at the northern edge of the bay. A gorgeous, expansive stretch of white sand fringed with coco palms, **Anaehoomalu Bay** fronts the Waikoloa Beach Marriott and is a perfect spot for swimming, windsurfing, snorkeling, and diving.

Don't Miss

Pu'ukohola Heiau National Historic Site is one of the most historic sites in all of Hawaii. It was here in 1810, on top of Pu'ukohola (Hill of the Whale), that Kamehameha the Great built the war *heiau*, or temple, that would serve to unify the Hawaiian Islands, ending 500 years of almost continual warring chiefdoms. ✉ *62–3601 Kawaihae Rd., Waimea, HI* 🌐 *www.nps.gov/puhe*

Best Beach Bar

The dining lanai at **Huggo's** overlooks the ocean's edge, and at night you can almost touch the marine life swimming below. Relax with cocktails and feast on fresh local seafood. On the Rocks, right next door, is a popular outdoor bar in the sand. ✉ *75–5828 Kahakai Rd., Kailua-Kona, HI* 🌐 *www.huggos.com*

Getting Here and Around

The Big Island's biggest airport lies smack in the middle of the region, and Routes 19 and 11 hug the coastline.

Hawaii's Cowboy Country, Big Island

Riding, Roping, and Rodeos

A half hour over the mountain from the Kohala Coast, **Waimea** offers a completely different experience than the rest of the Big Island. Lush green pastures dotted with cattle, men riding by on horseback, and signs advertising upcoming rodeos are common sights here in paniolo (cowboy) country. The spaces here are immense; for example, the 130,000-acre **Parker Ranch** is one of the largest privately held cattle ranches in the country. **Paniolo Adventures** offers horseback rides on a working cattle ranch, with spectacular views of three volcanoes and the coastline. 🌐 *www.panioloadventures.com*

Don't Miss

Near the birthplace of King Kamehameha, the charming towns of **Hawi** and **Kapa'au** thrived during the sugar-plantation days. Both are full of lovingly restored vintage buildings housing fun and funky shops and galleries, as well as noteworthy eateries. Another must-see is **Pololu Valley Beach**, which you reach via a 15-minute hike down a steep, rocky trail.

Best Restaurant

The signature restaurant of Peter Merriman, one of the pioneers of Hawaii regional cuisine, **Merriman's** is the home of the original wok-charred ahi. ✉ *65–1227 Opelo Rd., Waimea, HI* 🌐 *www.merrimanshawaii.com*

When to Go

This sunny part of the island is beautiful year-round. Because Waimea is at a higher elevation, it's cooler than the coast, making it a pleasant retreat on hot days.

Getting Here and Around

Waimea is at the northern end of the island, right at the junction of scenic Routes 19 and 190. From here, it's a beautiful, half-hour upcountry drive on Route 250 to Hawi.

When in Hawaii

IAO VALLEY STATE MONUMENT, MAUI

When Mark Twain saw this emerald expanse in the center of West Maui, he dubbed it the "Yosemite of the Pacific." An exaggeration, perhaps, but this is a lovely valley home to the curious Iao Needle, a natural stone pillar that rises some 1,200 feet above the park's junglelike topography. Ascend the stairs up to the Iao Needle for spectacular views of Central Maui. The park has some short strolls on paved paths where you can stop and meditate by the edge of a brook or marvel at the native plants. Mist often rises if it's rainy, which makes being here even more magical. Nonresidents need to make a reservation ahead of time. ✉ *Iao Valley Rd., Wailuku, HI* 🌐 *gostateparks.hawaii.gov/iao-valley*

Do This: A repository of the largest and best collection of Hawaiian artifacts on Maui, Hale Ho'ike'ike at the Bailey House contains objects from the sacred island of Kahoolawe. Erected in 1833 on the outskirts of Iao Valley on the site of the compound of Kahekili (the last ruling chief of Maui), the building was occupied by a family of missionary teachers until 1888. Surrounded by fragrant gardens, the museum contains missionary-period furniture offering a snapshot of the island during his time. ✉ *2375A Main St., Wailuku, HI* 🌐 *www.mauimuseum.org*

KALAUPAPA PENINSULA, MOLOKAI

One of the most remote areas in the Hawaiian Islands, the Kalaupapa Peninsula is a place of stunning natural beauty coupled with a tragic past. It's here on a strip of land hemmed in by the world's tallest sea cliffs that residents of Hawaii who displayed symptoms of Hansen's disease were permanently exiled between 1866 and 1969. A visit to Kalaupapa National Historical Park is a profound, once-in-a-lifetime experience. You must book a tour that arrives by plane to the isolated peninsula that backs up to 2,000-foot cliffs. Tours take you through the settlement and to several historic buildings and an excellent museum. ✉ *189 Kaiulani St., Kalaupapa, HI* 🌐 *www.nps.gov/kala*

Do This: Picnic at the Kalawao overlook, which takes in a breathtaking view of the cerulean ocean, two small islets just offshore, and the stunning northern Molokai sea cliffs.

KECK OBSERVATORY, BIG ISLAND

Located at 13,796 feet on the sometimes snowy summit of Maunakea, the pair of 10-meter optical/infrared telescopes at W.H. Keck Observatory are used by leading astronomers to make astounding discoveries, thanks in part to their location far above the turbulence of the atmosphere. ✉ *65–1120 Mamalahoa Hwy., Kamuela, HI* 🌐 *www.keckobservatory.org*

Do This: Because a four-wheel-drive vehicle is required to go beyond the 9,200-foot Onizuka Visitors Center, the best way to get here is by booking a stargazing tour. Several outfitters—Hawaii Forest and Trail and Mauna Kea Summit Adventures are a couple of excellent ones—offer guided trips, which include dinner, sunsets, and stargazing while you sip cocoa.

MAKENA BEACH STATE PARK, MAUI

Locals successfully fought to turn Makena—one of Hawaii's most breathtaking beaches—into a state park. This southwestern Maui stretch of deep golden sand abutting sparkling aquamarine water is 3,000 feet long and 100 feet wide. It's sometimes referred to as Big Beach, but locals prefer its Hawaiian name, Oneloa. For a dramatic view of the beach, climb Pu'u Olai, the steep cinder cone near the park's first entrance. Continue on to discover Little Beach, which draws one of the more free-spirited crowds of any beach in the state (it's an unofficial clothing-optional area). ✉ *4670 Makena Alanui, Kihei, HI* 🌐 *www.hawaiistateparks.org*

Do This: On your drive back from Makena Beach, you'll find arguably the best place for both oceanfront views and amazing food and drink. Morimoto Maui turns out modern Japanese fare at a scenic spot on the edge of the sleek Andaz Maui at Wailea Resort's lagoon pool. ✉ *3550 Wailea Alanui Dr., Wailea-Makena, HI* 🌐 *www.morimotomaui.com*

MAUI OCEAN CENTER

You'll get a full introduction to the sea life that makes Hawaii special at this aquarium, which focuses on creatures of the Pacific. One highlight is the acrylic tunnel that runs through the 750,000-gallon Open Ocean tank, providing an up-close, underwater look at more than 50 marine species, including sharks and stingrays. ✉ *192 Maalaea Rd., Maalaea, HI* 🌐 *mauioceancenter.com*

Do This: Shallow Reef and Living Reef exhibits enlighten you on the coral ecosystem, and a whale exhibit has interactive learning stations and a dome theater that uses 3D technology to give you a mesmerizing humpback-whale's-eye-view. Cultural exhibits focus on the First Hawaiians and their relationships with the sea and on the history of Kaho'olawe, a neighboring island that can be seen just across the Alalakeiki Channel.

SHANGRI LA MUSEUM OF ISLAMIC ART, CULTURE & DESIGN, OAHU

For more than 50 years, this home was a work in progress as heiress Doris Duke traveled the world, buying art and furnishings and picking up ideas for the estate that includes a Mughal Garden, a Playhouse in the style of a 17th-century Irani pavilion, and water terraces and tropical gardens. At the time of her death in 1993, Duke stipulated that her home just southeast of Diamond Head become a public center for the study of Islamic art. The house is open only by guided tour, through the Honolulu Museum of Art. Book early, as tours fill up very quickly. ✉ *900 S. Beretania St., Honolulu, HI* 🌐 *www.shangrilahawaii.org*

Do This: The excellent Honolulu Museum of Art is housed in a maze of courtyards, cloistered walkways, and quiet, low-ceiling spaces. There's an impressive permanent collection that includes an extensive collection of Hiroshige's ukiyo-e Japanese prints, Italian Renaissance paintings, and American and European art by Monet, van Gogh, and Whistler, among many others. ✉ *900 S. Beretania St., Honolulu, HI* 🌐 *www.honolulumuseum.org*

SNORKELING ON LANAI

Snorkel trips are a great way to see the island of Lanai (the smallest inhabited Hawaiian Island), above and below the surface, and scuba divers can marvel at one of the top cave-dive spots in the Pacific. Snorkeling requires nothing but a snorkel, mask, fins, and good sense. Borrow equipment from your hotel or purchase some in Lanai City if you didn't bring your own.

Do This: The best snorkeling on Lanai is at Hulopo'e Beach and Manele Small Boat Harbor. Hulopo'e, which is an exceptional snorkeling destination, has schools of *manini* that feed on the coral and coat the rocks with flashing silver. You can also easily view *kala* (unicorn fish), *uhu* (parrot fish), and *papio* (small trevally) in all their rainbow colors. Beware of rocks and surging waves. At Manele Harbor, there's a wade-in snorkel spot beyond the break wall. Enter over the rocks, just past the boat ramp. Do not enter if waves are breaking.

Cool Places to Stay

Falls at Reed's Island. Overlooking a dramatic waterfall in the largest and most historic (although also rainiest) town on the Big Island, this tranquil three-bedroom vacation home surrounded by the lush rain forest is one of the region's most romantic accommodations. ✉ *286 Kaiulani St., Hilo, HI* 🌐 *www.reedsisland.com*

Hana-Maui Resort. A destination in itself, this enchantingly remote and luxurious 75-room property at the end of the fabled Road to Hana still delivers the tropical Hawaii of your dreams. For additional peace and privacy, splurge with a stay in the Ocean Bungalows set on sprawling lawns overlooking the rugged coastline. ✉ *5031 Hana Hwy., Hana, HI* 🌐 *www.hanamauiresort.com*

Lava Lava Beach Club. Spend the day swimming at the beach just steps away from your private lanai and fall asleep to the sound of the ocean at one of four artfully decorated cottages on the sandy beach at Anaehoomalu Bay in Kauai. Bonus: Diners clamor for a table at the on-site restaurant, which serves up an eclectic menu of casual fare and fun drinks. ✉ *69–1081 Ku'uali'i Pl., Waikoloa Village, HI* 🌐 *www.lavalavabeachclub.com*

The Royal Hawaiian. There's nothing like the iconic "Pink Palace of the Pacific," which sits on 14 acres of prime Waikiki Beach in Oahu and has held fast to the luxury and grandeur that first defined it in the 1930s, when it became a favorite of the rich and famous. The Mai Tai Bar is Waikiki's most celebrated spot for sunset cocktails. ✉ *2259 Kalakaua Ave., Honolulu, HI* 🌐 *www.royal-hawaiian.com*

Sensei Lanai Four Seasons. Among the five different Four Seasons resorts in Hawaii—and they're all incredible—this adults-only wellness retreat, set among graceful pines at a crisp-aired elevation of 1,600 feet, stands out for its blissful, utterly relaxing spa services, peaceful setting, and personalized service. ✉ *1 Keomoku Hwy., Lanai City, HI* 🌐 *www.fourseasons.com/sensei*

Volcano House. Hawaii's only national park lodge is the ultimate destination if you want to spend the night on the edge of a volcanic crater in Maui. ✉ *1 Crater Rim Dr., Hawaii Volcanoes National Park, HI* 🌐 *www.hawaiivolcanohouse.com*

Waimea Plantation Cottages. Originally built in the early 1900s, these one- to five-bedroom sugar-plantation cottages are tucked among coconut trees along a lovely, walkable stretch of beach on Kauai's sunny West Side. ✉ *9400 Kaumualii Hwy., Waimea, HI* 🌐 *www.coasthotels.com*

About Our Writers

Anna Weaver was born and raised in Kailua, Hawaii. She's proud of her part-Portuguese heritage, as Portuguese immigrants to Hawaii were the ones who introduced both the delicious malassada and the ukulele to the state. She is a writer for a national nonprofit and several freelance projects, including *Fodor's Oahu* guidebook.

Essential Eats

Helena's Hawaiian Food. Prepare to wait for a table at this Honolulu establishment, serving up the best classic Hawaiian food in a simple dining room. Don't skip the Pipikaula (salted, dried, and fried) short ribs. ✉ *1240 N. School St., Honolulu, HI* 🌐 *www.helenashawaiianfood.com*

Kanemitsu's Bakery & Coffee Shop. Laid-back Molokai is perhaps the last island in Hawaii that you'd expect to find a James Beard–nominated restaurant. But here you'll find this quirky 1922 bakery, a veritable institution for morning coffee. During the day, regulars drop by for papaya bread, taro-glazed doughnuts, and cinnamon toast. But the real magic happens at night, every day except Monday, from 7:30 to 10 pm (11 pm on Friday and Saturday), when folks sniff their way down the alley to the hidden bakery window to pick up a loaf of hot bread, an insanely decadent confection that you can order with cream cheese, butter, sugar, cinnamon, and various fruit fillings. You can build your own with a combo of toppings or get "the works." One of these prodigious loaves is enough to share among several friends. ✉ *79 Ala Malama Ave., Kaunakakai, HI*

Mama's Fish House. This iconic, ocean-front Maui restaurant serves only fresh, island fish and many other artfully plated dishes and elegant cocktails concocted from local sources. Don't forget dessert, particularly the restaurant's crown jewel, the Black Pearl, a gorgeous, chocolate and lilikoi mousse in a wafer shell. Reservations are a must. ✉ *799 Poho Pl., Paia, HI* 🌐 *www.mamasfishhouse.com*

Merriman's/Monkeypod/Moku Kitchen. Hawaiian regional cuisine pioneer Peter Merriman has his namesake and renowned Merriman's restaurants on the Big Island, Kauai, Maui, and Oahu, as well as his more casual Monkeypod Kitchen and Moku Kitchen restaurants on Oahu and Maui. All showcase Hawaii's melting pot of cuisines in eye-catching dining rooms. 🌐 *www.merrimanshawaii.com* 🌐 *www.monkeypodkitchen.com* 🌐 *www.mokukitchen.com*

Oregon

Rugged beauty, locavore cuisine, and indie spirit are just some of Oregon's charms. The Pacific Northwest darling is home to hip Portland, whose happening food and arts scenes are anchored by an eco-friendly lifestyle. Smaller cities draw you in, too: you can sample microbrews in Bend, see top-notch theater in Ashland, and explore maritime history in Astoria. Miles of bike paths, hikes up Mt. Hood, and rafting in the Columbia River Gorge thrill outdoor enthusiasts. For pure relaxation, taste award-winning Willamette Valley wines and walk windswept Pacific beaches.

Capital: Salem

Population: 4,272,371

Area: 98,379 square miles

Statehood Date: February 14, 1859

Major Airports: Portland International Airport (PDX); Eugene Airport (EUG); Rogue Valley International-Medford Airport (MFR); Redmond Municipal Airport (RDM).

Travel and Tourism Information:
www.traveloregon.com

Famous Residents: Phil Knight (Nike founder); James Beard (chef); Matt Groening (*The Simpsons* creator); Carrie Brownstein (actress and singer); Elliot Smith (singer); Courtney Love (musician)

Fun Fact: Portland's name was determined by a coin toss. It could have been called Boston.

Downtown Portland's Parks

Lush Urban Spaces

One of the most unusual, and appealing, things about downtown Portland is its easy access to pristine nature. The city center fringes adjoining Forest Park and Washington Park, which contain several noteworthy attractions, including the **Oregon Zoo**, the **World Forestry Center**, and **Hoyt Arboretum.** The most glorious site of all is the **International Rose Test Garden**, which comprises three terraced gardens, where more than 10,000 bushes and some 550 varieties of roses flourish, peaking in June and July and again in September. Just a short stroll away, you can visit the serene **Portland Japanese Garden**, which unfolds over 12½ stunning acres. 🌐 *www.explorewashingtonpark.org*

Don't Miss

One of the nation's largest urban wildernesses, 5,157-acre **Forest Park** has more than 50 species of birds and mammals and more than 80 miles of trails through stands of Douglas fir, hemlock, and cedar. The 30-mile Wildwood Trail extends into adjoining Washington Park and to Pittock Mansion, with superb views of the skyline, rivers, and Mt. Hood and Mt. St. Helens.

While You're Here

A local legend, and rightfully so, **Powell's City of Books** is the largest independent bookstore in the world, with more than 1½ million new and used books along with a good selection of locally made gifts and goodies. ✉ *1005 W. Burnside St., Portland, OR* 🌐 *www.powells.com*

Getting Here and Around

You can reach Washington Park with a pleasant uphill stroll from downtown, by taking Bus 63, or via the Red or Blue Lines of the MAX light rail train.

Portland's East Side

A Foodie Haven

To fully experience Oregon's largest city, you need to bike, stroll, and eat your way through its most lively and distinctive neighborhoods where you'll find the city's world-renowned food scene and a vast bounty of cool shops and galleries. A must-visit is the **Alberta Arts District**, an eclectic neighborhood anchored by the shops and restaurants on Northeast Alberta Street. For the best people-watching, visit during a Last Thursday (of the month) art walk. Nearby are the similarly alluring North Mississippi and North Williams corridors, which buzz with sceney brewpubs, collectives, music venues, and an excellent food-cart pod, **Mississippi Marketplace.** Farther south, you'll find pockets of trendy food and retail in the Central East Side and Hawthorne.

Don't Miss

A playground on top of a volcano cinder cone? You'll find it in the East Side's most magical swatch of greenery, 190-acre **Mt. Tabor Park.** Picnic tables and sports make it popular for outdoor recreation, but plenty of quiet, shaded trails and wide-open grassy lawns with panoramic views of the Downtown skyline appeal to sunbathers, hikers, and nature lovers. 🌐 *www.portland.gov/parks/mt-tabor-park*

Best Food Carts

In a city famous for its distinctive food carts, **Hawthorne Asylum** is a standout, with almost two-dozen food carts representing cuisine from around the world, plus a central dining area with a firepit. ✉ *1080 S.E. Madison St., Portland, OR* 🌐 *www.instagram.com/hawthorne_asylum*

Getting Here and Around

These walkable East Side districts are easy to get to by bus or car, and it's usually easy to find street parking nearby.

The Columbia River Gorge

Drive the Pacific Northwest's Most Picturesque Gorge

Completed in 1922, the Historic Columbia River Highway is the first planned scenic road in the country built expressly for automotive sightseers. Serpentine U.S. 30 climbs to wooded bluffs, passes half a dozen waterfalls, and provides access to hiking trails leading to still more falls and gorgeous overlooks. Technically, it extends the entire 74-mile length of the beautiful Columbia Gorge, but much of that is along the modern interstate. It's the 22-mile western segment that's the real draw.

Don't Miss

The most famous attraction here is **Multnomah Falls**, a 620-foot-high double-decker torrent, the second-highest year-round waterfall in the nation. Historic Multnomah Falls Lodge overlooks the cataract and contains a popular restaurant famous for its Sunday champagne brunches.

Best View

A two-tier octagonal structure perched on the edge of 730-foot-high Crown Point cliff, **Vista House** offers unparalleled 30-mile views up and down the gorge. ✉ *40700 Historic Columbia River Hwy., Corbett, OR* 🌐 *vistahouse.com*

Best Brewery

On the Columbia River, in the lively and picturesque town of Hood River, **Pfriem Family Brewers** is all about the marriage of Belgium's brewing traditions and Oregon's distinctive, often hoppy, styles. ✉ *707 Portway Ave., Hood River, OR* 🌐 *www.pfriem-beer.com*

Getting Here and Around

The historic highway is accessed from the eastern edge of metro Portland as well as Interstate 84, the more direct path through the gorge.

Mt. Hood

Oregon's Tallest Peak

Technically an active volcano that's had very minor, lava-free eruptive events as recently as the mid-1800s, this 11,250-foot mountain is known for the thrilling challenge it poses to climbers and for the dozen glaciers and snowfields that make skiing possible nearly year-round. A few small resort villages form a semicircle around the north side of the mountain, offering après-ski bars and rustic lodgings, the most famous and scenic being Timberline Lodge. Black bears, elk, and the occasional cougar share the space with humans who come to hike, camp, and fish in this quintessentially Pacific Northwest wild ecosystem.

Don't Miss

Great fun after a day of hiking or skiing, the **Timberline Lodge** 's inviting restaurant has views of neighboring mountains. Or its atmospheric Ram's Head Bar overlooks a soaring 80-foot central fireplace and is popular for fondue and cocktails. ✉ *27500 E. Timberline Rd., Government Camp, OR* 🌐 *www.timberlinelodge.com*

Best Skiing and Snowboarding

The longest ski season in North America unfolds at Timberline Lodge & Ski Area, where the U.S. ski team conducts summer training. Thanks to the omnipresent Palmer Snowfield, it's the closest thing to a year-round ski area in the Lower 48.

When to Go

There can be snow on the ground outside Timberline Lodge even on the hottest summer days, and in winter, massive drifts of snow sometimes cover the building's entire first floor.

Getting Here and Around

Mt. Hood is a 90-minute drive east of Portland via U.S. 26.

Crater Lake National Park

America's Deepest Lake

Whether you drive, bike, or hike around all or part of the rim, book a cruise on the surface of the water, or swim in a designated area, you're sure to be entranced by this extraordinarily deep-blue and clear lake inside a massive volcanic caldera that formed about 7,000 years ago, when Mt. Mazama blew its top. The park is also famed for its pitch-black night skies. It's an easy 33-mile drive around the lake, with numerous pullouts and trailheads. ⊕ *www.nps.gov/crla*

Don't Miss

At the regal log-and-stone **Crater Lake Lodge**, the lobby serves as a warm, welcoming gathering place where you can play games, socialize with a cocktail, or gaze out of the many windows to view spectacular sunrises and sunsets by a crackling fire. ✉ *570 Rim Village Dr., Crater Lake, OR* ⊕ *explorecraterlake.com*

Best Tour

From July through September, **Crater Lake Trolley** offers tours aboard an enclosed "trolley" bus, driving the 33-mile Rim Drive—which encircles the lake—in around two hours, (including five to seven stops along the way to take photos. Trolleys depart and return from the Crater Lake Visitor Center and are wheelchair accessible. ⊕ *www.craterlaketrolley.net*

When to Go

The park's high season is July and August. From mid-October well into June, nearly the entire park closes due to heavy snowfall, but you can still get to Rim Village, as the South Entrance road is kept open.

Getting Here and Around

The year-round southern entrance to the park is off Route 62, 65 miles east of Medford and 44 miles north of Klamath Falls.

The Willamette Valley

America's Acclaimed Pinot Noir Wine Region

The Willamette (pronounced wil- *lam*-it) Valley is a wine lover's Shangri-La, particularly in the northern Yamhill and Washington counties between Interstate 5 and the Oregon Coast, a region that is not only carpeted with vineyards but abounds with small hotels and inns, romantic restaurants, and casual wine bars. The valley divides two mountain ranges (the Cascade and Coast), and contains more than 500 wineries, the majority specializing in earthy, elegant Burgundy-style Pinot Noir, although white grapes like Pinot Gris, Riesling, and Chardonnay also thrive in this cool climate. You'll find particularly prolific concentrations of wineries and tasting rooms in the charming towns of **Newberg, Dundee, Carlton,** and **McMinnville.** 🌐 *www.willamettewines.com*

Don't Miss

The Yamhill County seat, **McMinnville** lies in the center of Oregon's wine industry. The town's leafy and historic downtown area has a few shops and a growing number of tasting rooms set inside well-maintained 1890s–1920s buildings.

Best Restaurant

Enjoy hearty helpings of new Northwest fare at **Hayward Restaurant** in Carlton. ✉ *209 N Kutch St., Carlton, OR* 🌐 *www.haywardrestaurant.com*

Getting Here and Around

You'll need a car to get around the Willamette Valley. While self-driving is the easiest option if you have a designated driver, those wanting to imbibe are better off joining a tour. A Great Oregon Wine Tour is a long-standing and well-reputed choice and offers service from within the valley as well as day trips from Portland and select parts of the Coast. 🌐 *agreatoregonwinetour.com*

Bend

Oregon's Best Beer Town

A fast-growing former logging hub that's become one of the West's top recreational playgrounds, the largest city in central Oregon has several things going for it, including what may be the most impressive craft-beer scene in the Pacific Northwest. And what better way to unwind after a day of skiing sunny **Mt. Bachelor**, mountain biking around **Newberry National Volcanic Monument**, rafting on the **Deschutes River**, or climbing in **Smith Rock State Park**, than to hoist a mug of crisp IPA or velvety stout on a brewpub patio? For a list of options, download the **Bend Ale Trail** app or pick up a physical passport from the Bend Visitor Center. Once you've visited all the locations in one territory, drop by the visitor center to receive the prize: a 4-ounce taster cup specific to the territory. Visit all seven territories to collect glasses and get a taster tray to display them. 🌐 *bendaletrail.com*

Don't Miss

With so many notable options, it's hard to decide where to sip. Deschutes, 10 Barrel, Boneyard, and Worthy Brewing are all excellent choices. But perhaps the most interesting spot is **Crux Fermentation Project**, an experimental brewery with an ever-changing variety of pale ales and other craft brews. On-site food carts and a patio add to the fun. ✉ *50 S.W. Division St., Bend, OR* 🌐 *www.cruxfermentation.com*

Best Restaurant

Wild Rose serves delicious Northern Thai food, relying heavily on local ingredients when possible. ✉ *150 N.W. Oregon Ave., Bend, OR* 🌐 *www.wildrosethai.com*

Getting Here and Around

Downtown Bend is at the junction of U.S. 97 and U.S. 20.

The North Coast

Oregon's Most Stunning Beaches

From wide expanses of sand dotted with beach chairs to surf-shape cliffs, Oregon's 362 miles of public coastline is the backdrop for thrills, serenity, rejuvenation, and romance. The pristine sections along the north coast, from Cannon Beach to Pacific City, are especially stunning. In the shadow of glorious 235-foot-tall **Haystack Rock,** family-friendly **Cannon Beach** is wide, flat, and perfect for exploring tide pools and taking romantic walks in the sea mist. Each June the town's sand-castle contest draws thousands of visitors. Nearby **Ecola State Park** is the place to spot whales during the twice-yearly migrations.

Don't Miss

The **Three Capes Loop,** an enchanting 35-mile byway off U.S. 101, winds along the coast between Tillamook (take a tour and grab a dish of marionberry ice cream at the festive Tillamook Creamery) and Pacific City, passing three headlands: Cape Meares, Cape Lookout, and Cape Kiwanda.

Best Hike

At **Oswald West State Park,** hike a half-mile trail to dramatic Short Sand Beach, a spectacular beach with caves and tidal pools that's famous for surfing. If you wish, continue with the arduous 5½-mile trek to the 1,680-foot summit of Neahkahnie Mountain for dazzling views south for many miles toward the surf, sand, and mountains.

When to Go

Summer is high season and generally sunniest, but it's gorgeous here year-round, and storm-watching in winter is a highly popular pastime.

Getting Here and Around

It's about a 90-minute drive from Portland via U.S. 26 to the coast, which you can tour via stunning and rugged U.S. 101.

Oregon Dunes National Recreation Area

The Continent's Biggest and Wildest Sandbox

Along a 40-mile stretch of breathtaking, windswept coastline between Florence and Coos Bay, the largest expanse of coastal sand dunes in North America draws more than 1½ million visitors annually. For those who just want to swim, relax, hike, and marvel at the amazing expanse of dunes against the ocean, there are spaces off-limits to motorized vehicles. About 25 miles south, there's also **Bandon Dunes Golf Resort**, one of the most vaunted links courses in America. But the area also contains some of the best ATV riding around. **Honeyman Memorial State Park**, 515 acres within the recreation area, is a base camp for dune-buggy enthusiasts, mountain bikers, and more. ✉ *855 U.S. 101, Reedsport, OR* 🌐 *www.fs.usda.gov/siuslaw*

Don't Miss

The small but utterly enchanting town of **Yachats** (pronounced *yah*-hots) lies at the mouth of the Yachats River, not far north of Oregon Dunes. Its rocky shoreline includes the highest vehicle-accessible lookout on the Oregon Coast, **Cape Perpetua**, which towers 800 feet above the rocky shoreline.

Best Lighthouse

Some of the highest sand dunes surround **Umpqua Lighthouse**, a 65-foot tower near the small town of Reedsport. The Douglas County Coastal Visitors Center adjacent to the lighthouse can arrange tours.

Getting Here and Around

The dunes are located on the central Oregon coast. U.S. 101 connects all of the Oregon coast with roads that lead into the state's interior.

Depoe Bay

The West Coast's Best Whale-Watching

On Oregon's central coast, small but lively Depoe Bay is the whale-watching capital of the West Coast. With a narrow channel and deep water, its harbor is one of the smallest and most protected on the coast, making the charming beach town the place to spot massive whales migrating close to the shore. Get oriented at the small but excellent **Whale, Sealife, & Shark Museum**, whose marine biologist owner also operates the excellent Whale Research EcoExcursions tour company. The town's **Whale Watching Center**, run by the Oregon State Parks Department, is another valuable resource. Its observation deck offers fantastic views—you might see grays, humpbacks, and orcas along with a wide variety of seabirds and other sea mammals.

Don't Miss

In nearby Newport, the 4½-acre **Oregon Coast Aquarium** brings visitors face-to-face with the creatures living in offshore and near-shore Pacific marine habitats: frolicking sea otters, colorful puffins, pulsating jellyfish, and even a several-hundred-pound octopus. ✉ *2820 S.E. Ferry Slip Rd., Newport, OR* 🌐 *aquarium.org*

When to Go

You might spy resident gray whales off the Oregon Coast at any time of the year, but the winter (December) and spring (late March) migrations are the best periods for seeing other species.

Getting Here and Around

Scenic U.S. 101 hugs the central Oregon shoreline.

Oregon Shakespeare Festival

The Granddaddy of Shakespeare Festivals

From mid-February to early November, more than 100,000 Bard-loving fans descend on the sunny and picturesque mountain town of Ashland for some of the finest Shakespearean productions you're likely to see outside of London—plus works by both classic (Ibsen, O'Neill) and contemporary playwrights, including occasional world premieres. Eleven plays are staged in repertory in three venues, the most famous of which is an atmospheric re-creation of the Fortune Theatre in London. The festival, which dates to 1935, generally operates close to capacity, so it's important to book ahead. 🌐 *www.osfashland.org*

Don't Miss

Ashland is also a good gateway to the Rogue Valley wine country. **Weisinger Family Winery** is a long-established winemaker occupying a leafy hilltop and offering seating on a terrace with grand vistas of the surrounding mountains. ✉ *3150 Siskiyou Blvd., Ashland, OR* 🌐 *weisingers.com*

Best Pretheater Stroll

The festival theaters overlook **Lithia Park**, a 93-acre jewel filled with picnickers, joggers, dog walkers, and theatergoers.

When to Go

The Shakespeare Festival lasts from mid-February through mid-November, but Ashland is sunny and lovely all year round, popular for its hiking, winery-hopping, and great selection of restaurants and upscale inns.

Getting Here and Around

Ashland is the last town in Oregon on Interstate 5 before you reach the California border, and downtown and the theater complex are perfect for strolling.

Oregon Caves National Monument and Preserve

A Journey to the Center of the Earth

Marble caves, large calcite formations, and huge underground rooms shape a rare adventure in geology found in this massive cave network with around 15,000 feet of passages. The only way to see it for yourself is by joining a moderately strenuous ranger-led tour, which will take you through narrow passageways, twisting turns, and more than 500 stairs over the course of 90 minutes. If that's too daunting, you can still get a feel for the caves by visiting Watson's Grotto, the first room of the cave, around 75 feet from the entrance. ✉ *19000 Caves Hwy., Cave Junction, OR* 🌐 *www.nps.gov/orca*

Don't Miss

The preserve is an officially designated International Dark Sky Park due to its light-pollution-free skies that are ideal for gazing up at the Milky Way. For some of the best views, pack up a tent (and a telescope) and head to the **Cave Creek Campground**.

Best Lodging

Spend the night in the trees at the extraordinary **Out 'n' About Treehouse Treesort**, about 25 miles southwest of the park. One tree house has an antique claw-foot bath, and another has separate kids' quarters connected to the main room by a swinging bridge. ✉ *300 Page Creek Rd., Cave Junction, OR* 🌐 *treehouses.com*

When to Go

The caves are open from late spring until early fall, with tours running Thursday through Sunday. The caves are closed during the winter to allow resident bats to hibernate in peace.

Getting Here and Around

From Grants Pass, take U.S. 199 to Cave Junction and then head east on Route 46 for about 18 miles to the entrance of the park.

Wallowa Lake State Park

America's Steepest Aerial Tram

Although it receives far fewer visitors than the rest of the state, northeastern Oregon is a land of astounding beauty that's framed by enormous mountain peaks and borders America's deepest river gorge, Hells Canyon. The perfect town for its mix of lively businesses and access to stunning natural scenery is **Joseph.** The peaks of the Wallowa Mountains, typically snow-covered until July, tower 5,000 feet above this community whose Main Street is speckled with shops, galleries, brewpubs, and cafés. At gorgeous Wallowa Lake State Park, you can ride the **Wallowa Lake Tramway** on a memorable journey that rises 3,700 feet in 15 minutes, rushing you up to the top of 8,150-foot Mt. Howard. There's great hiking, expansive views, and a casual patio restaurant at the top. ✉ *59919 Wallowa Lake Hwy., Joseph, OR* 🌐 *www.wallowalaketramway.com*

Don't Miss

A relatively easy way to take in the natural splendor of the surrounding Eagle Cap Wilderness is by driving the **Wallowa Mountain Loop.** The three-hour trip from Joseph to historic Baker City, designated the Hells Canyon Scenic Byway, winds through the national forest and part of Hells Canyon Recreation Area, passing over forested mountains, creeks, and rivers.

Best Gallery

On Joseph's bustling Main Street, Valley Bronze of Oregon displays sculptures by the many artists who cast their work at the nearby foundry. ✉ *307 W. Alder St., Joseph, OR* 🌐 *www.valleybronze.com*

Getting Here and Around

The most direct route to Joseph is Route 82, a picturesque 70-mile journey from Interstate 5 in La Grande.

When in Oregon

ASTORIA

It's hard not to get a little awestruck the first time you experience the beauty of Astoria, Oregon, in person. Located near the place where the Columbia River meets the Pacific Ocean, the city offers breathtaking views everywhere you turn. Once you gain your bearings, a new feeling creeps in—familiarity. No, it's not déjà vu. You know the tiny town of Astoria from the movies—lots of them. The town is famously the setting for *The Goonies* and *Kindergarten Cop*, but its relationship with Tinseltown doesn't stop there. *Short Circuit*, *Teenage Mutant Ninja Turtles 3*, *The Ring Two*, the *Free Willy* movies, *Benji the Hunted*, and more were filmed there, too.

Do This: With a bit of Portland's hipster vibe, especially when it comes to shopping and nightlife, Astoria is also home to some first-rate attractions, including the superb Columbia River Maritime Museum, whose interactive exhibits illuminate the maritime history of the Pacific Northwest, and Fort Clatsop at Lewis and Clark National Historical Park, where the 30-member Lewis and Clark Expedition endured a rain-soaked winter in 1805–06. For the best view, scamper up the 164 spiral stairs to the observation deck atop the Astoria Column.

EUGENE

At the southern end of the Willamette Valley Wine Country, Oregon's second-largest city and home of the University of Oregon is a lively, youthful place with a counterculture edge. Full of parks and oriented to the outdoors, Eugene is famously popular for biking and—as the birthplace of Nike—is known as the Running Capital of the World. On the north edge of downtown, the Market District and up-and-coming Whiteaker neighborhood both boast stellar food scenes rife with artisan food and drink producers. Downtown's bustling Fifth Street Public Market is a good place to start, with its font of boutiques and crafts shops; a large gourmet food hub, Provisions Market Hall; and a trendy boutique hotel, the Inn at the 5th. Make your way west, stopping for a stroll through pretty Skinner Butte Park and a sip at Wildcraft Cider Works. At Blair Boulevard, you'll find the heart of Whiteaker's excellent eateries, among them El Buen Sabor Taqueria, Izakaya Meiji, and Territorial Vineyards & Wine Company.

Do This: Held every Saturday from April through mid-November, downtown's Eugene Saturday Market is a great place to browse for handicrafts, try out local food carts, or simply kick back and people-watch while listening to live music at the Market Stage. ✉ *126 E. 8th Ave., Eugene, OR* 🌐 *eugenesaturdaymarket.org*

JOHN DAY FOSSIL BEDS NATIONAL MONUMENT

The geological formations that compose this peculiar monument cover hundreds of square miles and preserve a diverse record of plant and animal life spanning more than 40 million years of the Age of Mammals. The national monument is divided into three units: Sheep Rock, Painted Hills, and Clarno—each of which looks vastly different and tells a different part of the story of Oregon's history. If you only have time for one unit of the park, make it Painted Hills, where the namesake psychedelic mounds most vividly expose the region's unique geology. ✉ *37375 Bear Creek Rd., Mitchell, OR* 🌐 *www.nps.gov/joda*

Do This: If you can, come to the Painted Hills at dusk or just after it rains, when the colors are most vivid. If traveling in spring, the desert wildflowers are most intense between late April and early May. Take the steep, ¾-mile Carroll Rim Trail for a commanding view of the hills or sneak a peek from the parking lot at the trailhead, about 2 miles beyond the picnic area.

PENDLETON ROUND-UP

More than 50,000 people roll into the town of Pendleton in mid-September for one of the oldest and most prominent rodeos in the country. With its famous slogan of "Let 'er Buck," the Round-Up features eight days of parades, races, beauty contests, and children's rodeos, culminating in four days of rodeo competition. Vendors sell beadwork and curios, while country bands twang in the background. At the Round-Up Hall of Fame Museum, you can learn about the rodeo's history from the collection of photos and memorabilia that dates back to 1910. ✉ *1205 S.W. Court Ave., Pendleton, OR* 🌐 *www.pendletonroundup.com*

Do This: Beyond the Round-Up, the town's most significant source of name recognition comes from Pendleton Woolen Mills, home of the instantly recognizable plaid wool shirts and colorful woolen Indian blankets. This location is the company's blanket mill; there's also a weaving mill in the Columbia Gorge town of Washougal, Washington. If you want to know more about the production process, take one of the engaging tours. The mill's retail store stocks blankets and clothing, with good bargains on factory seconds. ✉ *1307 S.E. Court Pl., Pendleton, OR* 🌐 *www.pendleton-usa.com*

TILIKUM CROSSING BRIDGE

Downtown Portland's collection of striking bridges gained a new member in 2015 with the construction of this sleek, cable-stayed bridge a few steps from the superb and very family-friendly Oregon Museum of Science and Industry (OMSI). Nicknamed "the Bridge of the People," the Tilikum is unusual in that it's the largest car-free bridge in the country—it's open only to public transit (MAX light-rail trains, buses, and streetcars), bikes, and pedestrians. The 1,720-foot-long bridge connects Southeast Portland with the South Waterfront district and rewards those who stroll or cycle across it with impressive skyline views.

Do This: Portland is famously bike-friendly, with miles of dedicated bike lanes and numerous rental shops. Also, some great companies offer guided rides around the city, covering everything from eating and brewpub-hopping to checking out local parks and historic neighborhoods. Cycle Portland Bike Tours and Rentals is one of the best, offering tours with themes that include Essential Portland, Foodie Field Trip, and Brews Cruise. The well-stocked on-site bike shop serves craft beer on tap. 🌐 *portlandbicycletours.com*

TILLAMOOK

More than 100 inches of annual rainfall and the confluence of three rivers contribute to the lush green pastures around Tillamook, probably best known for its thriving dairy industry and cheese factory. The Tillamook Creamery ships about 50 million pounds of cheese around the world every year. The town itself lies several miles inland from the ocean, but it is the best jumping-off point for driving the dramatic Three Capes Loop, which passes over Cape Meares, Cape Lookout, and Cape Kiwanda and offers spectacular views of the ocean and coastline. ✉ *4165 N. U.S. 101, Tillamook, OR* 🌐 *www.tillamook.com*

Do This: Cape Lookout State Park includes a moderately easy (though often muddy) 2-mile trail—marked on the highway as "wildlife viewing area"—that leads through giant spruces, western red cedars, and hemlocks, and ends with views of Cascade Head to the south and Cape Meares to the north. The section of the park just north of the trail comprises a long, curving stretch of beach with picnic areas and campsites.

Cool Places to Stay

Headlands Coastal Lodge & Spa. Luxurious lodging meets easy access to the outdoors at this Oregon Coast property that features sunny rooms with huge windows and seastack views. While the sleek spa and coast-inspired gourmet restaurant are enough to keep you busy, it's worth heading out on at least one of the Headland's many guide-led adventures, which range from mushroom foraging expeditions to romantic beachfront bonfires. ✉ *33000 Cape Kiwanda Dr., Pacific City, OR* 🌐 *www.headlandslodge.com*

Heathman Hotel. Dating to the 1920s, the Heathman Hotel is a downtown Portland institution. It's the oldest hotel in the city and has been drawing in locals with its afternoon tea service for generations. The Heathman's star attraction for bibliophiles is its private library, complete with floor-to-ceiling shelves and ladders and over 2,700 books, including an impressive collection of signed tomes from literary giants who've stayed at the hotel. ✉ *1001 S.W. Broadway, Portland, OR* 🌐 *www.heathmanhotel.com*

Heceta Head Lighthouse Bed & Breakfast. On a windswept promontory, this unusual late-Victorian property is one of Oregon's most remarkable bed-and-breakfasts. It's located at Heceta Head Lighthouse State Scenic Viewpoint and owned by a gifted chef who prepares an elaborate seven-course breakfast each morning, with seasonal offerings. ✉ *92072 Hwy. 1 S, Yachats, OR* 🌐 *www.hecetalighthouse.com*

Suttle Lodge. If the famously design-minded film director Wes Anderson built a wilderness lodge, it'd probably look something like this whimsically updated lakeside retreat in the Deschutes National Forest, where the vintage summer-camp vibes come with the finest craft cocktails you'll find between here and Portland. ✉ *13300 U.S. 20, Sisters, OR* 🌐 *www.thesuttlelodge.com*

Timberline Lodge. Guest rooms are simple, rustic, and charming (a handful of them lack private baths), so don't expect a cushy experience—the reason for staying in this gorgeous lodge built by the CCC in the 1930s is the magnificent setting high on the southern slope of Oregon's most storied peak, Mt. Hood. ✉ *27500 E. Timberline Rd., Government Camp, OR* 🌐 *www.timberlinelodge.com*

Vintages Trailer Resort. Just off the road that runs through the heart of the Willamette Valley Wine Country from Dundee to McMinnville, this quirky retro resort boasts 34 lovingly refurbished vintage trailers, most dating from the 1940s–60s, and each with a gas grill. ✉ *16205 S.E. Kreder Rd., Dayton, OR* 🌐 *www.the-vintages.com*

About Our Writers

Margot Bigg was born and (mostly) raised in Portland, Oregon. Her favorite thing about the state is its abundance of mineral-rich hot springs. She has contributed to publications all over the world and has co-authored numerous titles for Fodor's Travel.

Essential Eats

Kann. The creation of James Beard Award–winning celebrity chef Gregory Gourdet, Portland's Kann restaurant offers Haitian-inspired cuisine, much of it cooked right in front of diners using wood-fire cooking techniques. Crowds flock here for the creamy stews, grilled meats, and tasty vegetable dishes. Note that reservations get snapped up quickly—if you can't secure a seat, you can still experience some of Gourdet's culinary wizardry at Kann's sister lounge, Sousòl, in the basement of the same building. ✉ *48 S.E. Ash St., Portland, OR* 🌐 *www.kannrestaurant.com*

Oregon Pears. Oregon's thriving culinary scene is largely thanks to the state's abundance of fresh ingredients, from Pacific-caught albacore tuna to forest-foraged truffles. Oregon also has some of the tastiest pears in the country, from the crisp Bosc variety to sweet, buttery Comice pears. Southern Oregon's Rogue Valley is a great place to sample them for yourself, whether by picking them at Ashland's historic Valley View Orchard or by procuring a gold foil–wrapped pear from Harry & David in Medford. Can't make it that far south? The Hood River Valley, an hour's drive east of Portland, is a major pear-producing region, too.

Pinot Noir Pairings. Although Oregon wine once played second-fiddle to better-known wine regions in California, the state's wine scene is now well-known among wine lovers worldwide. Although Oregon's climatic diversity means that all sorts of great wines are grown in the state, the best-known varietal is Pinot Noir. Much of Oregon Pinot is produced in the Willamette Valley, where wineries such as Antica Terra offer multicourse dining experiences that pair seasonal dishes with Oregon wines. Another great place to pair Pinot with food is at Hood River's Hiyu Wine Farm, where meals crafted from farm-fresh produce are paired with estate-made wines.

Voodoo Doughnut. The long lines outside this Old Town 24/7 doughnut shop, marked by its distinctive pink-neon sign, attest to the fact that this irreverent bakery is almost as famous a Portland landmark as Powell's Books. The aforementioned sign depicts one of the shop's biggest sellers, a raspberry-jelly-topped chocolate voodoo-doll doughnut, but all of the creations here, some of them witty, some ribald, bring smiles to the faces of customers—even those who have waited 30 minutes in the rain. Order the Loop (covered in Fruit Loops cereal), the Grape Ape (vanilla frosting, grape dust, and lavender sprinkles), and the Voodoo Doll (doll-shape, with a pretzel "stake" stabbed into its raspberry-filled heart). ✉ *22 S.W. 3rd Ave. Portland, OR* 🌐 *www.voodoodoughnut.com*

Washington

Whether you're looking for hip cities, beautiful hikes, or laid-back beaches, Washington State has it all. In Seattle, you can sample farm-to-table treats at Pike Place Market and get a glimpse of the city lights at the top of the Space Needle, while outdoor adventurers can explore national parks like Olympic, North Cascades, and Mt. Rainier, as well as hike up to Mt. St. Helens and the Cascade Mountains. Beach lovers will find their bliss here too, with the San Juan Islands and Long Beach Peninsula offering plenty of swimming, surfing, and whale-watching.

Capital: Olympia

Population: 7,958,180

Area: 71,362 square miles

Statehood Date: November 11, 1889

Major Airports: Seattle-Tacoma International Airport (SEA); Spokane International Airport (GEG); Tri-Cities Airport (PSC); Paine Field Airport (PAE)

Travel and Tourism Information:
🌐 *www.stateofwatourism.com*

Famous Residents: Bruce Lee (martial artist); Jimi Hendrix (musician); Bill Gates (Microsoft founder); Kurt Cobain (musician); Anna Faris (actress)

Fun Fact: More Sasquatch (aka Bigfoot) sightings are reported in Washington than in any other state.

Mount Rainier National Park

PNW's Highest Volcanic Peak

Some say Mt. Rainier is the most magical mountain in America. At 14,411 feet, it is a popular peak for climbing, with close to 10,000 attempts per year—nearly half of which are successful. But this land of superlatives also includes about 35 square miles of glaciers and snowfields, more than 100 species of wildflowers that bloom in the park's high meadows all summer, and absolutely dazzling hiking along 260 miles of trails through old-growth forest, river valleys, lakes, waterfalls, and rugged ridges. Take time to visit the historic **Longmire Museum** and the contemporary **Jackson Memorial Visitor Center**. ✉ *55210 238th Ave. E, Ashford, WA* 🌐 *www.nps.gov/mora*

Don't Miss

The 5-mile **Skyline Trail** loop, one of the highest trails in the park, beckons day-trippers with a vista of alpine ridges and, in summer, meadows filled with wildflowers and songbirds. At 6,800 feet is Panorama Point, the spine of the Cascade Range.

Best Lodge

With its hand-carved Alaskan cedar logs, stone fireplaces, and glorious mountain views, the 1917 **Paradise Inn** is a classic example of a national park lodge. ✉ *52807 Paradise Valley Rd. E, Ashford, WA* 🌐 *www.mtrainierguest-services.com*

When to Go

Mt. Rainier is the Puget Sound's weather vane: if you can see it, skies will be clear. You're most likely to see the summit July through September.

Getting Here and Around

The park is relatively close to the Seattle–Tacoma Interstate 5 corridor, reached via a few different routes; the most direct is the 75-mile drive southeast on Route 7 from Tacoma.

The Space Needle

Washington's Most Famous Tower

The tallest building west of the Mississippi when it was constructed for the World's Fair in 1962, the 600-foot-tall Space Needle is as quirky and beloved as ever. A less-than-one-minute ride up to the observation deck yields 360-degree vistas of downtown Seattle, Elliott Bay, and the surrounding Olympic Mountains and Cascade Range through floor-to-ceiling windows, an open-air observation area, and a rotating glass floor. Below is the 74-acre Seattle Center, home to the kid-friendly Pacific Science Center, with more than 200 indoor and outdoor hands-on exhibits, two IMAX theaters, and a state-of- the-art planetarium. ✉ *400 Broad St., Seattle, WA* 🌐 *www.spaceneedle.com*

Don't Miss

For the best views of the Space Needle from afar, head to Kerry Park. And, while you're near the Space Needle, definitely spend time at **MoPOP**, a striking 140,000-square-foot complex designed by Frank Gehry with rock memorabilia from the likes of Bob Dylan and the grunge-scene heavies. ✉ *325 5th Ave. N, Seattle, WA* 🌐 *www.mopop.org*

Best Art Installation

Just steps from the base of the Space Needle, fans of Dale Chihuly's glass works delight in exploring the artist's early influences at **Chihuly Garden and Glass**. ✉ *305 Harrison St., Seattle, WA* 🌐 *www.chihulygardenandglass.com*

Getting Here and Around

The Seattle Center is on the northwest side of downtown, at the foot of Queen Anne Hill, and is easily reached on foot, bus, light-rail, and even monorail.

Pike Place Market

America's Iconic Market

This iconic structure with its famous neon red sign and a memorable setting overlooking Seattle's waterfront dates to 1907, when the city issued permits allowing farmers to sell produce from parked wagons. Today it buzzes with more than 200 restaurants, bakeries, coffeehouses, lunch counters, and eateries, plus crafts vendors, galleries, and cookery shops. A major expansion added artisanal-food purveyors, an on-site brewery, public art installations, seasonal pop-up vendors, and a 30,000 square foot plaza and viewing deck overlooking Elliott Bay. ✉ *85 Pike St., Seattle, WA* 🌐 *www.pikeplacemarket.org*

Don't Miss

The **Overlook Walk**, an elevated pedestrian pathway, connects the market with Seattle's redeveloped waterfront 100 feet below. With 60,000 square feet of park space, visitors can enjoy stunning 360-degree views of Puget Sound, the Olympic Mountains, Mt. Rainier, and the downtown skyline, see large-scale public art and lush native plants, and let the kids romp on the small playground.

Best Food

Attention foodies: for the best picnic supplies, head to **DeLaurenti Specialty Food and Wine**. This gourmet emporium has been doling out superb imported meats and cheeses and all sorts of other delicacies since 1972. Don't miss the excellent wineshop upstairs, too. 🌐 *www.delaurenti.com*

Getting Here and Around

Pike Place is in the heart of downtown Seattle.

Olympic National Park

A Stunningly Diverse Oasis

Covering nearly 1,500 square miles of the stunning peninsula for which it's named, Olympic National Park is home to some of the nation's most tranquil temperate rain forests, beautifully sculpted beaches, and dramatic coastal mountains. Beachcombers will discover miles of spectacular driftwood-strewn coastline hemmed with sea stacks and tidal pools. A dip in Sol Duc's natural geothermal mineral pools offers a secluded spa experience in the wooded heart of the park, while hardy hikers and climbers will want to spend time in the park's meadowed foothill trails and frosty peaks. ✉ *3002 Mt. Angeles Rd., Port Angeles, WA* 🌐 *www.nps.gov/olym*

Don't Miss

Considered one of the quietest places in North America, the park's **Hoh Rain Forest** is a place of utter tranquility, and hiking here is suitable for all abilities.

Best Camping

In addition to three beautiful, historic lodges, Olympic National Park is blessed with gorgeous campgrounds, but the most amazing place to pitch a tent is along one of the park's beaches. **Rialto Beach** is the most stunning with easy drive-in access, while up north among the park's alluring sea stacks is **Shi Shi Beach.** Remember to obtain a wilderness permit in advance.

When to Go

The Olympic Peninsula is most appealing weather-wise, but also most crowded, in summer.

Getting Here and Around

U.S. 101 nearly circumvents the entire park, and from this picturesque road, you can access all of its main areas.

North Cascades National Park

The Most Glaciers in the Lower 48

Outside of Alaska, this remote and wild park at the Canadian border contains more glaciers than any place in the country. Other joys of visiting North Cascades National Park include the chance to see bald eagles, elk, and other wildlife along nearly 400 miles of hiking trails, the ability to traipse meadows absolutely carpeted with colorful wildflowers in summer, and rafting and kayaking on beautiful Lake Chelan, Ross Lake, and the Stehekin River. You can access this 1,070-square-mile wilderness most easily via the North Cascades Highway. ✉ *810 Rte. 20, Sedro-Woolley, WA* 🌐 *www.nps.gov/noca*

Don't Miss

The only way to reach the **Lake Chelan National Recreation Area** portion of the park is by boat, and that's a big part of its appeal. A ferry and high-speed catamaran cruise between small waterfront villages along Lake Chelan, a pristine 55-mile-long fjord.

Best Tour

On the shore of turquoise-hued Diablo Lake, **North Cascades Environmental Learning Center** offers outstanding guided tours, including two-hour boat cruises of the lake. 🌐 *www.ncascades.org*

When to Go

Summer is peak season. North Cascades Highway closes from mid-November through mid-April, depending on snowfall.

Getting Here and Around

The park is traversed by the North Cascades Highway during the warmer months, and Stehekin can be reached by ferry along Lake Chelan year-round. Bellingham to the west and Winthrop to the east are the best bases for exploring the park.

Seattle's Waterfront

A Reinvented Hub for Seattle Culture

Seattle's reimagined waterfront, a 20-acre expanse transformed by the Waterfront Park project, opened after years of development following the 2001 Nisqually earthquake. The elevated Overlook Walk connects Pike Place Market to the waterfront with breathtaking views. Pier 58 features a jellyfish-inspired playground and the restored Waterfront Fountain while Pier 62 was renovated with a floating dock for events, games, and general gathering. Enduring features include the historic ferry docks at Colman Dock and the popular Seattle Great Wheel at Pier 57. Seasonal pop-up markets, a 1.2-mile bike path, and public art make Seattle's "front porch" a welcoming haven for visitors and locals alike. 🌐 *www.seattlewaterfront.org*

Don't Miss

The **Washington State Ferry System**—the largest ferry system in the United States and second-largest in the world—runs two of its 10 routes from the waterfront terminal; they connect to Bainbridge Island and Bremerton and carry nearly 6 million riders annually. With views of the city skyline, Mt. Rainier, and the active waterfront, a ferry ride is a "must-do" for first-time visitors.

While You're Here

At the north end of the waterfront, the **Olympic Sculpture Park** is a favorite destination for picnics, strolls, and quiet contemplation. ✉ *2901 Western Ave., Seattle, WA* 🌐 *www.seattleartmuseum.org/visit/olympic-sculpture-park*

Getting Here and Around

Several bus lines run close to the waterfront and a free summer trolley runs from downtown and Seattle Center.

The San Juan Islands

The West Coast's Prettiest Archipelago

One of the most enchanting island getaways in the western United States, the mountainous and lush San Juan Islands sit in the middle of Puget Sound, just off the coast of British Columbia and within easy weekending distance of Seattle. These utterly peaceful islands, the three largest of which—San Juan, Orcas, and Lopez—have regular ferry service, are filled with enjoyable outdoorsy diversions, including great whale-watching, as well as plenty of urbane charms like farm-to-table restaurants, exceptional art galleries, and cottages and B&Bs.

Don't Miss

The top place to spot whales isn't Orcas Island but rather San Juan Island, especially **Lime Kiln Point State Park,** where a rocky coastal trail leads to lookout points and a little 1919 lighthouse. The best time to spot whales is from the end of April through September. Several tour companies also offer whale-watching expeditions, including Maya's Legacy. 🌐 *www.sanjuanislandwhalewatch.com*

Best Hike

Offering a more peaceful, less crowded hiking and wildlife-watching alternative to Moran State Park, Orcas Island's 1,576-acre **Turtleback Mountain Preserve** comprises rugged ridges, wildflower-strewn meadows, temperate rain forest, and lush wetlands. Top trails include the steep trek up to 1,519-foot-elevation Raven Ridge and a windy hike to Turtlehead Point.

Getting Here and Around

Ferries serve the three main islands from the mainland town of Anacortes year-round; there's also a seasonal summer ferry between Friday Harbor and Port Townsend on the Olympic Peninsula.

Tacoma's Museum of Glass

A Uniquely Beautiful Museum

The showpiece of this spectacular complex of delicate and creative art-glass installations is the 500-foot-long Chihuly Bridge of Glass, a tunnel of glorious color and light that stretches above Interstate 705. Cross it from downtown to reach the museum's grounds, which sit above the Foss Waterway and next to a shallow reflecting pool dotted with large-scale sculptures. Inside, you can wander through quiet, light-filled galleries that present a fascinating and compelling array of rotating exhibits. ✉ *1801 E. Dock St., Tacoma, WA* 🌐 *www.museumofglass.org*

Don't Miss

The Museum of Glass is part of a cluster of superb downtown Tacoma museums. A highlight is the **Tacoma Art Museum** and its stunning, light-filled Benaroya Wing—designed by Olson Kundig—with its hundreds of contemporary art-glass works, including pieces by artists trained at the prestigious Pilchuck Glass School. ✉ *1701 Pacific Ave., Tacoma, WA* 🌐 *www.tacomaartmuseum.org*

Best Bar

The offbeat **McMenamins Elks Temple** consists of several colorful bars and restaurants and a 44-room hotel inside a dramatically refurbished 1916 Renaissance Revival landmark building adjacent to Tacoma's famous Spanish Steps. It's a memorable spot for drinks or a bite to eat after touring the city's museums. ✉ *565 Broadway, Tacoma, WA* 🌐 *www.mcmenamins.com*

Getting Here and Around

On the southern end of Puget Sound, about 30 miles south of Seattle, Tacoma is just off Interstate 5. The downtown museum district is quite pedestrian-friendly.

Mt. St. Helens

America's Most Famous Volcano

The site of the most devastating volcanic eruption in recent U.S. history, Mount St. Helens National Volcanic Monument gives you an up-close look at this striking peak 55 miles northeast of Portland, Oregon. On May 18, 1980, the massive eruption of this 9,667-foot peak launched a 36,000-foot plume of steam and ash into the air, leveling a 230-square-mile area and claiming 57 lives. The mountain now stands at 8,365 feet, and a horseshoe-shape crater forms the scarred summit. The modern and scenic Spirit Lake Highway carries travelers to the outstanding **Johnston Ridge Observatory,** about 5 miles from the summit. (Note that a landslide closed the highway and access to the observatory in 2023; road repairs and reopening are currently projected for 2026 or 2027.)

Don't Miss

Located 6 miles southwest of the summit, **Ape Cave** is the longest continuous lava tube in the continental United States.

Best Hike

Of the trails that lead to the summit of this legendary volcano, all of them requiring a permit, the most popular is the 10-mile round-trip **Monitor Ridge Trail,** which, though not for the faint of heart—it entails a 4,500-foot elevation gain—can be done in a day and requires no technical climbing.

When to Go

It's best to visit from mid-May through late October; many roads are closed the rest of the year.

Getting Here and Around

Johnston Ridge Observatory is at the end of the Spirit Lake Highway, 53 miles from Interstate 5. The trailhead for the Monitor Ridge Trail is Climbers Bivouac, a 14-mile drive from Cougar.

Walla Walla Wine Country

Washington's Premier Wine Region

Walla Walla Valley's sunny, fertile slopes began attracting grape growers in the 1980s, and this attractive town with sweeping views of the Blue Mountains is now one of America's most exciting wine countries. You'll find more than 130 wineries and tasting rooms here, many clustered among the attractive downtown's growing clutch of noteworthy bistros and bakeries—some musts include **Kontos Cellars**, **Browne Family Vineyards**, and **House of Smith**. It's also a treat to drive the region's back roads past acres of vines. Wineries with especially beautiful grounds and tasting rooms include **Waterbrook**, **Revelry Vintners**, **Abeja**, and **Long Shadows**. 🌐 *www.wallawallawine.com*

Don't Miss

Valdemar Estates, Walla Walla's first internationally-owned winery, was founded in 2019 by a fifth-generation Spanish winemaker, Jesús Martínez Bujanda. The winery features both Washington wines and Spanish wines from their family winery in Spain. ✉ *3808 Rolling Hills La., Walla Walla, WA* 🌐 *valdemarestates.com*

Best Wine Country Stay

In a rural setting 4 miles east of town, the **Inn at Abeja** is a 49-acre historic farmstead with gorgeous grounds and vineyards as well as stylish guest cottages and suites that are spacious and secluded. ✉ *2014 Mill Creek Rd., Walla Walla, WA* 🌐 *www.abeja.net*

Getting Here and Around

Walla Walla is on U.S. 12 in the south-eastern part of the state, about 50 miles east of the Tri-Cities.

Leavenworth

A Bavarian-Style Village Where It's Always Festive

This charming (if a touch kitschy) Bavarian-style village thrives with both old-fashioned and surprisingly urbane restaurants and inns, and it's also a hub for winter skiing and summer hiking. Formerly a railroad and mining center, Leavenworth fell on hard times in the 1960s, and civic leaders, looking for ways to capitalize on the town's alpine setting, convinced shopkeepers to add Black Forest–style trim to their buildings. The pedestrian-friendly village center bustles with tourists year-round, but Leavenworth truly comes alive during the holidays. There's an intricate maypole dance during spring's Maifest, oompah bands and delicious German food and beer during autumn's three Oktoberfest weekends, and carriage rides, caroling, and performances by the Marlin Handbell Ringers during the Christmastown festivities in December.

Don't Miss

More than 9,000 modern and antique nutcrackers—some of them centuries old—are displayed in the two-story **Nutcracker Museum and Shop**. ✉ *735 Front St., Leavenworth, WA* 🌐 *www.nutcrackermuseum.com*

Best Live Theater

Every summer since 1995, the hills come alive with summer performances of Rodgers and Hammerstein's *The Sound of Music*, enthusiastically performed by a cast of mostly college students and locals at an amphitheater with the Cascade mountains as the backdrop. The theater group also presents two other musicals each summer. 🌐 *www.leavenworthsummertheater.org*

Getting Here and Around

From Seattle, the 120-mile drive to Leavenworth over the Cascades and dramatic Stevens Pass, via U.S. 2, is one of the prettiest in the state.

Spokane's Riverfront Park

Washington's Coolest Urban Green Space

This beautifully maintained 100-acre park is what remains of Spokane's Expo '74. Sprawled across several islands in the Spokane River, the striking park was developed from old railroad yards, where the stone clock tower of the former Great Northern Railroad Station still stands. The modernist Washington State Pavilion, built as an opera house, is now the excellent **First Interstate Center for the Arts**. A 1909 carousel, hand-carved by master builder Charles I. D. Looff, is a local landmark. Another family favorite is the giant red slide shaped like a Radio Flyer wagon. The **Gesa Credit Union Pavilion** hosts concerts, festivals, and an eye-catching light display on weekends. For a great view of the river and falls, walk across Post Street Bridge or take the sky ride over Spokane Falls. ✉ *507 N. Howard St., Spokane, WA* 🌐 *www.spokaneriverfrontpark.com*

Don't Miss

Extend your time along the river by walking, biking, or skating on the **Spokane River Centennial Trail**, which runs 40 miles between the Idaho border to west of Spokane. Following the trail east from the park for a mile takes you to the modern Kendall Yards neighborhood to enjoy eateries, wineries, and shopping. 🌐 *www.kendallyards.com*

Best Restaurant

In a former flour mill with expansive Spokane River vistas, **Clinkerdagger** has been a Spokane favorite for decades. The seafood, steaks, and prime rib are excellent, but the setting is what really makes this spot special. ✉ *621 W. Mallon Ave., Spokane, WA* 🌐 *www.clinkerdagger.com*

Getting Here and Around

Interstate 90 cuts through downtown Spokane, within a few blocks of Riverfront Park.

Skagit Valley Tulip Festival

One of the World's Top Tulip Festivals

Five tulip farms in the Skagit Valley participate in this county-wide festival that runs throughout April. RoozenGaarde, the world's largest family-owned tulip-growing business, is the oldest and biggest of the farms and one of only two farms open year-round. Acres of greenhouses are filled with multicolored blossoms, and more than 1 million bulbs are planted each fall in its 7-acre display garden and 50 acres of daffodil and tulip fields. In the spring, the flowers pop up in neat, brilliant rows across the flat landscape, attracting upwards of 400,000 visitors. 🌐 *www.tulipfestival.org*

Don't Miss

Just a 15-minute drive northwest of Mount Vernon, the twin villages of **Bow-Edison** have become one of Washington's premier foodie destinations, with notable eateries and farm-fresh food purveyors.

When to Go

The Skagit Valley Tulip Festival takes place throughout April; a midweek visit can mean less traffic and crowds. The area's farms, fields, and scenic roads are beautiful throughout summer and fall.

Getting Here and Around

Tulip farms are a few miles west of Interstate 5 in Mount Vernon. Bow-Edison and Chuckanut Drive are 12 miles northwest, via U.S. 12.

Skydiving in Snohomish

The West Coast's Best Skydiving Destination

In a scenic river valley just 20 miles northeast of Seattle, the town of Snohomish has earned a reputation as a top destination for skydiving. Once you begin your descent from between 8,000 and 14,000 feet, you're rewarded with eye-popping scenery in every direction: Mt. Baker to the north, the jagged Cascade Range to the east, Seattle's sleek skyline to the south, and Puget Sound, the San Juan Islands, the Olympic Mountains, and Victoria, British Columbia, to the west. The highly respected outfitter Skydive Snohomish caters to everyone from first-timers to those with plenty of experience. ✉ *9906 Airport Way, Snohomish, WA* 🌐 *www.skydivesnohomish.com*

Don't Miss

Snohomish is a mere 12-mile drive from one of the loveliest towns in Washington. **Woodinville** contains more winery tasting rooms—some 130 in all—than any town in the Pacific Northwest.

Best Restaurant

For the ultimate post-skydiving celebration, head to the **Herbfarm** in Woodinville's tony Willows Lodge, where prix-fixe-only nine-course dinners take place over a few hours and feature at least six wine pairings. ✉ *14590 N.E. 145th St., Woodinville, WA* 🌐 *www.theherbfarm.com*

When to Go

Skydive Snohomish offers jumps year-round, although your likelihood of blue skies and panoramic views are greatest in summer.

Getting Here and Around

Skydive Snohomish is at Harvey Airfield, about 30 miles northeast of Seattle.

When in Washington

CAPE DISAPPOINTMENT STATE PARK

The cape and its treacherous neighboring sandbar—named in 1788 by an English fur trader who had been unable to find the Northwest Passage—has been the scourge of sailors since the 1800s. More than 250 ships have sunk after running aground on its ever-shifting sands. Now a 2,023-acre state park contained within the Lewis and Clark National Historical Park (which also has sections just across the Columbia River in Oregon), this dramatic cape with sheer sea cliffs and great stands of conifers offers 8 miles of trails leading to stunning beaches, two stately lighthouses, and the Lewis & Clark Interpretive Center, which sits atop a 200-foot cliff and has exhibits tracing the cape's human and natural history. ✉ *244 Robert Gray Dr., Ilwaco, WA* 🌐 *www.parks.wa.gov*

Do This: The adjacent Long Beach Peninsula consists of 28 continuous miles of broad, sandy beach bookended by two state parks and bounded by the Pacific Ocean and the Columbia River. This narrow stretch of land offers a series of oceanfront retreats, oyster farms, cranberry bogs, and beach after beach to comb. Kite flying, horseback riding, clam digging, and winter-storm watching are also popular pastimes.

LAKE WASHINGTON SHIP CANAL

For scenic strolls through waterfront greenery, check out the areas flanking this 8.6-mile canal that connects Lake Washington to Puget Sound. The top outdoor draws include 230-acre Washington Park Arboretum, with its rhododendrons, azaleas, and Japanese garden; Lake Union Park to the south, where you can visit the free Center for Wooden Boats; Gas Works Park, where the hulking remains of a 1907 gas plant lends quirky character to a green space overlooking Lake Union; and the Hiram M. Chittenden Locks, where you can watch boats take the "water elevator" between the lake and Puget Sound and see salmon and trout make the journey from saltwater to fresh each summer.

Do This: To explore the canal and Lake Union by water, there are plenty of boat rental options, including rowboats, kayaks, SUPs, electric boats, donut-shaped boats, and even hot tub boats. Or hop on a guided cruise, where your narrator will be sure to point out the iconic *Sleepless in Seattle* houseboat as they share other interesting facts about the city.

MARYHILL MUSEUM

A wonderfully eclectic collection is housed within the walls of a grandiose mansion built in the middle of nowhere by Sam Hill, the man who spearheaded the development of a scenic highway through the Columbia Gorge. Here you'll find the largest assemblage of Rodin works outside France; an impressive cache of Native American artifacts; furniture that belonged to Queen Marie of Romania; and posters, glasswork, and ephemera related to the modern-dance pioneer Loïe Fuller. The main Beaux Arts building dates to 1914, and a beautifully executed modern wing extends from the back, with a café and a terraced slope overlooking the Columbia River. The harmoniously landscaped grounds include a sculpture garden and pathways along the gorge. ✉ *35 Maryhill Museum of Art Dr., Goldendale, WA* 🌐 *www.maryhillmuseum.org*

Do This: The remarkable Stonehenge Memorial is a full-scale replica of England's legendary Neolithic stone creation. It was constructed in 1918 as the nation's first memorial to servicemen who perished in World War I. The memorial, a five-minute drive east of the Maryhill Museum, sits on a promontory with dramatic vistas overlooking the Columbia River.

NORTHWEST MARITIME CENTER

The Olympic Peninsula's Port Townsend is one of only three Victorian-era seaports on the register of National Historic Sites, and you can learn all about its rich heritage at the handsome Northwest Maritime Center. You can launch a kayak or watch sloops and schooners gliding along the bay from the boardwalk, pier, and beach that fronts the buildings. It's the center of operations for the Wooden Boat Foundation, which stages the annual Wooden Boat Festival each September, during which hundreds of wooden boats sail into Port Townsend Bay for a weekend of presentations, tours, and sea shanties. ✉ *431 Water St., Port Townsend, WA* 🌐 *www.nwmaritime.org*

Do This: With beautifully restored Victorian-era officers quarters that you can tour, 432-acre Fort Worden State Park is a fascinating history lesson. There are also hidden bunkers and expansive parade grounds. A sandy beach leads to the graceful 1913 Point Wilson Lighthouse, and touch tanks at Port Townsend Marine Science Center offer an up-close look at sea anemones and other creatures.

SEQUIM LAVENDER FESTIVAL

Fragrant purple lavender flourishes in the fields of this endearing old mill town and farming center between the northern foothills of the Olympic Mountains and the southeastern stretch of the Strait of Juan de Fuca. About 30,000 people flock here over a weekend in mid-July to attend the Sequim Lavender Festival. Local farms are open for tours and "u-pick" gathering, and events include crafts sales, cooking demonstrations, and an afternoon lavender tea. Pronounced "skwim," this beautiful community has witnessed a boom in urbane eateries and hip boutiques in its walkable downtown. 🌐 *www.lavenderfestival.com*

Do This: Curving nearly 6 miles into the Strait of Juan de Fuca, Dungeness Spit is the country's longest natural sand spit and is situated in a wild section of shoreline. More than 30,000 migratory birds stop here each spring and fall.

About Our Writers

Shelley Arenas was born in Seattle, raised in Spokane, and returned as a young adult to make Seattle her home. A true sunset chaser, she loves her favorite golden-hour spots: Edmonds Beach, where the sun's last light descends behind the Olympics and reflects on Puget Sound waters; the rugged Pacific coastline, with its vast horizon; and the North Cascades, bathed in alpenglow at twilight. She has written for Fodor's Travel for more than two decades.

Cool Places to Stay

The Finch. A former motel has been reborn as this hip hotel that hopes to be your base for exploring all that's wonderful about Walla Walla and its gorgeous wineries. If offers helpful maps to help guide your discoveries. ✉ *325 E. Main St., Walla Walla, WA* 🌐 *www.finchwallawalla.com*

Inn at the Market. From its heart-stopping views to the fabulous location just steps from Pike Place Market to its exceptional restaurants, this inviting boutique hotel is one you'll want to visit again and again. ✉ *86 Pine St., Seattle, WA* 🌐 *www.innatthemarket.com*

Kalaloch Lodge. Overlooking an absolutely dazzling stretch of the Pacific Ocean in Olympic National Park, Kalaloch has cozy rooms with beach views, cabins along the bluff, and an inviting restaurant. ✉ *157151 U.S. 101, Forks, WA* 🌐 *www.thekalalochlodge.com*

The Lodge at St. Edward. This upscale boutique hotel is set inside a transformed 1930s seminary building in 326-acre woodland St. Edward State Park, above the northeast shore of Lake Washington. Steep hiking trails lead down to the lake; an excellent restaurant, bars, and a spa are welcome indulgences after hiking back up. ✉ *14477 Juanita Drive NE, Kenmore, WA* 🌐 *www.thelodgeatstedward.com*

Salish Lodge & Spa. The stunning, chalet-style lodge—which you may recognize from the opening credits of *Twin Peaks*—sits dramatically over Snoqualmie Falls and offers a slew of creature comforts, including plush rooms with gas fireplaces, window seats, and a first-rate spa with sauna, steam room, and soaking tubs. ✉ *6501 Railroad Ave., Snoqualmie, WA* 🌐 *www.salishlodge.com*

Essential Eats

Fruit. Washington leads the nation in producing apples, sweet cherries, blueberries, and pears thanks to its volcanic soil, diverse climates, and long summer days. From late spring through fall, farmers' markets across the state overflow with ripe, local fruit, especially in the Yakima Valley and Wenatchee, known as the "apple capital of the world." For a hands-on experience, visit Green Bluff, a scenic farming community near Spokane where visitors can pick their own apples, berries, cherries, and peaches. 🌐 *www.greenbluffgrowers.com*

Oysters. Washington produces more oysters than any other state, and you can harvest your own pretty easily with the right tools and some practice. You'll also need a shellfish license, which costs $22 and lets you take up to 18 oysters per day. Hood Canal and South Puget Sound are popular destinations. For the freshest already-cooked oysters, check out the Oyster Saloon at Hama Hama Oyster Company, a sixth-generation oyster farm. It's open Friday through Sunday by reservation while the farm store is open daily (✉ *35846 N. U.S. Hwy. 101, Lilliwaup, WA* 🌐 *www.hamahamaoysters.com*). Another longtime oyster farming company, Taylor Shellfish Farms, has oyster bars throughout western Washington, including three in Seattle, one in Shelton, and one in Bow (🌐 *www.taylorshellfishfarms.com*).

Salish Lodge and Spa. Arguably the most iconic brunch in the state, the Salish Lodge and Spa's restaurant has been serving its four-course country breakfast for more than a century. Its signature tradition is "Honey from Heaven," where servers pour honey from high above your plate onto the warm biscuits below. These days, the honey is made from their own beehives, and you can also purchase it in the lodge gift shop to take home. The Restaurant and Terrace Bar has stunning views of Snoqualmie Falls, and dinner guests can sometimes catch a gorgeous sunset as well. ✉ *5401 Railroad Ave., Snoqualmie, WA* 🌐 *www.salishlodge.com*

Toshi's Teriyaki. In 1976, Toshihiro "Toshi" Kasahara opened this eatery in Seattle's Queen Anne neighborhood, the city's first stand-alone teriyaki restaurant. By adapting traditional Japanese flavors into a fast, casual meal of marinated grilled meats served over rice, he created a beloved Pacific Northwest specialty. Kasahara sold most of his locations over the years (many still have his name, including close to a dozen in the Seattle area), but he still owns and operates one location in Mill Creek, a Seattle suburb, where you can also buy bottled teriyaki sauce. ✉ *16212 Bothell-Everett Hwy., Mill Creek, WA* 🌐 *www.toshisgrill.com*

Chapter 7

THE SOUTHWEST

Updated by
Teresa Bitler, Andrew Collins,
Debbie Harmsen, Mike Weatherford,
and Tessa Woolf

WELCOME TO THE SOUTHWEST

TOP REASONS TO GO

★ **All-star parks:** The Southwest is home to a dozen national parks, including some of the most visited in the United States. Stand in wonder at the Grand Canyon, get away from it all at Great Basin, or even get underground at Carlsbad Caverns.

★ **Red rocks:** From Sedona's stunning formations and Bryce Canyon's hoodoos to Antelope Canyon's sweeping sandstone walls and Nevada's Valley of Fire State Park, this part of the country is awash in shades of ruby, red-orange, and maroon.

★ **Southwest cuisine:** Red hot chili peppers and Hatch green chilies bring the heat, but there's so much to love on every menu. You can find authentic Mexican food in border towns, and varieties, such as Tex-Mex, inland.

★ **The Old West:** It's been more than 100 years since Wyatt Earp landed in Tombstone, Arizona, and more than 150 years since the California Gold Rush began, but traces of the Old West culture of the 1800s live on.

1 Arizona. With its deserts and canyons below and wide-open dark skies above, the Grand Canyon State is a place for both adventure and relaxation.

2 Nevada. The bright lights of Vegas get all the hype, but don't forget about the Hoover Dam, Reno, and so much more in the Silver State.

3 New Mexico. Known for its adobe architecture and abundance of Native American art, New Mexico attracts artistic types to its towns and mountains.

4 Texas. From boomtowns, beaches, and border towns to major cities, scenic spots, and historic sites, the second largest state (after Alaska) has it all.

5 Utah. With its five national parks, including Bryce and Zion, plus world-class skiing and mountain biking, the Beehive State is the place to be outdoors.

MONTANA
SOUTH DAKOTA
IOWA
WYOMING
NEBRASKA
Salt Lake City
Park City
UTAH
5
Arches N.P.
COLORADO
KANSAS
Moab
Canyonlands N.P.
Capitol Reef N.P.
Grand Staircase-Escalante Nat'l Mon.
Monument Valley and the Four Corners
Antelope Canyon
Pueblo Ruins
Cumbres & Toltec Scenic Railroad
Taos
OKLAHOMA
Bisti Badlands
Georgia O'Keeffe Trail
Santa Fe
Amarillo
Albuquerque International Balloon Fiesta
Petrified Forest N.P.
Albuquerque
Palo Duro Canyon State Park
NEW MEXICO
3
1
Gila Cliff Dwellings
Roswell
Lubbock
Ft. Worth
Dallas
White Sands N.P.
Tucson
Abilene
Tombstone
Bisbee
Carlsbad Caverns N.P.
TEXAS
4
Waco
Arizona's Wild West
Bluebonnet Season
Presidential Libraries
Texas Hill Country
Marfa
Houston
Austin
Texas Rodeos
Galveston
San Antonio
MEXICO
Big Bend N.P.
IN SAN ANTONIO:
The Alamo
San Antonio River Walk
Corpus Christi
Gulf Coast Beaches
0
100 mi
0
100 km

WHAT TO EAT AND DRINK IN THE SOUTHWEST

Tex-Mex

TEX-MEX

You can't leave the region without diving into the cheesy, meaty, totally worth-the-calories dishes that derive from the border states of the Southwest, including nachos, enchiladas, chimichangas, and burritos (sometimes called burros in these parts). The major pillar of ingredients includes ground beef, black beans, and cheese. Don't miss Pelons Tex Mex in Austin.

BARBECUE

Texas is famous for putting its own stamp on the American favorite, especially in brisket, with variations in different regions of the Lone Star State. In South Texas, brisket and ribs are slathered with a thick molasses-based sauce. In West Texas, meats like pork and chicken are grilled directly over fire, giving it a smoky mesquite flavor. But Central Texas is the hub of the state's best barbecue, especially Austin.

WINE

Both Texas and Arizona have burgeoning wine regions where you can sip your way through award-winning reds and whites. Start your tour in Texas Hill Country, centering yourself on Fredericksburg with trips to Becker Vineyards and Texas Wine Collective. In Arizona, check out the wineries in Sonoita, about an hour south of Tucson, and Verde Valley, about an hour north of Phoenix.

UTAH HONEY AND SCONES

They don't call Utah the Beehive State for nothing. The state's delicious wildflower honey is sweet liquid gold. It's usually drizzled, along with powdered sugar, over Utah scones, fried pillows of doughnut-like goodness. Pick up a bottle at one of the many excellent farmers' markets around the state, including the Downtown Farmers Market in Salt Lake's Pioneer Park, the Park Silly Sunday Market in Park City, and the Farmers Market in Ogden.

PIÑON NUTS

This tasty variety of pine nuts is huge in New Mexico, Arizona, Utah, and Nevada and were traditionally harvested by the Navajo. They are sprinkled atop dishes like blue corn pancakes to give them texture and a rich nutty flavor. In Nevada's Great Basin National Park, you can fill three gunnysacks of piñon nuts you find in the park to take home. Piñon coffee is also popular.

KOLACHES

Famous in Texas (especially the tiny town of West, Texas) kolaches are pastries made of sweet yeast dough stuffed with savory sausage or sweet fillings like jam. The pockets were brought over by Czech immigrants and have been a hit ever since, especially along the very busy Interstate 35 corridor where people stop and wait in long lines to buy them.

TAMALES

Families order platters of this traditional Mexican dish by the dozen during the holidays, but you can enjoy them year-round. Much like burros or enchiladas, tamales feature a filling (usually meat but not always) surrounded by a shell. Tamales have a corn-based wrapper, and they're steamed in an actual corn husk, which you should unfold and discard before digging into the filling.

Tamales

Prickly Pear Margarita

PRICKLY PEAR

The Southwest's many towering cacti are the source of several food specialties, including cholla, nopales, and prickly pear. The prickly pear cactus produces the wonderful, sweet fruit that's used to accent beverages, desserts, and even entrées. Try it in a prickly pear margarita. When you take your first sip of the bright, magenta-hued drink, you'll wonder how the original ever existed without it.

TEXAS CHILI

The hearty classic is like a traditional chili save a few key ingredients. True Texans don't dare put beans or tomato sauce in chili: it's beef, beef, and more beef. Try it in Tex-Mex restaurants across the state, like Texas Chili Parlor in Austin.

HATCH CHILIES

You needn't fear the hatch chili, but you should respect it. These heat-seeking flavor bombs hail from the Hatch Valley of New Mexico, and are the chilies of choice around the region. Spicy, smoky, and a little sweet, they give a kick to dishes like pozole, salsa, and chili.

Arizona

From the vastness of the Grand Canyon to Sedona's red rocks and the living Sonoran Desert, Arizona's landscapes are awe-inspiring. The state's spectacular canyons, blooming deserts, raging rivers, petrified forests, and scenic mountains enthrall lovers of the outdoors in pursuit of hiking, rafting, golf, or picturesque spots to watch the sunset. But there is more to Arizona than beautiful vistas. World-renowned spas in Phoenix provide plenty of pampering, while Native American cultures thrive throughout the state.

Capital: Phoenix

Population: 7,431,344

Area: 113,655 square miles

Statehood Date: February 14, 1912

Major Airports: Phoenix Sky Harbor International Airport (PHX); Mesa Gateway Airport (AZA); Tucson International Airport (TUS)

Travel and Tourism Information:
www.visitarizona.com
www.arizonahighways.com

Famous Residents: Doc Holliday (Wild West gunfighter); Cesar Chavez (labor organizer and activist); Steven Spielberg (director); Michael Phelps (Olympic swimmer); Stevie Nicks (musician); Emma Stone (actress)

Fun Fact: Arizona adopted the bolo tie—a cord or leather braid with metal tips secured by an ornamental slide—as the state's official neckwear in 1971.

Grand Canyon National Park

America's Geological Superstar

It's the big one, the bucket list topper, and what President Teddy Roosevelt called "the one great sight every American should see." The Grand Canyon draws millions each year, to river raft, camp, ride a mule, take a ranger-led tour, and see wildlife, but most of all, to be awed at one heck of a canvas Mother Nature has crafted. The statistics—the canyon measures an average width of 10 miles, length of 277 river miles, and depth of 1 mile—don't truly prepare you for that first impression. ✉ *450 Rte. 64, Grand Canyon, AZ* 🌐 *www.nps.gov/grca*

Don't Miss

White-water rafting down the Colorado River from the depths of the canyon is an experience you won't soon forget. Most trips begin at Lee's Ferry near Page with one- and two-day trips offered by the Hualapai Tribe beginning in Peach Springs; sign up in advance. 🌐 *www.grandcanyonwest.com/things-to-do/colorado-river-rafting*

Best Hike

The **Rim Trail** runs along the edge of the canyon from Mather Point to Hermits Rest with several overlooks.

Getting Here and Around

There are two main access points: the South Rim—the most popular and easily accessible—is 60 miles from Williams and 80 miles from Flagstaff. The less-trodden North Rim is 220 miles from the South Rim and 265 miles from Las Vegas, and it's only accessible from mid-May to mid-October. Many South Rim visitors choose to spend the night in nearby Tusayan, in the park's lodges (El Tovar and Bright Angel) or on park campgrounds (Mather, Bright Angel, or Desert View).

Sedona

New Age Sophistication in the Desert

Surrounded by verdant pine forests and rugged red rock formations and filled with gourmet restaurants, art galleries, spas, boutiques, and wineries, Sedona is the ultimate place for outdoor adventure and a bit of desert sophistication. It also draws a New Age crowd looking for good vibes in the town's four major electromagnetic energy fields (or vortexes) said to be at **Airport Mesa**, **Cathedral Rock**, **Bell Rock**, and **Boynton Canyon**. Some locals say these spirals of energy make them feel energized and lighter. Of course, this also might be because they happen to afford some amazing, panoramic views of the red buttes. Regardless, you'll be in hiking heaven.

Don't Miss

The showstopper is **Cathedral Rock**, a 1,200-foot-high butte with towering, variegated spires that looms dramatically over town. The butte is best seen toward dusk from a distance, but you can also hike the 1.5-mile trail.

Best Tour

A jeep tour with **Pink Adventure Tours** is a popular choice for driving through the red rocks. Hang on as these seemingly gravity-defying vehicles clamber up and over boulders, giving you bursts of adrenaline in addition to panoramic views of the Coconino National Forest. 🌐 *www.pinkadventuretours.com*

Getting Here and Around

Sedona is about 30 miles from Flagstaff and about 120 miles from Phoenix. To explore on your own, rent a four-wheel-drive vehicle from an agency such as Barlow Adventures; most visitors opt for a jeep tour.

Phoenix

The Ultimate Desert Big City

With 300-plus days of sunshine each year, the Valley of the Sun more than earns its nickname. But warm weather and stunning sunsets aren't the only appeal to Phoenix, the nation's fifth-largest city. Year-round outdoor adventures, including hiking trails and world-class golf courses, plus outstanding museums, spas, and renowned restaurants make it a true oasis in the desert.

Don't Miss

The **Heard Museum** is a treasure trove of art and artifacts from Indigenous tribes. It's especially good to visit during the World Championship Hoop Dance Contest in February or the annual Indian Fair and Market in March. ✉ *2301 N. Central Ave., Phoenix, AZ* 🌐 *www.heard.org*

Best Hike

Named for its resemblance to a camel's hump, **Camelback Mountain** is not only Phoenix's most iconic natural landmark but also its most popular hiking destination. Two trails, Echo Canyon Trail and Cholla Trail, lead to stunning panoramic views.

Best Spa

With its meditation garden and indoor-outdoor treatment rooms at the base of Camelback Mountain, the **Sanctuary Spa** at the five-star Sanctuary Camelback Mountain Resort is a favorite for rejuvenation. ✉ *5700 E. McDonald Dr., Paradise Valley, AZ* 🌐 *www.sanctuaryaz.com*

Getting Here and Around

Fly into Phoenix Sky Harbor International Airport (PHX). It's best to rent a car to get around the sprawling town, although downtown Phoenix is served by a light rail and free DASH (Downtown Area Shuttle) bus service.

Antelope Canyon

A Stunning Sacred Canyon

Situated near the Utah-Arizona border, this narrow red-sandstone slot canyon stuns with its wondrous wavelike structure and convoluted corkscrew formations, dramatically illuminated by light streaming down from above. Like the steady hand of a master artist, wind and water carved the sandstone slot canyon over eons of time. The northern Arizona attraction is a sacred site of the Navajo, called Tsé bighánílíní (place where water runs through the rocks), and you can only visit as part of a guided tour. Nearby, lesser-known canyons like Cardiac Canyon, Antelope Canyon X, and Rattlesnake Canyon make equally impressive alternatives.

Don't Miss

Snapping photos of the canyon's natural formations (resembling a Navajo chief or a smiling shark, for example) is at the top of every photographer's bucket list. The best photos are taken at high noon, when light filters through the canyon surface.

While You're Here

Combine a visit to Antelope Canyon with a trip to nearby **Rainbow Bridge National Monument**, **Vermilion Cliffs National Monument**, or **Lake Powell**.

Good to Know

Because the canyon is on Navajo Nation grounds, the only way to experience it is through a guided tour with a Navajo-owned company. Several operate in Page, including Antelope Canyon Navajo Tours, Antelope Slot Canyon Tours, and Adventurous Antelope Canyon Tours. 🌐 *www.navajotours.com*

Getting Here and Around

Base yourself in nearby Page or book with a touring company that will transport you to the canyon from Phoenix, Sedona, Flagstaff, or Las Vegas. Page is a four-hour drive from either Phoenix or Las Vegas.

Arizona's Wild West

The Ultimate Wild West History Lesson

The Old West lives on in Arizona, especially in three towns: **Jerome**, **Bisbee**, and **Tombstone.** In these legendary Western towns, tours, shows, reenactments, and more bring legendary stories of sheriffs, saloons, silver mines, and shootouts to life. If you're a movie buff, be sure to visit Tucson's **Old Tucson Studios**, where over 500 movies and TV shows were filmed, including *Tombstone, Three Amigos* , and *Little House on the Prairie.*

Tombstone

Wyatt Earp and Doc Holliday made Tombstone famous with their quick draw near the **O.K. Corral,** and the town continues to re-create it among Allen Street's saloons and theaters. ✉ *326 E. Allen St., Tombstone, AZ* 🌐 *www.okcorral.com*

Bisbee

Explore the Bisbee Mining & Historical Museum and tour the Copper Queen Mine, where you don a hard hat, headlamp, and yellow slicker and descend 1,500 feet under the surface. ✉ *5 Copper Queen Plaza, Bisbee, AZ* 🌐 *bisbeemuseum.org*

Jerome

Once called the "wickedest town in the West," Jerome became a ghost town when its mine closed in 1953. Today popular attractions are the **Douglas Mansion**, the **Gold King Mine Ghost Town**, and ghost tours that include a stop at the supposedly haunted **Jerome Grand Hotel**.

Getting Here and Around

Tombstone is about an hour's drive southeast of Tucson, Bisbee is a 25-minute drive from Tombstone on Route 80 E, and Jerome is 295 miles northwest of Tombstone, closer to Sedona, which is 27 miles away.

Canyon de Chelly National Monument

Ancient Home of the Navajo

This national monument located on the Navajo tribal lands of the Colorado Plateau is one of the longest continuously inhabited landscapes in the continent, not to mention one of the most breathtaking natural wonders of the Southwest. On a smaller scale, it rivals even the Grand Canyon in beauty, featuring dramatic red sandstone walls soaring to the sky, ancient pictographs dotting the cliffs, and thousands of archaeological sites transporting you back in time. Among the features are **White House Ruins** and **Mummy Cave**, the remnants of ancient Pueblo villages. You can explore the canyon's rim on your own, hike into it with a ranger, or sign up for a tour with a Navajo guide. ✉ *Navajo Rte. 7, Chinle, AZ* 🌐 *www.nps.gov/cach*

Don't Miss

Spider Rock, a spectacular spire that rises more than 750 feet tall, can be viewed from an overlook on South Rim. The skinny needle of a rock is named for a character of Navajo legend, Spider Woman.

Best Tour

The Navajo-led Jeep tour is the way to go. Take in the spectacular scenery with a knowledgeable guide and learn about the culture of the people who have lived there for thousands of years. 🌐 *www.canyondechellytours.com*

Good to Know

Canyon de Chelly is pronounced "Canyon de Shay."

Getting Here and Around

Located in northeast Arizona, the park entrance is 2 miles east of Chinle. The canyon is 222 miles east of the Grand Canyon and 167 miles from Page.

Route 66

The Mother Road

Created in 1926, the Mother Road still draws travelers on road trips through yesteryear. Although it's not a continuous route anymore and the number 66 was decertified as a U.S. highway designation in 1985, much of the road connecting Chicago to Los Angeles is still drivable and sprinkled with spots of Americana. Arizona communities along the route embrace the kitsch, with 1950s-style diners, neon signs, roadside art, and shops with memorabilia. The route partially follows Interstate 40 and traverses the Petrified National Forest and such communities as **Winslow, Winona, Flagstaff, Williams, Seligman, Hackberry, Kingman,** and **Oatman.** *www.historic66az.com*

Don't Miss

Take your photo "standing on the corner of Winslow, Arizona," with a mural that immortalizes the Eagles' hit song and the famed route. Another great photo op is in front of the **Wigwam Motel** in Holbrook, the inspiration behind Cozy Cone Motel in the animated feature film *Cars*.

Best Pit Stops

Near Winslow, stop at the **Meteor Crater**, where an enormous meteorite struck the ground thousands of years ago. In Seligman, stop at **Delgadillo's Snow Cap Drive-In** for its ice cream, served with a side of quirky fun.

Best Shops

The **General Store** in Hackberry and **Angel & Vilma's Original Route 66 Gift Shop** in Seligman are worthy stops.

Getting Here and Around

For those visiting Petrified Forest National Park, Holbrook is a convenient starting point. For those driving from the Grand Canyon, Williams is the closest access town.

Saguaro National Park

USA's Largest, Oldest Cacti

The towering saguaro (pronounced sa– *wah*–ro) cactus grows only in the Sonoran Desert, so naturally it symbolizes the American Southwest like nothing else. Two distinct sections of Saguaro National Park (East and West) flank either side of Tucson and preserve some of the densest stands of these revered desert giants, which can live to be 200 years old, grow up to 50 feet tall, and weigh a whopping 6 tons. In the spring, white flowers with yellow centers pop up along the cacti's trunk and arms—the official state flower of Arizona. 🌐 *www.nps.gov/sagu*

Don't Miss

The park's West District (also called Tucson Mountain District) is smaller but more visited and has access to hiking trails, ancient petroglyphs, and **Bajada Loop Drive**, a scenic 6-mile drive through the densest growth in the park. The West entrance is near Tucson's **Arizona-Sonora Desert Museum**, so many visitors combine these two sites in one day.

While You're Here

Saguaro National Park's East District (aka Rincon Mountain District) has more than 100 hiking trails, including the accessible **Desert Ecology Trail**.

When to Go

Late April through June is when the saguaros bloom, with peak flowers in May. Fun fact: flowers only bloom on saguaros that are at least 35 years old.

Getting Here and Around

Saguaro National Park is situated on both sides of Tucson. The East District (Saguaro East) is 20 miles from Tucson International Airport (TUS), while the West District (Saguaro West) is 22 miles from Tucson proper.

Petrified Forest National Park

Arizona's Stunning Painted Forest

Step into an otherworldly lunar landscape where ancient trees look like they're made of colorful stone. One of Arizona's most unusual sites, Petrified Forest National Park is home to fossilized trees that date back to the Triassic Period, plus a stretch of the famed Route 66 protected within park boundaries. It's worth the trip just to see the park's beautiful Painted Desert—especially if you catch the brilliant colors of the landscape at midday. You could easily spend half a day or more viewing petrified logs as well as Pueblo rock art, hiking various trails, and enjoying views from the many overlooks. ✉ *1 Park Rd., Petrified Forest, AZ* 🌐 *www.nps.gov/pefo*

Don't Miss

Old Faithful, a roughly 44-ton log, lies along Giant Logs, a half-mile loop that begins behind **Rainbow Forest Museum** near the park's south entrance.

Best Drive

Winding 28 miles through the Painted Desert, the **Painted Desert Scenic Drive** is a must for seeing the park's flora and fauna, plus Newspaper Rock, a large boulder with petroglyphs carved into it, and several cone-shape teepees. The moderately steep 1-mile Blue Mesa trail loop can be accessed from the road. Listen to a free audio tour as you go either on the park's website or through the NPS's free app.

Getting Here and Around

Situated between Interstate 40 and U.S. 180, Petrified Forest National Forest is closest to the town of Holbrook, Arizona, about 25 miles away.

Stargazing

The Best Dark Skies in America

The heavenly bodies shine bright in Arizona's "dark sky" destinations, specially designated places that are far enough from city light pollution that you can see uninterrupted swaths of twinkling constellations up above the world so high. You might even see a planet or two. This happens nearly every night, given Arizona's roughly 350 clear-sky nights each year. The Tucson-based International Dark Sky Association deems 18 places in Arizona official "dark sky" destinations, including **Petrified Forest National Park**, **Oracle State Park**, **Flagstaff**, **Sedona**, **Camp Verde**, the **Village of Oak Creek**, **Kartchner Caverns State Park**, and the **Grand Canyon National Park**. Find them all at 🌐 *www.darksky.org*.

Don't Miss

To get a closer look with high-powered telescopes, head to the **Lowell Observatory** in Flagstaff, where Pluto was discovered in 1930 and **Kitt Peak National Observatory** in Sells outside Tucson, home to the world's largest solar telescope.

Best Stargazing Parties

In Tucson, Flandrau Science Center & Planetarium hosts a weekly astronomy program, and the Mt. Lemmon SkyCenter holds nightly stargazing programs. Each June, the Grand Canyon hosts a weeklong affair with constellation tours, telescope viewing, and free nightly astronomy talks.

Getting Here and Around

Stargazing is best in desert areas far from city light pollution. Flagstaff, Sedona, and the Grand Canyon are top places to stargaze. The Grand Canyon is a four-hour drive from Phoenix and its airport (PHX).

Scottsdale Golfing

The Best Golfing in the Country

The hot and dry climate of the Valley of the Sun, along with a wealth of high-end resorts, has made the upscale Phoenix suburb of Scottsdale an ideal playground for golfers. Scottsdale packs in 51 golf courses within its city limits and 200 more in its environs. Designed by such notable names as Robert Trent Jones, Phil Mickelson, Rees Jones, and Ben Crenshaw, Scottdale's sun-splashed courses provide golfers with a delightful cornucopia of Southwestern scenes, scents, and sounds—from rock formations, mountain vistas, and ribbonlike fairways lined with Sonoran Desert cacti to the aromas of eucalyptus, mesquite, and pine to the soft lullaby of cascading water. *experiencescottsdale.com/golf*

Don't Miss

Many of the courses have been ranked as top picks in the state and region by *Golf Magazine* and *Golf Digest*, including Boulders, Desert Forest, Estancia, We-Ko-Pa Golf Club (Saguaro), Scottsdale National (The Other Course), Desert Highlands, Whisper Rock (Upper and Lower), Talking Stick (O'odham), and Quintero.

While You're Here

After you've putted your way through Scottsdale's courses, retreat to one its many spas, pop into its art galleries, and visit Frank Lloyd Wright's winter home, **Taliesin West**, a UNESCO World Heritage site. *12621 N. Frank Lloyd Wright Blvd., Scottsdale, AZ* *franklloydwright.org*

Getting Here and Around

Scottsdale is about a 15-minute drive from Phoenix Sky Harbor International Airport (PHX). Touring downtown is easily done on foot, but you'll want a car to explore further.

Havasu Falls

An Epic Hike to An Epic Waterfall

One of the most spectacular waterfalls in Arizona is Havasu Falls (literally, "blue-green waters") part of the Havasupai tribal land of the Grand Canyon. This breathtaking beauty is hidden to most of the world, but hikers with the resources to complete the multiday 19-mile (round-trip) hike—including stamina, initiative, and proper backcountry gear and experience—are rewarded by the glorious sight of the falls' turquoise waters cascading over rugged red rocks and crashing down 100 feet into Havasu Creek below, all of it tucked into a paradisical red-rock setting.

Don't Miss

Camping at **Havasupai Campground**, located on Havasupai land between Havasu Falls and Mooney Falls, is a highlight of the hike. 🌐 *www.havasupaireservations.com*

Planning Your Trip

This is not a last-minute trip. A hard-to-come-by permit is needed, so aspiring hikers must make a reservation well in advance. It is also not a day trip. The minimum commitment is a three-night stay at the rustic Havasupai Falls Campground or at the basic lodge in the Supai Village; with either choice you will need to bring your own food. Permits are obtained online beginning February 1 each year.

While You're Here

Havasu Falls isn't the only waterfall on Havasupai land. It's also home to **Beaver Falls**, **Fifty Foot Falls**, **Little Navajo Falls**, and **Mooney Falls**.

Getting Here and Around

The Hualapai Hilltop trailhead is a 3½-hour drive from the South Rim of Grand Canyon National Park. Peach Springs is the nearest town to the trailhead.

When in Arizona

BEARIZONA

This 160-acre drive-through wildlife park and walk-through zoo within the Kaibab National Forest is home to more than two dozen animal species, including the arctic wolf, bison, jaguars, pythons, javelinas, mini donkeys, prairie dogs, elk, raccoon, deer, porcupines, foxes, reindeer, goats, and, of course, black bears and grizzlies. You can see the animals in their natural habitat as you drive through the park on your own or via a bus tour. Animals here are in the wild, so on the drive-through portion you are not allowed to touch or feed the animals. However, at Fort Bearizona, the portion of the park that follows the drive-through area, there is a petting zoo. ✉ *1500 E. Rte. 66, Williams, AZ* 🌐 *www.bearizona.com*

Do This: Learn about the animals from a knowledgeable guide on the park's "Wild Ride" bus tour, which stops to feed the bison and view a wolf-training session.

BISBEE ART SCENE

The independent spirit that once made Bisbee a rough-and-tumble kind of place in its old mining days now lends itself to artistic expression. Set in the Mule Mountains about 11 miles from the Mexico border and 95 miles south of Tucson, the town of just 4,900 has more than a dozen art galleries. Among the creations displayed are paintings, sculptures, ceramics, handmade furniture, photographs, contemporary art, jewelry, and specially crafted toys. An art walk occurs every second Saturday. Visual art pairs with wine tastings, live music, and antiques shopping.

Do This: Walk along the alleyway of Brewery Gulch after grabbing a pint at Old Bisbee Brewing Company and be treated to an eclectic collection of art lining the exterior wall. The pieces have come from a variety of sources and been obtained in all manner of ways, including dumpster dives. If you feel so inclined, make your own contribution.

LONDON BRIDGE

Remember the old nursery rhyme "London Bridge Is Falling Down"? Well, it was. In 1968, after about 150 years of constant use, the 930-foot-long landmark was sinking into the Thames. When Lake Havasu City founder Robert McCullough heard about this predicament, he set about buying London Bridge, having it disassembled, shipped more than 5,000 miles to northwestern Arizona, and rebuilt, stone by stone. The bridge was reconstructed on mounds of sand and took three years to complete. When it was finished, a mile-long channel was dredged under the bridge and water was diverted from Lake Havasu through the Bridgewater Channel. Today, the entire city is centered on this unusual attraction. ✉ *422 English Center, Lake Havasu City, AZ*

Do This: Take a self-guided walking tour, exploring the base before climbing 51 stairs to the top of the bridge. Stop and admire the antique lampposts. Lining the London Bridge, these historical structures were created from the cannons that the British took from Napoléon's army in 1815, spoils of war from the Battle of Waterloo.

SPRING TRAINING

You can watch practices and exhibition games for several teams during Major League Baseball's spring training each March in the Phoenix area, when the weather is fantastic. The Arizona Cactus League is composed of 15 different MLB teams: the Arizona Diamondbacks, Athletics, Chicago Cubs, Chicago White Sox, Cincinnati Reds, Cleveland Guardians, Colorado Rockies, Kansas City Royals, Los Angeles Angels, Los Angeles Dodgers, Milwaukee Brewers, San Diego Padres, San Francisco Giants,

Seattle Mariners, and Texas Rangers. Venues include Goodyear Ballpark, Peoria Sports Complex, Sloan Park, Scottsdale Stadium, Tempe Diablo Stadium, Camelback Ranch–Glendale, and Surprise Stadium. 🌐 *www.cactusleague.com*

Do This: Bring a blanket and picnic behind a fence on the sloped lawns just past the outfield (the Royals/Rangers, Guardians/Reds, Padres/Mariners, Angels, Giants, Cubs, and Diamondbacks/Rockies all have lawn seating) and let your kids collect any home-run balls that land nearby. And have your catcher's mitt at the ready, just in case.

About Our Writers

Teresa Bitler moved to Phoenix, AZ before her first birthday and has spent most of her life in its metro area. She loves the state's diversity, from its desert mountains to the world's largest contiguous Ponderosa Pine forest in the White Mountains, and she craves Sonoran Mexican food when she travels. She is a freelance travel writer.

Cool Places to Stay

Enchantment Resort. The energy from one of Sedona's major vortexes surrounds this luxury retreat, known for its award-winning Mii amo spa, full schedule of wellness classes, and guided hikes. The on-site Trail House keeps guests busy with add-on experiences including rock-climbing, mountain biking, and photography tours while the resort's Artist Cottage offers classes in painting, pottery throwing, pottery glazing, and wood burning. ✉ *525 Boynton Canyon Rd., Sedona, AZ* 🌐 *www.enchantmentresort.com*

Joshua Tree House Tucson. Bordering Saguaro National Park, this *posada*—Spanish for inn—takes advantage of its scenic and serene location with windows, patios, and rooftop balconies for glimpses of the flora and fauna as well as pleasant views of sunrises and star-filled nights. The desert-theme property features seven Spanish-styled suites that open into a shared living and dining area. ✉ *12051 W. Fort Lowell Rd., Tucson, AZ* 🌐 *www.thejoshuatreehouse.com*

Sanctuary Resort Camelback Mountain. Step into luxury, comfort, and serenity at this 53-acre Scottsdale-area property that has the scenic surroundings of Camelback Mountain as its backdrop. Enjoy a relaxing treatment at the Asian-inspired spa, face off on the tennis and pickleball courts, or lounge in the infinity pool. Elements, the on-site restaurant overlooking the Valley, satisfies with savory dishes inspired by earth, wind, fire, and air. ✉ *5700 E. McDonald Dr., Paradise Valley, AZ* 🌐 *www.sanctuaryoncamelback.com*

Wigwam Motel. Immerse yourself in the kitschy, 1950-era Americana vibes of Route 66 at this hard-to-miss village of concrete teepees along the Mother Road. Each cone-shape structure comes equipped with pine log furniture and either two twin beds or a queen bed and a small but full bathroom. There is also heat, air-conditioning, and cable TV. ✉ *811 W. Hopi Dr., Holbrook, AZ* 🌐 *www.sleepinawigwam.com*

Essential Eats

El Charro Café. Opened in 1922, this Tucson icon reigns as the oldest Mexican restaurant continuously run by one family in the United States and claims to have invented the chimichanga when its original owner accidentally dropped a burro in the fryer. Try the local favorite *carne seca*, marinated and sun-dried beef served with fresh tortillas, or the tamales, which are shipped around the world.✉ *311 N. Court Ave., Tucson, AZ* 🌐 *www.elcharro-cafe.com*

The Stockyards. A favorite dining spot for local cattlemen and politicians when it adjoined the local stockyards in the 1940s and 1950s, this steak house still grills premium steak but has broadened its menu to include elk medallions, bison meat loaf, Chilean sea bass, wild boar sausage, roast chicken, and salmon. Allow enough time for a drink at the hand-carved mahogany bar in the restaurant's saloon. ✉ *5009 E. Washington, Phoenix, AZ* 🌐 *www.stockyardssteak-house.com*

The Sugar Bowl. You can order a variety of sandwiches and salads, but ice cream is the main attraction at this parlor and soda fountain famous for its frequent appearance in local Bil Keane's *Family Circus* comic strip. Go all in and order a Sugar Bowl sundae with your choice of toppings or choose from four different banana splits, each crowned with a Maraschino cherry. ✉ *4005 N. Scottsdale Rd., Scottsdale, AZ* 🌐 *www.sugarbowlscotts-dale.com*

The Turquoise Room. Located inside La Posada hotel, this restaurant relies on seasonal ingredients for its Native American–inspired menu. Feast on Navajo-raised lamb, stuffed squash blossoms, grilled quail, pork chops, and prime rib. Guests can also opt for the Fred Harvey Experience, a prix-fixe three-course meal inspired by the glory days of train travel. ✉ *305 E. 2nd St., Winslow, AZ* 🌐 *www.theturquoiseroom.com*

Nevada

Nevada is a vast state with most of its population clustered in a certain Sin City in the southwest corner. Stark desert beauty and a bit of the Wild West is found in much of the rest of Nevada, particularly in Great Basin National Park, where high desert meets alpine forest. Straddling the California/Nevada state line is the Sierra Nevada resort region of Lake Tahoe and Reno, which beckons naturalists, campers, boaters, and those looking for similar action to Las Vegas in a more local setting.

Capital: Carson City

Population: 3,267,467

Area: 110,577 square miles

Statehood Date: Oct. 31, 1864

Major Airports: Harry Reid International Airport (LAS); Reno/Tahoe International Airport (RNO)

Travel and Tourism Information:
🌐 *www.visitlasvegas.com*
🌐 *www.nevadamagazine.com*

Famous Residents: Clara Bow (actress); Howard Hughes (businessman); Wayne Newton (musician); Andre Agassi (tennis player); David Copperfield (magician)

Fun Fact: One can both snow ski and water ski in one day on the edges of Las Vegas, moving from around 11,000 feet elevation at Mt. Charleston to 1,200 feet at Lake Mead.

Las Vegas Strip

America's Entertainment and Gambling Epicenter

A neon glow electrifies the 4.2 miles of 24/7 entertainment in the Las Vegas strip, the center of action for the 40 million people a year who come for glittering casinos, theaters, restaurants, rides, shows, shops, and everything over-the-top. The Strip disorients and delights; when you're here, you're all-in, and the "real world" seems far out. More than a dozen hotel-casinos are on the strip, including the **MGM Grand**, **Caesars Palace**, and the **Bellagio.** Professional football, hockey, and women's basketball franchises now play on the Strip alongside big-name concert acts, but there are still resident performers of all kinds, including acrobats, magicians, and comedians.

Don't Miss

Take a gondola ride at the **Venetian**'s rendition of Venice's Canalozzo. In addition to being serenaded on your boat ride, you can catch the gondoliers breaking out in song twice a day at the hotel. ✉ *3355 S. Las Vegas Blvd., Las Vegas, NV* 🌐 *www.venetianlasvegas.com*

Best Tour

The **Big Bus Open Top Las Vegas Night Tour**, a two-hour excursion on a double-decker bus includes both the Strip and Fremont Street and takes riders by famous city landmarks. 🌐 *www.bigbustours.com*

Getting Here and Around

Las Vegas's Harry Reid International Airport (LAS) is only 2 miles from the Strip, which is the portion of Las Vegas Boulevard that runs from Sahara Avenue on the north to Russell Road on the southern end. Free trams connecting three casinos and the Las Vegas Monorail (on the East side) can help you get around the Strip.

Hoover Dam

Industrial Wonder of the World

Straddling Nevada and Arizona, the Hoover Dam is an engineering feat that's been declared one of the industrial wonders of the world. The 6.6-million-ton, 724.6-foot-tall concrete dam was built as an arch-gravity dam, a type of barrier that uses an arch structure and the force of gravity to resist the pressure of the water against the dam—which, in the Hoover Dam's case, is 45,000 pounds per square foot at its base. Constructed by thousands of workers during the Great Depression between 1931 and 1936, the dam was built to control flooding and create a reservoir from the Colorado River that would supply water and electricity to the surrounding area. Today, the dam's stored water irrigates 2 million acres of farmland and goes to Los Angeles, Phoenix, and Tucson, while its power plant generates 4 billion kilowatt-hours of hydroelectric power to Nevada, Arizona, and California.

Don't Miss

Learn about the dam's history and engineering through exhibits at the interactive **Hoover Dam Visitor Center.** You can also take the guided dam tour, which includes admission to the visitor center, the power plant, and an elevator ride to the top of the dam. ✉ *81 Hoover Dam Access Rd., Boulder City, NV* 🌐 *www.usbr.gov/lc/hooverdam/service*

While You're Here

Visit the restaurants and shops in **Boulder City**, a community 7 miles away that was created for the workers erecting Hoover Dam. Inside the Boulder Dam Hotel is a free museum about the dam.

Getting Here and Around

Hoover Dam is 30 miles from Las Vegas, off Route 172. Parking is $10.

Fremont Street Experience

Vegas On Full Blast

Downtown Las Vegas has evolved dramatically in the past few years, seeing even more change than the Strip. Fremont Street pulses with its own beat and a slate of activities and entertainment, thanks to the canopy and its programmed LED light shows that closed vehicle traffic and transformed "Glitter Gulch" into the **Fremont Street Experience.** A zipline races above costumed characters, street performers, and two stages of free live music. With the exception of the towering Circa, the casinos along Fremont Street are not the mammoth structures with over-the-top features but are more the classic casinos that first made Las Vegas the country's gaming capital—think **Golden Nugget**, **Binion's Gambling Hall**, and **Golden Gate Hotel & Casino**, which opened in 1906. 🌐 *vegasexperience.com*

Don't Miss

The **Mob Museum** shines a light on the seedy world of organized crime and law enforcement's response to it. Be sure to head downstairs to the speak-easy and distillery—an add-on ticket will even get you a taste of moonshine and a lesson on how it's brewed. ✉ *300 Stewart Ave., Las Vegas, NV* 🌐 *www.themobmuseum.org*

Beyond Fremont Street

Not far from the northern terminus of the famous Strip, the Arts District sees a once-grungy Main Street and surrounding blocks transformed into a cool area for brewpubs, restaurants, live theater, and art galleries.

Getting Here and Around

Fremont Street is about 6 miles from Las Vegas's Harry Reid International Airport (LAS) and is easily walkable.

Great Basin National Park

A Quiet Slice of America's Largest Desert

One of the smallest national parks is also one of the least-visited. But that can add to the appeal of Great Basin National Park as a place to be away from the crowds seen at other national parks. The 77,180-acre northern Nevada park is remote, occupying a small portion of the 200,000-square-mile Great Basin Desert, the largest desert in America, covering 75% of Nevada as well as portions of Utah, Idaho, and California. A visit requires some forethought: the park's lone restaurant is open only part of the year (April through October), the campsites can be seasonally in demand, and the outlying community of Baker doesn't have the abundant lodging options of other parks. But Great Basin does reward you with some surprising gems: **Lehman Caves**, a limestone and marble cavern with a visitor's center, explored by guided tour only; groves of ancient and gnarly bristlecone pines, reached via **Bristlecone Pine Trail**, a 2.8-mile round-trip hike; and **Wheeler Peak**, best experienced by a scenic drive capped with panoramic views from 13,000 feet. ✉ *Rte. 488, Baker, NV* 🌐 *www.nps.gov/grba*

Don't Miss

Great Basin is an International Dark-Sky Park, so it's a great place to stargaze. If you're here at night, check out the view from **Mather Overlook**. Or book a trip on the **Nevada Northern Railway's Star Train**, a ranger-led trip where the night sky is literally the star of the show. The three-hour trip departs just before sunset from Ely, an hour west of the park. 🌐 *nnry.com/train-rides*

Getting Here and Around

The park is a 3¾-hour drive from Salt Lake City and a 4½-hour drive from Las Vegas.

Valley of Fire State Park

A Geologic Wonderland

Otherworldly rock formations and red Aztec sandstone highlight the 40,000-acre Valley of Fire State Park, a popular side trip from Las Vegas, about an hour north of the city. Visitors can hike several trails or take short drives to explore slot canyons, see petroglyphs from Native American communities from some 2,500 years ago, and marvel at structures like Arch Rock, Elephant Rock, Seven Sisters, Piano Rock, White Domes, Beehives, Silica Dome, Balanced Rock, and Atlatl Rock. Wildlife includes lizards, coyotes, and jackrabbits, as well as finches, sparrows, and roadrunners. Guided tours depart from Las Vegas. ✉ *29450 Valley of Fire Hwy., Overton, NV* 🌐 *www.parks.nv.gov*

Don't Miss

The easy, essential trail is **Mouse's Tank**, a short walk with petroglyphs and shade from the steep canyon walls. Stop at **Rainbow Vista** for panoramic views or **Fire Wave Trail** to see an incredible wavelike sandstone formation. For colorful fossilized wood from ancient pines, head to **Petrified Logs Loop** in the park's southwest quadrant.

When to Go

The sun-soaked, rocky landscape blooms in springtime with desert marigold, indigo bush, and desert mallow, and flourishes with burro bush, creosote brush, and a variety of cacti throughout the year.

Getting Here and Around

Valley of Fire State Park is about 60 miles from Las Vegas.

Red Rock Canyon

A Nature Escape From Vegas

The explosive growth of Las Vegas has pushed development to the very edge of Red Rock Canyon National Conservation Area, making the 195,819-acre refuge something akin to a city park for locals, while remaining a destination-tourism hub for serious rock climbers, hikers, and bikers. The red-sandstone rock formations, narrow canyons, and seasonal waterfalls have always offered a dramatic contrast to the Strip and a time-honored "morning after" breath of fresh air after a night of indoor sensory overload. 🌐 *www.redrockcanyonlv.org*

Don't Miss

The **Scenic Loop** is perfect for those with limited hiking abilities. The 13-mile one-way drive gives you the highlights of the park and several places to stop and hop out of the car to explore.

Good to Know

Calico Tanks is the most popular of the 26 trails, a 2.2-miler rated as "moderate-to-strenuous" and offering a short course in the canyon's diversity, from sandstone rocks for the kids to climb to a hidden water pocket.

While You're Here

Ice Box Canyon, is, as the name suggests, a popular hike that's refreshing in the warmer months, thanks to narrow canyon walls that keep it shaded. Nonetheless, the 2.2-mile trek is rated as "strenuous" so approach with caution.

Getting Here and Around

The canyon entrance is off Charleston Boulevard, about 22 miles from most Strip hotels. Timed reservations are required for the Scenic Loop from October through May. A modest visitor center inside the gate offers an air-conditioned view of the canyon, history of the region, and exhibits on local flora and fauna.

Lake Mead National Recreation Area

An Oasis in the Desert

Splash into 248 square miles of cool water at the nation's largest man-made lake and reservoir, Lake Mead, located in Lake Mead National Recreation Area. The larger area, which also includes Lake Mohave downstream from the dam, has 1.5 million acres of playground away from the desert heat. The terrain is mixed with surrounding beach-front—always changing, as the lake shrinks from years of drought, as well as mountains, valleys, and canyons. For water fun, there's houseboating, canoeing, kayaking, fishing, and swimming. You can even scuba dive in the fresh waters; underwater sights include a white gypsum reef. On the shore you can hike, bike, camp, horseback ride, and even hunt in a designated area. 🌐 *www.nps.gov/lake*

Don't Miss

Rent a houseboat on Lake Mead and you can pull into coves and explore the shoreline, relax on the beach, or play in the calm waters by day and stargaze by night.

While You're Here

Take a scenic drive along **Lakeshore Road**, which runs along a portion of Boulder Basin; **Pearce Ferry Road**, which winds through desert and Joshua trees near Grand Wash Cliffs; and 50-mile **Northshore Road**, which connects Callville Bay and Echo Bay.

Getting Here and Around

Lake Mead National Recreation Area has six main entrances: Boulder Beach, the most visited entry point, is near the Alan Bible Visitors Center 4 miles from Boulder City, which is 25 miles from Las Vegas's Reid International Airport (LAS). Other entrances are Lake Mead Boulevard, Lake Mead Parkway, Cottonwood Cove, Willow Beach (on the Arizona side), and Katherine Landing (at Lake Mohave Marina).

Lamoille Canyon Scenic Byway

A Dazzling Mountain Drive

This 12-mile drive through Humboldt National Forest might fool you into thinking you're no longer in Nevada. Climbing through 8,800 feet of a glacier-carved canyon, the paved road in the Ruby Mountains provides views of mountains and greenery in stark contrast to the desert scenery of much of the state and far from the bright lights of Las Vegas. Loosely following Lamoille Creek, the byway leads you past rock formations and through colorful alpine meadows filled with wildlife and wildflowers. You may see bighorn sheep, deer, and mountain goats.

Don't Miss

Pull over to picnic and hike. Any of the hiking trails will lead you to more gorgeous scenery, including little lakes with beaver ponds, serene waterfalls, and trickling streams (where you can fish), as well as to camping spots.

When to Go

The byway is seasonal, open May through October, with the dates on either end dependent on the weather. Springtime, when the wildflowers are in bloom and the snow is melting, is an ideal time to make the drive. The fall, when the aspen trees turn yellow, is also especially beautiful.

Getting Here and Around

Lamoille Canyon Scenic Byway, also called FS Road 660, is about 1 mile from Lamoille, Nevada, and 22 miles from the town of Spring Creek. Reach it via Lamoille Highway or Route 227. The scenic drive is not a loop; so when it ends, turn around and go back the way you came.

When in Nevada

AREA 51

Could this be the most popular place you can't visit? Since the mid-1950s, at the height of the Cold War, a mystery has shrouded this highly classified U.S. Air Force base. Myths have circulated for decades of alien sightings within the highly secured area, and Nevada State Route 375 has even become known as the Extraterrestrial Highway. The official statement is that any flying saucers spotted are specially crafted spy planes, but that didn't stop a legend from forming about the military facility. Its ominous signs warning visitors to stay away only add to the speculation. The location is tightly sealed up, and trespassing should not be attempted.

Do This: You can't step inside Area 51, but you can drive to the edge of it and have fun hitting the tourist traps nearby. The Little A'Le'Inn in the tiny town of Rachel is the essential stop for a burger, beer, and advice on how to get that photo opp near the gate without getting arrested. Check out the Alien Research Center between Hiko and Alamo, where you can learn more E.T.-related facts and fantasy.

BURNING MAN

Late every August, the temporary city of Black Rock emerges from the dust and draws thousands of pilgrims to Burning Man. More like an experimental community than a festival, Burning Man draws adventurers, artists, and partiers together under principles like "self-expression, communal effort" for larger-than-life art installations, impromptu performances, and wild parties. It's a spectacle you have to see to believe, but it's not cheap and requires complete self-reliance when it comes to camp planning and supplies. 🌐 *burningman.org*

Do This: In the "Temple Burn" a giant temple structure is burned to the ground at the end of the event, said to be almost a spiritual experience.

LAKE TAHOE

Lake Tahoe is one of the world's largest, clearest, and deepest alpine lakes, so spectacular that it takes two states to share joint custody. It's a premiere destination for hiking, camping, skiing, and boating. The Nevada side has Crystal Bay and the resort area of Incline Village on the north end, while the south end offers Nevada Beach, Zephyr Cove, and plenty of casinos. Most of them are in Stateline on the southern end of the lake, including Harrah's Lake Tahoe and Golden Nugget Lake Tahoe, offering Vegas-style shows and concerts along with fresher air.

Do This: Take the scenic 72-mile drive around the lake in the warmer months (when you don't have to worry about snow or tire chains). You'll see everything from beaches to elevated vistas if you travel Route 89 (southwest and west shores), Route 28 (north and northeast shores), and U.S. 50 (east and southeast shores).

NEON BONEYARD

Take a walk through the ghosts of Vegas signs past at the colorful 2-acre Neon Boneyard sitting behind the Neon Museum visitor center. You'll wind past walkways stacked with big, bold eye-popping signs that once dotted the Vegas landscape, from the iconic Golden Nugget and Stardust signs to the more modern guitar-shape Hard Rock Cafe sign. ✉ *770 Las Vegas Blvd. N, Las Vegas, NV* 🌐 *www.neonmuseum.org*

Do This: A guided tour of the boneyard, led by a historian, takes about one hour. The museum includes a North Gallery with signs from the 1930s to today. For obvious reasons, the museum can be more fun to visit at night, and it stays open until 11 pm.

RENO

Though sometimes called a less flashy version of Las Vegas, Reno has its own personality that sets it apart. This "biggest little city in the world," as the Reno arch will announce when you arrive, has its share of casinos, shows, and museums, but the town also has some Old West attractions, the Nevada Museum of Art, and a downtown Riverwalk District filled with shops and restaurants. That downtown area also has a college-town vibe, thanks to the University of Nevada, Reno campus being a short hop away.

Do This: Check out the National Automobile Museum, where you can see more than 200 classics, including those once driven by Elvis. ✉ *10 S. Lake St., Reno, NV* 🌐 *www.automuseum.org*

THE SPHERE

When it opened in 2023, the Sphere transformed the Las Vegas skyline with its animated exterior projections, but the 18,600-seat concert venue is equally impressive inside. Wraparound imagery offers a unique twist for veteran performers like the Eagles and Dead & Company and elevates the likes of the Backstreet Boys or electronic music DJs to new levels of interest. ✉ *255 Sands Ave., Las Vegas, NV* 🌐 *thesphere.com*

Do This: If you're not in town when someone you want to see is playing, check out the daytime film schedule. Custom productions, such as a reimagined version of *The Wizard of Oz,* put the 18K-projection and special effects—wind, fire, vibrating seats—to double-duty use.

Cool Places to Stay

Bellagio Hotel & Casino. Famously featured in *Ocean's Eleven*, the beautiful Bellagio, part of the MGM Resorts International chain of hotels, offers elegant rooms and suites with big-time views. Depending on which room you stay in, your window might frame mountain vistas, the Las Vegas Strip, or the famous Bellagio fountains. ✉ *3600 Las Vegas Blvd. S, Las Vegas, NV* 🌐 *bellagio.mgmresorts.com*

Houseboat on Lake Mead. Just 30 miles from Las Vegas, Lake Mead is the largest man-made lake and reservoir in the country. You can rent a houseboat and enjoy gazing at the stars at night and at the surrounding cliffs, canyons, and mountains during the day. Explore the shore, hit the beach, and splash in the calm waters. For those who don't feel at ease behind the wheel, Callville Bay has a "houseboat hotel" where you can stay on a docked one. 🌐 *www.callvillebay.com* 🌐 *www.houseboating.org*

Whitney Peak Hotel. The rare non-gaming hotel in Reno, this Hilton-affiliated, pet-friendly place near the Reno Arch caters to the outdoor enthusiast, with a free-spirit adventure vibe. In addition to its Sierra-theme rooms, the hotel sports a massive rock climbing wall. If you aren't scaling that wall, or relaxing in the sauna or steam room, you might be rocking out to live entertainment in the hotel's concert hall. ✉ *255 N. Virginia St., Reno, NV* 🌐 *www.whitneypeakhotel.com*

About Our Writers

Mike Weatherford grew up in Tulsa, OK, but got to Las Vegas before a lot of other people in 1987. Maybe that's why he gravitates to old-school places like the Bootlegger Italian Bistro that celebrate the classic, imploded era of Vegas, although he also loves how the once-sad downtown has been revived. He spent decades as an entertainment reporter-columnist at the *Las Vegas Review-Journal*, spanning the eras from Frank Sinatra to Bruno Mars.

Essential Eats

JJ's Pie Co. If you want to feel like a Reno local or a college student, you'll be surrounded by plenty of both in this pizzeria that's been feeding them since 1983. Join the generations of University of Nevada, Reno students who can't wait for the next pepperoni, salami, and sausage triple-whammy of a JJ's Special. ✉ *555 W. 5th St., Reno, NV* 🌐 *www.jjspieco.com*

Lotus of Siam. This James Beard Award–winning Thai restaurant has attained a cult status for its vast menu of Northern Thai, Issan-style dishes. Always start with the garlic prawns while pondering the wine list of 300 choices and a menu of dishes you may have never encountered before. There are three Las Vegas locations, including one inside Red Rock Resort. 🌐 *www.lotusofsiamlv.com*

Peppermill Las Vegas. This institution is a rarity for its longevity alone—it's been a fixture since 1972—and for surviving that time as a stand-alone, non-casino restaurant right on the Strip. The restaurant is popular for its supersize platters of Southern-fried steak and eggs and giant waffles, and it seats diners until 1:30 am when more and more of the better hotel restaurants close early. ✉ *2985 Las Vegas Blvd. S, Las Vegas, NV* 🌐 *www.peppermilllasvegas.com*

Piero's Italian Cuisine. Its location makes this a time-honored "expense account" tradition for those visiting the Las Vegas Convention Center just across the street. But the interior, the history, and, yes, the food make it a mecca for those fascinated by the classic mob era of Vegas. Indeed, Piero's has the dual honor of being both a filming location for the *Casino* movie and having hosted the real-life characters depicted in it. The labyrinth layout and dark-wood atmosphere resonate as much as the platters of linguini and clams. ✉ *355 E. Convention Center Dr., Las Vegas, NV* 🌐 *www.pieroscuisine.com*

Spago Las Vegas. Wolfgang Puck is widely credited for breaking the casino steakhouse mold and bringing celebrity chefs to Vegas when he brought Spago to the Strip (in a different location) in 1992. The signature pizzas, pastas, and farm-to-table produce now come with a view of the Fountains of Bellagio. ✉ *3600 Las Vegas Blvd. S, Las Vegas, NV* 🌐 *bellagio.mgmresorts.com*

New Mexico

Albuquerque is New Mexico's welcoming gateway, and its residents—like its food and art—reflect a confluence of Native American, Hispanic, and Anglo culture. Santa Fe is surrounded by mind-expanding mountain views and is filled with streets characterized by low-slung adobe architecture. Venture farther afield into New Mexico's stunning wilderness and you'll discover a land of exceptionally diverse scenery, from the dramatic limestone formations of Carlsbad Caverns to the towering dunes of White Sands National Park.

Capital: Santa Fe

Population: 2,130,25

Area: 121,590 square miles

Statehood Date: January 6, 1912

Major Airports: Albuquerque International Sunport (ABQ); Santa Fe Municipal Airport (SAF)

Travel and Tourism Information: *www.newmexico.org* *www.newmexicomagazine.org*

Famous Residents: Cormac McCarthy (author); Georgia O'Keeffe (artist); J. Robert Oppenheimer (scientist); George R. R. Martin (author); Demi Moore (actress); Neil Patrick Harris (actor)

Fun Fact: In traditional New Mexican restaurants, the server taking your order will almost always ask, "red or green?" This is a reference to the state's famously smoky and spicy chili sauce. If you want to enjoy them both, do as locals do and answer this question: "Christmas!"

Santa Fe

Oldest (and Artsiest) State Capital

On an inclined plateau at the base of the Sangre de Cristo Mountains—at an elevation of 7,000 feet—Santa Fe is both the highest and oldest capital city in the country. Its streets brim with reminders of four centuries of Spanish and Mexican rule, and of the Pueblo cultures that have thrived in the area for many centuries. The town is perhaps best known for its adobe homes and art. Artists and writers—from Willa Cather to George R. R. Martin—have been drawn to the rugged beauty and dry air of Santa Fe for generations. Compact though it is, the so-called City Different contains an astounding trove of museums that celebrate its creative traditions, including the **Georgia O'Keeffe Museum**, **Museum of International Folk Art**, **Museum of Indian Arts & Culture**, and contemporary **SITE Santa Fe**. Prominent art festivals as well as the renowned **Santa Fe Opera** take place throughout the summer months.

Don't Miss

More than 100 art galleries line **Canyon Road**, a famous nearly 1-mile stretch of pavement that was once a dusty burro path. Called "the art and soul of Santa Fe," the road is lined with adobe homes from the 18th century, most of which have been converted to house galleries, studios, boutiques, and a handful of notable restaurants.

Best Neighborhood

In the Railyard District, a popular indoor-outdoor farmers' market, a fun urban park, and hip restaurants, galleries, and indie shops keep things bustling in this redeveloped historic neighborhood.

Getting Here and Around

Most visitors fly into Albuquerque International Sunport (ABQ), an hour away.

Georgia O'Keeffe Trail

A Southwest Art Icon

Trace the footsteps of the Southwest's most celebrated painter at the homes that inspired the desert scenes and floral blooms of her abstract modernist works. While the artist grew up in Wisconsin, attended the Art Institute of Chicago, then studied painting in New York, she's most deeply associated with her later decades in the Southwest. After spending many summers in north-central New Mexico, she settled there full-time from 1949 until her death in 1986. At the area's several O'Keeffe attractions, you can see her works in museums and the breathtaking landscapes that she depicted.

Don't Miss

O'Keeffe's summer home, Rancho de los Burros, sits amid the remote red-rock wilderness of 21,000-acre **Ghost Ranch,** 15 miles from her main home in Abiquiú. Although the house is closed to the public, the ranch offers art workshops, horseback trail rides, and several O'Keeffe-focused tours. 🌐 *www.ghostranch.org*

O'Keeffe Home and Studio

The artist's main Pueblo Revival adobe home and studio sits on a dramatic bluff in the quiet, agrarian village of Abiquiú. ✉ *Rte. 554, Abiquiú, NM* 🌐 *www.okeeffemuseum.org/homes*

Georgia O'Keeffe Museum

This striking contemporary museum in downtown Santa Fe features 140 of O'Keeffe's drawings and paintings as well as personal items and related photographs and documents. ✉ *217 Johnson St., Santa Fe, NM* 🌐 *www.okeeffemuseum.org*

Getting Here and Around

Abiquiú lies about an hour's drive northwest of Santa Fe; it's another 20 minutes to Ghost Ranch.

White Sands National Park

The World's Largest Gypsum Dune Field

A massive beach without an ocean, the towering dunes of gypsum sand in the Tularosa Basin of New Mexico extend for 275 square miles. A portion of this enormous stretch of sand is preserved within White Sands National Park, the world's largest gypsum dune field. Bring chairs and sit on the pristine sand, which glimmers hot and bright in the sunlight. The desert looks like a vast sea of snow—it even inspires visitors to sled down the dunes on plastic boards. You can also hike one of the five designated trails, participate in ranger-led activities, walk through a native plant garden, and bike along 8-mile Dunes Drive. ✉ *U.S. 70 between Alamogordo and Las Cruces* 🌐 *www.nps.gov/whsa*

Don't Miss

Sunset is the most magical time to see White Sands. Hike a mile on the dunes in single file on a daily Sunset Stroll with a knowledgeable park ranger leading the way as the lowering sun sets the landscape aglow.

Best Trail

Dune Life Nature Trail, a moderate 1-mile hike through sloping dunes and heavier vegetation than you'll see in much of the park, is a great bet for seeing wildlife such as kit foxes, badgers, reptiles, and birds.

Getting Here and Around

White Sands is in the Chihuahuan Desert in south-central New Mexico, 52 miles northeast of Las Cruces, 15 miles southwest of Alamogordo, and 100 miles north of the nearest airport, ELP in El Paso.

Pueblo Ruins

New Mexico's Original Inhabitants

You haven't truly seen the Land of Enchantment until you've experienced it through the lens of its original inhabitants. New Mexico is home to 23 Native American tribes and sovereign nations from three groups: the Pueblo peoples, the Apache, and Navajo Nation. Most of the preserved sites in New Mexico relate to the rich Pueblo culture, including cliff dwellings, kivas (underground ceremonial chambers), and sacred symbols etched in rock.

Don't Miss

A compact and easily accessed national monument and UNESCO World Heritage site of the Ancestral Pueblos, **Aztec Ruins National Monument** contains well-preserved ruins that date back to between AD 1100 and 1300. ✉ *725 Ruins Rd., Aztec, NM* 🌐 *www.nps.gov/azru*

Petroglyph National Monument

Petroglyphs were carved into volcanic rocks with stone chisels and hammerstones 400 to 700 years ago by the Pueblo people and later Spanish settlers. Three canyon trails on the edge of suburban Albuquerque give access to hundreds of these designs and symbols. ✉ *Western Trail NW, Albuquerque, NM* 🌐 *www.nps.gov/petr*

Taos Pueblo

About 150 tribal members live full-time within the thick adobe walls of rambling Taos Pueblo, which has been continuously inhabited for more than 1,000 years. 🌐 *www.taospueblo.com*

Getting Here and Around

Petroglyph National Monument is on the west side of Albuquerque. From there, it's a three-hour drive to Aztec Ruins in far northwest New Mexico, near Farmington, and a 2½-hour drive to Taos.

Albuquerque International Balloon Fiesta

World's Largest Ballooning Event

More than 550 colorful hot-air balloons take to the skies of New Mexico's largest city each October. The event's signature two-hour Mass Ascension kicks off the nine-day festival at the 360-acre **Balloon Fiesta Park.** Most are powered by hot air, while others use gas (helium or hydrogen). Some whimsical creations—balloons shaped as a piggy bank, for example—don't fly but can be viewed during the Special Shape Rodeo. The event also includes fireworks and evening balloon "glows" when the balloons are lit up in the darkness. 🌐 *www.balloonfiesta.com*

Don't Miss

The **Rainbow Ryders** are the only company authorized to give balloon rides at the event, and rides book up well in advance. One-hour ride start from $525 per person. 🌐 *rainbowryders.com*

Where to Stay

Glamping in tents on the field of Balloon Fiesta Park outfitted with heated blankets, refrigerators, heaters, and queen beds at $1,600 for three nights is an epic (and convenient) location.

Good to Know

If you're unable to snag a spot with Rainbow Ryders, pick up business cards as you interact with the balloon crews during the event and make plans for your own high-flying adventure after the festival.

Getting Here and Around

Albuquerque International Sunport (ABQ) is served by most major airlines. Park & Ride shuttles run from designated lots to Balloon Fiesta Park.

Carlsbad Caverns National Park

Largest Cave Chamber in the Country

Tubular stalactites, soda straws, cave pearls, draperies, gypsum chandeliers, hydromagnesite balloons, subaqueous helictites, lily pads, stalagmites, and many other cave formations—known as speleothems—adorn the more than 120 caves in Carlsbad Caverns National Park. These impressive spaces were created by sulfuric acid dissolving the limestone, with water and minerals then added to the mix. Exploring the underground maze of geological activity for most visitors begins 75 stories below the surface in what is known as the Big Room, thanks to a floor size equaling 14 football fields—it's the largest cave chamber in the country. The Big Room is also high, with a 255-foot ceiling. It's no wonder actor Will Rogers once dubbed it "the Grand Canyon with a roof over it." ✉ 727 *Carlsbad Caverns Hwy., Carlsbad, NM* 🌐 *www.nps.gov/cave*

Don't Miss

There are several ranger-led cave tours of varying difficulty, with the challenging **Hall of the White Giant tour**, which requires belly-crawling into tight spaces, being especially popular. Due to federal budget cuts, all guided tours were suspended indefinitely as of this writing; check the park website for updates.

Good to Know

As many as 500,000 bats hang out (literally) in the caverns. Rangers offer an evening talk on bat flight.

Getting Here and Around

Carlsbad Caverns is about 27 miles southwest of Carlsbad, where a small airport (CNM) has flights to Albuquerque and Phoenix.

Taos

Best Skiing in the Southwest

Set in the southern Rocky Mountains, Taos draws plenty of fans of art and culture, but skiers and snowboarders know it as *the* place in New Mexico to embrace winter recreation. Drawing around 200 inches of snow a year, the four ski areas within an hour's drive of Taos are a playground for skiers who want to shred serious powder. The largest of the Taos-area ski destinations is **Taos Ski Valley**, which sits at a 9,200-foot elevation base and features 1,294 skiable acres and a 3,281-foot vertical drop. 🌐 *www.skitaos.com*

Don't Miss

The bustling center of downtown Taos, **the Plaza** is also filled with some of the town's most important history. Today, the plaza is the home to summer fiestas, family-friendly concerts, and other community events, and houses gift shops, galleries, and restaurants. Just two blocks away, the **Harwood Museum of Art** is an essential destination for all lovers of New Mexican art. ✉ *238 Ledoux St., Taos, NM* 🌐 *www.harwood-museum.org*

Best Tour

With Mountain Skills Guided Backcountry Ski Tours, intermediate and advanced skiers can hire a guide to carve through snow on the ungroomed slopes of Taos's backcountry. 🌐 *www.climbingschoolusa.com*

More Great Skiing

Angel Fire has three terrain parks for snowboarding and more than 80 runs for downhill skiers, plus night skiing, ski tubing, cross-country skiing, snowshoeing, and kid's sledding.

Getting Here and Around

About a 90-minute drive south, Santa Fe Regional Airport (SAF) is the nearest commercial airport to Taos.

Roswell

An Out of This World Town

In the summer of 1947, a mysterious object crashed at a ranch near Roswell and was retrieved by the U.S. military. Some believe it was a flying saucer, which is what the Roswell Army Air Field first reported, but the next day the RAAF said it was a weather balloon. Later, the U.S. government clarified that it was a nuclear test surveillance balloon. But the flying saucer theory still persists in this small central New Mexico town that has embraced its extraterrestrial reputation.

Don't Miss

Exhibits at the **International UFO Museum and Research Center** educate about UFO sightings, crop circles, and supposed alien abductions all over the world. ✉ *114 N. Main St., Roswell, NM* 🌐 *www.roswellufomuseum.com*

Best Tour

Two-hour **Roswell UFO Tours** will take you to 20 sites related to the 1947 UFO crash. 🌐 *www.roswellufotours.com*

While You're Here

Walk through an indoor blacklit path lined with kitschy spaceship and alien decor at the **Roswell UFO Spacewalk** to get into a UFO-spotting mood. ✉ *116 E. 2nd St., Roswell, NM* 🌐 *www.facebook.com/roswellufospacewalk*

Good to Know

The town has several fun UFO-related shops, including **Invasion Station**, **Alien Zone Area 51**, and **UFO Fizz** candy shop.

Getting Here and Around

The tiny airport, Roswell Air Center (ROW) airport, has flights from Dallas, or it's a three-hour drive from Albuquerque.

Cumbres & Toltec Scenic Railroad

An Epic Rocky Mountain Train Ride

Departing from the small village of Chama in the sparsely populated north-central reaches of the state, the Cumbres & Toltec Scenic Railroad climbs into the Rocky Mountains during a 64-mile journey through gorgeous changing scenery—from alpine meadows to mountain canyons to thickets of conifers—to Osier, Colorado, for a lunch stop, and then on to Antonito, Colorado. Crossing Cascade Creek Trestle and snaking along Tanglefoot Curve, the powerful, coal-fired steam locomotive carries passengers on a daylong escape to yesteryear. A National Historic Landmark, the railroad has been in operation since 1880. ✉ *500 S. Terrace Ave., Chama, NM* 🌐 *www.cumbrestoltec.com*

Don't Miss

Snap a photo as the train crosses **Cumbres Pass**. At 10,015 feet, it's the highest mountain pass in America traversed by train.

When to Go

Scenic rides are offered from early June through late October. Spring provides glorious wildflowers, while late September and early October are the ideal times to see the aspen leaves change colors. Special trips themed around geology, wine, beer, and other interests are offered.

Getting Here and Around

Chama is about a two-hour drive north of Santa Fe. At the end of your train ride, a bus returns you from Antonito to Chama.

Bisti Badlands

Hike Mars on Earth

"Unusual" and "surprising" don't even begin to describe the 45,000-acre Bisti/De-Na-Zin Wilderness badlands, in northwestern New Mexico's San Juan Basin. Rocks twist and turn and appear to have tumbled onto a moonlike landscape out of nowhere. Get out and hike among the sandstone, shale, silt, and coal pinnacles, spires, cap rocks, and more, continually reminding yourself that you're not actually on Mars. At one time, dinosaurs roamed here, including the "Bisti Beast," a 30-foot tyrannosaur that lived 34 million years ago and was excavated in 1998. Today eagles, hawks, falcons, lizards, scorpions, snakes, and porcupines are among the wildlife. 🌐 *www.blm.gov/visit/bisti-de-na-zin-wilderness*

Don't Miss

Spot rock formations, including **Conversing Hoodoos**, the **Alien Egg Hatchery**, and **Vanilla Hoodoos**.

Good to Know

This is undeveloped wilderness; there are no facilities or shade, so bring water and sun protection. Or hire a guided excursion through **Navajo Tours USA**. 🌐 *www.navajotoursusa.com*

When to Go

Visit in spring or fall to avoid the extreme heat of summer, but be prepared for wind in the spring and occasional late-afternoon thunderstorms in autumn.

Getting Here and Around

The Bisti Access Parking Area is 40 miles south of Farmington, which has a small airport (FMN) with service from Denver; it's about a three-hour drive to Albuquerque. Within the wilderness area, use a compass or your phone GPS (download maps in advance), because trails are not marked and it's easy to get turned around.

Gila Cliff Dwellings

Stunning Ancient Cliffside Homes

Around the late 13th century, nomadic people of the Mogollon Culture created temporary cliff-side dwellings in what is today southwestern New Mexico. These stunning abandoned homes (talk about prime real estate) can be explored within Gila Cliff Dwellings National Monument. Most people base themselves in the charming arts community of Silver City, about 90 minutes south, but you can also stay at four U.S. Forest Service campgrounds within a 10-minute drive of the park. 🌐 *www.nps.gov/gicl*

Don't Miss

A moderately strenuous hike along 1-mile **Cliff Dweller Trail** takes you up to the cave dwellings, which are cut into the rock and connected by catwalks. You can actually enter these rooms and imagine how the tribes must have lived.

Best Base

Silver City, at the foothills of the Pinos Altos Mountains, also invites you to step into the past, specifically the region's late-19th-century mining boom. The still-active Chino (aka Santa Rita) Mine, 15 miles east, is one of the world's oldest and largest open-pit copper mines. Silver City itself is a bustling college town with a bounty of welcoming eateries, art galleries, and boutiques.

Getting Here and Around

Budget a full day for a trip to Gila Cliff Dwellings from Silver City—the picturesque, mountainous drive takes a little over 90 minutes. The nearest airport is El Paso International Airport (ELP), 2½ hours southeast.

When in New Mexico

LINCOLN HISTORIC SITE

Explore the fascinating legacy of the Lincoln County War of the 1870s, involving larger-than-life figures like Billy the Kid, Pat Garrett, and others, in this picturesque site containing 17 period buildings, four of which are museums. You can walk through the Old Lincoln County Courthouse, from which Billy the Kid escaped after gunning down a pair of deputies. In this high-desert valley in the shadows of the dramatic Sacramento and Capitan Mountains, there are also a few quaint shops and eateries. ✉ *U.S. 380, Lincoln, NM* 🌐 *www.nmhistoricsites.org/lincoln*

Do This: Make a scenic two-hour side trip northeast to Fort Sumner, home of the Billy the Kid Museum and Bosque Redondo Memorial at Fort Sumner Historic Site, where you can view the outlaw's tombstone.

MEOW WOLF

Wander like Alice in Wonderland through more than 70 rooms filled with trippy and mind-bending immersive experiences and installations at the original location of this arts collective that can only be described as a feast for the senses. The arts complex and its permanent exhibition, the House of Eternal Return, have spawned other Meow Wolf outposts in Denver, Las Vegas, Houston, and more. ✉ *1352 Rufina Cir., Santa Fe, NM* 🌐 *www.meowwolf.com*

Do This: Give yourself at least a couple of hours to tour this 20,000-square-foot interactive space in which you'll encounter hidden doorways, mysterious corridors, ambient music, and clever, surrealistic, and often slyly humorous artistic renderings. It's a wonderfully bizarre experience, but it is absolutely family-friendly, and although occasionally eerie, the subject matter isn't frightening.

SANDIA PEAK

One of the world's longest aerial tramways, here tramway cars climb nearly 3 miles up the steep western face of the Sandias, giving you a dazzling close-up view (whatever the season) of the imposing rock formations and windblown wilderness.

Do This: From the observation deck at the 10,378-foot summit, you can scan some 11,000 square miles of spectacular scenery, including desert, volcanos, mountains, and more. An exhibit room at the top surveys the area's wildlife. ✉ *10 Tramway Loop NE, Albuquerque, NM* 🌐 *www.sandiapeak.com*

VERY LARGE ARRAY

The most versatile and widely used radio telescope in the world sticks out intriguingly with its large white radio dishes aimed at the sky of an otherwise remote high desert plain two hours from Albuquerque. It appears memorably in the movie *Contact,* whose lead actress Jodie Foster, provides the narration for an award-winning short documentary about the location, *Beyond the Visible,* which you can watch in the visitor center along with examining displays on radio astronomy and the Very Large Array telescope. ✉ *Old Hwy. 60, Magdalena, NM* 🌐 *public.nrao.edu*

Do This: Take a guided tour when available or a self-guided tour to the base of the dish antennas.

Cool Places to Stay

Inn of the Five Graces. In the heart of Santa Fe's historic downtown, near the tranquil Santa Fe River, this posh, imaginatively designed adobe inn and Relais & Chateaux property has plush colorful rooms with wood-burning kiva fireplaces, deep soaking tubs, and hand-laid tile mosaics. Stone courtyards have fountains and flowering foliage, and there's a spa with a variety of treatments. Breakfast is included. ✉ *150 E. DeVargas St., Santa Fe, NM* 🌐 *www.fivegraces.com*

Kokopelli's Cave. After exploring some of New Mexico's cliff dwellings, why not retire to a cliff of your own? Kokopelli's man-made cave is built into sandstone cliffs and gives you a breathtaking view of Shiprock Pinnacle and the Four Corners region. In your 1,700-square-foot room, enjoy views from your terraces, a waterfall shower set within rock walls, and a constant pleasant temperature in the cave between 68°F and 73°F. The cave is 70 feet below the surface, so be prepared to walk down a slope to reach it once inside the cliff. ✉ *87 Rd. 1980, Farmington, NM* 🌐 *www.kokoscave.us*

Riverbend Hot Springs Resort. Soak your cares away at this resort and spa's open-air hot springs on the banks of the Rio Grande, which were considered both healing and sacred by the Apache. The hotel rooms are done in either a delightful Southwestern motif or an upbeat Old West look, and RV sites are also available. Guests have complimentary access to the springs, while day visitors can enjoy them for $30–$40 per hour. There's a two-night minimum stay on weekends. ✉ *100 Austin St., Truth or Consequences, NM* 🌐 *www.riverbend-hotsprings.com*

Taos Earthships. Being off-grid doesn't mean sacrificing modern-day amenities at this out-there home that runs on solar and wind power. Earthship Biotecture earthship rentals include Wi-Fi, streaming on a flat-screen TV, a kitchen with hot water and propane oven, and more. The earthships are set on a high plateau west of Taos with expansive mountain views. ✉ *2 Earthship Way, Tres Piedras, NM* 🌐 *www.earthship.com*

About Our Writers

Andrew Collins spent five years living in Santa Fe, followed by three more in Albuquerque, during which he served as a travel columnist and copy editor for *New Mexico Magazine*. On his frequent travels back, he always plans at least one long road trip on one of the state's spectacular scenic byways, such as the High Road to Taos. A regular contributor to numerous Fodor's guidebooks, he also writes for the Points Guy and several other outlets.

Essential Eats

Campo at Los Poblanos. This casually chic restaurant with a James Beard Award–nominated chef presents gorgeously plated Mediterranean- and Southwestern-influenced dishes with a focus on local ingredients. It's part of the handsome and historic Los Poblanos Historic Inn & Organic Farm, along a cottonwood-lined stretch of the Rio Grande in northern Albuquerque. ✉ *4803 Rio Grande Blvd. NW, Albuquerque, NM* 🌐 *www.lospoblanos.com*

Izanami. Natural wood tones and paper lanterns create a serene vibe in this high-ceilinged contemporary izakaya specializing in creative bar bites—think spicy crab onigiri and hot-stone-grilled Wagyu beef ishiyaki. It's located at idyllic Ten Thousand Waves, a serene spa in the Santa Fe foothills where you can soak in outdoor tubs or enjoy a massage before or after your meal. ✉ *21 Ten Thousand Waves Way, Santa Fe, NM* 🌐 *www.tenthousandwaves.com*

Mad Jack's Mountaintop BBQ. You'll find quite a few purveyors of slow-smoked barbecue imported from neighboring Texas throughout the Land of Enchantment, and this rustic joint set amid the pine-scented breezes of Cloudcroft might just be the best. The tender sliced brisket is a perfect reward after a day of exploring White Sands National Park, 45 minutes down the mountain. ✉ *105 James Canyon Hwy., Cloudcroft, NM* 🌐 *www.madjacksbbq.com*

Orlando's New Mexican Cafe. This cheerful eatery with colorful painted walls, patio umbrellas, and views of Wheeler Peak ranks among the state's most beloved go-tos for classic New Mexican dishes like blue-corn chicken enchiladas, posole-smothered veggie burritos, and grilled carne adovada. ✉ *1114 Don Juan Valdez La., Taos, NM* 🌐 *www.orlandos.shop*

Sparky's Burgers & BBQ. Look to this quirky café festooned with vintage signs and colorful piñatas for some of the heftiest and juiciest green-chili cheeseburgers in New Mexico, plus luscious strawberry–red chili milkshakes. It's in the heart of Hatch, a small village in south-central New Mexico that's world-famous for growing and roasting chilies. ✉ *115 Franklin St., Hatch, NM* 🌐 *www.sparkysburgers.com*

Texas

The big and bold Lone Star State might just have it all. The Piney Woods of East Texas offers forests, ranches, and oil fields, while in West Texas, you'll find mountains and deserts as well as windmills, oil rigs, and beautiful Big Bend National Park. The panhandle features canyons and a cowboy heritage, while central Texas has both the scenic Hill Country as well as prairies, lakes, and the Interstate 35 corridor connecting Dallas, Austin, and San Antonio. Arid South Texas boasts a Hispanic culture, while in the Gulf Coast, there are beaches like South Padre and Galveston.

Capital: Austin

Population: 31,290,831

Area: 268,596 square miles

Statehood Date: December 29, 1845

Major Airports: Austin-Bergstrom International Airport (AUS); Dallas-Fort Worth International Airport (DFW); Dallas Love Field (DAL); George Bush Intercontinental/Houston Airport (IHC); William B. Hobby Airport; (HOU), San Antonio International Airport (SAT); El Paso International Airport (ELP)

Travel and Tourism Information: *www.traveltexas.com* *www.texasmonthly.com*

Famous Residents: Lyndon B. Johnson (president); Janis Joplin (singer); George H.W. and George W. Bush (presidents); Matthew McConaughey (actor); Beyoncé (singer)

Fun Fact: The Texas State Capitol is taller than the U.S. Capitol (302.64 feet tall versus 288 feet tall).

The Alamo

The Ultimate Symbol of Texas Freedom

An icon of Texas freedom fighting, this mission church turned military fort is the most celebrated building in Texas history. In 1836, Texas lost a major battle here against Mexico, and all inside died at the hands of Santa Anna's troops. Those slain included James Bowie, William B. Travis, and Davy Crockett. The defeat at the Alamo spurred Texans fighting in future battles for their independence to make sure they did not suffer the same fate. "Remember the Alamo" became the battle cry at San Jacinto, where Texas won its independence from Mexico with Sam Houston leading the charge. ✉ *300 Alamo Plaza, San Antonio, TX* 🌐 *www.thealamo.org*

Don't Miss

While the famous front of the mission is great for a photo op, many of the things to see are outside this treasured building. On the grounds you can stroll through the gardens, learn from the wall of history, and interact with guides at the living history encampment. At the Ralston Family Collections Center, view artifacts and exhibits, including weapons, original documents, and hundreds of other Alamo-related items from the collection amassed and donated by British singer Phil Collins.

Best Tour

Old Town Trolley Tours offers a narrated tour of San Antonio with a dozen hop-on/hop-off stops, making it a convenient and educational way to see top city's top sights. 🌐 *www.trolleytours.com/san-antonio*

Getting Here and Around

The Alamo is 9 miles from San Antonio International Airport (SAT).

Austin

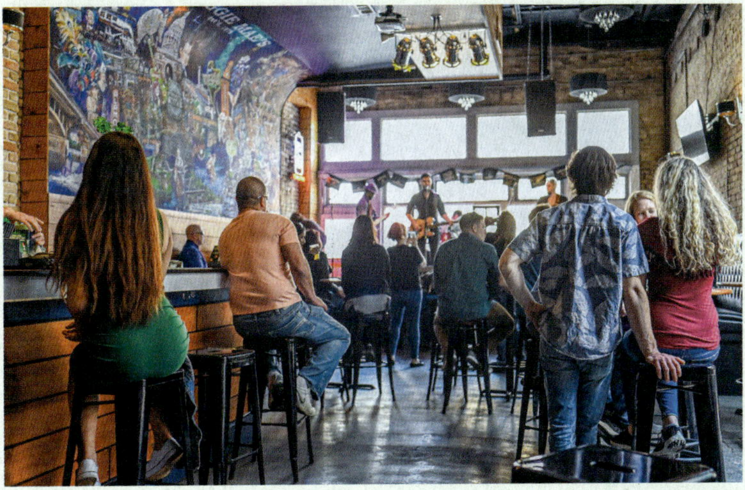

The City That Keeps It Weird

While Austin goes by many names—Live Music Capital of the World, Violet Crown City, Bat City, Hippie Haven—it's best known for its laid-back, individualistic, "keep it weird" vibe. Residents love their music, their outdoor pursuits, and the intellectual atmosphere of the behemoth University of Texas at Austin. The capital city continues to grow in both geographical size and population each year, drawing young professionals and adding even more opportunities to check out the music scene, eat delicious Southwestern food, snap photos next to artistic murals, and people-watch during bar hops.

Don't Miss

Nightlife in Austin is always memorable. Music spills out at popular downtown **Sixth Street** clubs; the same goes for the hip **South Congress** district south of Lady Bird Lake.

Best Murals

When you're on South Congress, stop by the famous "I love you so much" mural on 1300 South Congress Avenue before grabbing coffee and tacos at Jo's, and don't miss the "Greetings From Austin" life-size postcard mural on 1720 South 1st Street.

While You're Here

In Zilker Park, **Barton Springs Pool** is the place to enjoy a dip in spring-fed water. ✉ *2131 William Barton Dr., Austin, TX* 🌐 *www.austintexas.gov/department/barton-springs-pool*

When to Go

A fun time to be in town is during **South by Southwest** (SXSW), a huge annual music and film event held each March. 🌐 *www.sxsw.com*

Getting Here and Around

The Austin-Bergstrom International Airport (AUS) is 10 miles southeast of downtown.

Houston

The Biggest Texan City

Known for sports, oil, commerce, technology, and space exploration, Houston is the fourth-largest city in the country and the largest in Texas, with 2.3 million residents (7.8 million when you include its suburbs). So perhaps it's no wonder that this vibrant city personifies the "Everything's bigger in Texas" mentality, from its huge **Galleria** shopping complex with 3 million square feet of space and its massive medical center that covers 2 square miles to its jumbo-size megachurches like Joel Osteen's Lakewood Church, which holds 50,000 attendees each week, and its bigger-than-life sports arenas like the **Toyota Center**, which spans six city blocks.

Don't Miss

See world-class art in Houston's Museum District at the **Menil Collection**, known for its eclectic, Surrealist art, and the **Museum of Fine Arts Houston**, housing more than 70,000 works of art.

While You're Here

Just 25 miles south of downtown is **NASA's Space Center Houston** and the adjacent **Johnson Space Center.** Space aficionados can come here to learn about Apollo 13's mission and life with zero-gravity, and to explore Mission Control. ✉ *1601 E. NASA Pkwy., Houston, TX* 🌐 *spacecenter.org*

Did You Know?

Houston is the country's most ethnically diverse metropolitan area. At least one-fourth of residents are foreign born, more than 145 languages are spoken here, and there is no ethnic majority.

Getting Here and Around

Houston has two airports, George Bush Intercontinental Airport (IAH) and William P. Hobby Airport (HOU).

Dallas

Texas History and Culture

Dallas is a thriving city that has it all: arts and culture, professional sports, trendy restaurants and bars, and fabulous shopping. Whether you're strolling through the lovely Dallas Arboretum and Botanical Gardens, cheering on the Dallas Cowboys, or sipping a cocktail on a rooftop bar and enjoying the beautiful skyline studded with skyscrapers, there's always something to do in the Big D.

Don't Miss

Art lovers make a beeline to the Dallas Arts District, home to some of the city's most notable cultural offerings, including the **Dallas Museum of Art**, the **Nasher Sculpture Center**, the **AT&T Performing Arts Center**, **Dallas Theater Center**, and **Winspear Opera House**. 🌐 *www.dallasartsdistrict.org*

A Step Back

A favorite stop for history buffs and conspiracy theorists is the **Sixth Floor Museum** at Dealey Plaza, which covers JFK's assassination. ✉ *411 Elm St., Dallas, TX* 🌐 *www.jfk.org/the-museum*

Fun for All Ages

Great stops for those with kids in tow include the **Dallas World Aquarium**, **Six Flags Over Texas** in Arlington, and the **Ross Perot Museum of Nature and Science**.

When to Go

The fall is a great time to go if you like fried anything, auto shows, carnival rides, live music, and more because that's when the extravagant **State Fair of Texas** rolls into town. 🌐 *www.bigtex.com*

Getting Here and Around

Two airports serve Dallas—Dallas/Fort Worth International Airport (DFW), just west of Dallas, and Love Field (DAL), near downtown Dallas.

Big Bend National Park

The Most Beautiful Terrain in Texas

Set in the Chisos Mountains in West Texas, 1,252-square-mile Big Bend National Park has incredibly varied terrain, from desert landscape to bird-filled woods to natural hot springs to nearly 8,000-foot-high mountains. The scenic and wild Rio Grande River cuts through the park and has carved out a number of canyons, including Boquillas Canyon, where the limestone walls rise up to 1,500 feet high along the river. 🌐 *www.nps.gov/bibe*

Don't Miss

Big Bend is a terrific place for hiking, wildlife viewing, scenic driving, and camping under dark and starry skies. While exploring, be on the lookout for dinosaur fossils, caves with pictographs, and historic sites, including an abandoned mercury mine.

Best Hike

Hike the **Santa Elena Canyon Trail** near sunset; the setting sun turns the steep cliffs a beautiful red-chestnut color. The trek is 1.6 miles round-trip.

Best Scenic Drive

Ross Maxwell Scenic Drive, a steep 30-mile journey, takes you past ranches, an old Army compound, and heaps of volcanic ash from long-ago eruptions. And, best of all, it brings you to scenic overlooks such as Sotol Vista and ones where you can see Tuff Canyon and twin peaks resembling mule ears.

Best Thrill

The Lower Canyons, with Class II, III, and IV rapids, is a multiday, 82-mile trip of a lifetime for experienced kayakers. Summer is the best time for rafting.

Getting Here and Around

Big Bend is 39 miles south of Marathon, Texas, off U.S. 385. The nearest airport is in Midland, Texas, roughly 3½ hours' drive away.

Texas Hill Country

Dramatic Scenery in Wine Country

Sitting atop the Edwards Plateau and the Balcones Escarpment, the Texas Hill Country begins in Austin and extends north to roughly Route 29, west to U.S. 83, and south to northern San Antonio. The beautiful area is known for its rolling hills and the stunning vistas that come with the higher ground. The joy of visiting this area is driving the back roads that twist and turn through farmlands, small towns with German culture, and state parks and ranches. The Texas Hill Country also has several beautiful golf courses and lakes, in addition to vineyards in what's become the USA's fastest-growing wine region.

Don't Miss

Fredericksburg, full of wineries, antiques shops, and German restaurants, is a charming and popular area. For tours and tastings, popular wineries include **Becker Vineyards**, **Inwood Estates Vineyards Winery & Bistro**, and **Messina Hof Hill Country Winery**. For hearty German fare, there's **Otto's German Bistro**.

While You're Here

Lyndon B. Johnson National Historical Park close to Johnson City is where the former president's birthplace, home, ranch, and gravesite are located. ✉ *1048 Park Rd. 49, Stonewall, TX* 🌐 *www.nps.gov/lyjo*

Getting Here and Around

Austin and San Antonio are the region's gateway cities, and you can string along a few destinations on a weekend road trip. The area is especially pretty in spring when the bluebonnets dot the countryside.

The San Antonio River Walk

Best Urban Waterway

A whirl of colorful umbrellas, an array of tantalizing scents wafting from restaurants, and the sounds of mariachi bands blend together to make San Antonio's beautiful River Walk a feast for the senses. Winding 15 miles through the heart of the city, the pedestrian waterfront path is one of Texas's most visited attractions. In many ways hidden from the urban traffic above, shops, restaurants, hotels, museums, and more line the Paseo del Rio. At the northern end is the historic Pearl entertainment district and at the southern end is La Villita Historic Arts Village. 🌐 *www.thesanantonioriverwalk.com*

Don't Miss

The Riverwalk is popular for dining and nightlife, but it also provides access to excellent museums and performing arts venues. Along the route are such gems as the family-friendly and highly popular **Witte Museum**, the culture-rich **San Antonio Museum of Art**, the Spanish Mediterranean-styled **Majestic Theatre**, and the **Arneson River Theatre at La Villita**, a cozy space for outdoor productions.

Best Tour

A narrated riverboat ride is a delightful way to see the river from a different perspective. Purchase tickets from the Rio San Antonio Cruise kiosk at the Rivercenter. ✉ *809 E. River Walk, San Antonio, TX* 🌐 *www.goriocruises.com*

Getting Here and Around

The San Antonio International Airport (SAT) is the closest airport to the River Walk, which can be accessed from multiple points in the city. The River Walk website contains area maps under the Plan Your Trip tab.

Marfa

Mystery and Art in West Texas

The serenity and laid-back nature of wide-open West Texas meets mystery, myth, and minimalist art in Marfa. Called by some a paradise for hipsters, this small town of nearly 1,800 residents swells with tourists who come to see art, architecture, and, especially, the famous Marfa lights, a puzzling phenomenon in which red, blue, and white lights sometimes appear at night for no particular reason.

Don't Miss

Join the flock of people who come to look for the strange, colorful lights that have been glowing in Marfa's night sky since the 1880s. These mysterious lights are seen on clear nights between Marfa and Alpine as you look west toward the Chinati Mountains. The **Marfa Lights Viewing Area** with built-in telescopes is 9 miles from Marfa, off U.S. 90.

While You're Here

Strike a pose next to **Prada Marfa**, the sleekest piece of architecture you'll ever see in the middle of nowhere. Located 26 miles north of actual Marfa, the permanent art installation by artists Elmgreen and Dragset has become something of a pop culture legend and is particularly beautiful at sunset. ✉ *14880 U.S. 90, Valentine, TX*

When to Go

During the town's annual lights festival each Labor Day weekend, the population doubles as people come to see not only the lights but to enjoy food, music, a parade, crafts for sale, and live entertainment.

Getting Here and Around

At the junction of U.S. highways 90 and 67, Marfa is about 60 miles from the U.S.–Mexico border and 130 miles from Big Bend National Park. The nearest airports are in Midland or El Paso, both about three hours away by car.

Country Western Dance Halls

Line Dancing and Texas Two-Stepping

Country western dancing is alive and well in Texas and a fun way to spend an evening in those cowboy boots you've been wanting to wear. Some venues are small, others are large; some play classic country, at other's it's Texas swing. Inside they all have a similar sight: a wooden dance floor with couples crowded onto it two-stepping or individuals and groups line dancing.

Don't Miss

Billy Bob's is known as the world's largest honky-tonk. Able to hold 6,000 people at a time, the more-than-100,000-square-foot complex has a huge dance floor, pool tables, arcade games, a restaurant, multiple bars, and a gift shop. There also is a bull-riding area where professionals ride, but the rest of us can mount a fake bull and get our picture taken on it. ✉ *2520 Rodeo Plaza, Fort Worth, TX* 🌐 *www.billybobstexas.com*

Other Popular Spots

Austin and Fort Worth have several dance halls, but smaller towns feature noteworthy spaces, from **Gruene Hall** in New Braunfels, the oldest dance hall in the state, to **Luckenbach Dance Hall** outside Fredericksburg, made famous by a Waylon Jennings song.

Getting Here and Around

Billy Bob's is in Fort Worth's Stockyards National Historic District. The nearest airport is Dallas/Fort Worth International Airport (DFW).

Palo Duro Canyon State Park

The Grand Canyon of Texas

Dramatic vistas from far above the canyon floor as well as from within are the highlights of this canyon in Texas's Panhandle. Called the Grand Canyon of Texas by some, Palo Duro Canyon is 60 miles long and 800 feet deep and showcases layers of rock in varied hues along with hoodoos and other unusual rock formations. It is contained within the 16,402-acre Palo Duro Canyon State Park. People come to hike, mountain bike, bird-watch, and fish. Wildlife includes the diamondback rattlesnake, wild turkey, roadrunners, and wild pigs. ✉ *11450 Park Rd. 5, Canyon, TX* 🌐 *www.tpwd.texas.gov/state-parks/palo-duro-canyon*

Don't Miss

Take a scenic drive down the long, winding road into the canyon in the morning or evening to catch the gold colors the sun casts upon the ridges and pinnacles.

Where to Stay

For those who like to camp with modern conveniences, **Palo Duro Glamping** has the cabins for you. Equipped with tools for storing and prepping meals, including a refrigerator, a microwave, and a grill, the canvas-covered cabins even come with complimentary ice cream and s'more kits. The only thing that makes it not truly a glamping experience in some peoples' minds are the shared bathhouses. ✉ *11450 Park Rd. 5, Canyon, TX* 🌐 *www.paloduroglamping.com*

Getting Here and Around

Off Route 217, Palo Duro Canyon State Park, which contains Palo Duro Canyon, is 14 miles from Canyon, Texas, and 25 miles from Amarillo.

Texas Rodeos

The Official Sport of the Lone Star State

Sports are big in Texas—very big—but did you know that the official state sport of Texas is not football? It's the rodeo. Featuring barrel racing, steer wrestling, and bull riding paired with carnivals, concerts, and much more, rodeos are held throughout the state, in big cities and small towns alike. Some are held annually, some are held every weekend. Fort Worth has the oldest, while Houston has the largest and arguably the most popular. All celebrate a beloved part of Texas's history and culture.

Don't Miss

Drawing more than 65,000 people nightly during its 20 days of jam-packed excitement, the **Houston Livestock Show & Rodeo** is the ultimate Texas rodeo. The experience kicks off with a parade of cowboys and cowgirls riding in on horses along with colorful floats and marching bands. It continues with livestock exhibitions, seminars, shops, food vendors, live entertainment, a carnival, a barbecue contest, and competitions like a calf scramble, bareback riding, chuckwagon races, and mutton busting. 🌐 *www.rodeohouston.com*

Big-Name Entertainers

Gene Autry was a staple at early Texas rodeos, riding into the arena on Champion, the Wonder Horse. Well-known musicians have entertained rodeo crowds ever since, especially at the Houston rodeo, which has featured Sonny & Cher, the Jackson 5, Dolly Parton, Selena, Elvis, Beyonce, Brooks & Dunn, and Brad Paisley.

Getting Here and Around

The William P. Hobby Airport is about 15 miles from the NRG Stadium, home to the Houston rodeo. Buy tickets and parking in advance online.

Gulf Coast Beaches

The Texas Waterfront

Running from Beaumont down to South Padre Island, Texas's eastern border is home to the only oceanfront beaches in the Southwest. And with more than 600 miles of sand, the coast has plenty of places to build sandcastles and wade into sparkling water. Choose between the calmer bay side stretches or the more action-packed gulf-facing beaches.

Don't Miss

Padre Island is 100 miles long, starting near Corpus Christi and ending near where the Rio Grande empties into the gulf. Spring breakers have long known about South Padre, a popular beach town on Padre Island's southern end. Though boisterous around spring break time, South Padre is a favorite with families the rest of the year. In addition to swimming and sun-tanning, water-based activities on the island include fishing, parasailing, surfing, snorkeling, and scuba diving, along with horseback riding on the beach. ⊕ *www.nps.gov/pais*

Best Seashells

Corpus Christi is known for its variety of seashells. Your best bet is to search the shoreline after high tide or storms. Try Big Shell Beach for conchs, scallops, and ark shells. While in Corpus Christi, catch a dolphin training show and see the playful otters at the Texas State Aquarium. ✉ *2710 N. Shoreline Blvd., Corpus Christi, TX* ⊕ *www.texasstateaquarium.org* 🎟 *$49.95*

Getting Here and Around

South Padre Island is 28 miles northeast of Brownsville and 175 miles south of Corpus Christi. Airports include Brownsville South Padre International Airport (BRO) and Corpus Christi International Airport (CRP).

Galveston

A Victorian Seaside Resort in Texas

The roughly 30-mile-long island of Galveston has several beaches, a seaport museum, a popular shopping area called the Strand, a pier, a water park, and a cruise-ship terminal. But what it is best known for is its Victorian architecture, with several dozen of its buildings listed on the National Register of Historic Places.

Don't Miss

Broadway, a thriving street in the late 1800s, is where the city's Victorian splendor is on full display. Valued at $5.5 million today, the ornate **Bishop's Palace,** with stained glass windows, painted ceilings, and marble columns, was once home to railroad magnate Colonel Walter Gresham. The 32-room limestone-and-brick **Moody Mansion** with gilded trim was first owned by one of the country's most wealthy men, W. L. Moody, an entrepreneur in the insurance industry. Many of the family's heirlooms are inside. **Ashton Villa,** a 1859 Victorian Italianate home, was the first on the island. It was built in large part by enslaved people, and it served as headquarters for the Confederate Army. On June 19, 1865 (what would later become Juneteenth), Union general Gordon Granger stood on the balcony of Ashton Villa and declared all enslaved people to be free.

Where to Stay

Howard Hughes, Frank Sinatra, and Jimmy Stewart are among the past guests at **Hotel Galvez**, a six-story Spanish Colonial hotel once as "Queen of the Gulf" and "The Playground of the Southwest." ✉ *2024 Seawall Blvd., Galveston, TX* 🌐 *grandgalvez.com*

Getting Here and Around

Galveston is 50 miles from Houston. The nearest airport is Houston's William P. Hobby Airport (HOU).

Bluebonnet Season

Springtime's Star

Late March and early April is the season to take scenic drives in the Lone Star State, because that's when beautiful violet-blue flowers carpet fields, yards, cemeteries, railroad tracks, and even small patches of land along the interstate or medians in between lanes. The bluebonnet holds its own in the "truly gorgeous" category, but when it appears alongside pink Indian paintbrush (*Castilleja*) and Texas yellow stars (part of the sunflower family), it's even more glorious to behold. If you've come across a great patch of them, you're sure to see cars pulled over for pictures. You'll easily see why the bluebonnet was chosen as the Texas state flower.

Don't Miss

The bluebonnet can be found throughout the state, but some of the best places to see it are in central Texas towns like Brenham, north-central Texas in Ennis, Big Bend National Park in West Texas, and of course in the Hill Country—most notably in Austin, Burnet, Fredericksburg, Kingsland, Muleshoe Bend in Spicewood, and Turkey Bend Recreation Area.

Good to Know

To get updates on where to see the bluebonnets, call the Texas Department of Transportation Wildflower Hotline at ☎ *800/452–9292*.

When to Go

These beautiful flowers are only around for a short window of time each spring, usually beginning in mid- to late March and peaking in early to mid-April.

Getting Here and Around

Base yourself in Austin or San Antonio and drive through nearby Hill Country towns to combine a few bucket-list destinations into one trip. Fly into either Austin–Bergstrom International Airport (AUS) or San Antonio International Airport (SAT).

Waco

A Home Renovation Mecca

HGTV's *Fixer Upper* stars Chip and Joanna Gaines put the central Texas town of Waco on the map, educating a large TV audience about this midsize city on the Brazos River and attracting more than 1½ million visitors each year. But more than the fabulous press they've given Waco, the dynamic duo have been a huge driving force in renovating the city into a more hip, urban community. This is not your grandmother's (or mother's) Waco.

Don't Miss

After filming several seasons of their reality TV show, Chip and Joanna went full steam ahead with their entrepreneurial endeavors. They launched a home goods line, wrote a stack of books, came out with a magazine, started a TV network, kicked off a new cooking show, and opened multiple restaurants, shops, and home rentals. Their flagship property in Waco is **Magnolia Market at the Silos**, where visiting fans come to shop, sample a pastry, or enjoy a cup of coffee. Elsewhere in town is **Magnolia Table**, a sit-down restaurant serving breakfast, lunch, and dinner. 🌐 *www.magnolia.com*

While You're Here

Sports fans may enjoy the **Texas Ranger Hall of Fame & Museum** and the **Texas Sports Hall of Fame**, among Waco's attractions. The city is also home to the **Dr Pepper Museum**, the **Waco Mammoth National Monument**, and the **Mayborn Museum Complex** as well as **Baylor University** (Chip and Joanna's alma mater) and an economic engine of its own spurring growth and development in Waco.

Getting Here and Around

Off Interstate 35, Waco is about 90 minutes south of the Dallas–Fort Worth metroplex and 90 minutes north of Austin. It has its own airport, Waco Regional Airport (ACT).

Presidential Libraries

The Home State of Three Presidents

If you're a fan of attractions related to American history and specifically the role of its commanders in chief, Texas is the place for you. There are only 15 official presidential libraries and museums across the country, and the Lone Star State is home to three of them, more than any other state in the country. Texas puts the spotlight on America's 36th, 41st, and 43rd presidents through presidential libraries and museums in Austin, College Station, and Dallas, respectively.

Don't Miss

On the campus of the University of Texas at Austin, the **LBJ Presidential Library** holds phone recordings Lyndon B. Johnson made at the White House, more than 2,000 oral histories, and a large collection of photos and videos. ✉ *2313 Red River St., Austin, TX* 🌐 *www.lbjlibrary.org*

George H. W. Bush Presidential Library & Museum

George Herbert Walker Bush chose Texas A&M as the setting for his library, which contains documents, artifacts, and exhibits of his time in the military as well as in the Oval Office as vice president under Ronald Reagan and then as a one-term president. ✉ *1000 George Bush Dr. W, College Station, TX* 🌐 *www.bush41.org*

George W. Bush Presidential Library & Museum

This museum on the campus of Southern Methodist University features exhibits on the horror of 9/11, artifacts about the controversial 2000 election, legislation President Bush signed, and policy initiatives his administration enacted. ✉ *2943 SMU Blvd., Dallas, TX* 🌐 *www.georgewbushlibrary.smu.edu*

When in Texas

AUSTIN'S EPIC BAT FLIGHT

In the middle of downtown Austin, 1½ million Mexican free-tailed bats roost under the Ann Richards Congress Avenue Bridge. From March through October, people come from all around to watch these winged mammals take flight each night. There is a bat observation area on the southeast side of Congress Avenue, but you also can view their northwestward flight from a boat on Lady Bird Lake below, from along the sides of the bridge, or even from a hotel room that overlooks the lake on the west side of the bridge. ✉ *305 S. Congress Ave., Austin, TX*

Do This: To witness the spectacle of bats flying overhead, kayak at dusk on Lady Bird Lake or take a bat-watching boat ride. The best viewing months are July, August, and September. 🌐 *www.capital-cruises.com*

BLUE BELL CREAMERY

Vermont has Ben & Jerry's, but Texas has Blue Bell. The family-owned creamery in Brenham, Texas, is a fun place to visit, and a self-guided tour here is on the bucket list of many Texans. A museum features exhibits about the creamery's beginnings in 1907 as a dairy that churned out butter that evolved into making homemade ice cream that it delivered by horse and buggy to each home on the delivery route, much like an old-school milkman. ✉ *1101 S. Blue Bell Rd., Brenham, TX* 🌐 *www.bluebell.com*

Do This: Watch how ice cream is made and packaged from an observation deck that is open from 8 am to 2 pm Monday through Friday. Finish your tour with a dish of fresh ice cream at the adjacent parlor.

BUDDY HOLLY CENTER

On February 3, 1959, a plane carrying musicians Buddy Holly, Ritchie Valens, and J. P. "The Big Bopper" Richardson crashed in Iowa, killing all aboard. In his hit song "American Pie," singer and songwriter Don McLean calls it the day the music died. Known for songs like "That'll Be the Day" and "Peggy Sue," Holly was just 22 years old when he died. The rising star was from Lubbock, Texas, and his hometown recognizes his achievements and fame at the Buddy Holly Center. Located in the Lubbock Cultural District, it pays tribute to the musician's life through various exhibits, including his guitar, photographs, tour itineraries, one of his songbooks, and, of course, his famous eyeglasses. ✉ *1801 Crickets Ave., Lubbock, TX* 🌐 *ci.lubbock.tx.us/departments/buddy-holly-center*

Do This: Other Holly-related sites you can visit while in Lubbock include the Buddy Holly statue on the West Texas Walk of Fame, his childhood church and schools, and his grave at the City of Lubbock Cemetery. Inquire at the Buddy Holly Center for details on specific sites.

CADILLAC RANCH

Kitschy to the core, this roadside attraction outside Amarillo, along the famous Route 66 highway, is the site of 10 Cadillacs partially buried headfirst in the ground, their main bodies and back sides sticking up in the air. They have been spray-painted over and over again throughout the years with bright colors, and some visitors say you can smell the paint a football-field's distance away. ✉ *13651 I–40 Frontage Rd., Exit 60, Amarillo, TX*

Do This: If you want to add to the graffiti already adorning the exhibit, bring some rubber gloves and a few cans of spray paint. Make sure to snap your picture next to your masterpiece, because it will undoubtedly be covered by the next visitor.

FORT WORTH STOCKYARDS & CATTLE DRIVE

Want to see an authentic slice of Texas's cowboy history? There's no better place than at Fort Worth's stockyards, a historic district with an Old West ambience. In the late 1880s, drovers led longhorn cattle from Texas to Kansas on the Chisholm Trail, which began in South Texas and passed through Fort Worth. Today, Fort Worth relives its cattle era twice a day—at 11:30 am and at 4 pm—with reenacted cattle drives down East Exchange Avenue in the Stockyards. The 17 Texas Longhorns on the drive are known as the Fort Worth Herd. ✉ *131 E. Exchange Ave., Fort Worth, TX* 🌐 *www.fortworth-stockyards.org*

Do This: Each weekend in the summer from 1:30 to 2:30 pm, cowhands give free demonstrations at the Herd Observation Deck. There's grooming, saddling horses, roping, and more.

GUADALUPE MOUNTAINS NATIONAL PARK

Guadalupe Mountains National Park is a study in extremes: it has mountaintop forests but also rocky canyons, arid desert, white gypsum sand dunes, and a stream that winds through verdant woods. It also has the loftiest spot in Texas: 8,751-foot Guadalupe Peak. The mountain dominates the view from every approach, but it's just one part of a rugged landscape carved by wind, water, and time. 🌐 *www.nps.gov/gumo*

Do This: The main activity at the park is hiking its rugged, remote, and often challenging trails: 80 miles' worth that are nearly always free of crowds. The 8.4-mile Guadalupe Peak Trail takes you through several ecosystems and some great views, ending at top of Texas. The round-trip hike takes six to eight hours, but the trail is clearly defined and doesn't require undue athleticism.

NATIONAL MUSEUM OF THE PACIFIC WAR

The only one of its kind in the country, this museum looks specifically at World War II in the Pacific. Originally named after Admiral Chester W. Nimitz, the museum covers the life of this Fredericksburg native as well as the war's activity in Asia and the Pacific, from the attack on Pearl Harbor to the dropping of the hydrogen bombs. ✉ *328 E. Main St., Fredericksburg, TX* 🌐 *www.pacificwarmuseum.org*

Do This: Explore the exhibits and videos highlighting the Doolittle Raid, Midway, Iwo Jima, and more.

USS *LEXINGTON*

Docked in the bay of Corpus Christi, the USS *Lexington* is impossible to miss. The massive vessel is the longest-serving aircraft carrier in the history of naval combat, serving for 50 years, including in World War II. It is open now as a museum on water, so you can walk aboard and even go below deck. ✉ *2914 N. Shoreline Blvd., Corpus Christi, TX* 🌐 *www.usslexington.com*

Do This: Peruse the multiple exhibits and attractions, including a flight simulator, a 3D film, interactive games, and a sound and light show. There are also guided tours available.

Cool Places to Stay

Bloomhouse. A great place to embrace the signature "weird" of Austin is this unusual home built into the woodsy West Austin's hills. Resembling a white dragon-shape seashell and made out of polyurethane foam and cement plaster with cherry wood accents and a tiled floor, Bloomhouse looks like something out of a fantasy novel. Inside the curvy structure is a living space with TV and sleeper sofa, a dining area and small kitchen with a dishwasher, a bedroom with a queen bed, and one bathroom. There is also a delightful patio. ✉ *High Rd. in Westlake Highlands, Austin, TX* 🌐 *bloomhouse.live*

Dixie Dude Ranch. Bandera is known as Texas's Cowboy Capital, and there are many cattle ranches in the area where you can immerse yourself in the experience. One of Bandera's oldest dude ranches, and still a working ranch, Dixie Dude Ranch has plenty of activities, including hiking, volleyball, table tennis, pickleball, basketball, and, of course, trail rides. There is also a swimming pool and hot tub. Lodging is in cabins, cottages, a bunkhouse, or the lodge. Rates include two horseback rides per day and three family-style daily meals (except no dinner on Sundays). There is a two-night minimum stay (three nights on holiday weekends). ✉ *833 Dixie Dude Ranch Rd., Bandera, TX* 🌐 *www.dixieduderanch.com*

Hotel Emma. There are no superlatives left to describe the wonder that is Hotel Emma, located in the original 1894 Pearl brewhouse and providing luxurious guest rooms and exemplary service. Guest rooms and suites have baths featuring handmade Spanish porcelain tiles, beds with luxury linens, and a stocked Ice Box (an homage to South Texas neighborhood icehouses) and in-room pantry with South Texas treats. Enjoy chef John Brand's marvelous creations for breakfast, lunch, dinner, dessert, or brunch at on-site restaurant Supper, then relax at the dramatic city bar Sternewirth Tavern & Club Room off the lobby. ✉ *136 E. Grayson St., San Antonio, TX* 🌐 *www.thehotelemma.com*

La Cantera Resort & Spa. Set in the foothills north of San Antonio, La Cantera Resort & Spa is all about relaxation amid Hill Country beauty. It attracts day spa visitors as well as overnighters who want to enjoy the panoramic views, the spa, the golf, fine dining, and spacious rooms. It's an easy drive of about 20 to 30 minutes to San Antonio shopping and sightseeing. ✉ *16641 La Cantera Pkwy., San Antonio, TX* 🌐 *www.lacanteraresort.com*

About Our Writers

Debbie Harmsen went to college in Texas twice—first completing a B.A. from Baylor University, majoring in journalism and French, and then earning an MBA from Baylor several years later while working as Editor-in-Chief, Nonfiction for BenBella Books in Dallas. She is currently a writer and editor based in Iowa.

McGregor House. Showcased in season 3 of HGTV's *Fixer Upper,* the McGregor House is a charming slice of Joanna Gaines's signature style, complete with shiplap walls, chippy white paint, and a splash of country chic elements. The five-bedroom Airbnb property, accommodating up to eight guests, is in McGregor, Texas, about 30 minutes from Waco. ✉ *323 S. Madison Ave., McGregor, TX* 🌐 *www.airbnb.com*

Essential Eats

Cooper's Old Time Pit Barb-B-Que. This Hill Country restaurant established in 1962 is often touted as the best barbecue in the state, but that doesn't mean it's fancy. When you do barbecue in Texas, you go casual and eat family-style. What makes Cooper's top-notch is its tender meat with a smoky flavor, thanks to the mesquite charcoal used. Cooper's has multiple meat choices—brisket, chicken, chopped beef, goat, pork chops, pork loin, prime rib, rib eye, ribs (beef or pork), sausage (including jalapeño cheese sausage), sirloin, and turkey—as well as a slew of sides, from potato salad and coleslaw to beans and cornbread, and an array of cobblers for dessert. ✉ *604 W. Young St., Llano TX* 🌐 *www.coopersbbqllano.com*

Delia's. This is the go-to place for Rio Grande Valley residents when they want some amazing, homemade tamales to go. A tamale is traditional Mexican dish made of corn dough, stuffed with a filling, then wrapped with a husk and steamed. Delia's has seven locations throughout the Rio Grande Valley, and serves a variety of tamales, including bean and cheese, pork, chicken, and beef. If you're new to this authentic Mexican dish, note that you remove the corn husk before you eat the tamale. 🌐 *www.deliastamales.com*

Franklin Barbeque. If Central Texas is the hub of the state's best barbecue, then Franklin has become its favorite darling. The former food truck turned full-fledged, world-renowned restaurant, founded by pitmaster Aaron Franklin, attracts a daily throng of fans who wait in line for upward of three hours in hopes of devouring a tray of brisket, sausage, and pork ribs pulled straight from the smoker, alongside classic potato salad, pinto beans, and coleslaw. The hype is unmatched (President Obama even stopped by during an Austin visit) but so is the quality. People start lining up well before doors open at 11 am, but crowds dissipate when the meat sells out, which can be as early as 2 pm. ✉ *900 E. 11th St., Austin, TX* 🌐 *franklinbbq.com*

Mi Tierra Cafe y Panaderia. In San Antonio's colorful Market Square, this long-standing restaurant serves tasty Tex-Mex, from huevos rancheros for breakfast to chicken or beef enchiladas for lunch to chalupas, tamales, tacos, and more for dinner. And don't forget the margaritas. There is also a bakery on-site, where you can pick up some *pan dulces* to go. ✉ *218 Produce Row, Market Square, San Antonio, TX* 🌐 *lafamiliacortez.com/mi-tierra*

Pappas Bros. Steakhouse. This family-run establishment with three locations (in Dallas, Downtown Houston, and the Houston Galleria) has mouthwatering, tender steaks, from rib eyes to New York strips. It prides itself on using quality ingredients, preparing dishes from scratch, and aging its meats in-house. The Pappas chain also includes seafood, barbecue, and Tex-Mex restaurants in several Texas cities. 🌐 *www.pappasbros.com*

Veracruz All Natural. Veracruz wears a taco tiara in the Austin food scene and for good reason. Their migas taco lives up to the local lore, and the always-hopping original location in East Austin (there are several locations throughout the city) has a convivial patio seating area for enjoying tasty quesadillas, barbacoa, vegetarian and fish tacos on homemade tortillas, and fresh aguas frescas alfresco. ✉ *2505 Webberville Rd., Austin, TX* 🌐 *veracruzall-natural.com*

Whataburger. California brought the country In-N-Out and Texas brought it Whataburger, a locally loved fast-food joint that serves up mouthwatering burgers and honey-butter chicken biscuits under an orange-and-white-striped triangular arch that evokes 1950s-diner nostalgia. The original is in Corpus Christi, but you can find them across Texas. 🌐 *whataburger.com*

Utah

From mountain biking on slickrock to hiking past dinosaur fossils, Utah has thrilling adventures for everyone. The world-class ski resorts in Park City and Big and Little Cottonwood Canyons are a haven for those seeking perfect powder while national parks such as Arches and Zion offer colorful geology lessons with natural arches, hoodoos, and mesas in brilliant ocher and red. History lovers can ponder petroglyphs made by the area's earliest inhabitants or explore the Mormons' pioneer past in Salt Lake City.

Capital: Salt Lake City

Population: 3,503,613

Area: 84,899 square miles

Statehood Date: January 4, 1896

Major Airports: Salt Lake City International Airport (SLC)

Travel and Tourism Information:
🌐 *www.visitutah.com*

Famous Residents: Mitt Romney (politician); Donny Osmond (singer); Katherine Heigl (actress); Tan France *(Queer Eye* fashion expert); Post Malone (rapper)

Fun Fact: Utah consumes more Jell-O per capita than any other state in the United States.

Zion National Park

Utah's Most Popular National Park

The walls of Zion Canyon soar more than 2,000 feet above the valley below, but it's the character, not the size, of the sandstone forms that defines the park's splendor. Throughout the park, fantastically colored bands of limestone, sandstone, and lava in the strata point to the distant past. Stripes and spots of greenery high in the cliff walls create a "hanging garden" effect, and invariably indicate the presence of water seepage or a spring. Erosion has left behind a collection of domes, fins, and blocky massifs bearing the names and likenesses of cathedrals and temples, prophets and angels. Trails lead deep into side canyons and up narrow ledges to waterfalls, serene spring-fed pools, and shaded spots. 🌐 *www.nps.gov/zion*

Don't Miss

In addition to Zion Canyon, you'll find find three popular rock formations: **Court of the Patriarchs**; **The Watchman**; and the towering **Great White Throne**, one of the world's largest sandstone monoliths.

Best Hike

One of the most popular destinations in the park, and one of the most difficult and rewarding hikes, is a 5.4-mile trek up the 1,488-foot-tall **Angels Landing**. A permit is required and must be secured at least a day in advance; apply online.

When to Go

Visit in April, May, September, or October to avoid the extreme heat and the large summer crowds.

Getting Here and Around

Zion National Park is in the southwestern corner of Utah off Route 9 near Springdale. From April through October, a free shuttle transports you within the park.

Bryce Canyon National Park

Home of the Hoodoos

The world's highest concentration of hoodoos (tall, thin, weathered rock formations) can be found in this otherworldly national park, one of the most beloved in all of Utah. With its vivid colors, Bryce Canyon National Park is a feast for the eyes, especially when the light plays off the rocks and the brilliant colors pop. New hoodoos are continually formed as the rim of Bryce's amphitheater recedes, and old hoodoos affected by erosion eventually topple over, making this a living laboratory for geologists. 🌐 *www.nps.gov/brca*

Don't Miss

Sunrise Point, named for its stunning views at dawn, provides an overlook that's just a short walk from Bryce Canyon Lodge, 2 miles south of the park entrance. It's also the trailhead for the **Queen's Garden Trail** and the **Fairyland Loop Trail**. At **Sunset Point**, watch the late-day sun paint the hoodoos. You can see **Thor's Hammer**, a delicate formation similar to a balanced rock, from the rim, but when you hike 550 feet down into the amphitheater on the Navajo Loop Trail, you can walk through the famous and very popular **Wall Street**—a deep, shady slot canyon.

While You're Here

Nearby gems include **Red Canyon**, 14 miles northwest of the park on Scenic Byway 12, a favorite hideout for Butch Cassidy; and **Kodachrome Basin State Park**, home to colorful sand pipes and 22 miles southeast of the park.

Getting Here and Around

The nearest commercial airport to Bryce Canyon is 80 miles west in Cedar City, Utah, but many visitors fly into Las Vegas and road-trip the 267 miles from there. Many of the park's spectacular sights can be viewed from the 36-mile round-trip Main Park Road.

Arches National Park

The World's Largest Collection of Natural Arches

More than 1½ million visitors come to Arches annually, drawn by the red rock landscape and its teasing wind- and water-carved rock formations. The park is named for the 2,000-plus sandstone arches—the largest collection of natural arches in the world—that frame horizons, cast precious shade, and nobly withstand the withering forces of nature and time. The most famous arch is **Delicate Arch**, the largest freestanding arch in the park and a symbol of Utah (it appears on license plate designs). The park's longest arch is 306-foot, ribbonlike **Landscape Arch**, also the longest arch in North America. There are also fancifully named attractions like Tower of Babel, Three Gossips, and Sheep Rock to stir curiosity. The best way to see the arches is to hike to them. The park's Windows section has trails to Turret Arch, North Window, and Double Arch (which had a cameo in *Indiana Jones and the Last Crusade*). Not far from the Windows is Balanced Rock, off the Main Park Road. 🌐 *www.nps.gov/arch*

Don't Miss

Explore a maze of orange spires that look like tongues of flame at **Fiery Furnace**, either on your own or on a ranger-guided walk. It's about 14 miles from the park's visitor center. Access the viewpoint to see the iconic 52-foot-tall **Delicate Arch** on the way.

Getting Here and Around

Arches National Park is in southeast Utah, 5 miles north of Moab on U.S. 191. It is 26 miles from Canyonlands on Route 313. The nearest large airport is Grand Junction Regional Airport in Grand Junction, Colorado, 110 miles from Moab.

Capitol Reef National Park

Nature's Kaleidoscope

A natural kaleidoscopic feast for the eyes, Capitol Reef National Park is saturated in colors that are more dramatic than anywhere else in the West. The dominant Moenkopi rock formation is a rich, red-chocolate hue, and deep blue-green juniper and pinyon stand out against it. Other sandstone layers are gold, ivory, and lavender. Sunset brings out the colors in an explosion of copper, platinum, and orange, then dusk turns the cliffs purple and blue. The texture of rock deposited in ancient inland seas and worn by subsequent erosion is pure art. It's no wonder the Fremont people, whose culture dates back a thousand years and includes writing on the rocks in the park, called this part of the country the "land of sleeping rainbow." 🌐 *www.nps.gov/care*

Don't Miss

The park preserves the **Waterpocket Fold**, a giant wrinkle in the earth that extends 100 miles between Thousand Lake Mountain and Lake Powell. When you climb high onto the rocks or into the mountains, you can see this remarkable geologic wonder and the jumble of colorful cliffs, massive domes, soaring spires, and twisting canyons that surround it.

Best Surpise

The park has a surprising feature tucked among its slot canyons, arches, and slickrock wilderness: orchards. See the cherry, apricot, peach, pear, plum, and apple trees at Fruita Rural Historic District; you can eat as much of the fruit as you want.

Getting Here and Around

Capitol Reef is 4.6 miles from Torrey, Utah, via Route 24, which also runs through the park.

Canyonlands National Park

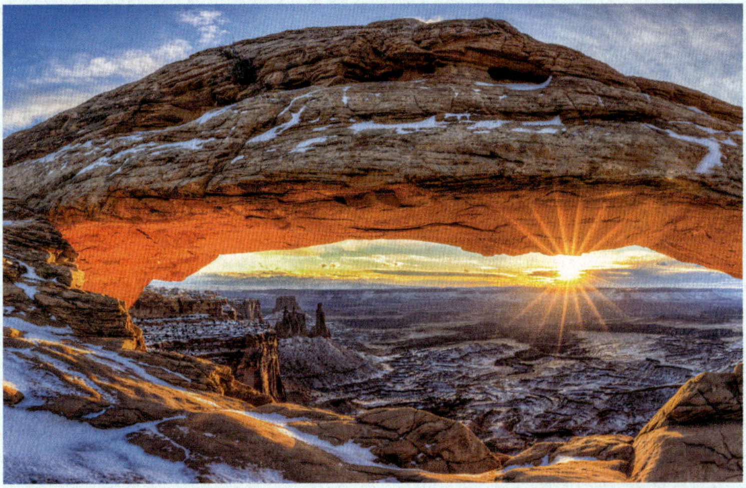

Utah's Ultimate Wilderness

Visiting spacious Canyonlands National Park in central Utah is a bit like walking on the moon thanks to its many mushroom-like rock formations in assorted shapes and colors. Chocolate-brown canyons and deep-red mountains highlight the northern part of the park, while red and white needles stand sentry in the southern part of the park, where there are also red mesas and buttes and grassy meadows. *www.nps.gov/cany*

Don't Miss

At **Grand View Point**, an overlook in the middle of the park, the panoramic view extends for miles. It's 12 miles from the Island in the Sky entrance and it's quite serene in winter.

Best Hike

The most popular trail is **Mesa Arch Trail**, a two-thirds of a mile loop that showcases a natural arch window sitting atop a cliff.

Good to Know

Canyonlands National Park is divided into three distinct land districts (**Island in the Sky**, **Needles**, and **the Maze**), as well as the separate **Horseshoe Canyon**, so it can be a little daunting to visit. It's exhausting, but not impossible, to explore Island in the Sky and Needles on the same day. For many, rafting through the waterways is the best way to see the park. The Green and Colorado Rivers, while very different today as a result of man-made dams from when John Wesley Powell explored them in the mid-1800s, are spectacular.

Getting Here and Around

Canyonlands National Park's Island in the Sky area is 28 miles from Arches National Park and 32 miles from Moab on Route 313.

Monument Valley and the Four Corners

Visit Four States at Once

Using two hands and two feet, you can be in Colorado, New Mexico, Arizona, and Utah all at once. The Four Corners is marked by a decorative cement and granite slab with a bronze disk in the middle noting where the state's borders touch. Because it's part of Native lands for the Navajo and Ute people, you can also browse booths with arts and crafts from Native American artists as well as learn more about the tribes' culture at the visitor center. There are also pueblos and other former Native homes throughout the region. The Four Corners area offers horseback riding and hiking trails, hot-air balloon rides, Jeep tours, and glorious sights of red rocks in nearby Monument Valley—from buttes and mesas to arches and needle-like spires.

Don't Miss

Within the 30,000-acre Monument Valley, a Navajo Tribal Park, stop at the Monument Valley Visitor Center on U.S. 163 for hiking permits, to pick up information, and to view artifacts from the old trading post, then take a two- to three-hour scenic drive through the valley. If it looks familiar, it's likely because you've seen it on the big screen in old westerns, *Forrest Gump*, and HBO's *Westworld*, to name a few. ✉ *U.S. 163 Scenic Hwy., Oljato-Monument Valley, UT* 🎫 *$20 per vehicle*

Best Tour

The best way to travel through Monument Valley and the Four Corners area, viewing rock art, ancient dwellings, and more, is with a Navajo guide. Tour lengths and prices vary depending on the operator. Some even offer overnight trips. 🌐 *www.navajonationparks.org*

Getting Here and Around

Monument Valley is 20 miles from Mexican Hat, Utah, and about 48 miles from Bluff, Utah. The Four Corners Monument is off U.S. 160.

Park City

Olympian-Approved Skiing

Top-notch skiing and snowboarding are found in the winter wonderland of Park City. With an average snowfall of more than 300 inches and lots of "power days," Park City has two main ski areas: **Deer Valley Resort** and **Park City Mountain Resort.** Deer Valley (🌐 *www.deervalley.com*) is a step into luxury, where there are ski valets, upscale lodging options, gourmet dining, and vacation planners at the ready to make your stay perfect. Thanks to the expanded East Village terrain, Deer Valley now boasts 203 runs, more than 4,300 skiable acres, and 31 lifts. It is a skiing-only mountain, catering to all levels of skiers. Meanwhile, Park City Mountain Resort features more than 7,300 skiable acres, 341 runs, seven terrain parks, 40 lifts, and world-class half pipes. The largest ski resort in America, Park City Mountain Resort (🌐 *www.parkcitymountain.com*) has 50% of its terrain for advanced skiers and snowboarders and only 8% for beginners. It's also where the U.S. Ski and Snowboarding Team trains.

Don't Miss

The 400-acre **Utah Olympic Park,** which hosted the 2002 Winter Olympics bobsled, skeleton, luge, ski jumping, and Nordic combined events, today contains the 2002 Olympic Games Museum. Visitors can don a helmet and take a bobsled ride or slide down a Nordic ski jump in an inner tube. ✉ *3419 Olympic Pkwy., Park City, UT* 🌐 *utaholympiclegacy.org/location/utah-olympic-park*

Getting Here and Around

Park City is about 38 miles from the Salt Lake City International Airport (SLC). Once in town, Park City Transit provides free bus rides throughout town.

Moab

Mountain-Biking Capital of the World

Moab has earned a well-deserved reputation as the mountain-biking capital of the world, drawing riders of all ages onto its rugged roads and trails. It's where the whole sport started, and the area attracts bikers from all over the globe to its red rocks and mountainous landscape. The towering cliffs and deep canyons can be intimidating and unreachable without the help of a guide. Fortunately, guide services are abundant in Moab.

Don't Miss

One of the many popular mountain bike routes is the **Slickrock Trail,** a stunning area of steep Navajo sandstone dunes a few miles northeast of Moab.

For Beginners

More moderate rides can be found on the Gemini Bridges or Monitor and Merrimac trails, both off U.S. 191 north of Moab. **Klondike Bluffs,** north of Moab, is an excellent novice ride.

Best Outfitter

In a town of great bike shops, **Poison Spider Bicycles** is one of the best. ✉ *497 N. Main St., Moab, UT* 🌐 *www.poisonspiderbicycles.com*

Best Tour

Head to Western Spirit Cycling Adventures for fully supported, go-at-your-own-pace, multiday mountain- and road-bike tours. 🌐 *www.westernspirit.com*

Getting Here and Around

From Moab, it's an easy drive to both Arches and Canyonlands national parks. The nearest large airport to southeastern Utah is Grand Junction Regional Airport in Grand Junction, Colorado, about 114 miles from Moab.

Grand Staircase-Escalante National Monument

Remote Cliffs and Switchbacks

This national monument got its name from its series of rugged cliffs and terraces that look like a giant staircase stretching across the glorious terrain in this remote part of the state. The layers of cliffs show a variety of sediment in the rock formations. Its three distinct sections—the Grand Staircase, the Kaiparowits Plateau, and the Canyons of the Escalante—offer remote backcountry experiences hard to find elsewhere in the Lower 48. Route 12, which straddles the northern border of the monument, is one of the most scenic stretches in the Southwest. ✉ *69 S. U.S. 89A, Kanab, UT*

Don't Miss

The showstopper is **Jacob Hamblin Arch** at Coyote Gulch, where you can splash in shallow water under a gigantic natural arch. The 2-mile Jacob Hamblin Trailhead is a relatively easy hike.

Make It a Road Trip

The Scenic Byway 12 winds 124 miles through alpine forests and wild landscape as well as through Grand Staircase-Escalante National Monument.

While You're Here

Continue your scenic drive along **Hells Backbone Road**, a 38-mile, mostly gravel road that takes you on a two-hour white-knuckle drive with steep drop-offs on either side and stunning views throughout.

Getting Here and Around

Grand Staircase National Monument is 16 miles from Kanab, Utah. The small towns of Escalante and Boulder offer outfitters, lodging, and dining.

Bonneville Salt Flats

Putting the "Salt" in Salt Lake

Did you know that the Great Salt Lake, the Western Hemisphere's largest saltwater lake, is saltier than the ocean? It's also part of what was once an ancient body of water that covered a third of Utah, Lake Bonneville. West of the lake is a souvenir from this lake: the Bonneville Salt Flats. This mind-bending, barren, 30,000-acre stretch along Interstate 80 formed when most of Lake Bonneville dried up, leaving behind salt deposits that stretch for miles. The crusted, white, salty surface features sodium chloride (table salt) as well as magnesium, lithium, and potassium.

Don't Miss

About 10 miles east of the town of Wendover is one of the best spots to view the salt flats. There's a rest stop here, where you can pause for a panoramic view and also walk onto the salt.

Good to Know

The salt desert is a harsh environment. Don't forget to apply sunscreen regularly, since the salt reflects the sun. Wear walking shoes and pack lots of water: the temperature can range from below freezing in winter to more than 100 degrees in summer.

While You're Here

About 100 miles to the east of Bonneville Salt Flats is **Great Salt Lake State Park**, where you can float in the salty waters of the western hemisphere's largest saltwater lake. ✉ *13312 W. 1075 S, Magna, UT* 🌐 *stateparks.utah.gov/parks/great-salt-lake*

Getting Here and Around

Bonneville Salt Flats is in the northwestern part of Utah near the state's border with Nevada. The distance on Interstate 80 between Salt Lake City and Wendover is about 121 miles.

When in Utah

DINOSAUR NATIONAL MONUMENT

Just 5 miles from Jensen, Utah, crossing over the Utah-Colorado border, is Dinosaur National Monument. While the dinosaurs are long gone, *Jurassic Park* lovers come to see the more than 1,500 fossilized dinosaur bones captured in a cliff wall. View them in the Quarry Exhibit Hall on the Utah side. The 210,844-acre monument also includes Native American rock art, old-time cabins, and plenty of wildlife viewing. The entrance to the remote monument is roughly 16 miles from Vernal, Utah, where there are more than 200-million-year-old dinosaur tracks at Red Fleet State Park. This area of the state has become known as Dinosaurland. 🌐✉ *www.nps.gov/dino*

Do This: If time allows, do a guided one-day or multiday white-water rafting trip on the Green River, departing from the Gates of Lodores. Enjoy incredible views as well as thrills—rapid names like Disaster Falls and Hell's Half Mile give you an idea of the level of excitement on a high river run.

LAKE POWELL

The Glen Canyon Dam forms this ultimate water playground and reservoir in southern Utah and northern Arizona. With almost 2,000 miles of shoreline, the lake provides plenty of chances to get on the water—whether you rent kayaks, paddleboards, and Jet Skis, swim, or fish. There is also incredible hiking and delightful bird-watching around the lake. 🌐 *www.lakepowell.com*

Do This: To enjoy a multiday trip at the lake, camp at Lone Rock Beach, Bullfrog Basin Campground near Kanab, or Stanton Creek Campground—a great base for a trip to Rainbow Bridge National Monument. Or, consider renting a houseboat for an on-water stay.

About Our Writers

Tessa Woolf was born and raised in Salt Lake City, Utah, and currently resides in the city's Avenues neighborhood. She thinks fry sauce (a mixture of mayo and ketchup that originated in UT) is a superior condiment, and, despite her love for skiing, she believes Utah's mountains are most beautiful in the colorful fall months. She is currently a freelance writer and the editor-in-chief of *Park City Magazine* in Park City.

SALT LAKE TEMPLE

In the mid-1800s, a group of thousands of Mormons led by Brigham Young and seeking religious freedom migrated west and settled in what today is the state of Utah. Young became the first governor of the territory. Today the religious group also known as the Church of Jesus Christ of Latter-day Saints has its headquarters in Salt Lake City. Built in the second half of the 1800s, the Salt Lake Temple is considered holy by members of the Church of Jesus Christ of Latter-day Saints and is therefore not open to the general public. But you can view the architecture from outside, walk through the grounds and gardens, and ask questions at the visitor center. ✉ *50 W. North Temple, Salt Lake City, UT* 🌐 *www.templesquare.com*

Do This: Attend a free recital by the Tabernacle Choir each Sunday morning or listen to them rehearse on Tuesday evenings.

Cool Places to Stay

Amangiri. Blending elegantly into its red-rock surroundings, this five-star resort is the place to find ultimate luxury in the desert. Everything about the building respects the unique landscape of southern Utah, with its glowing swimming pool built into rock; walls of glass and outdoor decks for easy viewing of the mesas, deserts, and ancient rock formations; and extensive work with Navajo artists. ✉ *1 Kayenta Rd., Canyon Point, UT* 🌐 *www.aman.com*

Capitol Reef Resort. If you love watching old *Little House on the Prairie* episodes, you may wonder what it's like to sleep in a covered wagon. Capitol Reef Resort lets you find out, sort of. The glamped-out Conestoga wagons here, which sleep up to six, include their own built-in bathrooms and bunk beds as well as modern-day amenities like air-conditioning. ✉ *2600 E. Rte. 24, Torrey, UT* 🌐 *www.capitolreefresort.com*

The St. Regis Deer Valley. Park City has several lodging options that offer luxurious getaways, and this upscale Marriott property is an especially good choice if you plan to ski while at Deer Valley Resort. At the St. Regis, temporary residents are pampered in posh surroundings, and the hotel's windows look out to the ski slopes. ✉ *2300 Deer Valley Dr. E, Park City, UT* 🌐 *www.marriott.com*

Sundance Resort. Founded by Robert Redford in 1969, this rustic, Michelin-rated retreat offers a dose of luxury tucked away at the base of Mt. Timpanogos in Provo Canyon. Originally an arts community, today Sundance is home to a ski resort, cozy cabins, award-winning restaurants, a spa, and an art studio (its famous film festival has recently left for Boulder, Colorado). ✉ *8841 N. Alpine Loop Rd., Sundance, UT* 🌐 *www.sundanceresort.com*

Talking Mountain Yurts. Perfect for those on an adventure in Utah's La Sal Mountain Range, these three yurts, operated by a Moab-based company, are located at various spots in the backcountry. Each of the yurts can sleep up to eight in shared beds and a futon or cots (bring your own linens or sleeping bags). Each has a kitchen with a wood-burning stove, cooking equipment, and a seating area. There is no electricity or plumbing, but each has a nearby outhouse. 🌐 *www.talkingmountainyurts.com*

Essential Eats

Hell's Backbone Grill. For more than 26 seasons, chef-owners Blake Spalding and Jen Castle have been serving delicious food in the small town of Boulder, Utah. Travelers journey from near and far to sample the restaurant's James Beard Award–nominated, farm-fresh fare (even Oprah is a fan). Featuring a rotating menu of Western and Southwestern flavors, every dish highlights organic, local, and seasonal ingredients, including produce from the on-site farm. ✉ *20 N. Rte. 12, Boulder, UT* 🌐 *www.hellsbackbonegrill.com*

Hires Big H. Established in Salt Lake City in 1959, Hires drive-in has been cooking up famous Big H burgers, fresh-cut fries, and homemade onion rings with its signature fry sauce (a combination of mayo and ketchup) to generations of hungry locals. Order a classic Big H combo and wash it down with a frosty mug of root beer or a refreshing cherry limeade. ✉ *425 S. 700 E, Salt Lake City, UT* 🌐 *www.hiresbigh.com*

Takashi. Sushi may not be the first food that comes to mind in a landlocked state, but if the nightly lines outside the door at Takashi in downtown Salt Lake City are any indication, this isn't your average sushi joint. Chef-owner Takashi Gibo and his wife Tamara have been serving unique sushi rolls for more than 20 years, including the Surf & Snow featuring Asian pear, avocado, and shiso inside with New Zealand salmon, Hirame, sliced lime, Thai chilis, and ponzu on top. ✉ *18 W. Market St., Salt Lake City, UT* 🌐 *www.takashisushi.com*

Chapter 8

THE ROCKIES

8

Updated by Gregory Hahn, Katie Jackson, and Kyle Wagner

WELCOME TO THE ROCKIES

TOP REASONS TO GO

★ **Modern-day Wild West:** Denver mixes Old West culture and big-city charm; Jackson Hole pairs ranching with glitz and glamour; Boise brings a thriving urban scene to life amid a wide-open landscape; and Cheyenne still feels like the frontier is alive and well.

★ **Outdoor adventures:** Getting into the backcountry is easier than ever, and activities abound, including skiing and other snow sports, rafting and other water sports, hiking, mountain biking, fishing, and hunting.

★ **National parks galore:** From Yellowstone and Grand Tetons in Wyoming to Rocky Mountain in Colorado and Glacier in Montana, there's no shortage of natural beauty to check off your list here.

★ **Cool mountain towns:** Enjoy the chill vibes of towns like Grand Junction and Durango that are set among the most idyllic mountain backdrops.

★ **Go wild:** Spot elk, bison, and grizzly bears in their natural habitat in the Wild West.

1 **Colorado.** The southernmost state of the Rockies, Colorado is known for Denver, its Mile High City, plus skiing mountains and four national parks, including Rocky Mountain National Park and Mesa Verde National Park.

2 **Idaho.** The "Gem State" has its fair share of crown jewels for outdoor lovers, including Craters of the Moon National Monument, Hells Canyon, Shoshone Falls, and Sun Valley skiing.

3 **Montana.** Mountains and plains that beg to be explored are scattered all across Big Sky Country, known for Glacier National Park as well as epic trout fishing.

4 **Wyoming.** The Cowboy State is mountain country, where high peaks—some of which remain snowcapped year-round—tower above deep, glacier-carved valleys. Stunners include the Grand Tetons and Jackson Hole.

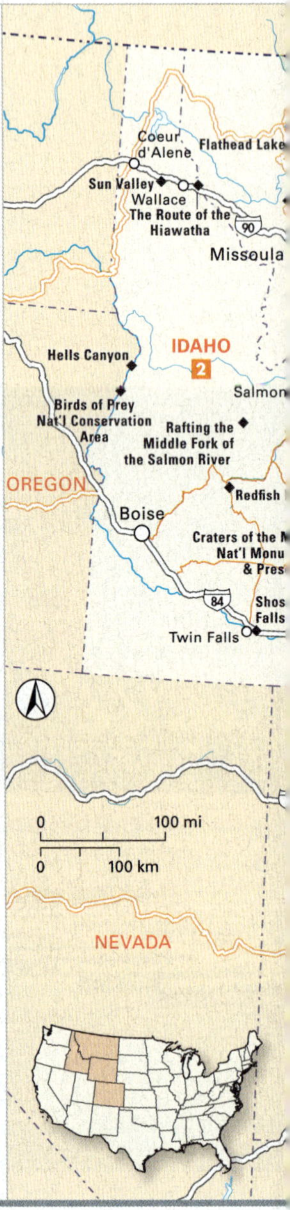

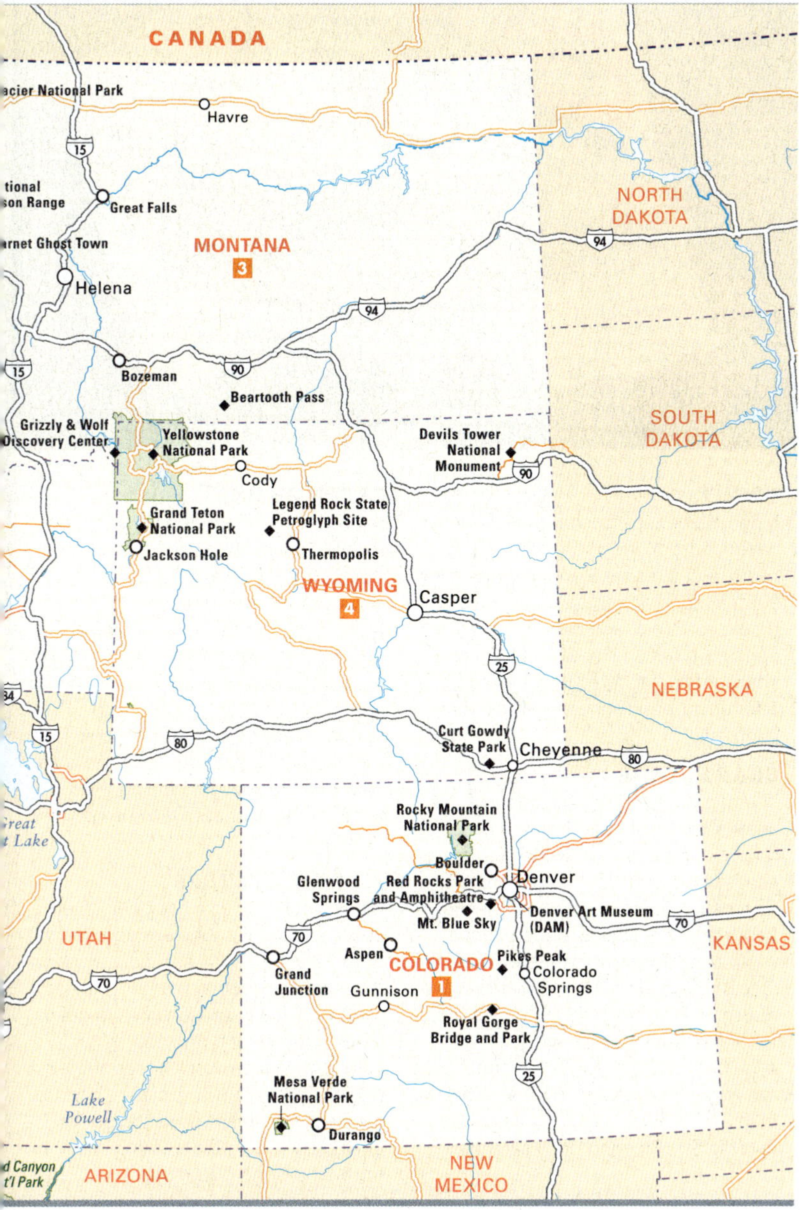
CANADA
acier National Park
Havre
tional
son Range
Great Falls
arnet Ghost Town
MONTANA
3
Helena
Bozeman
Beartooth Pass
NORTH
DAKOTA
SOUTH
DAKOTA
Grizzly & Wolf
Discovery Center
Yellowstone
National Park
Cody
Devils Tower
National
Monument
Grand Teton
National Park
Jackson Hole
Legend Rock State
Petroglyph Site
Thermopolis
WYOMING
4
Casper
NEBRASKA
Curt Gowdy
State Park
Cheyenne
reat
t Lake
Rocky Mountain
National Park
Boulder
Denver
Glenwood
Springs
Red Rocks Park
and Amphitheatre
Mt. Blue Sky
Denver Art Museum
(DAM)
UTAH
Aspen
Grand
Junction
COLORADO
1
Pikes Peak
Colorado
Springs
KANSAS
Gunnison
Royal Gorge
Bridge and Park
Lake
Powell
Mesa Verde
National Park
Durango
d Canyon
t'l Park
ARIZONA
NEW
MEXICO
15
94
90
25
80
70

WHAT TO EAT AND DRINK IN THE ROCKIES

Trout

TROUT

It doesn't get any fresher than when it's reeled in from one of the many lakes, rivers, and streams teeming with nearly a dozen species, including rainbow, brook, cutthroat, and brown, but you don't have to fish it in yourself, unless you want to. Most regional eateries offer up a trout dish, often smoked and panfried.

CRAFT BEER

The four states in this region rank among the top 11 states in the country for the number of breweries per capita, so it's fair to say that this is a prime destination for sampling a staggeringly wide variety of local beers produced by small and independent breweries. One of the most famous is Fat Tire, produced by New Belgium in Fort Collins, Colorado, but Odell Brewing's IPA is even better. Other solid craft options in the region include Grand Teton Brewing in Idaho; Melvin Brewing in Wyoming; and Big Sky Brewing Co in Montana.

GREEN CHILE

Spelled chile or chili, the slow-cooked, stewlike concoction originated in Mexico but traveled along the Santa Fe Trail into Colorado and parts beyond more than a century ago, transforming along the way into a unique chunky gravy. The base is roasted green chilies, of course, but guarded family recipes come in both pork and vegetarian versions, ideal for smothering a burrito or served solo with fresh tortillas for dipping. Find some of the best at El Taco de Mexico in Denver.

PRAIRIE OYSTERS

Many a bull's testicle has been eaten on a dare, but the Western delicacy is on so many menus because a properly done Rocky Mountain oyster (skinned, sliced, coated in seasoning, and deep-fried) is tender and tasty, and slightly gamier than the muscle meat of their origins. Try them with a side of cocktail sauce at the Albany, a quintessential cowboy bar in a 1905 building in downtown Cheyenne, Wyoming.

ROCKY MOUNTAIN EDIBLES

Colorado is famously the first state to have legalized cannabis, and the weed scene just continues to grow (pun intended). There's a dispensary on nearly every corner in most cities and towns—a few local favorites include Good Chemistry, Starbuds, Oasis Superstore, and Native Roots. To avoid couch coma from eating too much in edibles, start with 5 mg and wait four hours before adding more.

Palisade peaches

PALISADE PEACHES

The banana-belt climate of Colorado's Grand Valley, which includes the orchard-filled wine country of Palisade, also produces a first-rate peach, so juicy and sweet that folks flock to the area come harvest time. Cling peaches are available in mid- to late summer, while the freestone varieties are ripe and ready around the state come August and September.

ALL THE MEATS

Cattle and bison dot nearly every landscape throughout the region—from the Rocky Mountain valleys out to the Great Plains—and area universities' meat labs continually focus on creating better marbling and more environmentally friendly resource management, which explains why exceptionally produced meat from cattle and bison can be found everywhere here as steaks (often chicken-fried), burgers, stews, chili, jerky, and more.

Moose meat

POTATOES

The optimal climate in Idaho—hot days and cool nights through the summer together with the ashy volcanic soil—makes for a superior spud, fluffier when baked, crispier when fried, and not coincidentally, superb as a side for the mighty meats that also rule the region.

HUCKLEBERRY ANYTHING

Like a bigger, darker blueberry, the huckleberry has a similar sweetness when ripe, but also a tart edge that makes it perfect for pie, jams and jellies, wine and liqueur, ice cream, and other desserts. The official state fruit of Idaho, they're also native to Wyoming and Montana, and products containing huckleberries are so ubiquitous that you'll find them in gas stations.

Colorado

A playground for nature lovers and outdoor enthusiasts, Colorado has majestic landscapes, raging rivers, and winding trails perfect for activities from biking to rafting. The heart of the Rocky Mountains has scores of snowcapped summits towering higher than 14,000 feet and trails from easy to challenging for exploring them—as well as roads offering spectacular drives. Skiers flock to the slopes here for the champagne powder and thrilling downhill runs. Need a break from the outdoors? Urban adventures await in cool cities like Denver, Boulder, and Aspen.

Capital: Denver

Population: 5,957,493

Area: 104,185 square miles

Statehood Date: August 1, 1876

Major Airports: Denver International Airport (DEN); Colorado Springs Municipal Airport (COS); Aspen-Pitkin County Airport (ASE); Grand Junction Regional Airport (GJT)

Travel and Tourism Information: 🌐 *www.colorado.com* 🌐 *www.coloradolifemagazine.com*

Famous Residents: Molly Brown (socialite and *Titanic* survivor); John Elway (football player); John Denver (musician); Don Cheadle (actor), Amy Adams (actress); Matt Stone and Trey Parker (*South Park* creators)

Fun Fact: Originally named the "Black Cow" and inspired by the snowcapped peak of Cow Mountain in Cripple Creek, the root beer float was invented in 1893 by Frank J. Wisner, who owned the Cripple Creek Brewing Company.

Rocky Mountain National Park

Astounding Scenery and Wildlife Viewing

With more than 350 miles of trails, 30 miles of the Continental Divide, and 77 peaks jutting above 12,000 feet—including Longs Peak, the 14,259-foot flat-top monarch of the Front Range—Rocky Mountain National Park abounds with spectacular adventures for hardcore mountaineers and incredible scenery for nature and wildlife lovers. Hike to high-alpine lakes, picnic in wide-open meadows of wildflowers, or just drive along **Trail Ridge Road**, viewing the abundant wildlife along the way. The gateway to the park's East Entrance is charming **Estes Park**, a quintessential mountain town with an abundance of souvenir shops and eateries. 🌐 *www.nps.gov/romo*

Don't Miss

The **Alluvial Fan** is a massive boulder field created by a 1982 flood, with the Roaring River running through it and a scenic trail to the top.

Best Tour

Yellow Wood Guiding leads small groups for four to eight hours into the backcountry to find and learn to photograph wildlife. 🌐 *www.ywguiding.com*

When to Go

Late spring and early fall are the best times to visit, but they're also the busiest. Winter is considerably less crowded, but the main route through the park, Trail Ridge Road, often shuts down because of snow and ice.

Getting Here and Around

Denver International Airport (DEN) is 78 miles and Denver is 67 miles from the East Entrance to Rocky Mountain National Park.

Red Rocks Park and Amphitheatre

A Legendary Concert Venue

Massive slabs of ancient red sandstone jut out of the earth to form one of the world's most iconic and natural concert venues. Carved over millions of years, this open-air arena sits between the upright pillars known as Ship Rock and Creation Rock, offering unbeatable acoustics and breathtaking views. Denver's skyline sparkles in the distance at night, and during the day, hikers and mountain bikers explore the 27 miles of trails that meander through the pine-dotted hills and dramatic rock formations of the surrounding Red Rocks Park. The area is also a haven for runners (many of whom forgo the trails in favor of dashing up and down the steps inside the amphitheater), and yogis who gather at sunrise to soak up the quiet power of the place. A short drive brings you to the nearby town of **Morrison,** a quaint stop for post-hike burgers, live music, and local brews. ✉ *18300 W. Alameda Pkwy., Morrison, CO* 🌐 *www.redrocksonline.com*

Don't Miss

The **Red Rocks Hall of Fame**, which resides in the Heart of the Rock Theatre at the Visitors Center, showcases the legendary performers who have graced the red rock-framed stage over the decades.

Best Tour

You can go on a self-guided tour for free any time from one hour before sunrise to one hour after sunset, but to get the full scoop on the site itself and on past performers, **Aspire Tours** offers several options, including a morning hike and a driving tour that also takes in the Lariat Loop National Scenic Byway and the town of Golden. 🌐 *www.aspire-tours.com*

Getting Here and Around

Denver International Airport (DEN) sits 35 miles away.

Denver Art Museum (DAM)

Epic Art in the Mile High City

The Mile High City boasts some of the best art collections in the country, but the DAM, as it's known by locals, is the alpha museum here, housing one of the most impressive collections of art between Chicago and the West Coast. Set in a striking building in the Golden Triangle neighborhood downtown—the newer part of which was designed by architect Daniel Libeskind—galleries showcase more than 70,000 works by famed artists such as Vincent van Gogh and Winslow Homer, although the dazzling mountain views through hallway windows often compete for your attention. Plan to spend most of the day wandering the unique displays of Asian, pre-Columbian, Spanish, colonial, and Native American art. The museum is known for its buzzing energy, generated by a creatives-in-residence program for local artists from a variety of disciplines. ✉ *100 W. 14th Ave. Pkwy., Denver, CO* 🌐 *www.denverartmuseum.org*

Don't Miss

There are plenty of kid-friendly offerings here, including backpacks filled with games and puzzles to enhance the experience, as well as hands-on art projects.

Best Tour

As a counterpoint to First Fridays, the Denver Art Museum uses Final Fridays each month to team up with local creatives to offer late-night workshops, performances, and special tours.

When to Go

Final Fridays, weekends, and free Colorado days can be packed, so plan accordingly.

Getting Here and Around

Denver International Airport (DEN) is 24 miles away.

Pikes Peak

The Ultimate American Mountain

Composed of granite and shaped by glaciers over millions of years, Pikes Peak mountain—the highest summit of the southern Front Range of the Rocky Mountains—is a stunning backdrop for Colorado's second-largest city, Colorado Springs. When Katharine Lee Bates arrived at the summit of Pikes Peak in 1893, she immortalized the majestic mountain in her beloved anthem "America the Beautiful." There are several ways to reach the summit of this iconic Fourteener yourself, including hiking—it's a slog, so consider camping halfway—biking, driving, and as a passenger on the comfortable Broadmoor Manitou Pikes Peak Cog Railway, which has operated since 1891. 🌐 *www.pikes-peak.com*

Don't Miss

Sitting at the foot of Pikes Peak, Colorado Springs offers mild weather year-round, clean air, and access to such geologic marvels as the hiking favorite **Garden of the Gods**, the seven waterfalls at the aptly named **Seven Falls**, and the stalactite- and stalagmite-packed **Cave of the Winds.** Man-made attractions include the charming Cheyenne Mountain Zoo (uniquely set against a mountain) and the U.S. Air Force Academy.

Best Tour

The **Colorado Springs Sunrise Balloon Ride** through Rainbow Ryders offers a view of Pikes Peak and the Front Range that's hard to beat. 🌐 *www.rainbowryders.com*

Getting Here and Around

Nearby Colorado Springs International Airport (COS) is usually the best option, with fewer flights but also fewer traffic jams on the way out than Denver International Airport (DEN) 88 miles away.

Aspen

A Legendary Après-Ski Scene

Forever honored in the lyrics of John Denver, the Roaring Fork Valley—and Aspen, its crown jewel—is the quintessential Rocky Mountain high. A rampart of the state's famed Fourteeners (peaks over 14,000 feet) guard this valley, but Glitter Gulch, as Aspen is also known, is just as famous for its celebrities, its skiing, its luxury ski resorts, and perhaps North America's best après-ski scene. From see-and-be-seen spots like **Ajax Tavern** to Maroon Bells views at the cozy **Cloud Nine Bistro** to hot-tub drinks with a DJ and views at the W Hotel's rooftop **Wet Bar**, Aspen's après scene serves up high-class post-ski debauchery like no other.

Don't Miss

Two of the most photographed mountains in all of North America are the **Maroon Bells**, which sit about 12 miles west of town and serve as a backdrop for Maroon Lake and miles of hiking trails.

Best Tour

Ashcroft is a ghost town abandoned in the late 1880s after enjoying a brief heyday as a silver mining hub. Explore on your own in warmer months or with a naturalist guide in the winter, who can help you track snowshoe hares and avoid avalanches before depositing you for a pampering lunch or dinner at the **Pinecreek Cookhouse**, a cozy upscale log cabin. ⊕ *www.pinecreekcookhouse.com*

Getting Here and Around

There are only two ways to drive in or out: either over the precipitous Independence Pass (which closes in winter) or up the four-lane highway through the booming Roaring Fork Valley.

Mt. Blue Sky

The Highest Drive in North America

Colorado is famous for its Fourteeners, 58 mountains whose summits exceed 14,000 feet high. The most popular is Mt. Blue Sky (formerly known as Mt. Evans), partly because visitors can make the switchback-filled, 28-mile (round-trip) drive nearly to the top at 14,265 feet, although plenty of people park lower each year and hike up to "bag the peak." Plan to make your way up the highest paved road in North America slowly to wow over its sheer drop-offs and lakes along the way. Once at the parking area, join the other altitude-woozy walkers finding their way along the final few hundred feet to a literally breathtaking panoramic view of the Never Summer Range to the north and the Sangre de Cristo Mountains to the south. Get your reflexes and camera ready for the mountain goats and bighorn sheep that nimbly scramble all over the mountain.

Don't Miss

Visit **Echo Lake** and **Summit Lake** on the way up, and refuel in **Idaho Springs** afterward, home to one of Colorado's most famous pizza places (Beau Jo's) as well as one of its longtime breweries, Tommy Knocker.

Best Tour

The most relaxed way to get to the top of Mt. Blue Sky is by tour shuttle, and the **Colorado Sightseer** makes it even more pleasant by offering a local guide, providing lunch in Idaho Springs, and including a tour of a gold mine. 🌐 *www.coloradosightseer.com*

Getting Here and Around

Idaho Springs is the nearest town, 56 miles from Denver International Airport (DEN).

Mesa Verde National Park

The Largest Archaeological Preserve in the U.S.

With more than 4,000 archaeological sites and 3 million found objects, UNESCO World Heritage site Mesa Verde National Park is the preeminent destination for all things related to the Ancestral Puebloan culture (precursor to the Hopi, Zuni, and Pueblo tribes) that flourished in the area between 700 and 1,400 years ago. The cliff dwellings are mind-blowing—some carved into the sandstone cliff walls, some sitting atop the mesa—and hikes throughout the 80 square miles range from effortless to hard-core. The big houses, such as Cliff Palace and Balcony House, require purchasing extra tickets, but they're well worth it to try to get a handle on an unfathomable ancient lifestyle. 🌐 *www.nps.gov/meve*

Don't Miss

The **Chapin Mesa Archeological Museum**, built in the 1920s, features artifacts and dioramas of Ancestral Puebloan life.

Best Tour

Ranger-led hikes are the best way to fully appreciate how cliff dwellers navigated this unforgiving terrain. Hikes range from 90 minutes to eight hours and cover 1 to 8 miles to the lesser-visited and mostly non-excavated dwellings such as Mug House and Spring House.

Getting Here and Around

Just 18 miles from the park, the closest airport is Cortez Municipal Airport (CEZ), which has connecting flights through Denver International Airport (DEN), which sits 392 miles away. The Albuquerque International Sunport (ABQ), a 249-mile drive, is a bit closer.

Boulder

Where Adventure Meets Culture

Tucked against the Flatirons where the plains rise into the Rockies, Boulder blends dramatic views and outdoor adventures with a vibrant urban culture. This bustling college town is bookended by vast open space to the west and sprawling agriculture to the east, offering quick and easy access to hiking trails, bike paths, and the towering granite formations unique to this stretch of the Front Range. To the south, historic **Chautauqua Park** anchors the city's deep-rooted nature-driven culture, while to the north, **Flagstaff Mountain** points the way to a patchwork of canyons and forests. Boulder Creek winds through the heart of the city, perfect for tubing, kayaking, or just strolling along its scenic paths. A hike up Boulder Canyon reveals sheer rock faces and rushing waterfalls.

Don't Miss

The **Pearl Street Mall** is a popular pedestrian promenade, with outdoorsy shops, hip eateries, public art, and plenty of benches for prime people-watching packed into its four long blocks between 11th and 15th streets on Pearl Street. Buskers and musicians draw crowds in the warmer months.

Best Brewery

Boulder is a hub of Colorado's craft beer scene, and don't miss **Avery Brewing Company**, which has grabbed impressive awards for its innovative ales and lagers; the Avery IPA was Colorado's first packaged IPA. ✉ *4910 Nautilus Ct., Boulder, CO* 🌐 *www.averybrewing.com*

Getting Here and Around

Denver International Airport (DEN) is 41 miles away.

Royal Gorge Bridge and Park

North America's Highest Zipline

The highest suspension bridge in America, the Royal Gorge Bridge also spans one of the country's most stunning canyons, carved by the Arkansas River, a white-water rafting destination 956 feet below. In addition to the walkable bridge, aerial gondolas that traverse the gorge, and a quaint kids Playland modeled after a mining town, the park also offers North America's highest zipline, the **Cloudscraper ZipRider**, which allows intrepid visitors to soar 1,200 feet above the Arkansas hands-free. Also on hand are outdoor musical entertainment in summer, and the usual assortment of food and gift shops. ✉ *4218 County Rd. 3A, Cañon City, CO* 🌐 *www.royalgorgebridge.com*

Don't Miss

A ride on the **Royal Rush Skycoaster** ensures an adrenaline rush—you'll swing from a free-fall tower and momentarily hang over the gorge.

Best Tour

The **Royal Gorge Route Railroad** offers the best of both worlds by putting passengers at river level while also running beneath the bridge and through the gorge for a 2- to 2½-hour trip. 🌐 *www.royalgorgeroute.com*

When to Go

Open year-round, the park is most easily explored in warmer months, but winter means fewer crowds.

Getting Here and Around

Colorado Springs International Airport (COS) is 62 miles from the Royal Gorge Bridge and Park. Cañon City is the nearest city, 13 miles away.

Glenwood Springs

World's Largest Hot Springs Pool

The name Glenwood Springs is synonymous with hot springs in Colorado as this town between Vail and Aspen sports the world's largest outdoor natural hot springs pool (the eponymous Glenwood Hot Springs), along with several other soaking options, including Iron Mountain Hot Springs and Yampah Spa & Vapor Caves, where you will find naturally occurring mineral-steam baths. Originally inhabited by nomadic Ute Indian tribes and known as Yampah, or literally "Big Medicine," the mineral-rich waters are a healing wonder after a day of skiing at Sunlight Mountain Resort or biking the 20-mile round-trip paved path to Hanging Lake.

Don't Miss

Family-friendly **Glenwood Caverns Adventure Park** is a marvelous mix of corny and cool—it's home to the Historic Fairy Caves' subterranean caverns and labyrinths, as well as a gravity-powered alpine slide. ✉ *51000 Two Rivers Plaza Rd., Glenwood Springs, CO* 🌐 *www.glenwoodcaverns.com*

Best Tour

Out of the many tours **Glenwood Adventure Company** offers, the one- and two-hour horseback rides from Bair Ranch through 6,000 acres of private land in Glenwood Canyon are the most authentic Western experience. 🌐 *www.glenwoodadventure.com*

When to Go

Glenwood Springs comes into its own in the early summer, but there's a lot to be said for sitting in the springs as falling snow hits the steam.

Getting Here and Around

Glenwood sits along Interstate 70, Colorado's main east–west highway, which leads right out of Denver International Airport (DEN) 182 miles away.

Grand Junction

The Perfect Rocky Mountain Town

Here the mountains meet the desert at the confluence of the mighty Colorado and Gunnison rivers, hence the name Grand Junction. And it really is a grand junction, with lakes and forests to the east, the Colorado National Monument to the west, fertile farmlands with world-famous peaches and prolific vineyards to the south, and the sandstone Book Cliffs to the north. The charming downtown is a certified creative district with cafés, galleries, and a year-round outdoor sculpture exhibit with more than 100 sculptures. The great Colorado River flows from the Rocky Mountains down through the city, so you can take mild to wild river-raft rides, with several areas on the river offering Class IV rapids. Nearby **Rattlesnake Canyon** is worth a trip to see spectacular red-sandstone arches.

Don't Miss

Little Book Cliffs Wild Horse Range offers 36,113 acres of hiking in the canyons, as well as up to 150 mustangs wandering the sagebrush-covered hills.

Best Tour

Visitors find fresh fossils all the time by joining the **Museums of Western Colorado** on half-day or one- to five-day Dino Digs around northwestern Colorado. 🌐 *www.museumsofwesternco.org*

Getting Here and Around

Grand Junction Regional Airport (GJT) has direct flights to a few cities through several major airlines. Denver International Airport (DEN) is 269 miles away.

Durango

The Hollywood of the Rockies

Set against a scenic mountain backdrop with 2 million acres of wild national forest on its doorstep, Durango has served as a Hollywood go-to for Western movie sets, including *Butch Cassidy and the Sundance Kid, National Lampoon's Vacation, A Ticket to Tomahawk,* and *City Slickers.* The small city and former mining town is surrounded by the San Juan Mountains and many remote areas once inhabited by Ancestral Puebloans—including Chaco Canyon and Chimney Rock National Monument—as well as the Weminuche Wilderness, Colorado's largest wilderness area and a playground for outdoors enthusiasts. Professional skiers seek out Durango for its unrivaled terrain and spruce-lined trails, while fishermen flock to the many Gold Medal waters of the Animas River.

Don't Miss

Nestled in the mountains, **Vallecito Lake** sits 18 miles outside the city. Once home to the Ute Indians, it now serves as a getaway for boaters, water-skiers, and the fishermen seeking the Kokanee salmon run.

Best Tour

The **Durango & Silverton Narrow Gauge Railroad** offers a comfortable front-row seat to the San Juans during a five-hour excursion to remote and stunning Cascade Canyon, which is particularly scenic in winter. 🌐 *www.durangotrain.com*

Getting Here and Around

The regional Durango–La Plata County Airport (DRO) is 12 miles from Durango, while the nearest major airport, Albuquerque International Sunport (ABQ), sits 218 miles away.

When in Colorado

BISHOP CASTLE

The late Jim Bishop had been building his unusual and intriguing castle for more than 60 years, and now the curiosity that he always called "a work in progress" is being managed by his offspring. Purchased with paper route money in 1959, the property sits in the mountains west of Pueblo, surrounded by old-growth forest. The castle started as a one-room stone cottage but is now 16 stories high, all designed without blueprints by Bishop himself—and he did most of the work, too. Wrought-iron walkways, a sculpture of a fire-breathing dragon, stained glass windows, and just a general feeling of "what is going on here?" are among the highlights. Open daily from sunrise to sunset, the site offers no amenities and visitors enter the premises at their own risk. ✉ *12705 Rte. 165, Rye, CO* 🌐 *www.bishopcastle.org*

Do This: Bishop Castle sits just off the historic Frontier Pathways Scenic Byway, which is well worth continuing along as far as time allows. The paved, two-lane highway is 103 miles long, including the 16-mile spur to Westcliffe off the center of the horseshoe-shape drive that climbs to 9,400 feet. Keep your eyes peeled for pronghorn.

BLACK CANYON OF THE GUNNISON NATIONAL PARK

The Black Canyon of the Gunnison River is one of Colorado's most awe-inspiring places—a vivid testament to the powers of erosion, the canyon is roughly 2,000 feet deep. The steep angles of the cliffs allow little sunlight, and ever-present shadows blanket the canyon walls, leaving some of it in almost perpetual darkness and inspiring the canyon's name. While this dramatic landscape makes the gorge a remarkable place to visit, it also has prevented any permanent occupation—there's no evidence that humans have ever taken up residence within the canyon's walls. 🌐 *www.nps.gov/blca*

Do This: The 1½-mile round-trip Warner Point Nature Trail starts from High Point. It provides fabulous vistas of the San Juan and West Elk mountains and Uncompahgre Valley. Warner Point, at trail's end, has the steepest drop-off from rim to river: a dizzying 2,722 feet.

GREAT SAND DUNES NATIONAL PARK

Created by winds that sweep the San Luis Valley floor, the enormous sand dunes that form the heart of Great Sand Dunes National Park and Preserve are an improbable, unforgettable sight. North America's largest sandbox stretches for more than 30 square miles, solid enough to have withstood 440,000 years of Mother Nature. 🌐 *www.nps.gov/grsa*

Do This: Pack a picnic lunch and climb up to High Dune, followed by the more strenuous stretch over to Star Dune.

INTERNATIONAL CHURCH OF CANNABIS

While recreational cannabis use is now legal in almost half of U.S. states, Colorado was still the first. Just remember you still can't smoke weed in public spaces here. While a handful of members-only social clubs have cropped up and dispensary tours come and go, the nondenominational International Church of Cannabis—located in an actual church in Denver—welcomes anyone over 21 with a professed devotion to community and, yes, marijuana, which is often enjoyed right in the pews as folks congregate. Instead of a pastor or hymns, most "services" are either chats with locals in the biz or low-key rap sessions. To join, sign up as a "member" on the website, and remember, no buying or selling on-premises—it's BYO (you can buy in plenty of nearby dispensaries). ✉ *400 S. Logan St., Denver, CO* 🌐 *www.elevationists.org*

Do This: Stop by during one of the BEYOND guided meditations set to a laser light show ($25 per person), which happen at 20 minutes past the hour from noon to 8 pm Friday through Monday and 4 to 8 pm Tuesday through Thursday.

Cool Places to Stay

The Broadmoor. The expansive complex that is the Broadmoor in Colorado Springs is one of those destination resorts that you never have to leave once you've settled in. The original dusty-rose-color stucco buildings were constructed in 1918, but the 5,000-acre property has since grown to include three 18-hole golf courses, a full-service spa, dozens of cute little shops, a bowling alley, and multiple restaurants, including the excellent Penrose. ✉ *1 Lake Ave., Colorado Springs, CO* 🌐 *www.broadmoor.com*

Dunton Hot Springs. A circa-1800s ghost town and then cattle ranch has been transformed into a luxury resort tucked into the remote San Juan Mountains on 200 acres in southwest Colorado (near Telluride). It's all about the property's inviting hot springs, as well as the 14 fully restored original cabins replete with modern amenities, plus private plunge pools and wood-burning stoves. ✉ *8532 Road 38, Dolores, CO* 🌐 *www.duntondestinations.com*

Populus Hotel. With an eye-popping exterior design, this boutique hotel goes all in on the environment: everything about its thoughtfully curated design is nature-focused, from the natural textiles to the forest sounds on the elevator speakers. Nearly all the disposable material in public spaces and guest rooms is compostable, there's an on-site biodigester designed to ensure all food waste created is composted, and the hotel promises to plant a tree for every night every guest stays (achieving its coveted goal of becoming the first carbon-positive hotel in the country). ✉ *240 14th St., Denver, CO* 🌐 *www.populusdenver.com*

About Our Writers

Kyle Wagner has lived in Colorado since 1993, splitting her time between Denver and Trinidad. Soaking in the pools at Mount Princeton Hot Springs is her favorite way to relax and recharge after mountain biking, river rafting, and hiking around the state. After 30 years as a food, travel, and adventure sports writer for Denver newspapers, she now works for First Descents, a nonprofit that takes young adults with cancer and MS on outdoor adventures.

Vista Verde Guest Ranch. A beautifully situated Western-style ranch 23 miles north of Steamboat Springs, Vista Verde is a top-notch destination for many activities, including honing your horseback riding skills with one of their pro wranglers, learning how to cross-country ski, snowmobile, mountain bike, or fly-fish, or just wandering the 600-acre property that's surrounded by the 1.1-million-acre Routt National Forest. ✉ *58000 Cowboy Way, Clark, CO* 🌐 *www.vistaverde.com*

Yogi Bear's Jellystone Park Estes Park. Yogi Bear's Jellystone Park is just 10 minutes from the mountain town of Estes Park and offers a regular roster of family-friendly activities. Activities included in your stay range from movies after dark, ice-cream-float nights, and minigolf to two playgrounds, a game room, karaoke, and a seasonal heated swimming pool. Yogi Bear or Boo Boo Bear visit on a daily basis. ✉ *5495 U.S. 36, Estes Park, CO* 🌐 *www.jellystoneofestes.com*

Essential Eats

Casa Bonita. This beloved Colorado institution was saved by the creators of *South Park* in 2021 and it's still owned by them today (and is still Pepto-Bismol pink). Several free experiences include tarot card readings, a puppet show, a photo op with a *South Park* character, and a gift shop. Renowned Denver chef Dana Rodriguez has replaced the gloppy fare of the 1974 original eatery with fresh Mexican that makes good use of Colorado-style versions of red and green chilies. ✉ *6715 W. Colfax Ave., Lakewood, CO* 🌐 *www.casabonitadenver.com*

The Fort. A faithful adobe replica of the 1830s Bent's Fort located in southeastern Colorado, this restaurant brings frontier hospitality into the present. The period-style decor, teepee in the entrance, and Old West references on the menu evoke the pioneer spirit, but the food execution is solidly modern. If you were ever going to try Rocky Mountain oysters, this is the place to do it, but there are plenty of adventurous options here; starters include puff pastry stuffed with rabbit and rattlesnake, roasted bison marrow bones, and antelope sausage. ✉ *19192 Rte. 8, Morrison, CO* 🌐 *www.thefort.com*

Frasca Food and Wine. Since 2014, Frasca has been considered one of the top restaurants in the state, and a meal there quickly reveals why. The warm, neutral-toned dining room is intimate and elegant, the expansive wine list pulls primarily from the same Friuli-Venezia-Giulia region of Italy that informs the menu, and the food is simply revelatory. ✉ *1738 Pearl St., Boulder, CO* 🌐 *www.frascafoodandwine.com*

Rioja. The restaurant is hip and artsy, with exposed brick and blown-glass lighting, arched doorways, and textured draperies. Chef Jennifer Jasinski's intense attention to detail is evident in her tribute to Mediterranean food with contemporary flair. The wine list presents Riojas galore, and is well priced for Larimer Square. ✉ *1431 Larimer St., Denver, CO* 🌐 *www.riojadenver.com*

Idaho

Idaho is America's wild backyard. Almost two-thirds of the state's vast and geologically diverse landscape are public lands, giving residents and visitors alike unmatched access to big blue skies, pristine waters, and jagged snowcapped horizons that have been largely untouched by the masses. An outdoors enthusiast's paradise, rafters, kayakers, mountain climbers, backcountry skiers, and backpackers flock to Idaho's untamed wilderness.

Capital: Boise

Population: 2,001,619

Area: 83,557 square miles

Statehood Date: July 3, 1890

Major Airports: Boise Airport (BOI); Idaho Falls Regional Airport (IDA)

Travel and Tourism Information: *www.visitidaho.org* *www.idahomagazine.com*

Famous Residents: Lana Turner (actress); Ernest Hemingway (writer); Tom Hanks (actor); Aaron Paul (actor); Christina Hendricks (actress)

Fun Fact: The name "Idaho" has mysterious beginnings. Even back in the 1800s, there were false rumors of it being of Indigenous origin or meaning "Gem of the Mountains." Historians say it was simply made up—and it wasn't even referring to this part of the Northwest. A man in Colorado thought it up when they were looking to name that state, but when people discovered he invented it, they decided to stick with the Spanish word for "colored red." Steamboats bearing the catchy name brought miners to the gold and silver veins in this remote and mountainous area, and one theory says that led to the lodes being called the "Idaho Mines." However it happened, the made-up name stuck.

Craters of the Moon

A Stunning Lunar Landscape

Like the more famous calderas and geysers next door at Yellowstone National Park, much of Southern Idaho sits on a great volcanic rift. But the explosive activity here was much more recent: 2,000 years ago compared to the more than 600,000 for Yellowstone. The lava from these flows remains frozen in what was described by the presidential order that preserved them as a "weird and scenic landscape, peculiar to itself." Today you can hike and camp in the more than 1,000 square miles of jet-black flows, crags, and caves that make up Craters of the Moon National Monument and Preserve. Life, of course, can find a foothold in even the most extreme environments, and in early to mid-June each year, dozens of species of wildflowers bloom throughout the preserve, drawing photographers and visitors from all over. 🌐 *www.nps.gov/crmo*

Don't Miss

It wouldn't be Idaho if it didn't include a wild story about an iconoclastic adventurer, and at Craters of the Moon, that story is about Robert "Two-Gun Bob" Limbert, who documented the flows on a 17-day 80-mile trek through the desolate landscape in 1920. (He also built Redfish Lodge by Redfish Lake.) He went on to advocate for the valley's protection, and the visitor's center now bears his name. ✉ *1266 Craters Loop Rd., Arco, ID*

When to Go

Craters of the Moon is open year-round, but busiest in spring and fall.

Getting Here and Around

Idaho Falls Regional Airport (IDA) is 87 miles from the preserve; Boise Airport (BIO) is 167 miles away.

Shoshone Falls

The Niagara of the West

As the Snake River makes its way through Twin Falls to join the Columbia River in Magic Valley, it pauses in the most beautiful way to tumble over a wide swath of basalt cliffs, creating the mesmerizing Shoshone Falls. The powerful movement of the water is so thunderous that most visitors report physically feeling the reverberations—it's not called the "Niagara of the West" for nothing. And at 212 feet high, it's taller than Niagara, too. ✉ *4155 Shoshone Falls Grade Rd., Twin Falls, ID* 🌐 *tfid.org/309/shoshone-falls*

Don't Miss

Most visitors just walk the 75 feet from the car to the observation deck, but there are other vantage points to be found if you keep going. Check out Dierkes Lake and the Hidden Lakes behind it. The **Canyon Rim Trail**, a mostly flat and moderately strenuous paved trail, runs 8 miles west from the falls and is good for hiking or biking.

Nearby Sights

Just downriver from the falls—visible from the spectacular 486 foot **Perrine Memorial Bridge**—you can still see the earthen ramp construction for Evel Knievel's ill-fated 1974 attempt to jump the Snake River Canyon. Nearby **Auger Falls** features extensive hiking and biking trails while **Thousand Springs State Park** features crystal clear water that is estimated to have traveled underground for as long as 200 years or more before bursting out of the cliffside into the river. Bring a swimsuit, and end at one of the hot springs spots nearby; Banbury, Miracle, and 1000 Springs Resort all offer large, natural, and private swimming pools.

Getting Here and Around

Boise Airport (BOI) sits 129 miles from the entrance to the falls, which is less than 10 miles away from Interstate 84.

Sun Valley

One of America's Oldest Ski Resorts

Sun Valley has long been a playground for celebrities, athletes, and ski bums, but it's more than just a ski town—it's one of the coolest small towns in the United States. The beautiful Wood River Valley has been going through a little bit of a boom, bringing world-class music and arts and incredible dining and shopping to the year-round outdoor adventures that showcase some of the most jaw-dropping scenery in the Lower 48. Its famed Nordic skiing, mountain biking, angling, and backpacking has spawned a subculture of outdoors fanatics who call this place heaven. ⊕ *www.sunvalley.com*

Don't Miss

Towering over the small town of Ketchum, the world-famous **Bald Mountain** ski resort (or "Baldy") is known for its 3,400 vertical feet of consistent pitch, sunny skies, and celebrity sightings. Don't ski? No problem; you can buy a pass just to take a lift or gondola up and back. ✉ *2738 Bald Mountain Rd., Pierce, ID* ⊕ *skibaldmountain.com*

While You're Here

In a place known for its celebrities, Ernest Hemingway remains at the top of the list. His former home is now a writer's retreat owned by the local library and not generally open to the public, but you can visit his grave in the **Ketchum Cemetery** on the north edge of town and see a monument to the great writer on Trail Creek Road north of Sun Valley.

Getting Here and Around

You can drive from Boise (155 miles) or fly into Hailey's Friedman Memorial Airport (SUN), which is 14 miles from Sun Valley. The town is walkable and there is bus service to Ketchum and to Dollar and Bald mountains.

Hells Canyon

North America's Deepest River Gorge

Carved by the mighty Snake River, Hells Canyon in western Idaho is North America's deepest river gorge at 7,993 feet, almost 2,000 feet deeper than the Grand Canyon. Visitors usually find themselves with no one else around for miles, and tripping over mountain goats, bighorn sheep, mink, and otter, along with the occasional bobcat sighting. The recreation area encompasses more than 650,000 acres, 250,000 of which comprise the Hells Canyon Wilderness Area. More than a century ago, Native American tribes including the Nez Perce, called Hells Canyon home, and it's thrilling to happen upon pictographs and petroglyphs on the canyon walls, along with random abandoned homesteads. Hiking, rafting, fishing, hunting, and camping are the most popular pastimes in this vast geologic marvel.

Don't Miss

The challenging 30-mile loop around **Seven Devils** offers forests, ridges, lakes, and incredible views and takes about three days.

Most Unique Tour

For a century, ranchers, researchers, and other remote canyon residents have received their mail by boat, and you can join in on this amazing tradition (and maybe catch some fish) with **Beamers Hells Canyon Tours**, who have run the route in jet boats for more than 50 years. 🌐 *www.hellscanyontours.com/hells-canyon-us-mail-tour*

Getting Here and Around

Boise Airport (BOI) sits 216 miles away from the nearest border of the canyon.

Redfish Lake

Unspoiled Alpine Beauty

Situated at the headwaters of the Salmon River, the high-alpine Redfish Lake—about 60 miles north of Ketchum in the Sawtooth Mountains—is breathtaking, with crystal clear water, snowcapped mountain peaks, and pine trees bordering the lake shore. Named for the color of the sockeye salmon that once naturally proliferated here, the lake is now the beneficiary of a local hatchery devoted to reestablishing the fish. Midsummer, swimmers can brave what is still a frigid pool of crystal clear snowmelt. Lodging options include the vintage Redfish Lake Lodge and multiple campsites right on the water, as well as cabins for rent. But book early—this is a favorite destination for Idahoans from around the state.

Don't Miss

Redfish is a popular entryway to the 700 miles of backcountry trails in the 756,000 square mile **Sawtooth National Recreation Area.** Hardy day-hikers can navigate the 17.5 miles around the lake, a long but otherwise moderate trail that nets plenty of photo ops and the chance to see beavers, elk, and mule deer. Enjoy all the views and just half the hike by taking advantage of the water shuttle from the marina.

Best Tour

Groups of up to five can enjoy a catered and captained sunset appetizer cruise around the lake on the *Syringa*, a restored 1947 wooden Chris Craft. 🌐 *www.redfishlake.com*

Getting Here and Around

Boise Airport (BOI) sits 148 miles away, but it would be a shame to come all this way and not drive the full 350 mile loop that rounds the Sawtooth Mountains and takes you over the 8,700-foot Galena Summit and through Sun Valley.

Birds of Prey National Conservation Area

A Birder's Paradise

Bring the binoculars, because more than 800 pairs of hawks, owls, eagles, and falcons, including up to 200 pairs of prairie falcons, nest in the 485,000-acre Morley Nelson Snake River Birds of Prey National Conservation Area, most along an 81-mile stretch of the Snake River Canyon. Travel through the area by hiking, biking, or horseback riding, with views of the towering cliffs and river along the way. Camping and picnic spots are available in the Cove at CJ Strike Reservoir, or you can take a 56-mile loop driving tour beginning at the Kuna Visitor Center. 🌐 *www.blm.gov/visit/morley-nelson-snake-river-birds-prey-national-conservation-area*

Don't Miss

The Peregrine Fund runs the **World Center for Birds of Prey** outside Boise, where you can learn about efforts to revitalize raptors across the globe and come "face to beak" with exotic eagles, falcons, hawks, owls, and vultures, including the largest breeding flock of the California condor. ✉ *5668 W. Flying Hawk La., Boise, ID* 🌐 *www.peregrinefund.org/visit*

Best Tour

The Birds of Prey float trip takes rafters from Swan Falls Dam to Celebration Park in Canyon County. 🌐 *www.idahoguideservice.com*

When to Go

You can spot raptors in Snake River Canyon year-round, but in mid-March through June, birds are in the nests teaching their young to fly. Eagles are most visible in March.

Getting Here and Around

Road access to the eastern portion of the area can be found in the towns of Mountain Home, Grand View, and Bruneau. Boise Airport (BOI) sits 64 miles from Grand View.

Rafting the Middle Fork of the Salmon River

The Heart of the American Wild

The 2.3-million-acre Frank Church-River of No Return Wilderness is the largest designated wild area in the Lower 48 states, and don't let the name fool you—the best way to see it is from the river itself. The remote 100-mile stretch of Class III and IV-plus rapids on the Middle Fork of the Salmon River is truly a bucket-list experience even for the world's most accomplished whitewater enthusiasts. Private groups have a less than 2% chance of winning the annual lottery for permits, but you can skip the line and enjoy expert guides and catered meals through a number of established and respected outfitters. Along with its own unique Indigenous and pioneer history, the wilderness around the Salmon teems with wildlife including bighorn sheep, black bears, river otters, bald eagles, and much more.

Don't Miss

There are nearly as many hot springs along the Middle Fork as there are rapids, and nothing feels better than a restorative soak after a long day of adventure.

Best Tour

On a five- or six-day Middle Fork trip with **Idaho River Journeys**, you'll not only enjoy the adrenaline rush of shooting world-class rapids, side hikes to Indigenous pictographs and scenic vistas, and relaxing hot springs, but you'll also get the unrivaled pleasure of waking up in the wilderness to the smell of coffee and breakfast. 🌐 *www.idahoriverjourneys.com*

Getting Here

The town of Salmon is 245 scenic miles from the Boise Airport (BOI). Some guided trips include transportation to and from Boise. Gem Air provides round-trip and one-way shuttle flights as well.

The Route of the Hiawatha

An Epic Rails-to-Trails Bike Ride

One of the country's best rails-to-trails bike rides—created from the former Intercontinental Railroad route that ran from Chicago to Seattle in the early 1900s—the Hiawatha is a 15-mile (one-way, gently downhill) journey through nine train tunnels and over seven steel trestle bridges up to 230 feet high. The trail goes from Idaho into Montana, and the highlight for many visitors is the **St. Paul Pass Tunnel,** a 1½-mile dark tunnel that burrows under the state line. In Idaho, **Lookout Pass Ski Area** is the gateway to the route, where riders can rent gear, purchase a trail pass, and catch the shuttle for drop-off at the trailhead 12 miles away. 🌐 *www.ridethehiawatha.com*

Don't Miss

The nearby historic town of **Wallace,** Idaho, is the self-proclaimed "Center of the Universe," the location for the 1997 volcano thriller *Dante's Peak*, and home of the Oasis Bordello Museum (which was an operating brothel until 1988). The Old Mission State Park in Cataldo is a beautiful and serene place to learn about the meeting of Indigenous and European cultures in the mid-1800s.

Best Tour

A five-day rails-to-trails trek hits the Trail of the Coeur d'Alenes and the Route of the Hiawatha. You start and end in Spokane, Washington. 🌐 *www.rowadventures.com*

When to Go

The Hiawatha is open from late May to early October, weather permitting.

Getting Here and Around

The nearest airport is Washington's Spokane International (GEG), 94 miles away. It takes about two to three hours to complete the trail one way, but plan to spend a whole day.

When in Idaho

BOISE

Overlooked no more, the Boise metro area's population has nearly doubled since the turn of the century. The laid-back city still has a small-town feel and plenty of intriguing attractions, including the 29-mile riverside Boise Greenbelt, a vibrant downtown that features Freak Alley (several blocks of ever-changing street art), and a foothills trail system with 190 miles of high desert hiking, cycling, and horse riding trails. Low on chain eateries and shops, downtown Boise is easily navigated on foot. Bogus Basin is a mountain-biking hot spot in summer and a winter destination for skiing and snowboarding. The annual Treefort Music Fest takes over the town each March and often features emerging acts before they grace the stage at Coachella and other big-name festivals.

Do This: When summer temps hit triple digits, locals flock to float on the Boise River. The easy, 6-mile stretch from Barber Park to Ann Morrison Park is fast but low-key and takes about two hours.

BRUNEAU SAND DUNES

With killer views of the Snake River Canyon and the lake below and 4,800 acres to explore, Bruneau Sand Dunes features dunes as tall as 470 feet, as well as many options for enjoying them. For instance, $25 nets two rented "sandboards" for carving the sand waves from top to bottom, or you can hike the 6-mile self-guided trail that showcases the varied terrain. Camping, horseback riding around the base of the dunes, and fishing the lake or river are also popular ways to enjoy the endless sand. After the sun goes down on Friday and Saturday in mid-March to October, head to the Observatory, which offers telescopes for crisp, clear stargazing in an area that's remarkably free of light pollution. ✉ *27608 Sand Dunes Rd., Bruneau, ID* 🌐 *parksandrecreation.idaho.gov/parks/bruneau-dunes*

Do This: Just 30 minutes from the dunes, Bruneau Canyon Overlook feels like it's truly in the middle of nowhere. The 800-foot-deep desert canyon made of basalt and rhyolite is 1,300 feet wide and sports a breathtaking backdrop courtesy of the Owyhee Mountains. It's also an ideal spot for sunrise or sunset viewing.

IDAHO POTATO MUSEUM

Kitschy and quirky, the shrine to all things spud sits in a building that was originally a train depot for the Oregon Short Line Rail Road. It features not only the alleged largest collection of potato mashers in the world, but also the largest potato chip ever made (a 25-inch-long Pringle that's a Guinness Book of World Records holder). ✉ *130 N.W. Main St., Blackfoot, ID* 🌐 *www.idahopotatomuseum.com*

Do This: This place will make you hungry for taters, so thankfully the attached Potato Station Café serves them up baked, fried, dipped in chocolate, and many other delicious ways.

LIONHEAD NATURAL WATER SLIDES

Situated in the middle of a forest and found only by hiking 1½ miles from the little wooden sign at the end of the road, the natural waterslides near the Lionhead campground at Priest Lake make for a day of all-ages fun. Go on a weekday to have the place to yourself, and bring a yoga mat to avoid shredding your bathing suit or shorts. The campground sits 2½ hours north of Coeur d'Alene, Idaho; take a right at the entrance and follow the rutted gravel road for 5 miles to the trailhead, and then start hiking. 🌐 *www.priestlake.org*

Do This: About 10 miles from the slides, Eightmile Island is 8 miles from the south end of Priest Lake in Coolin. This 100-acre island is accessible only by boat (you can rent at the marina) and was once inhabited by two brothers who built a little homestead cabin in 1897. It's now on the National Register of Historic

Places, and offers a glimpse of Idaho's logging heritage.

MUSEUM OF CLEAN

The 74,000-square-foot Museum of Clean is a paean to the history of human attempts at controlling their environments. This laid-back place where you can touch everything doesn't take itself too seriously—don't miss the toilet collection, as well as the antique vacuum cleaners. ✉ *711 S. 2nd Ave., Pocatello, ID* 🌐 *www.museumofclean.com*

Do This: There's also an art gallery with more than 200 pieces devoted to the clean theme, with some dating back more than 2,000 years.

Cool Places to Stay

Coeur d'Alene Golf and Spa Retreat. A mainstay on the shores of one of the most beautiful lakes in America for over 40 years, this resort has something for every member of the family, whether they like to hit the links, sink into a massage, paddleboard the afternoon away, or just sip a cocktail overlooking the water. And golfers get ready: the famous Floating Green awaits on the 14th Hole. ✉ *115 S. 2nd St., Coeur d'Alene, ID* 🌐 *www.cdaresort.com*

Henry's Fork Lodge. Ever wonder how the other half fishes? Well you can find out here in the heart of some of the best trout waters in the world, where concierge service handles everything, from airports transfers to booking world-class outfitters and guides to making sure your favorite drink is ready for you at the end of a satisfying day on the water. And don't worry, the exquisitely crafted dinners are always timed to "match the hatch," so you will never miss the trouts' feeding time or yours. ✉ *2794 S. Pinehaven Dr., Island Park, ID* 🌐 *www.henrysforklodge.com*

Idaho Potato Hotel. Is there anything cozier than a big Idaho baked potato drenched in melted butter? Perhaps a big Idaho potato that you can sleep in? Billed as a farm stay on Airbnb, this one-of-a-kind lodging that sits 20 minutes outside of Boise was once a marketing tool for the Idaho Potato Commission, but now its home is 400 acres of farmland with views of the Owyhee Mountains, complete with a sweet Jersey cow to keep guests company. ✉ *Orchard, ID* 🌐 *www.idahopotatohotel.com*

The Modern Hotel. This renovated motor inn in downtown Boise isn't just the most stylish hotel in town, it also has one of the best bars and restaurants in the city. Locally owned and infused with local art, the Modern is a top choice for visiting artists, writers, musicians, and families hoping to experience the heart of Boise's creative culture. ✉ *1314 W. Grove St., Boise, ID* 🌐 *www.themodernhotel.com*

About Our Writers

Gregory Hahn got to know all 44 counties in Idaho in his two-decade career as a print and TV journalist based in Burley, Twin Falls, and Boise. He has definite opinions on where to find the best finger steaks (the Drift Inn in Rupert), the best French fries (Bar Gernika in Boise), and the best fly-fishing (like he would tell!). He has been lucky to work at some of Idaho's most essential institutions, including the *Idaho Statesman*, Idaho Public Television, and Boise State University.

Essential Eats

Amano. Chef Salvador Alamilla has earned multiple James Beard nominations—and a win in 2025—for his blend of traditional and unexpected Mexican food in this still-rural-feeling town about 30 miles from downtown Boise. Everything starts with tortillas made to order from heirloom Oaxacan corn hand-ground on-site (and, over the years, often made by Alamilla's aunts and other family members). ✉ *802 Arthur St., Caldwell, ID* 🌐 *www.amanorestaurante.com*

Kin. When Boise chef Kris Komori won the 2023 James Beard Award for best chef in the Northwest and Pacific region, he shut the restaurant down for a few days and traveled to the ceremony in Chicago with his entire staff. If he could have, he would have brought every farmer, rancher, and purveyor in the state. Kin is that kind of place. You'll know where all your ingredients are coming from, whether you opt for the formal multicourse prix fixe dinner, a more casual "late night" meal, high-end cocktails and bar food at the Art Haus (including Komori's locally famous "hot noods"), or just drinks and the best bar view in Boise at the tiny 14th-floor Ampersand Speakeasy. ✉ *999 W. Main St., Boise, ID* 🌐 *www.kinboise.com*

Pioneer Saloon. The "Pio" isn't the oldest restaurant in Sun Valley (if you want to sit at Hemingway's table, head to nearby Michel's Christiania). And it isn't the fanciest (that may be Vintage, also just around the corner) or the trendiest (Cookbook, say, or Flamma). But if you get a Manhattan at the bar while you wait for table and a rib eye once you are seated in this loud, cramped, friendly, and wonderful space, you are guaranteed to feel as Idahoan as possible. Ten-gallon hat optional. ✉ *20 N. Main St., Ketchum, ID* 🌐 *www.pioneersaloon.com*

Montana

Big Sky Country is more than just a nickname: Montana has huge expanses of rugged, pristine wilderness. It's a place to discover how beautiful the night sky can be and what "dark" truly is with limited city lights. But in addition to the natural beauty—stunning glaciers and ski slopes, trout-filled streams and high plains—you'll also find a welcoming place home to locals who love to share their state's natural beauty, mining history, and thriving cultural communities with others.

Capital: Helena

Population: 1,137,233

Area: 145,550 square miles

Statehood Date: November 8, 1889

Major Airports: Bozeman Yellowstone International Airport (BZN); Billings-Logan International Airport (BIL); Missoula International Airport (MSO); Glacier International Airport (FCA); Great Falls International Airport (GTF)

Travel and Tourism Information: *www.visitmt.com* *www.visitbigsky.com*

Famous Residents: Sitting Bull (Lakota leader); Gary Cooper (actor); Phil Jackson (NBA coach); Michelle Williams (actress); Jeff Bridges (actor)

Fun Fact: Yes, some locals here still ride horses around town. In fact, until recently, there was a state law that said if a student rode their horse to school, the principal had to take care of it during class (that said, it's illegal to bring a horse into a bar in Montana).

Glacier National Park

The Crown of the Continent

With its 1 million acres of glacier-carved peaks and valleys, pristine turquoise lakes and streams, and dense ancient forests, Glacier National Park—a designated UNESCO Biosphere Reserve and World Heritage site—is a true ecological wonder. It's also one of the few national parks that still offers a true wilderness experience, with more than 700 miles of hiking trails and the chance to spot grizzly bears, cougars, gray wolves, moose, and bighorn sheep, among many other animals. Rivers and lakes provide cooling waters to lounge by or play in, and there are plentiful campgrounds. Hiking options range from an easy 1-mile stroll on a boardwalk through a cedar forest to 10-milers that gain more than 2,000 feet in elevation. 🌐 *www.nps.gov/glac*

Don't Miss

The **Going-to-the-Sun Road**, one of the nation's most beautiful drives, connects Lake McDonald on the western side of Glacier with St. Mary Lake on the east. Turnoffs provide views of the high country and glacier-carved valleys. Logan Pass, elevation 2,026 meters (6,646 feet), sits at the Continental Divide, the highest point on the Going-to-the-Sun Road.

When to Go

Late June through September is best for snow-free visits. And if you want to drive up Going-to-the-Sun Road (reservations required), you may have to wait until mid-July for the snow plows to finish clearing Logan Pass.

Getting Here and Around

The west entrance, near West Glacier, is 19 miles east of Columbia Falls via U.S. 2; the east entrance, in St. Mary, is 22 miles northwest of Browning via U.S. 89. The closest airport is Glacier Park International Airport (FCA).

National Bison Range

See Bison in the Wild

One of the West's most famous residents, bison were slated for extinction until, ironically, Theodore Roosevelt started hunting them. He realized that they needed to be saved and joined the American Bison Society in New York in 1905, later committing three major chunks of land around the country for a reintroduction—among them the National Bison Range in the Mission Valley of northwest Montana. This 18,800-acre property, part of the Mission Mountain Range, is home to a herd of 350 bison, the descendants of the original 40-member herd. Drive the 19-mile, one-way loop that passes through four different habitats (grasslands, riparian, wetlands, and montane) or park and hike one of the four short (less than a mile each) trails, but always maintain a safe distance from the wild animals. ✉ *58355 Bison Range Rd., Charlo, MT* 🌐 *www.bisonrange.org*

Don't Miss

The bison rut occurs from June to September, and bison calves are born in the early spring and can be seen romping around among the adults.

Good to Know

More than a century after this land was seized to create a wildlife refuge, management of the 18,800 acres of grassland, woodland, and wildlife that comprise the National Bison Range have been returned to the Confederated Salish and Kootenai Tribes. It's officially part of the Flathead Reservation.

When to Go

The range is open year-round, with periodic closures on some roads in winter due to weather.

Getting Here and Around

The closest airport is Missoula International (MSO), 50 miles away.

Bozeman

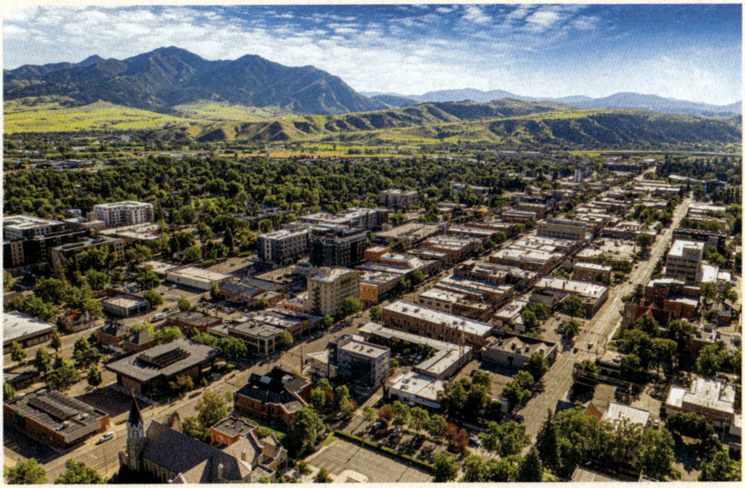

The Gateway to Yellowstone

Culture meets nature at this bustling university town in southern Montana, set in a valley at the foot of four different mountain ranges, just a little over an hour from Yellowstone National Park. Often topping lists of best places to live in the United States, Bozeman's bustling Main Street is filled with trendy cafés and restaurants as well as locals who enjoy easy access to hiking, mountain biking, fly-fishing, hot springs, skiing, and a variety of other snow sports. The **Custer Gallatin National Forest** surrounds the town, providing over 3 million acres of forest to explore throughout the year, and it's just an hour to **Big Sky Resort** where you'll find internationally acclaimed downhill skiing and snowboarding and nearly 6,000 acres of rideable terrain. It's the perfect base camp to explore the great outdoors.

Don't Miss

At the **Museum of the Rockies**, you'll find a celebration of the history of the Rockies region, with exhibits ranging from prehistory to pioneers, plus a planetarium with laser shows. Most renowned is the museum's Siebel Dinosaur Complex housing one of the world's largest dinosaur fossil collections. ✉ *600 W. Kagy Blvd., Bozeman, MT* 🌐 *www.museumoftherockies.org*

Best Tour

Montana Wilderness Outfitters has guests covered when it comes to fishing for trout in the blue-ribbon mountain streams. 🌐 *www.montanawildernessoutfitter.com*

Getting Here and Around

Bozeman Yellowstone International Airport (BZN) sits just 10 miles outside the city.

Beartooth Pass

The Highway to the Sky

Designated a National Scenic Byway, the 68-mile Beartooth Highway starts in the underrated mountain town of Red Lodge and climbs up the Beartooth Pass before topping out at nearly 11,000 feet and descending into Yellowstone via the park's northeast entrance. Take the many switchbacks slowly, as some have no guardrails. Plus, you'll want to soak up the screensaver-worthy views. If you have a hankering to get out and hike to an alpine lake, or simply stretch your legs, pack a jacket and boots. Even in late July, it's not uncommon to find yourself standing in 3 feet of snow.

Don't Miss

While there are many scenic lookouts, the aptly named **Vista Point** is the most popular. It boasts sweeping views of Rock Creek Canyon and beyond.

Best Hotel

Even those who swear it's haunted can't stay away from the **Pollard Hotel**, Red Lodge's first brick building that dates all the way back to 1893. Sleep in the same rooms that Buffalo Bill and Calamity Jane reportedly stayed in. ✉ *2 Broadway Ave. N, Red Lodge, MT* 🌐 *www.thepollardhotel.com*

When to Go

The Beartooth Highway is typically open to vehicles from Memorial Day through Labor Day. That said, intrepid cyclists and skiers like to venture up the pass in the shoulder seasons, too.

Getting Here and Around

The town of Red Lodge, at the beginning of the Beartooth Highway, is an hour from Billings and 2½ hours from Bozeman. You'll definitely need your own wheels as public transportation doesn't really exist here.

Flathead Lake

Western Montana's Waterfront Playground

Featuring more than 150 miles of shoreline, this popular place to swim, boat, ice fish, and even scuba dive is the Lower 48's largest freshwater lake west of the Mississippi. Once traversed by steamboat and home to Wild Horse Island (where there are still a few wild horses), Flathead Lake is found in a picturesque valley, approximately halfway between Missoula and Glacier National Park. Many Montanans from around the state spend their summers recreating in the crystal clear waters, while a hardy few can be found ice-fishing or ice-skating here in the winter. 🌐 *www.fwp.mt.gov/stateparks/flathead-lake*

Don't Miss

If you visit in late July or early August, make sure to stop at one of the roadside stands and pick up a pound or two of Flathead cherries. A few family-owned orchards still dot the lake's southern shores.

Good to Know

The southern half of Flathead Lake is located on Confederated Salish and Kootenai lands, so you'll need a tribal permit to recreate (fish, camp, hike, etc.) anywhere on the Flathead Indian Reservation. You can purchase one online at 🌐 *ols.fwp.mt.gov.*

When to Go

While summer is high season and winters here can be harsh, Flathead Lake is a year-round destination.

Getting Here and Around

Missoula Montana Airport (MSO) is 64 miles from the southern shore of Flathead Lake. Although it isn't served by as many flights, Glacier Park International Airport (GPI) is closer, approximately 18 miles from the lake's north shore.

Garnet Ghost Town

Montana's Best Preserved Ghost Town

Most abandoned mining towns have a story, and pretty Garnet Ghost Town, tucked away in the heavily forested Garnet Mountains east of Missoula, is no exception. In the 1890s, more than a thousand people lived in this thriving little gold town. There were four stores, four hotels, three livery stables, two barber shops, a union hall, a school, a doctor's office, and 13 saloons, but a series of unfortunate events caused the town to be deserted not once, but twice, and now all that remains are hints of what was clearly an austere existence (and tales of ghostly sounds of music and laughter at the former saloon). Wander around the 30 remaining buildings, which are in various stages of disrepair but are continually being restored for posterity. *www.garnetghosttown.org*

Don't Miss

Several moderate trails leave from the ghost town's parking lot, each between 2 and 3 miles round-trip. History buffs will love the **Sierra Mine Loop Trail**.

Best Place to Stay

The especially adventurous can rent one of two off-the-grid cabins in winter by contacting the Bureau of Land Management.

Get on Your Bike

Mountain bikers will find 30 miles of backcountry roads and trails in the **Garnet Range**, climbing up to about 7,000 feet.

When to Go

Garnet is open year-round, but in winter it's accessible only by snowmobile or cross-country skis/snowshoes.

Getting Here and Around

Missoula International Airport (MSO) is 40 miles away.

Grizzly & Wolf Discovery Center

Wildlife Rehabilitation at Yellowstone

Set on the edge of Yellowstone National Park, this not-for-profit wildlife park and rehabilitation and educational facility is dedicated to giving visitors the opportunity to observe magnificent wild animals while learning how to coexist with them. The priority is placed on not stressing out the animals, so they are rotated in and out of enclosures on a regular schedule. Most people come for the bears and the wolves, but there's also a Birds of Prey exhibit with eagles, as well as an otter habitat that offers the most consistent activity. Plan to spend an hour or two here before heading into Yellowstone (the West Entrance is mere blocks away). ✉ *201 S. Canyon, West Yellowstone, MT* 🌐 *www.grizzlydiscoveryctr.org*

Don't Miss

The Grizzly & Wolf Discovery Center is an active participant in product testing to determine how bear-proof products are. It's a hoot to see how the bears try to puzzle or muscle their way in. If after 60 minutes, the bears are defeated, the item gets a coveted "bear-resistant" designation.

Good to Know

On theme, the **Running Bear Pancake House** is just a few blocks from the center, and is known for its decadent cinnamon roll pancake. ✉ *538 Madison Ave., West Yellowstone, MT* 🌐 *www.runningbearwestyellowstone.com*

Getting Here and Around

Just one block from the West Entrance to Yellowstone, the center is a little more than 2 miles from the regional Yellowstone Airport (WYS) and 91 miles from Bozeman Yellowstone International Airport (BZN).

Great Falls

An Epic Lewis and Clark Pit Stop

The third-largest city in Montana, but one of the least-visited, Great Falls boasts Montana's first ski hill (Showdown), the most museums in the state, and yes, some great falls: Great Falls, Crooked Falls, Rainbow Falls, Colter Falls, and Black Eagle Falls. It was these falls that slowed down the explorers Lewis and Clark for a month in 1805, when their equipment and supplies, including canoes, had to be carried by hand or in makeshift wagons overland for 18 miles. Today, the famed portage route can be followed as part of the legacy left by the famed expedition. Surrounded by endless outdoor opportunities and plenty of Old West attractions and artifacts, Great Falls is an ideal base for present-day explorers of the Great Plains. Take a theme walking tour to learn about the area's railroad history and architecture, see the collection of cowboy artist Charles M. Russell at the **C. M. Russell Museum**, and learn everything there is to know about early exploration of the West at the **Lewis and Clark Interpretive Center.**

Don't Miss

The **Sip 'n Dip Lounge** at the circa-1962 O'Haire Motor Inn has a giant glass wall through which patrons can watch mermaids and mermen swimming. ✉ *17 7th St. S, Great Falls, MT* 🌐 *www.facebook.com/sipndiplounge*

Best Trail

The 60-mile **River's Edge Trail** connects many of the city's signature attractions, but with public art, scenic overlooks, and events, the trail is also an attraction in itself.

Getting Here and Around

Great Falls International Airport (GTF) sits just 5 miles outside of downtown Great Falls.

When in Montana

EARTHQUAKE LAKE

On a full-moon night in 1959, a one-minute earthquake blew 80 million tons of rock in the way of the Madison River as it flowed through the canyon, creating "Quake Lake," as locals call it, a 5-mile-long, third-of-a-mile-wide body of water. The quake had a magnitude of 7.5, shaking loose rocks, trees, and earth at the western end of the canyon to form a massive landslide. The slide went three-quarters of a mile north and spread a mile east to west, burying 19 people and killing nine more later.

Do This: Situated 27 miles northwest of West Yellowstone, today the peaceful alpine lake is known for some of the best fly-fishing for cutthroat and browns due to timber clogging the bottom, which creates ideal feeding and hiding spots. It's also surrounded by hiking trails, world-renowned ice-climbing areas, and horse camps.

HAVRE BENEATH THE STREETS

When a fire burned down the railroad town of Havre in 1904, the residents came up with a unique way to rebuild: underground. Built mostly by the Chinese workers who had constructed the railroad tracks, this six-block minitown was a bustling collection of the shops needed for day-to-day life a century ago: a meat market, a saloon, a bordello, a saddlery, a blacksmith, a smokehouse, a bakery, an ice-cream shop, a laundry, a pharmacy, a funeral parlor, and an opium den. After everyone moved aboveground again and Prohibition began, the tunnels were used to smuggle and store liquor. How anyone lived in such dimly lit close quarters is hard to fathom, but wandering around this beautifully preserved piece of history, looking as though everyone just left for a few minutes, is a fascinating way to try to imagine it. ✉ *120 3rd Ave., Havre, MT* 🌐 *www.havrebeneaththestreets.com*

Do This: On the same block as Havre Beneath the Streets, the Palace Bar has a back bar built in 1912 and a genteel feel. It echoes the old-timey atmosphere of the underground town, but with welcome modern "amenities," such as darts and TVs. ✉ *228 1st St., Havre, MT* 🌐 *www.facebook.com/palacebarbar*

KOOTENAI FALLS

Located between the cities of Libby and Troy in northwestern Montana, Kootenai Falls is the largest undammed falls in the state and is not only a spectacular reward for hikers in the Kootenai National Forest, but also a premiere white-water play area for kayakers. Famously serving as a setting for the movies *The Revenant* and *The River Wild*, the area is sacred to the Kootenai tribe as it is a meeting place for convening with the spirits.

Do This: The hike to the falls is only a mile round-trip, but it includes a unique 210-foot-long swinging bridge that sits 100 feet over the water and offers stunning views of the rapids and the falls as well as the many bird species along the river, including bald eagles, ospreys, and many types of waterfowl.

LITTLE BIGHORN BATTLEFIELD NATIONAL MONUMENT

When the smoke cleared on June 25, 1876, neither Lieutenant Colonel George Armstrong Custer (1839–76) nor 200 soldiers, scouts, and civilians were alive to tell the story of their part in the battle against several thousand Lakota-Sioux and Northern Cheyenne warriors inspired by Sitting Bull (circa 1831–90) and Crazy Horse (1842–77). It was a Pyrrhic victory for the tribes; the loss pushed the U.S. government to redouble its efforts to remove them to the Great Sioux Reservation in Dakota Territory. Now the Little Bighorn Battlefield, on the Crow Reservation, memorializes the warriors and the men of the Seventh Cavalry who took part in the conflict.

Do This: The interpretive exhibits explain the events that led to and resulted from the battle, as well as the deeper issues regarding the historical conflict between white and Native American culture. Talks by park rangers contain surprises for even the most avid history buff. ⊠ *Battlefield Rd., Busby, MT* ⊕ *www.nps.gov/libi*

MEDICINE ROCKS STATE PARK

Named for the "big medicine" practiced in the area by Native Americans, the 330-acre Medicine Rocks State Park in southeastern Montana features unique sandstone formations that have taken on a "Swiss cheese" look. This makes them the perfect hand- and footholds for scrambling to the tops of some of the larger formations—many of which have transformed into spires, caves, and arches—to get a better look at the surrounding peaceful plains. Amid the holes, thousands of petroglyphs were carved by the Sioux and Northern Cheyenne tribes that once camped here. ⊠ *1141 Rte. 7, Ekalaka, MT* ⊕ *www.fwp.mt.gov/stateparks/medicine-rocks*

Do This: Visitors can also camp in one of the eight designated sites, keeping an eye out for the golden eagles, antelope, mule deer, and sharp-tailed grouse that call the park home. Because of its far-flung locale, the park is usually nearly empty, so climb up a pockmarked boulder, close your eyes, and listen to the piercing cries of a falcon and the whisper of the prairie winds.

MONTANA STATE PRISON HOBBY STORE

At Montana State Prison, the incarcerated have the chance to learn a staggering variety of skills—from raising Angus cattle to training dogs to manufacturing wood furniture—but for over 40 years they also have been taught the ancient art form of braiding horsehair, which has earned them international acclaim. Horsehair belts—some of which take up to 100 hours to make using the limited tools allowed in prison—are just one of the many unique handcrafted items for sale at the Hobby Store, located in the Old Prison Museum complex in Deer Lodge. The shop also features intricate beaded jewelry, paintings and sculptures, and leather work such as wallets and purses. The incarcerated artists receive 75% of the commission on all purchases. ⊠ *1103 Main St., Deer Lodge, MT* ⊕ *cor.mt.gov/mce/productsandservices*

Do This: There are a bunch of quirky little museums near the Hobby Store, all part of the Old Montana Prison Complex (⊠ *1106 Main St., Deer Lodge, MT*), including the Auto Museum, with more than 200 vintage cars; the Frontier Montana Museum featuring cowboy memorabilia and weapons; Yesterday's Playthings with model trains, dolls, and toys; and the Powell County Museum, a small brick building filled with antique furniture and a mining exhibit. A ticket (🎫 *$18*) to one of the museums gets you into all of them. End a day of exploring at the Prison Cow Ice Cream Shop, where the milk comes from the prison's dairy operation.

About Our Writers

Katie Jackson is a fourth-generation Montanan who grew up on a cattle ranch just outside Lewistown. She's paid her mortgage in Billings for the past decade but dreams of one day owning a cabin in the aptly-named Beartooth Mountains. When she's not hiking, biking, skiing, and otherwise enjoying all four seasons in Big Sky Country, she's traveling the world (70-some countries and counting) while freelancing for Fodor's, *USA Today*, *Travel + Leisure*, and other outlets.

Cool Places to Stay

Field & Stream Lodge Co. The esteemed Field & Stream brand's first foray into the hospitality industry was a Holiday Inn in a past life, but don't expect cookie-cutter rooms or chain hotel vibes here. Instead, think family-friendly suites equipped with Pendleton blanket–covered bunks for the kids, plush dog beds for the pups, and a spacious communal yard with plenty of room for activities. Play a game of cornhole, take a dip in the hot tub, or hone your s'mores-making skills at the canoe-shape firepits. ✉ *5 Baxter La., Bozeman, MT* 🌐 *www.fieldandstreamlodgeco.com*

The Resort at Paws Up. A destination resort for celebs—the likes of Gwyneth Paltrow, Leonardo DiCaprio, and the Rolling Stones have stayed here—Paws Up is also famously the first place to have used the term "glamping," which in this case means giant, secluded, one- to three-bedroom safari-style tents with hardwood and (heated) slate floors, fancy linens on beds with heated mattresses, oversized showers, chef-created meals, and heating and a/c, along with a massive list of additional amenities. ✉ *40060 Paws Up Rd., Greenough, MT* 🌐 *www.pawsup.com*

Triple Creek Ranch. This adults-only Bitterroot Valley oasis offers remote outdoor adventures and five-star accommodations (it's a Relais & Châteaux property). Choose from a variety of luxury cabins and spacious ranch homes. All meals and most ranch activities—including horseback riding, fly-fishing, sapphire panning, and skiing—are included in the nightly rate. The property also has a spa, so you can treat yourself to a mountain man–worthy massage or facial after a long morning of mountain biking or dogsledding, depending on the season. ✉ *5551 W. Fork Rd., Darby, MT* 🌐 *www.triplecreekranch.com*

The Yodeler Motel. Opened in 1909 as apartments for European miners, then reimagined as a Bavarian-theme motor inn reminiscent of what you'd expect to find in the Alps, the Yodeler stands out in a state full of Old West–inspired stays. It's within walking distance of downtown Red Lodge and makes for the perfect base camp for exploring the Beartooth Highway. The pet-friendly property welcomes bikers in the summer, skiers in the winter, and pretty much every other traveler year-round. ✉ *601 S. Broadway, Red Lodge, MT* 🌐 *www.yodelermotel.com*

Essential Eats

The Huckleberry Patch. Located just outside of Glacier National Park but open year-round, this popular roadside eatery and one-stop gift shop with an on-site cannery pays homage to Montana's state fruit. The huckleberry is grown wild, so expect it to be on the tart side. Grab-and-go options here include huckleberry baked goods, candies, and other sweets. If time allows, get a table inside at the grill and order the Alpine Cristo Sandwich, served with huckleberry dipping sauce, of course. ✉ *8868 U.S. 2 E, Hungry Horse, MT* 🌐 *www.huckleberry-patch.com*

On the Rocks. Nothing is more Montana than this steak house, casino, bar, and liquor store combo owned by the Goggins, a local small-town family with city-size ambitions. Choose from any array of the signature certified Angus beef brand steaks or go rogue and order a bowl of Debi's famous chili, served with a cinnamon roll so huge you'll be begging for a doggie bag. ✉ *2441 Main St., Worden, MT* 🌐 *www.ontherocksworden.com*

Wyoming

While the days of the Wild West seem like history to many of us, Wyoming is still a land of cowboys and ranches. Even in high-end Jackson Hole, Western attire mixes with ski gear. True to that frontier spirit, it's a land perfect for exploration. The world's oldest national park, Yellowstone, brings scores of visitors to the state every year for the geothermal features and abundant wildlife. But don't miss out on the Grand Tetons, atmospheric towns like Cody and Jackson, and vast stretches of wide-open plains.

Capital: Cheyenne

Population: 587,600

Area: 97,088 square miles

Statehood Date: July 10, 1890

Major Airports: Jackson Hole Airport (JAC); Casper/Natrona County International Airport (CPR)

Travel and Tourism Information: 🌐 *www.travelwyoming.com* 🌐 *wyomingmagazine.com*

Famous Residents: Buffalo Bill Cody (Wild West cowboy); Jackson Pollock (artist); Harrison Ford (actor); Sandra Bullock (actress)

Fun Fact: You almost have a better chance of seeing Bigfoot here than you do an escalator; there are only two in the state (both in Casper).

Yellowstone National Park

The World's First National Park

The country's first designated national park, the 2.2-million-acre Yellowstone National Park is home to more geysers and hot springs than any other place on earth with about 10,000 hydrothermal features, including active geysers like Old Faithful and many far less famous gushers. More than 1,000 miles of trails offer plenty of opportunities to see (from a mandatory distance away) bison, bighorn sheep, elk, grizzly and black bears, moose, wolves, pronghorn, and trumpeter swans; wildlife is everywhere here, especially in the less-trafficked parts of the park. Fishing, canoeing and boating, horseback riding, and bus touring are also options. *www.nps.gov/yell*

Don't Miss

You can reach **Grand Prismatic Spring**, Yellowstone's largest hot spring (third-largest in the world) and arguably an even more dazzling sight than Old Faithful, by following a ⅓-mile boardwalk loop. The spring, in the Midway Geyser Basin, is deep blue with yellow and orange rings formed by thermophiles, heat-loving bacteria, that give it the effect of a prism. For a stunning perspective, view it from the overlook along the Fairy Falls Trail.

When to Go

Only one of the Montana entrances is open to cars year-round; the rest require over-snow vehicles. Summers see nearly impenetrable crowds.

Getting Here and Around

The West Entrance can be accessed by flying into West Yellowstone Airport. In winter, fly into Jackson Hole Airport (JAC) and then arrange for a snowcat or other over-snow means of entering the park's South Entrance, 57 miles north.

Grand Teton National Park

A Wild Mountainous Wonderland

Featuring some of the country's most dramatic scenery, Grand Teton National Park boasts 310,000 acres of lush valley floors, mountain meadows, alpine lakes, and the magnificent Teton Range. Hiking and climbing are top activities, and photographers flock here to catch iconic shots such as the old barn on Mormon Row (a remnant from the homesteaders who settled here in 1890). The melt from the stunning snowcapped peaks feeds the popular Jenny and Jackson lakes where you can rent a canoe or kayak for the day. Or drive the 42-mile road through the park, with optional spurs to Jenny Lake and the panoramic valley views at the summit of Signal Mountain and likely see some bison, bear, and moose. Towering above it all is the Grand Teton, dotted with climbers tackling the daunting peak. 🌐 *www.nps.gov/grte*

Don't Miss

The best hike in the park leads to both **Inspiration Point**, overlooking Jenny Lake, and **Hidden Falls**. Take the shuttle across the lake to access the trail, which is 2 miles out and back.

Best Tour

Jackson Hole EcoTour Adventures will help you cover way more of the park in one day than you could ever see on your own in a week. Guides are in constant communication with park rangers, so they know where the grizzlies are. 🌐 *www.jhecotouradventures.com*

When to Go

The best time to visit is mid-May to late September.

Getting Here and Around

Jackson Hole Airport (JAC) is just under 10 miles from the entrance.

Devils Tower National Monument

Wyoming's Most Unique Land Formation

The country's first national monument, the 867-foot-high Devils Tower in northeastern Wyoming is a unique butte created when cooling lava formed the columns of rock, although Native Americans have a much more interesting creation story for it involving two girls being chased by bears. Climbers flock here from around the world to sample the excellent routes to the top and for the hundreds of parallel cracks that make it one of the finest traditional crack climbing areas in North America. Hiking trails offer different vantage points and range from an easy two-thirds-mile stroll to a moderately strenuous 2.8-miler. 🌐 *www.nps.gov/deto*

Don't Miss

Look for signs pointing to overlooks along Route 110 where you can stop to watch the many inhabitants of **Prairie Dog Town** pop in and out of their homes.

Best Side Trip

A scenic 28-mile drive from Devils Tower, the town of **Sundance Kid** was named for the place where the famed outlaw successfully stole a lot of horses from a nearby ranch.

When to Go

Devils Tower is open year-round, but winter can bring unexpected blizzards and ice storms. Throughout June, the park asks visitors to refrain from climbing on the tower out of respect for area tribes.

Getting Here and Around

The closest airport is the Northeast Wyoming Regional Airport (GCC) in Gillette, Wyoming, 65 miles away. The closest major airport is Rapid City Regional Airport (RAP), 119 miles away.

Jackson Hole

A Luxurious Ski Resort and National Park Gateway

The gateway to Grand Teton National Park and one of the primary gateways to Yellowstone National Park, the ruggedly beautiful Jackson Hole is also a winter wonderland for skiers as home to **Snow King Mountain Resort**, **Grand Targhee Resort**, and **Jackson Hole Mountain Resort**. The latter is known as "the Big One," with the longest continuous vertical rise of any ski area in the United States, rising 4,139 feet from the valley floor to the top of Rendezvous Mountain. With the Snake River winding through it all, Jackson Hole is, not surprisingly, gorgeously and obsessively outdoors-oriented. But the valley (Jackson Hole) and the town (Jackson) also offer a remarkably cultured experience, with one of the country's most popular annual fine-arts festivals, noteworthy dining, and lots of Western-theme shopping.

Don't Miss

The **National Museum of Wildlife Art** 2½ miles north of town features more than 5,000 noteworthy artworks depicting animals from artists such as Georgia O'Keeffe and Andy Warhol. The building is inspired by the ruins of a castle in Scotland. A sculpture trail outside overlooks the **National Elk Refuge**, a 27,000-acre expanse boasting one of the world's largest populations of elk. In the winter, see the elk via sleigh ride. ✉ *2820 Rungius Rd., Jackson, WY* 🌐 *www.wildlifeart.org*

When to Go

The whole valley is a year-round destination.

Getting Here and Around

Jackson Hole Airport (JAC) is just under 10 miles from downtown Jackson.

Thermopolis

The World's Largest Mineral Hot Springs

What Thermopolis (population 2,740) lacks in residents, it more than makes up for with world-class hot springs. Soak for free at the **Wyoming State Bath House**, the crown jewel of Hot Springs State Park (although the park's resident bison herd and swinging bridge would like to have a word about that). It's open year-round, and you'll find picnic tables, hiking trails, and fishing access. If you want something more private and borderline posh, book a room at the **Hot Springs Hotel and Spa** where it's not uncommon to have a 20-person outdoor hot tub, filled with the same therapeutic mineral water, to yourself. 🌐 *www.thermopolis.com*

Don't Miss

Embrace your inner paleontologist and do the "dig for a day" program offered by the **Wyoming Dinosaur Center**. If you don't want to get dusty in the foothills, simply admire the 150-million-year-old fossils in the center's museum. ✉ *110 Carter Ranch Rd., Thermopolis, WY* 🌐 *wyomingdinosaurcenter.org*

Best Scenic Drive

A few miles south of town, you'll find yourself bewitched by a 2.8-billion-year-old canyon. Drive (or float the river) down to Shoshone (it takes about 40 minutes each way) on the **Wind River Canyon Scenic Byway**.

Getting Here and Around

Thermopolis is located 84 miles southeast of Cody on the eastern edge of the Wind River Indian Reservation. The nearest major airport is Casper/Natrona County International Airport (CPR), 123 miles away.

Legend Rock State Petroglyph Site

Marvel at Ancient Artwork

Legend Rock State Petroglyph Site is a 1,312-foot-long cliff that features 92 panels with more than 300 petroglyphs, some of which were carved nearly 10,000 years ago. The site is probably best known for its large, elaborate, and highly abstract anthropomorphic petroglyphs. There are depictions of humans as well as birds and animals such as elk, deer, bighorn sheep, horses, and buffalo. Trails with informative placards lead visitors around the rock walls, which helps to identify and offer the best interpretations of the figures and symbols incised and etched into the rock. ✉ *2861 W. Cottonwood Rd., Thermopolis, WY* 🌐 *wyoparks.wyo.gov/index.php/places-to-go/legend-rock*

Don't Miss

As seen on the Discovery Channel, you can rent a "ghost coach" from **Kirwin Ghost Town Adventures**, located in nearby Meteetse, and follow in Amelia Earhart's famous footsteps. The late aviator spent a lot of time in this part of Wyoming and even hired a contractor to build her a cabin here. 🌐 *www.kirwinghosttown.com*

While You're Here

Rocks, minerals, and gems (jade, agate, petrified wood, and geodes, to name a few) cover every surface inside and outside at **Ava's Silver and Rock Shop**. There are also dinosaur-themed souvenirs, locally made jewelry, and books on rockhounding in the area. ✉ *631 Shoshoni St., Thermopolis, WY*

Getting Here and Around

The site is located 29 miles northwest of Thermopolis, which has the regional Hot Springs County Airport (THP). The closest major airport is Casper/Natrona County International Airport (CPR) 123 miles away.

Curt Gowdy State Park

A Mountain-Biking Mecca

Sometimes state parks are just, well, another great park, but not Curt Gowdy (named for the beloved sportscaster who was born and raised in Green River) which sits halfway between Cheyenne and Laramie and offers endless recreational opportunities. With more than 35 miles of single- and doubletrack trails, four mountain-bike terrain playgrounds, and a skills area, the park was awarded the designation of "epic" by the International Mountain Biking Association (IMBA). Its log jumps, vertical drops, slab cruising, and meandering dirt paths continue to draw bicyclists of all levels. Boaters and fishermen also love the three reservoirs which offer a variety of fish, and in spring, bird-watchers flock here to catch sight of the many migrating, non-native birds who make stops here. In June, the Stone Temple Mountain Bike Camp allows teens to spend four days honing their fat-tire skills. ✉ *1264 Granite Springs Rd., Cheyenne, WY* 🌐 *wyoparks.wyo.gov*

Don't Miss

The park's 19.2-mile loop track wends through alpine and meadow settings and around the reservoirs, with moderately challenging technical sections and plenty of downhill to shake up those quads.

Insider Tip

The four cabins in the **Sherman Hills Campground** have a/c, heating, and views of the Granite Springs Reservoir.

Getting Here and Around

From Laramie or Laramie Regional Airport (LAR), take Interstate 80 to Route 210 (Happy Jack Road) to County Road 106; from Cheyenne or Cheyenne Regional Airport (CYS), take Happy Jack Road straight from town.

When in Wyoming

CHEYENNE

The capital of Wyoming, Cheyenne is also the state's biggest city, but at around 65,168 residents, it's small enough that you can check out its historical Western and railroad sites in a day or two. Considered the Railroad Capital of the country, Cheyenne boasts multiple train-theme attractions, including the restored Cheyenne Depot, the world's largest steam locomotive (Big Boy), and the Union Pacific Roundhouse Turntable. Because the city is still surrounded by an active ranching community, the cowboys here are real, and opportunities to buy locally crafted hats and boots abound.

Do This: If you visit in late July, the annual Cheyenne Frontier Days rodeo—the world's largest outdoor rodeo—has been in operation since 1896. Smaller rodeos strut their stuff throughout the season, too. 🌐 *cfdrodeo.com*

CODY'S OLD TRAIL TOWN

Just outside Cody along the Yellowstone Highway, you can take a step back in time by visiting the authentic Old West buildings that make up Old Trail Town. See the cabin where Butch Cassidy and the Sundance Kid hid out and the saloon where they and the rest of the Hole in the Wall gang did shots of whiskey and planned their escapades. The buildings were moved from their original locations around Wyoming and Montana and reassembled here in the form of a tiny town, in the spot that Buffalo Bill Cody originally surveyed for a "Cody City" in 1895. ✉ *1831 Demaris Dr., Cody, WY* 🌐 *www.oldtrailtown.org*

Do This: The Buffalo Bill Center of the Wild West sits just 2 miles away and is home to five museums: the Buffalo Bill Museum, Whitney Western Art Museum, Draper Natural History Museum, Cody Firearms Museum, and Plains Indian Museum. Each showcase a different aspect of the country's Native American and pioneering history. ✉ *720 Sheridan Ave., Cody, WY* 🌐 *centerofthewest.org*

COWGIRLS OF THE WEST MUSEUM

Located in downtown Cheyenne, the Cowgirls of the West Museum offers a welcome overview of the women who won the West just as handily as their male counterparts. Photos, newspaper clippings, clothing, and other artifacts are displayed with well-researched placards explaining their significance. The rodeo and women's suffrage sections are extensive (Wyoming was the first state to give women the right to vote). ✉ *205 W. 17th St., Cheyenne, WY* 🌐 *www.cowgirlsofthewestmuseum.com*

Do This: Next door to the museum is the Emporium, a shop that sells women's Western wear, cowgirl boots, silver and turquoise jewelry, and cowgirl-centric gifts and souvenirs. Most are locally made, and there are some vintage items, too. ✉ *203 W. 17th St., Cheyenne, WY*

FOSSIL BUTTE NATIONAL MONUMENT

Once covered in lakes, Fossil Butte—which sits about 9 miles west of Kemmerer—is now covered for 8,198 acres with the fossilized remains of extraordinary plant and animal specimens, some up to 56 million years old. You'll find originals and replicas of prehistoric fish species, as well as those of alligators, stingrays, and other sea creatures at the visitor center. Follow 4 miles of moderate to strenuous hiking trails for a close-up of a fossil quarry and scenic, rolling hills with their unique lake-bed-spawned flora and fauna. 🌐 *www.nps.gov/fobu*

Do This: Fishing in the surrounding Fossil Basin of southwestern Wyoming is a unique treat thanks to the the rich landscape and generously stocked reservoirs, including Fontenelle and Viva Naughton, as well as on the Hams Fork and Green Rivers. In winter, ice-fishing the reservoirs can yield some monster fish.

HELL'S HALF-ACRE

Don't let the name fool you: Hell's Half-Acre isn't a half acre—it's actually more than 320 acres of colorful canyons and rock formations. It's also not quite a hellscape: the longtime Wyoming Geological Survey study area is a type of badlands, a moonscape of sandstone and shale that makes for a great sunset stop. Adding to the confusion is that this isn't even the original Hell's Half-Acre, but instead got its name because a wrangler wandering around Casper thought he had stumbled upon the one in Idaho and the name stuck. 🌐 *natronacounty-wy.gov/240/hells-half-acre*

Do This: Famously the setting for the campy movie *Starship Troopers,* the area offers no hiking or amenities, but it's a cool roadside stop right off the highway as you travel between Casper and Thermopolis. The shocking stark landscape in the middle of miles of sagebrush makes for a beautiful sight.

Cool Places to Stay

Brush Creek Ranch. It's hard to imagine the term "elegant" applying to a working cattle ranch, but that's the best way to describe this 30,000-acre resort in south-central Wyoming's stunning North Platte River Valley, tucked between the Sierra Madres and the Medicine Bow National Forest. Three properties in one, the all-inclusive Brush Creek's lodging options include spacious, Western-theme rooms in The Lodge and Spa, and luxury cabins and cabin suites at Magee Homestead and the French Creek Sportsmen's Club. Activities include horseback riding (including cattle drives), fly-fishing the property's lakes, rivers, and streams, hunting, rock climbing, ATV riding, golf, mountain biking, hiking, and trail running in warm months. Skiing at the ranch's own Green Mountain ski area is possible in winter, along with snowshoeing, tubing, ice-skating, and snowmobiling. ✉ *66 Brush Creek Ranch Rd., Saratoga, WY* 🌐 *www.brushcreekranch.com*

The Lander Motel. This cheery motor inn with canary-yellow doors has been a Main Street landmark in the town of Lander since 1941. It takes pride in its innovative approach to contemporary convenience. Think: a "no check in, no check out" operation where guests can book a room, confirm reservations, and receive a passcode to enter their rooms without having to pick up the phone or wait in line at a reception desk. That said, the friendly owners are always around and happy to recommend a brew (or two) to try at the brewery next door. ✉ *569 Main St., Lander, WY* 🌐 *www.thelandermotel.com*

Old Faithful Lodge Cabins. With Old Faithful Geyser erupting just outside their cabin doors, guests at this historic Yellowstone National Park property (open early May through early October) enjoy

About Our Writers

Katie Jackson is a fourth-generation Montanan who has spent the last decade living about an hour north of Wyoming, where she likes to spend her weekends hiking and camping in the Absaroka–Beartooth Wilderness. She's road-tripped to every corner of the Cowboy State and for as much as she appreciates Jackson, Dubois is more her speed (and budget). Working as a freelance writer specializing in travel content is how she keeps chow in her 120-pound St. Bernard–mix's dish.

front-row seats to the action. The single-story lodgepole and stone structure was built in the 1920s, and it offers two types of cabin rooms: one with a private bathroom, and one with just a sink (but communal bathrooms are on-site). While both cabins lack creature comforts like air-conditioning, TVs, and cooking facilities, they are pet-friendly. Plus, there's a bake shop and cafeteria in the main lodge. ✉ *725 Old Faithful Lodge Rd., Yellowstone National Park, WY* 🌐 *www.yellowstonenationalparklodges.com*

Rusty Parrot Lodge & Spa. Like a phoenix rising from the ashes, the Rusty Parrot Lodge & Spa is proof that a property can emerge even better after a devastating fire. Guests can enjoy the luxurious rooms and suites—both of which boast fireplaces and balconies with Snake River views—and the Body Sage Spa. The floor-to-ceiling windows at the Wild Sage Restaurant look out at East Gros Ventre Butte. The Rusty Parrot's impressive art collection—some of which was rescued from the 2019 flames—is a testament to the owner's impeccable taste. ✉ *175 N. Jackson St., Jackson, WY* 🌐 *www.rustyparrot.com*

Essential Eats

Annie's Soda Saloon. Travel back in time at this family-friendly soda fountain found in Cody's former drugstore. Score a coveted stool at the counter if you want to watch your soda being prepared the old-fashioned way, with real cane sugar. Or grab a table out front, weather permitting, for some prime downtown people-watching. Hungry? Choose from an assortment of baked goods, soups, and piping hot paninis, best paired with ice-cold milkshakes. ✉ *1202 Sheridan Ave., Cody, WY* 🌐 *www.anniessodasaloon.net*

Born in a Barn. As seen on Food Network, this finger-licking-good Laramie sports bar is famous for its variety of wing sauces ranging from peanut butter and jelly (seriously) to a buffalo sauce so bold (think ghost chili meets molasses) you'll feel like you swallowed a blowtorch. Born in a Barn has also racked up accolades for its burgers. Try the Cowboy Joe, topped with candied jalapeños, and a side of torched tots or "barnchos." ✉ *100 E. Ivinson Ave, Laramie, WY* 🌐 *www.borninabarn307.com*

FIGS. Hotel Jackson pays homage to its Lebanese owners' heritage with FIGS. While this Eastern Mediterranean–inspired hot spot doesn't serve up wild game or your typical Wyoming fare, its few tables are always packed with locals and tourists hovering over the signature five-mezze shareable platter featuring falafel, za'atar fries, homemade hummus, baba ghanoush, and tabbouleh. Try not to fill up on the house-made pita bread, as you'll want room for the kafta kebabs. That said, vegetarians and vegans are welcome here, too. ✉ *120 S. Glenwood St., Jackson, WY* 🌐 *hoteljackson.com/eat-drink/figs*

Chapter 9

THE GREAT LAKES

Updated by
Robert Annis, Greyson Ferguson,
Amber Gibson, Kristine Hansen,
Natalia Mendez, and Kristan Schiller

WELCOME TO THE GREAT LAKES

TOP REASONS TO GO

★ **Lake life:** Whether you visit Lake Michigan, Erie, Huron, Ontario, or Superior, there are plenty of activities to try, from swimming to ice-skating to watching a sunrise or sunset over the water.

★ **Must-see cities:** In Chicago, Indianapolis, and Detroit, there are a wealth of standout museums, exceptional restaurants, stunning architecture, and buzzing nightlife.

★ **Spectator sports:** No need to travel far for good games in this region: Packers games are a big deal in Wisconsin, Ohio has the Cavaliers and Browns, and Chicago draws baseball fans to Wrigley Field.

★ **Winter wonders:** From ice fishing and exploring frozen falls to snow tubing and searching for the northern lights, the Great Lakes offer plenty of outdoor fun.

★ **Diverse cultures:** The region is home to lots of people originally from the Middle East, Somalia, Mexico, and many other places, which is reflected in the culture and excellent cuisine.

1 Illinois. Thanks to Chicago, the biggest city in the region, it's at the center of the Midwest action.

2 Indiana. From NCAA football to NASCAR racing, there's always an event to catch in this sports-obsessed state.

3 Michigan. With tons of idyllic towns and lakefronts, it's a prime place to hit the beach and explore natural attractions.

4 Minnesota. With hiking, skiing, ice-fishing, and more, the Land of 10,000 Lakes has plenty of outdoor adventures in store.

5 Ohio. The gateway to the Midwest has a number of midsize cities to explore and is beloved for its spectator sports and Rock & Roll Hall of Fame.

6 Wisconsin. Beers, brats, the Packers, and cheese give America's Dairyland a culture all its own.

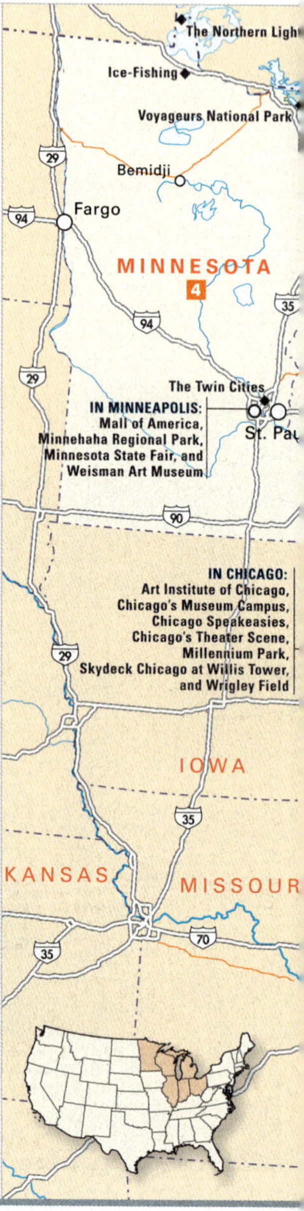

CANADA
Boundary Waters Canoe Area Wilderness
Isle Royale National Park
Grand Marais
North Shore Scenic Drive
Lake Superior
Apostle Islands National Lakeshore
Duluth
Pictured Rocks Nat'l Lakeshore
WISCONSIN
Mackinac Island
IN MILWAUKEE: Milwaukee Art Museum and Milwaukee Breweries
Sleeping Bear Dunes National Lakeshore
Lake Huron
6
Green Bay Packers
Door County
Traverse City
Green Bay
3
IN DETROIT: Belle Isle, Detroit's Museums, and Detroit's Motor History
IN GRAND RAPIDS: Michigan's Craft Breweries, Grand Rapids ArtPrize
Sheboygan
Wisconsin Dells
Kettle Moraine State Forest
Frankenmuth
MICHIGAN
Taliesin
Madison
Grand Rapids
Dane County Farmers' Market
Holland
Michigan's Wineries
Lansing
IN CLEVELAND: Cleveland Sports, and Rock & Roll Hall of Fame
Galena
Ann Arbor
Kalamazoo
Lake Erie
Frank Lloyd Wright Home and Studio
South Bend
Toledo
Cleveland
Ohio's Art Museums
Indiana Dunes Nat'l Park
Starved Rock State Park
Cuyahoga Valley Nat'l Park
Canton
OHIO
INDIANA
5
ILLINOIS
Boating in Indiana
2
Columbus
1
Ohio Air and Space Exploration
Dayton
Hocking Hills State Park
Springfield
Parke County Covered Bridges
Brown County State Park
Ohio Ice Cream Trail
Hopewell Ceremonial Earthworks
Cincinnati
Bloomington
WEST VIRGINIA
National Underground Railroad Freedom Center
St. Louis
IN INDIANAPOLIS: The Children's Museum of Indianapolis, Indianapolis Cultural Trail, and Indianapolis Motor Speedway
Shawnee National Forest
KENTUCKY
TENNESSEE

WHAT TO EAT AND DRINK IN THE GREAT LAKES

Chicago-style hot dog

HOT DOGS AND SAUSAGES

In Illinois, Chicago-style hot dogs come dressed with yellow mustard, white onions, electric-green relish, a pickle spear, tomatoes, sport peppers, and a sprinkle of celery salt, while in Wisconsin, bratwursts are cooked in beer with onions before being grilled and tucked into a bun. Coney dogs, hot dogs topped with beef chili, yellow mustard, and white onion, are the go-to style in Detroit, Michigan and Fort Wayne, Indiana.

DETROIT-STYLE PIZZA

Chicago's deep-dish pizza may get the name recognition outside the region (even though Chicagoans generally opt for tavern-style pizza themselves), but Detroit's rectangular, thick, crispy pies are worth seeking out. They feature tomato sauce layered on top of Wisconsin brick cheese (that order helps give the edges a cheesy crunch). The pies, which are baked in steel trays, are most commonly served with pepperoni. Try one at Buddy's Pizza, which invented the style in 1946, and has locations around the Detroit metro area.

PORK TENDERLOIN SANDWICH

This monster of a sandwich, found throughout Indiana, features a slice of pork loin that's pounded out so it's very thin but much larger than the bun it's served on. The meat is then breaded and fried so it has a crispy texture, and the sandwich is finished with toppings like sliced white onions, yellow mustard, pickles, mayonnaise, and lettuce.

BRANDY OLD-FASHIONED

Wisconsin's signature take on the old-fashioned is made by muddling cherries and oranges with sugar and bitters, pouring in brandy, and finishing it with a splash of soda (sweet, sour, soda water, or half sweet/half soda). It's a must to kick off a Friday-night fish fry at a supper club, a retro style of restaurant you'll find all over Wisconsin.

HORSESHOE

Springfield, Illinois is home to the horseshoe, an open-faced sandwich made by piling two slices of Texas toast with meat (a hamburger patty and sliced ham are common, but you'll also see chicken and pork tenderloin versions). Cheese sauce is poured over it all, and crispy French fries finish the dish.

JUICY LUCY

Minnesota's Juicy Lucy is a twist on the cheeseburger: two patties are formed around a slice of cheese, creating a burger with a gooey center. Two bars in Minneapolis claim to have invented it, Matt's Bar (where it's stuffed with American cheese and finished with pickles) and 5-8 Club (where you can opt for cheeses like blue or Swiss and your choice of garnishes).

CINCINNATI CHILI

Cincinnati chili, made with ground beef mixed with warm spices like cinnamon and cloves, is served over spaghetti (or hot dogs). Order it "three-way" and it comes with a mound of shredded cheddar, while "four-way" adds on chopped white onions or beans, and "five-way" adds both.

SHAWARMA

Dearborn, Michigan, has a large Middle Eastern population, and you'll find shawarma, beef and lamb or chicken roasted on a spit, then shaved off (some spots grill the meat instead) at restaurants there and in Detroit. Try it at Tuhama's or Hamido in Dearborn.

Detroit-style pizza

Frozen custard

FROZEN CUSTARD

Made with milk, cream, and egg yolks (the latter ingredient sets it apart from ice cream), thick, rich frozen custard is the definitive icy treat in the Great Lakes region. At spots like Scooter's Frozen Custard in Chicago, you can get it with mix-ins or turned into shakes.

SUGAR CREAM PIE

The filling in this Indiana-favorite pie is a mixture of pantry staples: sugar, butter, cornstarch, and milk, and flavored with vanilla and nutmeg. The result is a creamy, custardy pie that never goes out of season. Grab a slice at Wick's Pies in Winchester.

KRINGLE

Kringle is a round, flaky Danish pastry stuffed with fillings like almond or raspberry and finished with icing. It's popular in Racine, Wisconsin, where there's a large Danish-American population. Pick one up at O&H Danish Bakery.

Illinois

Home to Chicago and therefore the de facto capital of culture for the Midwest, Illinois is much more than its most famous city. Yes, of course, many visitors flock here for the Windy City and its art museums, architecture, blues clubs, comedy shows, and deep-dish pizza, but the rest of the state offers plenty in terms of history, culture, and the great outdoors. Explore the charms of smaller towns like Galena, see the houses designed by Frank Lloyd Wright in Oak Park, and learn what makes this the "Land of Lincoln" in Springfield.

Capital: Springfield

Population: 12,710,158

Area: 55,593 square miles

Statehood Date: December 3, 1818

Major Airports: Chicago O'Hare International Airport (ORD); Chicago Midway International Airport (MDW); Quad Cities International Airport (MLI); Peoria International Airport (PIA)

Travel and Tourism Information: 🌐 *www.enjoyillinois.com* 🌐 *www.choosechicago.com*

Famous Residents: Abraham Lincoln (president); Bill Murray (actor); John Cusack (actor); Pope Leo XIV (first American pope); Michelle Obama (first lady)

Fun Fact: From 1923 to 1969, American, rather than English, was the official language in Illinois.

Skydeck Chicago at Willis Tower

The Highest Observation Deck in the U.S.

At 110 stories and 1,451 feet high, the tallest building in Chicago's skyline—and third-tallest building in the Western Hemisphere—is the Willis Tower (formerly known as the Sears Tower). The tower mostly houses offices, but you can visit the Skydeck on the 103rd floor to take in a 360-degree view of the city and its architecture. If you're feeling especially brave, go out onto the Ledge, an observation deck—the highest one in the United States—with a glass floor to walk out onto, and peer below. In addition to an unparalleled bird's-eye view of Chicago, you'll see three states besides Illinois from the Skydeck: Indiana, Wisconsin, and Michigan. ✉ *233 S. Wacker Dr., Chicago, IL* 🌐 *www.theskydeck.com*

Best Tour

If you want to see the city's architecture from the ground level, the best tour is a river cruise from the pros at the **Chicago Architecture Foundation**. The 90-minute tour will tell you about the major architects who contributed to Chicago's world-class skyline, and you'll get a new perspective on the Willis Tower. 🌐 *www.architecture.org/tours*

Good to Know

Don't be surprised if you ask a Chicagoan for directions to Willis Tower and they don't know: many city residents still refer to it by its previous name, the Sears Tower.

Getting Here and Around

Chicago's Midway Airport (MDW) is an 11-mile drive to the tower, while Chicago's O'Hare International Airport (ORD) is 18 miles. At about a four-minute walk, Quincy is the closest CTA stop.

Wrigley Field

An Iconic Baseball Stadium

Few ballparks are quite as iconic (and historic) as Wrigley Field, home of the beloved Chicago Cubs. The team famously won the 2016 World Series after decades of being "cursed." Their North Side park was built in 1914 as Weeghman Park, making it one of the oldest ballpark stadiums in MLB. Between innings, appreciate the park's retro touches, including ivy-covered brick walls and a manually updated scoreboard. Be sure to participate in all the traditions, too: order a hot dog, sing along to a celebrity-led rendition of "Take Me Out to the Ball Game" in the seventh-inning stretch, and on game days, check for victory by spotting the "W" or "L" flag waving over the stadium. ✉ *1060 W. Addison St., Chicago, IL* 🌐 *www.mlb.com/cubs/ballpark*

Don't Miss

Statues of Cubs icons outside the park include famed announcer Harry Caray, located by the bleachers.

Best Tour

The off-season tour is the way to go, as game-day tours are more limited. During the 60-minute off-season tour, you'll visit the Cubs' dugout, visitors' clubhouse, and go out onto the field. 🌐 *www.cubs.com/tours*

Good to Know

Most Cubs games take place during the day with a 1 pm start time, so get there early to grab a Chicago-style hot dog or fancy sausage from the **Hot Doug's** kiosk for lunch before the first pitch.

Getting Here and Around

On the El, the Addison Red Line stop is a one-minute walk from the park.

Art Institute of Chicago

5,000 Years of World-Class Art

You could easily spend your entire Chicago visit exploring the Art Institute's 300,000 works. The museum, which was founded in 1879, is one of the oldest and largest art museums in the United States, and features holdings that span 5,000 years, with art from Southeast Asia, ancient Greece and Rome, and the European Renaissance, with a particularly strong impressionist program. The airy adjoining Modern Wing features 20th- and 21st-century artworks. There's also an outdoor sculpture garden; food trucks frequently post up outside the park, so pick up lunch and eat among the statues. ✉ *111 S. Michigan Ave., Chicago, IL* 🌐 *www.artic.edu*

Don't Miss

Three of the most famous works in the collection are Grant Wood's *American Gothic*, Edward Hopper's *Nighthawks*, and Georges Seurat's *A Sunday on La Grande Jatte*.

Best Exhibit

The Deering Family Galleries of Medieval and Renaissance Art, Arms, and Armor has an almost universal appeal. With armored knights and horses, jewelry, paintings, and treasures dating from from 1200 to 1600, there's plenty to see for kids and adults alike.

Good to Know

Download the museum's free app before your visit. It will give you access to audio tours in English, French, Spanish, Chinese, and Korean presented by a variety of experts, plus maps to help you explore the museum.

Getting Here and Around

On the CTA, you can take the Red Line to Monroe or the Pink, Green, Brown, Orange, or Purple Lines to State/Lake.

Chicago's Museum Campus

Acres of World-Class Institutions

Many of Chicago's best museums and institutions are clustered in a 57-acre park nestled along Lake Michigan just south of downtown. There, you'll find the **Adler Planetarium, Shedd Aquarium**, and **Field Museum of Natural History**, along with **Soldier Field** (home of the Chicago Bears football team) and the **Lakeside Center of McCormick Place** (a convention center). The area also features walking paths and parks, so stop for a picnic between museums. ✉ *1400 S. Lake Shore Dr., Chicago, IL*

Don't Miss

More than 400,000 square feet of exhibit space fill the Field Museum, which explores cultures and environments from around the world. It's also home to Máximo, a titanosaur modeled off fossils from the largest dino that ever lived. 🌐 *www.fieldmuseum.org*

Best Planetarium Show

Taking you on a journey through the stars to unlock the mysteries of our galaxy and beyond, the Adler tells amazing stories of space exploration through high-tech exhibits and immersive theater experiences. 🌐 *www.adlerplanetarium.org*

Best Aquarium Exhibit

One of the most popular aquariums in the country, the Shedd houses more than 32,500 creatures from around the world. A shark-filled 400,000-gallon tank is part of "Wild Reef," which explores marine biodiversity in the Indo-Pacific. 🌐 *www.sheddaquarium.org*

Getting Here and Around

The best way to reach the campus is via the CTA to the Roosevelt Red Line. From there, it's a 10- to 20-minute walk depending on which attraction you're heading to see. You can also take the 146 bus from Roosevelt.

Millennium Park

Chicago's Iconic Bean

The crown jewel of downtown Chicago, Millennium Park is best known as the home of Anish Kapoor's sculpture Cloud Gate (aka **the Bean**), but it also offers plenty of activities year-round, from movie screenings, festivals, and concerts in the summer to ice-skating in the winter. The park, which opened in 2004 (it was built to commemorate the start of a new millennium), also features artistic installations, such as the Crown Fountain video sculpture. ✉ *201 E. Randolph St., Chicago, IL*

Don't Miss

The 2½-acre **Lurie Garden**, located at the southern end of the park, features changing flora throughout the year, including colorful bulbs in the spring and ornamental grasses in the winter.

Best Activity

The Frank Gehry–designed **Pritzker Pavilion** hosts the Grant Park Music Festival, a series of evening concerts from the Grant Park Symphony Orchestra throughout the summer. Locals gather on the lawn to listen over elaborate picnics. 🌐 *www.grantparkmusicfestival.com*

Good to Know

For a beautiful view of the park from above, head to Cindy's at the **Chicago Athletic Association**; the outdoor patio space overlooks the park, giving you a bird's-eye view. It's also a good spot to meet for a drink after the Grant Park Music Festival. ✉ *12 S. Michigan Ave., Chicago, IL* 🌐 *www.cindysrooftop.com*

Getting Here and Around

From Chicago's Midway Airport (MDW), it's 12 miles to the park; Chicago's O'Hare International Airport (ORD) is 18 miles. From the CTA, take the Red Line to Lake, Blue Line to Washington, or Pink, Green, Brown, Orange, or Purple Lines to Washington/Wabash.

Frank Lloyd Wright Home and Studio

A Mecca for Modernist Architecture

The city of Oak Park, located just outside Chicago, has more Frank Lloyd Wright buildings than anywhere in the world, making it a must-stop for architecture buffs. Wright, who completed work on the building in 1889, lived with his family for 20 years in the home, which showcases open spaces and Japanese artwork. He designed many of his Prairie-style works in the adjoining studio space, and these homes and buildings are a short walk away. ✉ *951 Chicago Ave., Oak Park, IL* 🌐 *www.flwright.org*

Don't Miss

Visit **Unity Temple**, a Wright-designed building that was commissioned by the Oak Park Unity Church in 1905. It's available for tours, but you can also attend a weekly Sunday service. ✉ *875 Lake St., Oak Park, IL* 🌐 *unitytemple.org*

Best Tour

The **Frank Lloyd Wright Trust** offers two tours: a home and studio guided interior tour and an outdoor historic neighborhood audio tour. You can take each of these tours separately, but sign up for the combined 105-minute tour to get to know Wright's work and appreciate his artistic vision.

Best Lunch Spot

Grab an Italian beef and a lemon ice at **Johnnie's Beef**, an iconic cash-only stand located less than 2 miles away. ✉ *7500 W. North Ave., Elmwood Park, IL*

Getting Here and Around

Chicago's Midway Airport (MDW) and O'Hare International Airport (ORD) are both about 10 miles from the Home and Studio. The CTA Green Line has an Oak Park stop that is a 15- to 20-minute walk away.

Springfield

Abe Lincoln's Hometown

The president who preserved the Union during the Civil War and made history with the Emancipation Proclamation resided in Springfield from 1844 to 1861 with his wife, Mary, and three children, and you can take a tour of his home. Run by the National Park Service, the home tour includes the reception rooms and bedrooms. Take a stroll around the neighborhood, noticing how the surrounding four blocks have been restored to their 1860 appearance. Springfield also includes other must-visit Lincoln attractions, including the **Abraham Lincoln Presidential Museum & Library**. The **Lincoln's New Salem State Historic Site** is 20 miles away and features a reconstruction of the village where Lincoln lived from 1831 to 1837. ✉ *413 S. 8th St., Springfield, IL* 🌐 *www.nps.gov/liho*

Don't Miss

Lincoln is buried in **Oak Ridge Cemetery**; visit the elaborate tomb, which includes an obelisk, sculptures, and interior rooms with statues and plaques with Lincoln's speeches. ✉ *1500 Monument Ave., Springfield, IL* 🌐 *www.oakridgecemetery.org*

While You're Here

Springfield is the Illinois state capital. Tour the **Old State Capitol**, which is a reconstruction of the statehouse that stood from 1840 to 1876, as well as the current state capitol building, an Italian Renaissance Revival structure that dates to 1877.

Getting Here and Around

Abraham Lincoln Capital Airport (SPI) is located 4 miles from the Lincoln Home. An Amtrak station is located about a half-mile away.

Starved Rock State Park

Eagles, Waterfalls, and Canyons

In a state with no national parks, Illinois's state parks pull their weight in beauty. Located in central Illinois between Chicago and Peoria, Starved Rock State Park is a destination for its glacier-formed sandstone canyons, waterfalls, and beautiful hiking trails as well as the chance to spot America's national bird, the bald eagle. There are 13 miles of trails and 18 canyons in the park, so it's impossible to see everything in a day—take a free guided hike, offered on weekends throughout the year. ✉ *2678 E. 875th Rd., Oglesby, IL* 🌐 *www.starvedrock.org*

Don't Miss

French Canyon, which features a striking waterfall, is located less than half a mile from the visitor center. And if you're searching for eagles, keep your eyes peeled across from the park at **Plum Island**, home to a bald eagle sanctuary.

Best Hotel

The historic property **Starved Rock Lodge** includes a log lodge with wood-paneled hotel rooms as well as cozy cabins. All rooms come with modern amenities including microwaves, mini-refrigerators, and TVs, and the lodge also offers a swimming pool and a great room with a fireplace. ✉ *1 Lodge La., Oglesby, IL* 🌐 *www.starvedrock-lodge.com*

When to Go

The park is open year-round and winter is especially beautiful. Besides activities like ice-fishing and winter hiking, the waterfalls can freeze.

Getting Here and Around

From Chicago's Midway Airport (MDW), it's a 90-mile drive to the park; Chicago's O'Hare International Airport (ORD) is 95 miles. Peoria International Airport (PIA) is 70 miles away.

Shawnee National Forest

Stunning Hikes and Rock Formations

A hiking destination located in southern Illinois, Shawnee National Forest offers 403 miles of equestrian and hiking trails. The forest is set between the Mississippi and Ohio rivers, and serious hikers can trek the **River to River Trail**, a 160-mile route that stretches between the two and can take weeks to complete. There are plenty of shorter hikes as well, like the 3-mile **Little Grand Canyon Trail**, plus swimming and fishing at **Pounds Hollow Lake**. 🌐 *www.shawneeforest.com*

Don't Miss

Shawnee Forest's best-known attraction is **Garden of the Gods**, a part of the park with high sandstone cliffs, views of the hills, and striking rock formations, including Anvil Rock, Devil's Smoke Stack, and others. There's a ¼-mile observation loop you can walk along, as well as horseback riding trails.

While You're Here

Make sure to snap a photo with the Shawnee National Forest **Big Foot statue**, nicknamed "Sassy the Sasquatch" and located near the Garden of the Gods. There's even an annual Shawnee Sasquatch Festival in nearby Harrisburg.

Best Hotel

Camping is available, but for digs that are a little more luxe, the cozy **Willowbrook Cabins** offer amenities like Wi-Fi and laundry. ✉ *610 Eddyville Blacktop Rd., Golconda, IL* 🌐 *www.willowbrookcabins.com*

Getting Here and Around

St. Louis Lambert International Airport (STL) is about 90 miles from the western edge of the forest, while Evansville Regional Airport (EVV) is about 60 miles from the eastern edge.

Chicago's Theater Scene

The Broadway of the Midwest

With more than 250 theaters in Chicago (including five Tony Award–winning companies), you can see everything from splashy Broadway performances to indie shows at storefront theaters. The main theater district is in the Loop, where you'll find Broadway theaters like **James M. Nederlander Theatre**, but smaller options are scattered all across the city. The **Goodman Theatre**, the oldest and largest nonprofit theater, consistently stages excellent shows, while **Steppenwolf Theater** (which launched Nick Offerman's career) includes three stages and offers a regular series of plays geared toward young adults. For a real Chicago experience, see a show at an offbeat storefront theater, like **Victory Gardens**, a former movie theater in Lincoln Park.

Don't Miss

The Neo-Futurists is a lively, inventive experimental theater group that presents a number of short plays in a short amount of time (such as *The Infinite Wrench*). ✉ *5153 N. Ashland Ave., Chicago, IL* 🌐 *www.neofuturists.org*

While You're Here

Improv and comedy are also huge parts of Chicago's cultural scene, and no one leads the way like **Second City**, the comedy company that launched the careers of Tina Fey, Stephen Colbert, and many others. Catch nightly shows at the Chicago Main Stage, or sign up for a class to learn from the pros. ✉ *1616 N. Wells St., 2nd fl., Chicago, IL* 🌐 *www.secondcity.com*

Getting Here and Around

Chicago's Midway Airport (MDW) and O'Hare International Airport (ORD) are your best bet for landing you in the city. Most theaters and shows will be accessible via the CTA.

Chicago Speakeasies

Drink Like a Mob Boss

Chicago has a storied mob history, thanks to Al Capone and his Chicago Outfit. There are plenty of historical sites around the city with ties to the mob, but none are more fun than the speakeasies, which featured tunnels and secret entrances so patrons could enter them during Prohibition and get a drink. You can still drink in many of these today; a local favorite is **the Drifter**, which is located behind a door in the basement of the Green Door Tavern. Nowadays you don't need to hide your drinking, so order an excellent cocktail from the tarot card menu and watch a nightly performance, such as a burlesque show. ✉ *676–678 N. Orleans St., Chicago, IL* 🌐 *www.thedrifterchicago.com*

Don't Miss

The **Green Mill Lounge**, located in Uptown, is an iconic jazz club that offers nightly shows. The over-100-year-old bar has mob ties—it was a favorite spot of Capone, who had his own booth at the bar, and there are tunnels underneath to facilitate secretive comings and goings. ✉ *4802 N. Broadway, Chicago, IL* 🌐 *www.greenmilljazz.com*

Best Tour

The **Original Chicago Prohibition Tour**, an energetic 3½-hour bus tour, transports you to four different speakeasies, including Capone favorite the 226 Club (today it's the Exchequer Restaurant & Pub). It imparts knowledge about both the bars and the drinks of the era. A shorter downtown walking tour is also available, as is a group cocktail-making class. 🌐 *www.prohibitiontours.com*

Getting Here and Around

Chicago's Midway Airport (MDW) and O'Hare International Airport (ORD) will land you in the city; from there, most places are accessible by CTA trains and buses.

When in Illinois

GALENA COUNTRY

Galena Country comprises 11 different towns, from the historic city of Galena, which features a downtown composed of 19th-century architecture to Hanover, where you'll find a couple wineries. The area is also a draw for shopping and antiquing, hiking or biking the 8-mile Galena River Trail, and exploring nature at the Valley of Eden Bird Sanctuary, a 400-acre preserve. In the winter, it's a destination for Midwestern skiing; stay at the Chestnut Mountain Resort, which features slopes for skiers of all levels.

Do This: Ulysses S. Grant, the 18th president and Civil War general, moved to Galena before the war, and you can visit his Italianate-style home. The U.S. Grant Home State Historic Site features original furnishings; the house has been restored to look as it did in 1868. ✉ *500 Bouthillier St., Galena, IL* 🌐 *www.granthome.org*

GRACELAND CEMETERY AND ARBORETUM

This beautifully landscaped North Side cemetery, established in 1860, is the final resting place of many notable Chicagoans, such as architect Daniel Burnham, Chicago Cub Ernie Banks, boxing champ Jack Johnson, Arthur Ryerson (who perished on the *Titanic*), and even Augustus Dickens, Charles Dickens' brother, who immigrated to the United States. The cemetery features wide paved paths, a pond, and an array of elaborate tombs, from mausoleums to pyramids. ✉ *4001 N. Clark St., Chicago, IL* 🌐 *www.gracelandcemetery.org*

Do This: The cemetery has more than 2,000 trees and is also an arboretum. Take a tour (print out a map on the website or visit the office at the entrance for a guide) to spot the sycamore, hickory, Ohio buckeye, sweet gum, and other trees throughout the park and encircling the pond.

About Our Writers

Amber Gibson was born and raised in Naperville, Illinois. She doesn't care for deep-dish pizza, which is honestly more like lasagna, but her favorite places to get pizza in Chicago are Roots Pizza and Professor Pizza. Her work appears in the *Wall Street Journal*, *Travel + Leisure*, and the *Telegraph*.

Cool Places to Stay

Chicago Athletic Association. This chic hotel, located right across the street from Chicago's Millennium Park, is as much a draw for tourists as locals, thanks to delicious food and beverage offerings and a gorgeous rooftop bar and restaurant. Located in an old athletic association building, the hotel has a vintage sports vibe, from the pommel horses in guest rooms to a sprawling Game Room bar with bocce, billiards, and shuffleboard. ✉ *12 S. Michigan Ave., Chicago, IL* 🌐 *www.chicagoathletichotel.com*

Eagle Ridge Resort. Located on Lake Galena in one of the state's most charming small towns, this sprawling 6,800-acre golf and spa destination is surrounded by lush rolling hills. The Stonedrift Spa offers high-tech facials and excellent massages. Golfers can enjoy three 18-hole championship courses plus a shorter 9-hole East course. Villas and homes are great for multigenerational families. ✉ *444 Eagle Ridge Dr., Galena, IL* 🌐 *www.eagleridge.com*

The Has Bin Guest House. Who can say they've slept in a recycled grain bin? You can if you stay at this bed-and-breakfast. It's located on a working farm, so your choice of sweet or savory breakfast delivery will be fresh and local. ✉ *2*

Chicago St., Alvin, IL 🌐 *www.thehasbinguesthouse.com*

Park Hyatt Chicago. Chicago is Hyatt's global headquarters, and this is the flagship location of Hyatt's most luxurious brand. The skyscraper embodies understated elegance, with a museum-quality contemporary art collection on display in public spaces. Seventh-floor restaurant NoMI has curved floor-to-ceiling windows overlooking the historic Chicago Water Tower (one of the few buildings to survive the Great Chicago Fire in 1871) and an exclusive rooftop garden in the summer. ✉ *800 N. Michigan Ave., Chicago, IL* 🌐 *www.parkhyattchicago.com*

Essential Eats

Calumet Fisheries. Smoked fish was popular in Chicago in the mid-20th century, and although many of the smokehouses have since closed, you can still find some excellent ones. Calumet Fisheries, which was founded in 1948, is located along the Calumet River next to the 95th Street bridge. The restaurant is take-out only, so be ready to have a picnic. The smoked shrimp and pepper and garlic salmon are the restaurant's specialties. ✉ *3259 E. 95th St., Chicago, IL* 🌐 *www.calumetfisheries.com*

Chicago-Style Hot Dog. This particular style begins with a poppyseed bun and all-beef hot dog, which is then "dragged through the garden" with toppings that include yellow mustard, chopped white onions, neon green sweet pickle relish, a dill pickle spear, tomato slices or wedges, pickled sport peppers, and celery salt. No ketchup, ever. You can easily find one at Chicago Cubs and White Sox baseball games (at the latter they are called "Comiskey Dogs" after the ballpark's former moniker). Otherwise Gene & Jude's in River Grove is your best bet. ✉ *2720 N. River Rd., River Grove, IL* 🌐 *www.geneandjudes.com*

Daisies. Chef Joe Frillman takes farm-to-table to the next level here, partnering with his brother at Frillman Farms to source the freshest local produce. During the day, pastries, sandwiches, and coffee are available, showing off the talents of pastry chef and partner Leigh Omilinsky. Try the onion dip with house-made potato chips to start and any of the freshly made pastas, like beet agnolotti with smoked trout roe. ✉ *2375 N. Milwaukee Ave., Chicago, IL* 🌐 *www.daisieschicago.com*

Deep Dish Pizza. Created in 1943 at Pizzeria Uno, this hearty take on pizza is at least an inch deep and cooked in a cast iron pan, filled with layers of cheese, tomato sauce, and all manner of toppings. Honestly, it's more akin to lasagna than pizza. These days, Lou Malnati's (with various locations throughout the state) is the best classic deep dish with a super buttery crust, but Pequod's is a local favorite for its caramelized cheese edges. 🌐 *www.loumalnatis.com*

Esmé. Both an art gallery and a restaurant, Michelin-starred Esmé is a paragon of fine dining by husband-and-wife team chef Jenner Tomaska and Katrina Bravo in Lincoln Park. Each menu is a distinct collaboration with different local artists and creatives, extending to the plate ware and decor. ✉ *2200 N. Clark St., Chicago, IL* 🌐 *www.esmechicago.com*

Indiana

With its feet firmly planted in the heartland, Indiana is like one big small town, where locals take pride in their "Hoosier hospitality." The state is a healthy mix of rural and urban. Indianapolis, the state's largest city, features big-city culture like an opera and symphony orchestra, yet still retains charm and character. If you stop and ask for directions, chances are you'll also receive a tip on where to have dinner that night.

Capital: Indianapolis

Population: 6,920,00

Area: 36,418 square miles

Statehood Date: December 11, 1816

Major Airports: Indianapolis International Airport (IND); Fort Wayne International Airport (FWA); South Bend International Airport (SBN)

Travel and Tourism Information:
www.visitindiana.com

Famous Residents: David Letterman (talk show host); Kurt Vonnegut (writer); Larry Bird (basketball player); Michael Jackson (singer); Caitlin Clark (basketball player)

Fun Fact: Santa Claus, Indiana, receives more than a half-million "Dear Santa" letters from children every year.

Indianapolis Motor Speedway

The Greatest Spectacle in Car Racing

The **Indianapolis 500**, the largest one-day sporting event in the world, takes place at Indianapolis Motor Speedway at the end of May. But the 500 isn't the only time to soak up the excitement of the race and learn about its history. Throughout the month of May, you can check out practices, qualifications, and concerts. You can even attend other races throughout the year. Visit the grounds for free on non-event days to take in the museum or a guided tour. ✉ *4790 W. 16th St., Indianapolis, IN* 🌐 *www.indianapolis-motorspeedway.com*

Don't Miss

The **Indianapolis Motor Speedway Museum's** collection includes more than 300 vehicles, including vintage race cars, along with a Hall of Fame.

Best Tour

The popular "Kiss the Bricks" tour is a 30-minute narrated bus trip through the property, including a lap around the race track and a visit to the Yard of Bricks, the start and finish line of the Indy 500 race (winners typically bend down to "kiss the bricks," hence the name).

When to Go

The Indianapolis 500 is held annually on Memorial Day weekend, making it the most exciting time to visit (but also the busiest, so be sure to book tickets in advance). The museum and grounds are open year-round.

Getting Here and Around

Indianapolis International Airport (IND) is located 12 miles from the race track.

Indiana Dunes National Park

Towering Lakeside Sand Dunes

Stretching 15 miles along Lake Michigan in northern Indiana, Indiana Dunes may be best known as a fun beach escape from Chicago, but the dune-filled national park offers plenty of chances to get active as well. There are more than 50 miles of hiking trails over rugged dunes, including the Cowles Bog Trail, which takes you along wetlands. Bring your binoculars as there are notable bird-watching opportunities; you can spot more than 350 species, including sandhill cranes that migrate here in fall. Make sure to catch the sunset over Lake Michigan—you'll get to see the Chicago skyline set against the orange-hued sky. ✉ *1050 N. Mineral Springs Rd., Chesterton, IN* 🌐 *www.nps.gov/indu*

Don't Miss

To get your heart racing, the **Three Dune Challenge** is a 1.5-mile-long trail that loops you around to the three tallest dunes in the neighboring state park. Those three—Mt. Tom, Mt. Holden, and Mt. Jackson—are the equivalent of climbing 552 vertical feet (or 55 stories), so it's not a stroll for the fainthearted.

When to Go

Summer is the best time to visit, when you can take advantage of all the trails and beaches. In winter, you can cross-country ski, snowshoe, and look for animal tracks in the snow.

Getting Here and Around

From Chicago's Midway Airport (MDW), it's a 50-mile drive to the park, while Chicago's O'Hare International Airport (ORD) is 70 miles. From Indianapolis International Airport (IND), it's about 170 miles to the park.

Indianapolis Cultural Trail

Miles of Midwest Treasures

The Indianapolis Cultural Trail is an 8-mile path that connects many of the city's official cultural districts, which means you can see many of Indy's highlights in a single afternoon. Walk or bike along the path, which stretches from White River State Park to the Fountain Square neighborhood and covers many downtown attractions. The path will take you past the **Soldiers' and Sailors' Monument, NCAA Hall of Champions,** and the **Eiteljorg Museum of American Indians and Western Art,** and also includes nine commissioned art installations. The first part of an expansion project was completed in 2024, with more trail slated to be created in the coming years. 🌐 *www.indyculturaltrail.org*

Don't Miss

Fountain Square is a neighborhood packed with great places to eat and drink, including **Bluebeard,** a small-plates restaurant, and sister spot **Amelia's Bread** for pastries.

Best Tour

The nonprofit that manages the Cultural Trail offers walking and cycling tours with an advance reservation and a minimum of five people. You'll see all the highlights of the Trail, including Mass Ave and Fountain Square. 🌐 *www.indyculturaltrail.org/tours*

Good to Know

Many downtown hotels, such as the Conrad, offer complimentary cruisers and 10-speed bikes, or you can rent Indiana Pacers Bikeshare wheels at more than 50 stations around the city.

Getting Here and Around

Indianapolis International Airport (IND) is located 12 miles from White River State Park, where you can rent a Pacers bike and pick up the trail.

The Children's Museum of Indianapolis

The World's Largest Kid's Museum

The Children's Museum of Indianapolis is more than just a museum. It's an action-packed education center with five floors of exhibits and galleries, plus a planetarium, a theater with live shows, and a massive area devoted to outdoor sports activities. Dinosaur-loving kids can spot some on the facade of the building, explore the Dinosphere that's complete with skeletons and a play archaeological dig, and visit the R.B. Annis Mission Jurassic Paleo Lab in the basement where real paleontologists work with fossils and answer questions. Children of all ages will love exhibits devoted to pop culture, sports, puzzles, or travel (on Earth or in space). ✉ *3000 N. Meridian St., Indianapolis, IN* 🌐 *www.childrensmuseum.org*

Don't Miss

The Power of Children exhibit teaches kids about the lives of Anne Frank, Ruby Bridges, Malala Yousafzai, and Ryan White, and the contributions they made to the world through replica rooms and theatrical performances.

Best Exhibit

Beyond Spaceship Earth gives kids a chance to learn about the history of space exploration, see astronaut artifacts, try on space-walk costumes, and sit in a Soyuz spacecraft. There's also the Indiana Astronaut Wall of Fame, which honors state residents who have made notable contributions to astronomy.

Getting Here and Around

Indianapolis International Airport (IND) is located 22 miles from the museum.

Parke County Covered Bridges

The Covered Bridge Capital of the World

Indiana is proud of its charming covered bridges, and they're more than just a photo op—they bring the community together for festivities like one of the state's largest celebrations, the **Covered Bridge Festival**. Parke County, located in western Indiana, is home to the state's most covered bridges (31 to be exact) that were built from 1856 to 2006. Some bridges are drive-through, while others can only be walked or pedaled; download a map of the bridges on the county website to help plan your route. Biking and motorcycling are also popular ways to see the bridges. 🌐 *www.coveredbridges.com*

Don't Miss

The **Jackson Covered Bridge**, built in 1861, is the longest single-span covered bridge in Indiana.

Best Restaurant

Mecca Tavern has been serving bar fare since 1899 (it's the oldest bar in the county). Offerings include burgers and steak sandwiches, but you're going for the pork tenderloin sandwich, which is hand-pounded to order. ✉ *4854 Wabash St., Mecca, IN*

When to Go

The annual Covered Bridge Festival, held over 10 days in October, is the largest in the state. Nine communities in the county come together to offer arts and crafts vendors, plant sales, pig roasts, and more, all amid gorgeous fall foliage.

Getting Here and Around

Indianapolis International Airport (IND) is about 50 miles from Parke County; University of Illinois-Willard Airport (CMI), which is 75 miles from the county, has shuttle flights from Chicago, Dallas–Fort Worth, and Charlotte.

Bloomington

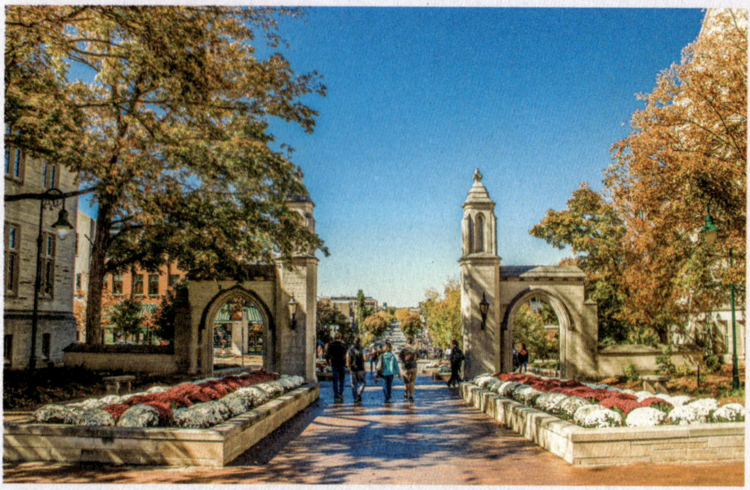

Where Art, Nature, and Community Come Together

Combining a small-town feel with an arts scene that rivals many major metropolitan areas, Bloomington is a unique gem in south-central Indiana. Home to **Indiana University**, the city is filled with scholars and free-thinkers, elite athletes and everyday locals. During evenings and the weekend, you'll find diverse groups of people rubbing shoulders on the town square, enjoying a drink at a pub, or attending one of the dozens of festivals that happen each year. Bloomington's multicultural flavor extends into its restaurant offerings, with favorites that include La Una Cantina, Marco and Polo, Little Tibet, and Samira. On hot summer days, locals flock to the water, like **Lake Monroe**, or neighboring **Hoosier National Forest**, taking refuge from the heat under a thick canopy of oak and sycamore trees. The B-Line bike trail allows visitors and residents both to get around the city and campus easily and safely.

Don't Miss

Being a college town, Bloomington has one of the best music scenes in the Hoosier state. Venues like **the Bluebird**, **Bishop**, and **Buskirk-Chumley Theater** not only present local artists to the masses, but also host nationally touring bands like Lucero and the Drive-By Truckers.

Good to Know

IU football draws fans from all over the Midwest to Saturday home games at **Memorial Stadium**. Be sure to book your hotel room early, as they can sell out quickly. ✉ *701 E. 17th St., Bloomington, IN* 🌐 *iuhoosiers.com*

Getting Here and Around

Located about 50 miles away from downtown Bloomington, Indianapolis International Airport (IND) is the nearest airport.

Brown County State Park

A Bit of the Smokies in South-Central Indiana

Indiana has a reputation for being a flat, boring state, but the rolling hills of Brown County State Park are filled with nearly unlimited outdoor fun and adventure. Often referred to as the Lil' Smokies due to its similarities to the Great Smokey Mountains, Brown County is the most visited state park in Indiana. Great hiking, biking, and paddling opportunities can be found throughout, and there are two lakes perfect for swimming, fishing, and kayaking. Be sure to climb the 113 steps up the fire tower for a bird's-eye view of the surroundings. To make a weekend out of the trip, book a campsite or room in the **Abe Martin Lodge**, which features both a kitchen serving Hoosier favorites and an inside water park for the kids. ✉ *1801 Rte. 46, Nashville, IN* 🌐 *www.in.gov/dnr/state-parks/parks-lakes/brown-county-state-park*

Don't Miss

Ranked as a silver-level Ride Center by the International Mountain Bicycling Association, BCSP boasts more than 30 miles of fast, flowy singletrack that stretches into nearby Yellowwood State Forest, and is good for all types of skill levels. Be sure to bring your helmet.

Best Restaurant

Less than 5 miles from the main entrance of Brown County State Park, **Hard Truth Distillery** offers a variety of barbecue and pub-inspired cuisine in addition to a selection of spirits. The Busted Knuckle Chili is a particular favorite when the temperature drops. ✉ *418 Old State Rd. 46, Nashville, IN* 🌐 *www.hardtruth.com*

Getting Here and Around

Indianapolis International Airport (IND) is about 50 miles away.

Boating in Indiana

Lakes for Days

Indiana has more than 100,000 acres of public lakes (not counting the Great Lakes shoreline in Indiana Dunes National Park), which makes boating a top Indiana summertime activity. **Patoka Lake,** the second largest in the state, has 10 launch ramps along with notable fishing and migratory bird-watching opportunities (including bald eagles!). Rent pontoon boats or take a sailing lesson in Indianapolis's Geist Reservoir.

Don't Miss

Clear Lake, so named for its crystal clear waters, is an 800-acre lake that was formed by a glacier. Rent a rowboat and peer down at turtles and other wildlife in the lake.

Best Lake for Boating

Monroe Lake, built in 1965 in Bloomington, is the state's largest inland lake. Bring your own boat or rent one there. (Lake Monroe Boat Rental allows you to book online.) You can rent a pontoon or double-decker boat for a group, a fishing boat if you're hoping to catch dinner, or a canoe or kayak for a leisurely option that allows for bird-watching and soaking up nature.

Good to Know

If you bring your own boat to a state park, you'll need a permit to put it on the water. Yearly permits are $25 for motorized boats and $5 for nonmotorized vehicles. See which lakes require permits and learn where to get them at 🌐 *www.in.gov/dnr.*

Getting Here and Around

Indianapolis International Airport (IND) is a good central location; it's located 58 miles from Monroe Lake and just over 110 miles from Patoka Lake.

When in Indiana

BUTLER BULLDOGS

Basketball is a way of life in Indiana, and Butler University's Hinkle Fieldhouse is one the oldest college arenas still in use. The brick fieldhouse, designed by Indianapolis architect Fermor Spencer Cannon, was built in 1928 and its design inspired gymnasiums for decades. Named for longtime coach Tony Hinkle, the 9,100-seat arena and National Historic Landmark has played host to the championship game in the movie *Hoosiers* as well as Butler University's basketball and volleyball games.

Do This: Seeing the crammed fieldhouse during a game is the best time to visit, but the building is also open during the week and on weekends for free, self-guided tours. The Bulldogs' women's volleyball season runs August to November, while the men's and women's basketball season runs November to March. ✉ *510 W. 49th St., Indianapolis, IN* 🌐 *www.butlersports.com*

EITELJORG MUSEUM OF AMERICAN INDIANS AND WESTERN ART

This downtown Indianapolis museum is one of only two museums east of the Mississippi to focus on art from both the American West and the Indigenous peoples of North America. The Western holdings, which range from the 1820s to the present, include paintings of landscapes by Georgia O'Keeffe and cowboys by Frederic Remington, while the Native American collection includes clothing, jewelry, carvings, and more. ✉ *500 W. Washington St., Indianapolis, IN* 🌐 *www.eiteljorg.org*

Do This: The museum's annual fine-art market and cultural festival (held each June on the weekend following Father's Day) brings together more than 100 Native artists from across the country who work in disciplines such as painting, pottery, and weaving. It also includes Native American music and dance performances.

SOUTH BEND

Best known as the home of the University of Notre Dame, South Bend is a city of 100,000 people that offers plenty of ways to get active. Start by taking a free tour of the Notre Dame campus, where you'll see the Grotto, Basilica of the Sacred Heart, the Golden Dome, and the "Touchdown Jesus" statue. Besides touring the university, you can visit the red pandas at the Potawatomi Zoo and see the vintage cars at the Studebaker National Museum.

Do This: Save time for wandering downtown, where you can dine at favorite local restaurants like fine-dining spot Café Navarre and modern Southern restaurant Fatbird.

About Our Writers

Robert Annis grew up in Indiana and has lived Indianapolis with his wife for the last 25 years. Although Indiana isn't known as an outdoorsy state, it does provide him some opportunities to escape into nature, like hiking local state parks and fishing for bluegill in the creek near his home. An award-winning journalist (and certified bear guide!), he also writes for *National Geographic*, *Outside*, AARP, and more.

Cool Places to Stay

The Alexander Hotel. With rain showers, mini-refrigerators, and extended-stay suites, the Alexander is a luxe spot to stay in downtown Indy. The design is sleek and artsy, with a coffee and cocktail bar that offers views of the skyline (and a rooftop deck) and an Italian restaurant, all walking distance from top destinations, including the Colts' Lucas Oil Stadium. ✉ *333 S. Delaware St., Indianapolis, IN* 🌐 *www.thealexander.com*

The Bradley. Located in Fort Wayne's downtown, this Vera Bradley–inspired hotel perfectly straddles the line between coziness and elegance. The stylish rooms include soft, comfortable beds and furnishings. Grab dinner in the acclaimed Arbor restaurant, then head up to Birdie's rooftop bar for a nightcap while gazing over the city lights. ✉ *204 W. Main St., Fort Wayne, IN* 🌐 *www.bradleyhotel.com*

Graduate Hotel Bloomington. The Indiana University–themed hotel isn't just a draw for returning alumni—the cute, cozy lodging is located close to campus and other downtown spots, like Cardinal Spirits. The pet-friendly rooms are decked out in plaid and include work stations and references to IU's Little 500 (a notable bike race). ✉ *210 E. Kirkwood Ave., Bloomington, IN* 🌐 *www.graduatehotels.com/bloomington*

Inn at Irwin Gardens. Although the Irwin family is best known for modern architecture, they called this Victorian mansion in downtown Columbus home for decades. Today, the massive manor is an inn catering to architecture lovers and well-heeled visitors. A stroll through the immaculate gardens is a must. ✉ *608 5th St., Columbus, IN* 🌐 *www.irwingardens.com*

Essential Eats

Bonge's Tavern. This rustic eatery near Perkinsville has achieved cult status among Hoosier foodies; patrons will even tailgate in the parking lot while waiting for their table to be ready. The rotating menu features fare from around the world, including Norwegian sea trout and New Zealand lamb chops. ✉ *9830 W. 280 N, Country Club Heights, IN* 🌐 *www.bongestavern.com*

Dawson's on Main. Practically sitting in the shadow of the famed Indianapolis Motor Speedway, this restaurant is known for another Hoosier tradition, the deep-fried pork tenderloin sandwich. If you've never had one, imagine a standard-size pork cutlet, pounded out to the size of a baby elephant's ear, breaded and deep-fried, then served between a standard bun. ✉ *1464 N. Main St., Indianapolis, IN* 🌐 *www.dawsonsonmain.com*

Oakleys Bistro. Chef Steven Oakley has earned a host of accolades over the years, including a James Beard nomination. Located in a fairly nondescript strip mall in northwest Indianapolis, his restaurant serves unpretentious meals that still burst with flavor (try the salmon fillet). ✉ *1464 W. 86th St., Indianapolis, IN* 🌐 *www.oakleysbistro.com*

St. Elmo Steak House. Easily the most famous restaurant in the Hoosier State, St. Elmo is known for perfectly prepared steaks, an extensive whiskey and cocktail menu, and a shrimp cocktail that comes with a cocktail sauce absolutely loaded with sinus-clearing horseradish. ✉ *127 Illinois St., Indianapolis, IN* 🌐 *www.stelmos.com*

Michigan

With over 3,000 miles of Great Lakes shoreline, Michigan is divided into two peninsulas: the Lower, which resembles a mitten and is the more densely populated, and the Upper, which is more rugged and rural. The state is graced with dramatic topography, ranging from waterfalls and forests to towering sand dunes and flat plains. From industrial cities like Detroit and Grand Rapids to resort towns like Traverse City and Saugatuck, visitors will find a little bit of everything in the Great Lakes State.

Capital: Lansing

Population: 10,140,459

Area: 97,716 square miles

Statehood Date: January 26, 1837

Major Airports: Detroit Metro Wayne County Airport (DTW); Grand Rapids Gerald R. Ford International Airport (GRR); Traverse City Cherry Capital Airport (TVC); Flint Bishop International Airport (FNT); Lansing Capital Region International Airport (LAN)

Travel and Tourism Information: *www.michigan.org* *www.exploremichigan.travel* *www.mibluemag.com*

Famous Residents: Henry Ford (car-maker); Stevie Wonder (musician); Diana Ross (musician); Madonna (singer); Eminem (rapper)

Fun Fact: Vernor's, the nation's oldest soda (or pop, as it's called in Michigan), was made inside a Detroit pharmacy between 1862 and 1866.

Mackinac Island

Explore a Car-Free Island

Mackinac Island, located in Lake Huron in northern Michigan, is a classic Midwest summertime destination. Cars aren't allowed, so the island has a leisurely pace. Spend your days biking around the island, riding horses, or exploring **Mackinac Island State Park**. With striking limestone bluffs and Arch Rock (a natural rock bridge), the park is a beautiful spot to hit the beach, go hiking, kayaking, or sailing. 🌐 *www.mackinacisland.org*

Don't Miss

Mackinac is known for fudge—13 shops on the island make 5 tons a day during high season from May to October, and there's even a Fudge Festival in August. With so much fudge on the menu, Mackinac Island is known as the "Fudge Capital of the World."

Best Attraction

British **Fort Mackinac** was founded in 1780 during the American Revolution, and the United States did not gain control of the fort until 1796. British forces retook the fort during the first land conflict of the War of 1812, where it remained under British control until its return to the United States in 1815, following the war's conclusion. In operation until the late 19th century, the fort has been restored to its appearance from that era. 🌐 *www.mackinacparks.com*

Getting Here and Around

Unless you spring for an air taxi, you'll need to take a ferry over to the island; the ride takes about 18 miles from either Mackinaw City (the closest airport is Pellston Regional Airport, 15 miles to the south), or St. Ignace (the closest airport is Chippewa County International Airport, 35 miles to the north). Get around the island by walking, biking, or taking a horse-drawn carriage.

Detroit's Museums

The Heart and Soul of the City

Detroit has a vibrant arts and culture scene, and many of the city's museums are clustered in the Cultural Center District, including the **Charles H. Wright Museum of African American History**; the **Michigan Science Center** (a kid-friendly museum and planetarium); the **Detroit Institute of Arts** (a standout art museum with 65,000 works); the **Detroit Historical Museum**; and the **Museum of Contemporary Art**. The **Motown Museum** (aka Hitsville, USA), the original house Berry Gordy used to record some of the most memorable Motown records, is located a few miles away.

Don't Miss

The **Detroit Institute of Art** has one of the largest art collections in North America. Don't miss the cathedral-ceiling courtyard adorned with Diego Riviera frescoes focusing on Detroit's industrial history. ✉ *5200 Woodward Ave., Detroit, MI* 🌐 *www.dia.org*

Best Exhibit

And Still We Rise: Our Journey Through African American History and Culture, a long-term exhibit at the **Charles H. Wright Museum of African American History**, powerfully traces the African American experience. ✉ *315 E. Warren Ave., Detroit, MI* 🌐 *www.thewright.org*

Best Tour

At the **Motown Museum**, take a lively, music-filled tour of the houses that formed Berry Gordy's original Motown offices and studio, where you'll see costumes and photos, and visit Studio A, where artists like Marvin Gaye and the Supremes recorded music from 1959 to 1972. ✉ *2648 W. Grand Blvd., Detroit, MI* 🌐 *www.motownmuseum.org*

Detroit's Motor History

America Runs on the Motor City

The Detroit area is home to the "Big Three" automakers of Ford, General Motors, and Chrysler (owned by Stellantis, a multinational auto corp that also owns Ram and Jeep). As the city's largest employer (the three combined employ over 250,000 metro residents) and a major influence on the city's history, Detroit was dubbed the "Motor City" in the 1920s. You can spend several days visiting all the attractions, including the **Henry Ford Museum of American Innovation** in Dearborn; **GM World,** with displays of the latest GM vehicles at the GM Renaissance Center; the **Ford Piquette Plant,** the birthplace of the Model T; and the world's first concrete mile on Woodward Avenue, which was built in 1909.

Don't Miss

The **Automotive Hall of Fame** traces the history of cars and motorcycles, from their debut to today, and how that's allowed for personal exploration and travel. On view are permanent and changing exhibits, as well as vintage cars and memorabilia. ✉ *21400 Oakwood, Dearborn, MI* 🌐 *www.automotivehalloffame.org*

Best Tour

The **Ford Rouge Factory Tour** gives you an overview of the company in the Henry Ford Museum of American Innovation, including a look at some vintage autos (like the 1929 Model A), several films, and a walking tour along an elevated walkway at the Dearborn Truck Plant, where you'll get to see a Ford F-150 truck assembled. ✉ *20900 Oakwood Blvd., Dearborn, MI* 🌐 *www.thehenryford.org*

Getting Here and Around

Flying into Detroit Metropolitan Wayne County Airport (DTW) will land you in Detroit; from there, all locations are a quick drive or cab away from each other.

Belle Isle

Cutest Urban Picnic Spot

An island located in the middle of the Detroit River (splitting the difference between the U.S. and Canada), Belle Isle is a 987-acre state park that's both larger and older than New York's Central Park (both were at least partially designed by landscape architect Frederick Law Olmsted). The island's woodsy spaces are ideal for picnicking away from the hustle and bustle of the city, while attractions such as the **Belle Isle Aquarium**, **Dossin Great Lakes Museum**, a half mile of beachfront, and wooded walking trails are also located on the island. The **Anna Scripps Whitcomb Conservatory**, featuring an outdoor lily pond, tropical house, cactus house, and more is perfect for nature lovers. 🌐 *www.belleisleconservancy.org*

Don't Miss

From Belle Isle, you'll have great views of both Detroit and Windsor, Ontario, skylines. It's also an excellent spot to take in Detroit's fireworks display on July 4.

Best Attraction

With an extensive collection of air-breathing fish (one of the largest in the world), **Belle Isle Aquarium** is housed in a Beaux Art–style building that dates back to 1904 (it was the third-largest aquarium in the world when it opened). The free collection now includes species from all over the world, as well as the Great Lakes.

Getting Here and Around

From Detroit Metropolitan Wayne County Airport (DTW), Belle Isle is a 25-mile drive. You can get there by walking or biking across MacArthur Bridge, which is less than half a mile. You can also take the No. 12 Conant bus, which stops in front of the aquarium.

Pictured Rocks National Lakeshore

Colorful Cliffs of the Upper Peninsula

Located on Lake Superior in the Upper Peninsula, Pictured Rocks National Lakeshore, the country's first national lakeshore, is an all-season destination for nature lovers. Named for the brightly colored sandstone cliffs (the colors are due to minerals in the rocks), the park also offers 100 miles of hiking trails, waterfalls, and the **Au Sable Light Station**, a working 19th-century lighthouse that you can tour and climb up for a view of Lake Superior, forests, and the Grand Sable Dunes. 🌐 *www.nps.gov/piro*

Don't Miss

The striking **Munising Falls** features a 50-foot drop over a sandstone cliff and is accessible via a paved walking trail. In winter, the falls transform into stunning ice formations.

Best Tour

The best way to see the rocks is by boat. From May through October, **Pictured Rocks Cruises** offers daily 2½- to 3-hour tours that take you along the cliffs. On the classic cruise, you'll see sights like the rock arch Lover's Leap and rock formation Miner's Castle. Tours that add on the Spray Falls waterfall at sunset are also available. 🌐 *www.picturedrocks.com*

When to Go

Summer is the best time to take advantage of the beaches and activities like kayaking and camping, but in winter you can go ice climbing at Sand Point, where the ice columns are 20 to 50 feet high.

Getting Here and Around

The closest airport is Sawyer International Airport (SAW), which has daily flights from Detroit. You'll need to rent a car; from the airport, it's about 45 miles to the entrance to the park.

Sleeping Bear Dunes National Lakeshore

Dunes You Can See From Space

Located in northwest Michigan along 65 miles of Lake Michigan, Sleeping Bear Dunes National Lakeshore is part of the largest freshwater dune system in the world—so large they're visible from space. The expansive, awe-inspiring lakeshore park is known for its stretches of sandy beaches and bluffs that rise 460 feet, along with 100 miles of hiking trails, canoeing and kayaking opportunities (including 21 lakes within the park boundaries), and the Sleeping Bear Heritage Trail, a 27-mile paved bike path. 🌐 *www.nps.gov/slbe*

Don't Miss

A chain of islands off the coast of the dunes, **North** and **South Manitou** are the two main islands, both accessible by ferry. With old-growth cedar forests and small villages, the islands are ideal for hiking and camping.

Best Base

If you aren't camping at the park, you may want to stay in **Traverse City** to soak up its culture scene (it hosts a major summer film festival) and have some memorable meals and drinks. Sample suds from the strong craft-beer community, and stop by the Cooks' House for a local, sustainable menu, or indulge with a sweet treat from Moomers Homemade Ice Cream.

Getting Here and Around

Sleeping Bear Dunes is 30 miles from Traverse City's Cherry Capital Airport (TVC). To reach the Manitou Islands, you'll need to take a ferry from Leland. The ferry is offered seasonally and can be booked through Manitou Island Transit. 🌐 *www.manitoutransit.com*

Michigan's Craft Breweries

America's Craft Beer Capital

With over 400 breweries recognized by the Brewers Association, Michigan is no stranger to craft beer. Several of the most decorated breweries in the country can be found here, with **Grand Rapids** frequently recognized as the top beer city in the United States. With more than 80 breweries making up the city's "Beer City Ale Trail," as well as brewing stalwarts Bell's and Founders located in its metro area, Grand Rapids can stand toe-to-toe with any beer-loving city in the United States. Beyond Grand Rapids, visitors will find exceptional breweries throughout the state.

Don't Miss

Bell's Brewing Company is not only the oldest craft brewery in Michigan, but the oldest east of Colorado. You've probably heard of its famed Oberon beer (a Belgian whit) or Two-Hearted IPA. ✉ *355 E. Kalamzoo Ave., Kalamazoo, MI* 🌐 *cafe.bellsbeer.com*

Most Popular Brewery

Founders Brewing Company open since 1996, is widely regarded as one of the best breweries not only in the state, but in the country. ✉ *235 Cesar E. Chavez Ave. SW, Grand Rapids, MI* 🌐 *www.foundersbrewing.com*

Traverse City Brews

Just outside Traverse City is Bellaire, home to **Short's Brewing Company.** While much of the brewery's production takes place in Elk Rapids (another neighboring city), you can enjoy the fruits of that brewing labor inside the Bellaire brewpub. ✉ *121 N. Bridge St., Bellaire, MI* 🌐 *www.shortsbrewing.com*

Michigan's Wineries

The Country's Best (and Only) Ice Wine

Michigan has more than 13,500 acres of vineyards, nearly 200 wineries, and 50 varieties of wine grapes grown. The state holds annual wine festivals and offers trails that group wineries into easy-to-travel routes. For instance, the **Leelanau Peninsula Wine Trail** features 24 wineries clustered around Traverse City. Michigan has five different appellations, including Fennville, Lake Michigan Shore, Leelanau, Old Mission Peninsula, and Tip of the Mitt. Wineries located along the Lake Michigan coastline have longer growing seasons as the massive body of water helps moderate the climate while protecting vines from premature frost. 🌐 *www.michigan.org/wineries*

Don't Miss

Michigan is one of the few places in the world where ice wine is made. Try the sweet dessert wine from producers like **Fenn Valley Vineyards**, paired with cheese. ✉ *6130 122nd Ave., Fennville, MI* 🌐 *www.fennvalley.com*

Best Tour

Fruitful Vine Tours offers tours through the region, which include visits to three wineries, tasting fees, and lunch as well as a wine-expert tour guide. 🌐 *www.fruitfulvinetours.com*

Getting Here and Around

If you're looking to visit wineries in the Fennville or Lake Michigan Shore areas, fly into Grand Rapids' Gerald R. Ford International Airport (GRR). If you're planning to visit wineries in Northern Michigan, fly into Traverse City's Cherry Capital Airport (TVC).

Isle Royale National Park

One of the Most Secluded National Parks

Accessible only by seaplane or boat, the secluded Isle Royale National Park consists of a main island, Isle Royale, and hundreds of smaller islands where solitude is king. Despite a closer proximity to mainland Minnesota and Ontario, Canada, the Lake Superior islands are part of Michigan. Due to the limited access, the national park is an outdoor lover's dream, as it receives fewer than 30,000 visitors annually. With the lack of human activity, wildlife, such as moose and wolves, live in abundance, and the isolated forest is perfect for outdoor activities, including kayaking, hiking, boat tours, and camping (there are 36 campgrounds on the main island). More of an underwater fan? You can scuba dive and visit 10 of the registered shipwrecks in the park, some of which date back to the 19th century. 🌐 *www.nps.gov/isro*

Don't Miss

Rock Harbor Lighthouse, which was built in 1855, is inactive, but you can tour it, see the view from the top, and learn about the park and its shipwrecks at a small museum.

Best Hotel

Rock Harbor Lodge offers a few different types of rooms, a main lodge, cottages with kitchenettes, and cabins without indoor plumbing. The hotel also books fishing charters and water taxis. 🌐 *www.rockharborlodge.com*

When to Go

The park is open April 16 through October 31.

Getting Here and Around

Reach Isle Royale through either Michigan or Minnesota. Ferries, seaplanes, or private boats are available. You can't bring your car (or any vehicle, including bikes) to Isle Royale, so plan to get around by hiking, canoe, or kayak.

Ann Arbor

The Quintessential College Town

Home of the University of Michigan, Ann Arbor is a classic Midwest college town, filled with museums, art galleries, shopping, great restaurants, and a favorite football team that plays in the largest stadium in the country. The best time to visit is the fall, when you can catch a game and see peak foliage, but there's plenty to do year-round. **The Ark**, a music venue that's been operating since 1965, is always a draw; in summer, go floating down the **Argo Cascades**. The food scene is led by restaurants like Cuban street-food spot **Frita Batidos**, legendary sandwich shop **Zingerman's Deli**, and local favorite **The Brown Jug**.

Don't Miss

The **University of Michigan Museum of Art** is a must-see free museum with cutting-edge exhibitions and a collection that includes African, Asian, and contemporary art. ✉ *525 S. State St., Ann Arbor, MI* 🌐 *umma.umich.edu*

Best Tour

Michigan Stadium, aka the Big House, is the home turf for the University of Michigan's Wolverines football team. Sixty- to 90-minute tours take you onto the field and through the locker room and press box. ✉ *1201 S. Main St., Ann Arbor, MI* 🌐 *umich.edu*

Good to Know

You're never too far from a great pint in Ann Arbor; top local breweries include **Arbor Brewing Company** (located in neighboring Ypsilanti), **Grizzly Peak**, **Mothfire Brewing Company**, and **HOMES.**

Getting Here and Around

From Detroit Metropolitan Wayne County Airport (DTW), Ann Arbor is a 25-mile drive. There's an Amtrak station located at 325 Depot Street, and a Greyhound station at 115 East William Street.

Frankenmuth

Michigan's Little Bavaria

Step foot in downtown Frankenmuth and you'll immediately realize you're someplace special. With authentic Bavarian architecture, the city feels as if it's been plucked straight out of Germany and dropped in Michigan. Frankenmuth was originally founded by German settlers who immigrated from Franconia, Germany. Translated, Frankenmuth means "courage of the Franconias." The town remained a destination for German migrants up until the start of World War II. Today, the city itself is small, with a population of around 5,000 residents, but it still hosts some of the biggest festivals in the state.

Don't Miss

If you can't make it to Munich for Oktoberfest, Frankenmuth's celebration is a solid alternative. In 1996, the **Frankenmuth Oktoberfest** was officially recognized by German Parliament as well as the city of Munich, making the first official Oktoberfest celebration outside of Germany. Combined with the German architecture and all the European shops inside the city, Oktoberfest in Frankenmuth is one of the most popular German festivals in the United States. 🌐 *frankenmuthfestivals.com/frankenmuth-oktoberfest*

Best Shop

No matter the time of year, you'll find something at Bronner's Christmas Wonderland. Recognized as the largest Christmas shop in the world, Bronner's is 7.35 acres of nonstop Santa, Rudolph, ornaments, and everything else you might want to jazz up your holiday season. ✉ *25 Christmas La., Frankenmuth, MI* 🌐 *www.bronners.com*

Getting Here and Around

Frankenmuth is about 90 minutes north of Detroit.

Grand Rapids ArtPrize

An Art Competition for the Ages

Initially conceived in 2009 as a way to increase tourism while touting the local art scene, the ArtPrize in Grand Rapids quickly became one of the largest and most important art competitions in the entire world. Unlike other art competitions, which are held in singular locations, ArtPrize is spread throughout the city, with over 160 venues taking part. This includes everything from more traditional art galleries to bars, auto shops, bridges, and outdoor open spaces. The festival, which takes place annually (usually around mid September until early October), welcomes nearly a million visitors every year. 🌐 *www.artprize.org*

Don't Miss

The beauty of ArtPrize is that a large portion of the city's businesses (especially those downtown) participate. You're just as likely to spot a new painting next to an ice cream stand as you are a massive sculpture overlooking a duck pond.

While You're Here

Founded in 1995, the **Frederik Meijer Gardens & Sculpture Park** is a draw for both art and garden lovers. The park includes a Japanese garden, farm garden, and annual butterfly garden, as well as nature trails to wander. There are about 300 sculptures on display, including art from renowned sculptors Auguste Rodin, Edgar Degas, Alexander Calder, Louise Bourgeois, and Ai Weiwei. ✉ *1000 E. Beltline Ave. NE, Grand Rapids, MI* 🌐 *www.meijergardens.org*

Getting Here and Around

The drive between Gerald R. Ford International Airport (GRR) and downtown GR is about 14 miles. You can easily take an Uber or taxi, and the city bus makes regular stops at the airport as well.

When in Michigan

DETROIT EASTERN MARKET

Founded in 1842, the Detroit Eastern Market is the place in Detroit for picking up fresh ingredients, prepared foods, and much more. The primary market is held year-round on Saturday and features more than 225 vendors, food trucks, and more. Two other markets run from June to September. The Sunday market includes local artists and musicians, and the smaller Tuesday market includes yoga and Zumba classes. ✉ *1445 Adelaide St., Detroit, MI* 🌐 *www.easternmarket.org*

Do This: Wander the market, then stop by one of the many nearby restaurants for lunch. Bert's Marketplace is all about the soul food (dishes include the Aretha Franklin World Famous Fried Chicken), Supino Pizzeria for a quick slice, or Zeff's Coney Island for breakfast anytime (and Coney dogs, of course).

GREAT LAKES SHIPWRECK MUSEUM

Over 500 ships have plunged into the icy depths of Lake Superior, 200 of which met their ends along the nefarious Shipwreck Coast, an 80-mile stretch of Upper Peninsula shoreline. A museum dedicated to these wrecks is located at the tip of Whitefish Point, which is near where the wreck of the *Edmund Fitzgerald*, a freighter that sank in 1975, taking with it its entire crew of 29, lies (none of whom were ever recovered). The museum covers this and other tragedies through exhibits and artifacts, including the Edmund Fitzgerald's bell. ✉ *18335 N. Whitefish Point Rd., Paradise, MI* 🌐 *www.shipwreckmuseum.com*

Do This: Take a tour of the 1861 lightkeeper's quarters, which are part of the Whitefish Point Light Tower, the oldest operating lighthouse on Lake Superior. The home features period furnishings, exhibits, and artifacts from the families who kept the lighthouse working and those who rescued ships.

HOLLAND

Nestled along Lake Macatawa about 6 miles from Lake Michigan, the town of Holland was originally settled and founded by Dutch immigrants. While it is possible to visit the various wooden windmills and lighthouses that appear as if plucked right out of the Netherlands throughout the year, May is when Holland is at its peak. The annual Tulip Time Festival, in operation since 1930, takes place in May, when over 5 million tulip bulbs sprout and transform the city.

Do This: Visit the Veldheer Tulip Garden, which is the epicenter of tulips during the annual festival. You can purchase bulbs while visiting the gardens, and even check in on how close the tulips are to blooming with the garden's live webcam stream. ✉ *12755 Quincy St., Holland, MI* 🌐 *www.veldheer.com*

About Our Writers

Greyson Ferguson was born and raised in East Lansing, Michigan. For Greyson, there was nothing like summertime bike rides with friends and coasting to a stop outside of Tasty Twist for a large vanilla cone dipped in chocolate. He now writes about his life and travels for publications including *Travel + Leisure*, *Business Insider*, Lonely Planet, and Fodor's, as well as his Medium and Substack accounts.

Cool Places to Stay

Detroit Foundation Hotel. Located in Downtown Detroit in a former historic firehouse, the DFH is the perfect combination of understated luxury and local-forward coolness. Hip, thoughtfully designed rooms are spacious and well-equipped while still maintaining their historic allure. The bar and restaurant, the Apparatus Room, has become one of the city's hottest tables with a fantastic wine and cocktail list. ✉ *250 W. Larned St., Detroit, MI* 🌐 *detroitfoundationhotel.com*

Lake Shore Resort. When Andrew Milauckas took over his family's lakefront mid-century motel, he added a dose of hipster cool. Rooms feature lake views (perfect for seeing the incredible sunsets), custom-made rugs, succulents, and solar shades for privacy. The rate includes continental breakfast along the lake, adult bikes to take and explore the town, kayaks, yoga classes, and more. ✉ *2885 Lakeshore Dr., Saugatuck, MI* 🌐 *www.lakeshoreresortsaugatuck.com*

Mackinac Island Grand Hotel. The place to stay on Mackinac Island, this 1887-built hotel has an old-world vibe with 400 rooms that are all uniquely decorated (stay in one of the "named rooms," which are designed to match a historic figure's tastes; the First Lady rooms include rooms named for Jacqueline Kennedy and Laura Bush). Even if you don't stay here, you can pay $10 to spend time relaxing on the porch (it's the world's longest porch at 660 feet and has 1,500 geraniums) and exploring the grounds. ✉ *286 Grand Ave., Mackinac Island, MI* 🌐 *www.grandhotel.com*

Mushroom Houses. "Mushroom" houses, a quirky design from architect Earl Young, are perfect for fans of *The Hobbit* (or anyone who wants an unexpected experience). The four houses, each entirely different in design, resemble hobbit abodes or mushrooms due to their roofs. The houses, which are located near the beach, include multiple bedrooms (with accommodations from 6 to 12 people) and amenities such as heated floors, grills, and washer-dryers. ✉ *Charlevoix, MI* 🌐 *www.vrbo.com*

The Siren. Located in downtown Detroit in the 1926 Art Deco Wurlitzer Building, the Siren is a glamorous hotel—think potted palms and fringed furniture, with just enough leopard print to keep things spicy. The rooms are decked out with vintage and custom furniture and terrazzo-tiled bathrooms. While the hotel is within walking distance to plenty of Detroit hot spots, there are plenty of reasons to not leave, including an on-site barber shop, the Siren Shop (specially curated magazines and other goodies), and a candy-pink cocktail bar, appropriately named Candy Bar. ✉ *1509 Broadway St., Detroit, MI* 🌐 *www.thesirenhotel.com*

Essential Eats

Cloverleaf Bar & Restaurant. Buddy's Pizza in Detroit is widely recognized as the birthplace of Detroit-style pizza. However, what's often left out of this history is that Gus and Anna Guerra, the creators of the pizza (and original owners of Buddy's), sold Buddy's and opened Cloverleaf Bar & Restaurant. So, if you want the original restaurant, go to Buddy's, but if you want the original pizza, go to Cloverleaf. ✉ *24443 Gratiot Ave., Eastpoint, MI* 🌐 *www.cloverleafrestaurant.com*

Harry's Place. For over 100 years, Harry's Place has existed inside an old residential home. The restaurant at one point in time was across the street from a major General Motors plant, and the plant closed decades ago, yet the restaurant remains. In a rust belt city like Lansing, a telltale sign of a good dive restaurant is when the factory restaurant outlives the factory. On the menu, there's a solid pizza (as long as you love cheese, because it's overflowing with it) and an all-you-can-eat Friday fish fry, but what put Harry's Place on the map was its olive burger. Olive burgers are a Michigan staple and feature a mayonnaise and olive-based sauce (it's not too far off from the Greek tzatziki sauce used on gyros). ✉ *404 N. Verlinden Ave., Lansing, MI* 🌐 *www.facebook.com/harrysplacelansing*

Pegasus Taverna. Really, you could pick a half-dozen different restaurants in Detroit's Greektown neighborhood, as this community has some of the best Greek food in the state (if not the country). Nestled close to the 19th-century Old Saint Mary's Catholic Church (worth popping in for a photo of the sanctuary), Pegasus Taverna features freshly made pita bread, gyros you'll dream about, and all the flaming cheese you could ever want. ✉ *558 Monroe St., Detroit, MI* 🌐 *www.pegasustavernas.com*

Quality Dairy Convenience Stores. Not exactly the mid-Michigan version of Wawa, but Quality Dairy convenience stores have a few staples you absolutely need to check out. There's nothing like the first batch of fresh apple cider when autumn hits, and on Fat Tuesday, you can find gut-busting paczki, a Polish doughnut on steroids. Not around either time of the year? Pop in year-round for a scoop of Superman ice cream. 🌐 *www.quality-dairy.com*

Sposito's Pasties. Throughout Michigan (specifically Northern Michigan and the Upper Peninsula), you'll find a take on Cornish pasties (basically an English empanada). The meat pocket was a popular meal for miners, as it allowed them to eat a hearty meal without getting coal-stained hands all over the food. While there are a number of great spots to grab classic pasties, Sposito's Pasties is at the top of the list. ✉ *1228 U.S. 2, St. Ignace, MI* 🌐 *www.spositopastie.com*

Zehnder's. Despite its history as a German immigrant town, Frankenmuth is known throughout the state as one of the best fried-chicken destinations. While many local inns and restaurants offer it, Zehnder's is regarded as the best. The all-you-can-eat restaurant has seating for up to 1,500 guests, and the chicken comes out with Thanksgiving-worthy sides of stuffing, mashed potatoes, and other goodies. ✉ *730 S. Main St., Frankenmuth, MI* 🌐 *www.zehnders.com*

Zingerman's Delicatessen. An iconic Ann Arbor deli, Zingerman's opened in 1982 and is a destination for sandwiches as well as specialty grocery offerings, from olive oils to teas to spices. In the decades since Ari Weinzweig and Paul Saginaw opened the deli, Zingerman's has expanded its tasty empire across the city to include a bakery, a creamery, a coffee company, a full-service restaurant (Zingerman's Roadhouse), and more. Having a corned beef Reuben at the deli is an Ann Arbor rite of passage, but you can put together a food crawl and try bites and sips from all their establishments, such as tangy pimiento cheese from Zingerman's Creamery, a latte at Zingerman's Coffee Company, sour cream coffee cake from Zingerman's Bakehouse, and a gelato-topped doughnut sundae at Zingerman's Roadhouse. ✉ *422 Detroit St., Ann Arbor, MI* 🌐 *www.zingermansdeli.com*

Minnesota

Minnesota's 11,842 lakes offer more shoreline than Florida, California, and Hawaii combined. If you travel all of Minnesota's 406 miles north to south from Canada to Iowa, you'll see three distinct terrains: to the west and south, you'll find plains and tallgrass prairies while eastern Minnesota is home to lush hardwood forests that burst into vibrant colors each fall as their leaves change. Heading north, visitors will encounter rockier landscapes dotted with coniferous trees that are better suited for the severe weather and thinner soil.

Capital: St. Paul

Population: 5,793,151

Area: 86,943 square miles

Statehood Date: May 11, 1858

Major Airports: Minneapolis–St. Paul International Airport (MSP)

Travel and Tourism Information: 🌐 *www.exploreminnesota.com* 🌐 *www.minnesotamonthly.com*

Famous Residents: F. Scott Fitzgerald (writer); Bob Dylan (musician); Judy Garland (actress); Charles Schulz (cartoonist); Prince (musician); Suni Lee (Olympic gold medalist)

Fun Fact: Scotch tape and Post-It Notes were invented in Minnesota, at the 3M headquarters located here.

Voyageurs National Park

A Watery Wonderland

Choose your own aquatic adventure at Voyageurs National Park, located at the very top of Minnesota near the Canadian border. With 84,000 acres of water, there's no shortage of enjoyment on and offshore with options for boating, paddling, fishing, swimming, camping, stargazing, birding, hiking, and more. Named for the French Canadians who traveled the waterways to trade furs, this untrafficked national park has no roads but does have 30 lakes and 1,200 miles of canoe routes, which you can explore with your own vehicle or on a tour through 🌐 *www.recreation.gov* (tours sell out, so be sure to book in advance). 🌐 *www.nps.gov/voya*

Don't Miss

The impressive **Ellsworth Rock Gardens** were designed by Jack Ellsworth, an artist and carpenter from Chicago, who created a terraced garden with 62 flower beds and more than 200 sculptures.

Best Hotel

Historic **Kettle Falls Hotel** offers a saloon and screened-in porch, along with both hotel rooms and villas with kitchens. It also offers boat, canoe, and kayak rentals. ✉ *12977 Chippewa Trail, Kabetogama, MN* 🌐 *www.kettlefallshotel.com*

When to Go

The park is open year-round, but the summer months are usually best for exploring the lakes. Snowfall averages 55 to 70 inches, so it's also a prime winter destination for snowmobiling, snowshoeing, or ice-fishing.

Getting Here and Around

International Falls Airport (INL) is the closest airport; it offers flights to and from Minneapolis/St. Paul International Airport (MSP) daily. The park is a five-hour drive from the Twin Cities and a three-hour drive from Duluth.

The Twin Cities

Cultural Gems of the Midwest

Looking for a way to experience the pulse of a city environment with the bonus of an abundance of nature tucked within its boundaries? From award-winning food to art, music, culture, diversity, sports, and numerous outdoor activities available year-round, flanking the roaring Mississippi River, Minneapolis and St. Paul have it all.

Don't Miss

A partnership between the Walker Art Center and the Minneapolis Park and Recreation Board, the 11-acre **Minneapolis Sculpture Garden** has about 60 sculptures, the most famous of which is Claes Oldenburg and Coosje van Bruggen's *Spoonbridge and Cherry*, a fountain sculpture. ✉ *725 Vineland Pl., Minneapolis, MN* 🌐 *www.walkerart.org/visit/garden*

Best Activity

The Twin Cities consistently rank among the top destinations for cycling nationwide, boasting nearly 550 miles of combined bike paths between the two.

Best Restaurant

James Beard Award–winning **Owamni** is a Native American restaurant that celebrates traditional Indigenous flavors from across North America. With a commitment to precolonial fare (that means no wheat, dairy, sugar, and proteins introduced by Europeans), each meal is a celebration of decolonized deliciousness. ✉ *420 S. 1st St., Minneapolis, MN* 🌐 *owamni.com*

Getting Here and Around

Fly into the Minneapolis–St. Paul airport (MSP) and hop on the light rail's Blue Line to get to downtown Minneapolis or switch to the Green Line to access St. Paul.

Mall of America

America's Mega Mall

With over 520 stores, from Apple to Zara, the Mall of America is the largest mall in the United States, spanning more than 96 acres in size (encompassing an area equivalent to seven Yankee Stadiums) and featuring over 4.3 miles of storefront. Nordstrom and Macy's department stores anchor it, but there's a variety of specialty shops offering gifts, books, and more. The Lego Store is fun for kids of all ages, thanks to its play tables, models, and a wall featuring dozens of specialty Lego pieces to purchase. And there's much more to do than just shop: the mall includes Sea Life Minnesota Aquarium, Minnesota's largest aquarium, with sharks, seahorses, and other creatures; an amusement park with rides; a mirror maze; and an escape room. ✉ *60 E. Broadway, Bloomington, MN* 🌐 *www.mallofamerica.com*

Don't Miss

Nickelodeon Universe, an amusement park with more than two dozen rides, is your chance to ride a roller coaster *inside* the mall.

Best Activity

The **Crayola Experience** features more than two dozen hands-on activities, including naming and wrapping a custom crayon and coloring page. 🌐 *www.crayolaexperience.com/mall-of-america*

Getting Here and Around

From Minneapolis–St. Paul International Airport (MSP), the mall is approximately a 7-mile drive, or you can take the light rail directly from the airport to the mall—it's the Blue Line's last stop.

Minnehaha Regional Park

A Gorgeous Urban Waterfall

One of the nation's first state parks, Minnehaha Regional Park is a must-visit for its beautiful Minnehaha Falls, a 53-foot rushing waterfall surrounded by limestone bluffs. While there are grander, taller waterfalls in the United States, few can match Minnehaha's accessibility (you can reach it by Minneapolis's light-rail, and there are bike paths that run directly to it) as well as its beauty in winter, when the falls freeze. Additionally, the 167-acre park offers Mississippi River overlooks, expansive gardens, hiking trails, an off-leash dog park, and a bike path. The park's now-defunct historic Minnehaha Depot was on the first railroad line west of the Mississippi River, and the Stevens House was the first wood-frame house in Minnesota. ✉ *4801 S. Minnehaha Dr., Minneapolis, MN*

Don't Miss

In winter, Minnehaha Falls often freezes, creating a stunning ice cave that makes for a striking photo op.

Good to Know

Minnehaha is sometimes incorrectly referred to as the "laughing waters" though its direct translation is "waterfall" in the Dakota language.

Best Activity

The park has a trio of gardens, **Song of Hiawatha Garden**, **Minnehaha Falls Pergola Garden**, and **Longfellow Gardens**, which feature woodland areas, prairie flowers like goldenrods, and other perennials.

Getting Here and Around

The park is located 3 miles from Minneapolis–St. Paul International Airport (MSP). Take the light-rail to 50th Street/Minnehaha Park.

Weisman Art Museum

A Museum That's A Work of Art Itself

Located on the University of Minnesota, Twin Cities campus in a striking Frank Gehry–designed building, this teaching museum has more than 30,000 works. The collection boasts strong holdings in ceramics, Korean furniture, and early-20th-century and contemporary American art, featuring works by notable painters such as Marsden Hartley and Milton Avery. Besides the permanent collection, the Weisman features rotating special exhibits, a student art showcase, gallery talks, and other events that allow you to engage with art. The museum also runs a Public Art on Campus program, which installs sculptures around the campus.
✉ 333 E. River Pkwy., Minneapolis, MN 🌐 wam.umn.ed

Don't Miss

Gehry's abstract architectural genius is on display before you even enter the museum. Take a moment to admire the building's brick facades and curved stainless steel sheets that resemble tin cans. Gehry added a brick extension to the building in 2011, significantly increasing the gallery space.

Best Collection

The museum has an exceptional collection of traditional Korean furniture, with works from the Choson and Silla dynasties, as well as folk art. The collection, a bequest from Dr. Edward Reynolds Wright Jr. in 1988, features works that encompass a range of woods, styles, and types of items, such as desks, rice storage chests, and tray tables.

Getting Here and Around

The museum is located 13 miles from Minneapolis–St. Paul International Airport (MSP). The East Bank stop on the Green Line light-rail is about a half mile from the museum.

Boundary Waters Canoe Area Wilderness

A Paddler's Paradise

Located in the farthest reaches of northeastern Minnesota's Superior National Forest along the Canadian border, the Boundary Waters is a canoer's dream. The huge preserve spans more than 1 million acres, featuring over 1,200 miles of canoe routes, 12 hiking trails, and many opportunities for camping, fishing, dogsledding, bird-watching, and more. There's ample wildlife to spot, from black-and-white loons on the water to wolves in the forest to birds of prey swooping in the sky. You'll need a permit for a specific entry point to visit, as well as border permits if you plan to explore the Canadian side. 🌐 *www.fs.usda.gov*

Don't Miss

Dogsledding is a popular winter activity in the preserve. Book a day trip to try it yourself or watch the area's **John Beargrease Sled Dog Marathon**, the longest sled dog race in the Lower 48.

Best Tour

Since it's so remote, a trip to Boundary Waters requires a ton of planning. Leave the work to the pros by booking either a single day canoeing trip or group overnight camping trip through the **Boundary Waters Guide Service** out of Ely. The experienced guides plan the itinerary, provide sleeping bags and gear, and cook all the meals, so you can focus on soaking up nature and taking great photos. 🌐 *www.elyoutfittingcompany.com*

Getting Here and Around

Fly into Duluth International Airport (DLH), which is 115 miles from Ely, a good home base for exploring the region.

Minnesota State Fair

The Great Minnesota Gathering

The Minnesota State Fair is frequently renowned as the best in the country, and for locals, the 12 days it spans at the end of August signal the end of summer. While most state fairs are somewhat more 4-H focused, Minnesota goes all out, featuring over 900 shows on its various stages, showcasing local livestock in 25 barns, and offering visitors a feast of over 275 food options, as well as nearly 650 service and product vendors. There's a little—or even a lot of something for everyone of all ages at the fair. ✉ *1265 Snelling Ave. N, St. Paul, MN* 🌐 *www.mnstatefair.org*

Don't Miss

Make sure to bring cash for the Corn Roast. While it sounds simple, it's a booth famous for its juicy, in-husk roasted sweet corn cobs dipped in vats of butter that are sure to leave your chin gleaming. Find it on the southeast corner of Dan Patch Avenue and Nelson Street.

Folk Art at the Fair

Explore the wide world of crafts in the Agriculture/Horticulture Building. Inside, you'll find the highly competitive crop art exhibit featuring pieces made from locally grown seeds and other plant parts. For more sculpture, head over to the Dairy building to view a live carving of the year's "Princess Kay of the Milky Way." That's the title given to the female ambassador of Minnesota's dairy farmers, and a life-sized likeness of her head is carved from a giant slab of butter.

Getting Here and Around

If coming from the Minneapolis-St. Paul airport, go north on I–35W, then east on I–94. Take Exit 237 for Snelling, and follow signs to the fair. There is free on-site bike and motorcycle parking, and several car parking options.

North Shore Scenic Drive

Explore an All-American Road

Stretching from Duluth to Grand Portage on the Canadian border, this 154-mile drive hugs Lake Superior and offers buckets of beautiful scenery and an array of activities along the way. You can stick to the road and drive north, admiring the wooded lakefront scenery and cliffs and stopping for lunch (try **Betty's Pies**, an iconic 1956 diner in Two Harbors that specializes in pasties as well as slices of pie). Or, visit one of seven state parks along the route, such as **Gooseberry Falls State Park** and **Temperance River State Park**, and go boating, fishing, hiking, or swimming.

Don't Miss

Split Rock Lighthouse, located in Split Rock Lighthouse State Park, opened in 1910 after a ferocious storm wrecked more than two dozen ships a few years earlier. Today, the decommissioned lighthouse is a National Historic Landmark that is open for guided tours. ✉ *3713 Split Rock Lighthouse Rd., Two Harbors, MN* 🌐 *www.mnhs.org/splitrock*

Best Stop

Artsy **Grand Marais** is a great village to spend the night since the town is filled with restaurants and bars, including local favorites World's Best Donuts and Voyageur Brewing Company. You can also spend time hiking up Eagle Mountain to take in an amazing view, or sit by the water and admire the sunrise or sunset.

Getting Here and Around

If you're starting at the southern end of the road, fly into Duluth International Airport (DLH); from the other direction, fly to Thunder Bay International Airport (YQT) in Ontario, which is located 43 miles from Grand Portage.

Ice-Fishing

The North's Great Pastime

Whether you're a seasoned angler or just want to try your hand at jigging with a spring bobber, Minnesota's many lakes make it a good spot to hit the ice and fish for walleye (the state fish), plus perch and northern pike. **Lake of the Woods** and **Lake Mille Lacs** are two of the top destinations, but you can find great ice fishing nearly anywhere in the state. If you're new to Minnesota ice fishing, book a guide, such as Grand Rapids Guide Service, to help steer you to the best fishing holes.

Don't Miss

If you're visiting the Twin Cities, try ice fishing at nearby **Lake Harriet** or **Medicine Lake**—either is close enough for a day trip.

Best Hotel

Lake of the Woods, situated in northwest Minnesota near the Canadian border, is a renowned destination for ice fishing and one of the largest freshwater lakes in the United States. Here, Ballard's Resort offers ice-fishing packages that include cabin lodging and meals, transportation to the lake, two holes in a fishing house, bait, and more. Guides track the best fishing spots each day. ✉ *3314 Bur Oak Rd. NW, Baudette, MN* 🌐 *www.ballardsresort.com*

Good to Know

Ice fishing season runs from early December through late March. You'll need to get a license (required if you're over 16), and be sure to check the Minnesota Department of Natural Resources (🌐 *www.dnr.state.mn.us/fishing*) to verify the limit of each kind of fish you're allowed to catch at a given time.

Getting Here and Around

International Falls Airport (INL) is the closest airport to Lake of the Woods, and Ballard's Resort is 80 miles away.

The Northern Lights

Nature's Big Show

While your chances of seeing the otherworldly and enchanting northern lights dramatically increase the farther north you go, you don't have to travel to the Arctic to cross this off your bucket list. Far northern Minnesota, away from bright lights and big cities, is an incredible spot to see the skies dance with swirls of greens, blues, purples, and yellows. **Boundary Waters Canoe Area Wilderness**, **Voyageurs National Park**, and **Northwest Angle**, the northernmost spot in the continental United States, are prime viewing locations, but if the conditions are right (that means no cloud cover) and magnetic activity is strong, you can see the charged solar particles in much of the state.

Don't Miss

Keep an eye on the Kp index, which tracks geomagnetic activity—it's on a scale of 1 and 10, and 6 is strong enough to see the aurora as far south as the Twin Cities.

Best Hotel

For guidance viewing the aurora, book the Northern Lights package at **Gunflint Lodge**, a Northwoods resort in Grand Marais. The booking includes a guided night hike. ✉ *143 S. Gunflint Lake Rd., Grand Marais, MN* 🌐 *www.gunflint.com*

When to Go

Though strong light displays are possible during any phase of the moon, lighter displays can be washed out by moonlight. Visit during the new moon phase for better visibility. The lights can appear year-round but they're most common in fall and winter.

Getting Here and Around

Ontario's Thunder Bay International Airport (YQT) is the closest airport to Grand Marais; Duluth International Airport (DLH) is 150 miles away.

When in Minnesota

DULUTH

Located on the shores of Lake Superior, Duluth is a waterfront city with tons to see and do, from the Great Lakes Aquarium to the Duluth Art Institute to the annual Bob Dylan Fest held each May (the rocker was born here). There are plenty of outdoor activities, including sailing, watching ships pass under the turn-of-the-century Aerial Lift Bridge from Canal Park, and strolling through gardens at Leif Erickson park. You may notice Erickson isn't the only Viking connection here; there's a strong sense of Nordic heritage throughout Minnesota (think Minnesota Vikings football), which is no wonder since the state has the largest population of Norwegians and Swedes outside of Scandinavia.

Do This: Sip aquavit, that favorite Minnesota spirit, at Vikre Distillery; visit the Nordic Center for cultural exhibits; and grab breakfast at Vanilla Bean Cafe, serving Scandinavian breakfast dishes such as Norwegian crepes and Swedish pancakes.

THE NORTH AMERICAN BEAR CENTER

Meet black bears and learn about their northern Minnesota habitat at this one-of-a-kind educational center, which features tours and exhibits showcasing mounted bears (including extinct species). The Northwoods Ecology Hall explores the animals with which black bears share their habitat and features aquariums, a reptile terrarium, mounted moose, and more. ✉ *1926 Rte. 169, Ely, MN* 🌐 *www.bear.org*

Do This: See the four black "ambassador bears" that make the center home; they live in a 2½-acre forested enclosure. Spot them from the viewing windows indoors or the outdoor balcony. Hourly tours highlight at least one of the bears with the chance for an up-close viewing.

PAISLEY PARK

Prince left behind a stunning estate and production studio outside the Twin Cities when he died in 2016; it's since been turned into a museum that you can visit and is also a spot for concerts, music festivals, and other events. Sprawling Paisley Park, which is as colorful and eclectic as the musician's wardrobe (you'll see his bright suits, hats, and jewelry on display) is a must for Prince fans, but it's a fun tour even if you're a newcomer to his music. For the most die-hard Prince fans, book a three-hour tour for an in-depth exploration of the property. You'll have access to special archives, a private video screening, and studio tours, plus see Prince's concert wardrobe, instruments, motorcycles, and more. Food and beverages are provided after the tour; it often sells out, so be sure to book in advance of your visit. ✉ *7801 Audubon Rd., Chanhassen, MN* 🌐 *www.paisleypark.com*

Do This: Each tour includes a stop at Studio A recording studio. Besides all the recording equipment, you can see the lyrics on a stand to the last song Prince was working on when he passed away.

PAUL BUNYAN AND BABE THE BLUE OX

A celebration of the American folk hero, you'll find an 18-foot-tall statue of Paul Bunyan and his faithful friend Babe the Blue Ox in the small city of Bemidji in northern Minnesota. Built in 1937 to promote tourism to the area, they've become a beloved roadside attraction and road trip pit stop. 🌐 *300 Bemidji Ave. N, Bemidji, MN*

Do This: The statues stand proudly in front of a Minnesota Tourist Information Center, which includes displays on the legend of Paul Bunyan and the Fireplace of States made of rocks from every American state and every Canadian province.

THE SOMALI MUSEUM OF MINNESOTA

Minnesota has the largest Somali population in the United States, and this museum, the only one of its kind in North America, explores Somali history and culture. The museum features over 700 items on display, including nomadic huts, kitchen utensils, woven textiles, and contemporary paintings by local artists. ✉ *2925 Chicago Ave., Minneapolis, MN* 🌐 *www.somalimuseum.org*

Do This: After visiting the museum, have lunch at Afro Deli, which has four locations around Minneapolis and St. Paul. The menu features Somali classics like Chicken Fantastic, chicken and vegetables in a Parmesan cream sauce served with saffron rice. 🌐 *www.afrodeli.com*

About Our Writers

Natalia Mendez (they/them) is from northeastern Wisconsin and has lived in Minneapolis for over 15 years. They think there's nowhere better to experience all four seasons outdoors than on bikes or at local state parks than in Minnesota, and while they are dubious of calling casseroles "hot dish," they can admit that the tater-tot hot dish is a perfect, albeit unhinged, culinary invention. They have been a freelance writer since 2011.

Cool Places to Stay

Alma. A must for food-loving travelers, Alma is an elegant seven-room hotel attached to the James Beard Award–winning Alma Restaurant. Each room is uniquely designed with queen or king beds with natural linens, flat-screen TVs with AppleTV and streaming services, vintage rugs, walk-in showers, and custom-made desks. Continental breakfast is provided each morning, as is complimentary wine and antipasti upon arrival. ✉ *528 University Ave. SW, Minneapolis, MN* 🌐 *www.almampls.com*

Hewing Hotel. This hip hotel in the North Loop neighborhood combines Scandinavian inspiration with Minnesota touches, including artwork from Minnesota artists and photographers, pine timber beams, and Faribault woolen blankets. Set in a historic building in a former farm implement warehouse, the hotel includes pet-friendly rooms that have an outdoorsy vibe, and an all-season rooftop lounge featuring city views. ✉ *300 Washington Ave. N, Minneapolis, MN* 🌐 *www.hewinghotel.com*

Merryweather Inn. In the late 19th century, Duluth was home to the most millionaires per capita, and the mansions in its historic Knob Hill district reflect this opulence. Take a step back in time above the shores of glittering Lake Superior at Merryweather Inn, a Georgian-colonial style home–turned–bed and breakfast built in 1904. Beautiful architectural details, fireplaces, and period fixtures have been maintained and blend smoothly with modernized amenities in the six large suites available for your stay. Don't skip the hearty homemade breakfast or pass up a nightcap from the rotating cocktail menu or a glass of wine from their Smiling Ferret speakeasy and wine cellar. ✉ *2316 E. 1st St., Duluth, MN* 🌐 *www.merryweatherinn.com*

Whistle Stop BNB. For "I spent the night somewhere wild" bragging rights, seek out this bed-and-breakfast, which features five restored train cars transformed into rooms. The cars, which are decorated with turn-of-the-20th-century antiques, include Murphy beds, whirlpool tubs, refrigerators, and fireplaces. The woodsy acre of property also includes a cottage and house with rooms, all of which include full breakfast each day. ✉ *107 E. Nowell St., Mills, MN* 🌐 *www.whistlestopbedandbreakfast.com*

Essential Eats

Hmong Sausage. Headily scented lemongrass, chili pepper, and herb-filled links exist in Minnesota thanks to an influx of Hmong immigrants and refugees after wars in Vietnam and Laos. Experience the real deal in St. Paul's Hmongtown Village, or at restaurants in Northeast Minneapolis like Diane's Place and Vinai.

Juicy Lucys. There are few things better than molten cheese oozing from a juicy, flattop-seared patty, which you'll discover upon trying one of the iconic Minnesota burgers. Two Minneapolis restaurants claim to be the origin of the dish (Matt's Bar and the 5-8 Club), both with their own distinct takes.

Tater Tot Hotdish. Everyone else calls it casserole, but in Minnesota, hotdish is king. This specific thrifty staple is a blend of cream-based soups, ground beef, and frozen vegetables, and is studded with crispy tots on top. Find riffs of it at the Minnesota State Fair (deep-fried tater tot hotdish on a stick? You betcha!) and at Crooked Pint Alehouse locations across the state.

Ohio

Known as the "Gateway to the Midwest," the Buckeye State is a beautifully balanced blend of not only everything Midwestern but also everything American. From college and pro sports to ballet and theater, Ohio's got plenty to entice folks from out of town. There are history, science, art, and children's museums. Food lovers relish the abundance of restaurants highlighting culinary traditions from around the world. Indoor and outdoor concerts pull in the biggest names around, while natural attractions and outdoor activities can be found in parks and along lakes and rivers throughout the state.

Capital: Columbus

Population: 11,825,255

Area: 44,825 square miles

Statehood Date: March 1, 1803

Major Airports: Cleveland Hopkins International Airport (CLE); John Glenn Columbus International Airport (CMH); James M. Cox Dayton International Airport (DAY)

Travel and Tourism Information: 🌐 *www.ohio.org* 🌐 *www.travelohio.com*

Famous Residents: Paul Newman (actor); Neil Armstrong (astronaut); Toni Morrison (writer); Gloria Steinem (feminist activist); Guy Fieri (chef); Lebron James (basketball player)

Fun Fact: A small liberal arts college founded in Oberlin, Ohio in 1833, Oberlin College was the first interracial and coeducational college in the United States.

Rock & Roll Hall of Fame

The Ultimate Stop for Music Fans

A must-visit for music fans, the Rock & Roll Hall of Fame is loaded with memorabilia, photographs, costumes, instruments, and much more from artists like Elvis Presley, Whitney Houston, and the Beatles. As you'd expect from a museum dedicated to music, the exhibits are packed with films, interactive kiosks, and videos, so you can watch and listen to iconic performances. The museum includes the main exhibit hall, which traces the beginnings and evolution of rock and roll, and the Hall of Fame level, with panels honoring each inductee. The architecture of the building itself is worth a look: designed by world-renowned architect I. M. Pei, it features pyramids and a tower and is meant to look like a record player from above. ✉ *1100 E. 9th St., Cleveland, OH* 🌐 *www.rockhall.com*

Don't Miss

The Hall of Fame has curated a variety of tours, from Women Who Rock to an instrument-focused tour, but to see the best of the artifacts and memorabilia on display, follow the Staff Picks Tour, which takes 2½ hours and leads you to all the highlights, from Joey Ramone's black leather jackets to Run-D.M.C.'s Adidas sneakers.

Just Nearby

Just a five-minute walk away is **Great Lakes Science Center,** home to the historic 618-foot steamship William G. Mather, and **NASA Glenn Visitor Center,** which is filled with kid-friendly space exhibits, interactive experiences, and unique artifacts.

Getting Here and Around

From Cleveland Hopkins International Airport (CLE), the Hall of Fame is a 15-mile drive.

Cuyahoga Valley National Park

The Midwest's Best Waterfalls

Located halfway between Cleveland and Akron, the 33,000-acre Cuyahoga Valley National Park (CVNP) is an easy day trip from both cities. Known for its waterfalls (there are over 100 in the park), CVNP also offers 140 miles of trails for hiking, biking, and horseback riding; the Ohio & Erie Towpath Trail is a notable path that traces the route of the Ohio & Erie Canal. Paddling and picnicking are popular activities, and the park is also a good spot to stargaze and see Mercury, nebulae, eclipses, and the aurora borealis. 🌐 *www.nps.gov/cuva*

Don't Miss

Brandywine Falls, a striking 60-foot waterfall popular for its accessible boardwalk and gorgeous views, is the most popular location in the park. Get there by parking nearby and walking along the boardwalk, or hiking in from the Boston Mill Visitor Center, about a 5-mile hike.

Best Activity

One of the most relaxing ways to see the park is by rail on the **Cuyahoga Valley Scenic Railroad**. This leisurely train trip through the park goes through the Cuyahoga Valley and along the rushing Cuyahoga River. You'll see wildlife like bald eagles, great blue heron, white-tailed deer, and Eastern coyotes. Sit in the upper dome panoramic observation car for the best view. 🌐 *www.cvsr.org*

Getting Here and Around

From Cleveland Hopkins International Airport (CLE), the park is 22 miles; from Akron-Canton Airport (CAK), the park is about 28 miles.

Lake Erie

Ohio's Best Beach Destination

Much of Ohio's northern border is on Lake Erie, a major summer destination for beaches and water activities like kayaking. The shallowest of the Great Lakes, Lake Erie is also the warmest, which means it's perfect for swimming. Visit sandy spots like **East Harbor State Park** in Lakeside-Marblehead and **Headlands Beach State Park** in Mentor. From here you can also check out the **Merry-Go-Round Museum** in Sandusky; the highlight is a restored working carousel with a collection of carved carousel figurines dating back to 1915.

Don't Miss

Try a Lake Erie Monster IPA, produced by **Great Lakes Brewing Co.** of Cleveland; it's named after Lake Erie's mythical lake monster, South Bay Bessie. ✉ *2516 Market Ave., Cleveland, OH* 🌐 *www.greatlakesbrewing.com*

Best Day Trip

Kelleys Island, located off the coast, showcases the effects of glaciers on the rocks and land; you can reach it by ferry. Head over to visit the 677-acre state park and go swimming, boating, and fishing, or in winter, cross-country skiing or ice fishing. Grab lunch at the Village Pump, a popular spot for Lake Erie perch and a Brandy Alexander (a boozy milkshake). 🌐 *www.kelleysislandferry.com*

Best Tour

Rent a kayak, paddleboard, canoe, or hydrobike and hit the water on your own, or book a Harbor Yak Kayak Tour. 🌐 *www.harboryak.com/tours*

Getting Here and Around

Cleveland Hopkins International Airport (CLE) is located at about the Lake Erie midpoint, while Toledo Express Airport (TOL) is located at the western edge; you can fly into either depending on your lake destination.

National Underground Railroad Freedom Center

A Poignant Look into History

Built in 2004 on the banks of the Ohio River near the Cincinnati side of the John A. Roebling Suspension Bridge which crosses over into Kentucky, this 158,000-square foot center illustrates the role Ohio played in helping enslaved people escape to freedom on the Underground Railroad through personal narratives, rare documents and artifacts, and interactive experiences. Its location is symbolic in that the bridge, completed during the Civil War, was a passage for escapees between the states to the south of the Ohio River, which allowed slavery, and those to the north, which did not. The center also has the world's first permanent exhibition on modern-day slavery and human trafficking.
✉ *50 E. Freedom Way, Cincinnati, OH*
🌐 *freedomcenter.org*

Don't Miss

The 25-minute film *Brothers of the Borderland* relays in gripping detail the story of John Parker and Reverend John Rankin, two abolitionists from Ripley, Ohio, who help a woman flee a life of slavery.

While You're Here

Stroll across the **John A. Roebling Suspension Bridge,** about a half-hour round-trip walk just outside the Freedom Center's front door. When the bridge opened in 1867, its 1,075-foot span made it the longest suspension bridge in the world. Today, it has walkways on either side and offers beautiful views of the Cincinnati cityscape.

Getting Here and Around

The center is located in downtown Cincinnati.

Hopewell Ceremonial Earthworks

Masterpieces of Landscape Architecture

The Hopewell Ceremonial Earthworks consist of eight earthen monuments, each covering several acres, built between 1,600 and 2,000 years ago along tributaries of the Ohio River by a network of Native Americans known today as the Hopewell. The Earthworks became a UNESCO World Heritage site because they were deemed to be complex masterpieces of landscape architecture and are exceptional among ancient monuments worldwide in their enormous scale, geometric precision, and astronomical alignments. ✉ *16062 Rte. 104, Chillicothe, OH* 🌐 *hopewellearthworks.org*

Don't Miss

Fort Ancient is often considered the most impressive of the Hopewell sites for its sheer size. Built on a bluff at the edge of the Little Miami River in Oregonia, Ohio, it consists of a 126-acre enclosure with over 3½ miles of embankment walls that are almost 25 feet high.

Good to Know

Serpent Mound is an internationally known National Historic Landmark built by Native Americans but not the Hopewells. It is an effigy mound along the Hopewell route in the shape of a snake with a curled tail. ✉ *3850 Rte. 73, Peebles, OH* 🌐 *www.greatserpentmound.com*

Getting Here and Around

The eight Hopewell sites are best visited by allowing for a half day in each of the three Ohio cities—Newark, Chillicothe, and Oregonia—in which they are grouped. Start in Columbus, then take the 45-minute drive east to Newark, where you can visit two sites. Drive for about 1½ hours southwest to Chillicothe, spend the night, and visit the five sites there. End your tour on day three by taking the 1-hour drive west to Oregonia and visiting the final Hopewell site.

Ohio Air and Space Exploration

The Birthplace of Aviation

Ohio is full of museums and sites that honor the state's contributions to space exploration because the Wright brothers, who invented the airplane, hail from Dayton, and no less than eight NASA astronauts are from Cleveland. John Glenn and Neil Armstrong are both Ohioans as well. You can visit the **John & Annie Glenn Museum** (Glenn's boyhood home) in New Concord to learn about their lives or the **Armstrong Air & Space Museum** in Wapakoneta to see artifacts like space suits and full-size aircraft flown by Armstrong. You can also learn about the space race and how Ohio has influenced space travel.

Don't Miss

The **Neil Armstrong Space Exploration Gallery** at the Cincinnati Museum Center is a permanent exhibition that explores the Apollo 11 mission, during which Armstrong and Buzz Aldrin walked on the moon (that's one small step for man, one giant leap for Ohio). The exhibit includes a replica of Armstrong's space suit from the mission and a moon rock he collected. ✉ *1301 Western Ave., Cincinnati, OH* 🌐 *www.cincymuseum.org*

Best Stargazing

Stare into infinity and beyond with a close-up view of the night sky at **Nassau Astronomical Station** in the 1,100-acre Observatory Park in Montville Township, the only dark-sky park in Ohio. 🌐 *www.geaugaparkdistrict.org/park/observatory-park*

Getting Here and Around

From John Glenn Columbus International Airport (CMH), the Armstrong Air & Space Museum is 90 miles away and the John & Annie Glenn Museum is 70 miles. Nassau Astronomical Station is 55 miles from Cleveland Hopkins International Airport (CLE).

Ohio's Art Museums

America's Most Underrated Art Scene

Ohio's art museums are some of the finest in the country, if not the world. The **Cleveland Museum of Art** (✉ *11150 East Blvd., Cleveland, OH* 🌐 *www.clevelandart.org*) has excellent Impressionist, Postimpressionist, and modern European and American painting collections while its Egyptian collection is one of the best of its kind. Further west, the Frank Gehry–designed **Toledo Museum of Art's** (✉ *2445 Monroe St., Toledo, OH* 🌐 *www.toledomuseum.org*) Center for Visual Arts is a work of art unto itself, a giant body of geometric forms swathed in lead-coated copper, while its postmodern Glass Pavilion houses a world-renowned glass art collection. In Cincinnati, the Zaha Hadid–designed **Contemporary Arts Center** (✉ *44 E. 6th St., Cincinnati, OH* 🌐 *www.contemporaryartscenter.org*) is famous for art from around the world that addresses political and cultural themes; here, visitors are encouraged to interact with the art, not just view it.

Don't Miss

The Cleveland Museum of Art includes a spectacular Arts of Africa gallery with a sizeable collection of traditional and contemporary works from various regions of the continent.

Good to Know

At the Toledo Museum of Art's Glass Studio, you can observe and take part in the art of glassblowing.

Getting Here and Around

The Cleveland Museum of Art is a 25-minute drive from Cleveland Hopkins International Airport (CLE), while the Toledo Museum of Art is about an hour and 45-minute drive. Farther south, the Contemporary Arts Center in Cincinnati is about an hour and 45-minute drive from John Glenn Columbus International Airport (CMH).

Hocking Hills State Park

Ohio's Best State Park

About an hour's drive southwest of Columbus, you'll find a forested sanctuary with more than 25 miles of hiking trails winding past a lake, waterfalls, caves, and gorges. Hocking Hills State Park is where weary Midwesterners go to unwind and commune with nature. Old Man's Cave is the park's most popular attraction, with several hiking trails nearby providing ample views. Six miles south of Old Man's Cave, you'll find Cedar Falls, a scenic waterfall reached by traversing a half-mile trail bordered by steep rock walls. Wear good hiking shoes; the terrain is varied. The park's visitor center, next to the parking lot for Old Man's Cave, offers trail maps and exhibits on the unique geology of the area which at times feels like something straight out of a Harry Potter book. 🌐 *www.hockinghills.com*

Don't Miss

The park's hidden gem is **21 Horse Cave**, also known as Chapel Cave. There's no signage for it and it's not on any of the park's maps. To get there, start at the northern end of the Hocking Hills Climbing and Rappelling Area parking lot at 24798 Big Pine Road in Logan, Ohio and begin hiking on the bridle trail marked with white blazes. The trail follows Long Hollow Stream for just under a mile, then you'll come to a hill. Head up the hill and turn right at the base of the large rock outcrop and you'll find Chapel Cave. You may have to cross a few small creek beds along the bridle trail, but you'll be rewarded on arrival with magnificent views.

Getting Here and Around

The closest major airport to Hocking Hills State Park is John Glenn Columbus International Airport (CMH), located about an hour to 90 minutes away by car.

Cleveland Sports

Cheer for O-H-I-O

Spectator sports reign supreme in Ohio, which is home to iconic professional teams—and good ones at that—in all major leagues. A few of the greats are conveniently clustered together in downtown Cleveland, including the Cavaliers NBA team, Browns NFL team, Guardians MLB team, and Monsters AHL team. That means no matter the season, it's easy to catch a game or two. The Cavs and Monsters share the **Rocket Arena,** while the Browns play at **Huntington Bank Field,** and the Guardians make their home at **Progressive Field.**

Don't Miss

The **Pro Football Hall of Fame** is located in Canton, about 60 miles south of downtown Cleveland. Visit to see the Hall of Fame Gallery, with bronze busts of each enshrined player, Super Bowl rings, the Vince Lombardi Trophy for Super Bowl LV, and a gallery devoted to exploring contemporary issues in the National Football League. ✉ *2121 George Halas Dr. NW, Canton, OH* 🌐 *www.profootballhof.com*

Best Activity

Tailgating at a Cleveland Browns game is a time-honored tradition. Hours before the game kicks off, Browns fans bedecked in orange and brown gather at the Muni Lot at 1500 South Marginal Road, the Pit at 1101 West 9th Street, and elsewhere in the area.

Getting Here and Around

Fly into Cleveland Hopkins International Airport (CLE); it's 12 miles from the airport to Progressive Field. From Progressive, Huntington Bank Field is a mile away, and Rocket Arena is ¼ mile. The Pro Football Hall of Fame is 60 miles from the airport.

Ohio Ice Cream Trail

America's Best Dairy Farms

With more than 1,450 dairy farms, it's only natural that Ohio has become such an ice-cream destination—the state even has its own ice-cream trail, which guides you to no less than 150 spots across the state for a scoop. **Jeni's Splendid Ice Creams**, which started in Columbus, and **Graeter's,** which started in Cincinnati, are two of the best-known purveyors, but you'll find many other worthy spots. **Toft's** in Sandusky is Ohio's oldest dairy, churning out flavors like black sweet cherry and cotton candy, while **Mitchell's Ice Cream** in Cleveland, opened in 1999, now has eight small-batch shops in the city with seasonal favorites like lavender honey, caramelized chocolate, and fresh peach. 🌐 *ohio.org/home/seasons/summer/ohio-ice-cream-trail*

Don't Miss

Graeter's, which started in 1870 when Louis Graeter began selling his ice cream at Cincinnati street markets, is arguably the most famous producer in Ohio and has dozens of shops across the state. It's famous for its chocolate chip ice creams, like mocha, mint, and black raspberry filled with thick, yet pliable, chocolate chunks. 🌐 *www.graeters.com*

Best Buckeye Treat

The Utica-based company **Velvet Ice Cream** has been a family-run business since 1914; you can eat lunch at their café and for desert treat yourself to the Buckeye Classic, inspired by the Ohio-favorite peanut butter and chocolate candies. ✉ *11324 Mt. Vernon Rd., Utica, OH* 🌐 *www.velveticecream.com*

Getting Here and Around

Ice-cream makers are located all across the state, but flying into John Glenn Columbus International Airport (CMH) will give you a good home base. Velvet's factory is located about 35 miles from the airport and Toft's is just over 100 miles to the north.

When in Ohio

CEDAR POINT

Sandusky's Cedar Point, the second-oldest operating amusement park in the United States (it opened in 1870), packs in the rides: it has 67 in total, including 19 roller coasters, the second most of any park. It's set along Lake Erie, and includes a mile-long beach, as well as a water park with waterslides and wave pools. ✉ *1 Cedar Point Dr., Sandusky, OH* 🌐 *www.cedarpoint.com*

Do This: With so many coasters, there's a ride for everyone, but the record-breaking Steel Vengeance is beloved among thrill-seekers. It's the fastest, tallest hybrid coaster in the world and includes a 90-degree 200-foot drop and four inversions.

A CHRISTMAS STORY HOUSE

The famous house from *A Christmas Story* is located in Cleveland; take a tour of the home, which looks just as it did in the movie, right down to the leg lamp. Visit the A Christmas Story Museum across the street to see costumes and memorabilia from the film, including Randy's snowsuit and the family's car. ✉ *3159 W. 11th St., Cleveland, OH* 🌐 *www.achristmasstoryhouse.com*

Do This: Die-hard fans of the movie can spend the night at the house; the top floor features a private loft, and you have access to the entire house from an hour after closing until 9 am the next day. The Bumpus House, where the next-door neighbors live in the film, has two suites available for rent.

CLEVELAND'S WADE OVAL

Wade Oval, a 7-acre park on the east side of the city, is lined with attractions like the Cleveland Museum of Art, Cleveland Natural History Museum, Museum of Contemporary Art, Severance Hall (where the Cleveland Orchestra plays), and the Cleveland Botanical Garden. This larger area is called University Circle, and it's also home to Case Western Reserve University, several libraries, historic homes, and more. Pick up a CirclePass, which gets you 25% off admission to the Cleveland History Center, the Cleveland Botanical Garden, and Cleveland Museum of Natural History. 🌐 *www.universitycircle.org*

Do This: WOW! Wade Oval Wednesdays, held Wednesday evenings from June to August, features live-music performances, food trucks, local beer, and more. In the winter, the oval turns into a skating rink.

CLEVELAND'S WEST SIDE MARKET

Cleveland's historic West Side Market, which got its start as an open-air market in 1840, is a living embodiment of America's diverse tapestry of cultures. Seventy vendors—including many family-owned businesses—showcase cuisines from Polish to Cambodian to French and more, all under one roof. Aisles are packed with stalls selling items like spices, produce, cheeses, meats, baked goods, and candy, with a mix of ingredients and ready-to-eat dishes. The market has been modernized since the brick building (with its iconic 137-foot clock tower) opened in 1912, but its vintage feel remains. ✉ *1979 W. 25th St., Cleveland, OH* 🌐 *westsidemarket.org*

Do This: Put together a picnic by hitting vendors like Sebastian's Deli for smoked meats, the Cheese Shop for domestic and imported cheeses, and Mediterra Bakehouse for freshly baked bread. There are some benches outside, or take your lunch to the Market Square park across the street or a lakefront spot like Edgewater Park.

Cool Places to Stay

The Casa at Gervasi Vineyard. Located on a 55-acre estate, this elegant hotel features 24 suites, with fireplaces and covered verandas, as well as continental breakfast with fresh croissants and fruit delivered each morning. The vineyard has several dining and drinking options, and 5 acres of vines; they grow three different types of grapes suited to the Ohio climate. ✉ *1700 55th St. NE, Canton, OH* 🌐 *www.gervasivineyard.com/stay/the-casa*

The Fidelity Hotel. Within easy walking distance of major sights, Cleveland's Fidelity Hotel oozes old school glamour with its Hollywood Regency–meets–Art Deco aesthetic. The ground-floor restaurant, the Club Room, is run by chef Dan Young, who worked with Michael Symon at no less than three of his restaurants. As for the rooms, well-heeled guests can luxuriate in the 695-square-foot Fidelity Suite, which includes a large wet bar and separate dining and seating areas in addition to Bellino Italian linens. ✉ *1940 E. 6th St., Cleveland, OH* 🌐 *www.fidelityhotelcle.com*

Frank Lloyd Wright's RiverRock. Frank Lloyd Wright fans will be thrilled to learn that they can book an overnight stay at RiverRock, located in the Cleveland suburb of Willoughby Hills, about a 30-minute drive from downtown. When Wright died in 1959, he had just completed the blueprints for RiverRock, but the building wasn't completed until 2025. The three-bedroom dwelling was constructed with stone harvested from the Chagrin River, which inspired its name, and it sits on a forested swath of land with the river running through it. ✉ *2217 River Rd., Willoughby Hills, OH* 🌐 *www.riverrockhouse.com*

Getaway Beaver Creek. These tiny cabins encourage unplugging for the weekend—stocked with cell-phone lockboxes, a queen bed, a bathroom, a tiny kitchenette, and big windows to peer into nature, they have everything you need for a cozy break. Located 90 minutes from Cleveland, this outpost is near hiking trails as well as grocery stores if you're cooking for yourself (and restaurants if not). ✉ *45529 Middle Beaver Rd., Lisbon, OH* 🌐 *getaway.house/pittsburgh-cleveland*

The Mohicans Treehouse Resort. Get back to nature at these eco-friendly tree houses in the Mohican Valley. Nine uniquely designed tree houses offer full indoor bathrooms (and warm-weather outdoor showers), kitchenettes and charcoal grills, living areas, and decks. ✉ *23164 Vess Rd., Glenmont, OH* 🌐 *www.themohicans.net/treehouses*

About Our Writers

Kristan Schiller grew up in Shaker Heights, Ohio, where she currently resides after spending 23 years in New York City and two years in London. A die-hard fan of Cleveland, Kristan hopes to surf Lake Erie this winter and live to write about it. She is an award-winning journalist who has traveled to over 80 countries and has been published in the *New York Times*, *New York Magazine*, CNN, Afar, and Bloomberg, among other outlets.

Essential Eats

Agni. Columbus-based Agni is known for its multicourse tasting menu of Bangladeshi-American dishes centered on live-fire cooking. Led by acclaimed chef Avishar Barua, high-caliber dishes include Bengali shrimp tacos, crisp ribs, and Thai Malay curry scallops. And while the restaurant is relaxed and unpretentious, its tasting menu makes it the ideal option for a special occasion, focusing on an immersive experience with palate cleansers and storytelling. ✉ *716 S. High St., Columbus, OH* 🌐 *www.dineatagni.com*

The Aperture. Located in the Cincinnati's emerging Walnut Hills neighborhood and led by chef-owner Jordan Anthony Brown, the highly acclaimed Mediterranean menu here includes standouts like glazed hamachi collar and tomato spaghetti swirled with candied chilies. Other interesting dishes include leek with gribiche sauce and white anchovy, and saffron rigatoni with lamb ragù, cherry tomato, whipped pecorino, and rosemary. Don't forget to save room for dessert; order the coriander lemongrass ice cream, a subtly spicy frozen treat to finish off your five-star feast. ✉ *900 E. McMillan St., Cincinnati, OH* 🌐 *www.theaperturecinci.com/menu*

Tony Packo's Restaurant. With five locations around the Toledo area, the old-school restaurant Tony Packo's is an institution. Founded in 1932, the restaurant specializes in Hungarian-inspired dishes like hot dogs with spicy chili sauce, chicken paprikash with Hungarian dumplings, crispy pierogi with smoked paprika ranch sauce, and a variety of pickles, like the sweet-hot pickles and peppers. ✉ *1902 Front St., Toledo, OH* 🌐 *www.tonypacko.com*

Zhug. Cleveland native Doug Katz has a handful of stellar eateries scattered across the city; arguably the most exceptional is Zhug in Cleveland Heights, an elegant, Middle Eastern tapas restaurant that has drawn praise from restaurant critics and foodies from across the country. A few favorites are the smoked calamari with saffron aioli, purple potato, and olive and the eggplant moussaka with tomato, feta, lentils, mushrooms, and oregano. Other tasty plates include harissa peanut hummus; honey roasted beets with spiced labneh; and garlicky green beans served with citronette, almonds, and pomegranate molasses. Zhug is pricey but worth the splurge for its unique twist on Mediterranean mezze. ✉ *12413 Cedar Rd., Cleveland Heights, OH* 🌐 *www.zhugcle.com*

Wisconsin

Welcome to America's Dairyland, famous for its cheese, beer, the beloved Green Bay Packers, and some stunning natural attractions. From Door County's shoreline and Kettle Moraine's glacial forest to the Wisconsin Dells' water parks and Milwaukee's cool neighborhoods, there's truly something for every visitor. Most of Wisconsin's landscape was formed some 10,000 years ago by a great glacier that left in its wake 15,000 lakes, 12,624 rivers and streams, pristine prairies, and some of America's finest examples of glacial topography.

Capital: Madison

Population: 5,960,975

Square Miles: 65,498 square miles

Statehood Date: May 29, 1848

Major Airports: General Mitchell International Airport (MKE); Dane County Regional Airport (MSN); Appleton International Airport (ATW); Austin Straubel International Airport (GRB)

Travel and Tourism Information:
www.travelwisconsin.com

Famous Residents: Orson Welles (director); Frank Lloyd Wright (architect); Chris Farley (comedian); Mark Ruffalo (actor); Oprah Winfrey (media mogul)

Fun Fact: A hodag is a folklore critter discovered in Rhinelander, Wisconsin, and featured in Paul Bunyan tales.

Door County

The Midwest's Most Stunning Peninsula

Door County, the long, narrow peninsula that juts out from Green Bay into Lake Michigan, is a year-round destination for exploring the outdoors, whether that's hiking to take in the foliage at **Peninsula State Park** or visiting beaches (and quaint ice-cream shops) during the summer. The small towns that dot the peninsula, like **Sister Bay** and **Ephraim,** each have their own feel, and there's a growing food and drink scene led by places like Thyme and Island Orchard Cider.

Don't Miss

A fish boil, in which big pots full of whitefish and red potatoes are set aflame, is as much a show as a meal. Catch it at the **White Gull Inn**, among other spots on the peninsula. ✉ *4225 Main St., Fish Creek, WI* 🌐 *www.whitegullinn.com*

Best Day Trip

A 30-minute ferry ride from Ellison Bay's Northpoint Pier, the 22-square-mile **Washington Island** is known for its large Icelandic community. Check out School House Beach, a beautiful stretch made of gray stones, and Stavkirke Church, a striking wooden church modeled after a Scandinavian design.

Getting Here and Around

Green Bay's Austin Straubel International Airport (GRB) is located at the base of the peninsula. From there, it's 99 miles to Gills Rock, at the very tip of the peninsula. You'll need a car to get around between towns.

Apostle Islands National Lakeshore

Sea Caves and Dramatic Cliffs

The Apostle Islands National Lakeshore, a remote destination on Lake Superior in northern Wisconsin, consists of a stretch of shoreline on the mainland with walking trails, along with 21 islands that are only accessible by water, where you can see rock formations, ice caves, and 19th-century lighthouses. Wildlife is a draw, with bald eagles and black bears in abundance, and camping is available on 18 of the islands for adventurous souls who prefer to spend the night. ⊕ *www.nps.gov/apis*

Don't Miss

The sea caves, striking arches, and cutouts in the cliffs on **Devils Island** are a must-see by boat.

Best Tours

Book a tour with **Apostle Islands Cruises** (⊕ *www.apostleisland.com*), which offers multiple options for seeing the islands from the water. The Grand Tour, a 55-mile scenic narrated tour, takes you past lighthouses, sea caves, and wildlife. **Apostle Island Rustic Makwa Den** (⊕ *www.apostle-islandsrusticmakwaden.com*) offers kayaking tours, which include kayaking around the cliffs for two hours.

When to Go

Summer is the easiest time to visit and offers the most activities, although the islands are open year-round. In the winter, you can visit the ice caves.

Getting Here and Around

Gogebic–Iron County Airport (IWD) is the closest airport; access it by flying Boutique Air from Chicago O'Hare (ORD) or Minneapolis–St. Paul (MSP). From the airport, it's 66 miles to Bayfield, where you can catch a shuttle boat, take your own vessel, or even rent a kayak to reach the islands.

Green Bay Packers

Cheesehead Pride at Lambeau Field

Of all the major league professional sports teams in the United States, there's only one that's community-owned, by its loyal fans—the Green Bay Packers. The third-oldest team in the National Football League, Green Bay is also dubbed "Titletown" for its NFL wins (including four Super Bowl championships). The best way to experience the big small-town love is by visiting the team's home turf at **Lambeau Field**. While game tickets are hard to come by, you can take a tour that brings you onto the field or visit the Hall of Fame to see artifacts and exhibits devoted to the team's history. The Hall of Fame is self-guided and includes the fan-favorite replica office of legendary coach Vince Lombardi. Even if you can't make it to the field, make like a local and head to the corner bar to watch the game any Sunday in season. ✉ *1265 Lombardi Ave., Green Bay, WI* 🌐 *www.packers.com/lambeau-field*

Don't Miss

The **Packers Heritage Trail** highlights locations around the city that represent key moments in Packers history, from the Packers practice fields to team founder Curly Lambeau's grave site. A trolley tour of the trail is available as well. If you get hungry along the way, stop by **Al's Hamburgers**, a vintage 1934 diner, for classic burgers and shakes. 🌐 *www.packershofandtours.com/explore/heritage-trail*

When to Go

The stadium is open for tours and Hall of Fame visits year-round, but if you visit during the NFL season, you can tailgate and try to score tickets for a game.

Getting Here and Around

Green Bay's Austin Straubel International Airport (GRB) is about 4 miles from Lambeau Field.

Dane County Farmers' Market

Sample America's Dairyland

The Dane County Farmers' Market, held outdoors at the Wisconsin State Capitol building in Madison every Saturday morning from mid-April to early November, is America's largest producers-only farmers' market, with more than 100 vendors. That means you'll find an unparalleled selection of locally grown fruits and vegetables, plus jams, baked goods, meats, eggs, fresh beans, maple syrup, popcorn, and Wisconsin's famous cheese. Pick up prepared foods, like Stella's hot and spicy cheese bread, to snack on as you walk around the square. ✉ *2 E. Main St., Madison, WI* 🌐 *www.dcfm.org*

Don't Miss

You can't go to Wisconsin without trying the cheese (it is America's Dairyland after all). Dairy vendors at the market frequently bring samples of their sharp cheddars, creamy spreads, and squeaky curds, so you can find your favorite. **Hook's Cheese**, which makes exceptional cheddars and blue cheeses, is a standout.

While You're Here

The market is held surrounding the **Wisconsin State Capitol**, so be sure to admire the architecture. You can also go inside for a free tour, and, between April and December, you can walk up to the sixth-floor observation deck to get a view of the city. 🌐 *legis.wisconsin.gov/about/visit*

Good to Know

The market is held year-round, but it moves indoors in mid-November to the Garver Feed Mill. ✉ *3241 Garver Green, Madison, WI*

Getting Here and Around

The Dane County Regional Airport (MSN) will get you to Madison; from there, it's just under 5 miles to the capitol building.

Milwaukee Breweries

The Beer Capital of America

Beer is in Milwaukee's DNA—the city has been a brewing destination since the mid-19th century, when European settlers to the region began making beer. It became home to Pabst, Schlitz, and Miller, and even as other cities' beer scenes have surpassed it in size, the association has endured (the city's baseball team is called the Brewers, after all). Plenty of excellent new breweries have joined the lineup in recent years, from **Supermoon Beer Co.**, where you can get farmhouse beers, to **Hacienda Beer Co.**, where the food is a perfect pairing to the beer (try a Guava Milkshake IPA with a brisket sandwich).

Don't Miss

Miller Brewery's tour includes a visit to the underground beer caves where beer baron Frederick Miller used to chill beer in the 1880s. ✉ *3897 W. State St., Milwaukee, WI* 🌐 *www.millerbrewerytour.com*

Best Tour

The nearly 40-year-old **Lakefront Brewery** is known for its laid-back 50-minute tour that focuses on the samples (four to be exact), so it's especially fun if you aren't there for all the technical details about how beer is made. ✉ *1872 N. Commerce St., Milwaukee, WI* 🌐 *www.lakefrontbrewery.com*

Getting Here and Around

General Mitchell International Airport (MKE) or Milwaukee Intermodal Station (Amtrak) are easy jumping-off points for exploring the beer scene. You'll want to skip a rental car, of course, but it's easy to take rideshares between breweries.

Taliesin

Frank Lloyd Wright's Summer Home

Taliesin, renowned architect Frank Lloyd Wright's summer home and studio, features buildings he designed from the 1890s to the 1950s. A UNESCO World Heritage site, Taliesin is set on an 800-acre estate on a hill in the Wisconsin River valley. There's plenty to explore, from Wright's 37,000-square-foot house to Hillside Home School, run by his aunts, to the rolling landscape, which helped inspire some of his designs. ✉ *5481 County Rd. C, Spring Green, WI* 🌐 *www.taliesinpreservation.org*

Don't Miss

The **Riverview Terrace Cafe** is Wright's only restaurant design, and the menu features local cuisine made with ingredients grown at neighboring farms.

Best Tour

Taliesin offers a number of different tours, but for true Frank Lloyd Wright fans, the Estate Tour is the only way to go. The four-hour tour takes you to the Romeo and Juliet Windmill Tower, Hillside Home School, and the studio. You'll also get to relax on the terrace with provided snacks.

While You're Here

Combine a trip to Taliesin with a show at **American Players Theatre**. Located a mile from Taliesin, the outdoor amphitheater is set in a wooded meadow and focuses on Shakespeare's plays. ✉ *5950 Golf Course Rd., Spring Green, WI* 🌐 *www.americanplayers.org*

Getting Here and Around

The Dane County Regional Airport (MSN) in Madison is just over 40 miles from Taliesin. From General Mitchell International Airport (MKE) in Milwaukee, Taliesin is about 120 miles away.

The Great River Road

Wine, Dine, and Hike the Mississippi

Wisconsin's stretch of the Great River Road runs 250 miles alongside the Mississippi River in the western part of the state. The road, which you can drive or bike, features beautiful mountains and views of the river, and offers plenty of opportunities to hike, fish, and camp at five state parks, including **Wyalusing State Park.** The road stops in 33 towns, so there are many options for shopping and dining. **La Crosse** is home to an outpost of the University of Wisconsin and has some memorable pit stops, including Pearl Ice Cream Parlor, with 1930s decor. 🌐 *www.wigrr.com*

Don't Miss

The **Great River Road Wine Trail** features 10 wineries set along the Mississippi River. Stops are mostly located in Wisconsin and just across the river in Minnesota. Visit **Maiden Rock Winery & Cidery**, which offers wine and cider tastings, as well as a river wine cruise, where you can also admire the cliffs of the coastline. 🌐 *www.greatriverroadwinetrail.org*

Good to Know

Birders should head to the **Trempealeau National Wildlife Refuge** along the Mississippi River to spot warblers, pelicans, eagles, and more. ✉ *W28488 Refuge Rd., Trempealeau, WI*

Getting Here and Around

Minneapolis–St. Paul Airport (MSP) is just under 30 miles from the northern start of the road in Prescott, Wisconsin. Dubuque Regional Airport (DBQ) is 16 miles from the southern edge of the road in Kieler, Wisconsin.

Wisconsin Dells

The Water Park Capital of the World

Wisconsin Dells is both the name of a city along the Wisconsin River and a 5-mile gorge that cuts through it. For Wisconsinites though, "the Dells" is a family-friendly summer destination packed with water parks, pancake restaurants, minigolf, and boat tours through the gorge. Get up close to the towering sandstone cliffs of the gorge by taking to the water in a kayak, canoe, or tube. Those who prefer a less active way to enjoy the scenery can stroll down the quarter-mile walking path that offers views of the cliffs.

Don't Miss

The largest and arguably the most popular water park in the Dells is **Noah's Ark Water Park,** with 70 acres of waterslides, surfing, restaurants, and more. ✉ *1410 Wisconsin Dells Pkwy., Wisconsin Dells, WI* 🌐 *www.noahsarkwaterpark.com*

Best Tour

The **Original Wisconsin Ducks**, the oldest duck-boat operator in the Wisconsin Dells (they debuted in 1946), offers hour-long tours of the Wisconsin River and Lake Delton, plus woodsy trails. They'll zip you through Red Bird Gorge and give you a great view of the sandstone cliffs. The company also runs nighttime ghost boat tours for the truly adventurous. 🌐 *www.wisconsinducktours.com*

When to Go

Summer is the time to visit the Dells, as all the restaurants and outdoor water parks are open for the season.

Getting Here and Around

Dane County Regional Airport (MSN) in Madison is just over 50 miles from the Wisconsin Dells. You can also take Amtrak or Greyhound from Chicago, which takes 3½ hours by train and 5½ hours by bus.

Milwaukee Art Museum

Wisconsin's Best Museum

Founded in 1888 as Milwaukee's first art gallery, the museum includes more than 30,000 works, spanning from ancient Mediterranean sculpture to contemporary painting. Areas of particular focus include American decorative arts, German Expressionism, and Haitian art, but the museum's winged architecture is often considered one of its showstoppers. Spread across three distinctive buildings (designed by Eero Saarinen, David Kahler, and Santiago Calatrava), the museum, which is located right on Lake Michigan, also includes a geometrically designed garden. ✉ *700 N. Art Museum Dr., Milwaukee, WI* 🌐 *www.mam.org*

Don't Miss

The Burke Brise Soleil, the striking, white, 217-foot architectural "wings" on the building's exterior, were designed by Santiago Calatrava (the architect of New York's Oculus). They open each day at 10 am, flap at noon, and close at 10 pm; make sure you head outside to catch the show.

Best Collection

The collection of art from painter and Wisconsin native Georgia O'Keeffe is among the largest holdings of her work in the country.

Good to Know

The museum is very kid-friendly. If you're traveling with children, pick up ArtPacks with paper for sketching plus books and other materials. Stop by the first Saturday of each month at 10:30 am for storytime.

Getting Here and Around

General Mitchell International Airport (MKE) is located 10 miles from the museum. From the Milwaukee Intermodal Station, where Amtrak operates, it's just over a mile to the museum. From Chicago's O'Hare International Airport (ORD), it's an 80-mile drive.

Kettle Moraine State Forest

Wonders From the Ice Age

The big geographic feature of this 56,000-acre forest is a large moraine (basically, what's left after a significant glacier moved through the area many thousands of years ago). The resulting landscape consists of hills, lakes, and prairies, which means the forest is a prime location for swimming, hiking, cross-country skiing, and fishing. The terrain is also a draw for equestrians, and an equestrian campground is available, as are RV campgrounds. Prefer to take in the sights from your car? The 115-mile **Kettle Moraine Scenic Drive** winds through the forest and offers scenic stops to picnic along the way. ✉ *S59 W36530 County ZZ, Dousman, WI* 🌐 *dnr.wisconsin.gov*

Don't Miss

Parnell Observation Tower, the highest elevation in Kettle Moraine, offers a 25-mile panoramic view of the surrounding forest.

Best Canoe Trail

The 17-acre lake doesn't allow motorized boats, which makes it a calm, clear lake for a quiet paddling adventure. The **Ottawa Lake Canoe Trail** takes 30 to 40 minutes to complete, and you can pick up a pamphlet on-site that will guide you to numbered buoys and highlight the natural features of the lake. There's also excellent fishing, with walleye, muskie, trout, bass, and other species in the waters.

Getting Here and Around

Dane County Regional Airport (MSN) in Madison is 61 miles to the west of the forest's Southern Unit, while Milwaukee's General Mitchell International Airport (MKE) is 37 miles to the east. MKE is 50 miles to the south of the forest's Northern Unit, while MSN is 75 miles to the southwest.

When in Wisconsin

HOUSE ON THE ROCK

Spring Green may be best known for Frank Lloyd Wright's Taliesin, but Alex Jordan's House on the Rock is another worthy pilgrimage. Like something from Zillow Gone Wild, the home, which opened in 1959, has a seemingly endless array of theme rooms, which have expanded over the years to include a massive carousel, rooms filled with model airplanes and dollhouses, a *Titanic* display, Japanese gardens, and more. ✉ *5754 Rte. 23, Spring Green, WI* 🌐 *www.thehouseontherock.com*

Do This: You'll want your camera out as much as possible, but save the selfie for the Infinity Room, a long corridor made of tiny glass windows that extends out over the forested valley below.

JOHN MICHAEL KOHLER ARTS CENTER

Tucked into downtown Sheboygan since 1967 and located on the grounds of the former Kohler family homestead (yes, of luxury-plumbing fame), this is not your normal art museum. Instead of paintings in gilded frames or collections exhibited in glass cases, you'll experience a mix of contemporary art from self-taught artists as well as artist-built environments, with most stemming from Wisconsin. Of note is the 14,000-piece collection of works by Wisconsin-born artist Eugene Von Bruenchenhein. It might sound silly, but be sure to go into the men's and the women's bathrooms, as these are also works of quirky art. ✉ *608 New York Ave., Sheboygan, WI* 🌐 *www.jmkac.org*

Do This: A visit to this art corner of Wisconsin would not be complete if you didn't swing by the Art Preserve (closer to I–94 but still in Sheboygan). Walking through the artist-built environments, painstakingly reconstructed from their original sites, is as close to being in their homes as one can be. ✉ *3636 Lower Falls Rd., Sheboygan, WI*

Cool Places to Stay

Anaway Place. A cut above your average woodland cabin, these beautiful lodgings in southwestern Wisconsin embrace Scandinavian hygge aesthetics, with wood-burning stoves, cozy reading lofts, and patios. A stay is about the quality of the house as much as the outdoors, with cabins ranging from two-person escapes to large spaces that can accommodate a dozen. ✉ *21558 Candlewood La., Richland Center, WI* 🌐 *www.anaway.com*

The Iron Horse Hotel. Motorcycle aficionados can ride up to this downtown Milwaukee hotel, which is located a half mile from the Harley-Davidson Museum and features covered on-site parking for your wheels and gear storage. Built into a 100-year-old warehouse, the rooms are spacious and dog-friendly, with views of the city, and there's a spa for those days you'd rather stay in. ✉ *500 W. Florida St., Milwaukee, WI* 🌐 *www.theironhorsehotel.com*

About Our Writers

Kristine Hansen has lived in Wisconsin for 25 years and currently resides in Milwaukee. She's a die-hard Packers fan and thinks Wisconsin cheese is way tastier than California cheese. As a freelance travel and design writer, she contributes to national outlets and is the author of *Wisconsin Cheese Cookbook* and *Frank Lloyd Wright's Wisconsin*.

Seth Peterson Cottage. Spend the night in a Frank Lloyd Wright–designed cabin in Mirror Lake State Park. The one-bedroom cabin has huge windows with views of the forest, a full kitchen, stone walls, and a large fireplace you can cozy up next to in the winter. In summer, take advantage of the canoe that goes along with the property. ✉ *E9982 Fern Dell Rd., Reedsburg, WI* 🌐 *www.sethpeterson.org*

Essential Eats

Cheese Curds. The best cheese curds (curdled-milk pieces) should be so fresh that, when you bite into one, they squeak. Curds are so common here they're sold at gas stations but for some of the best, hit up Carr Valley Cheese's seven retail stores (🌐 *www.carrvalleycheese.com*) or try Fromagination in Madison, which sells Cedar Grove Cheese's curds (✉ *12 S. Carroll St., Madison, WI* 🌐 *www.fromagination.com*).

Ishnala Supper Club. Supper clubs are a Wisconsin tradition: they're vintage-y, loaded with surf-and-turf menu options, and designed for lingering. At this Lake Delton restaurant, perched above Mirror Lake in Mirror Lake State Park, there's a line out front just to get in, and even if all you have time for is an Old Fashioned (Wisconsin's official state cocktail) at the bar, it's worth the stop. The restaurant's open between April and October. ✉ *S2011 Ishnala Rd., Lake Delton, WI* 🌐 *www.ishnala.com*

Milwaukee Public Market. Akin to Seattle's Pike Place Market, this is a one-stop shop for Wisconsin's best foods, groceries, and drinks, including award-winning cheese from West Allis Cheese & Sausage Shoppe, craft beer at Thief Wine Shop & Bar, and spices from the Spice House, which dates back to the 1950s. A variety of eateries also operate stands. Grab a table on the second floor or at Thief Wine Shop & Bar's tasting room to enjoy your culinary finds with a glass of wine. ✉ *400 N. Water St., Milwaukee, WI* 🌐 *www.milwaukeepublicmarket.org*

Pizza Farms. Wisconsin has many culinary claims to fame, but none are more offbeat than pizza farms, a tradition in the western part of the state. As the name implies, the experience includes eating pizza on a working farm, but it's more than that: it's a summertime weekend tradition in which friends and neighbors can gather for a casual evening over pizzas made with fresh ingredients straight from the farm, like house-made fennel-maple sausage. Stoney Acres Farm hosts pizza nights April to November. They also have a beer and wine garden with suds and ciders from their own brewery, as well as a farm stand to stock up on produce to take home with you. ✉ *245728 Baldwin Creek Rd., Athens, WI* 🌐 *www.stoneyacres.farm*

Index

A

B

M

N

O

P

Q

R

S

T

Photo Credits

Front Cover: Mike Kline/Notkalvin Photography/GettyImages [Descr.: A view of the Gateway Arch in St. Louis, Missouri from within the park. Fall colors adorn the deciduous trees in the foreground and a blue sky completes the scene. The arch is inside Gateway Arch National Park, and was designed by Eero Saarinen.] **Back cover, from left to right:** Tusharkoley/Shutterstock. Steve Heap/Shutterstock. Lorcel/Shutterstock. **Spine:** Dean_Fikar/iStockphoto. **Interior, from left to right:** AlexKane/GettyImages (1). OverlandTheAmericas/Shutterstock (2-3). **About Our Writers:** All photos are courtesy of the writers except for the following. Adam H. Callaghan courtesy of Stasia Brewczynski. Stratton Lawrence courtesy of Claire van der Lee. Teresa Bitler courtesy of Rick D'Elia. Katie Jackson courtesy of Eric Baumann. Kristine Hansen courtesy of Troy Freund Photo LLC. **Chapter 1: Experience Bucket List USA:** Songquan Deng/Shutterstock (6-7). Tsyu87/Dreamstime (10). Karandaev/iStockphoto (10). SL_Photography/iStockphoto (10). Oleg Albinsky/GettyImages (10). Heyengel/iStockphoto (11). Ingus Kruklitis/Shutterstock (11). R.C. Bennett/Shutterstock (11). Boarding1Now/iStockphoto (11). Skreidzeleu/Shutterstock (12). TRphotos/Shutterstock (12). Sara Winter/Shutterstock (12). Kan_khampanya/Shutterstock (12). Biolifepics/Dreamstime (13). BlueBarronPhoto/Shutterstock (13). Don Mammoser/Shutterstock (13). Kavram/shutterstock (13). Lembi/Shutterstock (14). Saro17/iStockphoto (14). Ablokhin/iStockphoto (14). Jim Mallouk/Shutterstock (15). Daniel_Goldin/iStockphoto (15). F11photo/Dreamstime (16). Konstantin L/Shutterstock (16). RomanSlavik.com/Shutterstock (16). Jorgeantonio/Dreamstime (16). Krblokhin/GettyImages (17). Dbvirago/Dreamstime (17). Dononeg/Dreamstime (17). Gabby Lovelace/Shutterstock (17). Matthew Connolly/Shutterstock (18). Kirkikisphoto/Dreamstime (18). Zack Frank/Shutterstock (18). Zrfphoto/iStockphoto (18). Wirestock/Dreamstime (19). Rymasheuskaya Volha/GettyImages (20). LnP images/Shutterstock (20). F11photo/Shutterstock (20). AlexandreFagundes/iStockphoto (20). Phagenaars/Dreamstime (21). Enrico Della Pietra/iStockphoto (21). Georgia O'Keeffe Museum (21). Negro Leagues Baseball Museum, Inc. (21). Mia2you/Shutterstock Brendamunsterman/Dreamstime (22). Alexey Stiop/Shutterstock (22). Hoover Tung/Shutterstock (23). Jimmy W/Shutterstock (23). Mikericci/Dreamstime (24). Tbintb/Dreamstime (24). In Dancing Light/Shutterstock (24). Michael Gordon/Shutterstock (24). Adeliepenguin/Dreamstime (25). F11photo/Dreamstime (25). Wangkun Jia/Shutterstock (25). Zhukova Valentyna/Shutterstock (25). Tiago_Fernandez/iStockphoto (26). Northlight/Shutterstock (26). EQRoy/Shutterstock (26). Nagel Photography/Shutterstock (26). Jo Hunter/Shutterstock (27). Edgar Lee Espe/Shutterstock (27). Marekuliasz/Shutterstock (27). Susan Vineyard/iStockphoto (27). JhvePhoto/Shutterstock (28). Mitten Crate (28). Shriver's (28). Peterboro Basket Company (28). Amana Society, Inc (29). **Chapter 2: New England:** Mike Ver Sprill/Shutterstock (33). Brent Hofacker/Shutterstock (36). AnastasiaKopa/Shutterstock (37). Magdalena Kucova/Shutterstock (37). Faina Gurevich/iStockphoto (39). Ian Dagnall/Alamy (40). Sean Pavone/Shutterstock (41). Malley Photography/Shutterstock (42). Shanshan0312/Shutterstock (43). Jeremy D'Entremont/GettyImages (44). Try Media/iStockphoto (49). Photo Italia LLC/iStockphoto (50). Sean Pavone/iStockphoto (51). James Griffiths Photography/iStockphoto (52). Scott McManus/Shutterstock (53). Esposito Photography/Shutterstock (54). E.J.Johnson Photography/Shutterstock (55). IronLifeMoney/Shutterstock (56). David Rajter/Shutterstock (57). Seacoastmountainphoto/iStockphoto (58). Jsnover/iStockphoto (59). Pat/Alamy (60). Wangkun Jia/Shutterstock (61). Sean Pavone/Dreamstime (66). Eric Broder Van Dyke/Shutterstock (67). F11photo/Dreamstime (68). LnP images/Shutterstock (69). Harmony Waldron/Shutterstock (70). Mbastos/Dreamstime (71). Christopher Seufert/iStockphoto (72). Georgios Antonatos/Shutterstock (73). Jay Yuan/Shutterstock (74). Allan Wood Photography/Shutterstock (75). T photography/Shutterstock (76). Alexander Sviridov/Shutterstock (77). Mauritius images GmbH/Alamy (78). T photography/Shutterstock (79). Heidi Besen/Shutterstock (80). JMP Traveler/iStockphoto (86). Appalachianviews/Dreamstime (87). J. S. Wolf Photography/Shutterstock (88). YuziS/Shutterstock (89). Patrick Herlihy/Shutterstock (90). Kevin Burkholder/GettyImages (91). Dan Lewis/Shutterstock (92). Wangkun Jia/Shutterstock (93). AlexandreFagundes/iStockphoto (98). Danita Delimont/Alamy (99). Sanghwan Kim/GettyImages (100). Randydellinger/iStockphoto (101) Laura Stone/Shutterstock (102). Carl Beust/Shutterstock (103). Kirkikisphoto/Dreamstime (104). FashionStock.com/Shutterstock (109). AlbertPego/iStockphoto (110). Eric Dale/Shutterstock (111). Frank Grenon/Shutterstock (112). Reimar/Shutterstock (113). James Casil/Shutterstock (114). Doug Kerr/Flickr (115). Dbimages/Alamy (116). Jay Yuan/Shutterstock (117). **Chapter 3: The Mid-Atlantic:** Paul Hanley Photos/iStockphoto (121). Rawf8/iStockphoto (124). MSPhotographic/iStockphoto (125). Hihitetlin/Shutterstock (125). Jon Bilous/Shutterstock (127). Cmoulton/Dreamstime (128). Randy Duchaine/Alamy (129). Tolbert Photo/Alamy (130). James Gilbert/Stringer/GettyImages (131). Kruck20/iStockphoto (135). Valentyn75/Dreamstime (136). Ewy Media/Shutterstock (137). Nathaniel gonzales/Shutterstock (138). Abriggs21/iStockphoto (139). Vito Palmisano/iStockphoto (140). Woodsnorthphoto/Shutterstock (141). Thomas Marchessault/Alamy (142). Vikvad72/Dreamstime (143). Mary Salen/iStockphoto (147). EQRoy/Shutterstock (148). Gary C. Tognoni/Shutterstock (149). Vlad G/Shutterstock (150). Mihai_Andritoiu/Shutterstock (151). EleanorAbramson/Shutterstock (152). Aoldman/Dreamstime (153). Brian Logan Photography/Shutterstock (154). D. Pimborough/Shutterstock (155). John A. Anderson/iStockphoto (161). Spyarm/Shutterstock (162). Roman Babakin/Shutterstock (163). Tinnaporn Sathapornnanont/Shutterstock. (164). Barbaraaaa/iStockphoto (165). Selcuk Oner/Shutterstock (166). Cdominguezbasalo/Dreamstime (167). Francisco Blanco/iStockphoto (168). Alessio Catelli/Shutterstock (169). Rarrarorro/iStockphoto (170). Saletomic/Dreamstime (171). Francois-roux-photography.com/iStockphoto (172). Saronix/ Dreamstime (173). Felix Lipov/Shutterstock (174). Peterspiro/iStockphoto (175). Leonard Zhukovsky/Shutterstock (176). Haveseen/Shutterstock (177). Bukharova/iStockphoto (178). Sean Pavone/Shutterstock (184). MontenegroStock/Shutterstock (185). Appalachianviews/Dreamstime (186). Nagel Photography/Shutterstock (187). Daniel Price/GettyImages (188). Gscott54/Dreamstime (189). Desha Utsick/Shutterstock (190). Vadim 777/Shutterstock (191). Drewthecreative/Dreamstime (192). MH Anderson Photography/Shutterstock (193). Zack Frank/Shutterstock (194). Olivier Le Queinec/Shutterstock (195). Jon Bilous/Shutterstock (200). Studiodr/iStockphoto (201). Orhan Cam/Shutterstock (202). Kristi Blokhin/Shutterstock (203). Ultima_Gaina/iStockphoto (204). Sherry V Smith/Shutterstock (205). Andrew Repp/Shutterstock (206). Sean Pavone/Shutterstock (210). Sean Pavone/Shutterstock (211). Tverdohlib/iStockphoto (212). Steve Heap/Shutterstock (213). Eurobanks/iStockphoto (214). Mihai_Andritoiu/Shutterstock (215). Prakash Patel/International Spy Museum (216). Steveheap/Dreamstime (222). Pat/Alamy (223). MarkVanDykePhotography/Shutterstock (224). Tristanbnz/Dreamstime (225). Breck P. Kent/Shutterstock (226). PT Hamilton/Shutterstock (227). **Chapter 4: The Southeast:** Steve Bower/iStockphoto (231). Bhofack2/iStockphoto (234). Cavan-Images/Shutterstock (235). Olyina/Shutterstock (235). Adele Heidenreich/Shutterstock (237). Mrolands/Dreamstime (238). Sean Pavone/Shutterstock (239).

Photo Credits

Michael Gordon/Shutterstock (240). James Kirkikis/Shutterstock (241). Public domain sourced/access rights from Alpha Stock/Alamy (242). Carmen K Sisson/iStockphoto (243). Niwat panket/Shutterstock (248). Brandon Olafsson/GettyImages (249). Damon Shaw/Shutterstock (250). Kitleong/Dreamstime (251). Zrfphoto/Dreamstime (252). Doug Fox/Shutterstock (253). Kitleong/Dreamstime (254). Jennifer Lynn/Flickr (259). Littleny/iStockphoto (260). Sandrafoyt/Dreamstime (261). Vito Palmisano/iStockphoto (262). Gabby Lovelace/Shutterstock (263). Michael Marko/Ball & Chain (264). NaughtyNut/Shutterstock (265). Thierry Eidenweil/Shutterstock (266). Joshua Lehew/Shutterstock (267). Craig Hinton/Shutterstock (268). William Rodrigues Dos Santos/Dreamstime (269). Parick Farrell and Peter W. Cross (270). Rafal Michal Gadomski/ Shutterstock (271). Andriy Blokhin/Shutterstock (272). Jaimie Tuchman/iStockphoto (273). Sean Pavone/Shutterstock (274). F11photo/ Shutterstock (279). Michael Gordon/Shutterstock (280). Felix Mizioznikov/Shutterstock (281). Jshanebutt/Dreamstime (282). Hanny1224/ Shutterstock (283). Wilsilver77/iStockphoto (284). Brandy Wright/Shutterstock (285). Nicole Kibert/Flickr (286). Jeffrey M. Frank/Shutterstock (287). Elan7t50/iStockphoto (288). B Cruz/Shutterstock (289). Irina Mos/Shutterstock (294). Try Media/iStockphoto (295). Alex Slitz/ GettyImages (296). PEO Acwa/WikimediaCommons (297). Joe Hendrickson/Shutterstock (298). Oliclimb/Shutterstock (299). Roman Zaiets/ Shutterstock (300). Phil Denton/Flickr (301). Alexey Stiop/Shutterstock (302). Steve Robinson/Shutterstock (307). GTS Productions/ Shutterstock (308). Steveheap/Dreamstime (309). William A. Morgan/Shutterstock (310). Brian Lauer/Flickr (311). Alisa_Ch/Shutterstock (312). Page Light Studios/Shutterstock (313). Brent Hofacker/Shutterstock (314). IrinaK/Shutterstock (315). Tiago Lopes Fernandez/Peek Creative Collective/iStockphoto (320). James Kirkikis/Shutterstock (321). C5Media/Dreamstime (322). Deebrowning/Dreamstime (323). Carmen K. Sisson/Shutterstock (324). Sean Pavone/iStockphoto (325). Magraphy/Shutterstock (326). KpaigePhotography/Shutterstock (327). Sean Board/iStockphoto (331). Nolichuckyjake/Shutterstock (332). Anthony heflin/Shutterstock (333). Levai/Shutterstock (334). Coralimages2020/Dreamstime (335). Denis McDonough/Shutterstock (336). Toribio93/Shutterstock (337). Kmm7553/Dreamstime (338). Susanne Pommer/Shutterstock (344). Donna Brooks/iStockphoto (345). Warren LeMay/Flickr (346). MargaretW/iStockphoto (347). Will Kunkel/Shutterstock (348). Sean Pavone/Shutterstock (349). Alex grichenko/iStockphoto (350). Sean Pavone/iStockphoto (351). Digidreamgrafix/Shutterstock (352). Sean Pavone/Shutterstock (356). Dwhob/iStockphoto (357). Jejim/Shutterstock (358). Nicholas Lamontanaro/Shutterstock (359). F11photo/Shutterstock (360). Rolf_52/Shutterstock (361). Alizada Studios/Shutterstock (362). Jonathan Ross/iStockphoto (363). **Chapter 5: The Great Plains:** Alex Potemkin/GettyImages (367). Lulugirl5/Dreamstime (370). Courtesy of Travel South Dakota (371). Bhofack2/Dreamstime (371). David Papazian/Shutterstock (373). Courtesy of Iowa Tourism Office (374). Courtesy of Riverboat Twilight (375). Judidthann59/Dreamstime (376). Camerashots/Dreamstime (377). Reb/Dreamstime (378). Bruce Leighty/Alamy (379). Iowa Tourism Office (380). Iowa Tourism Office (381). Jacob Boomsma/Shutterstock (382). RaksyBH/Shutterstock (386). Brent Coulter/ iStockphoto (387). Vincent Parsons/Flickr (388). APN Photography/Shutterstock (389). CLP Media/Shutterstock (390). Dave Drum/iStockphoto (391). Courtesy of Cosmosphere (392). Sean Pavone/iStockphoto (396). Stljb/Shutterstock (397). Mohammad-amin asareh/Shutterstock (398). Zuma Press, Inc./Alamy (399). Water Street/Shutterstock (400). Photos BrianScantlebury/Shutterstock (401). JeremyMasonMcGraw.com/ GettyImages (402). Lost_in_the_Midwest/Shutterstock (406). Kent Weakley/Shutterstock (407). Steven Branscombe/GettyImages (408). Martin Mora (409). Ken Schulze/Shutterstock (410). Nebraska Tourism (411). Aspects and Angles/Shutterstock (412). Martin Hobelman/ Shutterstock (413). Drewthehobbit/Shutterstock (414). Ammodramus/WikimediaCommons (415). Randall Runtsch/Shutterstock (420). Pjworld-tour/Dreamstime (421). Northlight/Shutterstock (422). DC_Colombia/iStockphoto (423). Plains Art Museum (424). John Finney Photography/ GettyImages (425). Americanspirit/Dreamstime (426). Chad Kainz/WikimediaCommons (427). Dee Browning/iStockphoto (431). Joshua McDonough/iStockphoto (432). Doubleclick7/Dreamstime (433). Allison Meier/Flickr (434). Ehrlif/Dreamstime (435). EyeEm Mobile GmbH/ iStockphoto (436). Zrfphoto/iStockphoto (437). G. Edward Johnson/WikimediaCommons (438). Dean_Fikar/iStockphoto (442). Joseph Sohm/ Shutterstock (443). SL_Photography/iStockphoto (444). Capt' Tom/Shutterstock (445). Ashmephotography/Dreamstime (446). ThePonAek/ Shutterstock (447). Photostravellers/Shutterstock (448). Jacob Boomsma/Shutterstock (449). Sopotnicki/Shutterstock (450). Chaden Roggow/ iStockphoto (451). **Chapter 6: The West Coast and the Pacific:** NKneidlphoto/Shutterstock (455). FloridaStock/Shutterstock (458). Guajillo studio/Shutterstock (459). Thejamez/Dreamstime (459). Glebtarro/Dreamstime (461). Denemiles/Dreamstime (462). Sekarb/ Dreamstime (463). Gentilcore/Dreamstime (464). Rex Lisman/Shutterstock (465). Npgal77/Dreamstime (466). Image Source Trading Ltd/ Shutterstock (467). Tashka/iStockphoto (468). Jim Lambert/Shutterstock (469). Jefwod/Dreamstime (470). Michael Rosebrock/Shutterstock (471). Troutnut/Dreamstime (472). ESB Professional/Shutterstock (477). Bannosuke/Shutterstock (478). Dancestrokes/Shutterstock (479). Francesco Ferrarini/Shutterstock (480). Michael Urmann/Shutterstock (481). Tryder/Dreamstime (482). Gary C. Tognoni/Shutterstock (483). Marcorubino/Dreamstime (484). Stephen Moehle/Shutterstock (485). Dancestrokes/Shutterstock (486). Julie Caron/iStockphoto (487). Viewapart/Dreamstime (488). Checubus/Dreamstime (489). Walter Cicchetti/Shutterstock (490). Pauloqfernandes/Dreamstime (491). BlueBarronPhoto/Shutterstock (492). Stephanie Braconnier/Shutterstock (493). CSNafzger/Shutterstock (494). Rumata7/Dreamstime (495). Brian Swanson/Shutterstock (496). Engel Ching/Shutterstock (497). Jimekstrand/Dreamstime (498). Kit Leong/Shutterstock (499). Andrew Zarivny/Shutterstock (500). Bennymarty/Dreamstime (507). George Burba/Shutterstock (508). Linda Bair/iStockphoto (509). Pierre Leclerc/ Shutterstock (510). Hiroyuki Saita/Shutterstock (511). Pung/Shutterstock (512). Maridav/Shutterstock (513). Demerzel21/Dreamstime (514). Art Boardman/Shutterstock (515). Gnagel/Dreamstime (516). Theodore Trimmer/Shutterstock (517). Janaph/iStockphoto (518). Damienverrier/ Dreamstime (519). Nancy Erger/Big Island Visitors Bureau (BIVB) (520). Paula Cobleigh/Shutterstock (526). Artyooran/Dreamstime (527). Cgardinerphotos/Dreamstime (528). Victoria Ditkovsky/Shutterstock (529). Zhukova Valentyna/Shutterstock (530). Chiyacat/Dreamstime (531). Joshuaraineyphotography/Dreamstime (532). Tusharkoley/Shutterstock (533). Nadia Yong/Shutterstock (534). Kelly vanDellen/Shutterstock (535). Kim Budd (536). Wirestock/GettyImages (537). Unclejay/Dreamstime (538). Galyna Andrushko/Shutterstock (544). Sean Pavone/ Shutterstock (545). Mlharrisphotography/Dreamstime (546). Laurens Hoddenbagh/Shutterstock (547). Galyna Andrushko/Shutterstock (548). 400tmax/GettyImages (549). Monika Wieland Shields/Shutterstock (550). Irina88w/Dreamstime (551). Roman Khomlyak/Shutterstock (552). Christiannafzger/iStockphoto (553). Strekoza2/Dreamstime (554). Kirk Fisher/Shutterstock (555). Pierre Leclerc/Shutterstock (556). Skydive Snohomish (557). **Chapter 7: The Southwest:** Ronnybas/iStockphoto (561). Zoryanchik/Shutterstock (564). Rose Ressner/Shutterstock

Photo Credits

(565). Msphotographic/Dreamstime (565). Pat Tr/Shutterstock (567). Derrick Neill/Dreamstime (568). Likephotography/Dreamstime (569). NaughtyNut/Shutterstock (570). CrackerClips Stock Media/Shutterstock (571). Zack Frank/Shutterstock (572). Jon Chica/Shutterstock (573). Nate Hovee/Shutterstock (574). Cheri Alguire/Shutterstock (575). Raphoto/iStockphoto (576). Bcfc/iStockphoto (577). Varina And Jay Patel/ Dreasmtime (578). RomanSlavik.com/Shutterstock (583). Sean Pavone/iStockphoto (584). Sean Pavone/Shutterstock (585). Beth Ruggiero-York/Shutterstock (586). Filip Fuxa/Shutterstock (587). Dmodlin01/Shutterstock (588). CrackerClips Stock Media/Shutterstock (589). Gerald Corsi/iStockphoto (590). Amadeustx/Shutterstock (595). Adam-Springer/iStockphoto (596). Sunsinger/Shutterstock (597). Traveller70/ Shutterstock (598). Zhukova Valentyna/Shutterstock (599). Name_Thats_Not_Taken/iStockphoto (600). Blake Jorgensen/Taos Ski Valley (601). Steve Lagreca/Shutterstock (602). Brian Welker/Dreamstime (603). Lightphoto/iStockphoto (604). Traveller70/Shutterstock (605). Sean Pavone/Shutterstock (610). Rolf52/Dreamstime (611). Tom Durr/Shutterstock (612). Sean Pavone/Shutterstock (613). Zrfphoto/iStockphoto (614). Terri Butler Photography/Shutterstock (615). Sean Pavone/Shutterstock (616). Anitatakespictures/Shutterstock (617). TLF Images/ Shutterstock (618). Zrfphoto/Dreamstime (619). JhvePhoto/Shutterstock (620). RoschetzkyIstockPhoto/iStockphoto (621). Fotoluminate LLC/ Shutterstock (622). Brian Luke/Shutterstock (623). Sebastian Ruzycki/Shutterstock (624). Jacqueline F Cooper/Dreamstime (625). Evenfh/ Shutterstock (631). Dibrova/Shutterstock (632). Fyletto/iStockphoto (633). TomKli/Shutterstock (634). Colin D. Young/Shutterstock (635). Stefano Borsa/Shutterstock (636). Irene Skvorzowa/iStockphoto (637). VisualCommunications/iStockphoto (638). Kojihirano/Shutterstock (639). Hotaik Sung/iStockphoto (640). **Chapter 8: The Rockies:** Sean Pavone/Shutterstock (643). Goskova Tatiana/Shutterstock (646). Phillip Rubino/Shutterstock (647). Saastaja/Dreamstime (647). JFunk/Shutterstock (649). Sepavo/Dreamstime (650). Gnagel/iStockphoto (651). John Hoffman/Shutterstock (652). Csnafzger/Shutterstock (653). Hikeflyshoot/Shutterstock (654). Sopotnicki/Shutterstock (655). Pgiam/ GettyImages (656). Mile High Aviator/Shutterstock (657). Jon Arnold Images Ltd/Alamy (658). Josh Campbell/GettyImages (659). WorldPictures/Shutterstock (660). Jonathanwcohen/Dreamstime (665). Benny Marty/Shutterstock (666). CodyHaskell/iStockphoto (667). Danita Delimont/Shutterstock (668). Csnafzger/Shutterstock (669). Bureau of Land Management/Flickr (670). Christiannafzger/iStockphoto (671). JordanRT/Shutterstock (672). Dan Breckwoldt/Shutterstock (677). Debraansky/iStockphoto (678). JimKruger/GettyImages (679). Alan Majchrowicz/GettyImages (680). Bmswanson/iStockphoto (681). Sue Smith/Shutterstock (682). Dennis Stogsdill/iStockphoto (683). Michael Gordon/Shutterstock (684). Lorcel/Shutterstock (689). Kwiktor/iStockphoto (690). Hale Kell/Shutterstock (691). TenleyThompson/iStockphoto (692). Nichimar/Shutterstock (693). Larry Porges/Shutterstock (694). Jayme Burney/Shutterstock (695). **Chapter 9: The Great Lakes:** John Lupu/Shutterstock (699). Brent Hofacker/Shutterstock (702). Igor Sokolov/Dreamstime (703). Stu_spivack/WikimediaCommons (703). James Kirkikis/Shutterstock (705). FiledImage/Shutterstock (706). Tinamou/Dreamstime (707). Wirestock Creators/Shutterstock (708). Juliengrondin/ Dreamstime (709). Thomas Barrat/Shutterstock (710). Grindstone Media Group/Shutterstock (711). Todd Ryburn/GettyImages (712). Eddie J. Rodriquez/Shutterstock (713). Joe Hendrickson/GettyImages (714). Anthony Farinas (715). Grindstone Media Group/Shutterstock (719). Delmas Lehman/Shutterstock (720). Sean Pavone/iStockphoto (721). James Kirkikis/Shutterstock (722). Keifer/Dreamstime (723). Susan Vineyard/iStockphoto (724). Wildnerdpix/Shutterstock (725). Ncschneider Images/Shutterstock (726). Michael Deemer/Dreamsime (730). Smontgom65/Dreamstime (731). Monica Wells/Alamy (732). Sean Pavone/Alamy (733). Adeliepenguin/Dreamstime (734). John McCormick/ Shutterstock (735). Bell's Brewery (736). Jeffrey Isaac Greenberg 5+/Alamy (737). Steven Schremp/Shutterstock (738). Paul Brady Photography/Shutterstock (739). GummyBone/iStockphoto (740). Bmosh99/Dreamstime (741). Devon Greenburg/iStockphoto (746). Sean Pavone/iStockphoto (747). Jeff Coleman/Dreamstime (748). GummyBone/iStockphoto (749). Sophie James/Shutterstock (750). Wildnerdpix/ Shutterstock (751). Joe Christensen/GettyImages (752). Lonnie Paulson/Shutterstock (753). Dan Thornberg/Shutterstock (754). BlueBarronPhoto/Shutterstock (755). Sean Pavone/Shutterstock (760). Michael Shake/Shutterstock (761). Sara Winter/Shutterstock (762). Pthamil2/Dreamstime (763). Zack Frank/Shutterstock (764). David Davis Photoproductions/Alamy (765). Eniko Balogh/Shutterstock (766). Helgidinson/Dreamstime (767). Jetcityimage/Dreamstime (768). RianeR/Flickr (769). Nejdet Duzen/Shutterstock (774). Apostle Islands Cruises (775). Roger Gerbig/Flickr (776). MarynaG/Shutterstock (777). Raymond Maiden/Shutterstock (778). Jim Roberts/Dreamstime (779). Joe Ferrer/Dreamstime (780). Charles Hester/Dreamstime (781). Cundy Bird/Dreamstime (782). Adam Wineke/Dreamstime (783).

**Every effort has been made to trace the copyright holders, and we apologize in advance for any accidental errors. We would be happy to apply the corrections in the following edition of this publication.*

Fodor's BUCKET LIST USA

Publisher: Stephen Horowitz, *General Manager*

Editorial: Douglas Stallings, *Editorial Director;* Jill Fergus, Alexis Kelly, Amanda Sadlowski, *Senior Editors;* Brian Eschrich, *Editor;* Angelique Kennedy-Chavannes, Yoojin Shin, *Associate Editors*

Design: Tina Malaney, *Director of Design and Production*; Jessica Gonzalez, *Senior Designer;* Jaimee Shaye, *Graphic Design Associate*

Production: Jennifer DePrima, *Editorial Production Manager*, Elyse Rozelle, *Senior Production Editor;* Carol Seigler, *Production Editor*

Maps: Rebecca Baer, *Map Director*, Mark Stroud (Moon Street Cartography), *Cartographer*

Photography: Viviane Teles, *Director of Photography;* Namrata Aggarwal, Neha Gupta, Ashok Kumar, *Photo Editors;* Zamantta Larios Salazar, Shanelle Jacobs, *Photo Production Interns*

Business and Operations: Chuck Hoover, *Chief Marketing Officer;* Robert Ames, *Group General Manager*

Public Relations and Marketing: Joe Ewaskiw, *Senior Director of Communications and Public Relations*

Fodors.com: Jeremy Tarr, *Editorial Director;* Rachael Levitt, *Managing Editor*

Editor: Amanda Sadlowski

Production Editor: Jennifer DePrima

2nd Edition

ISBN 978-1-64097-903-1

ISSN 2768-3974

PRINTED IN TURKEY

10 9 8 7 6 5 4 3 2 1